Paris 1889

American Artists at the Universal Exposition

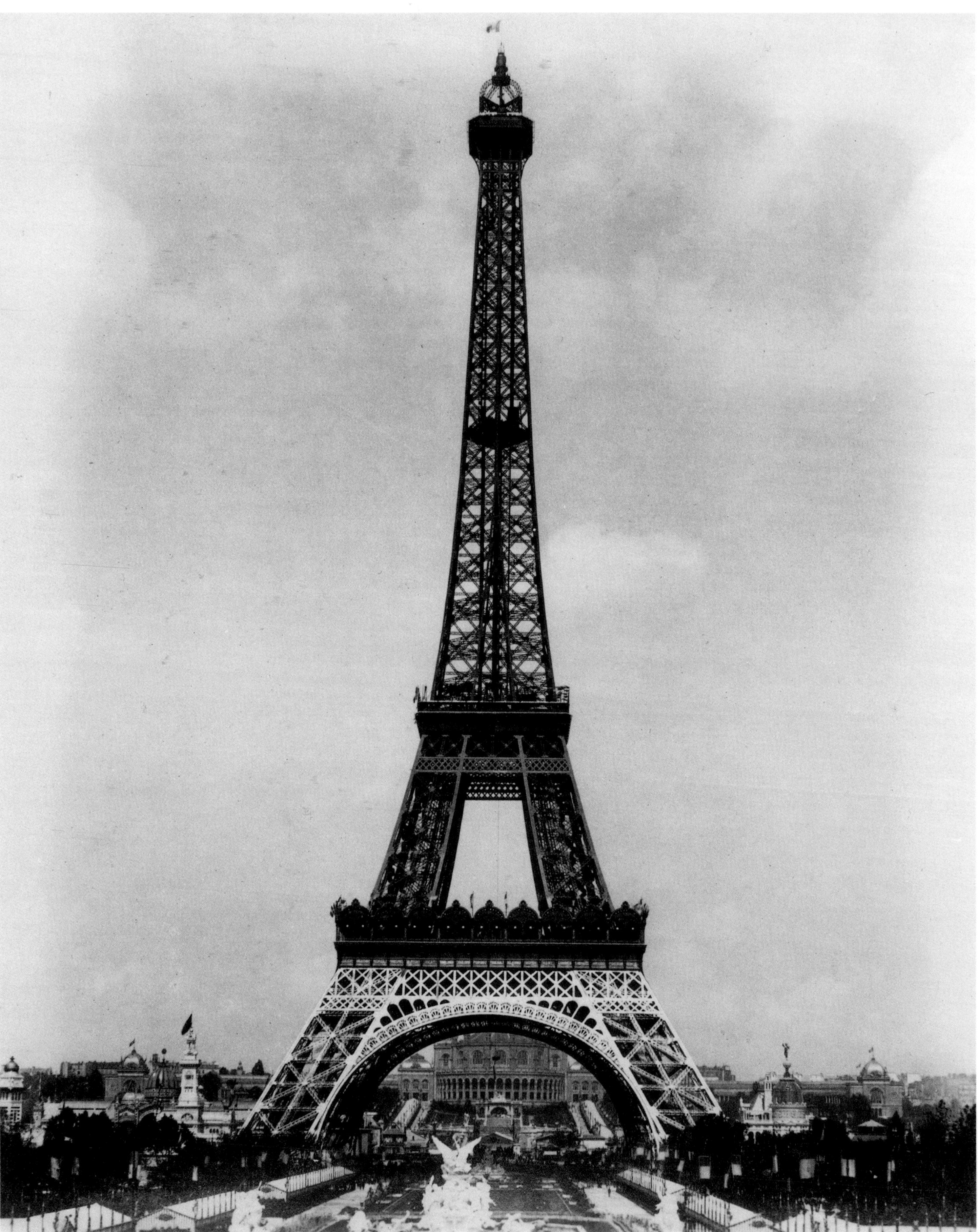

Paris 1889

American Artists at the Universal Exposition

Annette Blaugrund

with essays by
Annette Blaugrund
Albert Boime
D. Dodge Thompson
H. Barbara Weinberg
Richard Guy Wilson

Pennsylvania Academy of the Fine Arts, Philadelphia
in association with
Harry N. Abrams, Inc., Publishers, New York

The exhibition was organized by the Pennsylvania Academy of the Fine Arts and made possible by generous grants from the Pew Charitable Trusts and the National Endowment for the Arts, a Federal agency.

Exhibition itinerary:

Chrysler Museum, Norfolk, Virginia
September 29–December 17, 1989

Pennsylvania Academy of the Fine Arts, Philadelphia
February 1–April 15, 1990

Memphis Brooks Museum of Art, Tennessee
May 6–July 15, 1990

Editor: Ruth Eisenstein

Designer: Jody Hanson

Library of Congress Cataloging-in-Publication Data

Paris 1889: American artists at the Universal Exposition/Annette Blaugrund; with essays by Annette Blaugrund . . . [et al.]. p. cm.
Issued to accompany an exhibition, organized by the Pennsylvania Academy of the Fine Arts; to be held at Norfolk's Chrysler Museum Sept. 29–Dec. 17, 1989, at Pennsylvania Academy of the Fine Arts Feb. 1–Apr. 15, 1990, and at the Memphis Brooks Museum of Art May 6–July 15, 1990.
Bibliography: p. 266
Includes index.
ISBN 0–8109–3703–4
1. Painting, American—Exhibitions 2. Painting, Modern—19th century—United States—Exhibitions. 3. Exposition universelle de 1889 (Paris, France) I. Blaugrund, Annette. II. Pennsylvania Academy of the Fine Arts. III. Chrysler Museum. IV. Memphis Brooks Museum of Art.
ND210.P27 1989
759.13'074'74—dc20 89–3898
ISBN 0–943836–12–3 (pbk.)

Published in 1989 by Harry N. Abrams, Incorporated, New York.

A Times Mirror Company

Printed and bound in Japan

Frontispiece
Eiffel Tower, Exposition Universelle de Paris, 1889
Gustave Eiffel (1832–1923), with Emile Nouguier and Maurice Koechlin (1856–1946), associate engineers, and Stephan Sauvestre (1847–?), architect
The Library of Congress, lot 6634

Contents

List of Lenders

Aberdeen Art Gallery and Museums, Scotland
Archives of American Art, Smithsonian Institution, Washington, D.C.
The Art Institute of Chicago
The Berkshire Museum, Pittsfield, Massachusetts
Berry-Hill Galleries, New York
JoAnne Bowie
The Brooklyn Museum, New York
The Carnegie Museum of Art, Pittsburgh
Jane and John D. Caruthers
Phillip Dennis Cate and Family
The Century Association, New York
The Chrysler Museum, Norfolk
Cincinnati Art Museum
The Cleveland Museum of Art
The Corcoran Gallery of Art, Washington, D.C.
Cornell University, Ithaca
Allen P. Crawford
Dr. and Mrs. Demosthenes Dasco
Dr. and Mrs. James E. Deitz
Essex Club, Newark
The Fine Arts Museums of San Francisco
The FORBES Magazine Collection, New York
George Haigh
Heckscher Museum, Huntington, New York
Ipswich Public Schools, Massachusetts
The Library of Congress
The Manney Collection
Manoogian Collection
Memphis Brooks Museum of Art
The Metropolitan Museum of Art, New York
The Minneapolis Institute of Art
Musée des Beaux-Arts et d'Archéologie de Rennes
Musée Municipal de Brest
Musée National de Blérancourt
Musée National du Château de Versailles
Musée d'Orsay, Paris
Musée Vivinel, Compiègne
Museum of Fine Arts, Boston
The Museum of Fine Arts, Houston
National Academy of Design, New York
National Museum of American Art, Smithsonian Institution, Washington, D.C.
The Newberry Library, Chicago
Mr. and Mrs. Eddy G. Nicholson
The Peabody Institute of Johns Hopkins University, Baltimore
Pennsylvania Academy of the Fine Arts, Philadelphia
Philadelphia Museum of Art
Stuart Pivar
Alexander R. Raydon, Raydon Gallery, New York
Frederic Remington Art Museum, Ogdensburg, New York
Hazel Patrick Rickenbacher
Rifkin-Young Fine Arts, New York
San Antonio Museum of Art
Sheffield City Art Galleries, England
Hardwick Simmons
The Paul Singer Foundation, New York
Terra Museum of American Art, Chicago
The Toledo Club
Trinity College, Hartford
Union League Club of Chicago
Valparaiso University Museum of Art
William Vareika Fine Arts, Newport, Rhode Island
Virginia Museum of Fine Arts, Richmond
Mr. and Mrs. Richard M. Waitzer
Mr. and Mrs. Benjamin L. Walbert
Walters Art Gallery, Baltimore
Watson Gallery, Wheaton College, Norton, Massachusetts
Nelson Holbrook White
Chris Whittle
Grayce Patrick Wray
Yale University Art Gallery, New Haven
Larry Zim World's Fair Collection
Nine Anonymous Lenders

Foreword

"I would rather go to Europe than go to Heaven," declared William Merritt Chase. This was the cry of many of the more ambitious American artists in the years after the Civil War. While the grand tour had been part of the education of American artists since the mid-eighteenth century, it was during the last quarter of the nineteenth century that they flocked to Europe—mostly to Paris—in ever greater numbers, in search of antiquity and tradition, enlightenment and subject matter, and in the hope of winning recognition and patronage. The highly developed French atelier system, which emphasized a more formalized curriculum of drawing, perspective, and the study of anatomy from the nude model (as opposed to antique statuary), and which encouraged students to compete for prizes, absorbed Americans in seemingly unlimited numbers. Some returned home and introduced this system of education to the more progressive art schools, such as the Art Students League in New York, the School of the Museum of Fine Arts in Boston, and the Pennsylvania Academy of the Fine Arts in Philadelphia.

This unique transitional moment in American art history when French and American artists were so interdependent was dramatically represented by the American display at the Universal Exposition of 1889 in Paris. Celebrating the Centennial of the French Revolution, that great world's fair, the most visible reminder of which is the once controversial Eiffel Tower, included a retrospective exhibition of a century of French painting and a formidable display of contemporary art, to which nations worldwide were invited to submit works. After the French, the greatest number of paintings on view in this fine arts display were by Americans—the largest showing of contemporary American art held in Europe up to that time.

As part of the current celebration of the Bicentennial of the French Revolution, the Pennsylvania Academy has undertaken to recreate the American display at the 1889 Exposition. Ninety works by 67 artists have been brought together here for the first time in 100 years. To illuminate more clearly the inspiration of the Americans, 13 works by selected French masters have been included.

Many of the American artists are familiar figures important in any historical survey. Others, well known in their time, have fallen into relative obscurity—as have, until recently, many of their French masters. The Americans' styles, subjects, and concerns were as diverse as those of their European colleagues: there were the society portraits with the flashy brushwork of John Singer Sargent, the intimate impressions of nature by William Merritt Chase, and the linear and abstracted symbolist works of Elihu Vedder. Three quarters of the exhibiting American artists had studied with French masters, and while some observers criticized the American works for being entirely too derivative from the French, the exhibition proved significant for the Americans, who received numerous medals and won appreciation in the context of the international marketplace.

As American art has matured since World War II, there has been increasing interest in studying its history in greater depth. Universities and colleges have added American art history, formerly relatively neglected, to their curricula, and museums are eagerly expanding their collections of American art of all periods, with renewed interest in the more academic traditions represented in this exhibition and its companion volume. Both will serve as important documents in achieving a greater understanding of our American artistic heritage.

The cooperation and participation of a large team of individuals have been essential to the realization of this project. To begin, I salute D. Dodge Thompson, who—aware of the importance of the American section at the Universal Exposition of 1889—conceived the idea of the present exhibition and recognized the appropriateness of its being undertaken by the Pennsylvania Academy of the Fine Arts. The logic of this connection is everywhere apparent, starting with the National Historic Landmark status of the 1876 building of the Pennsylvania Academy and its spacious period galleries, designed by George Hewitt and Frank Furness. Indeed, many of the Pennsylvania Academy's annuals of the latter part of the nineteenth century included paintings by American artists working in Paris, and three works shown in the Exposition of 1889 are in its collection: Robert Vonnoh's *Companion of the Studio*, Alexander Harrison's *The Wave*, and Daniel Ridgway Knight's *Hailing the Ferry*. In the late nineteenth century and the early twentieth, several Pennsylvania Academy instructors were hired from the rolls of exhibitors at the Universal Exposition: Robert Vonnoh, Theodore Robinson, Cecilia Beaux, William Merritt Chase, J. Alden Weir, and Edward Howland Blashfield.

This venture has been carried forward with consummate skill by Annette Blaugrund, Guest Curator at the Pennsylvania Academy. Her scholarship and the tireless exercise of her talents for organization and diplomacy have been integral to the creation of both exhibition and catalogue. I join with her in acknowledging with profound appreciation the assistance of the many persons who have advanced the undertaking. High on the list are the scholars whose essays, along with Annette Blaugrund's, constitute a major contribution to this volume: H. Barbara Weinberg, D. Dodge Thompson, Albert Boime, and Richard Guy Wilson. They have all, in addition, rendered invaluable service as consultants to the exhibition. The authors of the catalogue entries—Holly Pyne Connor, Judith Hayward, Susan James-Gadzinski, Maureen C. O'Brien, and Karen Zukowski—also deserve special thanks.

The Pennsylvania Academy is indebted to the many individuals and institutions that have graciously lent their works of art to "Paris 1889: American Artists at the Universal Exposition." The project is supported in part by a grant from the National Endowment for the Arts, and, like many of the other activities of the Pennsylvania Academy, it has benefited greatly from the generous and continuing support of the Pew Charitable Trusts in Philadelphia.

Linda Bantel
Director of the Museum, Pennsylvania Academy of the Fine Arts

Preface

"Never before in such variety and quantity have the productions of the arts and manufactures been brought together," summarized Rush C. Hawkins, United States Fine Arts Commissioner, in his report to Congress on the 1889 Universal Exposition. In this international array, representing the decorative and liberal arts, industry, agriculture, science, and architecture, the fine arts were just one component. But the great number of entries sent to the paintings section demonstrated that Americans were ready to compete in the cultural as well as the commercial and scientific spheres.

That paintings far outnumbered sculptures and graphics governed the decision of the Pennsylvania Academy of the Fine Arts to concentrate on the 336 paintings submitted to the Exposition by 189 artists. Although the search to find works actually exhibited in 1889 was somewhat hindered by radical shifts in taste, by changes in title, and by nonspecific titles such as *Landscape* and *Portrait*, more than 125 examples have been located. Despite the fact that some paintings were unavailable because of condition problems, some were subject to prior commitments, some had been deaccessioned, some were in collections that do not lend, and some had been destroyed, we were able to assemble a rich and diverse display of subjects and styles that convincingly illustrates the broad range of late-nineteenth-century American art.

Our aim has been to include at least one work by each artist and, where possible, in order to approximate the original ratio, to include two or three works by artists who sent multiple entries to the fair. Overall, the goal of exhibiting only paintings shown at the 1889 Exposition has been adhered to. We have deviated only by accepting a study or a replica made by the artist when the original was unobtainable.

The exhibition "Paris 1889: American Artists at the Universal Exposition" represents a sampling of the works chosen in 1889 by two juries of American artists, one in New York and one in Paris. Their selections acknowledged the academic standard that predominated in the art galleries of most nations participating in the fair, for the avant-garde paintings of the period—Impressionist and Post-Impressionist works—were mostly seen in galleries outside the fairgrounds. It was in the nature of world's fairs to feature conventional art that appealed to the taste of a broader audience. Works by several of the important French academic artists who were the teachers of American art students are included in the exhibition.

This book augments the Pennsylvania Academy of the Fine Arts exhibition in several ways. Five major essays provide a background for understanding the relation between the American exhibitors and their European, primarily French, mentors and illuminate both the physical and the sociocultural context of the Exposition. Each painting in the exhibition is reproduced in color, and the illustration is accompanied by a short essay on the work and the artist. The original 1889 catalogue of the American paintings section, annotated and illustrated, brings to light lost and little-known works shown at the fair. It is our hope that the publication of this volume will not only foster a better understanding of the development of American academic art, and encourage the appreciation of it, but will stimulate further research and spur the recovery of lost works.

One of the great pleasures in working on this book has been the opportunity to collaborate with my fellow authors—Albert Boime, D. Dodge Thompson, H. Barbara Weinberg, and Richard Guy Wilson. Each has provided much more than an essay. Their contributions have taken many forms: they have offered ideas, picture sources, facts, and advice as needed, and they have never been too busy to share with me their experience and knowledge. The catalogue entry writers—Holly Pyne Connor, Judith Hayward, Susan James-Gadzinski, Maureen C. O'Brien, and Karen Zukowski—have cheerfully undertaken research and curatorial chores in the face of imminent deadlines and last-minute additions and substitutions.

For giving me the opportunity to work on this project, I want to thank Linda Bantel, Director of the Museum of the Pennsylvania Academy of the Fine Arts, whose astute counsel throughout has been my mainstay. Deep appreciation goes to the staff of the Pennsylvania Academy, without whom this book and exhibition could not have been accomplished. Robert Arthur Harman, Associate Registrar, in addition to arranging for all the paintings, compiled the list of lenders and exhibition data; Elyssa Kane, Assistant to the Registrar, ordered and kept track of the innumerable photographs; Inez Wolins, Curator of Education, helped me to conceptualize exhibition ideas for grant proposals; and Jacolyn Mott, the Academy's Editor, guided this publication early on. For performing the myriad unseen labors that go into endeavors such as this, I am also indebted to Mark Bockrath, Marietta Bushnell, Susan Danly, Carolyne Hollenweger, Cheryl Leibold, Helen Mangelsdorf, James Martin, Gale Rawson, Jane M. Schmidt, Judith Stein, James Voirol, and other museum personnel associated with the exhibition.

A hundred years ago, when the American artists who are the subject of this book sent their paintings to the great Exposition in Paris, they were participating in the centennial celebration of the birth of the French Republic. These American artists are once again part of the celebration of that momentous event, for this book and exhibition have been designated an official project of the United States Commemoration of the Bicentennial of the French Revolution and the Declaration of the Rights of Man and the Citizen. In this connection we have had the aid of Patrick M. Talbot, Cultural Counselor, and Leith Symington, Coordinator of Special Projects for 1989, of the French Embassy in New York, and I thank them for their enthusiastic support.

Many people in the museum world have earned my gratitude: Betty Blum, Archives of American Art Chicago Project; William McNaught, Archives of American Art, New York; Catherine Denning, Annmary Brown Memorial Library, Brown University; Milo M. Naeve, Art Institute of Chicago; Debra Bricker-Balken, Berkshire Museum; Véronique Weissinger, Musée de Blérancourt; Thomas Bruhn, William Benton Museum of Art, University of Connecticut at Storrs; Linda S. Ferber, Barbara Dayer Gallati, Sarah Faunce, Elizabeth Easton, and Christina Usefero, The Brooklyn Museum; Annegreth Nill, The Carnegie Museum of Art; Roger D. Clisby, The Chrysler Museum; William Bodine, The Corcoran Gallery of Art; Nancy E. Allyn, Herbert F. Johnson Museum, Cornell University; Ilene S. Fort, Los Angeles County Museum of Art; Joan Barnes, Manoogian Collection, Taylor, Michigan; William Heidrick, Memphis Brooks Museum of Art; John K. Howat, Kathleen Luhrs, Doreen Bolger, Pamela Hubbard, Catherine Hoover Voorsanger, Lewis

I. Sharp, and Stephen Rubin, The Metropolitan Museum of Art; Pierre Rosenberg, Musée du Louvre; Carol Troyen and Trevor J. Fairbrother, Museum of Fine Arts, Boston; Abigail B. Gerdts, National Academy of Design; Lois Marie Fink, Elizabeth Broun, George Gurney, William Treuttner, and Karol Lawson, National Museum of American Art, Washington, D.C.; Mary P. Wyly, the Newberry Library; Elizabeth Schaaf, The Peabody Institute of Johns Hopkins University; Joseph Rishel and Darrell Sewell, Philadelphia Museum of Art; Anthony Janson, John and Mable Ringling Museum of Art; Martha Hoppin, Springfield Art Museum; Mark Simpson, M. H. de Young Memorial Museum; and Helen Cooper, Yale University Art Gallery.

Scholarly assistance was made readily available to me by William H. Gerdts, who gave me access to his personal library and helped identify paintings, and by Dianne Pilgrim, who always lends an understanding ear. For freely sharing information and expertise I am grateful to Madeleine Fidell Beaufort, Jennifer Martin Bienenstock, John Davis, Lee M. Edwards, Kathleen Foster, Susan Grant, Peter Hassrick, Maria Chamberlin Helman, Patricia Hills, Elizabeth Johns, Norman Kleeblatt, Merle M. Moore, Jr., Maria Naylor, Barbara Novak, Lucy Oakly, Francis V. O'Connor, Richard Ormond, Ronald G. Pisano, Gary A. Reynolds, Herbert Reynolds, David Sellin, Katherine Shano, Cynthia Siebels, Annette Stott, Tara Tappert, and Denny Young.

The tasks of locating lost paintings, acquiring information, and obtaining loans from private collectors were greatly facilitated through the assistance of a number of art dealers in New York and other cities: James Hill, Frederick Hill, and Bruce Chambers of Berry-Hill Galleries; Jeffrey Brown and Katherine Corbin of Brown-Corbin Fine Art, Boston; Robert Preato of Grand Central Galleries; Bergen Kirk of Hammer Galleries; Kathleen Burnside of Hirshl & Adler Galleries; Vance Jordon of Jordon-Volpe Gallery; Mary Ran of Mary Ran Gallery, Cincinnati; Alexander Raydon of Raydon Gallery; Laurene Banks and David Henry of Spanierman Gallery; Abbott W. and Robert C. Vose, Jr., of Vose Galleries, Boston; Richard York and Eric Widing of Richard York Gallery; and Thomas Rearick of Maxwell Galleries, San Francisco.

On the domestic front, help and encouragement were in constant supply from family, friends, and assistants: Andrea Blaugrund, the late Linda Galub, Marc Gobé, Leemour Pelli, Thelma Polanco, Betty Rauch, and Cherie Smith. As always, the empathy and devotion of my husband, Stanley M. Blaugrund, have been a continuing source of strength.

I have found the association with the staff of Abrams wonderful from start to finish. Paul Gottlieb, president and publisher, was not only receptive to the idea of the book but in fact amplified its scope. I mention with fondness and respect Ruth Eisenstein, our outstanding editor, who has handled the manuscripts of ten contributors with wisdom and patience. Margaret Donovan, who generously donated odd hours borrowed from her own busy schedule, deserves a word of thanks, as do Rebecca Tucker and free-lance editor Brenda Gilchrist for their steadfast assistance. It has been a great benefit to have had the precise, professional help of Barbara Lyons, Director of Photo Research, Rights, and Reproductions, and to have had at work in the shaping of the book the imagination and creativity of designer Jody Hanson.

If my acknowledgments are in any respect incomplete it is because so many people have assisted me; to all of them I am truly grateful.

Annette Blaugrund
Guest Curator, Pennsylvania Academy of the Fine Arts

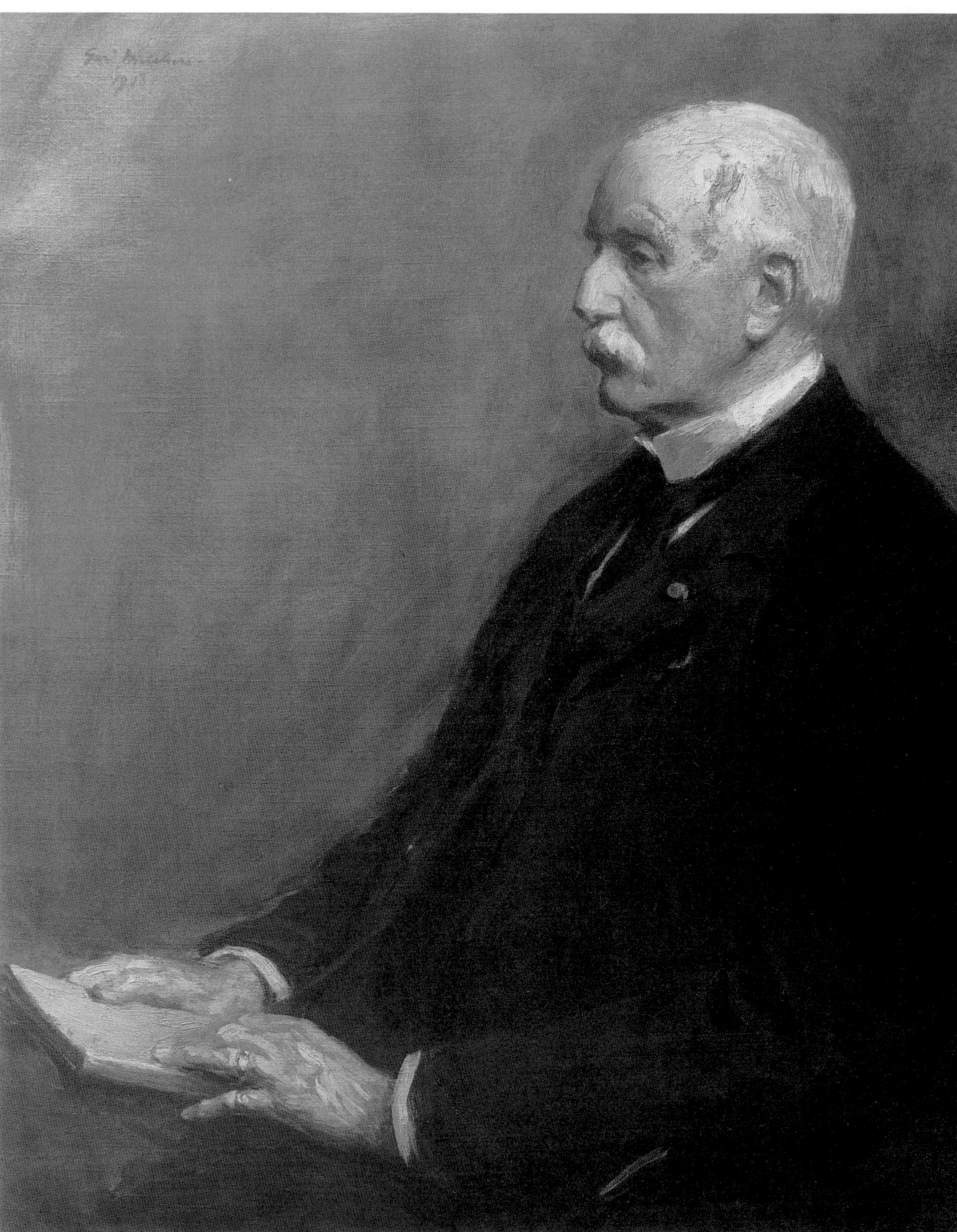

ANNETTE BLAUGRUND

Behind the Scenes: The Organization of the American Paintings

1.
(Julius) Gari Melchers (1860–1932)
Portrait of Rush C. Hawkins, 1908
Oil on canvas, 37¾ x 30½" (95.9 x 77.5 cm)
Annmary Brown Memorial Library, Brown University, Providence

Just as the Eiffel Tower—that mythic symbol built to commemorate the centennial of the French Revolution—commanded attention and provoked controversy, so too did America's contribution to the fine arts section of the 1889 Universal Exposition. Of all the foreign participants, the Americans, in an effort to be recognized as contenders in the international arena, sent the largest number of paintings. The politics surrounding the selection and installation of these works is the subject of this essay.

France hosted universal expositions, also called world's fairs, approximately every eleven years from 1855 through 1900. Americans were not as well represented in the fine arts at the first fair, where the Salon was part of the Exposition, as they were at later fairs. In 1855 only 39 American paintings, lent by ten artists living in France, were exhibited.[1] As more artists became interested in participating in the international forum, the American fine arts contribution increased: in 1867 the number of American paintings was 82. The entries, which many European critics considered provincial, were selected by a committee of collectors, connoisseurs, and art dealers from New York and Philadelphia, including collector-turned-dealer Samuel P. Avery, who was designated Commissioner of Fine Arts. Even the Commissioner-General, well-known publisher Frank Leslie, was of the opinion that the United States was not represented by a full range of styles and themes. Yet America had sent its very best: landscapes by Frederic E. Church, Albert Bierstadt, and Sanford R. Gifford, for example, along with genre scenes by Winslow Homer and Eastman Johnson.[2]

At the 1878 fair, French critics, expecting a repetition of the national styles seen in 1867, were surprised by the increased number of American paintings that manifested European influence. David Maitland Armstrong, Commissioner of the American fine arts section, with the assistance of the sculptor Augustus Saint-Gaudens, solicited, selected, and installed the American works.[3] An advisory committee in New York selected 87 of the 127 oil paintings sent abroad, and the remainder were chosen by Armstrong and Saint-Gaudens, together with C. E. Detmold, in Paris. Along with Church, Gifford, and John Kensett, names that no longer appear in 1889, were John La Farge, Walter Gay, and Mary Cassatt, all of whom had worked in France. Frederick Bridgman, who was to play an important role in 1889, won the highest award in 1878.

During the years between the fairs of 1878 and 1889, America's patriotism and pride in its accomplishments—industrial and artistic—grew significantly. When invited to participate in the 1889 fair, the American government accepted with greater promptness, and enthusiasm, than it had previously.[4] The speedy reply was an indication of approval of the French Republic and endorsement of the centennial celebration of the French Revolution—a gesture matched by few other nations.[5] According to a contemporary source, "Neighboring monarchical States looked with disfavor upon the project and discountenanced it as political in character. . . ."[6] America's "hearty cooperation" was "warmly appreciated" by the French, and rewarded in many ways.[7]

For American artists, many of whom had studied in Paris or Munich, participation was more than a political gesture. It afforded them the dual opportunity of affirming their own and their nation's ability to compete artistically in an international setting. While displaying their skill, they were also making a bid for the world art market. In this setting, which encompassed industrial products, scientific displays, and consumer goods, art was made available to a wider audience than ever before. The 1889 Exposition, which ran from May 5 to November 5, surpassed all previous nineteenth-century world's fairs in size and diversity. It was so popular that it was extended for a week. Over 32 million people visited 61,722 exhibits, of which more than 1,750 were from the United States. To many of these visitors art was another commercial product. The American fine arts section comprised 572 works—336 paintings by 189 painters, 117 drawings and grisaille paintings by 32 artists, 16 sculptures (mostly busts) by 11 sculptors, 102 engravings, etchings, and lithographs by 21 graphic artists, and an architectural drawing. These works, many of which revealed the American assimilation of French themes and techniques, were meant to enhance the cultural reputation of the United States.

Rush Christopher Hawkins (1831–1920) was appointed Commissioner of Fine Arts. General Hawkins (fig. 1) was described as "the right man in the right place" by a friend, who wrote: "Your correct knowledge of the Fine Arts acquired during so many years of travel quite fit you for your position but I do not envy you the task of rejecting paintings, it always creates ill feeling."[8] Hawkins had proved himself an able leader as organizer and commander of a regiment of Zouaves during the Civil War. Independently wealthy, he had traveled a great deal, visiting art collections and libraries all over Europe.[9] While a young lawyer in New York, having developed an interest in early printing and wood engraving, he formed an extensive collection of fifteenth-century books and engravings and wrote a standard text on the subject.[10] In 1905 he established the Annmary Brown Memorial Library at Brown University to house his incunabula and paintings, naming it after his recently deceased wife, the granddaughter of the school's founder. Letters to and from Hawkins stored in this library, where he and his wife are entombed, reveal the nature of the formidable task of organizing the American fine arts section at the 1889 fair. They provide a more or less chronological record of the behind-the-scenes preparation of the American display and illuminate Hawkins's role in the selection, insurance, shipment, installation, and ultimately the dispersal of the paintings. Included among his papers are early circulars soliciting works of art and specifying rules and regulations. These were sent to art institutions in November 1888 and were reproduced in publications such as the *Boston Transcript* and the *Art Amateur*.[11] Group I, the fine arts, was categorized as follows in Circular 3:

CLASS I.—Oil Paintings.—*Paintings on canvas, panels and various grounds.*

CLASS II.—Paintings of different kinds and Drawings.—*Miniatures; paintings in water-colors; pastel and drawings of all kinds; paintings on enamel, earthenware and porcelain; cartoons for stained-glass windows and frescoes.*

CLASS III.—Sculpture and Engravings on Medals.—*Statuary, bas-relief, repoussé work and chiselled work, medals, cameos, engraved stones, inlaid enamel work.*

CLASS IV.—Architectural Drawings and Models.—*Studies and fragments. Representations and plans of buildings, restorations from ruins or documents.*

CLASS V.—Engravings and Lithographs.—*Engraving in black; polychromatic engravings. Lithographs in black, in chalk and with brush; chromo-lithography.*

Inevitably the regulations, which applied to American artists on both sides of the Atlantic, did not cover some issues adequately. For example, the Commission offered what it deemed a reasonable amount of insurance, but many artists requested higher valuations. (Any extra insurance had to be paid for by the artist.) J. Carroll Beckwith wrote to Hawkins asking whether a work lent by a collector could be insured for its buying price; he also wanted assurance that damage to the painting or frame would be covered.[12] Edwin Blashfield wrote asking for the name of the insurance company because he had just sold one of his entries, *Inspiration*, for $2,550 and thought the painting should be covered for that amount; in the same letter he thanked the Commissioner for granting him an extension of time at this "moment when you must have been simply up to your neck in business and work."[13] Hawkins, in keeping with his military background, seemingly adhered to the rules and made few exceptions.

The regulation requiring artists to pay for the transportation of paintings with no assurance of their acceptance also elicited many letters. Though such risks were commonly taken when entering the National Academy of Design annuals or the Salon exhibitions, Thomas Allen, representing the Boston artists, informed Hawkins that artists there would be reluctant to send paintings to New York at their own expense. He requested that a jury be appointed in Boston, but to no avail.[14] Despite objections, a good number of Boston artists participated.

Procedures for American artists living in France differed only in submission dates. However, French artists were initially asked to itemize the works they wished to enter, and the lists were ruled on between June 1 and July 1, 1888; immediately afterward, French artists were advised which works would be acceptable. The actual selection of the paintings took place between January 5 and January 20, 1889. Works chosen were to be delivered between March 15 and March 20. Entry forms, similar to those issued to American artists, required name of artist, date of birth, permanent and local addresses, names of teachers, itemization of previous prizes, and, for each work, title, description, date, medium, and size.[15] These entry forms were the basis of the official record published by the French government; they were also used for the individual catalogues that each country was authorized to produce in its own language.[16] It is the American catalogue, annotated and illustrated, that is reproduced at the back of this book (see pages 267–97). Hawkins's French counterpart, Antonin Proust (1832–1905), was the Deputy Commissioner of Fine Arts in France (see fig. 2). A childhood friend and champion of Edouard Manet, a critic and a politician, Proust wielded great authority.

2.
Edouard Manet (1832–1883)
Portrait of Antonin Proust, 1880
Oil on canvas, 51 x 37¾" (129.5 x 95.9 cm)
The Toledo Museum of Art, Gift of
Edward Drummond Libbey

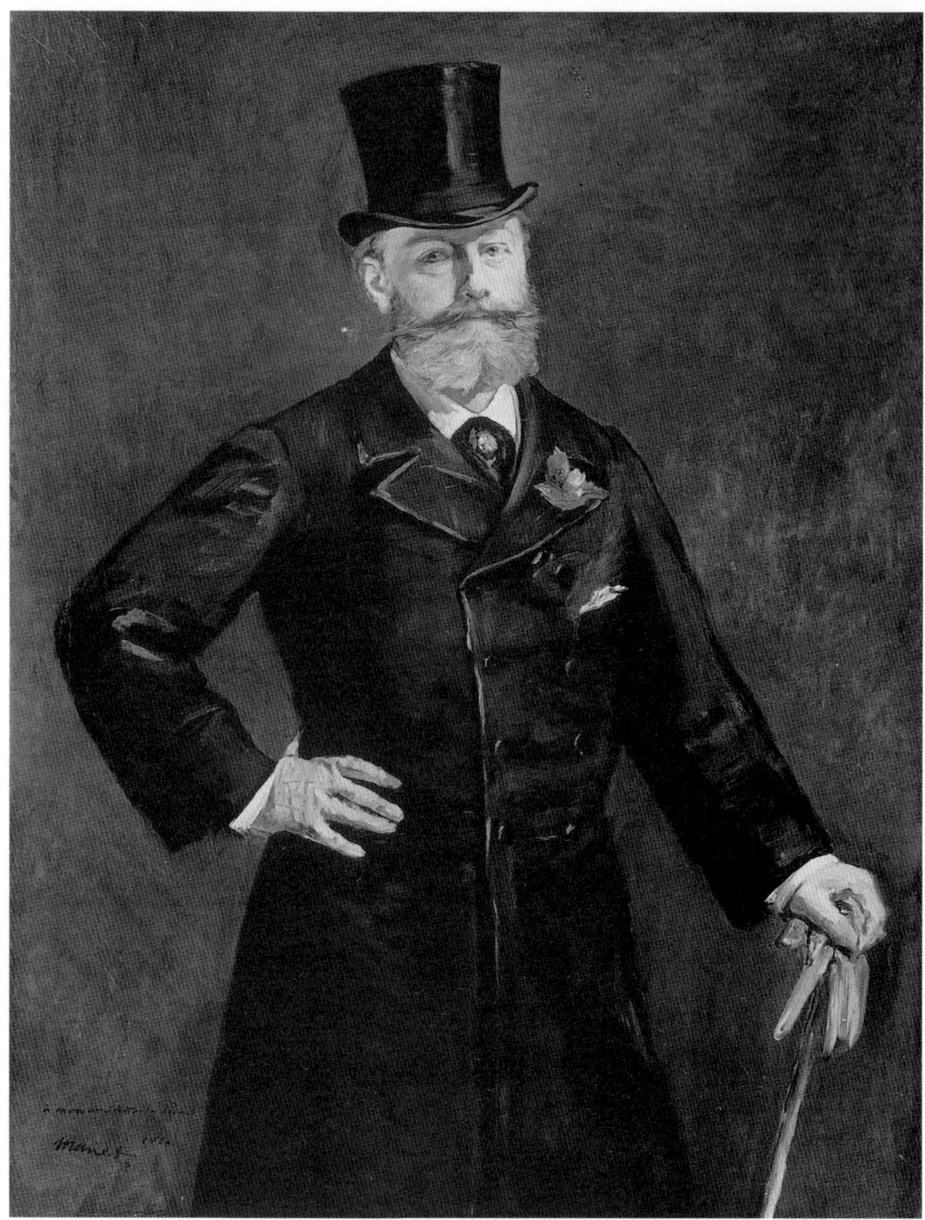

In America, applications were submitted to the Assistant Commissioner-General, Somerville P. Tuck, who maintained an office in Manhattan from which he generated circulars and dealt with prospective exhibitors. As early as November 1888, he wrote to Hawkins that applications were already coming in.[17] When applications were received, he informed artists that their exhibits would be picked up in New York, Brooklyn, or Jersey City, and that works by artists outside these cities should be sent to the New York storeroom at 1 West 14th Street before February 10, 1889.[18] He reiterated the rule that shipping charges would be paid only for items accepted by the jury and specified that each piece was to be labeled with the title, the name and address of the artist and/or owner, the return address, the price, if for sale, and the market or insurance value. Boldface print stressed that there would be no extension of time—a rule not always observed.

Simultaneously with soliciting applicants through announcements in periodicals, Hawkins approached the most important art organizations in New York: the National Academy of Design (NAD), the Society of American Artists (SAA), and the Society of American Wood Engravers (SAWE). He proposed that they choose delegates to the New York jury. Written into the minutes of the NAD's council meeting of November 5, 1888, is Hawkins's proposal for an "open expression of views as to the methods to be employed to secure the best results and also, for the further purpose of selecting a jury to pass upon exhibits which may be presented for acceptance and exhibition." From the NAD, Hawkins requested the names of twelve artists, including one from Boston and one from Philadelphia and two alternates. The SAA was asked to submit five names.[19]

The NAD selected five figure painters—J. G. Brown, Walter Shirlaw, Frank D. Millet, Edgar M. Ward, and George W. Maynard (along with alternates Charles Y. Turner, George B. Butler, and Wordsworth Thompson, who painted figures and landscapes)—and five landscape painters—William Hart, H. Bolton Jones, Jervis McEntee, Thomas Moran, and Worthington Whittredge (with J. R. Brevoort as alternate). Thomas Allen was chosen from Boston and Thomas Hovenden from Philadelphia.[20] The SAA submitted the names of J. Carroll Beckwith, William A. Coffin, Kenyon Cox, Augustus Saint-Gaudens, and J. Alden Weir.[21] By approaching these two organizations, Hawkins ensured that the New York jury would be composed of both advanced and conservative artists. That two of the men chosen by the NAD had worked abroad, and that William Merritt Chase, president of the SAA, was elected an associate of the NAD that year, testifies to the infiltration of avant-garde artists into the Academy, forecasting its eventual merging with the SAA in 1905. Worthington Whittredge (NAD) was elected president of the jury and Kenyon Cox (SAA) secretary. By encouraging the participation of the two organizations, Hawkins assembled the broadest possible representation; departing from the procedure at previous fairs, where the works had been chosen by collectors and dealers, he placed the selection in the hands of the artists themselves.

Not everyone asked to serve on the New York jury was enthusiastic about participating. Jervis McEntee pleaded that he was busy with "private affairs"; only because Whittredge and others urged him to accept did he reluctantly agree to serve. All the other nominees replied in the affirmative between November 23 and 24, 1888, but they soon found reasons for missing meetings. McEntee, who often complained about the encroachment of French painting in America, gave up his chance to choose works that would show Europeans what was going on in the United States; he never made the preliminary meeting on December 15 and eventually resigned.[22] He was replaced by Arthur Parton.

The jury pared down the more than 300 submissions to 190, which "in the opinion of those in a position to know . . . will be the most creditable to American art of any ever sent out of the country."[23] If the 190 paintings selected in New York were indeed sent to the Exposition, it means that the majority of the 336 paintings in the United States section came from the painters at home. However, since reviews from Paris indicate that the work of the expatriates dominated the exhibition, some of the 190 must have been paintings by expatriates. Two such cases were *The Amateur* by Alexander Harrison, from the collection of the Art Institute of Chicago, and William Dannat's *The Quartette*, from the collection of the Metropolitan Museum of Art, both of which came directly from the States to the Paris jury at the request of the artists, both expatriates.

Generally speaking, American artists resident in the United States sent a maximum of three paintings each, whereas Paris-based artists sent as many as six. The differential may have been due in part to the expense of shipping pictures abroad. Two jury members, William Hart and Thomas Moran, did not enter any paintings. Daniel Huntington, president of the NAD, submitted only one work, a historical genre piece, and Whittredge, president of the jury, contributed two Barbizon-tinged landscapes. The jury members were predominantly conservative academicians whose landscapes and genre paintings were considered old-fashioned in comparison with the nonnarrative, figurative work of SAA affiliates. Seven of them contributed only one painting each, four entered two works, and five sent three. Cox and Chase were the exceptions. Cox sent four, while Chase entered eight, more than any other artist at home or abroad. His plethora of entries did not go unnoticed. One reporter deduced that many artists must have withdrawn in favor of Chase, "which is very kind of them."[24] It may be that so many of Chase's paintings were accepted for exhibition because the jury thought his work would have great appeal overseas. His Munich-styled portraits and brightly colored landscapes, prefiguring his approach in the 1890s, were more avant-garde than the works of most other artists in New York. Unlike the exuberant, prolific Chase, most artists did not have suitable paintings on hand; it was a recurrent lament among them that, given the short notice, they lacked time to prepare works appropriate for the Exposition.

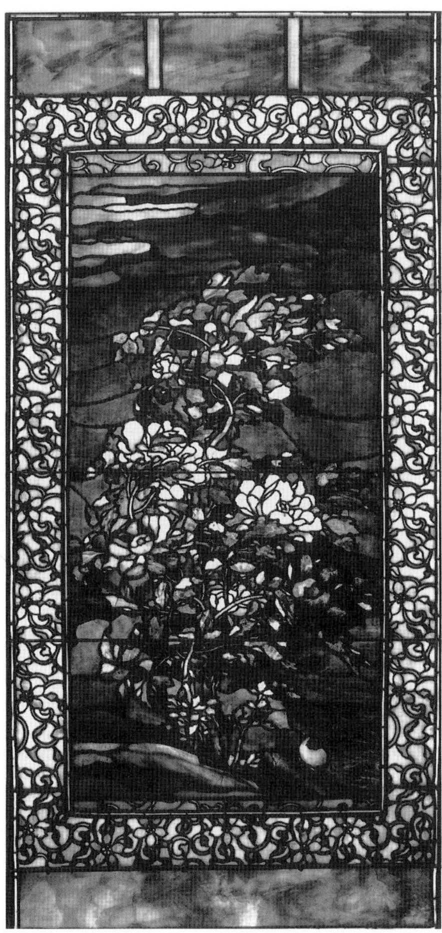

3.
John La Farge (1835–1910)
Peonies Blown in the Wind, c. 1889
Leaded glass window, 56½ x 26½″
(143.5 x 67.3 cm)
The Nelson-Atkins Museum of Art, Kansas City, Missouri. Photograph courtesy Christie's, New York

In giving the major art organizations the opportunity to select a jury from their own ranks, Hawkins's objective was to be equitable, but no jury is entirely satisfactory to everyone. This jury was beset with problems of absenteeism and with requests for exceptions. Because of a clause in Circular 3 giving the Commissioners the power to override jury decisions, solicitation of the Commissioners for personal consideration was constant, as Hawkins's letters record. One unaffiliated artist complained to Hawkins that he and others like him had been given short shrift by the jury.[25] The Commissioner, as usual, upheld the jury's decision. People peripherally associated with the Commission petitioned for special dispensations,[26] and in some cases exceptions were made. Commissioner-General William Buel Franklin wrote to Hawkins explaining that John La Farge had been ill and therefore could not get his paintings in on time. "I will be very glad if something of his can go. I like him, and if any of his productions would do us credit, I hope they will get in."[27] None of La Farge's paintings were included in the Exposition, but stained-glass windows such as the *Watson Window* (Trinity Church, Buffalo) and *Peonies* (Nelson-Atkins Museum of Art, Kansas City) won him a first-class medal in Group III, class 19 (see fig. 3).[28]

One problem that arose in New York was whether paintings in America by expatriate artists should be judged by the New York jury in order to save shipping expenses and help to balance the European and American applications. It was the opinion of the committee in Paris that any paintings by American expatriates sent from the States should be judged in Paris. Somerville Tuck, working with Hawkins, made an exception for expatriate Elihu Vedder's four paintings and submitted them to the New York jury, which accepted the lot.[29]

The selection process was not easy. Objections arose not only within the ranks of the artists but also among outside observers. James Fairman, a correspondent for the *Tribune*, regarded the management of the jury as "chaotic blundering" and suggested that a "complete default would be preferable to deliberate disgrace"; not enough representative painters were being chosen because of "the indifference of American artists to the Paris exhibition," owing to dissatisfaction with the insurance provisions and the lack of guarantee of acceptance.[30]

"Some of the American artists are not satisfied with the way in which they have been treated by the committee on American art at the Paris International Exposition, and talk of a 'bolt,'" said a reporter in the *Boston Transcript*. He listed the artists who would not be represented: "Bierstadt, De Haas, William Hart, the Morans, Homer, F. E. Church, Inness, La Farge, Lippincott, Shirlaw, Dielman, Millet, Warner and Saint-Gaudens. The list might be longer, and not prove anything to the prejudice of the committee. It is not to be expected that all, or even a majority, of the American artists will be represented at Paris. Many would abstain from exhibiting under any circumstances. It is to be expected naturally that those Americans who reside in France will be more interested than those who stay at home."[31] In point of fact, Edward Moran, Walter Shirlaw, Frank Millet, Mauritz De Haas, George Inness, and Olin Warner were represented. Thus, although some critics were quick to insinuate that the jury was prejudiced, America's most renowned and influential artists participated.[32] It was the less well known, home-based artists who were left out.

Two artists who declined to participate—George Inness and Alexander Wyant—were represented nonetheless. Inness had resolved not to enter because he was gathering work for a solo exhibition. Hawkins, who felt strongly that Inness should contribute, took matters into his own hands and, without consulting the artist, borrowed one of his paintings from the American Art Association. Although some disapproved of Hawkins's action, others, like J. Carroll Beckwith, held that Hawkins was within his rights to make sure that America showed the best and broadest range of its artists. The *Art Amateur* suggested that Hawkins's behavior in the Inness case was "rather high-handed" but defended the general, saying that "it was his duty to get a proper representation of American artists." Incensed by Hawkins's action, Inness persuaded Alexander Wyant not to participate.[33] Hawkins, his appeals to Wyant apparently unsuccessful, borrowed one of the artist's works from a private collector. Another reluctant participant, Eastman Johnson, yielded to Hawkins's entreaties. Thomas Moran, regarded as a spokesman for the malcontents, sent only an illustration—probably his way of protesting the treatment of Inness.[34]

The absence from the American paintings display of a few well-known artists was mainly due to extraneous circumstances. Winslow Homer, probably because he had not painted many oils at the end of the eighties, submitted only a grisaille version of his watercolor *Looking Over the Cliff* (shown in the drawing section). As for the absence of Frederick Stuart Church, popular for his watercolors and illustrations, his statement that he had been informed by the Commissioner that no watercolors or etchings would be shown can be discounted because Eakins sent *Negro Boy Dancing* (then titled *The Dancing Lesson*) and Weir showed *Preparing for Christmas* (unlocated), both highly finished watercolors that were exhibited among the oil paintings.[35] More serious was Church's political reason for withholding work: "Any nation that put a 30% duty on foreign works of art and refused to pass an international copyright law had better take a back seat in the matter of foreign exhibitions."[36]

The article in the *New York Herald* in which Church was quoted devoted a full paragraph to the unrepresented artists, mentioning Maynard, who, although he was on the jury, sent nothing because he did not have appropriate works available. And the renowned elder master Frederic E. Church, handicapped by rheumatoid arthritis, was more or less inactive by 1889. Frank Duveneck, a member of the American committee in Paris, did not submit a picture because his wife had died in 1888 and he was preoccupied with creating her memorial tomb. Although Mary Cassatt had exhibited in 1878, she did not show in the

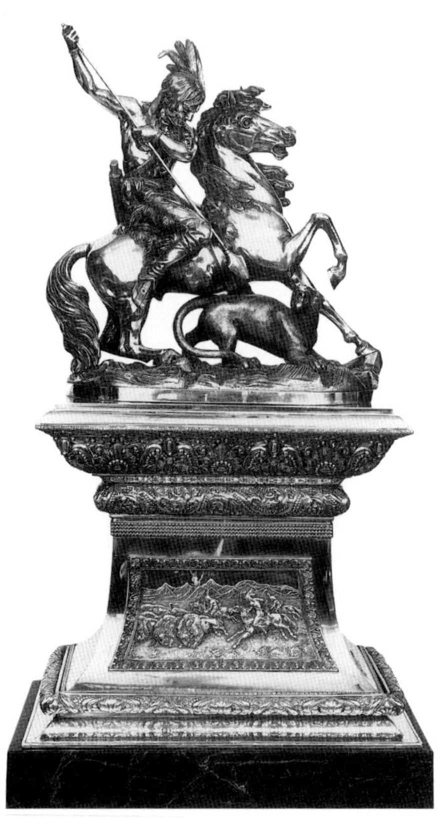

4.
Theodore Baur (1835–after 1902) for Meridian Britannica Co.
Indian Spearing a Mountain Lion, c. 1880
Silvered-bronze equestrian sculpture on parcel-gilt stand, height 37¾" (96 cm)
The Paul Singer Foundation, New York

1889 fair, probably because she had spent much of the previous year recuperating from a serious riding accident.[37] There were corresponding lacunae in the French fine arts section, which included the Exposition Centennale, a display of 100 years of French art, as well as in the Exposition Décennale, the display of contemporary French art. Although in the Centennale there were a few paintings by some still controversial Impressionist artists like Monet and Pissarro, others, like Degas and Renoir, were not represented. Degas had declined because by the end of the 1880s he was sufficiently well established to forgo participation in group exhibitions; Renoir felt that nothing of his was worthy of the Exposition.[38]

Despite some resistance, Hawkins was instrumental in assembling an impressive group of American paintings to represent this country abroad. Collectors such as William T. Evans, who generously lent at least eight paintings, greatly aided the Commissioner. In contrast, so famous a patron of American art as Thomas B. Clarke, according to the *New York Herald*, "was acting like an enemy and refused to lend anything from his collection." The *Herald* suggested that Clarke resented not having been appointed Commissioner of Fine Arts.[39] Clearly Hawkins's taste and judgment helped to shape the exhibition. He insisted that a full range of artistic examples be included in order to show the art of the United States to advantage.

In addition to those who were pressured into participating, there were some who willingly submitted paintings but were rejected. The *Art Amateur* reported, "This is one side of the situation: artists refusing to be represented at the Paris Exposition. Another phase is the jury's refusal to accept pictures by men who by virtue of their position, if for no other reason, should have been considered 'hors concours' [allowed to enter without jury review because of past accomplishments]." This issue came up frequently, especially for the American jury in Paris. "And what can the jury say in justice of rejecting Bierstadt's *The Last of the Buffalo* . . . ?" asked the *Art Amateur*'s critic, who called himself Montezuma. "Being thoroughly American, it, doubtless, would have proved highly interesting to the foreign visitors to the Exposition; but this fair-minded jury, which had allowed some of the younger painters to send as many as half a dozen canvases each, and has placidly admitted the work of mere novices, puts itself on record as deciding that Mr. Bierstadt, a veteran of established reputation, cannot paint well enough to earn a place even in such a miscellaneous collection of pictures as has been sent over to represent the United States at the Exposition."[40]

One of the jurors, J. G. Brown, said that the painting was rejected because it was too big and also because it did not represent Bierstadt at his best.[41] In other quarters the jury's decision was defended as "perfectly in accordance with the aims of the cosmopolitan show. Only pictures painted since 1878 and representing the advance made in American art since that period were desired by the committee in charge of the exhibit at New York. Neither [William Wetmore] Story as a sculptor, nor Bierstadt as a painter has contributed to the progress of American art for many years and even in America they have had their day."[42] Yet the "Wild West" was of interest to foreigners, and the subjects of Indians and buffalo hunting were combined in a silvered bronze sculpture displayed in the American decorative arts section (see fig. 4).

Story's work was eventually accepted, but Bierstadt's was not. Nor was this Bierstadt's first experience with rejection; his paintings had been turned down at other exhibitions.[43] Bierstadt is representative of the many painters of the Hudson River and Rocky Mountain schools whose works had, by the mid-seventies, become unfashionable. The 1889 rejection proclaimed the demise of

Bierstadt's career. Some Hudson River painters, among them Whittredge and McEntee, while criticizing the preference for French painting, superimposed Barbizon characteristics on their former, more exacting, style in order to conform to current taste. That one of the aims of the Paris Exposition was to show what was new perhaps motivated the likes of Whittredge and McEntee to submit large-scale updated landscapes to this global art market.

As well as conspicuous omissions, the *New York Herald* listed, albeit incompletely, the paintings chosen to go to Paris. The artist J. B. Bristol wrote to Hawkins suggesting that a comprehensive selection list be published, but so far as is known it never appeared.[44] Boston singled out its own representatives: Frank Benson, J. Foxcroft Cole, George Fuller, Walter Gay, Benjamin C. Porter, Edmund Tarbell, and Frank H. Tompkins; for sculpture, Daniel Chester French; and the architectural firm of McKim, Mead and White for a perspective of Bates Hall in the Boston Public Library.[45] Ultimately over 400 works of art in all categories by 116 artists were packed into 61 crates, stored on February 22, and shipped a month later, on March 23. On March 9, with less than two months to opening date, Hawkins had left for Paris.[46]

While an exposition in Paris may have seemed remote to painters based in the United States, for American artists living in Europe this was a convenient chance to demonstrate their achievements in an international arena. The expatriates met on April 7, 1888, at the Grand Hotel in Paris, seven months earlier than their colleagues in New York. They resolved that a committee of 19 American artists working in Paris would constitute the sole jury to judge the work of American artists abroad. This committee, which eventually became the jury, agreed to work in conjunction with any other committees of American artists at home or abroad in order to "secure as large and representative a collection of American art as possible," and "to make the American Art Department of the International Exhibition at Paris of the year 1889 the equal of any foreign Art Department there."[47]

Frederick Bridgman was elected president of the Parisian committee, Ridgway Knight and Alexander Harrison vice-presidents, and George Hitchcock secretary. The highly successful expatriate Bridgman, who at the 1878 fair had not only won a silver medal but also been named a Chevalier of the Legion of Honor, was a natural choice as leader. The jury comprised painters William Dannat, Frank Duveneck, Walter Gay, George P. A. Healy, Gari Melchers, Henry Mosler, Charles S. Pearce, Charles Reinhart, John S. Sargent, Edward Simmons, Julius L. Stewart, Eugene Vail, Edwin L. Weeks, and the sculptors Paul W. Bartlett and Henry H. Kitson; most of these artists had exhibited and won awards at the Salon. Alternate members were Charles Davis, Henry Bacon, Frank Boggs, Clifford Grayson, William Howe, Julius Rolshoven, Julian Story, and Robert Vonnoh. It was thought that a large committee, following the example of the Salon jury, would ensure sufficient attendance at meetings, would distribute responsibility, and would prevent personal prejudice from playing a role in the selection of paintings. A large committee also meant that many more artists would participate.[48] The officers of the committee, acting on behalf of the American artists in Europe, kept Hawkins apprised of their activities. By December 1888, the committee was writing home for circulars to distribute among the expatriate artists and was also working to secure adequate space at the Exposition.

The correspondence between Hawkins and the Paris committee gives the impression of impartial treatment, but after the American galleries at the Exposition were opened, letters to the editor of the Paris edition of the *New York*

Herald pointed out injustices. One irate writer reported that there were "members of the jury that are not speaking as they pass by. . . ."[49] The scandal erupted when the installations were viewed, because the committee had placed their own enormous, canvases in the best positions. In addition, artists who were not members of the committee protested on several grounds: they had been excluded by the "ring" that had been formed before the first meeting, at the Grand Hotel; at that meeting they had allegedly been presented with two alternative ballot slates which in fact hardly differed; and they suspected foul play in the tally of votes. A letter to the Paris *Herald* signed "Vigil" characterized the jury as including "some whose intense selfishness and disregard for the rights of others finally grew to be the common scandal of the studios" and described how they "very leisurely in a body visited each other's studios and went through the farce of passing judgement on themselves. It is notorious now that only in the case of one of the seventeen [*sic*] was any demur made to anything offered by these gentlemen. . . ."[50] Although the French dealer Georges Sedelmeyer "kindly offered one of his large galleries to the committee of American artists for use in examination of pictures by the jury of admission to the Universal Exhibition," the jury apparently used it to judge everyone else's work but their own.[51]

The 1889 catalogue of paintings (see pages 267–97) reveals that most of the "gentlemen" on the Paris jury entered as many as six paintings each, while non-jurors entered only three or four. In New York, except for Chase and Cox, jurors and others sent only three. And as "Vigil" specified, many of the paintings submitted by the jury were enormous; in addition, some had recently been exhibited at the Salon or at previous expositions, such as the one in Munich the year before. Other letters, concurring and contradicting, appeared. While most writers used noms de plume, Alexander Harrison, vice-president of the Paris committee, wrote under his own name, defending the jury's actions. He said its primary goal was to make a good showing but that "unavoidable mistakes due to exactions of limited space, of symmetry in hanging the pictures, and—as man is mortal—of some clashing of individual interests" were made. But a writer signing himself "Hors Concours" persisted. Two days later he wrote that regardless of what Harrison thought, "a ring had rejected pictures which have artistic values much greater in several instances than had some of those accepted."[52]

How much of the controversy was based on fact and how much was due to petty jealousy is difficult to determine. The *Boston Transcript*'s regular correspondent, who thought that Hawkins was more abused by dissatisfied artists and their supporters in the press than any other commissioner, came to this conclusion: "There can be no doubt whatever that the exhibition has presented a very remarkable display of American art, and it is almost equally certain that its success would have been very much less had no member of the jury been allowed to hang more than one or two pictures, and all the space thus gained had been given to works which, matters being arranged as they were, have been left out in the cold. It is not surprising that there should have been lamentation and gnashing of teeth among those who had sent or brought their pictures from Munich, Dresden and all parts of the continent and were given to understand that they had better take them back, inasmuch as the Parisianized Americans wanted all or nearly all the available space; but is there not the same gnashing of teeth among hundreds of *refusés* every year just before the Salon opens?"[53] Faultfinders turned up among the French as well, causing Commissioner Proust to reflect, "The secret of satisfying everybody has not yet been discovered."[54]

5.
William Wetmore Story (1819–1895)
Salome, 1871
Marble, height 57" (144.8 cm)
© The Metropolitan Museum of Art, New York, Gift of William Nelson, 1896. 97.9

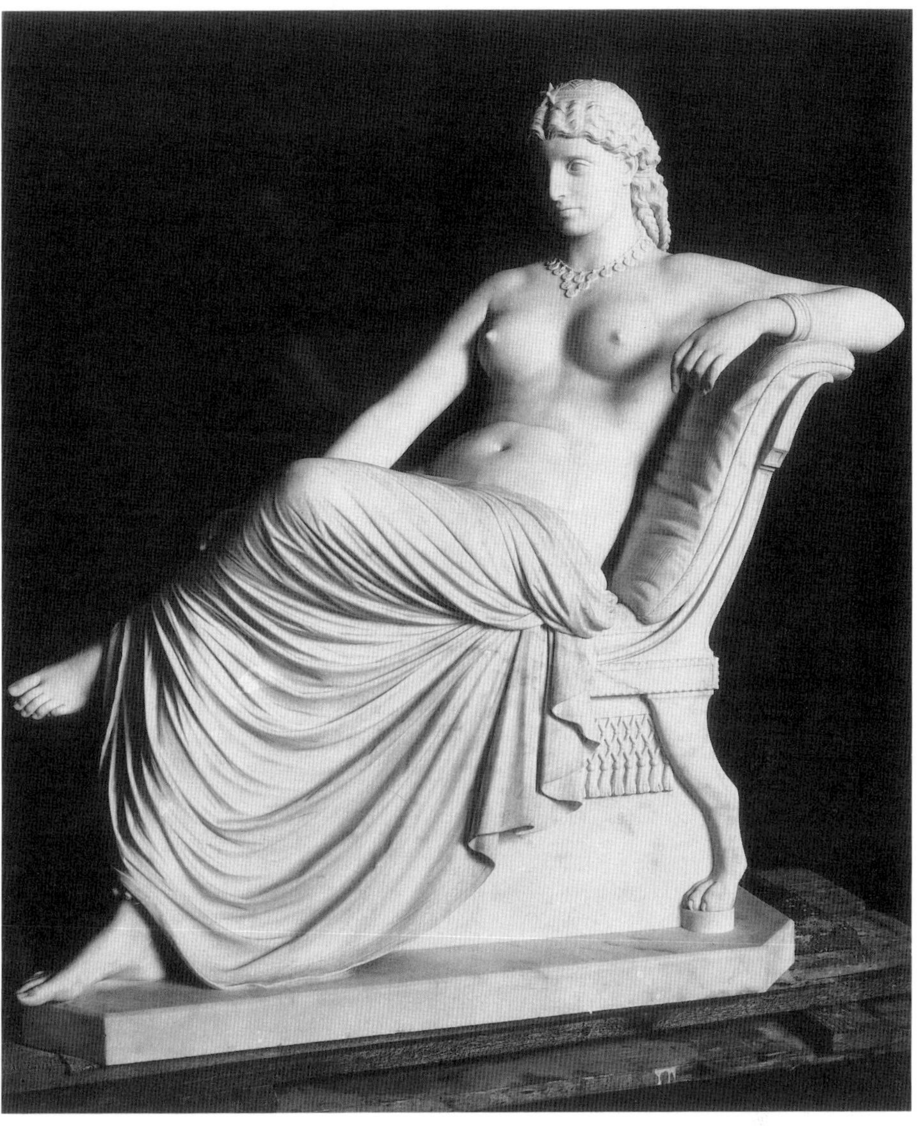

In general, Hawkins refrained from interfering in jury selections, maintaining that the artists had elected their peers to represent them and therefore had to accept their decisions. Two cases in which Hawkins and the jury were persuaded to change their minds involved the painter Elizabeth Jane Gardner and the sculptor William Wetmore Story.[55] Not much is known about the Gardner turnabout, but her status as *hors concours* at the Salon and her association with William Bouguereau, whom she married in 1896, probably aided her. The Story case is documented by letters in the Hawkins archives. Julian Story, the sculptor's son, and others argued that the rejected marble statue, *Salome*, 1871 (fig. 5), which had already been shipped to Paris, should be exhibited because of the sculptor's renown and his advanced age. Hawkins was petitioned but answered that he would abide by the jury's decision, "believing, as ever, that its action will surely be for the best interest of all concerned."[56] To the jury he said that if they changed their minds they should publish a statement explaining that Story's work was not being accepted "on its merits as a work of art."[57] Sargent, Dannat, and Melchers were jury members who were influential

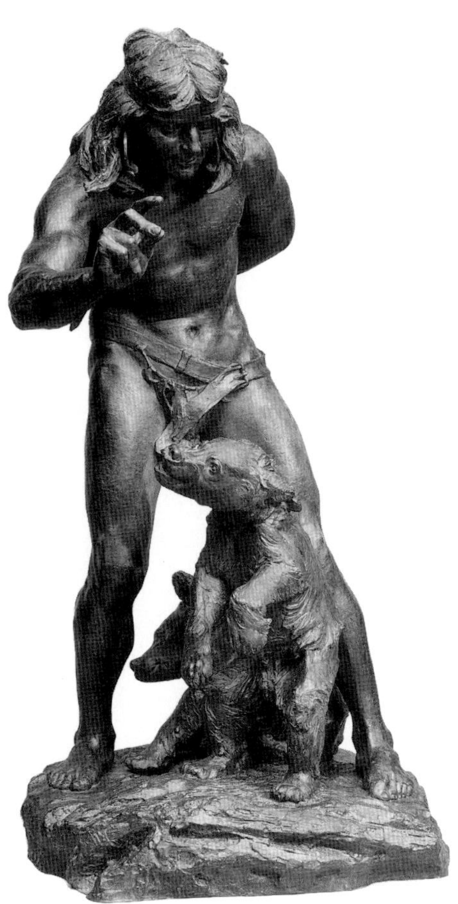

6.
Paul Wayland Bartlett (1865–1925)
The Bohemian Bear Tamer, 1887
Bronze, height 68½" (173.2 cm)
© The Metropolitan Museum of Art, New York, Gift of an Association of Gentlemen. 1891. 91.14

in the decision to exhibit the large statue even "if it should be a little old fashioned."[58] The acceptance of a retardataire piece of such huge dimensions was quite a concession, especially considering that there seems to have been only one other major sculpture, Paul Bartlett's *Bohemian Bear Tamer* (fig. 6), in the American exhibit.

Other exceptions were made on the basis of good connections. Alice D. Kellogg, while a student in Paris, wrote home that paintings and sketches sent by students at the Académie Julian were accepted at the Salon because the teachers at Julian's saw to it that their pupils' works were admitted.[59] Such bias existed in connection with the Exposition as well. Agnes O'Halloran, a pupil and paramour of George Hitchcock, secretary of the Paris jury, definitely was accepted because of her relationship with him.[60] Interestingly, of the sixteen women who contributed to the American section, not one, no matter how successful, was on the Paris committee/jury—but neither were such well-known expatriate artists as Charles "Shorty" Lasar (who taught many Americans in his classes at Concarneau and Paris), William P. W. Dana, and Charles Forbes.

Indeed an inner clique of zealous men concerned about America's artistic reputation made up the jury, and they claimed special privileges. Partly this was because they believed that their work would make the best showing in this international setting. However, they endeavored to acquire a broad sampling. Bridgman even wrote to Hawkins on March 24, 1889, requesting an extension so that works delayed in transit or not yet finished could be included.[61] He argued that the fine arts galleries would probably not open until June 1, there being delays in the French section as well. Although the American section was not fully installed by the official opening day, May 5, it was ready soon after, and well before June 1.

Letters between Bridgman, Hitchcock, and Hawkins reveal that the Paris jury had, along with political problems, more logistical problems than its New York counterpart. Changes in announcements, time extensions, and problems of space were some of the issues they handled. William John Hennessy, whose paintings were delayed in transit from England, asked for an extension because the circumstances were beyond his control. He also asked to be considered *hors concours* because his pictures had "already passed juries in London . . . , had good places *on the line*," and had "passed the juries of the *salon*, and other continental exhibitions."[62] But, since each painting was judged on its merits and not accepted because of past awards, the Exposition jury had a greater degree of control than the Salon jury, which had to accept any work by an *hors concours* artist. On April 7, Bridgman wrote to Hawkins that the jury had made its last revision and would not consider any other changes.[63] The catalogue of the American paintings was then compiled, just one month before the opening.

Just as the selection of paintings provoked disputes, so did the size and location of the galleries and the installation of the paintings. The United States was assigned four galleries, one very large, and a portion of the stairway leading to its space, which was on the second floor at the north end of the Palace of Fine Arts (fig. 7).[64] When Hawkins arrived in Paris, he was shocked to find that the space allotted to the Americans was upstairs and adjacent to the galleries of Belgium, Sweden, and Greece, instead of on the main floor, where Great Britain, Russia, and even Spain and Italy were located. The French occupied one entire side of the building, while the other side was reserved for foreign art.[65] America's disadvantageous placement "was the mistake of the representative of the United States, who was on the ground before the arrival of General Hawkins, who came too late to correct the blunder," declared Montezuma.[66]

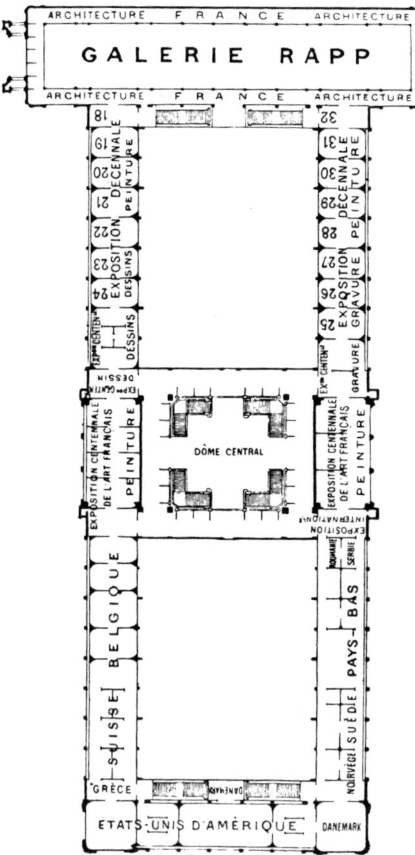

7.
Plan of the American Galleries
Second floor, Palais des Beaux-Arts
Exposition Universelle de 1889

Visitors complained that the location was inconvenient and that after walking through all the galleries of French art they arrived at the American section tired and satiated.

To make matters worse, the French authorities, as Montezuma reported, gave away part of the space outside the main American gallery to "some of the petty Balkan states. Then the American eagle did scream and no mistake." Hawkins threatened to withdraw the entire American exhibit if the space was not restored. "This firmness had the desired effect, and after that the Commissioner and his associates on the Jury had only to meet the enmity of their own countrymen, which has lasted unremittingly almost to the present writing. Without any reserve, the American newspapers in Paris seem to have given the freedom of their columns to every disaffected artist whose picture has been rejected, or has been hung differently from the way desired by him." Hawkins was criticized by the press because of "the chaos that reigned in that department a little while before the opening . . . but I hardly know of another man who would have had the nerve he has shown in defending the rights of the artists of the United States against the official annoyances to which they have been subjected."[67]

Again Hawkins had to come to the rescue of his artistic charges. But even the stalwart general had no control over the battle for space. A. Bailly Blanchard, secretary of the United States commission in France, had written to Commissioner-General Franklin on December 10, 1888, that Antonin Proust, who was in charge of the apportionment of space, was familiar with the work of American expatriate artists because he had seen it at the Salons, but not with the work of artists from the States. Nevertheless, he recognized the importance of representing both contingents fairly. The American artists in Paris requested 1,800 square meters (19,375.7 sq. ft.), while the group from home asked for 2,500 square meters (26,910.7 sq. ft.). But the Fine Arts Palace was not big enough to meet these demands.[68] Somerville Tuck wrote to Hawkins on the same day, December 10, informing him that Proust had allotted the entire American contingent only 1,750 square meters (18,837.5 sq. ft.) of wall surface.[69] On January 26, 1889, Blanchard wrote to Franklin, "Although I have not been successful in securing the amount of space desired by you, still by persistent and repeated efforts, I have obtained for our exhibit one third more space than has been allotted to any other country."[70] In the event, the Americans were assigned more space than any other foreign nation—1,950 square meters (20,990.3 sq. ft.) of wall area, which included the space above each door.

By the time spatial limitations became known, too many paintings had been selected, and members of the jury were asked to reduce the number of their entries. Some balked while others cooperated, suggesting which of their works should be eliminated. Walter Gay requested "that the large picture of 'La Charité' [see page 153] be exhibited as it is my last work and in the opinion of the artists would do me credit at the Exposition. I would rather have any of the others taken away before this one."[71] William Dana agreed to "unite in this self-sacrifice" even though he had submitted only four works and, because of the Exposition, had not sent anything to the Salon that spring. Davis resented being asked to give up a picture, since he had sent only four whereas others had sent six; he suggested that the sizes of the works determine the number.[72] Alexander Harrison offered to withdraw *The Amateurs* and *Le Crépuscule*, "although I honestly think if these works were hung they would help to sustain the standard of the exhibition. . . . I think it would be a pity if in our section any good work were replaced by any mediocre or bad one."[73] Most of the jury's work was eventually accommodated; Davis and Dana showed four each, Gay and Harrison six. The *Boston Transcript* reported, "The American section, which is exceedingly creditable to the nation, occupies two large rooms with oil paintings alone. If all the pictures sent in had been hung, much more wall space would have been needed for them than that allotted to the section."[74] If any paintings were in fact eliminated during the installation, it cannot be determined from existing documents and photographs.

As with everything else, the business of installation was complicated by politics, and Hawkins was once again on the firing line. In planning the arrangements for the American paintings section, he had suggested early on that American art would be seen to advantage if the work of artists residing in the States was separated from the work of those residing in Europe. This would enable each jury, the one in New York and the one in Paris, to hang the pictures it had chosen. The plan was discussed and apparently agreed to by the NAD, the SAA, and the expatriates in Paris.[75] Hawkins wrote to Hitchcock asking his advice about this matter, and on April 17, 1889, Hitchcock replied, quoting the bylaws of the committee of American artists in Paris: "For the purpose of hanging pictures the jury shall be divided into sections to consist of not more than four or less than three members whose action shall be subject to a revision by the whole body of the jury."[76] Each group of jurors would hang one wall; thereby the responsibility and the work would be distributed. The consensus was that members of the jury were best qualified to install because they were most familiar with the pictures.

Installation photographs used to illustrate Hawkins's report to Congress depict three walls of the expatriate artists' gallery and one wall of the smaller gallery where the works of artists from home were hung. In the larger gallery are seen enormous Salon-size machines in prominent positions, with smaller pieces crammed into corners and between other paintings (see figs. 20–23). The photograph of the stateside gallery features the work of SAA members Cox, Beckwith, and Weir and of other artists, such as Eastman Johnson, who were influenced by French painting. Thus, for photographs intended for permanent record, and to document the American contribution, paintings in the international style were clearly favored. The works of the more retardataire Daniel Huntington, Whittredge, and McEntee, it can be assumed, were either on the unphotographed walls or in locations outside the main gallery.

While the plan to separate the two contingents of American artists was adhered to, the idea of grouping all the works by one artist together was not entirely feasible, probably because of spatial limitations. No more than two or three of the paintings by artists who had multiple entries were clustered. In fact, the installation photographs reveal that in many cases all the paintings by one artist were not even hung in the same room. Individual artists did not complain about the lack of clustering but rather about placement. Carl Gutherz, whose painting *Lux Incarnationis* (see page 162) was skied above a door, wrote to Hawkins a few days after the opening that he resented not being placed on the line. "I now claim for my picture a first class place, because it is not only a first class work, but because it is also a large and unusual subject, because it is one of the most original works in the entire exhibition."[77] Another disgruntled artist griped that the five members of the hanging committee, "the sacred five," had favored their own works and surrounded them with "inoffensive wall coverings."[78]

General criticism of the installation was mixed, with the majority favoring the expatriates' gallery. Theodore Child thought the separation of expatriate and stateside artists invited a comparison disastrous to the artists living in America; Mariana van Rensselaer concurred: "Only the American painters living abroad were well represented. The shipment from home very inadequately showed what is really being done at home."[79] But an examination of NAD and SAA exhibition records reveals that Mrs. van Rensselaer's statement was not entirely accurate. Most well-known stateside artists were represented, partly owing to Hawkins's intervention. "Vigil" maintained that the gallery with pictures from America was the best and most unbiased room: "Here someone had been at work whose taste, judgement, and honesty were equal to caring for the rights of all and making a satisfactory *ensemble*."[80] On the whole, careful study of the photographs and written reports supports the opinion that the installation favored the work of European-influenced artists.

An international jury was chosen to decide on the awards to exhibitors. As early as February 1889, Hitchcock, as secretary of the Paris jury, sent Hawkins the following resolution: "The jury having been elected by the American artists in Paris feel that they should have a voice in the selection of a member of the international jury of awards." There were three positions open to Americans on this jury, and "one of the members," Hitchcock wrote, "ought to be our nominee."[81] From New York, Beckwith appealed to Hawkins: "It is to be hoped that a proper representation of the residents here and abroad can be made. Mr. [William] Coffin is to be in Paris late in May and would be a good representative from this side. Of course if one of the older men of the Academy can be attained he would be most acceptable to the men here."[82] In the end, the American representatives to the international jury were Hawkins, Dannat, and Pearce for painting, Julius Stewart for wood-engraving, and Paul W. Bartlett and Henry Bisbing as alternates for painting and wood-engraving, respectively—clearly all expatriates and none of the "older men of the Academy." At the first meeting of the international jury the French painter Ernest Meissonier was elected president, the Dutch genre painter Daniel Adolf Constant Artz vice-president, the critic and painter Georges Lafenestre reporter, and the American expatriate William Dannat secretary. In view of the size and importance of the United States exhibit, Hawkins had been nominated for vice-president, but he received only seven votes because he was not an artist. Dannat was elected unanimously.[83]

The international jury met on June 12, and the awards were presented on June 24. America earned a total of 57 awards and 24 honorable mentions. Grand prizes were awarded to Melchers and Sargent; gold medals (1st class) to Alexander Harrison, Vail, and Weeks; silver medals (2nd class) to 14 artists; and bronze (3rd class) to 38.[84] Winners of silver and gold medals had to pay for their medallions but bronze medals were complimentary (see fig. 8). Almost half of the American painters, 81 out of the 189, won recognition in some form. Those who received the highest honors were predominantly artists working abroad; their successful assimilation of European styles was rewarded by the international jury. But some old-fashioned NAD members were recognized as well—Whittredge, Brown, Henry, and McEntee, for example. Recipients were compensated further by the favorable publicity, which led to sales and commissions. One purchaser was the French government, which already owned four paintings in the American section—Gay's *Le Benedicité*, Mosler's *The Return*, Birge Harrison's *Novembre*, and Boggs's *Place de la Bastille*—and later bought three of the exhibited works—Vail's *Fishing Harbour, Concarneau*, Dannat's *A Study in Red*, and Alexander Harrison's *In Arcadia*.

Never before and never again would American art be so closely related to that of the French—in subject, style, and general sensibility—a closeness perceived as positive by some and negative by others. A French critic summed it up: "What is a little wanting in this American Exhibition is native painting on native subjects . . ." as found in the work of Ulrich, Inness, and Whittredge. Others, he continued, naming a number of expatriates, are "good recruits for the young American school and everything tells us that we must take it more and more into serious consideration."[85] Within a short time, many of these talented "recruits" returned to the United States to concentrate on "native subjects" and, more important, to pass on the legacy of French academic instruction.

Like all the other aspects of this American venture, the awards aroused mixed reactions: some artists were elated, while others were dissatisfied. Ridgway Knight complained to Antonin Proust that his high standing, acquired after twenty years of work in France, was compromised by the second-class medal he received in competition with his compatriots; *Hailing the Ferry* had already attained equal or higher recompense at the Salon. Since he lost by only two votes, he appealed to Proust for support.[86] Proust's reaction to this sort of complaint can be gathered from the statement he made two years later that the system of rewards was childish.[87] The issue of the medals may seem trivial, but it did determine status in later exhibitions and was important for the marketing of paintings. Although Knight was disappointed with his silver medal, the young John Douglas Patrick was delighted with his bronze, which in fact marked the pinnacle of his career.

In the long run, the most prized forms of recognition were those bestowed by the Legion of Honor. Of the four Legion of Honor designations—Grand Officier, Commandeur, Officier, and Chevalier—Franklin, as Commissioner-General, was named Commandeur, the next-to-highest award. Tuck and Hawkins were named Officiers and Dannat was named Chevalier. Hawkins, to his credit, recommended all American members of the international jury to the Legion of Honor's committee because as jurors they were ineligible to receive medals. He had also recommended Knight and Edwin Austin Abbey, although they were not on the international jury.[88] Bisbing, an alternate juror, complained about being left out in the cold. Alexander Harrison was named Officier d'Académie for his outstanding abilities as a teacher and received the accompanying Palmes Académiques from the French government, but he was dissatisfied and returned the award. He thought of it as a lesser honor and also objected to his being the only American artist to receive one of these awards.[89] There were even those who thought that Dannat, to protest the fact that he was the only American artist to receive the Legion of Honor award in October 1889, should decline the Chevalier. So many artists complained about the paucity of Legion awards that it would appear that the French reconsidered and named two other American artists in November—John Singer Sargent and Alexander Harrison. The Americans did not seem to know that groups of people were honored consecutively, one group (which included Knight, and Whistler for the British) on September 27, 1889, one on October 30, and one on November 27.[90]

Pearce, who complained to Hawkins that he was left with nothing, believed that the scarcity of Legion of Honor awards to Americans was the French way "to reply directly to our tariff on works of art."[91] But artists like Pearce acted as if Legion of Honor awards were a right and not a courtesy. Meissonier, as president of the international jury, was said to have a hand in the choice of artists to be decorated, but it was probably Antonin Proust who made recommendations to the Legion of Honor committee, and even among French artists he was accused of treating the Americans unfairly.[92] It should be remembered that

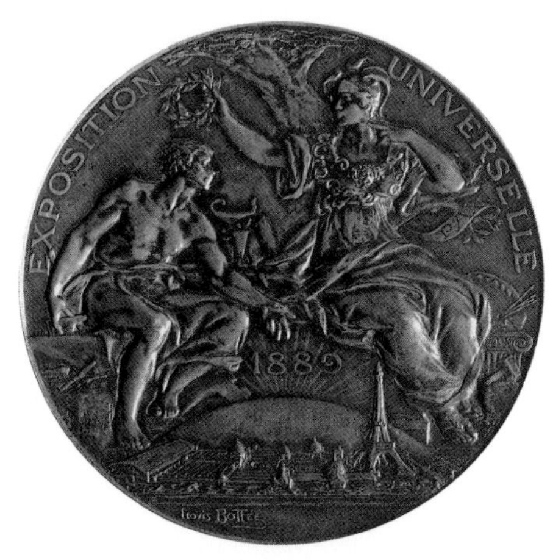

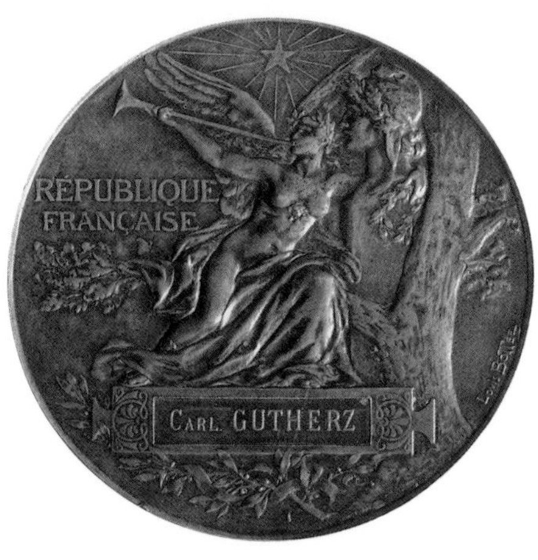

8.
Louis Alexandre Bottée (1852–1941)
Exposition Universelle 1889 third-class medal awarded to Carl Gutherz
Bronze, diameter 4½″ (11.4 cm)
Memphis Brooks Museum of Art,
Gift of Marshall and Elizabeth Goodheart

although Proust had given more space to the Americans than to any other foreign nation, they considered themselves short-changed, since they had applied earlier than any other country. Proust's chauvinistic attitude most likely affected both his decisions about space and his recommendations for awards. Like Hawkins, he was concerned about what was best for his own country, and he was as much criticized as Hawkins by the press and discontented artists.

Overall, most of the American artists considered their experience at the fair advantageous. Almost half of them had a new citation or honor to add to their résumés. Expositions were the international counterparts of the Paris Salons and the exhibitions at London's Royal Academy and New York's National Academy of Design and were significant art markets. That seven American pictures from the 1889 Exposition found their way into French museums confirms not only recognition by the French but also the value of such exposure. Private collectors in France also purchased paintings directly from the galleries at the fair. Letters in the Hawkins archives disclose that some of the paintings purchased at the fair were sold for less than their original asking price. The French government certainly paid less: it was a privilege for an artist to be represented in the national museums, and the publicity and prestige made the lower price acceptable.[93]

Many of the paintings that returned to the States were soon exhibited at museums and made available to them for purchase. Within two years of the fair, three of the paintings were bought by the Pennsylvania Academy of the Fine Arts. Other works were purchased by such famous collectors as Potter Palmer. A number of artists chose to hold on to their exhibition pieces, recycling them at every major fair. Over fifty of the paintings exhibited in 1889 were seen again, four years later, at the World's Columbian Exposition in Chicago.

At the end of the Exposition, Hawkins and his associates supervised the sale of paintings, the dismantling of the galleries, and the shipment of the works to the proper destinations. Hawkins then returned to the United States and wrote a summary of the fine arts section of the fair which was published by Congress in the *Reports of the United States Commissioners to the Universal Exposition*.

Despite mudslinging by aggrieved artists, in retrospect Hawkins proved to be evenhanded. He withstood the pressures of various factions and succeeded in presenting a broad range of American painting. Several of the exhibiting artists, among them Melchers and Pearce, remained his lifelong friends, and in 1908 Hawkins chose Melchers to paint his portrait (fig. 1). Hawkins, along with the juries, selected for the American display in Paris mainstream conventional art comparable with that seen in the French and other foreign sections. The 1889 Universal Exposition was the last world's fair at which this academic aesthetic predominated. While many of the paintings shown there reappeared at the World's Columbian Exposition, they were eclipsed by works that reflected the increasing appreciation of Impressionism. A number of the artists had returned to America, shed their academic approach in favor of a lighter palette and freer brushwork, and influenced future generations through their teaching and exhibitions of their work. Thus, while the organizational triumphs and failures of the 1889 Exposition served as useful examples for the Chicago fair, which was being launched even before the Paris fair opened, artistic preferences moved in new directions.

Notes

1. It was Napoleon III who decided to include art as well as industry, according to Maurice Brincourt, "Paris, The Coming Exhibition—International Exhibitions, Their Genesis and History . . . ," *American Architect and Building News*, 25 (March 23, 1889), p. 39.
2. For more about the 1855 and 1867 expositions, see the *Complete Official Catalogue of the Paris Universal Exhibition 1867* (London and Paris, 1867); Patricia Mainardi, *Art and Politics of the Second Empire: The Universal Expositions of 1855 and 1867* (New Haven and London, 1987); and Carol Troyen, "Innocents Abroad: American Painters at the 1867 Exposition Universelle, Paris," *American Art Journal* 16 (Autumn 1984), pp. 3–29.
3. *Reports of the United States Commissioners to the Paris Universal Exposition, 1878*, vol. I, Appendix G, p. 10. Armstrong suggested in his report that in the future American artists be given sufficient notice so that they, like the French, could prepare from five to fifteen pictures to be exhibited together. A catalogue of the American section was published at Armstrong's expense.
4. For the 1867 fair, President Lincoln had accepted the French invitation as early as 1865, but Congress delayed appropriation of funds until the last minute (recovery from the Civil War and public interest in Reconstruction made events in Paris seem remote and costly). Members of the American selection committee raised $10,000 for crating and shipping. See "Report of the Commissioner-General," *Paris Universal Exposition, 1867: Reports of the United States Commissioners* (Washington, D.C., 1870). For 1878, Congress again appropriated funds late (Dec. 1877), so that American artists did not have the opportunity to produce works expressly for the fair. Although Congress acted faster in 1889, there were still complaints of tardiness. See Theodore Stanton, "America at the Paris Exhibition," *Boston Daily Evening Transcript*, June 29, 1889, p 5. On May 10, 1888, Congress authorized $250,000 to cover general expenses, some of which went to pay for shipping and insuring the paintings.
5. Merle Curti, "America at the World Fairs, 1851–1893," *American Historical Review*, 55 (July 1950), p. 836. I am grateful to Judith Hayward for bringing this article to my attention.
6. M.P.K., "In Paris Next Summer," *Boston Daily Evening Transcript*, Nov. 27, 1888, p. 4.
7. Theodore Stanton, "The Paris Exhibition," *Boston Daily Evening Transcript*, June 1, 1889, p. 5.
8. W.C. Cooper to Hawkins, April 11, 1889, Hawkins Scrapbook 13, Annmary Brown Memorial Library, Brown University, Providence, R.I. Letters and documents from this repository will hereinafter be cited by writer, date, and scrapbook number. The Annmary Brown Library was brought to my attention by Dodge Thompson, and I found there Hawkins's Scrapbooks, containing an important cache of letters documenting the organization of the Exposition. "The Note Book," *Art Amateur*, 20 (Dec. 1888), p. 2, reported that Hawkins "seems to give satisfaction to all concerned."
9. Hawkins was born in Pomfret, Vermont, and began his education at the state military academy. During the Civil War he was made Brevett Brigadier General for his leadership of the Zouaves (so named because they adopted the Algerian uniform of the Zouaves in the French army, particularly the tasseled hat and balloon pants). In 1872, Hawkins served in the New York Legislature, and he remained an activist and reformist all his life.
10. Rush C. Hawkins, *Titles of the First Books from the Earliest Presses Established in Europe Before the End of the Fifteenth Century* (New York, 1884). For more about Hawkins, see Margaret Bingham Stillwell, *General Hawkins as He Revealed Himself to His Librarian* (Providence; reprinted from the Papers of the Bibliographical Society of America, 1923). See also "General Franklin Here," *New York Herald Tribune* (Paris ed.), April 16, 1888, p. 1, and *Dictionary of American Biography*, vol. 8, pp. 415–16.
11. "American Art at the Paris Exposition of 1889," *Boston Daily Evening Transcript*, Nov. 7, 1888, p. 10; "Notes from Montezuma," *Art Amateur*, 20 (Dec. 1888), p. 2.
12. Beckwith to Hawkins, Jan. 31, 1889, Hawkins Scrapbook 13.
13. Blashfield to Hawkins, March 1889, Hawkins Scrapbook 13.
14. Allen to Hawkins, Jan. 29, 1889, Hawkins Scrapbook 13.
15. French National Archives, Paris, F21–4058, Folder 3a.
16. Both in the French National Archives and among Hawkins's papers there are letters from the Commissioners and from individual artists correcting data to be included in the American catalogue. Between the French and American versions of the paintings catalogue there exists a discrepancy: Julian Story and Rosina Emmet Sherwood are, in error, listed twice in the French version.
17. Tuck to Hawkins, Nov. 10, 1888, Hawkins Scrapbook 13.
18. According to an undated newspaper clipping in Thomas Hovenden's scrapbooks (Archives of American Art, Roll P 13, frame 11), this was the address of Budworth's storerooms above the Old Guard Armory. The judging process apparently took place there over a period of two days.
19. Between Nov. 10 and Nov. 20, 1888, Hawkins received letters from William A. Coffin of the SAA, William Merritt Chase, President of the SAA, Daniel Huntington, President of the NAD, and Jonathan P. Davis of the SAWE, stating that they would comply with the request to send a list of potential jurymen (Hawkins Scrapbook 13). For the response from the SAWE, see "Life and Works of Elbridge Kinsley," Archives of American Art, Roll 48 (no frame number).
20. Huntington to Hawkins, Nov. 20, 1888, Hawkins Scrapbook 13.
21. Chase to Hawkins, Nov. 21, 1888, Hawkins Scrapbook 13.
22. McEntee to Hawkins, Dec. 5, 1889, Hovenden to Hawkins, Dec. 6, 1889, and Millet to Hawkins, n.d., Hawkins Scrapbook 13. According to an undated newspaper clipping in the scrapbooks of Thomas Hovenden (Archives of American Art, Roll P13, frame 11), McEntee went to Mexico with F.E. Church at this time.
23. "Art and Artists," *Boston Daily Evening Transcript*, Feb. 21, 1889, p. 7.
24. "Art Notes," *Boston Daily Evening Transcript*, April 2, 1889, p. 6.
25. C.G. Wyllis (?) to Hawkins, Feb. 9, 1889, Hawkins Scrapbook 13.
26. H. Howe to Hawkins, Feb. 15, 1889, Hawkins Scrapbook 13, asked that the watercolors by the brother-in-law of the man in charge of the Compagnie Générale Transatlantique be given proper attention by the jury.
27. Franklin to Hawkins, Feb. 28, 1889. J. G. Brown to Hawkins, March 4, 1889, Hawkins Scrapbook 13, agreed that one of La Farge's works should be included because "he is one of our big men in Art. . . ."
28. "Our Artistic Show at Paris," *New York Herald*, March 8, 1889, p. 1, recorded that La Farge's *Saint John at the Foot of the Cross* was sent. It is unclear why this work was not exhibited.
29. Tuck to Hawkins, Jan. 5, 1889, Hawkins Scrapbook 13, wrote he had already promised Mrs. Vedder that the New York jury would examine the pictures and advised Hawkins, "We can keep [this] to ourselves."
30. Fairman was quoted in E.W.H., "New York Notes," *Boston Daily Evening Transcript*, March 4, 1889, p. 6.
31. "Art Notes," *Boston Daily Evening Transcript*, Feb. 28, 1889, p. 4.
32. According to an article titled "America's Immortals" in the *Philadelphia Inquirer* of Oct. 11, 1890, American artists agreed that Inness, Johnson, Chase, Hovenden, and Homer were the best painters in the United States. All were represented in the 1889 Exposition, albeit Homer showed only a grisaille.
33. "Notes from Montezuma," *Art Amateur*, 21 (April 20, 1889), p. 98. Nicolai Cikovsky, Jr., in his Ph.D. dissertation, *The Life and Work of George Inness* (New York: Garland, 1977), chronicles this episode in Inness's career, citing some articles that cast aspersions on Inness's patriotism.
34. It is possible that Moran planned to send a painting and changed his mind to protest Hawkins's treatment of George Inness (see p. 173). He signed Inness's petition to prevent Hawkins from exhibiting *A Short Cut, Watchung Station*. Moran was also preoccupied with his forthcoming print exhibition. I am grateful to Anne Morand for helping me deduce Moran's reasons for not exhibiting.
35. Highly detailed watercolors were often framed and treated like oils; see page 147 for further discussion. I found proof that Eakins's *The Dancing Lesson* was indeed the watercolor *Negro Boy Dancing* in "Our Artistic Show at Paris," *New York Herald*, March 8, 1889, p. 1.
36. "Our Artistic Show at Paris," *New York Herald*, March 8, 1889, p. 1. Although the article is unsigned, according to James Yarnell the author may be Royal Cortissoz, who often wrote for the *Herald*.
37. I am grateful to Lee M. Edwards, curator of the forthcoming Mary Cassatt exhibition at the Whitney

Museum of American Art, for her insights on Cassatt.

38. John Rewald, *Post-Impressionism: From van Gogh to Gauguin* (New York, 3rd. ed. rev., 1978), p. 256. Rewald suggested that Renoir was depressed and filled with self-doubt, but "Latest Art Gossip from France," *Boston Daily Evening Transcript*, Jan. 31, 1889, p. 6, reported that Renoir "had been stricken with paralysis."

39. "Our Artistic Show at Paris," *New York Herald*, March 8, 1889, p. 1.

40. "Notes from Montezuma," *Art Amateur*, 21 (April 1889), p. 98. *The Last of the Buffalo* was shown at the 1889 Salon.

41. Gordon Hendricks, *Albert Bierstadt: Painter of the American West* (New York, 1974), p. 284.

42. "Monthly Record of American Art," *Magazine of Art*, 12 (July 1889; London), p. xxxi.

43. See Elizabeth Broun, "American Paintings and Sculpture in the Fine Arts Building of the World's Columbian Exposition" (Ph.D. dissertation, University of Kansas, 1976), p. 80.

44. Bristol to Hawkins, March 8, 1889, Hawkins Scrapbook 13.

45. "Art Notes," *Boston Daily Evening Transcript*, March 11, 1889, p. 7.

46. "Art and Artists," *Boston Daily Evening Transcript*, April 1, 1889, p. 6, reported that the paintings were shipped on *La Bretagne*, but the *New York Herald* of March 8 said that Hawkins sailed on that steamer on March 9 and that the paintings were to be shipped on March 23 on *La Champagne*.

47. A printed notice in Hawkins Scrapbook 13 records the resolutions passed by the committee, beginning "At a General Meeting of American Artists Resident in Paris Held at the Grand Hotel Paris April the Seventh 1888 It was Resolved That. . . ."

48. George Hitchcock, as secretary of the Paris committee, wrote to Hawkins (Nov. 15, 1888, Scrapbook 13) stating that 220 artists had applied and were asking for 3,000 square meters of space.

49. "Exhibition Rambles. Further complaints that the show is still incomplete. American artists have a few Words to say about the management of their section," *New York Herald* (Paris ed.), May 22, 1889, p. 1.

50. "Artists Complain: letter to the editor from 'Vigil,'" *New York Herald* (Paris ed.), May 24, 1889.

51. "Art and Artists," *Boston Daily Evening Transcript*, Jan. 11, 1889, p. 6. A letter from Lt. Buckingham, Paris, to Hawkins (Feb. 5, 1889; Scrapbook 13) also mentions the offer of free gallery space. Sedelmeyer often sold paintings to American collectors.

52. "The Art Controversy," *New York Herald* (Paris ed.), May 28, 1889, p. 2.

53. E.B., "The Exhibition Closes," *Boston Daily Evening Transcript*, Nov. 8, 1889, p. 6.

54. Antonin Proust, *The Salon of 1891* (Paris, 1891), p. 51. Proust tried to institute installation reforms but was unsuccessful.

55. "The Fine Arts," *Boston Daily Evening Transcript*, June 5, 1889, p. 5. Gardner succeeded in winning a bronze medal.

56. Hawkins to Hitchcock, April 19, 1889, Hawkins Scrapbook 13.

57. Hawkins to Bridgman, April 13, 1889, Hawkins Scrapbook 13.

58. Bridgman to Hawkins, April 12 and April 19, 1889, Hawkins Scrapbook 13. Most of the other sculptures were portrait busts.

59. Letter to her sister Kate, Feb. 19, 1888. Archives of American Art, Washington, D.C. Kellogg was studying at the Académie Colarossi at the time of the Exposition, and the same conditions held true.

60. See page 288 for details.

61. Bridgman to Hawkins, March 24, 1889, Hawkins Scrapbook 13.

62. Hennessy to Hawkins, March 27, 1889, Hawkins Scrapbook 13.

63. Bridgman to Hawkins, April 7, 1889, Hawkins Scrapbook 13.

64. William Walton, *The Paris 1889 Chefs-d'Oeuvre* (Philadelphia, 1889), Book 7, p. 28.

65. "L'Architecture à l'Exposition," *Gazette des Beaux-Arts*, 1, ser. 3 (Nov. 1889), p. 476.

66. "Notes from Montezuma," *Art Amateur*, 21 (Aug. 1889), p. 46.

67. Ibid., p. 47.

68. A. Bailly Blanchard to General William B. Franklin, Dec. 10, 1888, Hawkins Scrapbook 13. Blanchard also mentioned that because America was an early applicant Proust had agreed to allow French paintings in America sent to the Exposition to be readmitted duty-free.

69. Tuck to Hawkins, Dec. 10, 1888, Hawkins Scrapbook 13.

70. Blanchard to Franklin, Jan. 26, 1889, Hawkins Scrapbook 13. "Latest Art Gossip From France," *Boston Daily Evening Transcript*, Jan. 31, 1889, p. 6, noted that applications for the art section were so numerous that the building had to be enlarged.

71. Walter Gay to Hawkins, April 21, 1889, Hawkins Scrapbook 13.

72. Dana and Davis to Hawkins, April 21, 1889, Hawkins Scrapbook 13.

73. A. Harrison to Hawkins, April 1889, Hawkins Scrapbook 13.

74. E.B., "America in Paris," *Boston Daily Evening Transcript*, June 5, 1889, p. 5.

75. Hitchcock to Hawkins, Dec. 22, 1888, Hawkins Scrapbook 13, and "Art and Artists," *Boston Daily Evening Transcript*, Dec. 19, 1888, p. 11.

76. Hitchcock to Hawkins, April 17, 1889, Hawkins Scrapbook 13.

77. Gutherz to Hawkins, May 14, 1889, Hawkins Scrapbook 14.

78. "Artists Complain," *New York Herald* (Paris ed.), May 24, 1889.

79. Theodore Child, "American Artists at the Paris Exhibition," *Harper's New Monthly Magazine*, 79 (Sept. 1889), p. 518; M. G. van Rensselaer, "Open Letters: Impressions of the International Exhibition of 1889," *Century Magazine*, 39 (Dec. 1889), p. 318. William Walton, op. cit., p. 28, expressed similar sentiments.

80. "Artists Complain," *New York Herald* (Paris ed.), May 24, 1889.

81. Hitchcock to Hawkins, Feb. 15, 1889, Hawkins Scrapbook 13.

82. Beckwith to Hawkins, March 8, 1889, Hawkins Scrapbook 13.

83. "Notes from Montezuma," *Art Amateur*, 21 (Sept. 1889), p. 67.

84. The recipients of silver medals were: Boggs, Bridgman, Chase, Davis, Dewing, Donoho, W. Gay, B. Harrison, Howe, Knight, MacEwen, Mosler, Reinhart, and Weir. Bronze medal winners included Allen, Beckwith, Bell, Blashfield, Blum, Brandegee, Butler, Coffin, Cox, Dana, Delachaux, Dodge, Farney, Forbes, Fowler, Gardner, Gaul, Gutherz, Gifford, Inness, Hart, Hassam, Johnson, Jones, Klumpke, Minor, Moore, Patrick, Peters, W. T. Richards, Simmons, Story, Thayer, Thompson, Truesdell, Ulrich, Vonnoh, and Walker. Those who received honorable mention were Breck, Bristol, Brown, Butler, Curtis, Denman, Dow, Gross, De Haas, Hayden, Henry, Koehler, McEntee, de Meza, Nicoll, Parton, Plumb, Shirlaw, Theriat, Turner, Vedder, Whiteman, Whittredge, and Wyant.

85. André Michel, *Journal des Débats*, Sept. 22, 1889, as quoted in Rush C. Hawkins, *Reports of the United States Commissioners*, vol. 2, pp. 110–11.

86. Knight to Proust, July 23, 1889, Hawkins Scrapbook 14. Knight was disobeying the rules by appealing to Proust directly.

87. Antonin Proust, op. cit., p. 51.

88. Franklin to Hawkins, Oct. 7, 1889, Hawkins Scrapbook 14.

89. Walton, op. cit., p. 29.

90. The Archives of the Legion of Honor in Paris confirms that Rush Hawkins and William Dannat received their citations on Oct. 30, 1889. (I am grateful to Susan Grant and to Mme. Claude Jacir, Archivist at the Musée National de la Légion d'Honneur, for supplying this information.) Most of the letters in the Hawkins Scrapbooks discussing the Legion of Honor decorations are written after this date. I found no mention of Knight's, Sargent's, or Harrison's receiving a Legion of Honor award.

91. Pearce to Hawkins, n.d., Hawkins Scrapbook 14. Between Nov. 3, 1889, and Jan. 25, 1890, several artists wrote to Hawkins on the subject of the Legion of Honor awards. Susan Grant, "American Paintings Acquired by the French Government, 1879-1900" (master's thesis, George Washington University, 1983), discusses the tariff and its reception in France. I am grateful to her for sharing her essay with me and the other authors and for all her help and support in the organization of this exhibition.

92. Pearce to Hawkins about the Legion of Honor awards, Nov. 9, 14, 27, Dec. 5, 1889, and Jan. 25, 1990, Hawkins Scrapbook 14. Pearce was named a Chevalier of the Legion of Honor in 1894.

93. For more on this subject, see Grant, op. cit.

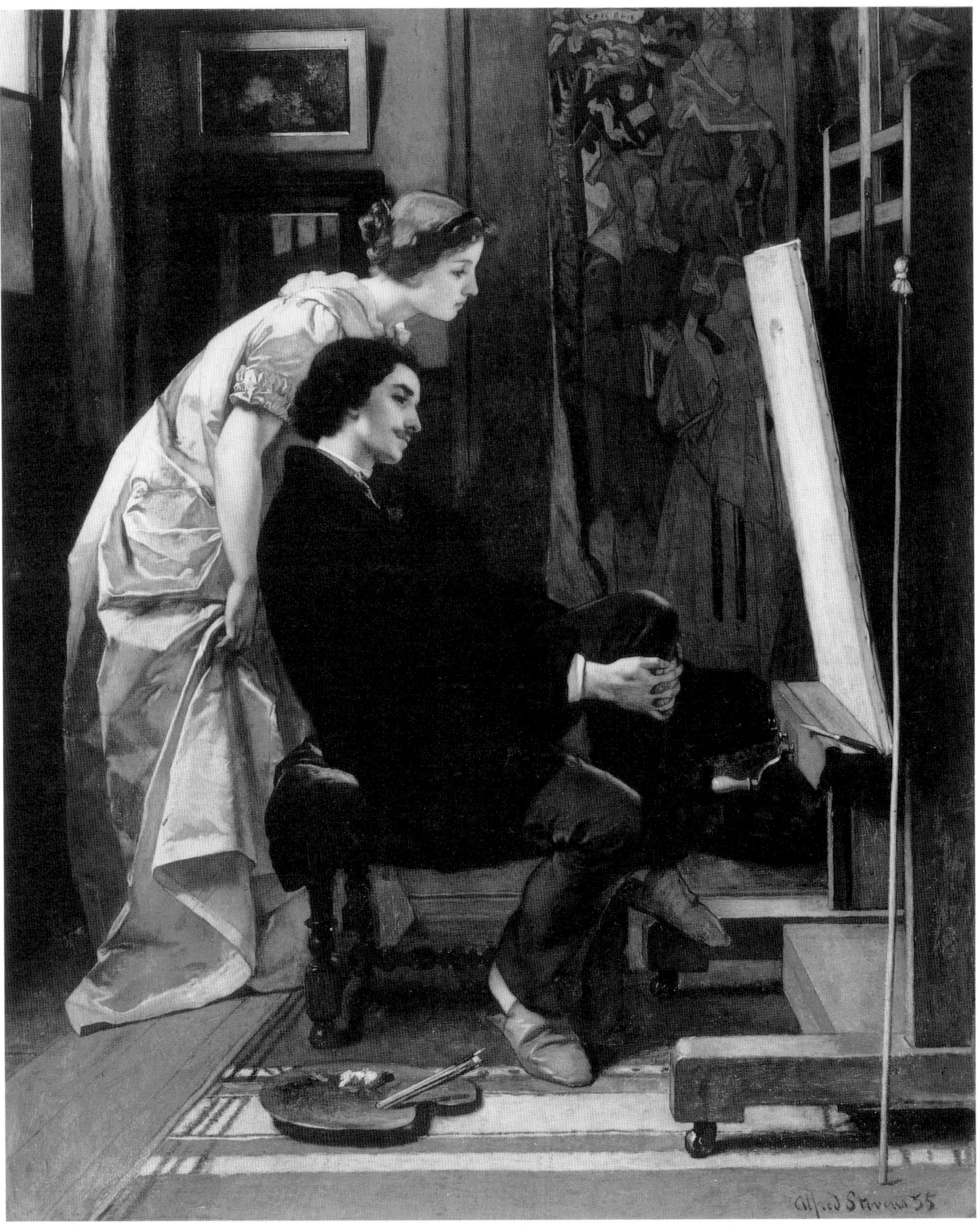

H. BARBARA WEINBERG

Cosmopolitan Attitudes: The Coming of Age of American Art

9.
Alfred Stevens (1823–1906)
The Painter and His Model, 1855
Oil on canvas, 36⅜ x 29″ (92.3 x 73.7)
The Walters Art Gallery, Baltimore

In 1887, Henry James explained why he would designate John Singer Sargent an American artist despite his foreign birth, his expatriate life, and the fact that "in the line of his art he might easily be mistaken for a Frenchman." James argued: "It sounds like a paradox, but it is a very simple truth, that when to-day we look for 'American art' we find it mainly in Paris. When we find it out of Paris, we at least find a great deal of Paris in it."[1] Indeed, late-nineteenth-century American painters and sculptors, and architects as well, avidly emulated contemporary French models, demonstrating a marked artistic Francophilia. Few observers would have disputed with the expatriate painter Edwin Lord Weeks when he said, in 1890, "Paris is to the artist what Wall Street is to the broker, the centre of all life."[2]

The influence of current Parisian ideals on late-nineteenth-century American art was as new as it was strong. True, Jacksonian and mid-century artists had enriched their vocabularies with European references, but these had derived from a retrospective taste and from informal contacts—inspection of old master paintings at home and during the grand tour and friendly associations with foreign artists—rather than from total immersion or programmatic instruction. Although foreign influence was undeniable, outright imitation of contemporary foreign styles was rare. An exception was the style associated with Düsseldorf, whose academy attracted several dozen American students in the late 1840s and the 1850s. In Düsseldorf, some artists, among them Albert Bierstadt, reinforced the taste for precise landscape renderings of the Hudson River School and its patrons, and others, such as Emanuel Leutze, were inspired to essay history painting in the grand manner.

At mid-century, a limited number of Americans were enrolled in Parisian studios for instruction. Their periods of study with such masters as Thomas Couture, François Picot, and Charles Gleyre were simply part of the grand tour or were added to the brief training they had received in Düsseldorf—occasionally serving as an antidote to the mechanical academic manner advocated there. What was available in Parisian studios, and in the French government's Ecole des Beaux-Arts (where some Americans matriculated for additional drawing instruction under a rotating team of critics), was an unalloyed emphasis on working from the human figure. Once having served an apprenticeship in drawing from plaster casts of antique sculptures, a student would concentrate on drawing and, ultimately, on painting single-figure studies from the living nude model. Week in and week out, the production of such *académies* was the central curricular concern, with the execution of multifigured compositions a skill to be developed outside the master's studio and used at the Ecole only in the context of its frequent competitions.

The growth of American interest in art study in Paris was quickened by the reform in 1863 of the curriculum at the Ecole des Beaux-Arts. This reform added three studios for painting to the facilities and consolidated drawing instruction under a single teacher, Adolphe Yvon (1817–1893). The school, remaining tuition-free and open to men of any nationality, now became more fully professional, attracting the world's art students and serving as the international model in artistic pedagogy.

Postbellum American interest in Parisian art study was also stimulated by practical developments. Transportation and communication had entered a phase of relative accessibility and ease. The end of the Civil War marked the beginning of unprecedented American expansion—material, territorial, and urban. Increased wealth and leisure, wider international contacts, and an enlarged and more sophisticated art press intensified the demand for art, especially for French works, which critics recommended for their technical superiority and as sound investments.[3] The newly rich formed the first great American art collections, purchasing European paintings in huge quantities in accordance with the demands of fashion. American collectors—particularly in New York and Philadelphia—recognized the French academics as the *dernier cri* in figure painting, and—especially in Boston—praised and patronized the Barbizon painters. The presence of so many imported works and the obvious preference of influential collectors for contemporary European art awakened in American artists a desire to secure patronage by emulating the works that the new millionaires were buying. These developments, about which much more could be said, were profoundly important as symptoms of vital changes in American taste and cultural aspirations.

Increasingly, American artists recognized the attractions of late-nineteenth-century Paris. They came by the dozens to experience its spirit—and to study at its newly reformed government school and in private studios. Many enrolled in the Ecole's three ateliers for painting, especially under the popular Jean-Léon Gérôme and Alexandre Cabanel. Others sought instruction outside the government school, joining the *ateliers des élèves* of Léon Bonnat and Carolus-Duran, although they may have also matriculated in the government school for drawing instruction. Yet others—indeed, the greatest number—avoided any entrance requirement other than the ability to pay the tuition by enrolling in the private academies that competed with the Beaux-Arts school. These—especially the Académie Julian—offered instruction that was entirely in accord with Beaux-Arts technical standards but was accessible to artists, including women, who were not admitted to the Ecole.

As awareness of the technical superiority of French painting grew, and as its emphasis on the human figure began to have a greater influence on American painters, a new, more varied sort of figure painting began to attract the most ambitious American artists. Many Jacksonian and mid-century painters had channeled their energy into grand-scale landscapes that bespoke their pride in America as the "new Eden." Most painters who essayed history painting confined their search for texts to American history, even when they painted abroad, as in the case of Leutze. By contrast, their successors, increasingly reflecting French attitudes, explored a wide range of themes with a greater technical sophistication and with an expanded world view, catering to an audience whose tastes transcended the earlier provincial limits. Even painters who remained committed to landscape altered their art according to French ideals, echoing the intimate tonal poetry of the Barbizon School rather than the bombastic prose of Cole, Church, and Bierstadt.

No group of American paintings could have more clearly revealed the results of American painters' Parisian studies—could have more amply validated James's perception of the "Gallicization" of American art in the decades after the Civil War—than that shown at the 1889 Exposition Universelle. The forum, after all, was Paris, the undisputed center of the international art world. The occasion was the centennial celebration of French independence from monarchical rule—won in a revolution that paralleled our own. American painters had been participating in ever-increasing numbers in the annual Salons, and had sent larger and larger groups of works to the universal expositions held in 1855, 1867, and 1878. They had grown accustomed to testing themselves on the Parisian stage, to which the world's eyes regularly turned.

The extraordinary Frenchness of the American display in 1889 reflected the facts that three-fourths of the artists who showed paintings had studied in France and that four-fifths of the works shown were by these artists. Predictably, the artists who had had their most extensive training in France best documented the Gallicization of American art in the years since mid-century, but even those whose training had been to some extent mixed reflected French stylistic traits. Some painters had through subsequent Parisian study modified or divested themselves of styles learned at competing European centers—especially Düsseldorf and Munich. In evidence, too, was the impact of French styles upon Americans who had never studied in France—of the Barbizon approach to landscape deduced from paintings by Corot, Millet, and others that had entered American collections; of French techniques and taste absorbed at second hand by artists who studied with artists who had studied in Paris; of the academic style of figure painting acquired in Antwerp and Munich but ultimately rooted in Parisian standards.

American assimilation of French ideas was underlined in the 1889 display of American paintings by the fact that it was the artists who had most fully assimilated them and who had become expatriates living in Paris that dominated its organization and management. Led by such masters of the Salon style as Frederick Bridgman, William T. Dannat, Walter Gay, Alexander Harrison, and Henry Mosler, the Parisian residents arranged to show twice as many works as did their repatriated colleagues, French-trained or not. The separate hanging of the works of the Paris-based artists also attracted critical attention to a specifically Franco-American subcommunity. While the hanging scheme had been initiated with the approval of the New York jury (see page 26), it was an apparent assertion of privilege that would generate persistent hard feelings in the American art world.[4] The more positive result of the segregation of Franco-American from American artists at the 1889 fair was a curious consolidation of nationalism in both groups. This led to the founding of the American Art Association of Paris in 1890 and to the emphasis on home-based paintings at the 1893 World's Columbian Exposition in Chicago.

Its art-politics notwithstanding, the display at the 1889 Paris fair presented significant patterns of evolution in late-nineteenth-century American painting. American artists born as much as a half century apart—from George P. A. Healy, born in 1816, to William de Leftwich Dodge, born in 1867—were represented. Their works reflected their exposure to a nearly complete catalogue

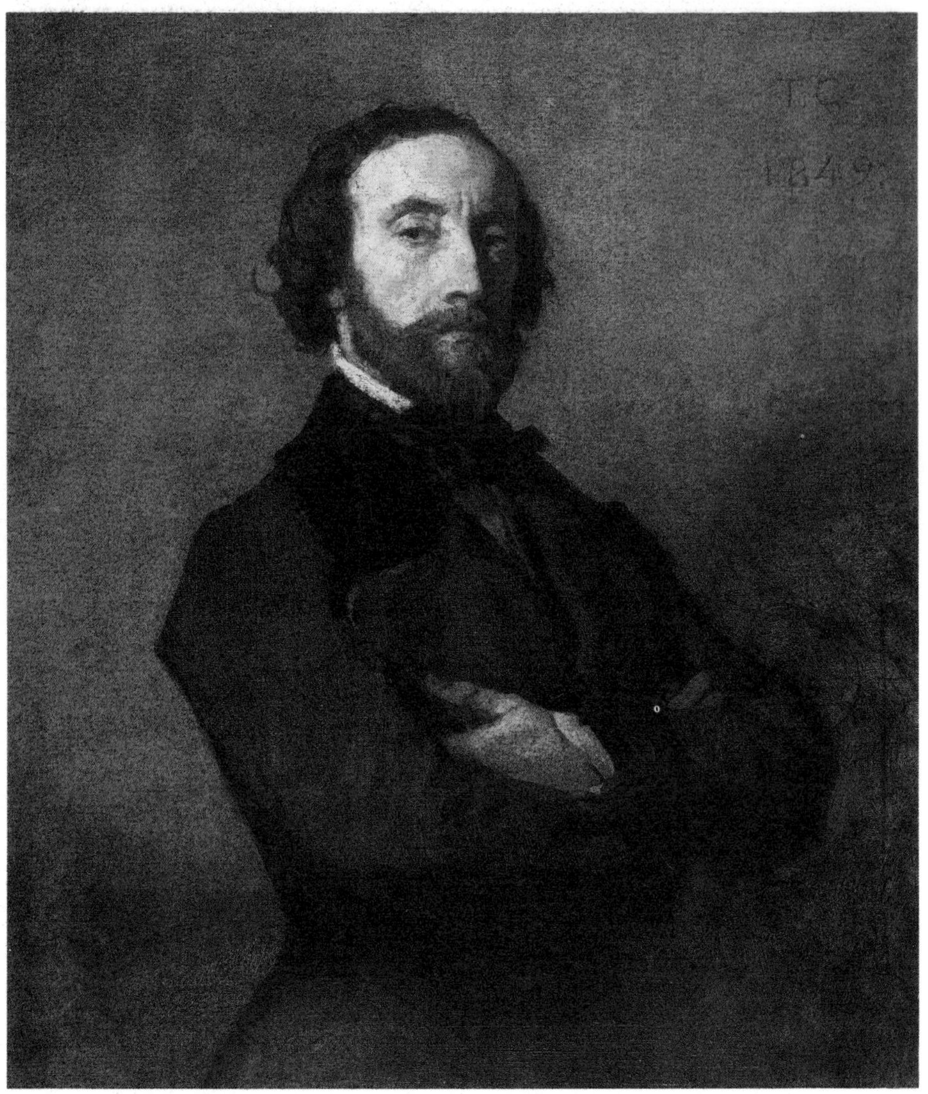

10.
Thomas Couture (1815–1879)
Portrait of M. Paul Barroilhet, 1849
Oil on canvas, 38 x 31⅛" (96.5 x 54.6 cm)
The Harvard Art Museums, Cambridge,
Bequest of Grenville L. Winthrop

of European—especially Parisian—teachers and art schools between the mid-1830s and the late 1880s—from Baron Antoine-Jean Gros and Couture, who taught Healy, to the reformed Ecole des Beaux-Arts and the Académie Colarossi (the Académie Julian's leading rival), where the twenty-two-year-old Dodge was still studying at the time of the fair. In general, the American display demonstrated a maturation of technique and a muting of the national voice with respect to choice of subject. The exhibition was in some ways virtually indistinguishable from that of other participating countries, featuring paintings that were interchangeable with those of the hundreds of French, English, Swiss, Scandinavian, and other nationals who had learned most of their lessons in Parisian studios.

Like the other national displays—including the French—the American exhibition was conservative in its overall aspect. This was art endorsed by official juries, essentially retrospective in style even if most of the works had emerged in the decade since the previous Paris exposition. There were only a few intimations among the Americans who showed in 1889 of the influence of Impressionism, whose French founders had had their last group exhibition three years before. (American Impressionism would debut at the Chicago fair in 1893.)

The two oldest of the Americans to show in 1889, George Peter Alexander Healy and Daniel Huntington, presented works that reflected the manner of Thomas Couture—Healy in five portraits and a figure study and Huntington in a historical costume piece. Couture's style was based on the coloristic Venetian tradition, preserving the freshness of the sketchy underpainting rather than seeking academic high finish (see fig. 10). It had deeply impressed American painters—almost forty of whom came to study with Couture between 1846 and 1879—and had found favor with American patrons as well.[5]

On going abroad in 1834, Healy had entered the studio of Gros, but his study under Gros was cut short by his teacher's suicide in 1835. It was in Gros's studio that he had first encountered Couture, as a fellow student. By 1840, Healy had met Couture again and had begun to grow close to him, both personally and stylistically. As he had in several Salon catalogues, he designated Couture as one of his teachers in the catalogue of the paintings section of the 1889 Paris fair. Healy was the only American who had shown in all three prior universal expositions.

Healy's 1863 painting *Orestes A. Brownson* (see page 167) offers as apt a demonstration as any of the American portraitist's position as a leading disciple of Couture. Typical of the influential patrons whom Healy documented during a long and productive international career, the bearded minister confronts the viewer with an easy, affable dignity, enlivened by powerful, energetic hand gestures. Passages such as the scumbling of brown paint in the foreground books echo the characteristic surfaces of Couture's works. Healy's devotion to Couture's style, strength as a portraitist, and manifest appeal to an international clientele were also evident in the four other portraits he showed at the fair.

The enduring influence of Couture is seen in the work of Enoch Wood Perry and Eastman Johnson although both had studied in Düsseldorf before entering Couture's Paris studio. Perry spent two years under Couture, from 1854 to 1856, and Johnson a few months in the summer and fall of 1855. Both artists added to armatures based on academic traditions of solid, sculpturesque figure description and lucid composition, Couture's more sensuous approach to paint handling. This dualism appears in Perry's *Mother and Child* (1881; Manoogian Collection), a gentle genre scene that is reminiscent of the classicizing tendencies of such Dutch little masters as Peter de Hooch in its rectilinear organization of figures and space but creates a poetic mood through a tonal veneer indebted to the practice of Couture.

Far more ambitious in scale, Johnson's *The Funding Bill* (see page 175) alludes only in its title to current concerns about a Congressional act to refund the national debt. With its historical allusions embedded in a blend of portraiture and genre painting, the work partakes of the general late-nineteenth-century academic tendency to deflate historical themes, to stress their most everyday aspects. Technically, *The Funding Bill* reflects Düsseldorfian emphasis on the construction of convincing volumetric figures and their disposition on a classically organized stage. The dramatic chiaroscuro and the painterly veneer recall Johnson's exposure to Dutch works, especially those of Rembrandt, during the three years in The Hague that followed his study in Düsseldorf. But the spontaneous, energetic paint application—still evident despite the painting's poor condition—discloses Johnson's debt to his brief contact with Couture.

Older than Couture but still active at mid-century was François Edouard Picot (1786–1868), an orthodox academic, a durable contemporary and rival of Ingres, who attracted a handful of American students. Among them was William Parsons Winchester Dana, who had studied briefly with Picot in 1852

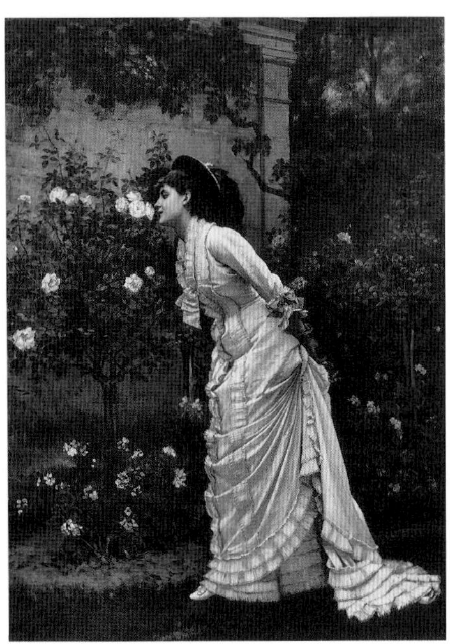

11.
Auguste Toulmouche (1829–1890)
A Girl and Roses, 1879.
Oil on canvas, 24½ x 17¹¹⁄₁₆" (62.2 x 45 cm)
Sterling and Francine Clark Art Institute, Williamstown, Massachusetts

before spending nearly a decade with the seascape painter Eugène LePoittevin (1806–1870). It is a dismaying testament to the transience of reputation that none of the four works that Dana showed in 1889—works that brought him a bronze medal like the one he had won at the 1878 fair—could be located for inclusion in the present exhibition.

Picot's best-known and most successful American pupil was Elihu Vedder, who worked in Picot's Parisian atelier in 1856–57 before pursuing additional studies in Florence and back home in New York. Traces of the French academic emphasis on linear definition are easily detected in the paintings that Vedder showed in 1889. Also linked to academic impulses is Vedder's dependence upon canonical old masters, especially Michelangelo, for the poses of such figures as the reposing male in the foreground of *The Last Man* (1886; unlocated) and for the androgynous physiognomies of *The Fates Gathering In the Stars* (see page 220). Although Vedder's later susceptibility to the more mannered tendencies in English painting and illustration—especially the styles of William Blake, of the Pre-Raphaelites, and of Walter Crane—may have exaggerated the wiry, metallic linearity of his style, the origins of that style in his study under Picot cannot be discounted.

At least as committed as Picot to an orthodox academic style, bespeaking a devotion to the long tradition of Raphael, Poussin, and David, was Charles Gleyre (1806–1874), a third important mid-century teacher. Yet, by contrast to Picot's, his approach to subject more fully reflected the inclination to deflate the heroic and the moralizing, to search for the human realities in traditional narratives, and even to minimize the force of narrative altogether. These tendencies, manifest in the works of most academics, constitute a conservative analogue to the revolutionary realism and the rejection of narrative concerns associated with such radical painters as Courbet. The interest of Gleyre and other academic teachers in the everyday, or genre, components of historical subjects provided a foundation for a younger group of artists (including Gérôme), known as neo-grecs, to paint classical genre in an academic style with little concern for narrative; for others, such as Marie-François Firmin-Girard and Auguste Toulmouche, to serve the taste of the Second Empire for contemporary genre in a similarly conservative style (see fig. 15); and even for the Impressionists, who were also committed to the contemporary, to radically repudiate traditional academic high finish. Of the Impressionists, four—Monet, Renoir, Sisley, and Bazille—were students in Gleyre's atelier in the early 1860s. They may have been nourished by his humanizing approach to subject and may have founded their style upon his practice of rendering free and fluent academic sketches and underpaintings. Though these were essential components of the academic process,[6] no orthodox artist would have exhibited them as completed works—as the Impressionists did.

Of Gleyre's ten recorded American pupils, five showed works in the 1889 Paris fair: William Mark Fisher, Edward Lamson Henry, Daniel Ridgway Knight, Alfred Wordsworth Thompson, and James Abbott McNeill Whistler. The first American to enter Gleyre's studio (in 1856), Whistler contributed two paintings—*Arrangement in Black, #7, Portrait of Lady Archibald Campbell* (see page 227) and *Variations in Flesh Color and Green: The Balcony* (1865; Freer Gallery of Art, Washington, D.C.)—to the British section, for reasons that are described elsewhere (see pages 228–29). *The Yellow Buskin* may be viewed in terms of its debt to the process of broad, tonal underpainting characteristic of academic practice, including Gleyre's. Its monochromatic palette—its subtle description of the dark-gray dress against the black background—may also be linked to Gleyre's preferences. While the subjectlessness of *The Balcony* is indebted to Whistler's contact with the English painter Albert Moore, its disregard of narrative also accords with that in Gleyre's works and in the works of such of Gleyre's English students as Sir Edward Poynter.

More distinct stylistic connections with Gleyre are evident in the highly finished works of Knight, especially in a painting like *Hailing the Ferryman* (see page 180). Here the stagelike composition, monochromatic palette, and immaculate surface plainly reflect traits in the works of Gleyre, with whom Knight studied from 1861 to 1863, before returning home to serve in the Union army. The minutely articulated detail and almost photographic finish also echo the practice of Ernest Meissonier (see fig. 17), with whom Knight worked in 1874–75, when he settled in Poissy, north of Paris. Knight's graceful figures—models dressed up as peasants and posing in the suburban setting of the artist's Poissy studio—are akin to the elegant Second Empire ladies depicted by some of Gleyre's French students. Though suggesting an additional debt to the popular paintings of Jules Bastien-Lepage in its peasant subject and flat, gray light, Knight's work speaks much less to the reality of peasant travail and much more to a nostalgic, voyeuristic interest in the peasant-picturesque.

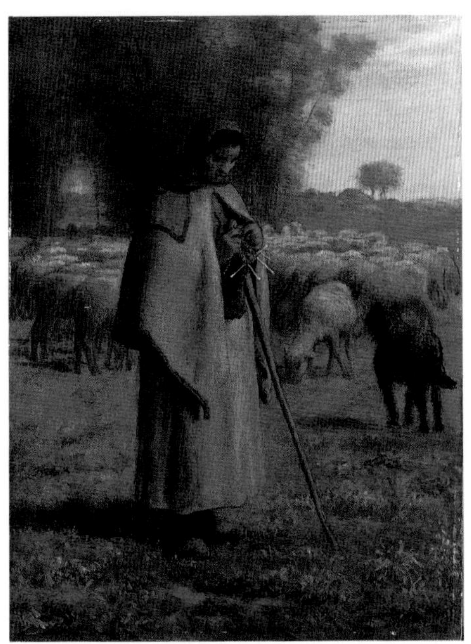

12.
Jean-François Millet (1814–1875)
The Shepherdess: Plains of Barbizon, c. 1862
Oil on panel, 14 15/16 x 10 3/4" (38 x 27.3 cm)
Sterling and Francine Clark Art Institute, Williamstown, Massachusetts

At mid-century, when Couture, Picot, and Gleyre began to attract small groups of American pupils, the Barbizon manner of generalized, poetic landscape began to affect American landscape painting.[7] Some painters made pilgrimages to Barbizon and worked there in the company of the leading Barbizon painters, especially Jean-François Millet (see fig. 12). These included William Morris Hunt, who had studied with Couture from 1846 to 1852 before spending three years with Millet at Barbizon. Although Hunt would inculcate in his own students in Newport and Boston the technical principles of Couture, he would be an even more significant agent for Barbizon taste, encouraging influential collectors to acquire works by Millet, Corot (see fig. 13), and other members of the Barbizon group. Such acquisitions, which were especially conspicuous in Boston collections but were not absent in New York and Philadelphia, prompted American painters to mirror Barbizon landscapes' somber tonalities, intimate scale, and subjective moods. Enough paintings were available as models to enable Americans to adopt the Barbizon mode without going abroad; they could reinforce their lessons later through journeys to France.

Barbizon influence is the common denominator of almost all the landscapes that Americans showed at the 1889 Paris fair; it made itself felt in various ways and in varying degrees. Direct contact with Barbizon painters influenced Alfred C. Howland and Alfred Wordsworth Thompson, who had studied with Emile Lambinet (1815–1878) in the early 1860s, and Joseph Foxcroft Cole, who had worked with Lambinet between 1860 and 1863 and with Charles-Emile Jacque (1813–1894) in 1866. George Inness and Hugh Bolton Jones absorbed Barbizon influence by consulting paintings during foreign travel. Arthur Parton merely studied the many Barbizon paintings imported to the United States. Other practitioners of the American Barbizon mode that was so much in evidence at the 1889 fair had studied under artists who had themselves adopted the Barbizon manner. Robert Van Boskerck was a student of Alexander Wyant and R. Swain Gifford. (Both Wyant and Gifford were also represented in the American display.) Multiple infusions of Barbizon influence were experienced by Horace Wolcott Robbins, who had followed study with the Barbizon-influenced James Hart (also represented in the 1889 exhibition) with work under Théodore Rousseau (1812–1867) in 1865, and by Robert Crannell

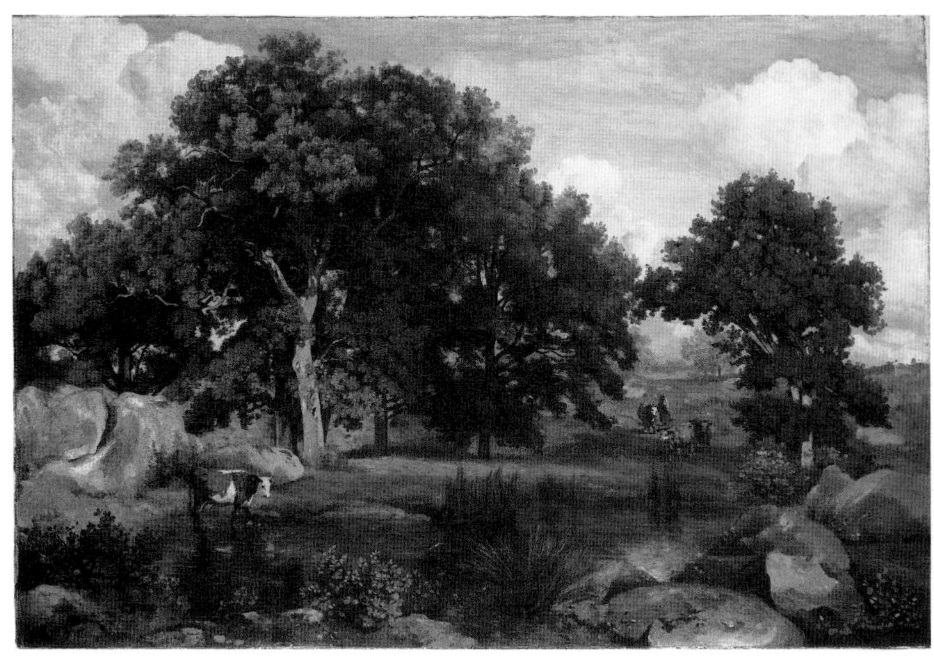

13.
Jean-Baptiste-Camille Corot (1796–1875)
Forest of Fontainebleau, Salon 1846
Oil on canvas, 35⅝ x 51" (90.5 x 129.5 cm)
Museum of Fine Arts, Boston,
Gift of Mrs. Samuel Dennis Warren

Minor, who had reinforced study under Parton with work in the company of Narcisse Virgile Diaz de la Peña (1807–1876) at Barbizon.

Even artists like Jervis McEntee and Worthington Whittredge (the latter trained in Düsseldorf), who had exchanged their earlier concern with geographic and botanical description for the compositional strategies and generalized surface treatments of Corot and Rousseau, were affected by Barbizon landscapes. The metamorphoses of these artists, and of other members of the Hudson River School "old guard," were undoubtedly motivated by their desire to appeal to patrons attracted to the more up-to-date Barbizon style.

Some of the American landscape painters who showed in 1889 had studied in French ateliers, where figure painting was the central instructional concern and high finish and meticulous detail were technical goals. When they turned to landscape—as did Fisher, who had studied with Picot, and Charles Harold Davis and John Leslie Breck, who had studied at the Académie Julian—they also made a change in techniques, modifying their expectably academic strategies by reference to Barbizon painterliness and tonalism. The results are in contrast to the more technically conservative style seen in seascapes by Alexander Harrison and Edward Emerson Simmons. Harrison had been a pupil of Gérôme in the late 1870s and early 1880s, and Simmons was a student at the Académie Julian at about the same time. Both preserve in their works—especially their paintings of waves in the open sea—an academic concern for structure and finish, despite the use of unusual compositional formats.

The influence of Barbizon, so noticeable in landscape painting, also affected figure painting. It was conspicuous in the American display in George Fuller's painting *The Quadroon* (see page 152). This work demonstrates the self-taught Fuller's initial dependence on Washington Allston's enigmatic painterly romanticism, updated by his appreciation of Millet's melancholy peasants and of the evocative textured paint surfaces from which they emerge. And the related—and even more powerful—influence of the French peasant painters Bastien-Lepage

14.
Jean-Léon Gérôme (1824–1904)
La Terrasse du Serail
Oil on canvas, 32½ x 48″ (81.8 x 121.9 cm)
Private Collection
Photograph courtesy Gerald M. Ackerman

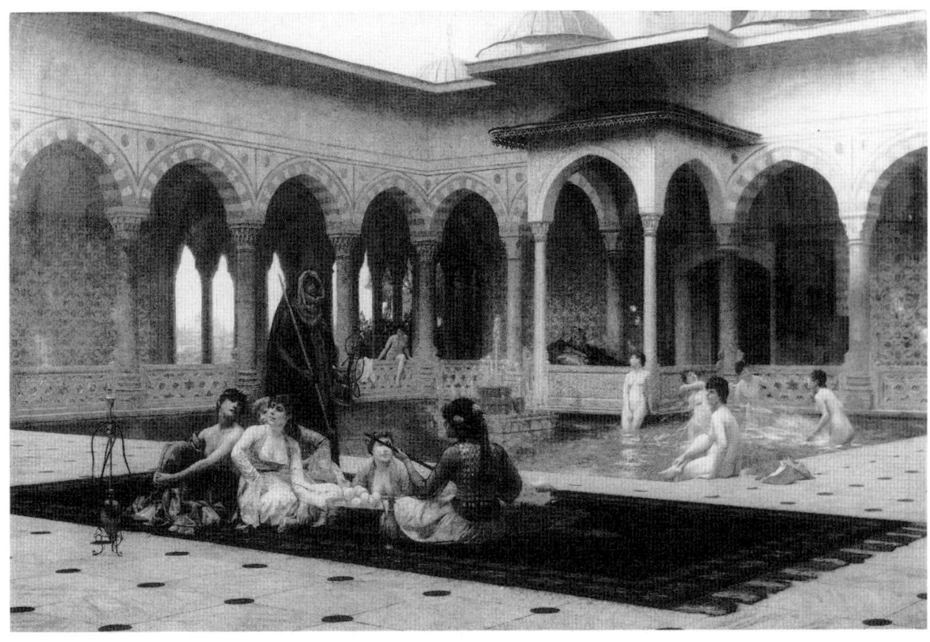

and Jules Breton is evident in the works of Knight, Charles Sprague Pearce, Birge Harrison, and others who had had extensive exposure to academic ideals.

Perhaps the strongest Parisian magnets for aspiring painters in the 1860s and 1870s were the three ateliers established at the Ecole des Beaux-Arts in 1863 under the direction, respectively, of Gérôme, Cabanel, and Isidore Pils (1813–1875). Of these, it was certainly Gérôme's that enjoyed the greatest popularity among the Americans.[8] Gérôme, who had studied under Paul Delaroche and Gleyre, successfully applied a lapidary academic style to a variety of subjects: classical and French history, whose episodes he described with an eye to actualities rather than to moral lessons; classical genre, in the manner of his fellow neo-grecs in Gleyre's studio; and exotic genre, especially images of North Africa and the Near East (see fig. 14). The consistency of his rigorous academic style, the fluidity of his subject interests, and his durability as a teacher made him a significant resource for dozens of American students of painting. Several artistic generations of Gérôme's students contributed to the 1889 American display, ranging from Harry Humphrey Moore and Thomas Eakins, who began study in the Gérôme studio in 1866, to Dewitt Clinton Peters and Charles Francis Browne, who entered it twenty or more years later.

Moore appears to have been one of Gérôme's most consistent imitators, judging by documentary photographs, descriptions of lost works, and a few preserved paintings analogous to those that he showed in 1889. His *Glimpse into the Pleasure Quarters, Yoshiwara* (see page 192) is a Japanese analogue of Gérôme's popular Near Eastern harem scenes—his highly finished, detailed voyeuristic images of the seraglios in Constantinople and the grand baths in Bursa. Moore shared an interest in Japanese subjects with Robert Blum and with the extremely obscure Eugene Armand La Chaise, both of whom showed such works in the 1889 American display. These, and similar costume genre works by such French artists as Firmin-Girard (see fig. 6), exemplify academic *japonisme*, the con-

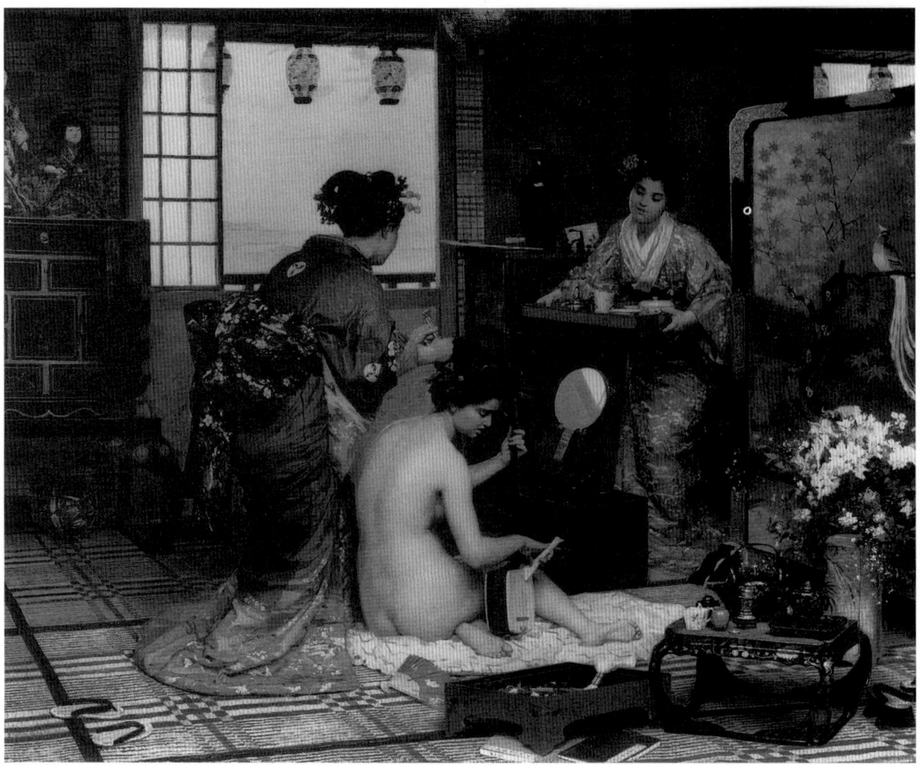

15.
Marie-François Firmin-Girard (1838–1921)
Toilette Japonaise, 1873
Oil on canvas, 21¼ x 25¾" (54 x 65.4 cm)
Museo de Arte de Ponce, Puerto Rico,
The Luis A. Ferré Foundation

servative counterpart to the interests of Manet, Whistler, and other experimental painters. Moore's works are exceptional as deriving from the artist's experience of actually spending time in Japan in the early 1880s rather than from his merely painting Parisian models dressed up in kimonos.

Some Americans who studied with Gérôme at an early date compromised his manner by adopting stylistic tendencies contradictory to his. Bridgman, who worked in Gérôme's Beaux-Arts studio from 1867 to 1871, is an example: while his paintings of the seventies so fully emulated those of his teacher that critics remarked that Gérôme might as well have signed them, in later works Bridgman seems to have added to his stylistic tools an interest in the painterly orientalism of Eugène Delacroix. An example of this more fluent manner of Bridgman's is his *Horse Market at Cairo* (see page 124), a sumptuous display of color and sinuous forms. An expatriate living in Paris, a faithful exhibitor and frequent prizewinner at the annual Salons, recipient of a Legion of Honor award at the 1878 Paris fair, Bridgman has suffered from the twentieth-century rejection of academic orientalism—European and American—that prevailed until the mid-1970s. Like Weeks, Dana, Moore, Charles Stanley Reinhart, and other acclaimed contributors to the 1889 display, he forfeits fair and complete appraisal because so many of his works are unlocated.

Weeks never enrolled for instruction under Gérôme, studying instead in Bonnat's private atelier. But he gradually divested himself of Bonnat's more painterly manner, absorbing a great deal from Gérôme's example and informal advice and increasingly imitating his technical tendencies. By the 1880s, Weeks had transposed Gérôme's scrupulous anthropological academic orientalism to India, as was evident in the five paintings he submitted to the 1889 fair. For example, *The Last Journey, Souvenir of the Ganges* (see page 224), depicting the hasty excursion enabling a dying man to breathe his last in the holy city of Benares, recalls Gérôme's river scenes and his occasional tendency to melodrama. *The Rajah of Jodhpare* (see fig. 26) and *Hindoo Marriage Procession, Ahmedabad* (unlocated) are even more photographic in their overall focus, their carefully ordered stage settings, and the meticulous detail with which exotic figures and costumes and curious customs are described.

In contrast to Moore, Bridgman, and Weeks, who shared Gérôme's interest in exotic genre, some American students echoed his portrayals of classical genre. Abbott Thayer, who had worked under Gérôme from 1876 to 1879, invented a race of allusive winged figures, based essentially on single-figure female *académies*. Typical of these is Thayer's *Angel* (see page 216), which demonstrates the possibility of a devoted student's departing from academic constraints with respect to high finish and exploiting instead the freedom of the study in his painting's final surface.

After studying with Gérôme from 1879 to 1882, Kenyon Cox had renounced the painterly manner of his first Parisian teacher, Carolus-Duran, in favor of the linear rigor of Gérôme's style. Cox's self-consciously classical *Painting and Poetry*, known only from an illustration, appears to have been one of only two examples of such allegorical imagery to appear in the 1889 American display, the other being Edwin Blashfield's *Inspiration* (unlocated). Like Weeks, Blashfield had been a student of Bonnat but was counseled informally by Gérôme. Blashfield's command of the contrasting techniques of the two masters was evident in the works he showed in 1889: the high seriousness, Renaissance allusions, and metallic linearity of *Inspiration* served as a foil to the more painterly portrait of his wife (see page 117).

While Blashfield's portrait style departed from academic practice, Cox applied the lucid, tight manner of Gérôme, for example in his *Portrait of Augustus Saint-Gaudens* (see page 133), a work that also echoes Gérôme's—and other academics'—interest in portrayals of artists in their studios. The painting depicts the leading American sculptor of the period working on a relief of a leading painter, William Merritt Chase. Saint-Gaudens appears at half length in profile, like a figure in one of the Renaissance reliefs that he is adapting in clay. Documenting the integration of the arts, the new commitment to bronze rather than stone and to study from life rather than from the antique, Cox's portrait is a comprehensive distillation of Beaux-Arts attitudes.

Douglas Volk, who had studied in the master's Beaux-Arts studio from 1873 to 1878, duplicated Gérôme's interest in a wide range of subjects. At the 1889 fair, Volk showed genre paintings relating to both the past and the present—*The Puritan Captives* (1882; unlocated) and *After the Reception* (see page 221). Alexander Harrison also applied his academic skills to diverse subjects: the clearly detailed seascapes that have been mentioned; landscapes, such as the allusive *Castles in Spain* (see page 163), populated by peasants; and academic nudes, exemplified by *In Arcadia* (see page 164). Wyatt Eaton, who had worked with Gérôme from 1872 to 1876, and had simultaneously been attracted to Barbizon peasant genre, recommitted himself to a more academic course in the 1880s, turning his attention to portraiture and to ideal nudes such as *Ariadne* (see page 152), which echo the classicizing images of Cox and Harrison.

Contemporary genre, which, if not a specialty of Gérôme himself, had been the specialty of such of Gérôme's fellow students in Gleyre's atelier as Firmin-Girard and Toulmouche, found its American exponent in Julius L. Stewart. The son of a prominent Philadelphia collector and patron of Gérôme, Stewart had added instruction under the French master to lessons learned from

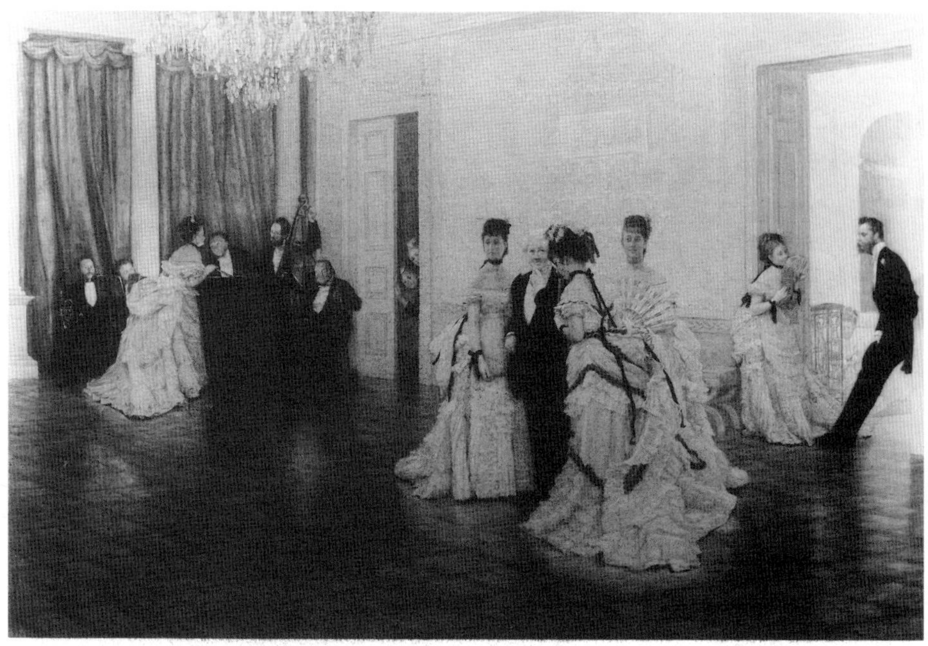

16.
James Jacques Joseph Tissot (1836–1902)
Too Early, 1873
Oil on canvas, 28 x 40″ (71.1 x 101.6 cm)
Guildhall Art Gallery, London

Spanish genre painters Eduardo Zamacois (1842–1871) and Raimondo de Madrazo y Garreta (1841–1920). The products of Stewart's varied but generally conservative instruction, and of his admiration of the works of James Tissot (see fig. 16) and Jean Béraud (1849–1936), were sumptuous large-scale portrayals of the pleasures of contemporary upper-class life, especially in the American cosmopolitan and expatriate communities. Of these characteristic paintings, Stewart showed two particularly fine examples at the 1889 fair: *A Hunt Ball* and *The Seine at Bougival* (see page 212).

Aside from Gérôme's informal advising of American painters enrolled in other studios—among them Blashfield and Weeks (and artists, such as Mary Cassatt, who as women were excluded from the Ecole altogether)—his influence was felt through the example of his works. Thomas Hovenden, who worked in the Beaux-Arts studio of Cabanel in 1874–75, reveals in his *Last Moments of John Brown* (see page 174) more of Gérôme's journalistic, humanizing approach to history than of the approach of his own teacher, which tended toward the melodramatic and the erotic. Neglecting episodes of Brown's heroism at Harper's Ferry in favor of portraying a sentimental moment—Brown's legendary farewell to a black child—Hovenden displays an impressive command of academic stylistic traits, including a photographic verisimilitude.

Study under Cabanel at the Beaux-Arts, reinforced by instruction at the Académie Colarossi, equipped Eugene Lawrence Vail with the academic skill to construct lucid spatial settings and to populate them with volumetric figures. The monumental Breton fisherfolk who appear in *The Widow* (unlocated) and the London workers seen in *On the Thames* (see page 217) are academic analogues of the types portrayed by Winslow Homer. Vail and Homer pursued similar themes. Homer's commentaries on the struggles of men and women against nature were evoked by his experiences on the English coast in 1881–82 but were domesticated to New England upon his return; the high esteem in which they have been held in the twentieth century is attributable not only to their unquestionable visual and emotional strength but also to their association with the American scene and even to Homer's relative stylistic naïveté. Vail brought to similar subjects—which were not at all unfamiliar among French and British painters of the period[9]—a far more extensive academic training. Born in France of American parents, raised in New York, eventually an expatriate living in Paris, and a recipient of numerous international honors and awards (including a gold medal at the 1889 fair), Vail has been lost to twentieth-century art history because of his cosmopolitanism.

Although the ateliers of the Ecole des Beaux-Arts had attracted many American students of painting, beginning in the late 1860s, independent studios continued to exercise their appeal. Groups of students seeking alternatives to the Beaux-Arts emphasis on draftsmanship and on the classical tradition had organized two such studios, in which Bonnat and Carolus-Duran were visiting critics. Founded in 1865 and 1873, respectively, these two *ateliers des élèves*, which served students into the early 1880s, numbered dozens of Americans in their ranks. (Fernand Cormon [1854–1924] took over Bonnat's studio in 1883.) In these studios, and in others similarly run, students took responsibility for renting space, hiring models, and collecting fees to cover expenses. The critics, who usually visited twice a week, did so with no recompense other than their students' loyalty and gratitude.

Bonnat (1833–1922), who had based his style on a combination of Parisian academic and Spanish baroque influences, applied it to gruesomely realistic biblical themes, which recalled the interests of Ribera, and painted portraits reminiscent of those of Velázquez. By the mid-1870s he had subordinated these realist tendencies to an interest in society portraiture. The influence of Bonnat's academic-painterly manner, evident at the 1889 fair in the works of Weeks and Blashfield, was even more apparent in the works of Thomas Eakins.

Eakins, in fact, recapitulated Bonnat's stylistic development, establishing an academic armature by study at the Pennsylvania Academy of the Fine Arts and under Gérôme in Paris, and then adding Spanish realism through a few months of study under Bonnat and a visit to Spain. Eakins's portraits *Professor George F. Barker* and *The Veteran* (see page 149) derive in part from Bonnat's lessons and paintings. They reveal a characteristic veneer of expressive paint laid over carefully studied, solidly developed volumes and a suggestive chiaroscuro reminiscent of Rembrandt, whom both Bonnat and his pupil admired. However, the special eloquence of Eakins's image of Reynolds is attributable solely to Eakins's sensibility. A portrayal of a friend, not a commissioned portrait, it was inevitably more intimate. It may also reflect a closeness between artist and sitter arising from the fact that both were grappling at the time with difficulties in their lives: Eakins professionally, in his dispute with the Pennsylvania Academy and Reynolds personally, in the recent death of his wife.

Bonnat's more fashionable portrait manner resonates in the image that Charles Sprague Pearce showed of his wife in the 1889 fair. A student of Bonnat from 1873 to 1876, Pearce had produced several ambitious works that recalled his teacher's melodramatic interpretations of biblical episodes. Also, in his quest for figure subjects, he pursued the exotic, following the lead of Bonnat's occasional excursions into orientalism and finding additional inspiration in Brittany peasants. For these works, including *Shepherdess* (unlocated) and *Evening* (see page 200), he relied, too, on stylistic inspiration from the analogous subjects of Jules Breton and Bastien-Lepage, especially the latter's exploitation of an even, diffused, shadowless light, a high horizon line, and a monochromatic palette.

Like Pearce, whom he followed in Bonnat's studio, working there from 1876 to 1879, Walter Gay demonstrated a dual interest in works shown at the

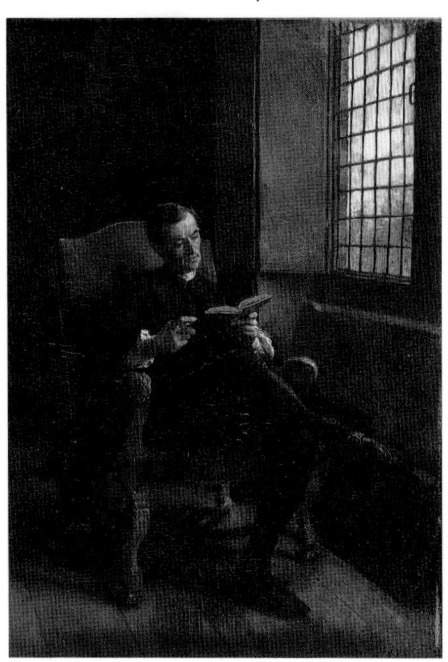

17.
Jean-Louis-Ernest Meissonier (1815–1891)
Man Reading, 1855
Oil on panel, 8½ x 6″ (20.8 x 15.2 cm)
Wadsworth Atheneum, Hartford,
Gift of James Junius Goodwin

1889 fair. Under the influence of Bonnat, Gay had absorbed lessons from Spanish art, both traditional and current, developing an affection for the charming small-scale costume pieces by Mariano Fortuny y Marsal (1838–1874). These popular vignettes of exotic and old-time characters, and others painted by Fortuny's French counterpart, Meissonier (see fig. 8), inspired Gay to similar efforts, such as *The Book-worm* and *A Dominican* (both unlocated). In 1884, however, Gay abandoned this charming genre form in favor of monumental portrayals of Brittany peasants, typified by the four large canvases that dominated the group of six paintings he showed in the 1889 display. Inspired fundamentally by Bonnat's early realism, in part by Jules Breton, Bastien-Lepage, and other French painters of peasant life, and finally by Pearce's recent success with similar subjects, Gay commented in paint upon the rural labors and the piety of the peasant and on the waning era of handicraft, still preserved in Brittany.

Carolus-Duran (1838–1917) rivaled Bonnat as a popular portraitist in the Third Republic, practicing a manner even more seductively vivacious and flattering, one that appeared to be especially appealing to women sitters. After a brief period of academic instruction in his home city of Lille, Carolus-Duran had eschewed additional formal instruction, basing his art on personal study of masters of the painterly tradition: Titian, Murillo and Velázquez, Gainsborough, Reynolds, and Lawrence. The teaching method that he evolved was at odds with the academic system. He did not favor long and rigorous study in cast and life drawing but advocated painting from the live model as early as possible. Apparently more willing than their French counterparts to take a chance with a stylistic dissident and apparently eager to acquire a fluent style rapidly, many Americans gravitated to Carolus-Duran. His *atelier des élèves* was well represented at the 1889 fair: twenty-one of his students exhibited. The most prominent in the display, the quintessential stylistic clone of the master and the leading product of the studio, was John Singer Sargent.

Entering the studio of Carolus-Duran in 1874, at the age of eighteen, Sargent was a prodigy; he submitted works to the Salon as early as 1877 and won an honorable mention the following year. The eighties marked Sargent's attainment of maturity, and the events of the decade are summarized in the works he showed at the 1889 fair: his travels to confirm contact with Spanish and Dutch baroque traditions produced *The Daughters of Edward D. Boit* (fig. 19); his debut in Paris as a fashionable portraitist was linked with his *Mrs. Henry White*, depicting the wife of the American ambassador (who hung the portrait prominently in the embassy); the *succès de scandale* of the 1884 Salon, Sargent's ensuing move to London, and his cultivation of English sitters are reflected in *The Misses Vickers* (see page 205). Technically, this group of portraits and others document Sargent's debt to the virtuoso manner of his Parisian teacher as well as his own willingness to defy tradition in the interest of lively composition and his personal verve in characterization.

By the 1870s, the pressure on Parisian facilities for art instruction was so great that institutions other than the Beaux-Arts school and its studios, and the nonprofit student-run *ateliers des élèves*, flourished. These included small private schools, in which an individual teacher or two might charge tuition and offer instruction, and larger schools similarly run for profit. The largest, most ambitious, and most durable of these private institutions was the Académie Julian, which had been founded in 1868 to assist students in preparing for the matriculation examinations at the Ecole des Beaux-Arts. Reorganized after the Franco-Prussian War along more professional lines, Julian's began to compete with the overcrowded Ecole, employing teams of critics to provide instruction fully consistent with Beaux-Arts technical standards. With only financial requirements for admission and an unlimited ability to expand its premises, Julian's became an immense, multibranched resource for hundreds of art students from the United States and elsewhere, including numerous aspiring women artists (who did not gain access to the government school until 1897).

The most popular teams of critics at Julian's during the late 1870s and the 1880s were Gustave Boulanger and Jules-Joseph Lefebvre, and William Adolphe Bouguereau (1825–1905) and Tony Robert-Fleury (1837–1912). The teams would make studio visits in alternate months and each team was responsible for instructing in the school's women's studios during certain periods. A similar system was in effect at the rival Académie Colarossi, where Gustave Courtois (1853–1923), Raphael Collin (1850–1916), P. A. J. Dagnan-Bouveret, and other younger artists offered criticism. The leading critics in both schools were exemplary practitioners of the academic style, the artistic alter egos of their counterparts at the Beaux-Arts. As students at the government school themselves, several of them had won the Prix de Rome, the Beaux-Arts' highest honor. They were frequent contributors to and jurors for the Salon exhibitions (a matter of no small interest to their students), recipients of many official prizes, and beneficiaries of extensive public and private patronage. The instruction that they offered was conservative, stressing figure drawing and scrupulous study of the model as preparation for painting.

As at the Beaux-Arts, students at Julian's and Colarossi's proceeded, upon the recommendation of their instructors, from cast drawing to life drawing and ultimately to painting from life. Technical standards were essentially identical with those of the government school's ateliers. In the weekly production of the inevitable single-figure *académies*, naturalistic rendering of the appearance of the model at hand was emphasized. These exercises were supplemented by weekly composition assignments to be completed in the students' own quarters and brought to the academy for judging. Such competitions and other regular *concours* constituted a second level of instruction, providing opportunities for approbation and for cash prizes—both of considerable interest to students who had made significant emotional and financial investments in their Parisian studies. In contrast to the Beaux-Arts, the independent academies operated year-round, provided additional instruction in accord with the trade school tradition (for example, classes in illustration, watercolor, and miniature painting), and accommodated in evening classes students employed during the day.

In the American display at the 1889 fair, the predominance of paintings from the 1880s—when Julian's and Colarossi's attracted so many American pupils—makes the influence of study under Boulanger, Lefebvre, and their confrères a prominent visual keynote—as well as a much-reiterated reference in the 1889 catalogue notes. Almost fifty participants had been students of Boulanger and Lefebvre, more than ten of Bouguereau and Robert-Fleury. Some worked in more than one studio and even in more than one school, so the variations with respect to designated teachers are numerous. (There are also some instances in which a student known to have studied with certain teams at Julian's or Colarossi's did not so specify in the fair catalogue.)

Study at the independent Parisian schools was the primary source of French academic ideals for a few of the Americans who showed in 1889. Elizabeth Jane Gardner and Thomas Dewing, for example, had had only rudimentary instruction at home before going to Paris. Although Gardner worked briefly with other Parisian artists in the mid-1860s, the most profound stylistic influence upon her was Bouguereau, with whom she appears to have begun study at Julian's in 1875. Gardner would not only re-form her style in close imitation of Bouguereau's—as is evident in her entries in the 1889 fair—she would become her teacher's constant companion and eventually, in 1896, his wife. Dewing, who had had some drawing instruction at the Lowell Institute in Boston, had also presented a *tabula rasa* to his teachers at Julian's, Boulanger and Lefebvre, from 1876 to 1879. In the classicizing works done after his return from study in Paris, Dewing would echo Lefebvre's predilection for a highly refined, mannered type of female figure. Residues may be discerned in a work such as his *Lady in Yellow* (Isabella Stewart Gardner Museum, Boston).

By contrast with Gardner and Dewing, most of the American students of the independent Parisian art schools and studios had received multiple dosages of French academic training. They had begun work at home, in schools such as that of the Museum of Fine Arts in Boston, the National Academy of Design and the Art Students League in New York, and the Pennsylvania Academy of the Fine Arts in Philadelphia—all of which had been founded, or reformed, on the Beaux-Arts model. Having worked under alumni of the studios of Gérôme and Cabanel, they had come to Paris for additional training, occasionally under their teachers' teachers at the Beaux-Arts, but most often at Julian's or Colarossi's. Sorting out individual influences from within the relatively subtle range of their teachers' stylistic and subject preferences in this later period is an especially delicate task. Analysis of the effect of individual teachers is also complicated by the fact that some students pursued multiple affiliations while in Paris, working either with a succession of teachers, or supplementing instruction received in one studio—even at the Beaux-Arts—with study at Julian's or Colarossi's in the evening or during school vacations.

In general, the academic traits evident among the students of Gérôme and Cabanel in the 1870s differ little from those evident in the works of artists who studied in Paris in the eighties. These younger artists—Hitchcock, Melchers, Gutherz, Klumpke, and dozens of others—were all equipped with formidable skills in figure drawing and painting and would range far and wide for subjects in which they could demonstrate those skills: traditional historical and religious, symbolic, and allegorical themes; historical and exotic genre, including peasant and oriental images; even contemporary genre, foreign and domestic. Ultimately some of those attracted to the contemporary—artists such as Hassam and Tarbell—would even use the academic armatures evident in their 1889 fair entries as substructures for Impressionist patinas. In the 1889 display the most striking premonitions of American painters' interest in Impressionism appear in works by students of Gérôme: Kenyon Cox's *Flying Shadows* (see page 133) and J. Alden Weir's *Lengthening Shadows* (see page 226). The reasons for American academic painters' commitments to the varied subjects that they examined—other than their merely finding something curious or convenient to paint, which seems to have been the case for many—invite further inquiry.

The American display of paintings at the 1889 fair included not only works that recorded American painters' direct contact with a variety of French teachers and influences but also works that were executed at home by the students of former students in Paris. Although the experience of French training of these artists was at second hand, their works are best understood within the French tradition. Frederic Remington, for example, was fully aware of French art and studio methods through his study at the Yale School of Fine Arts with John H. Niemeyer and John F. Weir from 1878 to 1880. Niemeyer had worked under Gérôme for four years in the late 1860s, and Weir had been in close touch with

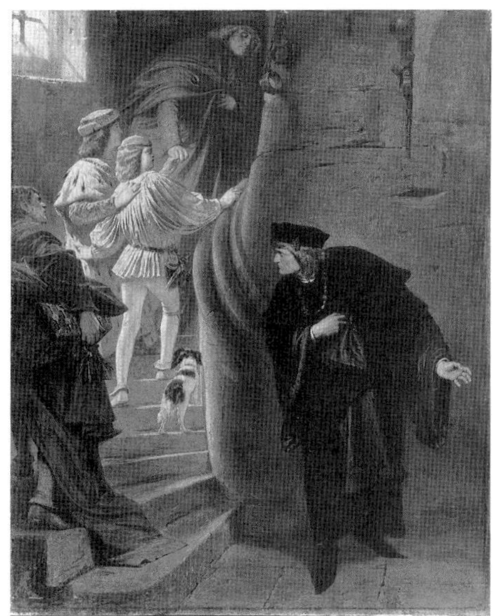

18.
Karl von Piloty (1826–1886)
The Imprisonment of Princes Edward and York in the Tower of London
Oil on canvas, 53¼ x 43" (135 x 109 cm)
Bayer: Staatsgemäldesammlungen, Munich

his brother, J. Alden Weir, when the latter was studying under Gérôme, in the mid-1870s. Remington resumed his art instruction in 1886 at the Art Students League in New York, where two former pupils of Gérôme—Eakins and George de Forest Brush—were teaching. In the light of this exposure, and of manifest interest in similar subjects on the part of Brush and Eakins, it is not difficult to link Remington's commitment to the "exotic" genre of the American West with the concerns of his teachers and of their teacher, Gérôme.[10]

Although Paris was the most potent influence upon late-nineteenth-century American painters, several other European art centers attracted American students. The most competitive was Munich, especially for Americans of German ancestry. Vestiges of Munich training can be discerned in some of the works shown by Americans in 1889. It should be understood that the style advocated by the Royal Academy in Munich scarcely differed from the style associated with the Ecole des Beaux-Arts. Indeed one of the leading Munich instructors, Karl von Piloty (see fig. 18), had been a fervent admirer of Delaroche and a student of Gleyre—both teachers of Gérôme—and had adopted and espoused traits that French academics would have endorsed: dramatic, journalistic reportage, lucid, stagelike presentation, and high finish. There were subtle differences between the approach of Piloty and those of his colleagues, but the chief differences between academic instruction in Munich and that in Paris were closer personal contact between the French teachers and their students and a relative de-emphasis on study from the nude in the German school.

In the 1870s, instruction available in Munich was enriched and complicated by the presence of Wilhelm Leibl (1844–1900). He became a mentor to many artists although he taught no classes. Leibl stood in relation to the Munich Royal Academy as his friend Courbet stood in relation to the Beaux-Arts—as a dissident preferring common subjects and a rough painterly style. He ignored linear definition and high finish in favor of the flashy manner of Hals. Many Americans who studied in Munich in the 1870s were attracted to Leibl's example, often despite their concurrent enrollment in the Royal Academy.

The manner of Leibl, which became the foundation for the signature style of William Merritt Chase, one of the most prominent contributors to the 1889 American display, is seen in *The First Portrait* (see page 129). Chase imparted the virtuoso style based on the northern baroque tradition to his many American pupils, among them Rosalie Lorraine Gill and Rosina Emmet Sherwood, both of whom also showed in 1889. He shared his enthusiasm for the Belgian painter Alfred Stevens (see fig. 9) with such pupils as J. Louis Webb, whose *A Studio Corner* (unlocated) echoes interiors by both Chase and Stevens. A master eclectic, Chase had not failed to absorb the influence of Carolus-Duran and Sargent, as is evident in *Lady in Black* (see page 129). During the 1880s Chase lightened his palette in a series of New York park scenes that are indebted to the works of Giuseppe de Nittis (1846–1884); they anticipate Chase's fuller commitment to Impressionism in the 1890s.

The impact of the academic Munich style is apparent in the works of such artists as Robert Koehler and Charles Ulrich, who arrived in Munich for study after 1880. By that time, Leibl himself had abandoned the manner of Hals in favor of that of Holbein, whose effect—like that of the concurrent interest in the Dutch little masters—was to reinforce academic precision. Koehler's *The Strike* (see page 181) and Ulrich's *In the Land of Promise* (Corcoran Gallery of Art, Washington, D.C.) are ambitious genre scenes recorded with a meticulousness of technique that would have elicited as much praise among academics in Paris as in Munich. Their content, however, was as unusual for Munich as it was for conservative Paris; to find an analogue one has to turn to English social realism as practiced by Hubert von Herkomer.[11]

With respect to English influence, one should consider the case of Francis Davis Millet, who showed in both the English and the American section. Millet's early training had been undertaken in Antwerp, whose academy was devoted to the painterly tradition of Rubens, but his style was re-formed by his increasing contact with such English Victorian painters as Sir Lawrence Alma-Tadema and Sir Frederic Leighton. While High Victorian painting was based on the art of classical antiquity and of Renaissance Italy, these foundations were buttressed by French influence such as the training that several English artists had under Gleyre. Thus, while Millet's costume pieces—whether classical, seventeenth-century, or eighteenth-century, American or English—may rely on English examples, they are not inconsistent with French models.

The multiple, diverse, overlapping, and reinforcing influences on Millet and on the others examined here are typical of the eclectic artistic experiences of many late-nineteenth-century American painters. American artists who exhibited at the Exposition Universelle of 1867 had been criticized for the provincialism of their styles and subjects. In the ensuing years they had sought to remedy their perceived shortcomings; responding to the growing attraction of Europe, especially of Paris, for art training, they had begun to equip themselves by study there to compete for international approbation and patronage. The results of American artists' efforts to assimilate European—particularly French—stylistic traits began to be apparent in the Salons and in the Exposition Universelle of 1878. They were fully in evidence at the 1889 fair and were rewarded by prizes, by purchases—including several by the French government—and by favorable critical commentary. In the degree that it emulated European models, American art was perceived to have come of age.

Seeing the current recreation of the American display of paintings at the 1889 Exposition brings home to us the wealth of sheer competence and talent that Americans had developed. But this exhibition also makes clear the debt that late-nineteenth-century American painters owed to European—especially French—ideals. So pervasive is French influence that the suspicion arises that at the original display the sign ETATS-UNIS over the door was necessary to assure visitors that they were in the American section.

In the presence of these paintings we can understand more fully than ever before the strong reaction against cosmopolitan academicism that surfaced around the time of World War I. Critics searching for what was American in American art found little to praise in the Salon manner that the leading painters of the late nineteenth century had mastered, in works that responded to international artistic imperatives—the stylish, the curious, the picturesque—rather than to native traditions and values. Bolstered by the midwives to modernism who condemned the teachers that the Americans had studied under, cultural nationalist commentators defamed the leading lights of the late nineteenth century almost in direct proportion to their earlier success. Cultural nationalism was nourished by the isolationism of the period between the world wars and by efforts to find a reassuring national past in the face of the Great Depression. The durable effects of this peculiar xenophobia in the history of American art have been meaningfully challenged only since about 1970.[12] The present exhibition, mining that revisionist vein, presents a fascinating cross section of the highest accomplishments of American artists of the heart of the Gilded Age, as measured by their own standards. It cannot help but illuminate, and provoke further inquiry into, the cultural, political, and economic forces that generated an American art that was not very American at all.

Notes

1. Henry James, "John S. Sargent," *Harper's Magazine* (Oct. 1887), reprinted with emendations in *Picture and Text* (1893); reprinted in John L. Sweeney, ed., *The Painter's Eye: Notes and Essays on the Pictorial Arts by Henry James* (London, 1956), p. 216.
2. "Our Artists at Home: Mr. Edward *[sic]* Lord Weeks . . . in the Avenue Wagram," *New York Herald* (Paris ed.), Aug. 3, 1890, suppl., p. 2, quoted in Susan Grant, "American Paintings Acquired by the French Government, 1879–1900" (master's thesis, George Washington University, Washington, D.C., 1983), p. 90.
3. See Lois Marie Fink, "French Art in the United States, 1850–1870, Three Dealers and Collectors," *Gazette des Beaux-Arts*, 6ième période, 92 (Sept. 1978): pp. 87–100; Alexandra R. Murphy, "French Paintings in Boston: 1800–1900," in Anne L. Poulet, *Corot to Braque: French Paintings from the Museum of Fine Arts, Boston* (exhib. cat., Museum of Fine Arts, Boston, 1979), pp. xvii–xlvi.
4. For a later instance of such separatism in the interest of attracting European patronage see Jennifer A. Martin Bienenstock, "From Yankee Ingenuity to Yankee Artistry: American Artists at the Antwerp World's Fair of 1894," *Museummagazine, Koninklijk Museum voor Schone Kunsten, Antwerp*, no. 7 (1987), pp. 36–48.
5. See Albert Boime, *Thomas Couture and the Eclectic Vision* (New Haven and London, 1980), chap. 15.
6. See Albert Boime, "The Instruction of Charles Gleyre and the Evolution of Painting in the Nineteenth Century," in Rudolf Koella, René Berger, Michel Thévoz, et al., *Charles Gleyre ou les illusions perdues* (exhib. cat., Kunstmuseum, Winterthur, Switzerland, 1974), pp. 102–25.
7. For a full treatment of the issue, see Peter Bermingham, *American Art in the Barbizon Mood* (exhib. cat., National Collection of Fine Arts, Washington, D.C., 1975).
8. See H. Barbara Weinberg, *The American Pupils of Jean-Léon Gérôme* (Fort Worth, Texas: Amon Carter Museum, 1984).
9. See William H. Gerdts, "Winslow Homer in Cullercoats," *Yale University Art Gallery Bulletin*, vol. 36, no. 2 (Spring 1977), pp. 18–35.
10. For a fuller discussion of Remington in relation to his teachers, see Doreen Bolger Burke, "Remington in the Context of His Artistic Generation," in Michael Edward Shapiro, Peter H. Hassrick, et al., *Frederic Remington: The Masterworks* (exhib. cat., St. Louis Art Museum, 1988), pp. 38–67.
11. See Michael Quick, Eberhard Ruhmer, and Richard V. West, *Munich and American Realism in the 19th Century* (exhib. cat., E. B. Crocker Art Gallery, Sacramento, Calif., 1978).
12. See especially Lois Marie Fink, "The Role of France in American Art, 1850–1870" (Ph.D. dissertation, University of Chicago, 1970), and related articles; Michael Quick, *American Expatriate Painters of the Late Nineteenth Century* (exhib. cat., Dayton Art Institute, 1976); H. Barbara Weinberg, "Nineteenth-Century American Painters at the Ecole des Beaux-Arts," *American Art Journal* vol. 13 no. 4 (Autumn 1981), pp. 66–71; David Sellin, *Americans in Brittany and Normandy 1860–1910* (exhib. cat., Phoenix Art Museum, 1982); *The Quest for Unity: American Art Between World's Fairs 1876–1893* (exhib. cat. with essay by David C. Huntington, Detroit Institute of Arts, 1983); Jennifer A. Martin Bienenstock, *The Forgotten Episode: Nineteenth Century American Art in Belgian Public Collections* (exhib. cat., American Cultural Center, Brussels, 1987). Scheduled for Fall 1990 publication is H. Barbara Weinberg, *The Lure of Paris: Nineteenth-Century American Painters and Their French Teachers*, Abbeville Press, Inc., New York.

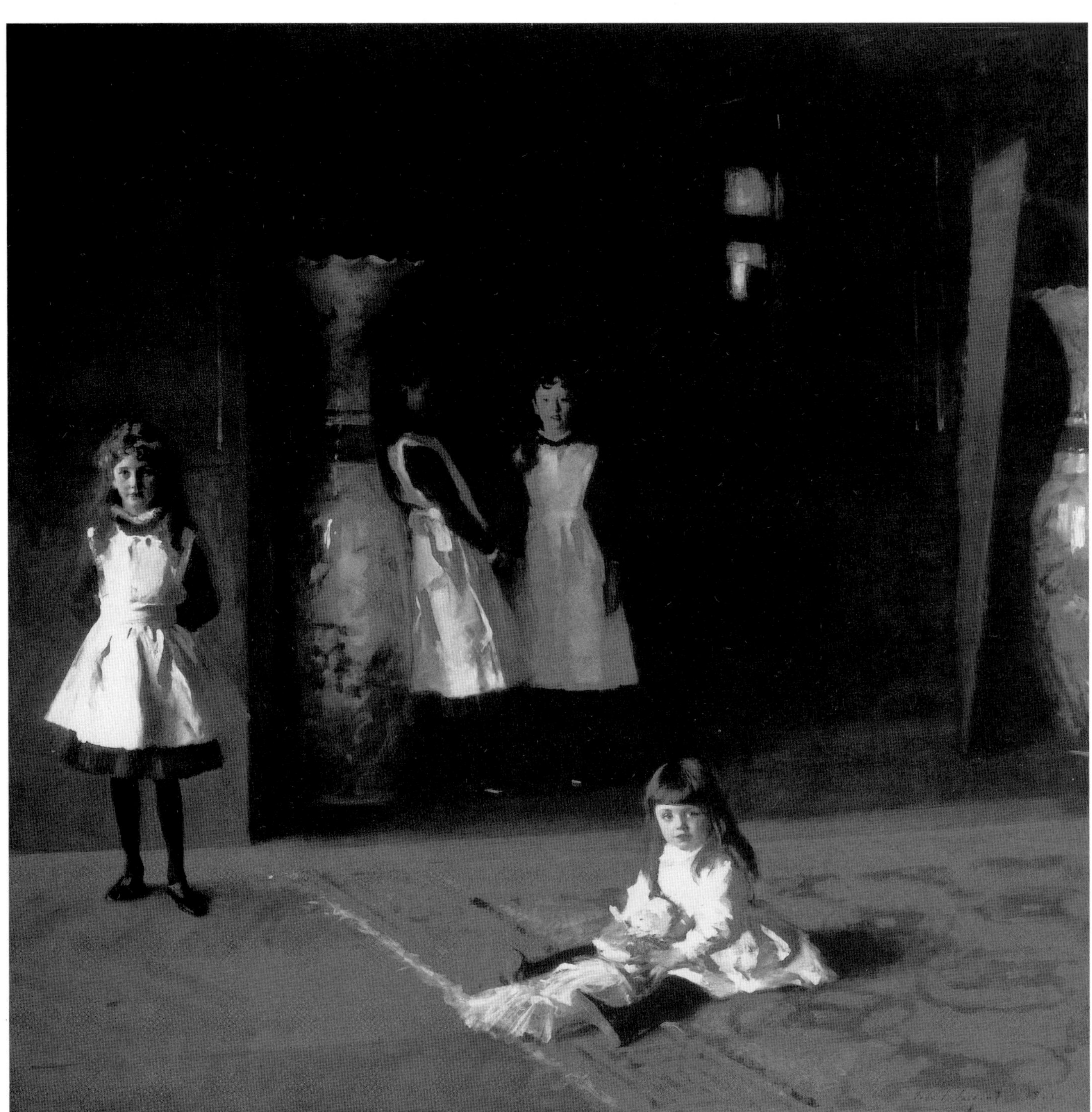

D. DODGE THOMPSON

"Loitering Through the Paris Exhibition": Highlights of the American Paintings at the Universal Exposition of 1889[1]

19.
John Singer Sargent (1856–1925)
The Daughters of Edward D. Boit, 1882
Oil on canvas, 87 x 87" (221 x 221 cm)
Museum of Fine Arts, Boston,
Gift of the daughters of Edward D. Boit,
in memory of their father

The American contribution to the 1889 world's fair surprised the critics in "the variety of temperaments represented and the diversity of the pictures," reported Theodore Child in *Harper's Monthly*.[2] The reviewers were typically at a loss to formulate an analytical framework to describe the American paintings section of the fair. Harold Frederic, commentator for the *New York Times*, reported that his mission "was not unlike the task of an amateur turned loose in a picture dealer's attic."[3] With 336 paintings by 189 American artists, many of whom studied in France, no wonder the reviewers were unable to summarize succinctly the tendencies or national characteristics of an "American School." The reviewer in the *Atlantic Monthly* wrote:

There never was a time in which there were so many diversities of style; contrasts could hardly go further in conception and treatment of the same subject in every school of painting,—portraits, landscapes, religious, marine, military. One would like to say, "My brethren, be not many masters," but the difficulty is rather that there are too many pupils.[4]

In the *Catalogue Général Officiel* the American painters proudly listed their teachers in the customary French fashion (for example: *William S. Allen . . . élève de MM. Bouguereau, J. Lefebvre, et Claude Monet*), and it was evident that compared to the previous Paris world's fairs, in 1867 and 1878, the American section was particularly international in its training and cosmopolitan in outlook.

The selection process itself (see pages 13ff.), with artists proposing their own works and with final decisions divided between an expatriate and a stateside jury, inevitably resulted in a heterogeneous representation. Faced with this artistic omnium-gatherum—an exhibition of almost incomprehensible diversity of style and subject matter—the commentators on the American section reviewed the selection in Baedeker fashion.[5] Critics would commence with the most celebrated works in the collection, and then move on to other works in proximity to them in the galleries. Fortunately, there exist good photographs of the two galleries devoted to oil paintings in the American section, used as illustrations in the official reports of the United States Commissioners, to assist the viewer a century later to replicate this experience.[6] Three of the photographs (figs. 20–22) reproduce most of the main gallery of the American paintings section,

20.
Main ("Expatriate") Gallery, United States Section, Exposition Universelle, Paris, 1889.
Memphis Brooks Museum of Art,
Gift of Marshall and Elizabeth Goodheart

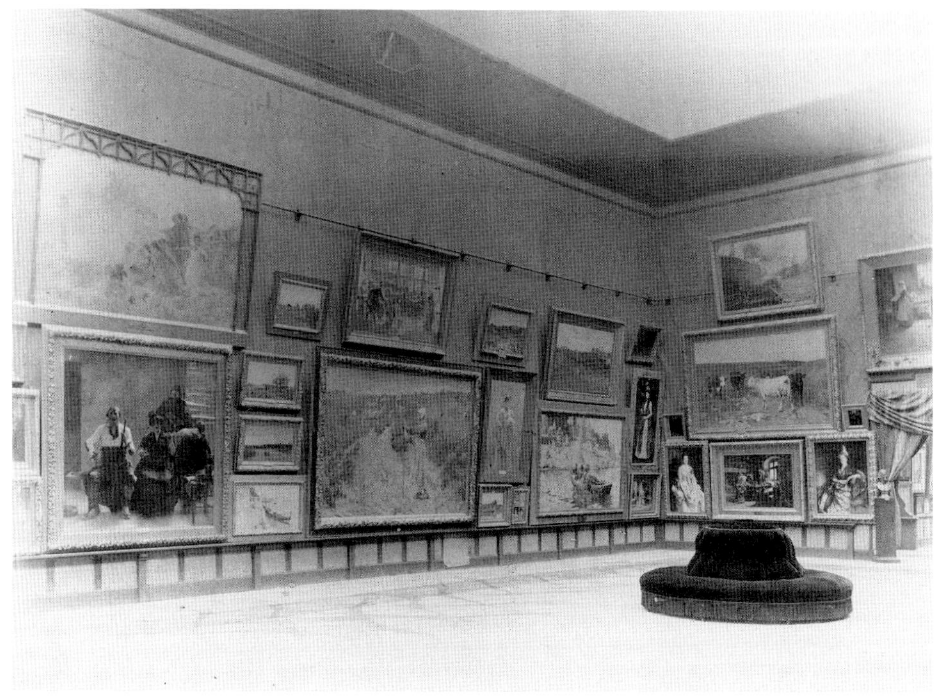

21.
Main ("Expatriate") Gallery, United States Section, Exposition Universelle, Paris, 1889
National Academy of Design, New York.

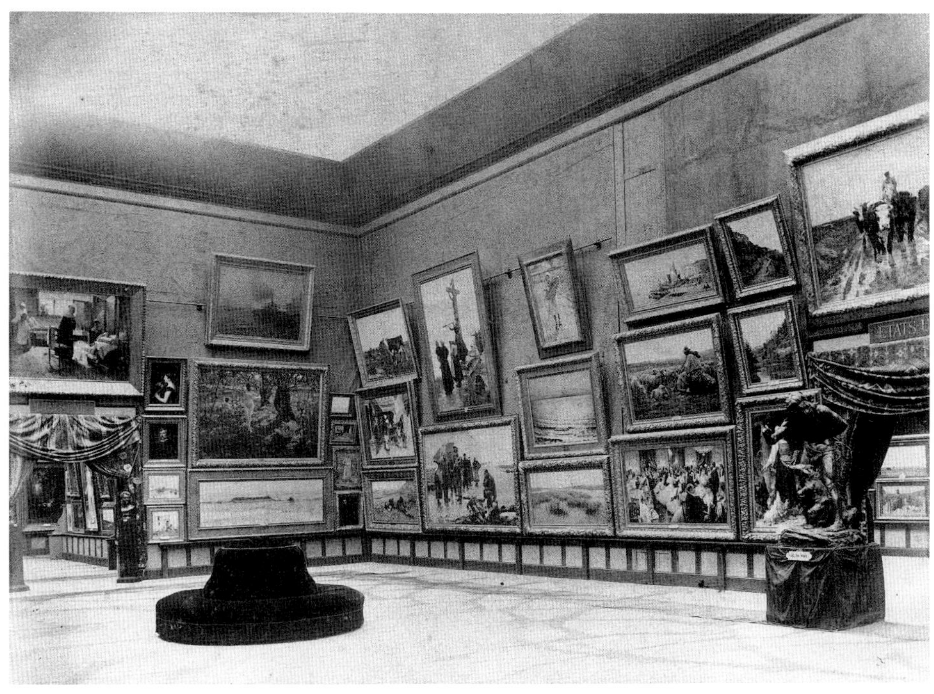

22.
Main ("Expatriate") Gallery, United States Section, Exposition Universelle, Paris, 1889
National Academy of Design, New York

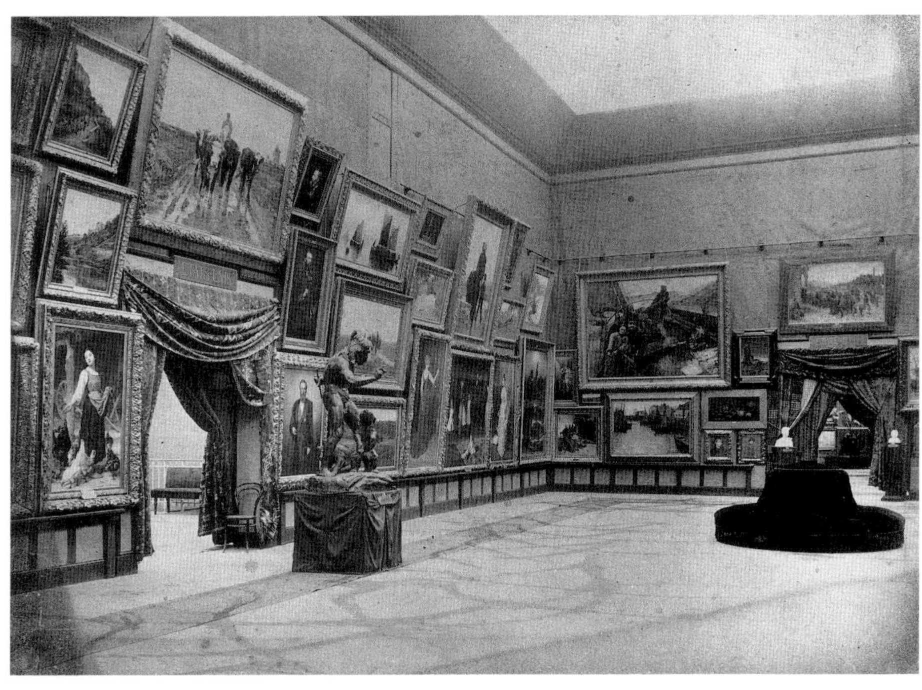

23.
Lateral ("Resident American") Gallery, United States Section, Exposition Universelle, 1889
National Academy of Design, New York

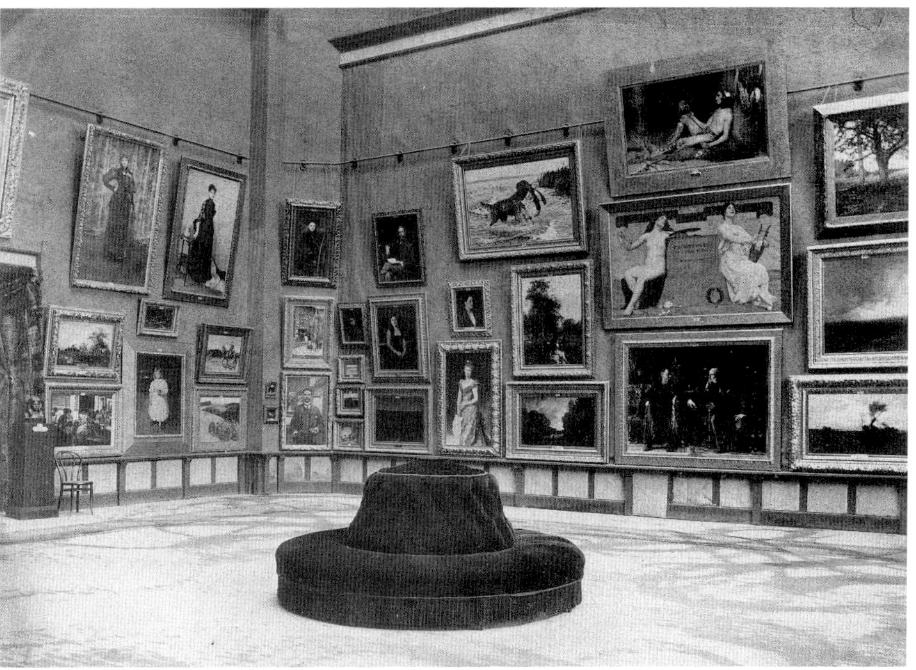

24.
William Turner Dannat (1853–1929)
The Quartette, 1884
Oil on canvas, 94⅛ x 91¼" (240 x 23.1 cm)
© The Metropolitan Museum of Art, New York, Gift of Mrs. William H. Dannat. 87.26

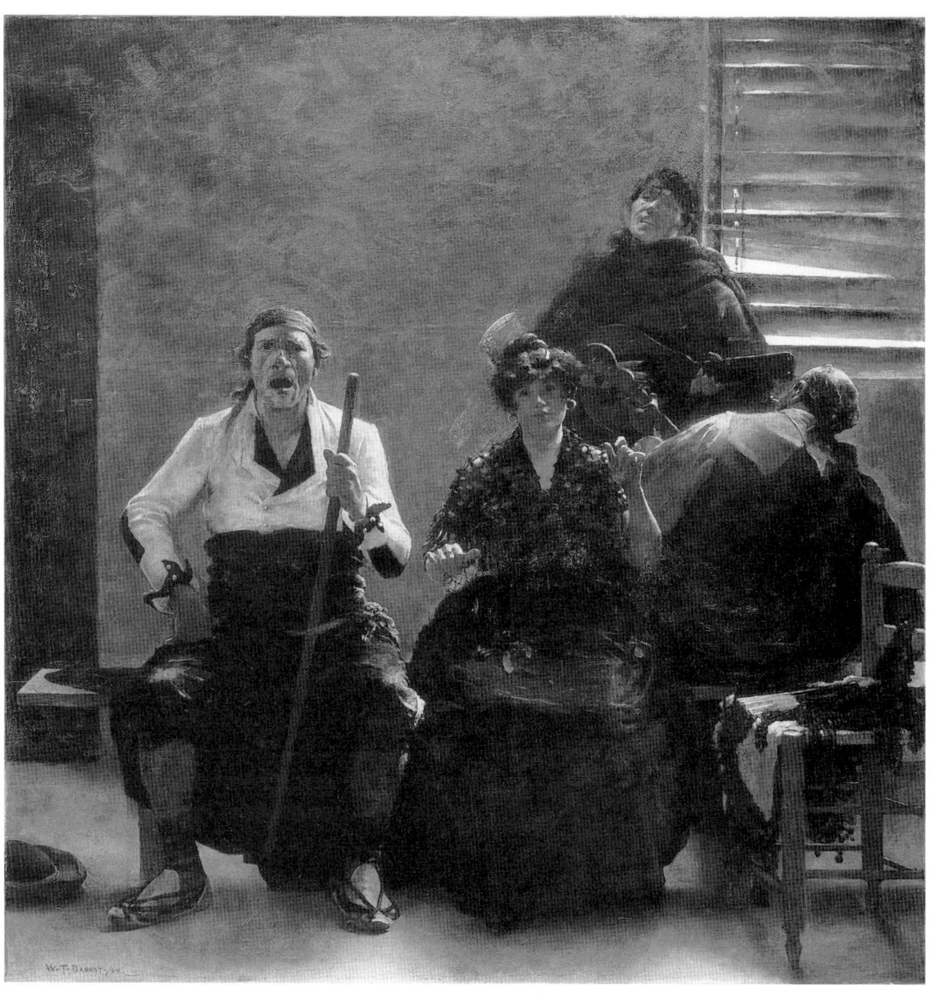

dominated by the Paris-based American artists; a fourth photograph (fig. 24) records about one-third of the installation of the somewhat smaller gallery occupied by the stateside artists.

The critics agreed that the "place of honor" in the American paintings section in 1889 was accorded by the United States jury to William T. Dannat's *The Quartette* (figs. 20, 24), a Spanish genre scene.[7] Dannat's *tableau vivant* was installed in the center of the most prominent wall of the main gallery documented in the period photographs. Dannat was represented by two other paintings in the main gallery, a selection that highlighted his study of the old masters. If *The Quartette* was an ambitious exercise in the Spanish baroque, the *Portrait of Miss H.* (see fig. 22) was an essay in the Dutch manner. Dannat's forthright portrait of Eva Haviland recalled the portraits of Rogier van der Weyden; United States Commissioner of Fine Arts Rush Hawkins remarked that it "seems to take us back to the best period of the Dutch school."[8] Although a modest canvas by comparison with many works surrounding it in the main gallery, the *Portrait of Miss H.* attracted a great deal of attention and was purchased by the French government for the Luxembourg Museum. A year later, Dannat persuaded the Luxembourg to exchange the *Portrait of Miss H.* for *A Study in Red* (see fig. 22 and page 137), which also hung in the main gallery.[9]

While Dannat's *The Quartette* was installed in the place of honor, most contemporary critics acknowledged that the crowning achievement of the

American section was the six portrait compositions of John Singer Sargent.[10] Dannat had entered Carolus-Duran's atelier five years after Sargent, and he begged comparison with his older compatriot through such ambitious Spanish works as *The Quartette*. With *A Study in Red*, Dannat entered a new stylistic phase characterized by a softer, enveloping atmosphere and delicate color harmonies, far removed from Sargent's bravura style based on the art of Velázquez and Hals. The comparison between the two American expatriates was encouraged by the American jury through the juxtaposition in the gallery (see fig. 22) of Dannat's full-length portrait with two of Sargent's most magisterial creations, *The Daughters of Edward D. Boit* (fig. 19) and *Mrs. Henry White*. Curiously, while the portraits of both artists were warmly praised by the critics, Dannat's and Sargent's relative merits and styles were not directly compared.

From the far end of the main gallery, Mrs. Boit attentively kept an eye on her daughters. *Mrs. Edward D. Boit* (see fig. 20 and page 205), a three-quarter-length likeness of the matron by Sargent, was paired with yet another portrait of a grande dame by Sargent, *Mrs. Benjamin Kissam*, depicting a member of the Vanderbilt clan. Many critics were puzzled by Sargent's conservative showing, marked by none of the sensational originality that had accompanied his earlier appearances at the Salon.[11] It is apparent that Sargent wanted to avoid reviving the memory of the scandal of *Madame X*, in 1884, and was determined to use the Exposition to promote patronage for his female portraits. There were several other ambitious female portraits, among them two portraits of artists' wives—Edwin H. Blashfield's (see page 117) and Edmund Tarbell's (see page 213). But none of the depictions of women compared with Sargent's for originality and *virtuosité*.

If Sargent had no peer as a portrayer of feminine charms at the Paris Exposition, George P. A. Healy was the most widely recognized formal portraitist of men. Healy was the oldest of the American artists exhibiting at the Exposition, a historic link with the ateliers of Baron Gros and, especially, Thomas Couture, whose portrait style he perpetuated. Two of Healy's portraits were prominently displayed next to the door of the main gallery (see fig. 22). At eye level was installed the artist's stately rendering of Her Britannic Majesty's ambassador to France. Above *Lord Edward Robert Bulwer-Lytton* (see page 167) was positioned Healy's even more swagger portrait, *King of Roumania*. Despite the redoubtable prestige of the sitters, neither of these beribboned state portraits was as sympathetic as Healy's more informal likeness of a great adventurer: *Sir Henry M. Stanley* (see fig. 21) was located on another wall of the main gallery.

The hallmark of portraiture at the Exposition was informality and intimacy, and throughout the American section were extremely successful portraits whose authors chose not to rely on established formulas. Eastman Johnson's *Two Men* (see page 175), also known as *The Funding Bill*, was a blend of genre and portrait painting (see fig. 23, bottom row). The life-size double portrait in a dimly lit interior reflected Johnson's study of the Dutch masters. No portrait could be in greater contrast to it than James Carroll Beckwith's high-valued, broadly painted *Portrait of William Walton* (see page 116), a few paintings away. Beckwith's portrait of a fellow artist and critic was displayed effectively on the canted surface between two walls of the stateside artists' gallery. Beckwith, like Johnson, combined genre with portraiture, perhaps taking his cue from Manet's famous portrait of Zola (Musée d'Orsay, Paris). While Sargent's portraits won the honors of the exhibition, Beckwith's portrait received its share of critical attention, reminding the two friends that their teacher, Carolus-Duran, once called the *Portrait of William Walton* "the best portrait that ever came from America".[12] One other informal male portrait might be mentioned. At the top of the line of paintings to the right of *William Walton*, where it was seen to little advantage, was Thomas Eakins's *The Veteran* (see page 149). This portrait of George Reynolds—among Eakins's most somber, moving, and personal works—was hardly mentioned by the critics in their discussion of large-scale public portrait compositions in the American section.

Portraiture was the bread and butter of many American artists. To ensure an eventual livelihood, American students who studied in Paris often enrolled with a history or genre painter and also took instruction from a portraitist. Thus Thomas Eakins, Edwin Lord Weeks, and Edwin Blashfield had the benefit of study with Léon Bonnat, whose reputation as a portrait instructor was second to none among American expatriates, and of study with Jean-Léon Gérôme for history and genre painting. The visitor to the main gallery of the United States section was immediately aware of a large number of portraits, one in five works, representing 20 percent of the entire American contribution.

The largest category in the United States section was genre painting, nearly half (49 percent) of all the works shown. Landscape was the next most numerous category, at slightly more than a fourth (26 percent) of the American entries. A generation earlier, at the Exposition Universelle of 1867, the relative proportion of American genre and landscape pictures exhibited was virtually reversed (29 and 46 percent, respectively).[13] The primary emphasis on studying from the human figure encountered in European, especially French, art education encouraged Americans to compete with their European fellow students and instructors in the field of figure painting. Looking around the main gallery, the 1889 visitors, struck by the large number of genre paintings in the room, must have been hard pressed to determine which nation's exhibit they were viewing. On these walls could be seen Spanish musicians, Venetian gondoliers, Breton shepherds, Norman fisherfolk, Dutch weavers, English lightermen, Algerian felaheen, and Indian fakirs.

Within the category of genre painting the favorite subject matter was the depiction of the rustic life of the European peasant. It would be difficult to overestimate the prevalence of this theme at the time of the 1889 Exposition. The sources of the peasant motif in nineteenth-century art have been explored by a number of scholars.[14] In the *New York Times* Harold Frederic recorded his personal preference for the peasant subject by stating that a leading American exponent of the theme, Charles Sprague Pearce, deserved "the real honors of the show," with another, Daniel Ridgway Knight, having "perhaps the next best showing."[15] Pearce's largest composition, *Shepherdess* (see figs. 20 and 25), was placed, in direct competition with Dannat's *The Quartette*, on the long wall of the main gallery, where its more refined sentiment and range of gray atmospheric effects gave it an advantage over Dannat's coarse Aragonaise performers. In the main gallery Pearce's *Shepherdess* was joined by a host of French peasants, including shepherds by Gaylord S. Truesdell (see fig. 21) and Charles Henry Hayden (see fig. 20), cowherds by William Henry Howe (see fig. 21), a farmer's daughter by Elizabeth Gardner (see fig. 22), and a baker's child by Theodore Robinson (see fig. 21).

It was not only in the villages and fields but also on the rugged, elemental shorelines such as the coast of Normandy that the occupations and emotions of peasants were portrayed. Charles S. Reinhart was represented in the main gallery (fig. 21) by two large narrative compositions, *Awaiting the Absent* and its pendant, *Washed Ashore*, which together depicted the aftermath of a shipwreck near Dieppe witnessed by the artist. "It is the life of the common people of the coast,

25.
Charles Sprague Pearce (1851–1914)
Shepherdess (unlocated) c. 1886
Engraving after the painting, from George William Sheldon, *Recent Ideals of American Art*, p. 27

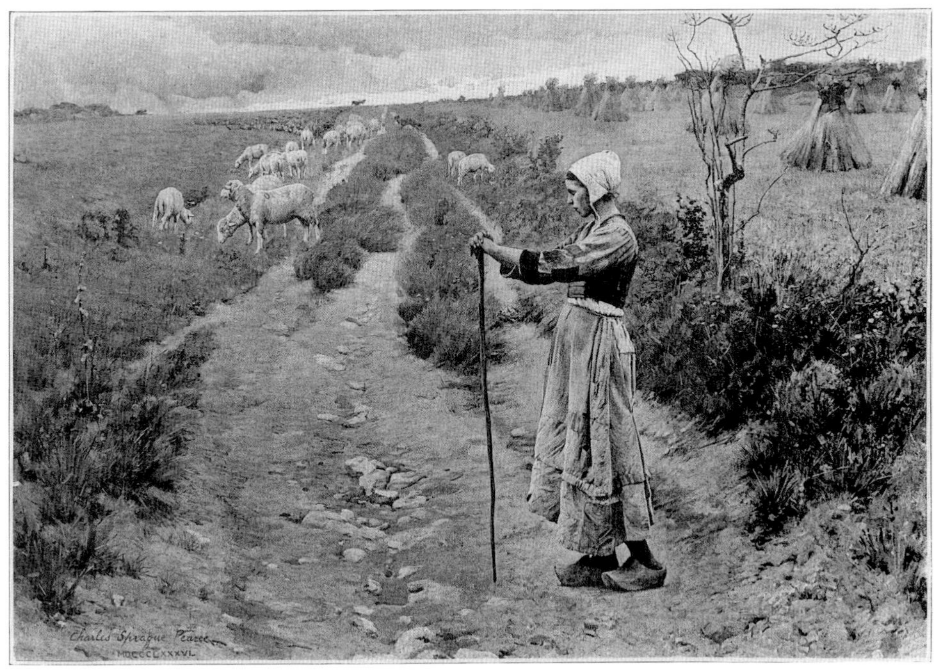

the drama of the sea that repeats itself year after year, as long as its breakers beat against the rocks and the poor fishermen go down into the sea in ships," reported Reinhart with evident sympathy for the Norman fisherfolk.[16] "I have told my story simply, as Nature tells it, without melodrama. . . . Some tender souls may be shocked, but who has not a profound impression in the presence of Death?" Reinhart's rendering of the story was more anecdotal and linear in style than most of the peasant scenes in the American section, suggesting his principal occupation as an illustrator of magazines and books.

Another artist of the seacoast was Eugene Vail, and several of his paintings appeared together in a corner of the main gallery (see fig. 22). Vail was represented by a trilogy of paintings, each in a different mood: the poignant figure study of a young widow of the sea and her son; the exertions of three sailors in a fishing smack in a hard breeze; and the port of Concarneau on a gray day. The last, a view of a Brittany fishing village, was purchased by the French government, a signal tribute to pay a foreign artist.

Some painters of peasants combined the figure with landscape, as did John Leslie Breck, Pearce, and Truesdell; others, such as Reinhart and Vail, portrayed the rustic fisherfolk in marines; still others depicted the peasant in indigenous interiors. Thus Henry Mosler dedicated himself, with great success, to the rendering of the Breton peasant's household. Mosler was the first American honored by the purchase of a work by the French government for the Luxembourg Museum. General Hawkins said of Mosler's peasants: "He portrays with equal force their joys and sorrows, and many of his works suggest that he must derive a solemn pleasure from depicting the pathetic side of their lives."[17] Mosler's *The Last Moments* (see fig. 20), charged with great pathos, was conspicuously but incongruously displayed in the main gallery between two of Sargent's grande dames, while the catalogue directed the visitor to the Luxembourg Museum to view his celebrated painting *The Return*.

Walter Gay likewise specialized at this time in Breton interiors, and four examples were accepted for the United States section. Gay's *The Spinners* was appropriately installed next to Eugene Vail's *Fishing Harbour* (see page 217), since Gay at this time lived in that fishing village in Brittany. Gay's *Le Benedicité* was bought by the French government for the Luxembourg Museum before the Exposition, and the artist borrowed it back to show in the American section.

The portrayal of the peasant was a trans-European phenomenon, observable from Sweden to Sicily. Americans studied in many artistic communities outside France in the latter half of the nineteenth century, and a common activity was the depiction of "the rural peoples who lived outside of time."[18] One of the most appealing locales for Americans to study was Holland. George Hitchcock went to Holland in 1881 to study with The Hague School marine painter Hendrick Willem Mesdag, and was joined in the Egmonds for a time in 1883 by Walter MacEwen and by Gari Melchers in 1885. Neither Hitchcock nor Melchers appears to have been featured in the installation photographs of the main gallery, despite the facts that Melchers was one of only two Americans (the other was Sargent) to be awarded a grand prize and that Hitchcock was secretary of the American committee in Paris.

MacEwen was represented by two large canvases in the main gallery. The first, *Returning from Work* (see fig. 22 and page 184), depicts young Dutch peasants crossing the polder at the end of the day. It was displayed above the door—probably without irony, near William Henry Howe's depiction of cows crossing the polder. MacEwen's second narrative was a history painting, *Town Hall of New Amsterdam (New York) 1650* (see fig. 20). It was commonplace for American artists to use an analogous European setting to provide the backdrop for an American history composition, and since depictions of seventeenth-century Dutch interiors survived in abundance, it was natural for MacEwen to employ them in recreating a Nieuw Amsterdam interior. Samuel Richards, likewise, created a historical setting for his transcription of Longfellow's *Evangeline* (see fig. 21), as did Julian Story in his outsize *The Black Prince*.

The appeal of the peasant to the artist, as well as to the patron, was based on a nostalgia for the preindustrial past, for the simplicity and self-sufficiency of the pastoral life-style. However, as a number of scholars have documented, from the 1840s on, artists increasingly recognized and forcefully depicted the plight of the poor and the dispossessed.[19] Since Robert Koehler's *The Strike* (see fig. 22 and page 181) portrayed angry factory workers in Pittsburgh, it is not surprising that the Paris jury chose to display it inconspicuously above one of the three doors to the main gallery, lest Mr. Frick or Mr. Carnegie, visiting the American section, take offense. Similarly expressive of a social point of view, Charles F. Ulrich's *In the Land of Promise* challenged the myth of America as the golden door of opportunity for the immigrant, making its point with an ironic title.

The rapid development of long-distance transportation and significant advances in illustrated journalism abetted the artistic quest for exotic subject matter, which had begun with the European colonization of North Africa at the beginning of the century and accelerated with the opening of the Suez Canal, in 1869.[20] Many American artists trained in Paris embraced *orientalisme* at some point in their career. Frederick Arthur Bridgman, president of the Paris-based American committee, entered the largest number of scenes of North Africa. Charles Theriat's *Souvenir of Biskra* (see fig. 21), could be seen in the bottom row to the right of a door to the main gallery. On an adjacent wall was installed Edwin Lord Weeks's *Hindoo Marriage Procession, Ahmedabad* (see fig. 21), extending the scope of the exotic from North Africa to even more distant Hindustan. The adventuresome Weeks, one of the few orientalist artists who

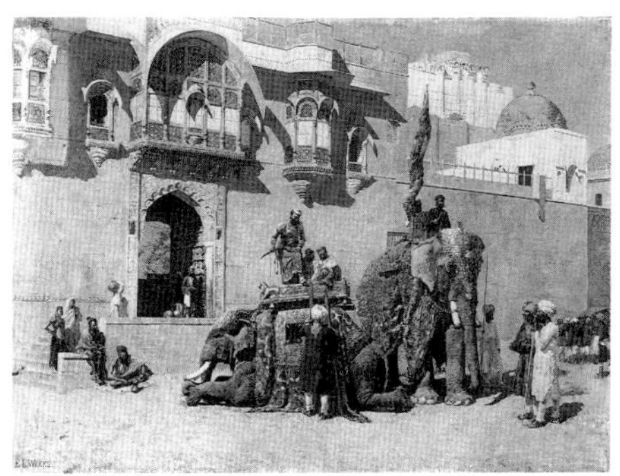

26.
Edwin Lord Weeks (1849–1903)
The Rajah of Jodhpare, c. 1888
Oil on canvas, 56 x 74" (143 x 188 cm)
Nationalgalerie, Staatliche Museen zu Berlin

ventured as far east as India, produced the largest and most compelling pictorial album of that country of any Western painter of his day. His prodigious *The Last Journey: Souvenir of the Ganges* (see page 224) competed on the wall with the *chefs-d'oeuvre* of Dannat and Pearce. Weeks's *The Rajah of Jodhpare* (see figs. 21, 26) was later bought by Kaiser Wilhelm of Germany. General Hawkins was unstinting in his praise: "He paints with rare fidelity and artistic effort, and it is doubtful if the works of any artist convey better pictures of Eastern life."[21] The judges likewise took notice of Weeks's near-photographic ability to record picturesque architecture and ritual and awarded him a gold medal.

Another student of Gérôme, the New Yorker Henry Humphrey Moore, journeyed even farther afield than his fellow students under that master, Bridgman, and Weeks. After specializing in North African subjects during the 1870s, Moore ventured to Japan in 1881, one of the earliest American artists to do so; he produced a number of genre and landscape paintings, including the three *vues japonaises* shown at the Exposition. General Hawkins was comparing Moore favorably with the large number of Paris-trained painters who experienced Japan primarily through ukiyo-e prints or photographs when he commented, "Several of these [Moore's studies] are singularly artistic in treatment, and they have the advantage of being actual scenes drawn on the spot by a careful observer."[22]

The partition of the United States paintings section into two separate galleries, one for Paris-based artists and the other for stateside artists, resulted in a virtual segregation of American history themes in the stateside gallery. Here were seen Eastman Johnson's *The Funding Bill*, Thomas Hovenden's *The Last Moments of John Brown* (see page 174), and Douglas Volk's *The Puritan Captives*. In a similar manner, the native landscape painters were isolated from the expatriate practitioners of the genre, despite the fact that many of the Americans employed a thoroughly French, Barbizon School style. Thus on either side of Johnson's *Funding Bill* in the stateside gallery was a landscape in a Barbizon mood: on the left Robert Swain Gifford's *Near the Coast* and on the right Robert C. Minor's *Close of Day*.

Traditions of patronage—state, church, and private—account in part for the different emphasis of subject matter by exhibiting nations. For example, the French government supported the production of military painting, shown at the world's fair by such partisans as Edouard Detaille and Ernest Meissonier, whereas the United States government felt no comparable need to encourage the commemoration of the deeds of its armed forces. On the contrary, Americans viewed the Civil War as a source of divisiveness and banned its representation from the country's own world's fair in Philadelphia in 1876. Military depiction in the United States was largely left to the magazine illustrators, and from this tradition came the only two scenes of the Civil War in the Exposition, *Charging the Battery* and *The Wounded Officer* by William Gilbert Gaul.

Reticent about the depiction of the Civil War, American artists were even more tentative about the representation of the life and culture of black Americans. The condition of black Americans was scantily portrayed in the American paintings section of the 1889 exposition—and only by white artists. In contrast to the heroic *Last Moments of John Brown* by Hovenden, William Verplanck Birney presented two stereotypical genre scenes, *Dolce far Niente* and *The Labor Question in the South*; George Fuller presented a brooding, mysterious portrait of a young female fieldworker, *The Quadroon*; and Thomas Eakins showed his watercolor of a father and son, *The Dancing Lesson* (see page 149).

27.
Frederic Remington (1861–1909)
The Last Lull in the Fight. Descriptive of an Affair on the Staked Plain (Texas), in 1861, as Told by a Comanche "Brave" who Participated (unlocated), c. 1889
Wood engraving after the painting, from *Harper's Weekly*, March 30, 1889, pp. 244–45
Frederic Remington Art Museum, Ogdensburg, New York

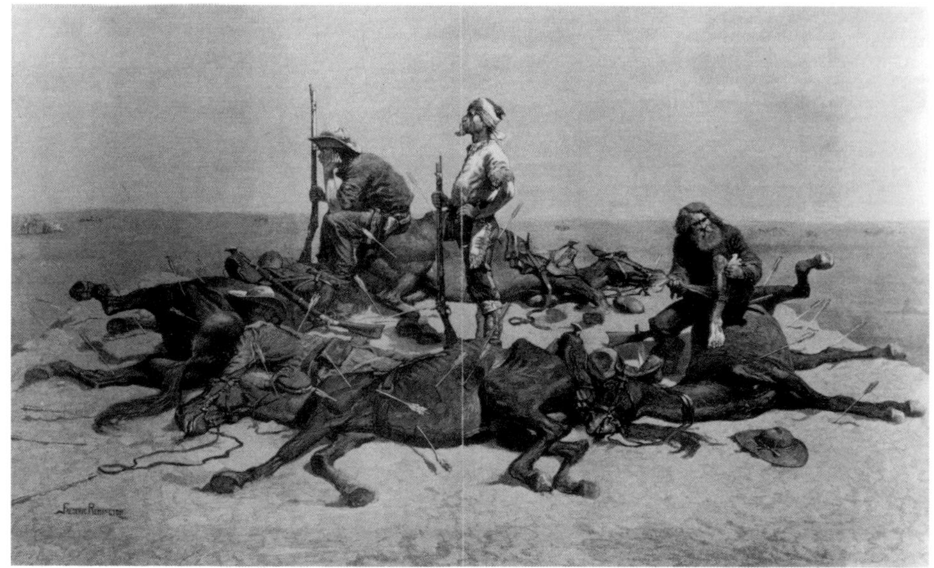

Also assigned to the stateside gallery were the painters of North American Indian themes. The painters of these subjects felt obliged to explicate for European viewers the mysteries of Native American history and custom, and in discharging this obligation they achieved the distinction of accompanying their works with the longest titles. Frederic Remington gave his sole contribution the explanatory title *A Lull in the Fight. Descriptive of an Affair on the Staked Plain (Texas), in 1861, as Told by a Comanche "Brave" Who Participated* (fig. 27), and De Cost Smith was equally detailed in the case of *Conflicting Faiths, Representing an Iroquois Holding a Shamanic Mask, Symbolizing Paganism, and a Priest with a Rosary, Symbolizing Christianity during the Period of the French Jesuit Missions Among the Iroquois in Canada in the XVIIIth Century* (see fig. 23). In contrast, a third Indian subject, the work of Henry F. Farny, had a mercifully brief and poignant title, *Danger*.

Other discrete categories of paintings represented in the United States fine arts section were marines, city views, animal pictures, still lifes, nude figure studies, and religious subjects. The *Atlantic Monthly* reviewer remarked on the progress of American maritime painting, observing that "a beautiful sea-piece by T. W. [*sic*] Richards [*After a Storm*] and one or two more studies of the same subject by painters not yet famous, gave promise that we shall soon have a fine marine school."[23] Two poetic marines were exhibited in close proximity in the main gallery (see fig. 21). These two marines—by Alexander Harrison and Edward Emerson Simmons—primarily studies of light, water, and clouds, derive from the "sea landscapes" *(paysages de mer)* painted by Whistler and Courbet when they were working together in Trouville, Normandy, in 1865. Other examples of this type of marine include Harrison's *Twilight*, Simmons's *Night, St. Ives Bay* (see page 209), and James Craig Nicoll's *Sunlight on the Sea*. Traditional maritime painting, in which seagoing vessels are the central focus, was represented by Carlton T. Chapman's *Early Morning in a Harbor*, William Merritt Chase's *Gowanus Bay*, William P. W. Dana's views of the Thames, Maurits F. H. De Haas's *On the Fishing Grounds*, Edmond Moran's *City and Harbor of New York* (see page 193), James G. Tyler's *Off Cape Ann*, and Lionel Walden's scenes of shipping activity on the Thames.

Scholars have described how Manet and the Impressionists in the 1860s and 1870s transformed the tradition of the pictorial representation of Paris and other modern cities, formerly the province of topographers and illustrators, into a source of inspiration for major artists.[24] Manet's own panoramic view of a previous Exposition Universelle, *The World's Fair of 1867* (1867; Nasjonalgalleriet, Oslo), was one of the key examples in the revitalization of city views as a modern subject category. A few adventuresome Americans acknowledged the developments of the Impressionists in their city views. Frank Myers Boggs offered three modern cityscapes, including a perspective of the Place de la Bastille, which had established the artist's reputation when it was purchased by the French government in 1882. Childe Hassam's *Rue Lafayette; Winter Evening* was closer to genre than topographical painting. Reflecting his recent residence in Paris, the painting demonstrated a familiarity with a type of urban street scene popularized by Jean Béraud, Luigi Loir, and other exhibitors in the French section. Charles Gifford Dyer showed two rather conventional views of Venice in the fashion of the current revival of eighteenth-century *vedute*, whose best-known proponent, Martin Rico y Ortega, exhibited three examples in the nearby Spanish fine arts section.

Animal pictures were surprisingly numerous. Paintings by Thomas Allen, Henry S. Bisbing, William Henry Howe, and Ogden Wood presented pastoral scenes with cows. Robert Hatton Monks, Charles Sprague Pearce, and Gaylord S. Truesdell focused on flocks of sheep, while Horatio Walker depicted a litter of pigs. The New York animal painter John H. Dolph entered into the spirit of the French celebration with an illustration of one of La Fontaine's fables, *The Rat Who Retired from the World*. Rather more prosaic was William B. Baird's rendering of a hen with her chicks, *En Famille*. There was evident only one sporting subject, John M. Tracy's *Chesapeake Bay Dog Retrieving a Wounded Goose* (see fig. 23), a large canvas installed in the upper row of paintings in the stateside gallery. Still lifes were few in number; Eleanor Greatorex and Louise Catherine Pearce joined Abbott Graves as the only proponents.

In one salient aspect American artists, revealing their Puritan background, distinguished themselves from their French teachers: studies of nude figures in the United States section at the 1889 Exposition were much less numerous than in the French section. The only nude figure compositions were Kenyon Cox's *Painting and Poetry* (see fig. 23), Wyatt Eaton's *Ariadne* (see page 152), Sarah P. B. Dodson's *Morning Stars*, Frederick W. Freer's *Nude Study*, Alexander Harrison's *In Arcadia* (see page 164), Arthur F. Mathews's *Pandore*, Walter Shirlaw's *Rufina* (see page 209), and Elihu Vedder's *The Fates Gathering In the Stars* (see page 220), *The Last Man*, and *Love Always Present*. Of the eight painters, only Frederick Freer did not give his work the aura of respectability lent by a classical or literary title. A few years earlier, Thomas Eakins had wryly told his father, in a letter from Paris, about the practice of providing nude figures with the fig leaf of classical allusion. "The rest of the painters," he wrote, "make naked women, standing, sitting, lying down, flying, dancing, doing nothing, which they call Phrynes, Venuses, nymphs, hermaphrodites, houris, and Greek proper names. The French court is become very decent since Eugénie had fig leaves put on all the statues in the Garden of the Tuileries."[25]

Six of the eight American artists who showed nudes at the 1889 Exposition had been represented in a recent genteel manifesto about American figure painting, an expensively produced volume published in Philadelphia in 1886 under the title *Book of American Figure Painters*. The anthology reflected the rise of figure painting as a primary area of creative endeavor among American artists of the time, noted the popular and astute critic Mariana van Rensselaer in her introduction. "Such a book" she added, "could not well have been given us even a few years ago."[26] This volume demonstrated the tendency of New World painters to treat their subjects decoratively rather than realistically, and a comparison of American efforts with French figure painting at the Exposition confirmed this difference in attitude. For example, Kenyon Cox's allegorical *Painting and Poetry*, dominating one wall of the stateside gallery (see fig. 23), was more architectural than flesh-and-blood in effect, anticipating the artist's later practice as a mural painter of institutional buildings. Cox's allegory was a thinly veiled reworking of Titian's *Sacred and Profane Love* (Villa Borghese, Rome), and thus possessed a further layer of reference and propriety.

Only Alexander Harrison's *In Arcadia*, despite its classical title, placed the nude in a realistic landscape with a minimal degree of contrivance. Harrison's figure composition, a work regarded, when it was exhibited in the Salon in 1886, as audaciously avant-garde for its bold combination of figure study and realistic landscape, unabashedly demonstrated the educational bias of the life drawing classes at the Ecole des Beaux-Arts.

Reticent about the presentation of nude-figure studies, American artists were even more reluctant to promote overtly religious subjects. Kenyon Cox's *Jacob Wrestling with the Angel*, William P. W. Dana's *Christ Walking on the Sea*, William de Leftwich Dodge's *David and Goliath*, Sarah P. B. Dodson's *Meditation of the Holy Virgin* (see page 144), and Carl Gutherz's *Lux Incarnationis* (see fig. 20 and page 162) were the only works with biblical subjects. Yet American artists admired the simple devotion they found among the faithful in Europe, and they sympathetically portrayed the pious at worship, as in Walter Gay's *Le Benedicité*, William J. Hennessy's *Expiation Pilgrimage, Calvados*, Gari Melchers' *Communion* (see page 185) and *The Sermon*, and Henry Mosler's *The Last Sacraments* (see page 196).

All in all, the United States section was distinguished by a remarkable range of subject matter, and the critics proclaimed the American contribution to the Exposition Universelle of 1899 a success. Mrs. van Rensselaer, one of our more acute observers of the Paris exposition, wrote in summary:

The foundation [of American art] is well laid, and the prospects for further development seem good, at least in certain directions. Portraiture promises extremely well; genre *painting only needs to be more national in subject-matter to show its strength and individuality better; and landscape gives sure signs of incarnating those very qualities which, in the French school, it threatens to lose—those personal, poetic qualities which made the glory of the French generation just extinct. The least hopeful branches are those of historical and idealistic painting and the painting of the nude.*[27]

"The collection as a whole," said the *New York Times* critic, "is the best that has ever been made of American art—or what is called American art."[28] The reviewer in the *Atlantic Monthly* surmised: "The excellence of the United States department of painting must have been a joyful and proud surprise to a great many diffident Americans, if such there be." She continued with an observation that is no less apposite today: "It might be . . . objected that such names as Dannat, Rheinhart *[sic]*, Klumpke, De Meza, and many more equally foreign do not represent native American talent; but they would represent a vote at our elections, and if the genius of our people derives some of its quality from an infusion of foreign blood, no doubt some of our progress in art comes from the same element."[29]

Another American critic, J. Eugene Reed, was not overly concerned about the Gallic accent of the United States section, predicting: "What there is distinctly American about the exhibit is most worthy, but there is too much of the manifest influence of the French school, in which a great majority of the exhibitors have studied; but this will have to be borne for a long time, just as the French school for a long time bore the character of their early taste for the Italians."[30]

By 1893, when the World's Columbian Exposition was held in Chicago, a native voice had emerged in the guise of an Americanized Impressionism, one that maintained the armature acquired at the French academies and superimposed on it a brighter palette and broader brushwork. With the perspective of a century, today's observer can readily see that American art, no longer speaking with a foreign accent as it did at the 1889 Exposition, has developed its own distinct syntax and vocabulary. Although American art did not reach its maturity until after World War II, it came of age at the 1889 Exposition.

Notes

1. The title "Loitering Through the Paris Exposition" is borrowed from an unsigned review of the Exposition (written by Sarah Butler Wister) published in the *Atlantic Monthly*, 65 (March 1889), pp. 360–74.
2. Theodore Child, "American Artists at the Paris Exhibition," *Harper's New Monthly Magazine*, 79 (Sept. 1889), p. 489.
3. Harold Frederic, "American Art in Paris: Work Our Artists Have Sent to the Exhibition," *New York Times*, June 16, 1889, p. 11.
4. [Wister], op. cit., p. 371.
5. See, for example, Frederic, op. cit.
6. Rush C. Hawkins, "Fine Arts," *Reports of the United States Commissioners to the Universal Exposition of 1889 at Paris* (Washington, 1891).
7. See, for example, Child, op. cit., p. 502, and Frederic, op. cit.
8. Hawkins, op. cit., p. 64.
9. For an analysis of the history and importance of patronage of American artists by the French government, see Susan Grant, "American Paintings Acquired by the French Government, 1879–1900" (master's thesis, George Washington University, 1983).
10. See Child, op. cit., pp. 502–3.
11. See Frederic, op. cit.
12. "My Note Book," *Art Amateur*, 17 (Sept. 1887), p. 72.
13. Carol Troyen, "Innocents Abroad: American Painters at the 1867 Exposition Universelle, Paris," *American Art Journal*, 16 (Autumn 1984), pp. 2–29.
14. See, for example, Richard R. and Caroline B. Brettell, *Painters and Peasants in the Nineteenth Century* (Geneva, 1983).
15. Frederic, op. cit.
16. For Reinhart's own description of the circumstances, see George William Sheldon, *Recent Ideals of American Art* (New York, 1888) pp. 154–56.
17. Hawkins, op. cit., p. 67.
18. Brettells, op. cit., p. 8.
19. For example, Julian Treuherz, *Hard Times: Social Realism in Victorian Art* (London and New York, 1987).
20. See D. Dodge Thompson, "American Artists in North Africa and the Middle East, 1797–1914," *Antiques*, 126 (Aug. 1984), pp. 303–12.
21. Hawkins, op. cit., p. 71.
22. Hawkins, op. cit., p. 67.
23. [Wister], op. cit.
24. Theodore Reff, "The City Viewed," *Manet and Modern Paris* (exhib. cat., National Gallery of Art, Washington, D.C., 1982), pp. 32–51.
25. Quoted in Lloyd Goodrich, *Thomas Eakins* (Cambridge, Mass., and London, 1982), vol. 1, p. 28.
26. M. G. van Rensselaer [Mrs. Schuyler van Rensselaer], *Book of American Figure Painters* (Philadelphia, 1886), n.p.
27. Mrs. Schuyler van Rensselaer, "The International Exhibition of 1889," *Century Magazine*, 39 (Dec. 1889), p. 318.
28. Frederic, op. cit.
29. [Wister], op. cit.
30. J. E. Reed, *Selected Paintings from the Paris Exhibition, 1889* (Philadelphia, 1889), p. 6.

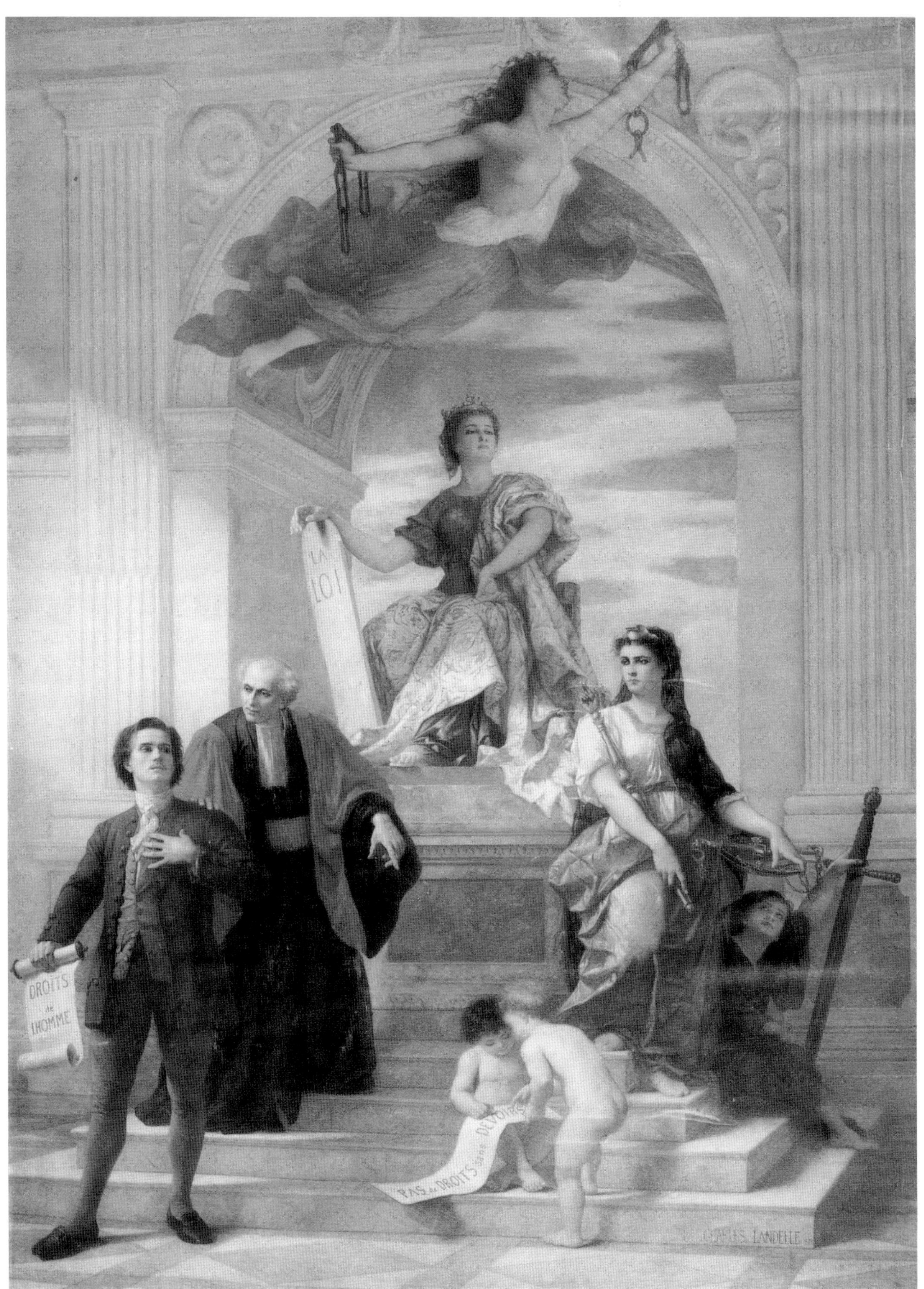
LA LOI
DROITS de L'HOMME
PAS de DROITS sans DEVOIRS
LANDELLE

ALBERT BOIME

The Chocolate Venus, "Tainted" Pork, the Wine Blight, and the Tariff: Franco-American Stew at the Fair

28.
Charles Landelle (1812–1908)
Le Droit moderne;—1789, 1885
Musée-Ecole de la Perrine, Laval

World's fairs blaze across the horizon of the nineteenth century as a series of cosmopolitan self-portraits of the resourceful industrial bourgeoisie on the make.[1] On these sites the governments of the world openly acknowledged their ties with the business community and demonstrated solidarity of outlook in trade, science, education, and the arts. To lure the public into celebrations of the ideology and accomplishments of the industrial elite, the expositions were made into entertaining pageants. Here the industrialists and financiers prepared the public for the expansion of their technology and furnished the pretext for their economic and political domination; the fairs nurtured an environment in which they could amass greater and greater pools of capital and thereby increase their command over the economic and political domains. Complex and dazzling to the public, on examination these exhibitions rather fascinatingly reveal the interrelations between the economy and government, domestic and international trade policy, warfare and technology, nationalism and internationalism.

The international specialization of labor, analogous to the domestic division of labor and known as the "comparative advantage" of individual nations, is the foundation of international trade. By definition, international trade means trade with foreigners, and foreigners, from the perspective of the indigenous population, always seek to outsmart the home country. This attitude explains the generally desultory efforts of American exhibitors at the Exposition of 1889. A spokesperson for the United States Commission attempted to explain the poor performance with the statement "Our people realize that an exhibition is, as a rule, a much better undertaking for the country which promotes it than for those who send exhibits."[2]

The economic expression of nationalist competitiveness is the protective tariff. Domestic propaganda was required to mobilize the various sectors of a nation behind tariff and tax policies that favored producers over consumers, and diplomatic negotiations and power politics were needed to persuade other governments to lift their embargoes. The painful contradictions of international trade and their toll on the pocketbooks of consumers required major efforts to foster a climate of support for the entrepreneurial elite. One strategy for achieving the acquiescence of the populace in economic schemes that did not serve their best interests was played out behind the glitzy gateways and facades of the fairs.

The encyclopedic and interdisciplinary nature of these shows, embracing all aspects of society and culture, rhetorically advanced the rationalist faith in the perfectibility of the human species and the ultimate goal of a unified world civilization under the aegis of benign free enterprise. In their association of material progress and well-being with democracy and liberty the fairs forecast a rosy future and broadcast a heady sense of optimism, but they also suggested that these utopian projections ultimately depended on the fate of the industrialists. The 1889 Exposition mapped out a suggestive visual and conceptual space: at one end of the main grounds on the Champ-de-Mars perched the arches of the Eiffel Tower, serving as gateway to the fair, and at the other stood Charles-Louis-Ferdinand Dutert's vast Palais des Machines.[3] Sandwiched between these two architectural marvels of iron and glass was a space partitioned for exhibitions devoted to the liberal and the fine arts and for manufacturing processes. Thus the visitor proceeded along a mythologized path that traced the bourgeois view of evolutionary progress. The other major portion of the show on the Esplanade des Invalides comprised a prominent military display, colonial exhibits, and an exhibit of housing and hygienic facilities for working-class families. The juxtaposition of these three exhibits metaphorically pointed to the external and internal controls on the potentially unruly sectors of the French republic-empire.

At every stage, the Exposition visitor passed through a concentration of primitive or exotic dwellings of ancient or modern colonialized centers before confronting the edifices built specifically for the show. The History of Human Habitation display ran along the width of the fair grounds directly in front of the Eiffel Tower, while at the fringes of the Palais des Machines, along the Avenue de Suffren, were stationed the "exotic pavilions" and booths of Egypt, Siam, Morocco, Persia, and Japan. The Retrospective History of Labor was the last display in the Palais des Beaux-Arts that one saw before entering the Palais des Machines. These calculated and schematized contrasts of modern Western civilization with its evolutionary antecedents and "retarded" societies of the present encoded the subtext of the Exposition's sign system. Alfred Picard, who wrote the official French report on the Exposition,[4] insisted that the fair commemorated an event important not only for France but also for the "history of humanity." The official catalogue for both the Retrospective History of Labor and the Anthropological Sciences declared that the aim of the exhibit was to retrace "the stages of human genius"—that is, leading to the Paris Exposition of 1889.[5] This progression could be clarified only by joining the study of the evolution of artifacts with the study of the evolution of the human being exemplified in the physiques of the various races.

While the world's fairs demonstrated individual nations' economic and artistic resources, these were played down in favor of the broader shared views of race, nationalism, and progress that shaped these extravaganzas into coherent programs proclaiming the authority of corporate political, military, industrial, scientific, and cultural leadership. Their very scale and scope created an aura of prestige and accomplishment that awed spectators into acknowledging the superiority of the dominant elite. By creating the sense of omnipresence and omniscience, the fairs—and this would apply as well to modern-day automobile shows and seemingly playful Disneylands—functioned optimally as a pacific means used by industrial and financial elites to promote support for their idea of social order (backed up, of course, by the show of arms in the military exhibits).

The ultimate irony of these massive and universal displays of material accomplishment was their obvious dependence on racist and nationalist rivalries. Individual nations, especially sponsoring ones, exploited the fairs to measure their achievements against those of the other participants, and these achievements were partly symbolized by colonial exhibits consisting of native peoples on display. Colonialization and the expansion of world trade were seen as inseparable, and in the last quarter of the century they were justified on the basis of current scientific and evolutionary theories of race and culture. The rise of anthropology in Europe and the United States takes off with the publication of Darwin's *On the Origin of Species* in 1859, and its legitimation as a science coincides with the movement toward empire. While physical anthropology did not necessarily involve belief in racial inferiority or superiority, it could imply this when linked to the study of the evolution of humans on the basis of the prehistoric fossil record. Darwin could be exploited to show that some existing races or social classes were inferior because they typified an earlier stage of biological evolution or of sociocultural evolution or both.[6] Anthropological explanations by an academic elite trickled down to the public through the mediating filter of the world's fairs. The organization and classification of the colonial exhibits were arranged not by the indigenous peoples themselves but by the anthropologists and natural scientists of the sponsoring nations. The sciences were thus called upon to reinforce the notion of "progress" emphasized in the conquest of the material world, a progress possible through the exploitation and suppression of colonialized peoples. Visitors to the fairs were orchestrated to feel superior to the exotic Asians, Africans, Native Americans, and other nonwhite peoples and to measure these peoples' quaint habitations, their "primitive" arts and curios, against the colossal technological advances of the whites. In this way the fairs helped promote public support for colonial and international trade policies based on the hierarchical theory of race.

A French critic was struck by the Marines standing guard before the North American installations at the 1889 Exposition. They were blond, tall, and young and demonstrated an "astonishing military bearing under arms."[7] This display of a certain racial type was inseparable from the cultural expression of the American elite representing itself to the public. The organizers encouraged the public to identify industrial production with the superior civilization attained by a particular racial and geographical group. What many white visitors may not have realized at the time was that the same hierarchical structure was in place to discriminate against selected classes, nationalities, and ethnic minorities represented among them. Indeed, this discrimination was deliberately built into the structure of the Paris fair of 1889 and the Chicago fair of 1893.

The proximity in time of the 1889 and 1893 fairs, and the similarity of their physical and ideological schemata, make them useful coordinates in mapping out Franco-American relations in the period. The French fair served as the model for the World's Columbian Exposition. The Chicago organizers carefully followed the pattern of glaring contrasts between rude colonial villages and new technological structures set up in Paris. They established live ethnological displays of Native Americans and other peoples of color in fake habitats to contrast with the displays of modern machinery. Materiel was even conveyed to the fair grounds for a tower to rival the Eiffel, but at the last moment the idea was abandoned as unworkable and as a substitute a gigantic Ferris Wheel incorporating some of the structural innovations of the French engineer was erected. The adherence of the Chicago group to the 1889 model is also evident in their showing a large proportion of the paintings exhibited by the Americans at the 1889 fair.

At the World's Columbian Exposition, special days were set aside for particular ethnic groups. African-Americans (who in this period in the South were declared unfit and unqualified to vote) had not even been considered until their spokespersons demanded a special day for them. (The black community in

Chicago divided bitterly over the issue, many rejecting the resulting offer of a Colored Jubilee Day—including free watermelon—as patronizing and demeaning.) Discrimination against blacks at the fair in all but menial employment was so egregious that Frederick Douglass and the anti-lynching crusader Ida B. Wells felt called upon to publish a pamphlet, *The Reason Why the Colored American Is Not in the World's Columbian Exposition*. Africans on display on the Midway were confounded with African-Americans, which gave rise to speculation on the political and economic situation of African-Americans being the result of their "savage" origins. Douglass and Wells denounced the organizers of the Exposition for bringing Dahomeans to Chicago "to exhibit the Negro as a repulsive savage" and for expecting them "to act the monkey." They seized the occasion of the Colored Jubilee Day to call attention to the flagrant contradiction between the outrages committed against people of color and the flaunting of "American liberty and civilization" at the fair. They pointed out that the appalling exploitation of blacks was being rationalized by the same anthropological arguments as those advanced at the world's fairs in the name of empire.[8] Here again, in a fictionalized setting obscuring class differences, the oppressed white ethnic minorities could participate with a false sense of sharing in the national purpose as defined by the dominant elite.

The desire to outdo the French by magnifying the scale of the Chicago fair and the close dependence of Americans on French culture pointed to the basic contradiction of the world's fair as an institution. Despite their rhetoric of fraternalism and international cooperation, the universal expositions were commercial and cultural battlegrounds on which the nations of the world played out their rival strategies. The inevitable ambivalence, rooted in the very nature of the fairs, pervades the Franco-American relations of the period.

The love-hate relationship of France and the United States in these years belied the fraternal aims stated at their respective expositions, as in the remarks of Pierre-Emmanuel Tirard, the prime minister, at the opening ceremony of the Paris 1889 fair:

> *Let us receive and joyfully entertain the foreigners who are already crowding here: let us prove to them that Republican France is hospitable and generous; that she loves and honors the workmen of all nations, and sees in them, not rivals of whom she is jealous, but fellow-workmen who labor with her for the happiness of humanity and the peace of the world.*

This lip service to the "workmen of all nations" formed part of the rhetoric designed to ensure the allegiance of the working classes to the brand of nationalism created by the establishment. The signification of nationalism had to be limited lest it be interpreted to imply a larger role for the underclasses in the control of production and open the way to increased identification with workers and exploited people in other corners of the world. Their shared bombast and shibboleths about progress and liberty barely masked the voracious appetites of both fairs for global resources and markets.

In Paris and in Chicago there was the same degrading of colonialized peoples in favor of the triumphant civilization embodied in the Beaux-Arts style. The unmistakable similarity between the painting, sculpture, and architecture of the two countries attests to the dominance of the Beaux-Arts style in American culture. The predominance of French taste and the rejection of a more modern alternative vision by local architects was tied to the look of imperium envisioned by the organizers of the Chicago fair. Called the "White City" for its neoclassical

Beaux-Arts architectural scheme, the fair meant to project a bright utopian future; but this was no Oz but a "simon-pure lily-white" product hinting at the "white man's burden" of empire.

The year 1889 was a critical one for the French Republic. The heavy antigovernmental vote in 1885, the popular support for the threatened coup d'état of Georges Boulanger in 1888–89, and intense labor agitation were among the difficult problems facing the conservative Republic.[9] Yet between 1885 and 1889, with the govenment in a state of crisis, the French parliament was almost totally barren of reforming legislation. Labeled by the opposition as a diversionary tactic of Opportunist politics, the fair did represent a desperate ploy for survival. The Exposition was a case of magnificent window dressing; its organizers managed to pull off an impressive propaganda coup at a crucial time. Without question, it was a political expedient created to shore up the foundations of the fledgling government, an attempt to project a symbolic triumph over party politics and demonstrate that the principles of 1789 were firmly in the saddle. The boycott of the fair by monarchies such as England and Germany, on the grounds that it celebrated the overthrow of monarchy, and the conspicuous absence of royalist deputies at the opening ceremonies did the fair no harm, indeed probably contributed to its success.

The Exposition was organized by moderate Republicans eager to emphasize the achievements of 1789 and not the excesses of 1793.[10] The inaugural festivity of the centennial took place at Versailles on May 5 in commemoration of the opening of the Estates-General, and a plaque was placed in the Salles des Menus-Plaisirs to recall the formation of the National Assembly. Nothing on the main fair grounds recalled the sanguinary events of the Terror; this side of the Revolution was commemorated in a separate exhibition located on the site of the Tuileries destroyed during the Commune.[11] That the organizers set out to play up the era of moderate reform, and not the Jacobin era of radical reform, is evidenced by one of the few art works actually treating the revolutionary theme shown at the Exposition: Charles Landelle's *Le Droit moderne;–1789* (fig. 28). The allegory depicts a young man in eighteenth-century garb with his left hand on his heart and his right holding a scroll with the inscription DROITS de L'HOMME. With burning enthusiasm he steps forward before an altar to bring his message to the world but is restrained by a stately magistrate personifying Rights, who points to another scroll, being studied by two putti, on which is inscribed PAS de DROITS sans DEVOIRS (No rights without duties). The Law is represented by a woman seated on a pedestal on the altar, while hovering overhead is Liberty, bearing the broken chains of former captives, a reference to the unrestrained character of the events of 1793–94. The Law sits patiently, secure in the knowledge that after the turmoil and bloodshed her rule will prevail. Her minister, Justice, carrying sword and scepter, steps down from the altar while casting a stern glance at the misguided youth. It is not surprising that American robber barons like Leland B. Stanford profoundly admired the work. He considered it "the most accurate expression of the social ideas of the United States" and ordered a smaller replica, in which his recently deceased son was to figure as the sword bearer of Justice.[12]

Ironically, the revisionist position advanced by Landelle was picked up by official French historians in the 1980s in the midst of preparations for the bicentennial celebration.[13] The National Commission of Historical Research for the Bicentennial took an analogous approach that would have selectively treated the Revolution as a mainstream and consensual event, downplaying the events of 1793 once again. This gave rise to fundamental debate over the definition of the

Revolution, in some ways recapitulating the Left–Right cleavage of 1789.

The ambiguity of the enterprise in 1889 further reveals itself in the attitudes of French critics to the foreign exhibitors, most notably the United States, which, in contradistinction to the monarchies, had eagerly accepted the French nation's invitation to participate. Indeed, Americans felt slighted in the inaugural festivities, despite the fact that the mainstream press treated the United States and France as "sister Republics" celebrating a year of importance for both of them.[14] (The festive centennial celebration of the inauguration of Washington—and therefore of the institution of the American republic—centered in New York on April 30 and May 1, 1889.) Following the fair, the Americans complained that they were discriminated against as a body in the assignment of space and in the distribution of the official Legion of Honor awards, despite their excellent showing among the juried medalists. Both the Americans and the French indulged in chauvinist exchanges, and while these attitudes are never explicitly spelled out, they reveal themselves between the lines of the commentaries.[15]

Despite their digs at each other, the two fledgling republics had similar and overlapping goals in 1889. Among the ten principal industrial nations, France was listed fourth, just behind the United States, its closest rival. The long international depression that had begun in the 1870s afflicted both nations with chronic overproduction and dramatically falling prices, and they resorted to the tariff to protect home markets. They stimulated the home industries by drastically curtailing imports, a policy that Picard lauded as the genius behind the striking French display at the Exposition of 1889 and that to him demonstrated the success of the government's fiscal policies.[16] In 1886 the industrial and financial elites on both sides had negotiated the gift of the Statue of Liberty, emblematic of imperialistic and expansionist policies.[17] It turned up again in 1889: Bartholdi's terra-cotta maquette was shown at the Exposition, and on July 4, with Whitelaw Reid, the American ambassador to France, acting as spokesperson, the American colony donated to the municipality of Paris a reduced replica in bronze, which was unveiled on the Ile des Cygnes in the middle of the Seine.[18] The Liberty project was exploited by Jules Ferry, then prime minister (who originally conceived of the Exposition of 1889), as part of France's quest, spurred by the crash of 1882, for new markets. He feared that the United States threatened old French markets, such as those in South America. As rivals for the trade of South America, both France and the United States had special plans for a canal through Central America.

Two international heroes of French enterprise figured prominently in the Liberty project. One was engineer Gustave Eiffel—shortly to achieve world renown for his tower at the Exposition of 1889–who used his experience in railway and bridge construction to design the trusswork for the support of the copper sheathing of the statue. His combination of engineering skills, managerial talent, and vast entrepreneurial ambitions epitomized the ideal of the elite members of the Franco-American Union, which worked out the arrangements for the shipping of Liberty. The other hero was Ferdinand de Lesseps, the intrepid builder of the Suez and Panama canals, who became chairman of the Franco-American Union in 1883. De Lesseps continually linked the Liberty project to his scheme for the Panama Canal, for which he needed American support. When de Lesseps' company went bankrupt, the ensuing exposure of the bribery of politicians that had accompanied the parliamentary authorization and the raising of funds became a national scandal. Many of the Republican deputies implicated, including the powerful Commissioner-General of Fine Arts,

Antonin Proust, had been directly involved in the organization of the 1889 fair.[19] Proust belonged to the faction of moderate Republicans condemned by their critics as Opportunists. It was they who had built up France's great colonial power and they exploited the fair of 1889 as a showcase of their achievements.

The president who accepted the French invitation to participate in the fair was Grover Cleveland, a moderate republican in his own right.[20] Although as a Democrat he was a member of the party that declaimed in stentorian tones against the power of trusts and monopolies, Cleveland hastened to assure industrialists that his election should not disturb them: "No harm shall come to any business interest as the result of administrative policy so long as I am President . . . a transfer of executive control from one party to another does not mean any serious disturbance of existing conditions." The absence of decisive issues and clarifying divisions of class interest in the presidential contest of 1884 (which foreshadowed the campaigns of the 1980s) had prompted a disillusioned Henry Adams to write to an English friend:

We are here plunged in politics funnier than words can express. Very great issues are involved. . . . But the amusing thing is that no one talks about real interests. By common consent they agree to let these alone. We are afraid to discuss them. *Instead of this the press is engaged in a most amusing dispute whether Mr. Cleveland had an illegitimate child, and did or did not live with more than one mistress. . . .*[21]

When Cleveland was declared the winner in a close contest, robber baron Jay Gould telegraphed to congratulate him, declaring that "the vast business interests of the country will be entirely safe in your hands."[22]

Both in France and in the United States the moderates had to fight off an increasingly organized Left. In France the passing of the law of 1884 authorizing the formation of trade unions, or *syndicats*, was evidence that the Opportunists recognized the existence of a new force in their midst. They put their weight behind the *syndicats* to neutralize the anarchists and the socialist Parti ouvrier founded by Jules Guesde in 1883. In a similar move, Cleveland had announced in favor of tax and tariff reform in his 1887 State of the Union message, with this warning: "Opportunity for safe, careful, and deliberate reform is now offered; and none of us should be unmindful of a time when an abused and irritated people . . . may insist upon a radical and sweeping rectification of their wrongs."[23] Cleveland felt the pressure of the Noble Order of the Knights of Labor, by 1886 embracing 700,000 members, as well as the growing labor unrest, which led to the Haymarket riot of May 4. Anarchist newspapers in France closely monitored the ensuing trial of the eight anarchists in Chicago.[24]

Both Cleveland and Chauncey Depew—the silver-tongued president of the New York Central Railroad, who delivered the American Centennial Oration on April 30, 1889, in Wall Street, and would be in the forefront of the group trying to get the 1893 fair for New York—spoke at the dedication of the Statue of Liberty in 1886, and both alluded to the Haymarket affair. For the railway magnate, the monument implied that "the problems of labor and capital, of social regeneration and moral growth, of property and poverty, will work themselves out under the benign influence of enlightened lawmaking and law-abiding liberty, without the aid of kings and armies, or of anarchists and bombs."[25] A similar perspective informed the public pronouncements of Prime Minister Tirard and the President of the Third Republic, Sadi Carnot. At the closing ceremony of the 1889 Exposition, Tirard declared:

29.
Alfred Roll (1846–1919)
Miners' Strike (La Greve des mineurs), 1880
(destroyed during World War II)
Formerly Musée des Beaux-Arts, Valenciennes

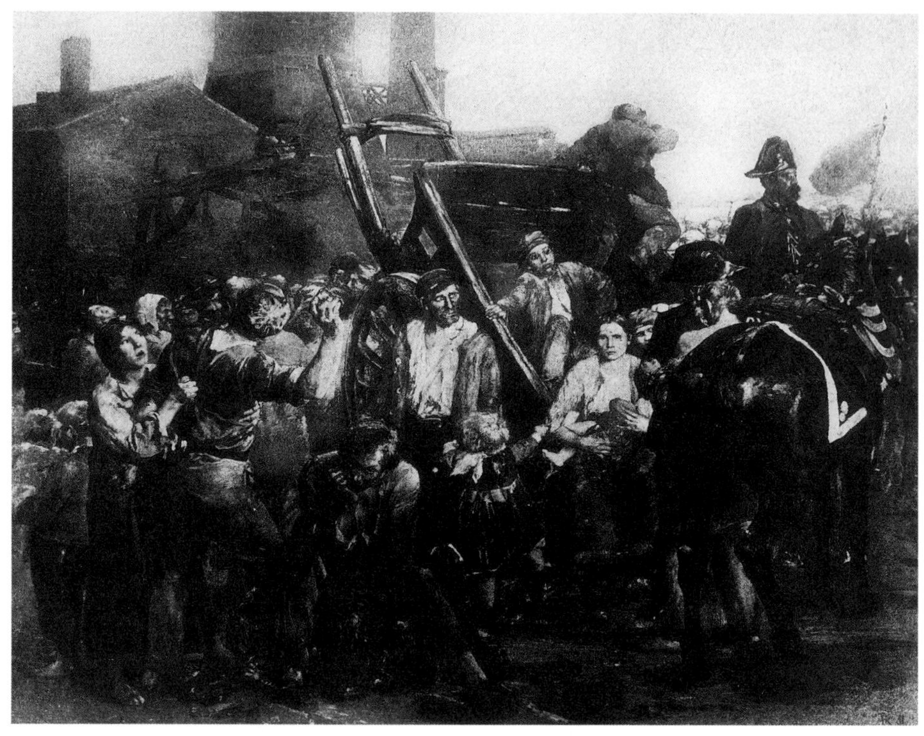

We shall wisely and resolutely continue the work of 1889 without permitting the constantly recurring exactions of new ideals to weary and discourage us. We will remember that the social reforms dimly seen by our fathers, and whose outcome we realize, are obtained neither by surprise nor by violence, and that to produce sure and durable results, they must be patiently and progressively attained. Thus, gentlemen, will France continue its ascending march in the direction of progress and civilization, with the worship of liberty, with the love of labor, which is to-day the master of the world.[26]

For all the rhetoric about the "love of labor" on both sides of the Atlantic, and notwithstanding the fair's Retrospective Exhibition of the History of Labor (a mixed bag, including everything from human skulls to musical instruments), there was remarkably little evidence of this concern in the subjects of the art works displayed by the two countries; except for the predictable scenes of peasant and fishing activities, there was scant attention paid to the laboring class, which had been so active in organizing major strikes at Décazeville and Vierzon in 1886 and frequent work stoppages throughout the decade. Two exceptions were Alfred Roll's *Miners' Strike* (fig. 29) and Robert Koehler's *The Strike* (see page 181), but even in these two cases the workers were treated with so little sympathy that it is difficult to grasp the thematic emphasis. Other exceptions were the paintings of the French artist Fernand Pelez, whose depictions of proletarian misery and poverty had been praised even by the anarchist press.[27]

Lack of concern for labor animates a working-class theme of a kind accepted by the Salon and Exposition jurors—a theme that made the protagonist the butt of humor or cruelty. The bizarre work entitled *The Intruder* (fig. 30)

30.
Louis-Joseph Anthonissen (1849–1913)
The Intruder (Un Intrus), Exposition Universelle of 1889
From *L'Illustration*, August 24, 1889, p. 157

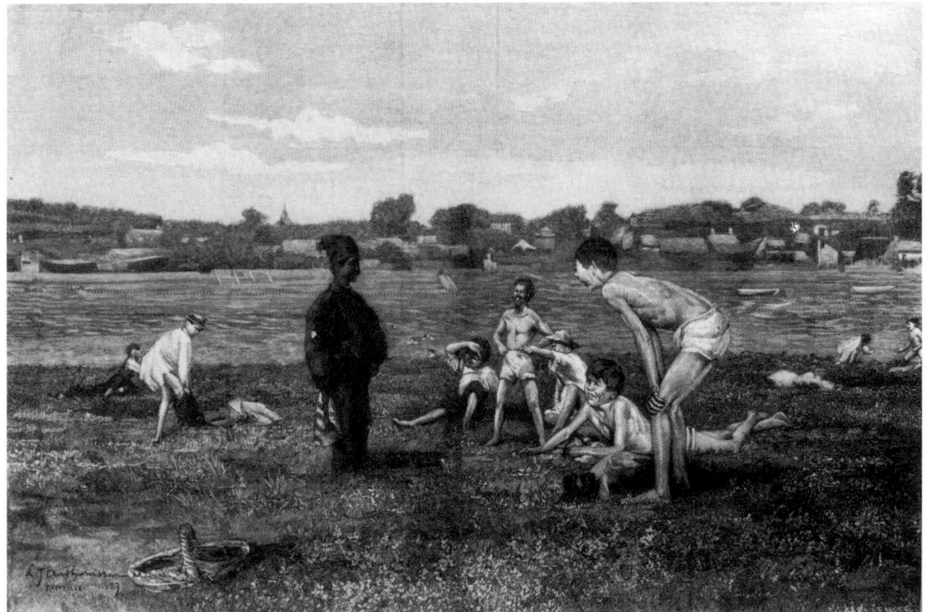

by Louis-Joseph Anthonissen, a Belgian trained in Paris, depicts a grotesque-looking chimney sweep covered with soot from head to toe standing on the beach at the fashionable resort of Trouville surrounded by astonished bathers. Some gaze in horror at the strange creature, while others double over in laughter. The object of all this attention smiles embarrassedly, his white teeth conspicuous in his blackened face. One reviewer took this smile to mean that the chimney sweep shared in the general laughter directed at him, confident that "people with a good sense of humor are incapable of malevolence or injustice."[28] This scene of alienation and oppression encodes the upper-class ideal of workers excluded from the cultural and social edifice constructed by their labor happily accepting the position assigned to them by the privileged. Another example was the controversial picture *Brutality* (see page 197)[29] by the American John Douglas Patrick, showing a French cabbie beating his horse. The picture angered Parisians in general as casting aspersions on their humaneness, but their anger was focused primarily on the working-class drivers. While there were instances of individual drivers maltreating their horses (see fig. 31), most of the maligning of cabbies in this period sprang from opposition to their demands for higher rates for their services from the cab owners, who ruthlessly exploited them. The fact that the drivers struck during the height of the Exposition, leaving the privileged without means of transportation, brought them under sharp attack.[30] The painting understandably infuriated the drivers, and they tried to prevent its being shown.

Although critics in the two countries spoke of the triumph of "realism" and "modernity" in contemporary art, they did not extend their analyses to embrace the manifold problems in labor–capital relations that constituted the core of "reality" at the time. Closer to reality was Depew's Columbian Oration, delivered in 1892 at the dedication ceremonies of the World's Columbian Exposition, which reiterated some of the basic themes he addressed at the inaugural ceremony of the Statue of Liberty in 1886:

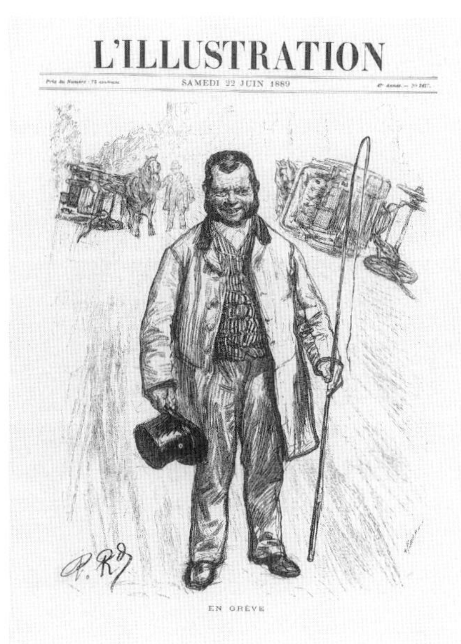

31.
En Grève
From *L'Illustration*, June 22, 1889, p. 517

The time has arrived for both closer union and greater distance between the Old World and the New. . . . Unwatched and unhealthy immigration can no longer be permitted to our shores. We must have a national quarantine against disease, pauperism and crime. We cannot admit those who come to undermine our institutions, and subvert our laws. But we will gladly throw wide our gates for, and receive with open arms, those who by intelligence and virtue, by thrift and loyalty, are worthy of receiving the equal advantages of the priceless gift of American citizenship. The spirit and object of this Exhibition are peace and kinship.[31]

What Depew—who, as William Vanderbilt's right-hand man on the New York Central Railroad, violently opposed trade unions—meant by "kinship" was nothing short of total identification with the ideology of the entrepreneurial elite.

Republican Benjamin Harrison, who succeeded Cleveland as president in 1889, was a lawyer who had previously gained a reputation for strikebreaking and siding with the owners of production against their employees. The major reform of his term was the Sherman Antitrust Act, passed in the following year. Although the act made it illegal to form a "combination or conspiracy" to restrain trade in interstate or foreign commerce, its real purpose, as summed up by the author himself, was to conciliate the critics of monopoly: "You must heed their appeal or be ready for the socialist, the communist, the nihilist. Society is now disturbed by forces never felt before. . . ."

Thus far we have seen striking evidence of the overlapping interests of France and the United States as exemplified in their respective fairs. Yet the managers of the World's Columbian Exposition tried to make a fundamental distinction between the two shows. Originally set for 1892, the fair in Chicago would commemorate an event as far-reaching as the French Revolution but without its pointed political significations. The Americans predicted that the celebration of the discovery of the continent by Columbus would appeal even to the monarchical governments that boycotted the 1889 Exposition.[32] Nevertheless, like their French rivals they had their own "Terror" from which to distance themselves: the systematic extermination of Native Americans, the ongoing violence against blacks, and the ruthless suppression of labor agitation and working-class movements.

On the French side, the concern for commercial expansion took on a complex and nuanced xenophobia in the drive for wealth and territorial extension. It surfaced largely in the decade of the 1880s. For several years after the Franco-Prussian War and the Commune, which ended French hegemony on the Continent and exposed its glaring political and social contradictions, the French elite had indulged in a kind of effervescent cosmopolitanism. The growing use of anglicized or outright American and English terms was an important index to this new receptivity. But the crash of the Union Générale bank in 1882 touched off a long depression that compromised this cultural openness. Latent hostility in the French community—aroused by English and North American economic power, agricultural competition, the setback to the wine industry caused by the phylloxera blight, leading to demands for protection, and colonial rivalries—flared up dramatically after 1882. And it was directed to a new kind of American, one recognized as culturally sophisticated. Critics complained of the growing "Americanization" of French culture, a term that encoded their alarm over Yankee economic power.[33] Symbolically, this anxiety took the form in 1889 of an unreserved flaunting of the Eiffel Tower as an example of French industrial prowess inaccessible even to the Yankee upstarts.

It had been noted in 1882, the year of the stock market crash, that the

American colony in Paris was rapidly expanding, and this is reflected in the statistics: by the mid-1880s the United States group had become the most numerous foreign enclave in the Parisian art community.[34] In the late 1870s and early 1880s, American artists received wide praise and even critical enthusiasm for their Salon exhibits. In 1883, however, a French critic asserted that French supremacy in art was being challenged by foreigners in the Salon, and developed the theory that painters like Whistler, Sargent, Story, and Pearce had studied under French masters in the hope of surpassing them.[35] Three years later a group of French students at the Ecole des Beaux-Arts published a brochure complaining of the displacement of native artists by foreigners, who enjoyed most of the advantages and suffered none of the disadvantages of the French students; since Americans made up the majority of the foreigners in the Parisian art community, they were the targets of the most abusive comments.[36]

In retrospect the almost complete dismissal of American painting as imitative at the Exposition of 1889 appears as a calculated attempt to reduce the importance of the Americans as a national group vis-à-vis the French. Commissioner-General Proust, for example, wrote disdainfully that it was especially in the American rooms that one could imagine oneself to be "in an excellent French gallery. Messieurs Sargent, Dannat, Melchers, Gay, Knight, Chase, Vail, Davis, Bridgman, Boggs, MacEwen, and Mosler almost invariably attach themselves to one of our famous masters."[37] In his official report, Picard observed that "the section of the United States was only a brilliant annex of the French section."[38] Maurice Hamel, writing in the prestigious *Gazette des Beaux-Arts*, complained that he could not "discover a national character in American art." According to him, American artists possessed the skill of assimilation, quickness of hand, and the taste for sensational effects, but their aesthetic "gymnastics" were not balanced by original invention, passion, and deep reflection. In the end, they preferred to emulate the superficial aspects of European art rather than establish a new point of view.[39]

This belittling of the American display pervaded the reviews of the commercial products as well. Emile Monod's authoritative multivolume report on the Exposition manifested mild amusement at the "take-charge" attitude of the Yankees (which he described in English as "go ahead") in the way they organized their booths and installations. He expressed astonishment but also amusement at their obsession with machinery whose unique aim seemed to be "to invent unceasingly new means to produce more quickly or more easily this or that object. Further reflection on their behavior leads one to conclude that they have a double aim; on the one hand, they wish to astonish each other, and on the other to astonish old Europe." In summing up his observations of the displays of the United States, he noted that "the impression which remains with us from our visit is that the North Americans are a great people of prodigal sons who sometimes startle us by the admirable audacity of their inventions and sometimes cause us to smile by their gigantic puerilities."[40] Here the critic functioned as a French father figure to the American prodigals, who in his estimation could have used a heavy dose of Old World maturity. In the same patronizing fashion he placed French art in a superior position in relation to the work of the Yankees—a master–pupil, parent–child connection.

One display that fused American know-how with Old World culture earned Monod's scornful laughter: the full-scale Venus of solid chocolate fabricated by the firm of Henry Maillard. As he put it, "Only a Yankee could have conceived of the idea of creating an edible Venus de Milo." The obsession of most of the French critics with this exhibit signified a level of anxiety that none of them seemed ready to admit. Black people were often described as chocolate-colored, both in France and in America, and a popular African-American entertainer in Paris in the 1890s was nicknamed "Chocolat."[41] Further, a parodic strain in the Anglo-European literature of racism recounted the voyages of an alluring "Sable Venus," whose physical charm was comparable to that of the famous classical statue the Medici Venus.[42] The conversion of a French national treasure of classical antiquity into an edible chocolate-brown female figure would have touched a chord deep in the national psyche. Much of the world's supply of cocoa derived from the Portuguese possessions of São Tomé and Principe, off the west coast of Africa, and the Gold Coast and Nigeria, British colonies in West Africa, where, despite emancipation, labor conditions remained just a notch above slavery.[43] The exploitation of the blacks in these cocoa-growing areas was justified by the same kinds of anthropological arguments as were advanced at the world's fairs.

Ironically, in this period North European scholars tried to keep black Africans as far away as possible from the history of European civilization. Philologists posited Indo-European roots of the Greek language and culture and rejected Egyptian and Semitic connections. The denial of the Afro-Asiatic sources of Greek civilization was inseparable from imperialism and the sense of national solidarity fostered in the metropolitan nations against "uncivilized" non-European peoples.[44] In this context the presence of the chocolate Venus would have conjured up associations and resonances of the very history that Europeans were trying hard to suppress in the name of empire. Crowning these anxieties was the fact that, as the product of an upstart industrial nation, the confectionary Venus played on the fear of competition for global markets.

This response to American products represented an attempt to distance the Old World from the New World that threatened everyday to overturn it. The frustration with the "Americanization" of French culture, the introduction of the new tempo of life associated with modernity and identified with the United States, expressed itself primarily in the realm of culture, where the French had the edge and their North American protégés acknowledged it. In contrast to their innovative activity in the realm of technology, Americans demonstrated caution in the cultural domain and looked to Europe for models. Here the French could maintain a paternalistic attitude and emphasize the dependence of the Yankees. Thus they wholeheartedly backed the division of the American fine arts section into two parts—one primarily reserved for artists resident in Paris and the other for those resident in the United States—and then proceeded to systematically disregard the second category.[45]

However, although acknowledging the influence of their masters, and even the superiority of French culture generally, Americans were not swayed by the "imitative" charge. Ambitious for success, they perceived themselves as the heirs of a grand and universal tradition that would eventually enable them to assume worldwide cultural leadership. American artists living in Paris stated their aim modestly in print: to make their showing at the Exposition "the equal of any foreign Art Department there."[46] Their apologists hit upon various strategies to get around the "French look" of the work; one distinguished between national "French art" and cosmopolitan "Parisian art," placing the Americans in the latter group, while another emphasized that no matter how strong the influence of the master "the American sees his subject with the eyes of an American."[47] Indeed the definitional problem became patently absurd, with the Americans living in Paris described as the "Paris Americans" or "Franco-Americans," as distinguished from the "American Americans."[48]

Aside from their notorious chocolate Venus,[49] what drew intense French scorn down upon the Americans in the period of the 1889 Exposition was the tax on works of art imported from abroad.[50] Together they symbolize the curious ambivalence of the French attitude toward the United States republic in the centennial celebration of the French Revolution and reveal the contradictory nature of the French position on their own national history and current status.[51] The ongoing question of the tariff went right to the heart of the nationalist discourse so pervasive in the period. Nationalism and free trade were deemed incompatible, and the so-called democratic republics—in their efforts to mobilize the masses behind their programs—chose the tariff and restriction of free trade.

A rationale for the official line was formulated by the conservative historian and economist Emil Schalk, who couched the justification for the tariff in anthropological terms. Aligning himself with the Social Darwinists, Schalk identified protection—"applied to every sphere of life"—as the "distinguishing feature of civilization." Elaborating further, he asserted: "Without protection society and civilization cannot exist; barbarism, savage life, the life of a brute, alone prevails. Protection is the slow-working agency which gradually lifts man to higher planes of civilization." For Schalk, free trade implied the "very reverse of protection and civilization. It is a return to the methods of barbaric life. It is the fight of each against all; of individuals against the species, and of entire organized species against the individual. It means want of forethought and reflection in the individual, and society as a whole."[52] In this view, anthropology is pressed into service as a handmaiden to the tariff and becomes another instrument of global conquest.

Foreigners, however, openly objected to the blatant American imperialism, especially as it impinged on their cultural exports. America was considered a cultural pariah for its taxing of imported works of art, then an anomaly in the Western world. In 1883 these duties had been raised from 10 to 30 percent.[53] Although Grover Cleveland, the first Democrat to win the presidency since James Buchanan's election in 1856, stressed tariff reduction in order to contain the populist wing of his party, he could not override the protectionists among the Republicans, who controlled the Senate, and the Democrats, who controlled the House. In his annual addresses to Congress of 1885, 1886, and 1887, Cleveland championed a reduced tariff and, except in the last-mentioned year, recommended the abolition of the duty on the paintings of foreign artists.[54] For this recommendation he received a special note of thanks from the membership of the official society of painters and sculptors in Belgium, the Cercle Artistique Littéraire et Scientifique of Antwerp.[55]

Starting in 1887, the Democrats and Republicans divided sharply over the tariff, but often the differences were more rhetorical than substantial. The Democrats would have allowed some imports of raw materials duty-free, but they agreed with the Republicans on the need to expand exports abroad and maintain a protectionist system for the home market. It was in this period that the government transformed its tariff into an active instrument of foreign policy to gain leverage in the international market.[56] The Congress justified the tariff on art, as it did other tariffs, by pointing to its protection of indigenous painters. But since the vogue in the 1880s greatly favored the French, French-trained Americans—who often studied in the free ateliers of the state-sponsored Ecole des Beaux-Arts—disapproved of the tariff on their masters.[57]

President Chester Arthur had earlier, in a message to Congress, expressed the fear that the import duties would result in "the practical exclusion of our painters and sculptors from the rich fields for observation, study, and labor, which they have hitherto enjoyed." Evidence for the validity of this forecast was not immediately forthcoming; except for letters and petitions from the art institutions and governments, no formal measures of retaliation seem to have been instituted. Americans did believe, however, that the French ban on American pork represented retaliation for the tax on art.[58] Furthermore, the attitudes expressed by the French in 1889 suggested to many of the North American participants that the tariff may have been an influential factor in what they read as the unfavorable reception of their work at the Exposition.[59]

Although American artists won a large number of medals for their exhibits, this apparently resulted from the unexpected generosity of Meissonier, the president of the Exposition jury. Meissonier wanted to open the annual French Salon to as many unaffiliated painters as possible in order to wrest control from those who had heretofore dominated the Salon juries—Bouguereau and his colleagues and their students of the Académie Julian. Meissonier's victory in this power struggle meant that henceforth medal-winning Exposition participants would be exempt from juried evaluations and would be given automatic admission to the Salon and the right to vote for the jury. Thus the principal cause of the epochal schism in the Salon that occurred the following year—the division into separate official exhibitions under the auspices of the old Society of French Artists and the new Société Nationale des Beaux-Arts—turned on the power struggle fought out between Meissonier and Bouguereau over the large number of medals conferred at the Exposition of 1889.[60] The complaints by Americans of unjust treatment with regard to the Legion of Honor awards and the allocation of space have to be kept separate from the bestowal of the medals, which took place under a different administrative jurisdiction. Decisions on the Legion of Honor and the question of space fell directly to the state as represented by Proust and were more likely to have been biased in reaction to the United States tariff.[61]

American artists as a body deplored the discrimination against their fellows working abroad.[62] In 1883, when the new tariff was instituted, no less than 300 native artists signed a petition in favor of the free admission of works of art into the ports of the United States. The following year, the Union League Club of New York undertook to systematically gauge the sentiment of American artists by gathering data from a large sampling of artists, art teachers, and art institutions (collectors and dealers excluded). The Club then reported the result—near unanimity for abolition—to Congress, adding a legal interpretation filed by Charles B. Curtiss, a noted lawyer. He argued that high import duties could be justified only for manufactured objects; that painting, sculpture, and related arts are not manufactures in the commercial sense but a means of education and culture; that the elevation of taste brought about by exposure to works of art actually promoted home industries by increasing the skill and ennobling the aims of American workers and by creating a demand for such improvements as add to the beauty and convenience of homes, costume, and practically everything that gives pleasure to the mind and comfort to the body.[63]

The report reminded Congress that the United States was the only nation in the civilized world that levied heavy duties to keep works of art outside its borders; that the law of 1883, which raised the duty to 30 percent, was not called for by artists, not advocated by the press, not demanded by the people, and that as a measure of financial policy it had proved to be a failure, since it had restricted trade and diminished the public revenue. The report concluded that the measure succeeded only in incurring the enmity of nations such as France, Belgium, and Italy, which registered their protests with the State Department.

The views expressed by the French master Jean-Léon Gérôme in a letter to a patron in New York summed up the feelings of the American painters as well:

In the huge budget of the United States the sum arising from duties on pictures is but a drop of water to the ocean. But there is a moral aspect to this question. It is in France and Germany, but more especially in France, that your young painters have been taught. . . . Is it just to treat the works of these foreign artists, these educators, with such severity? . . . People will one day say: "It was at the close of the nineteenth century, in the full flush of civilization, that the strange, odd idea cropped up of likening the products of the mind to sardines in oil and to smoked hams. All over the world works of art were duty free. In one country alone were they saddled with excessive tax, and that country was the youngest, the greatest, and the wealthiest of nations."[64]

Here Gérôme, who made his fortune in large part by selling his work to Americans, was sounding his personal economic alarm. Yet his ironic linking of sardines in oil and smoked hams with works of art brings us back to the French astonishment at the sight of the chocolate Venus and their conviction that the idea of creating an edible work of art could only have come from the mind of Yankees who taxed works of art like canned food. Art, for a Congress with a sense of cultural inferiority, had to be conceived of as a commodity to make it understandable. At the same time, by levying heavy duties on art works, the Congress served the interests of the wealthiest collectors, who achieved status through the possession of prestigious French art. Under the impact of the tariff, only the wealthiest—such as the department store magnate A. J. Stewart, who bought Meissonier's *Friedland* for $80,000 after the painter deliberately jacked up the price for a work previously earmarked for Sir Richard Wallace at $60,000—could afford the "latest" French exports in art. The 33⅓ percent markup by Meissonier exemplifies the general impact of the tariff on the international art market. Thus the whole world began to see art works as commodities like hams, sardines, and chocolate but with the precious advantage of a longer shelf life. The translation of the classical artifact into an edible—read "consumable"—commodity constituted a threat to the very ideal of the world's fairs, which aimed to separate culture and commerce into distinct spheres that could be bridged but not fused.

The Exposition of 1889 stimulated the debate over the tariff once again, especially in the context of American participation. The year before, the painter Charles Reinhart had complained of the jealousy of French artists toward "their American brethren" in Paris. He contended that the Salon jurors refused to award honors to Americans "because of the duty on pictures in America, which was only put on to counterbalance that on (U.S.) pork in France. In France the American only has a right to learn painting. But he must not paint anything saleable or sell it when painted."[65]

There is no question that the refusal of Congress to remove the high tariff on works of art annoyed French officialdom, including Commissioner-General Proust. On the United States side, the discussion assumed an unexpected complexity, since it cut across political lines: protectionists and free traders could be found joining hands for or against the art tariff. Some Southern free traders, for example, favored the retention of the tariff to gain leverage in abolishing duties on ordinary items, maintaining that works of art were easily definable luxuries of the rich and therefore prime targets of taxation, and that it would be grossly unfair to admit free of duty the robber barons' pictures while taxing the coats, shoes, and tools of the laboring poor. Then there were the "America for Americans" protectionists, inveighing against the influx of foreign objects and the consequent encouragement of native artists to go abroad for their training: "If an artist is to preserve his originality, and retain the power frankly and freely to express himself, he must decline to submit his brush to the inspiration of European masters and European scenes."[66]

Opposing these arguments—labeling them as "demagogic" and warning the unwary not to be deceived by those in Congress posing as champions of the poor—were both free traders and protectionists. Is art a luxury like wine, silk, and lace? Does it minister only to the pleasure or ostentation of the rich, without benefiting the community at large? The then moderate periodical *The Nation* asked these questions and answered no, drawing a distinction between art works and the luxuries with which they are unfairly grouped: the work of art is not consumed by the purchaser; it lives long after the purchaser passes from the scene and may therefore enter a public institution and serve the public. Even in the purchaser's own lifetime many people will view it, "and a work of art truly belongs to him who enjoys it, not to him who owns it."[67]

The Nation was espousing the aesthetic doctrines of Ruskin and other Victorian thinkers who emphasized the democratic enjoyment of the work of art as a morally uplifting agent for all:

The first quality in which a work of art differs from a luxury is its permanence; the second is its productiveness. It not only gives pleasure to thousands and for ages, but it gives much more than pleasure—it gives education. The history of art is the history of civilization. Art, in one form or another, is the great beautifier and ennobler of life, and a nation without art—without poetry or painting, architecture or sculpture or music—is a nation of barbarians, though it possess the steam-engine and electricity.

The writer also pointed to the economic value of French artisans. Did the supporters of the tariff know how many millions of dollars the taste of its artisans—formed by the liberal government's support of the fine arts—is worth annually to France? "Has it ever occurred to them that in hundreds of industries the market of the world is not open to him who makes cheapest, but to him who makes most beautifully?. . . Bring everything down to the mere brutal test of money's worth, and art is productive." Appealing to the entire spectrum of party affiliations to abolish the tax, "worthy only of a race of savages," *The Nation* asked, "Why should not all men of culture, all men of intelligence, all lovers of art and of beauty, Democrats and Republicans, protectionists and free-traders, be of one mind to erase from our statute-book this abominable relic of barbarism?"

The question had been raised in Congress on May 19, 1884, over a 10 percent compromise bill introduced by New York Democrat Perry Belmont, whose father, August, was a prominent collector of French art. In the debate, Democrat Poindexter Dunn of Arkansas emphasized the discrepancy between the high taxes on salt and coarse woolen goods heaped on the poor and the low tax proposed for costly pictures and statuary: "Tax the salt of the humblest laborers of the land and take off the tax from the one hundred thousand dollar painting and other works of art of the millionaire! Is that Justice?" Angrily denouncing the proposed tariff reform as "a Trojan Horse with an army of spoilsmen concealed within it" who wish to tax the implements of industry of the laborers and give the wealthy their luxuries for free, Dunn stood firm:

So long as I stand here you shall never with my consent, remove taxation from whiskey nor from works of art, from luxuries, nor from silks, nor from fine raiment of any kind until you reduce it on all the articles consumed by the toiling poor and over-taxed people of this country—for them I for one shall stand firm to the last until relief is given.[68]

The complexities of the issue are shown in the curious alignments for or against it: the more socialist or populist-minded of the South and Midwest—normally free traders—favored the luxury tax, while some Democrats in the North could concert with Republicans against it.[69] Socialists and populists could support the tariff on luxury goods because it was not meant to protect industry but to raise revenue.[70] Most Northern Democrats, especially manufacturers, lined up with Republicans in favor of some form of protectionist tariff, with the exception of a group known as the Gold Democrats—mainly financiers and importer-exporters concentrated in New York and Boston—who gathered around Cleveland and pushed for free trade. Nevertheless, on the issue of luxury tax the free traders and the protectionists could join forces in protest. Those most vociferous in the call for abolition consisted of robber baron collectors and art dealers and the artists deeply imbued with the current French style. They felt a missionary call to spread good—that is, their own French-influenced—taste to American shores and harped on the need to elevate the aesthetic standards of the laboring masses. They attacked the philistines, the nouveau-riche industrialists who displayed gaudy furnishings and gingerbread decor in their mansions. They saw themselves as an elite, but an elite sympathetic to the poor and under-privileged. They were mainly Republican, but they were supported by the Democratic Grover Cleveland in the call for abolition of the tariff on foreign art.

One of the most outspoken critics of the tariff was Rush C. Hawkins, the American Commissioner of Fine Arts for the Universal Exposition of 1889. Hawkins seized the opportunity provided by his official report on the world's fair to take American society to task not only for the tariff but for all its cultural faults and blemishes. He confessed that the task (to which he felt assigned) of reforming and regenerating the national taste was "not an easy one." Hawkins began by noting the uneven distribution of wealth in the country and expressed despair about elevating the public taste:

The crushing power of unprecedented enormous wealth concentrated in the possession of a comparatively small number of our population, and the conceit it engenders in the minds of its possessors, constitutes a sort of intangible Chinese wall, which stands as a barrier against general improvement in matters of taste and artistic adornment.

Hawkins condemned American taste generally, claiming that of the thousands of public monuments in the United States "it is safe to assert that there are not more than twenty-five which, from an art standpoint, are fairly good." He referred to "bronze monstrosities of unprecedented hideousness" and the lack of decent-looking bank notes, coins, and stamps, which remain at the level of the "lowest commonplace."[71]

Of the many obstacles standing in the way of progress, he cited the statutory restriction upon the importation of works of art and the tendency of the new rich from Maine to California to "overdo" decoration. The ugly, excessively furnished residences of a large wealthy class demonstrate a "semi-barbaric desire for show that is indifferent to sham." The arrogance that leads the "new-made man of millions" into thinking that he is superior culturally as well as economically has created a Frankenstein in our social structure. It is precisely this ignorant body of plutocrats that made it an urgent necessity to lift the duty upon the importation of works of art. The restriction has encouraged the collaboration of forgers and dishonest dealers, who easily pass off fakes to these millionaires as the real thing. Thus the pernicious law "may be regarded as an extreme illustration of the emptiness of our pretension to occupy a higher position in the history of the civilization of the nineteenth century."

In any plan to upgrade artistic standards, the right to purchase works of art takes precedence. The argument that such works are luxuries for the rich and purchased primarily for personal gratification is a specious one. It would be preferable if the government obtained them for public collections, but this is not going to happen in the realm of "practical politics." What the government must do is to encourage citizens to enrich their collections, since it is mainly from private collections that most public galleries in the United States have been formed. Hawkins concluded that the repeal of the 30 percent duty would do more to improve the national taste than his Exposition report on the condition of art in other nations.

Hawkins enthusiastically praised France's representation at the Exposition as a model for other countries, saying that in their exhibition the French surpassed all the other nations and made the success of the Exposition of 1889 "one of unparalleled splendor and completeness." The high standard of excellence in the arts is reflected in the studied simplicity of French industrial, architectural, and interior design. Hawkins was not just thinking of aesthetic standards, however; his critique extended to the effect of the visual environment on morals and public health. Indeed, proper surroundings

make men and women more considerate, kind, and reserved in their intercourse with each other, and help to give refinement to the transactions of everyday life. Prize-fighters, wife-beaters, and tobacco-chewers are not results which flow from the source that irrigates the arts. No doubt the salon *has furnished its share of characters whose names are to be found in the world's record of crime, but their misdeeds have scarcely been on the level of the brutal murderer's, or those of the sneaking cut-purse.*

It is not surprising that in his report Hawkins also considered the working class—the failure "to raise the morals and ameliorate the physical condition of this burdensome class of human beings." His solution was to build working-class housing subsidized by philanthropists "benevolently disposed to think about the best method to be employed in order to secure the substantial improvement of the classes intended to be benefited." Other aspects of Hawkins's social views come through in his discussion of the links between art education and the recruitment of a managerial elite to fill the places in the state's bureaucratic infrastructure:

Our people are now forming what might be appropriately called in social geology the palace strata. What better business can our National or State Governments engage in than that of educating not only our fast-growing class for the palace strata, but likewise all classes of our people, up to a certain standard of knowledge concerning art values, as necessities which ought to find expression in our everyday surroundings?

Although Hawkins had left to the juries the vital selection of work to be shown at the Exposition, the choice of East Coast institutions, more or less biased in favor of French art, to designate stateside jury members (American artists living in or near Paris formed their own jury) inevitably gave a French look to the American exhibits and inadvertently provided grounds for Parisian art critics to dismiss them as an extension of local schools. Hawkins clearly belonged to that elite which, frightened of the changing cultural patterns of the last quarter of the century, asserted their leadership through the sponsorship of French and French-influenced work. The current barbarians at the gate were the immigrants and the rich newly emerged from immigrant status, and they threatened not only the elite's cultural leadership but also their political power.

Since his taste moved more in the direction of the elegant seaside resort than the forest of Fontainebleau, Hawkins did not embrace the whole of French painting. He despised Millet and could not understand how his works—so "devoid of grace, interest, imagination, or beauty of any sort"—could command the enormous prices they did. (Ironically, here Hawkins disagreed with his French counterpart, Fine Arts Commissioner Antonin Proust, who considered Millet one of France's seminal painters and worked assiduously behind the scenes in the summer of 1889—at the risk of his reputation and his reelection to the Chamber of Deputies—to keep the *Angelus* out of American hands at any price and to install it in the Louvre.[72]) Hawkins regarded Millet's subjects as unworthy of a true master—most often "idiots or monsters" engaged in such trivial activities "as carrying sick calves, hog-sticking . . . in which the majority of mankind do not take the least interest." (So much for Hawkins's concern for workers and work-related issues.) His ideal was clearly the prettified peasants painted by such American students of the French academicians as Daniel Ridgway Knight and Charles Sprague Pearce.[73]

Like the organizers of the new Musée d'Orsay in France, Hawkins believed that the culmination of the grand tradition inaugurated by Jacques-Louis David was Thomas Couture's *Romans of the Decadence*. Calling it an "immortal work," Hawkins saw it as the last great painting of the modern epoch—a "story of debauchery and dissipation, sapping the physical vitality and destroying the morale of a great people, as it was never told before. . . . "

Yet for all his praise of the influence of the antique on French painting, Hawkins's unsympathetic view of the events of 1789 commemorated by the Exposition suggested that he conveniently forgot the classicism of the art of the Revolution. His sympathies were wholly on the side of the elite institutions that were overthrown in 1789, as is shown by his pithy comment on the closing of the Académie Royale des Beaux-Arts: "In 1793 the wild spirits who controlled the affairs of France arrived at the conclusion that the nation had greater need of guillotines than pictures and statues." Summed up in Hawkins's report is his artistic and social ideology, as well as his anxieties over what he sees as the moral decay of the present and the wellsprings of his program for reform.[74]

There were other events and issues central to the exchange between France and the United States, some on the seemingly lighter side, others debated at the highest diplomatic levels. While the Wild West show (fig. 32) of Buffalo Bill ("Colonel" Cody) appealed profoundly to the masses of French people (Rosa Bonheur was one of his many admirers and painted his portrait[75]), some French critics took a dim view of the spectacle and expressed skepticism about the number of villages in the United States "inhabited entirely by colonels."[76] One writer seized on the show to mount a scathing attack on American morals and to debunk the romance of the cowboy. He observed that the violence of the West was mainly caused by the palefaces, much "more savage" than the Indians, "since they carry with them into Indian territory all the savagery of their civilization," and noted that the so-called civilized whites chase the Native Americans from

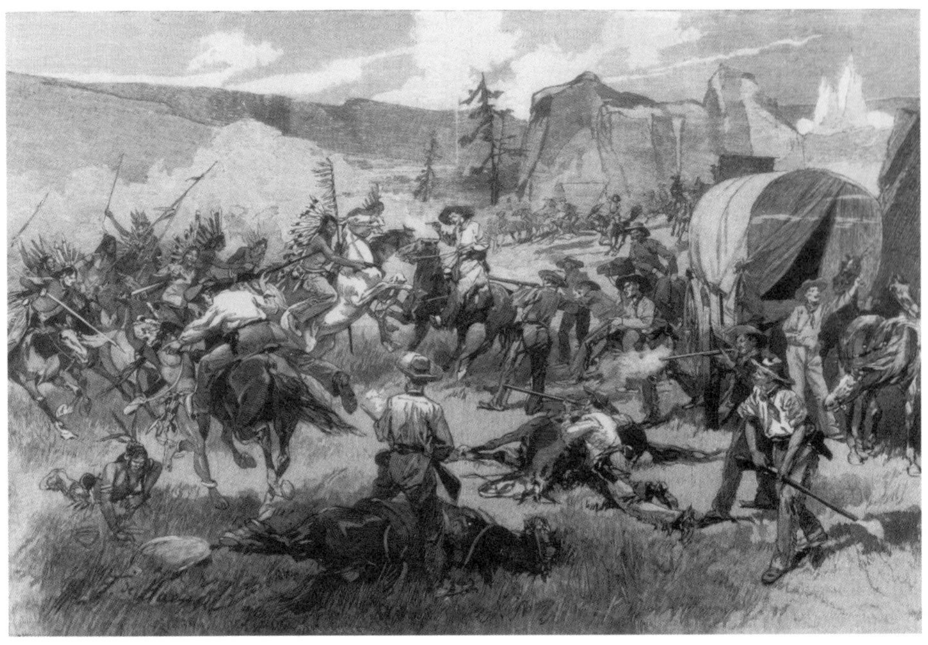

32.
La Troupe du Colonel Cody (Buffalo Bill)
From *L'Illustration*, June 22, 1889, p. 533

their lands and force them to keep pushing west. The Indians "die with the nostalgic memory of their abandoned lands before their eyes; they are unable to comprehend the beauties of the struggle for life, and those who do grasp them are reduced to parodying Buffalo-Bill and to engage in their petty exercises before admiring audiences."[77] This writer proved to be prophetic: near the end of the following year, on a cold winter day, United States Army troops attacked Sioux Indians camped at Wounded Knee, South Dakota, and killed 300 men, women, and children. Colonel Cody's entertaining reenactments of Indian attacks on emigrant trains and dramatic rescues by the infantry were not simply a nostalgic look back at the pioneer past and the heyday of the by then "vanishing Redman"; they were an example of popular culture operating as an agent on behalf of the mopping-up phase of Manifest Destiny.[78]

Buffalo Bill repeated his Wild West show, complete with Indian massacres and army rescues, at the World's Columbian Exposition four years later. During the inaugural ceremonies several Oglala Sioux braves in full ceremonial garb watched the tumultuous opening from the highest balcony of the Administration Building. At the moment when President Cleveland pulled the switch that set off the machinery and signaled the raising of the flags, and a huge chorus began to sing "My Country, 'Tis of Thee," an observer—a fervent admirer of Buffalo Bill as a "real American" type—noted a detail that

gave an unexpected American tinge to the climax of the interesting ceremonies: the braves in their blazing war paint, gorgeous necklaces and representative American savagery appeared on the north abutment of the building, a blazing line of character moving along with high, flaunting crests of feathers and flaming blankets which stood out against the gleaming white of the staff dome like a rainbow cleft into remembrances of a lost, primitive glory. Nothing in the day's occurrences appealed to sympathetic patriotism so much as this fallen majesty slowly filing out of sight as the flags of all nations swept satin kisses through the air, waving congratulations to cultured achievement and submissive admirations to a new world.[79]

In contrast to this report are eyewitness accounts of the chaotic behavior of the crowd and the trampling of people underfoot at the opening events. By a reversal, the writer turns the dignified Indian observers into metaphorical aggressors whose elimination as a force from the national scene coincides with the birth of a "new world"—a classic case of blaming the victim. This contradiction is conspicuously present on the first page of Rossiter Johnson's monumental history of the Columbian Exposition:

Of all the secular events that have taken place since the dawn of history, the discovery of this Western Hemisphere in 1492 was by far the most important. Even if conquest were to be classed with discovery—the mere change of rulers with the opening of new fields for industry and civilization—the rank of that great achievement would still remain unchanged. When we consider the density of Europe's population to-day, it is appalling to think what it might be had not this vast domain been welcoming immigration for four centuries. We should still have but about three hundred thousand savages roaming over the continent . . . .[80]

If French urban audiences delighted in the shenanigans of Colonel Cody, their rural counterparts expressed anger that the insect destructive to their wines had come from the United States, and they were even more outraged by their dependence on the grafting of American species—much more resistant to the phylloxera—onto their own vines.[81] In 1888 there were 93,000 hectares of American vines in the department of Hérault. An entire bureau in the ministry of agriculture was devoted to phylloxera, and at the 1889 Exposition a special section of the French exhibit of vine cultivation and wine making on the Quai d'Orsay displayed the methods used to control vine maladies, particularly the destruction of the injurious phylloxera. Not fortuitously, the French played down their widespread grafting of native vines onto American roots, in direct contrast with the United States' wine exhibit, which stressed the importance of American vine stocks in the regeneration of French vineyards.[82]

Bearing directly on the problem of the tariff was the French ban on pork. The year 1888 witnessed the Great Tariff Debate and the first presidential campaign in which the tariff was the central issue. In a classic argument predicting a glutted home market and stressing the need to maintain a high level of employment, President Cleveland urgently recommended reducing the tariff to make American manufacturers more competitive in foreign markets. Although it was his administration that accepted the invitation of the French government to participate in the Exposition, when the Exposition opened, a Republican occupied the White House. Businessmen rallied to the Republicans out of fear that Democrats would reduce the tariff too drastically. Benjamin Harrison, the new president, was a devout protectionist and advocated the tariff as a major factor in the creation of a strong domestic market. He had the advantage that his party now dominated both executive and legislative branches.

Harrison believed in economic expansion, and he early concentrated on the passing of the first federal meat inspection act, with the primary purpose of eliminating the European embargo on pork products imported from the United States (which had been excluded from French ports since 1881 on the grounds that they contributed to the spread of trichinosis). Ambassador Whitelaw Reid made the issue his principal diplomatic focus. The economic consequences of the ban are seen in the statistics: in 1880 the exports of American pork products into France had amounted to $3,900,000, while in 1889 they amounted to around $5,000. Reid took advantage of the goodwill generated by United States participation in the Exposition to persuade French officials that American pork was safe and to push for the lifting of the embargo. Reporting to the president on the favorable attitude of the members of the new French cabinet on the pork question, the ambassador wrote: "They all have a kindly feeling also because of our attitude towards their exposition while Europe was boycotting it;—and on their success with the exposition their offical lives depend." Thus informed, the Chicago firm of Armour & Co., through their French agents in Le Havre, made every effort during the Exposition to induce the French government to withdraw the restrictive duties against American pork products.

Himself an ardent protectionist, Reid suggested to the president that Congress try to penetrate the strongly protectionist screen of the Chamber of Deputies by threatening legislation of an increased duty on French wines, following the French example of blaming the unhealthfulness of the product. By adducing examples of the adulteration of French wines, the Congress might get the French, motivated by fear of the inevitable protests from their constituents, to reverse their policy. Reid added the suggestion that the Congress could also offer a "carrot" in the form of a revised law on the duties on art:

If we could then approach the Government with a suggestion that the best way to avoid the threatened action of Congress would be to show a rational spirit on the subject of pork, and if we could add that prompt and friendly action on this subject might lead to a law admitting French pictures free, there might be a better chance for reaching a satisfactory result than at present.[83]

As a diplomat involved in American foreign policy, Reid agreed with artist Charles Reinhart and others that there existed a strong link between the American tariff on art and the French ban on pork.[84]

The prodigious popular enterprises known as universal expositions became the battlegrounds on which nationalist and internationalist rivalries were played out. Each fair represented an attempt to freeze for an instant the pace of dynamic change and to give it definition. The industrial and technological advances seemed to justify optimistic visions of infinite progress, but the tragic by-products of the uneven distribution of wealth sharpened the painful dissonance between the rhetoric of liberty and progress and everyday reality. The organizers of the mammoth fairs attempted to contain literally and figuratively the facts of change and their social and political effects, but international rivalries disrupted the show of harmony to reveal the confusions and contradictions within the respective domestic spheres.

The most conspicuous of the contradictions resides in the hierarchical and racist symbolism of the exhibitions and its attendant rhetoric. The word "savage" recurs frequently as a means of justifying territorial expansion on the part of the dominant political elites: over and against the "savage" or "barbaric" consciousness, they posit the "spiritual" and "civilized" values revealed in their own "higher" culture. The weakness of this position as taken by the Americans was clearly spotted by the French in the Yankees' ruthless extermination of Native Americans; the French revealed their own soft spot in their harsh repression of indigenous peoples in Oceania, Asia, and Africa. All this is vividly demonstrated by the way Emmanuel Frémiet's sculpture *Gorilla Carrying Off a Human Female* (fig. 33),[85] which created a sensation at the Salon of 1887 and again at the Exposition of 1889, was perceived. For the elites everywhere the ape was a metaphor for the "savage" of colonialized territories; Hawkins saw it as a vision "of the lowest side of human nature."[86] The French dramatist and critic Philippe Gille imagined it as representing the victory of bestiality over humankind, a victory that is only momentary, however, since Providence soon intervenes in the form of a bullet that stops the beast and releases the woman. Gille saw the sculpture as pointing to France's own victory over a "terrible past" and concluded that "France is alive and well and that the spiritual always ends by triumphing over matter." The appeal of Frémiet's work lay in its capacity to encode social Darwinism and colonial oppression, a process that enabled both the North American and the French elite to project onto native peoples and their own working classes the very barbarism into which they had plunged. The terrifying prospect of the Dark Continent emanated from the deepest recesses of the Western imagination, and its sublimation assumed the dazzling guise of the world's fairs of 1889 and 1893.

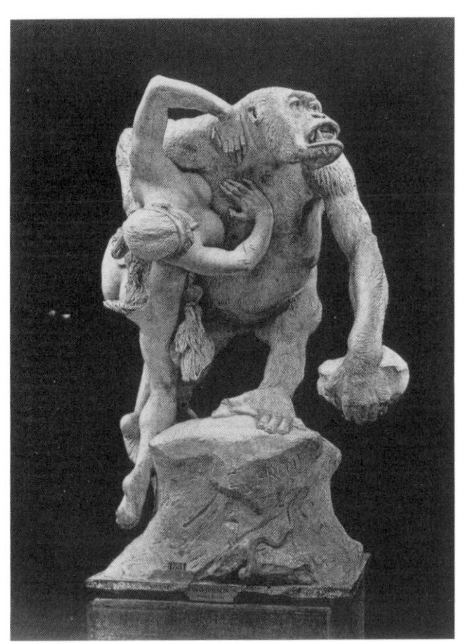

33.
Emmanuel Frémiet (1824–1910)
Troglodytes Gorilla, 1887
Sculpture shown at the Palais des Beaux-Arts, Exposition Universelle, 1889. Steel engraving illustrated in *Figaro–Exposition* 1889. Helga Photo Studio, New York

NOTE. *I am beholden to a number of wonderful people who made this essay possible. Annette Blaugrund gave unstintingly of her time, knowledge, and documentary resources. Ronald J. Mahoney made his home, as well as the rich special collections at the Henry Madden Library, California State University, available to me. Other friends and colleagues who led me to elusive sources and through inaccessible material and helped in innumerable ways include: Denise Bratton, Edward Berenson, Carolyn Carr, Patricia Carranza, Jean Coffey, Lois M. Fink, George Gurney, David Lake, Bernard Legendre, Merle M. Moore, Jr., and Debora Silverman.*

Notes

1. There is a voluminous literature on the world's fairs. See Bibliography.
2. Theodore Stanton, "America at the Paris Exhibition," *Boston Daily Evening Transcript*, June 29, 1889, p. 5.
3. For the plan of the fair, see Debora Silverman, "The 1889 Exhibition: The Crisis of Bourgeois Individualism," *Oppositions*, 8 (Spring 1977), pp. 71–91.
4. Alfred Picard, *Exposition Universelle Internationale de 1889 à Paris: Rapport générale* (Paris, 1891–92), vol. 1, p. 303.
5. *Exposition Universelle Internationale de 1889 à Paris. Catalogue général officiel. Exposition rétrospective du travail et des sciences anthropologiques* (Lille, 1889), p. 9. The same philosophical outlook prevailed in the 1893 world's fair at Chicago; see James G. Blaine et al., *Columbus and Columbia, A Pictorial History of the Man and the Nation Embracing a Review of Our Country's Progress, a Complete History of America, a New Life of Columbus and an Illustrated Description of the Great Columbian Exposition* (Omaha and Denver, 1892).
6. Ministère du commerce, de l'industrie et des colonies, *Congrès international des sciences ethnographiques, tenu à Paris du 30 septembre au 7 octobre 1889. Procès-Verbaux sommaires* (Paris, 1890), pp. 31–32.
7. C.-L. Huard, *Livre d'or de l'exposition* (Lisbon, 1889), vol. 2, p. 483.
8. Frederick Douglass and Ida B. Wells, *The Reason Why the Colored American Is Not in the World's Columbian Exposition* (Chicago, 1893), p. 9; E. M. Rudwick and A. Meier, "Black Man in the 'White City': Negroes and the Columbian Exposition, 1893," *Phylon: The Atlanta University Review of Race and Culture*, 26 (1965), pp. 354–61.
9. This is how one American correspondent perceived the situation: "Everybody agrees that to deliver France over to the tumult and uncertainty of a great electoral struggle, involving the very principle and form of government, at the eve of the International Exhibition, would be most unpatriotic, though exactly the same argument was used six months ago against dissolution. Now there is force in it, but it is far from certain that the exhibition will save the Chamber from collapse at a moment still more inconvenient than the present one. It is impossible to disguise the fact that although the Chamber lives it is in an advanced state of decomposition." R. B., "The Exhibition and Party," *Boston Daily Evening Transcript*, March 13, 1889.
10. Charles de Mazade, "Chronique de la quinzaine," *Revue des deux mondes*, ser. 9, vol. 93 (May 15, 1889), pp. 465–67; Sophia Beale, "A Last Look at the Paris Exposition," *Universal Review*, 6 (1890), pp. 113–14; Pierre Paget, "Le Salon de 1889," *L'Illustration*, April 27, 1889. For a view of the way the French interpreted foreign responses to the Revolution, see the allegorical piece by Anatole Leroy-Beaulieu, "Le Centenaire de 1789," *Revue des deux mondes*, ser. 9, vol. 93 (June 15, 1889), pp. 860–904.
11. [Sarah Butler Wister], "Loitering Through the Paris Exposition," *Atlantic Monthly*, 65 (March 1889), pp. 364–65.
12. See Casimir Stryienski, *Charles Landelle 1821–1908* (Paris, 1911), pp. 129–30. The replica,

known as *Liberty Regulated by Law*, remained in the Stanford University Art Museum until the early 1970s, when it was deaccessioned and sold. See C. M. Osborne, *Museum Builders in the West; The Stanfords as Collectors and Patrons of Art 1870–1906* (Stanford, 1986), p. 56.

13. The projects for the abortive fair of 1989 sound remarkably similar to the program of 1889, except that the crude anthropological concepts are replaced by the theme of "genetics." Analogously, the projected fair aimed at "la valorisation de l'industrie française à l'occasion de l'Exposition Universelle." See *Projets pour l'Exposition universelle de 1989 à Paris: Livre Blanc* (Paris, 1985), pp. 11, 16–17, 112, 163.

14. G. W. S., "The French Exposition," *New York Tribune*, May 5, 7, 1889, p. 1.

15. Guillaume-Louis Figuier, *L'Année scientifique et industrielle* (Paris, 1890), p. 452; Rush C. Hawkins Scrapbook 13 (Annmary Brown Memorial Library, Brown University): letter from Somerville P. Tuck to Hawkins, Dec. 10, 1888; letter from William B. Franklin to Hawkins, Jan. 26, 1889; letter from Hawkins to Franklin, Oct. 6, 1889. Although their government refused to participate officially, the English were given a much larger overall space in the fair than the United States. See H. T. Wood, "Exposition of 1889," *Journal of the Society of Arts*, (Dec. 13, 1889), p. 57.

16. Picard, op. cit., vol. 9, pp. 393–94.

17. Albert Boime, *Hollow Icons: The Politics of Sculpture in Nineteenth-Century France* (Kent, Ohio, 1987), pp. 113–39.

18. Bingham Duncan, *Whitelaw Reid* (Athens, Ga., 1975), p. 117.

19. Antonin Proust, *L'Art sous la République* (Paris, 1892), pp. 164–82; M. R. Levin, *Republican Art and Ideology in Late Nineteenth-Century France* (Ann Arbor, Mich., 1986), pp. 4–5, 86–87, 178–79.

20. For Cleveland I have used Allan Nevins, *Grover Cleveland* (New York, 1962).

21. Quoted in Matthew Josephson, *The Politicos 1865–1896* (New York, 1966), p. 364.

22. Ibid, p. 373.

23. G. F. Parker, ed., *The Writings and Speeches of Grover Cleveland* (New York, 1892), p. 84.

24. "L'Effet de la bombe," *La Révolte*, May 15–21, 1886; "Les Condamnés à mort de Chicago," *La Révolte*, Oct. 15–21, 1887.

25. "France's Gift Accepted," *New York Times*, Oct. 29, 1886, p. 1. The French anarchists countered that the "Statue of Liberty of the American bourgeois" was a lie, as demonstrated in the case of the Haymarket prisoners. They suggested that images of child labor should be carved on its pedestal, as well as the miseries of big-city slums caused by the exploitation of the Vanderbilts and the Mackays. See "La Liberté," *La Révolte*, Nov. 6–12, 1886.

26. *Reports of the United States Commissioners to the Universal Exposition of 1889 at Paris* (Washington, D.C., 1890–91), vol. 1, p. 21.

27. François Hoffman, "La Question sociale au Salon de 1888," *La Révolte*, June 9–15, 1888.

28. Louis d'Hurcourt, "Nos Gravures," *L'Illustration*, 94 (Aug. 24, 1889), pp. 157, 160.

29. "The Home Coming of the Famous Painting 'Brutality'... First Exhibition in America Beginning Wednesday, February 12, 1908" (Jones Dry Goods Co., Kansas City, 1908).

30. For details of the strike, see "Les Oeuvres et les hommes," *Le Correspondant*, 155 (June 25, 1889), pp. 1189–90; Louis d'Hurcourt, "La Grève des cochers," *L'Illustration*, 93 (June 22, 1889), p. 524. For an anti-driver view see "Paris Drivers," *New York Herald* (Paris ed.), June 5, 1888, and "Crowded Paris," *Boston Daily Evening Transcript*, June 28, 1889, p. 6.

31. Chauncey M. Depew, "The Columbian Oration," *Memorial Volume. Dedicatory and Opening Ceremonies of the World's Columbian Exposition* (Chicago, 1893), p. 183.

32. "World's Fair in New York," *New York Herald* (Paris ed.), Aug. 1, 1889; J. R. Hawley, "The Value of International Exhibitions," *North American Review*, 149 (Sept. 1889), pp. 312–13.

33. See Albert Boime, "Sargent in Paris and London: A Portrait of the Artist as Dorian Gray," in Patricia Hills, ed., *John Singer Sargent* (New York, 1986), pp. 75–109. The subject of the Americanization of European culture came up stridently in the context of the 1889 fair: see Charles Crosnier de Varigny, "L'Exposition des Etats-Unis," *L'Exposition de Paris, 1889* (Paris, 1889), vol. 2, pp. 90–91.

34. I am grateful to Lois Marie Fink for allowing me to read the manuscript of her forthcoming publication *American Art at the Nineteenth-Century Salons*.

35. Charles Bigot, "Le Salon de 1883," *Gazette des Beaux-Arts*, 2nd per., vol. 28 (1883), p. 23.

36. L. Vérax, *De l'Envahissement de l'Ecole des Beaux-Arts par les étrangers. Réclamations des élèves français* (Paris, 1886), pp. 15 ff.

37 Emile Monod, *Exposition universelle de 1889. Grand ouvrage illustré historique, encyclopédique, descriptif publié sous le patronage de M. le Ministre du Commerce, de l'Industrie et des Colonies* (Paris, 1890), vol. 1, p. 607.

38. Picard, *Rapport général*, vol. 4, p. 111.

39. Maurice Hamel, "Les écoles étrangères," *Gazette des Beaux-Arts*, 3rd per., vol. 2 (1889), pp. 382–84.

40. Monod, op. cit., vol. 2, p. 596.

41. Rossiter Johnson, in *A History of the World's Columbian Exposition*, (New York, 1897), vol. 3, pp. 443–44, recalls the Dahomean village on the Midway and the action of the "chocolate-hued West African barbarians." For the African-American entertainer, see Hugh Honour, *The Image of the Black in Western Art* (Cambridge, Mass., and London, 1989), vol. 4, part 2, pp. 213–14.

42. Honour, op. cit., vol. 4, part 1, pp. 33–34.

43. Iolo A. Williams, *The Firm of Cadbury* (London, 1931), pp. 191–215.

44. See Martin Bernal, *Black Athena: The Afroasiatic Roots of Classical Civilization* (New Brunswick, 1988), vol. 1, pp. 1–73, 337–99.

45. Theodore Child, "American Artists at the Paris Exhibition," *Harper's New Monthly Magazine*, 79 (Sept. 1889), pp. 518–19.

46. Printed minutes of the meeting of "American Artists, Residents in Paris," April 7, 1888 (Hawkins Scrapbook 13, Annmary Brown Memorial Library, Brown University).

47. "Glimpses of Parisian Art," *Scribner's Monthly*, 1, (Dec. 1880), p. 169; G. W. Sheldon, *Recent Ideals of American Art* (New York and London, 1890), pp. 141–46.

48. W. C. Brownell, "The Paris Exposition. Notes and Impressions," *Scribner's Magazine*, 7 (Jan. 1890), p. 34; G. W. Sheldon, *Ideals of Life in France or How the Great Painters Portray Woman in French Art* (New York and London, 1890), p. 143.

49. Maurice Brincourt, *L'Exposition universelle de 1889* (Paris, 1890), pp. 58–61; Arsène Alexandre, "Promenades aux sections étrangères. Angleterre—Etats-Unis," in F. G. Dumas and Louis de Fourcaud, *Revue de l'Exposition universelle de 1889* (Paris, 1889), vol. 2, p. 217.

50. American tariff policy is analyzed by Claudio Jannet, "Les Faits économiques et le mouvement social en Amérique," *Le Correspondent*, 158 (Jan. 25, 1890), pp. 348–78. See also Charles Crosnier de Varigny, "Un Homme d'état américain. James G. Blaine et le Congrès des Trois Amériques," *Revue des deux mondes*, 9th ser., vol. 97 (Jan. 15, 1890), pp. 433–62.

51. For a sampling of writings of the period fostering the stereotype of the American as venal and materialist, see Charles Crosnier de Varigny, "La Femme aux Etats-Unis," *Revue des deux mondes*, 9th ser., vol. 93 (May 15, 1889), p. 441, and "L'Amérique à l'Exposition universelle," *Revue des deux mondes*, 9th ser., vol. 95 (Oct. 15, 1889), pp. 842–48; Auguste Laugel, "Un Ouvrage récent sur les Etats-Unis," *Revue des deux mondes*, 9th ser., vol. 98 (March 15, 1890), pp. 432–33; Albert de Chenclos, "Les Yankees chez eux," *Le Correspondant*, 157 (Dec. 25, 1889), pp. 833–59, 1026–48.

52. Emil Schalk, "The Logic of Protection: The Distinguishing Feature of Civilization," *New York Daily Tribune*, May 9, 1888, p. 4.

53. *The Statutes at Large of the United States of America from December, 1881, to March, 1883, and Recent Treaties, Postal Conventions, and Executive Proclamations* (Washington, D.C., 1883) vol. 22, pp. 513, 522–23. For a general study of the Tariff Act of 1883, see F. W. Taussig, *The History of the Present Tariff 1860–1883* (New York and London, 1888), pp. 76–102.

54. Parker, ed., op. cit., p. 341.

55. *The Statutes at Large of the United States of America from December, 1881, to March, 1883*, vol. 22, pp. 32–33.

56. D. A. Lake, *Power, Protection, and Free Trade* (Ithaca, N.Y., and London, 1988), pp. 91–92, 98.

57. "The Artists Speak Again," *Boston Daily Evening Transcript*, June 5, 1883, p. 6; Albert Boime, "America's Purchasing Power and the Evolution of European Art in the Late Nineteenth Century," in F. Haskell, ed., *Saloni, Gallerie, Musei e loro influenza sullo sviluppo dell'arte dei secoli XIX e XX, Atti del XXIV Congresso Internazionale di Storia dell'Arte* (Bologna, 1981), pp. 126–27; Susan Grant, "American Paintings Acquired by the French Government, 1879–1900" (master's thesis, George Washington University, 1893), pp. 47–48.

58. "The History of the Tariff on Art," *The Studio: A Journal of the Fine Arts*, 3 (April 1889), p. 78.

59. Sheldon, *Recent Ideals of American Art*, p. 133.

60. Sheldon, *Ideals of Life in France*, pp. 17–18.

61. Proust was also personally disappointed by the loss of Millet's painting *L'Angelus* to the Americans, following the wild auction scene at the sale of the Secrétan collection on July 1, 1889. See n. 72.
62. "The Artists Speak Again," *Boston Daily Evening Transcript*, June 5, 1883, p. 6.
63. "The History of the Tariff on Art," *The Studio*, 3 (April 1889), pp. 76–78.
64. See Sheldon, *Recent Ideals of American Art*, pp. 32–34; Emile Durand-Gréville, "La Peinture aux Etats-Unis. Les galeries privées en Amérique," *Gazette des Beaux-Arts*, 2nd per., vol. 36 (1887), p. 69.
65. "Americans on Art," *New York Herald* (Paris ed.), May 9, 1888; quoted in Susan Grant, op. cit., pp. 46–47.
66. Sheldon, *Recent Ideals of American Art*, pp. 37–38.
67. "Art No Luxury," *The Nation*, 1255 (July 18, 1889), p. 46.
68. "The History of the Tariff on Art," *The Studio*, 3 (April 1889), pp. 77–78; "Duties on Works of Art," *Congressional Record*, 48th Cong., 1st sess., vol. 15 (1884), pp. 4294–98.
69. In the breakdown of the vote on Democrat Belmont's 10 percent compromise proposal, the majority of the 52 yeas derived from Northern and Ohio Republicans, while the majority of the 179 nays derived from the predominantly Democratic South and Midwest. One notable exception to the latter was Charles Boutelle of Maine, an ardent Republican protectionist.
70. At one point in the debate, Dunn of Arkansas declared: "It is unfortunate that no man can speak for the tax-payer here without being howled against as a communist or a demagogue. Sir, that denunciation has no terrors for me. . . ." *Congressional Record*, 48th Cong., 1st sess., vol. 15 (1884), pp. 42–96.
71. Hawkins was not the only American critic of American design; it was observed that at the 1889 fair the United States stood way "behind England" in this category: "America at the Exhibition," *Boston Daily Evening Transcript*, May 13, 1889.
72. The sale of the Secrétan collection on July 1, 1889, and the wrangling of the French (represented by Proust) and the Americans (mainly represented by James Sutton of the American Art Association) created an international sensation and sparked debates in the major newspapers of Paris and New York. Proust triumphed over his rival at the auction, but when the French Chamber refused to vote the funds necessary to supplement the private sum raised by Proust's consortium, he had to cede the picture to Sutton. Sutton, recognizing that the 30 percent duty would raise the price of the work by nearly $35,000, asked Congress for a special exemption on the grounds that his primary purpose in importing the *Angelus* was to exhibit it to the public, arousing the ire of New York art dealers, who recognized this proposal as a disguise for mercantile aims. Their analysis proved to be accurate when Sutton sold the work to the French department store magnate Alfred Chauchard, in November 1890. See R. L. Herbert, *Jean-François Millet* (Paris, 1975), no. 66, pp. 103–6; Antonin Proust, op. cit., pp. 173–82; "The 'Angelus' Is All Right," *New York Daily Tribune*, Aug. 1, 1889, p. 7.
73. William Dean Howells portrayed the French-trained painter hero Ludlow in similar terms: struggling to reconcile the French style with American subject matter, he "believed that if the right fellow ever came to the work, he could get as much pathos out of our farm folks as Millet got out of his Barbizon peasants. But the fact was that he was not the fellow; he wanted to paint beauty not pathos; and he thought, so far as he thought ethically about it, that the Americans needed to be shown the festive and joyous aspects of their common life. To discover and to represent these was his pleasure as an artist, and his duty as a citizen." See W. D. Howells, *The Coast of Bohemia* (New York and London, 1901 [1893]), p. 6.
74. For the full text of Hawkins's report, see "Report on the Fine Arts" in *Reports of the United States Commissioners to the Universal Exposition of 1889 at Paris*, vol. 2, pp. 3–104.
75. Anna Klumpke, *Rosa Bonheur, sa vie, son oeuvre* (Paris, 1900), pp. 6, 8; W. F. Cody, *An Autobiography of Buffalo Bill* (New York, 1923), p. 325. For a sense of Buffalo Bill's vast appeal to the Parisian public, see Art Young, *Art Young: His Life and Times* (New York, 1939), p. 8.
76. Rastignac, "Courrier de Paris," *L'Illustration*, 93 (May 11, 1889), p. 394.
77. P. Artout, "Au pays des Indiens," *L'Illustration*, 93 (June 15, 1889) pp. 506–7.
78. Albert de Chenclos, "Peaux-Rouges et visages-pales," *Revue des deux mondes*, 9th ser., vol. 93 (June 15, 1889), pp. 858–59. It may be noteworthy in this regard that the American jury rejected Albert Bierstadt's *Last of the Buffalo*, whose symbolic reminder of the white man's destruction of the Indian peoples may have been considered too much of an admission even for the 1889 fair. See page 00.
79. Amy Leslie, *Amy Leslie at the Fair* (Chicago, 1893), p. 13.
80. Johnson, op. cit., vol. 1, p. 1.
81. Pierre Viala, *Les Maladies de la vigne* (Montpellier and Paris, 1893), pp. 523–25. See also P. de Lafitte, *Quatre Ans de luttes pour nos vignes et nos vins de France* (Paris, 1883); A. Millardet, *Histoire des principales variétés et espèces de vignes d'origine américaine qui résistent au phylloxera* (Paris, 1885).
82. See *Reports of the United States Commissioners to the Universal Exposition of 1889 at Paris*, vol. 5, pp. 312, 328, 453–59.
83. Royal Cortissoz, *The Life of Whitelaw Reid* (New York, 1921), vol. 2, pp. 136–51. Reid did manage to negotiate the lifting of the embargo, on Dec. 5, 1891.
84. During the 1884 debate on the 10 percent compromise bill for the duty on art, Congressman Hurd of Ohio, one of its proponents, declared: "We have the assurance from our own minister [to France] that this discrimination against French artists is one of the principal obstacles in the way of a satisfactory adjustment of our commercial relations. . . . An excuse for maintaining prohibitions against American pork and restrictions upon importations of other agricultural products of this country is found in our high duties on French works of art and discrimination against French artists. In this way the farmers of America are made seriously to suffer." *Congressional Record*, 48th Cong., 1st sess., vol. 15 (1884), p. 4297.
85. Philippe Gille, "L'Exposition des Beaux-Arts," *Figaro–Exposition 1889* (Paris, 1889), p. 313.
86. *Reports of the United States Commissioners to the Universal Exposition of 1889 at Paris*, vol. 2, p. 47.

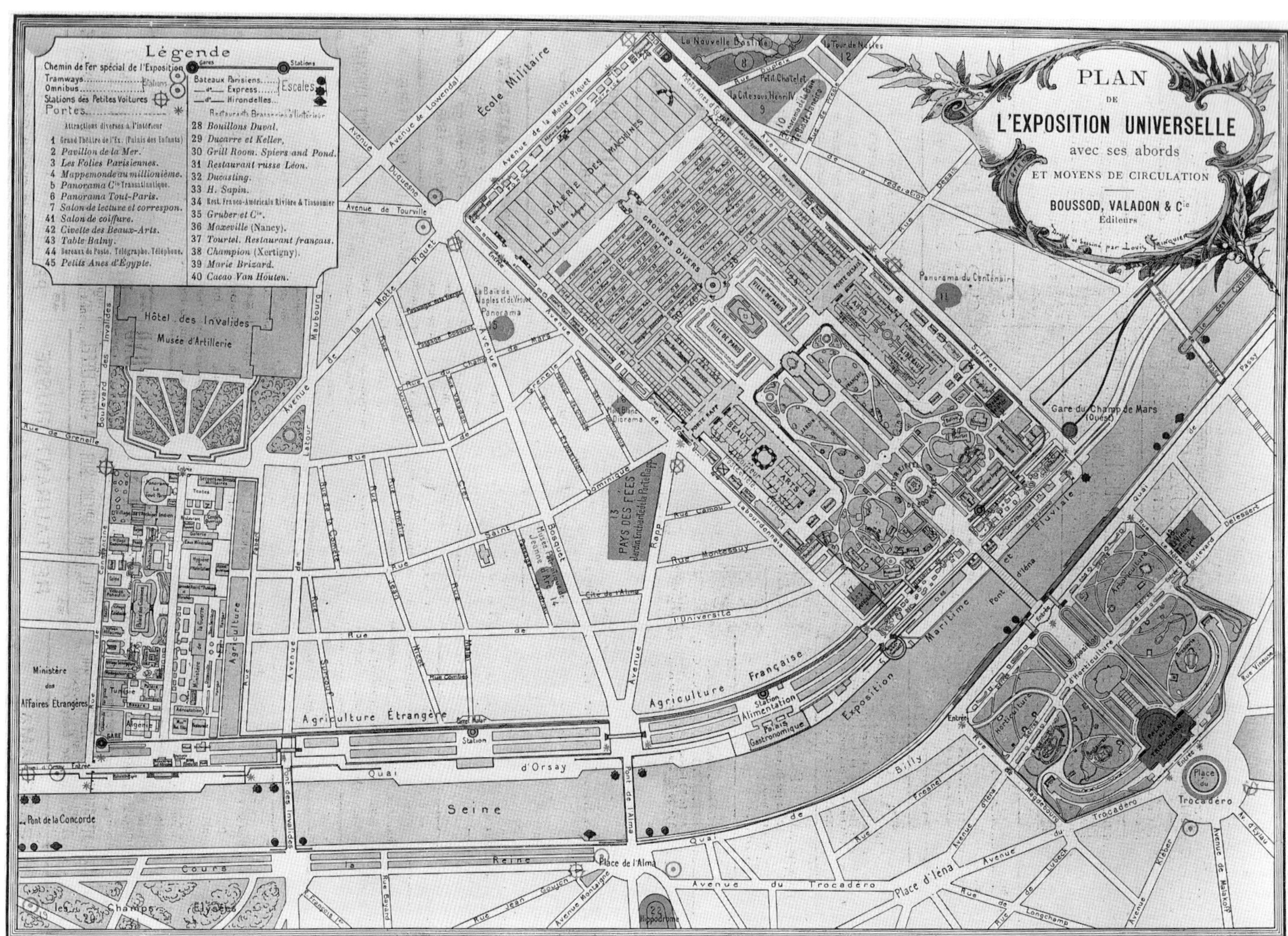

34.
Plan of the Exposition Universelle de Paris, 1889
Figaro–Exposition 1889
Helga Photo Studio, New York

RICHARD GUY WILSON

Challenge and Response: Americans and the Architecture of the 1889 Exposition

L'Exposition Universelle de 1889 (see fig. 35) marked for many Americans a rude awakening and a great challenge. World's fairs such as the Paris Exposition represent many things: they exhibit art and display goods; they communicate, educate, and seduce; they are the material inventories of nations, and manifestations of nationalistic hubris.[1] Americans came to the 1889 world's fair hoping to find America triumphant; instead they found only a few partial successes and plenty of cause for "Mortification."[2] For some Americans the Exposition became the opening engagement in a campaign of architectural and artistic imagery: a battle of the fairs, of competitions between towers and white cities, iron and staff, statues and mural paintings—all proclaiming the artistic hegemony of one nation over another.

The entire Exposition Universelle de 1889 had nationalistic implications, to the approximately 150,000 Americans who came to Paris in person and also to the millions more of Americans who experienced it vicariously through magazines, pamphlets, letters, photographs, and oral accounts.[3] The possible meanings of the Paris world's fair of 1889 are many, but unmistakable is the fact that the French creators of the ensemble intended to assert French supremacy in all areas, from the arts to manufacturing. That specific challenge was understood by many Americans.

The first and most apparent challenge to Americans—and indeed to any visitor—rose over the roofs of Paris, observable from nearly every corner: the Eiffel Tower (frontispiece). There it stood, 1,000 feet tall, on the Champ-de-Mars, already an indelible, universally recognized landmark. Controversial, it had been both hailed and condemned almost from its inception. Fabricated out of giant iron lattice trusses and web beams, the Tower stood firmly planted on huge angled feet, soaring upward in a great sweeping arc. Left behind were traditional structures of masonry and wood, appearing puny, weak, and earth-hugging. Along with the Tower, the other building at the Exposition about which visitors raved was the Palais des Machines; together they appeared to synthesize new technology and structural systems in a quest for a new architecture that would touch the heavens and enclose great volumes of space. The Tower and the Machinery Palace seemed to have abandoned the history of built forms and styles and to proclaim that henceforth the creators of monuments would be those individuals who stood at the center of the scientific and industrial premises of the

35.
Bird's-Eye View of the Exposition Universelle de Paris, 1889
Lithograph, 25¼ × 38½" (64.1 × 97.8 cm)
Collection Phillip Dennis Cate and Family

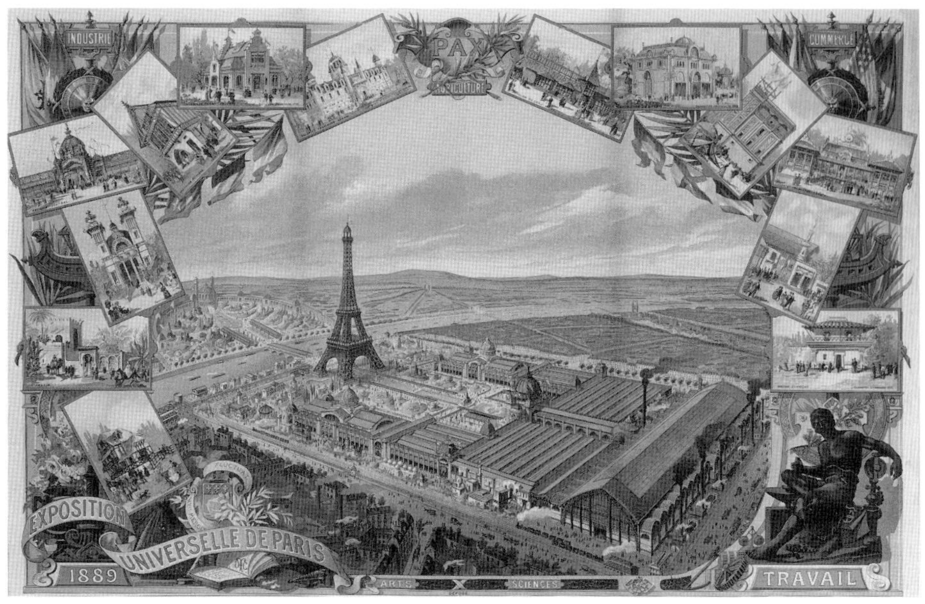

modern age. The engineer/architect who understood new materials and needs would displace the traditional architect relying on worn-out styles taught by history books.

The Eiffel Tower, like the giant Palais des Machines (fig. 36) and the other exhibition pavilions, with their contents, stood as both material objects and symbols of many types for the visitors in Paris during 1889. But what sort of symbols? Blank, as Roland Barthes has suggested with regard to the Eiffel Tower—so absolutely useless, so absolutely new, so empty, so ineluctable that it can mean everything or nothing?[4] Or was the 1,000-foot (actually 300-meter, or 986-foot) tower with its frame of perforated trusses the first mature example of the creation of modern space—open, transparent, and continuous? What was it like to rise up in the Eiffel Tower for the first time and feel the disorientation of free space? Or just to see it on the horizon of Paris—something perhaps imagined but still new to human eyes? Or to enter the vast hall of the Machinery Palace—a vast, luminous space that stretched nearly a quarter mile in length and rose to a height of nearly 150 feet? Its massive iron members seemingly were balanced—like Degas ballet dancers—*en pointe*.

Four years later, and nearly 6,700 miles away, the challenge of the iron Eiffel Tower and the Palais des Machines begat another memorable image: the Court of Honor, or White City, at the World's Columbian Exposition in Chicago (fig. 37). The Court of Honor looked not scientific or modern; with its classical colonnades, porticos, and domes, it recalled ancient civic forums and religious complexes. A tower and a white city—the two images have manifold meanings. A few are similar in that their initial purposes were for international expositions, but their ultimate implications are at wide variance. These two images resonate far into the future. Extremely different in appearance, they are tied together by an umbilical cord: the American involvement in the Exposition Universelle de 1889 in Paris produced the Court of Honor at the World's Columbian Exposition in Chicago.

The world's fairs were grand displays. The pavilions of the Paris Exposition of 1889 were crammed with material possessions, categorized and

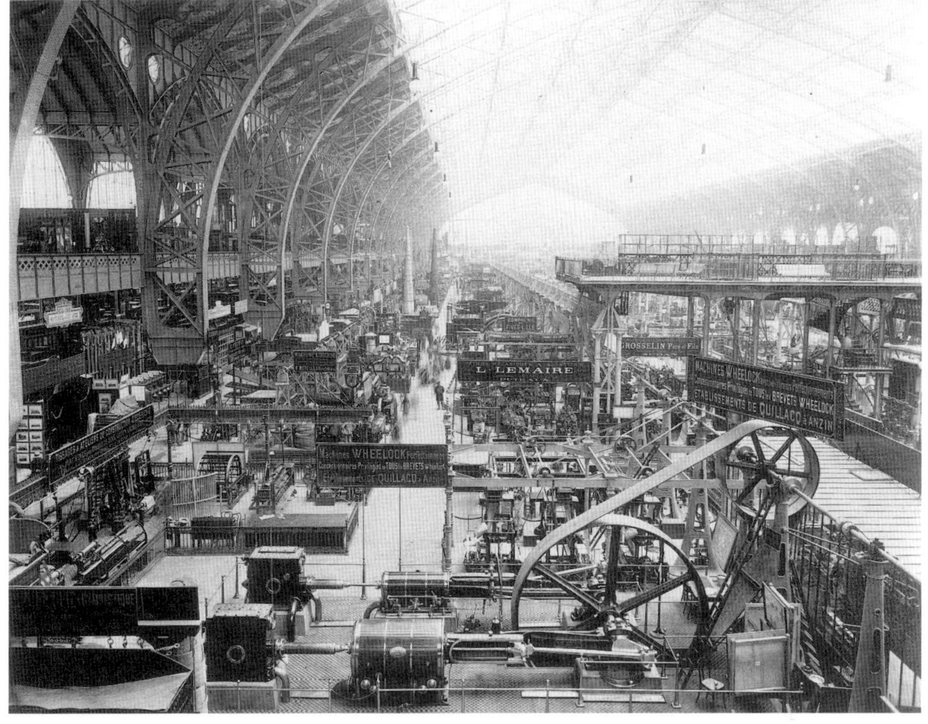

36.
Interior, Palais des Machines, Exposition Universelle de Paris, 1889
Ferdinand Dutert (1845–1900), architect; Victor Contamin (1840–1893), of Contamin, Pierron, and Charton, engineers
The Library of Congress, lot 6634

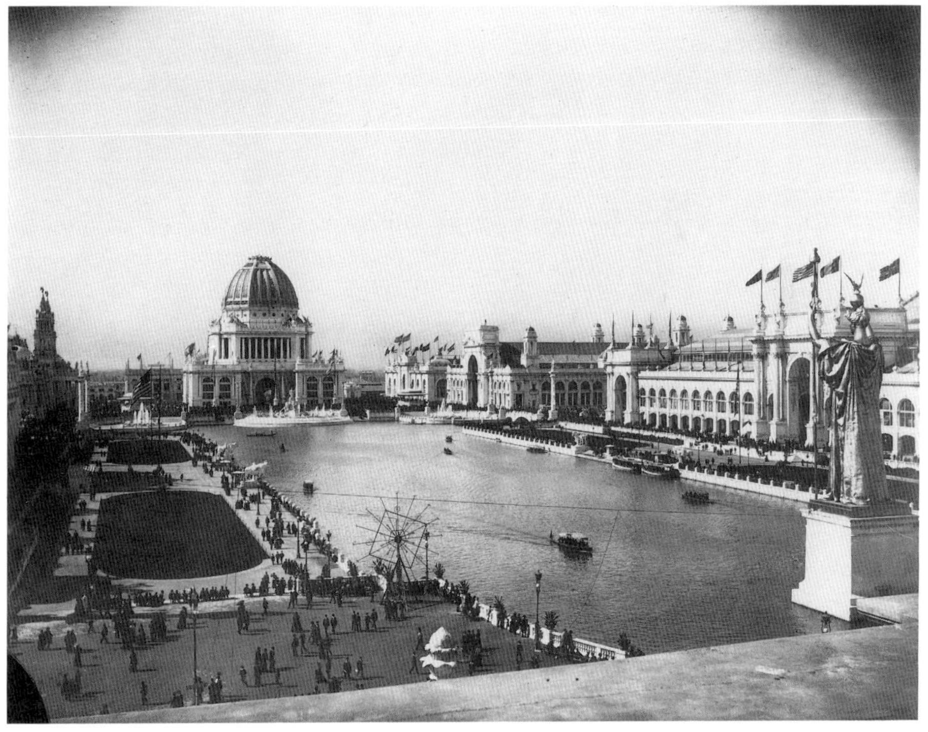

37.
Court of Honor, World's Columbian Exposition, Chicago, 1893
Photograph by Frances Benjamin Johnston
The Library of Congress

systematized in order to show the upward progress of civilization. Art was shown, from large shows of traditional academic and genre paintings to a small smattering of the advanced Impressionists. The French galleries were accorded the greatest accolades, the most popular works being Emmanuel Frémiet's *Troglodytes Gorilla* (see fig. 33) and Gabriel Ferrier's *Salammbo*, male erotic fantasies passed off as high culture. And there were commercial and manufacturing exhibits—from Tiffany silver of New York to Sèvres porcelain and from cognac to McCormick plows. Over seventy international congresses were held in many fields as adjuncts to the fair. Richard Morris Hunt of New York came as the American delegate to the World Congress of Architects and was elected a vice-president.[5] Visitors came away numbed, overloaded with information, for the Exposition seemed like a giant department store of both goods and ideas; everything seemed to be there![6]

American comments on the Paris Exposition were extensive and varied, ranging from nearly instantaneous—next-day—accounts via the Atlantic cable of the opening ceremonies at Versailles to a letter complaining of a "deluge of dirty water containing grease and what appeared to be kitchen refuse" poured on the heads of visitors underneath the Eiffel Tower.[7] Some writers viewed the Exposition negatively: a Boston correspondent reported eyes aching from the "gaudy coloring" and rated the architecture "scarcely above the level of Chinese conceptions."[8] But many more would have agreed with another Boston correspondent that the Exposition was "built on the most fantastic principles" and that the Eiffel Tower "deserves to be ranked among the wonders of the world."[9] This fair was the first of the great international exhibitions to be lighted at night and to remain open into the evening, and the effect was stupendous: "Imagine a piece of glowing charcoal rising ten thousand feet into the air and you will see in fancy the Eiffel Tower as it was on Monday night."[10] A city of color, fantastic hues, and brightness, both at night and in the day, was a common assessment. Everything seemed to have multicolors, even the Eiffel Tower, which was painted in five shades of red, from a dark "'Barbedienne' bronze" tint at the base to a golden-yellow tint at the top.[11] Americans loved the exhibits of the French colonies, of Javanese girls in native costumes, and the Street of Cairo.[12] William Walton, in an extensive account of the art work for American audiences, admitted: "Undoubtedly, however, it is the architects and the engineers who have carried off the principal honors of the Exposition."[13] This was echoed by Chicago businessman Edward T. Jeffery, who pronounced the Eiffel Tower "a combination of engineering skill and artistic beauty unsurpassed in any modern work of magnitude."[14] The Americans not only came, looked, and reported back home; they were extensively involved, from the successful painters and sculptors to Buffalo Bill and Annie Oakley, who restaged the recent Oklahoma land rush.[15]

America sent exhibits and occupied more space—nearly 113,000 square feet—than any other country, with the exception of France and its colonies, Great Britain and its colonies, and Belgium.[16] And Americans captured prizes, although the results overall were disappointing, for of the nearly 33,000 awards given out Americans received only 1,044. It was some cause for joy that Americans got 515 grand prizes and 214 gold medals.[17] Americans triumphed in the art galleries, where, after the French, they received the highest number of awards. There was success in other areas: John La Farge's window was awarded a medal and he received a citation from the French Legion of Honor. The French thought that Americans were clearly superior in agricultural exhibits.[18] For Americans the Paris fair of 1889 was a testing ground, a chance to see how they looked—whether in painting or farm equipment—in the rivalry of an international exposition. The usual American boosterism can be found in reports such as that of Mariana Griswold van Rensselaer, who asserted that "an American could walk through his own [art] galleries without shame." Still, she felt compelled to proclaim, "Once again, the capital of France was unquestionably the capital of Western civilization."[19] Other Americans were even less enthusiastic. Chauncey Depew recalled entering the fair grounds with "the Stars and Stripes flying, but came out with the flag in his pocket!"[20] Americans had some success, but still a long road lay ahead to match the French triumph.

The world's fair as the scene of international rivalry and competition goes back to the London Exhibition of 1851 and its great Crystal Palace.[21] Both the building and the exhibits of 1851 were specifically intended to promote—and also to inspire and improve—British industrial prowess and the arts and to demonstrate that just as England dominated the world militarily so it had superior culture and industry. In quick succession came Paris 1855; London 1862; Paris 1867; Vienna 1873; Philadelphia 1876; Paris 1878—as well as smaller regional expositions. The international exposition was one of the most important and lasting legacies of nineteenth-century nationalism and the development of the concepts of patriotism and allegiance to the homeland. The world's fairs might be "friendly rivalry," as one American said, but they were competitions.[22]

Prime Minister Jules Ferry had begun in 1880 to plan a universal exposition for 1889.[23] His agenda were specifically political: to demonstrate to the world that France led in the arts and manufacturing and to boldly confirm the achievements of the liberal Third Republic, one hundred years after the great Revolution of 1789. The Exposition Universelle of 1878 had been unsuccessful, and French political life was in disarray. Needed was a great national event to put into the past an emperor, the Commune, the formation of the anarchist and the socialist parties, a militant trade-union movement, and even the continuing presence of a right wing of royalists, antiparliamentarians, clergy, and conservatives. In 1885, Ferry, the initiator of the Exposition, fell from power, and four successive governments were responsible for its actual erection. Economic prosperity would, it was hoped, be restored by a world's fair showing the glories of a liberal modern bourgeois republic.[24] The fair would parade the products of the machine and of artists, along with the social accomplishments in the institutionalization of education in the Third Republic. In other areas would be exhibited workers' houses and a new, and much commented on, display, L'Economie Sociale, devoted to industrial workers and their welfare.[25] Certainly not to be commemorated, or mentioned, was the descent into terror of a century before. This blatant political commemoration of modern republicanism was not to the taste of a monarchy such as Germany, which decided to forgo the Exposition.

The actual opening of the celebration of 1889 took place not at the Exposition but at Versailles, on May 5, 1889, when President Sadi Carnot commemorated the opening of the Estates-General one hundred years earlier, in 1789. The next day, May 6, a procession led by the president came up the Champs-Elysées, crossed on the Pont d'Iéna, and assembled on the axis of the central complex on the Champ-de-Mars underneath the arches of the Eiffel Tower (see fig. 38). They then proceeded across the Cour d'Honneur created by the wings of the Palace of Fine Arts and the Palace of Liberal Arts and entered the great portico of the Central Dome, which was capped by Eugène Delplanche's enormous statue of the Republic of France distributing crowns to nations. Inside, surrounded by a large mural frieze by Jean Baptiste Lavastre and his assistant T. M. M. Carpezan, showing "all the nations coming to pay their respects to France," speeches were made, the "Marseillaise" was sung, and the military passed in review.[26] That night, with the Eiffel Tower outlined in

38.
View looking north from underneath the Eiffel Tower, Exposition Universelle de Paris, 1989
From left to right: corner of Palais des Arts Liberaux, Jean-Camille Formigé (1845–1927), architect; Le Pavillon de la Bolivie, Fouquiau, architect; Le Palais de la République Argentine, A. Ballu (1849–1939), architect
The Library of Congress, lot 6634

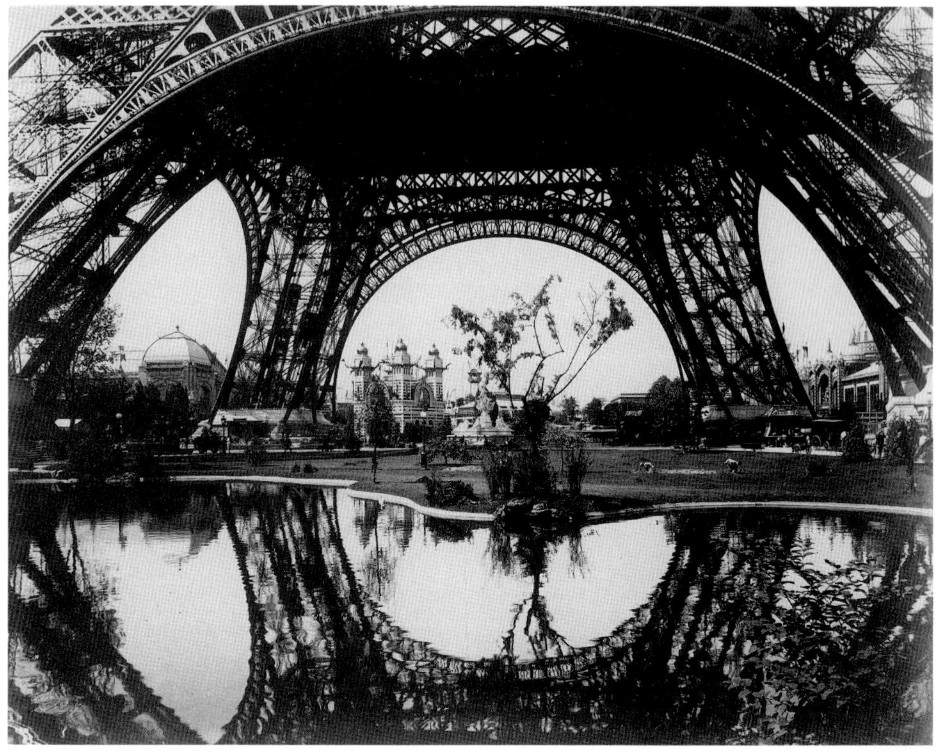

lights of red, white, and blue, a great fireworks show of 500,000 bombs and 200,000 rockets announced that the Exposition was officially open.

The quasi-religious nationalism of the Exposition and its layout was widely understood. The upper two-thirds of the Eiffel Tower bore a striking resemblance to Notre Dame's spire, while its base, the great spread piers, were a triumphal arch modeled on the Arc de Triomphe. Eiffel claimed the Tower was a "triumphal arch for science," and on the frieze at the first level, legible from the ground, appeared names of "men who have honored French Science."[27] Beyond the Tower, the Court of Honor leading to the Central Dome was, like the forecourt at St. Peter's, lined with statues that both measured and forced the perspective. Behind the dome lay the great horizontal sweep of the transept of the Palais des Machines, which Frantz Jourdain, critic and architect and a great supporter of the new iron structures, acclaimed as "a work of art as beautiful, as pure, as original, as elevated as a Greek temple or a cathedral."[28]

The Universal Exposition of 1889 encompassed 228 acres laid out in three distinct areas (see fig. 34). The first, creating "most striking effects architecturally," was the central focus of the axis from the Trocadero Palace (designed for the Exposition of 1878 by Gabriel Davioud) on the Right Bank, across the Pont d'Iéna to the Champ-de-Mars on the Left Bank, where the Eiffel Tower, the other large exhibition buildings constructed out of iron, and some smaller pavilions were located.[29] A second area was a narrow strip along the river Seine on the Quai d'Orsay, the site of various agricultural pavilions and other exhibits. In the third area, at right angles to the Seine, in the esplanade of the Hôtel des Invalides, were agriculture exhibits, the French colonial pavilions, the Ministry of War, various native villages (see fig. 39) from Senegal, the Congo, and Indo-China, and other exhibits, including L'Economie Sociale. The Exposition was a small city, some Americans noted, attracting over 300,000 visitors on some days and a grand total of nearly 32,000,000.

The tower by Gustave Eiffel had already been decided upon by 1886, when the major planning began. The idea of a tower had a long history: cited in the various arguments for and against it were not only biblical predecessors but the recently completed Washington Monument (at 555 feet), various British projects of the mid-nineteenth century, and even a 1,000-foot Centennial Tower proposal in Philadelphia in 1874.[30] In 1884 two engineers in Eiffel's employ, Emile Nouguier and Maurice Koechlin, made a preliminary sketch for a 300-meter (986-foot) tower of iron. They asked Stephen Sauvestre, the head of Eiffel's architectural office, to give the idea architectural form, and he inserted arches at the base, added an onion-shaped dome, and scattered some sculptures over it. Eiffel was then at the peak of his career as a designer and builder of bridges and structural systems, among them the armature for the Statue of Liberty in New York. Initially, Eiffel showed minimal interest in the project, but then, sensing its possibilities, he purchased the right to the idea from his employees, patented it (in late 1884), and began promoting the concept of a 300-meter tower as the centerpiece of the upcoming exhibition.[31] His rendering, showing the projected tower soaring above Notre Dame and the Arc de Triomphe, was widely published, in the United States as well as elsewhere.[32] Eiffel convinced Edouard Lockroy, who had been Minister of Commerce in 1886 and was the cabinet minister in charge of the Exposition, of the feasibility of the tower. A graduate of the Ecole des Beaux-Arts and a *littérateur*, the author of comedies and operas, Lockroy recognized the explosive and powerful appeal of a tower. And he pointed out that the U-shaped complex on the Champ-de-Mars—the Palace of Fine Arts, the Palace of Liberal Arts, the Central Dome, and the Palace of Machines—"would take the form of an Arch of Triumph laid out on the ground."[33]

A competition was suddenly announced in May of 1886, and while several other interesting entries were submitted, the result was a foregone conclusion: the chairman of the jury and the Exposition's Director-General of Construction, Jean Alphand, announced that Eiffel would build his (and his employees') tower. A by-product of the competition was the assignment of other buildings to several of the unsuccessful contestants: Charles L. F. Dutert, also a graduate of the Beaux-Arts, became the architect of the Palace of Machines, and Jean-Camille Formigé received the commission for the twin palaces of fine and liberal arts.[34] The tower idea raised a storm of protest; most notable was a lengthy letter of 1887 describing the tower as "profane," "grotesque," and "hideous" and declaring, "The Eiffel tower, which even commercial America refuses, is, rest assured, a dishonor to Paris." The signatories included such leaders in the arts as the architects Charles Garnier and J. A. E. Vaudremer, the authors Dumas fils and Guy de Maupassant, the composer Charles Gounod, and the painters William Bouguereau and Ernest Meissonier. This letter and the protest in general were well known in America.[35] After some redesigning by Eiffel, a contract was let; construction began on January 26, 1887. The Tower's upward rise was avidly followed in the international press during the two years and two months until its completion, on March 31, 1889.

The other structures—all since destroyed—on the Champ-de-Mars portion of the Exposition grounds provided a context of both contrast to the Tower and continuation of certain themes. Immediately upon crossing the Seine from the right bank one encountered the History of Human Habitation (fig. 40) designed by Charles Garnier, the architect of the Paris Opéra. Obviously inspired by Viollet-le-Duc's book of nearly the same title, Garnier had constructed a long row of forty-four dwellings, ranging from the stone age through the Pharaohs, Incas, and Greeks, up to the current time. Appropriately costumed natives occupied many of the houses.[36] The habitations exhibit provided a telling contrast with the Eiffel tower looming overhead. National pavilions such as those of Argentina, Bolivia, Nicaragua, and Norway, along with restaurants and other structures, were also scattered around the base of the Tower. The Latin American pavilions (see fig. 41) excited much comment, especially for their wild eclecticism and novel usage of materials. Under the Tower stood a large statue by Francis de Saint-Vidal representing "Night vainly endeavoring to restrain the Genius of Light, who advances, her wings displayed." Beyond the Tower was the Cour d'Honneur formed by the main exhibit halls, filled with statuary and large illuminated fountains. The centerpiece was by Jules-Félix Coutan: the City of Paris (fig. 42), a female figure standing erect in a "vessel of progress" and surrounded by Fame with her trumpet and twenty-two other allegorical figures personifying modern life. Fifteen of the figures were "colossal" in size, measuring nearly 12 feet in height. An observer noted, "The silhouette is agreeable, full of movement and very decorative."[37]

The main exhibit halls surrounding the Court of Honor were, to the left and right respectively, the Palace of Fine Arts and the Palace of Liberal Arts by Jean-Camille Formigé, and then, on axis with the Tower, the Palais des Industries Diverses by Jules Bouvard. Bouvard's structure connected to the Palais des Machines by an enclosed gallery, the Galerie de Trente Mètres (see fig. 43). For the interior of the Industries Diverses, architects had been engaged to design the *portes*, or gates, to the various exhibit sections (see fig. 44); the results were extravaganzas of various motifs.[38] The exteriors of these structures had a "festal" air, an almost stage-set quality, with their overdone surfaces a promiscuous display of colors and frilly ornament, "rococo" in character.[39] Glazed brick, polychrome terra-cotta, and staff (a mixture of plaster of Paris and horsehair that could be molded) threatened to overwhelm the slim, contrapuntal ironwork of the structures. The Industries Diverses, with a high Central Dome of 225 feet (68.58 meters) and a diameter of 100 feet (30.48 meters), acted as the main focus. Crowned by Eugène Delplanche's huge statue of France, it was sheathed in dusky gold bronze and decorated with large standing ribs, cartouches, winged sphinxes, lion's heads, and garlands. Its gigantic gaping portico created a void that undercut the stability of the weighty dome overhead. Two statuary groups, Jean Gautherin's *Commerce* and Charles Gauthier's *Industry*, guarded the entrance pylons, which were surmounted by large idealized human visages. The two wing structures, the Palais des Beaux-Arts and the Palais des Arts Liberaux, were appropriately subdued, their decoration of garlands and putti muted, though still extensive. Their colors of gold, fawn, and salmon were set off by the pale flat blue of the iron frame and the white of the statuary.[40] In front of the Palace of Fine Arts stood Rodin's heroic *Architecture*, with Jean-Paul Aubé's *Printing* across the court. The domes of the two lateral palaces were appropriately less elaborate than the Central Dome. Hemispherical in shape, they were covered in a delicate blue-green faience picked out with fretwork of yellow and white.

The interiors in the Palace of Fine Arts presented problems, since the architect had included too many windows and not enough wall space; many of the windows had to be covered in order to make room to hang pictures. A display of French sculpture on the ground level and outsize canvases on the balcony con-

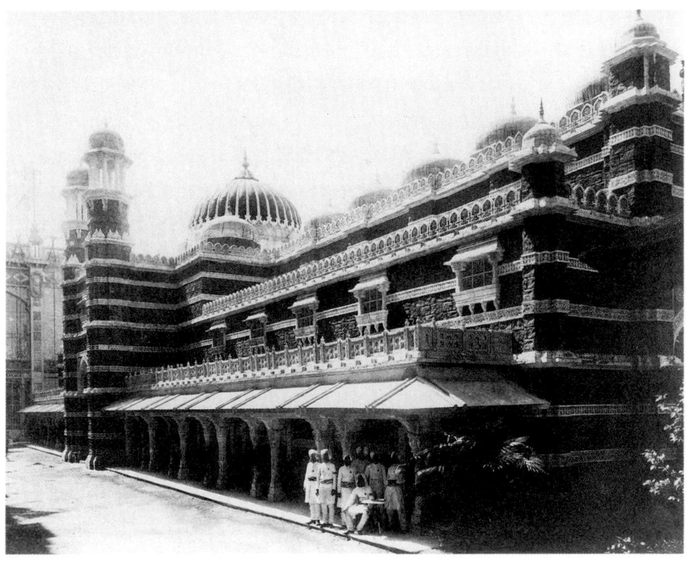

39.
Le Sérai Indien, Exposition Universelle de Paris, 1889
Purdon Clarke, architect
The Library of Congress, lot 6634

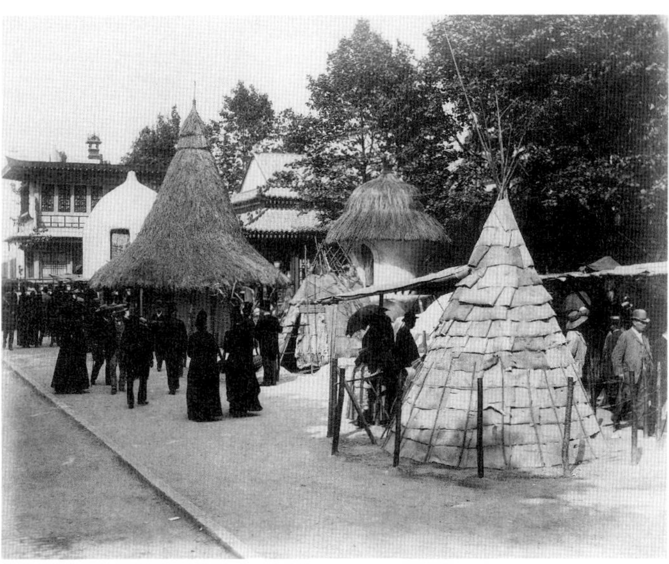

40.
Histoire de l'Habitation, Exposition Universelle de Paris, 1889
Charles Garnier (1825–1898), architect
The Library of Congress, lot 6634

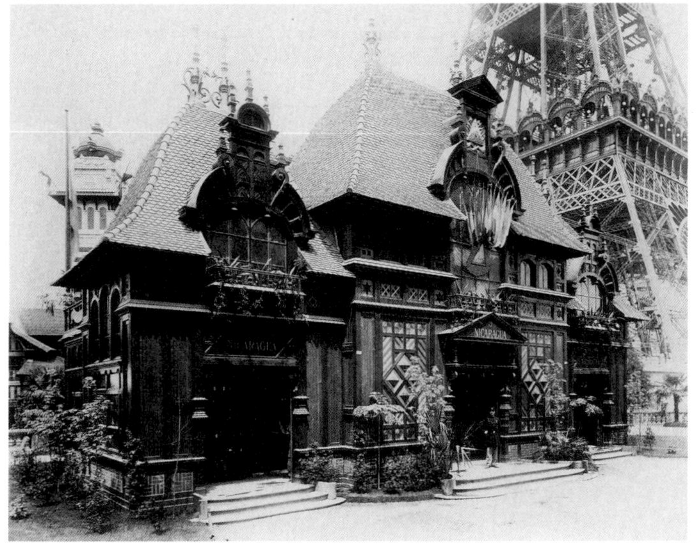

41.
Le Pavillon du Nicaragua, Exposition Universelle de Paris, 1889
Stephan Sauvestre (1847–?), architect
The Library of Congress, lot 6634

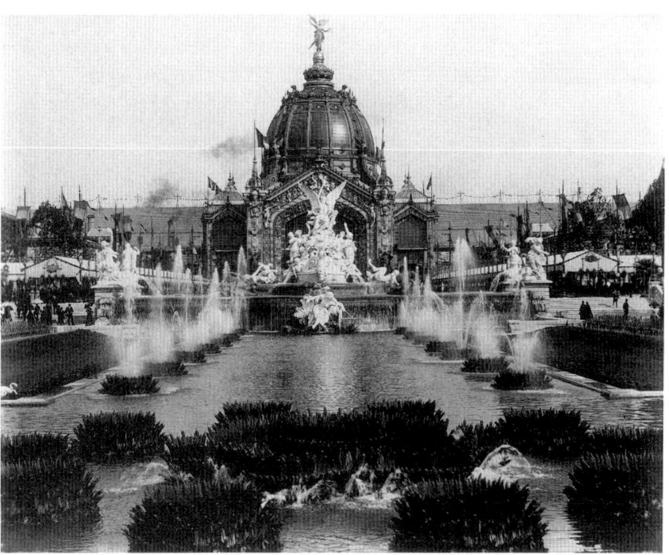

42.
The City of Paris, on her barge environed by Science, Industry, Agriculture, and Art, enlightening the world with Flambeau, by Jules-Félix Coutan (1848–1939), in front of the Dôme Central, Palais des Industries Diverses, Jules Bouvard (1840–1920) architect. Exposition Universelle de Paris, 1889
The Library of Congress, lot 6645

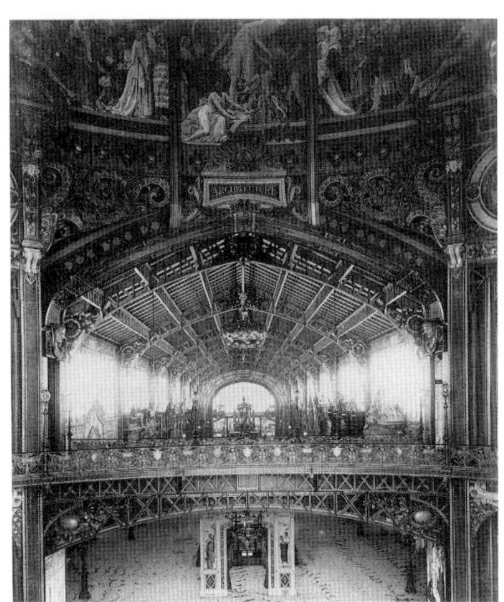

43.
Interior, Dôme Central and La Galerie de Trente Mètres, Exposition Universelle de Paris, 1889, Jules Bouvard (1840–1920), architect. Mural by Jean Baptiste Lavastre (1834–1891) and T.M.M. Carpezan
The Library of Congress, lot 6634

trasted with the large industrial-iron columns in the palace's rotunda. Except for the elaborate rotunda, the interior was a large undifferentiated space. The exhibitors provided their own installation. The American galleries appeared very crowded, in contrast to those of other countries.

The Palais des Machines loomed up as a gray, swelling volume behind the Central Dome. Certainly the structure most commented on, after Eiffel's tower, the Machinery Palace was singled out by the United States Government Commissioners as "the boldest work of the exhibition."[41] The French, as an American observer noted, dubbed it "the Palace of Force."[42] Nearly every account remarked on the great interior span—the "widest . . . ever erected"—and the absence of central supports; the great span was carried on twenty transverse arches.[43] For technical expertise, architect Dutert teamed up with the engineer Victor Contamin of Contamin, Pierron and Charton, but both the idea of a great glazed hall and the curve of the arches were his. The arches were huge lattice web joists, hinged at base and apex for movement. The span was 111 meters (364.2 feet), the height was 43.5 meters (147.5 feet), and the length was 429 meters (1,387 feet). On either side of the main space were two-story galleries, bringing the overall width to 150 meters (492 feet).[44] Glazing covered much of the structure, creating a great luminous interior. Dutert had originally designed glazed apses for the ends; however, for economy they were deleted. Frequently pictured as an empty space of almost Boulléeian dimensions, the hall was actually filled with engines and machines from various countries that transformed it into a Piranesian drama of action. Four steam generators for powering the machinery were located at the corners, and an elevated railroad, a *pont roulant*, encircled the hall so that the spectators could take in the awesome scale of both space and machinery.

Contemporary photographs emphasized a bare-bones industrial aesthetic, though the Machinery Palace had extensive ornament and decoration on the interior and the exterior (see fig. 45). The cornice was surmounted by acroteria, and the huge arch was decorated with a foliated design showing implements of labor between the leaves and vines. On the lintel over the main entrance was spelled out in colorful faience the inscription PALAIS DES MACHINES. Flanking this eastern entrance, stood gigantic sculptural nudes in plaster: *Steam* by Henri-Michel Chapu and *Electricity* by Louis-Ernest Barrias. The great glass roof was tinted in a shade described as a "rosy yellow."[45] The colored windows at the eastern end of the hall contained "emblozonments" (*sic*) in a semiabstract pattern incorporating the seals of the principal countries contributing to the Exposition, while the west opening was filled with an immense representation of the battle of Bouvines. Multicolored ceramic bricks, mosaics, stencils, paintings, sculptures, and coats of arms (of the major exhibitors) covered many of the interior surfaces. Various French artists contributed panels. Abstract serpentine and floral decorations appeared on the ramp ironwork, made by Henri Louvet, and two large bronze figures, each bearing a cluster of twenty incandescent lamps, stood at the foot of the staircase.[46]

The Palace of Machines and the Eiffel Tower, along with some of the other Exposition structures, became widely regarded as influential, but the exact nature of their impact has been little studied. Both the Machinery Palace and the Eiffel Tower seemed to indicate that the age of the engineer/architect had arrived, that bare-bones mass-produced buildings would be the direction of the future. And both structures became enshrined in the history books as icons of the modern movement in architecture; new, ahistorical, lightweight, and open, they seemed to have escaped from the style manuals.[47] The Eiffel Tower, in par-

44.
Vêtements porte, Palais des Industries Diverses, Exposition Universelle de Paris, 1889, Emmanuel Bertrand (1856–1920), architect
The Library of Congress, lot 6634

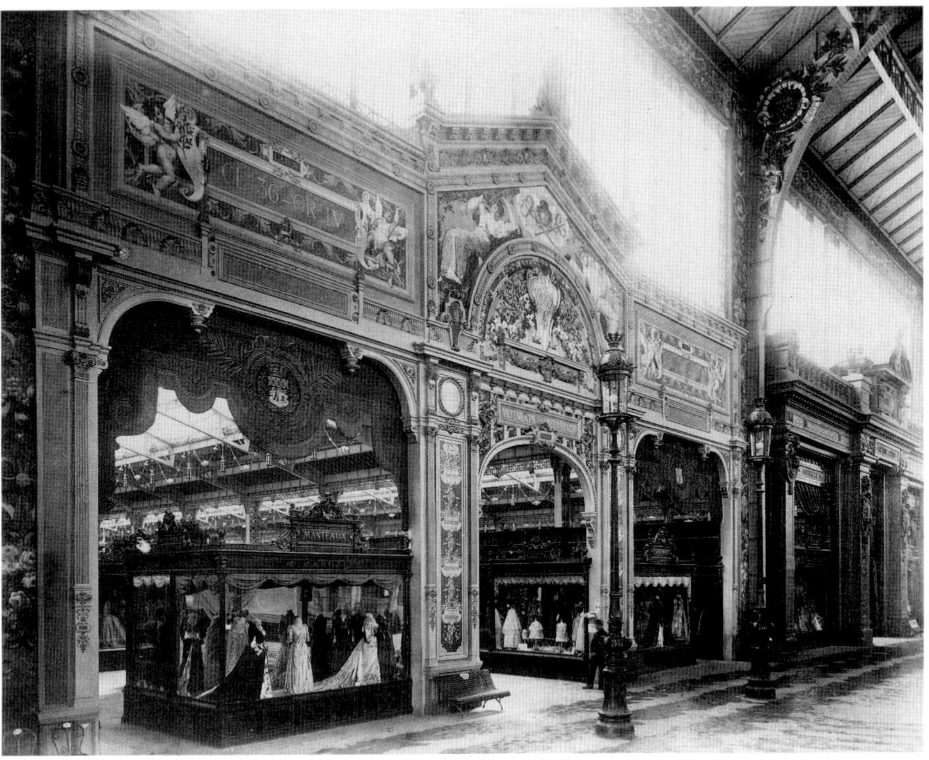

45.
Exterior, Palais des Machines, Exposition Universelle de Paris, 1889
The Library of Congress, lot 6001.

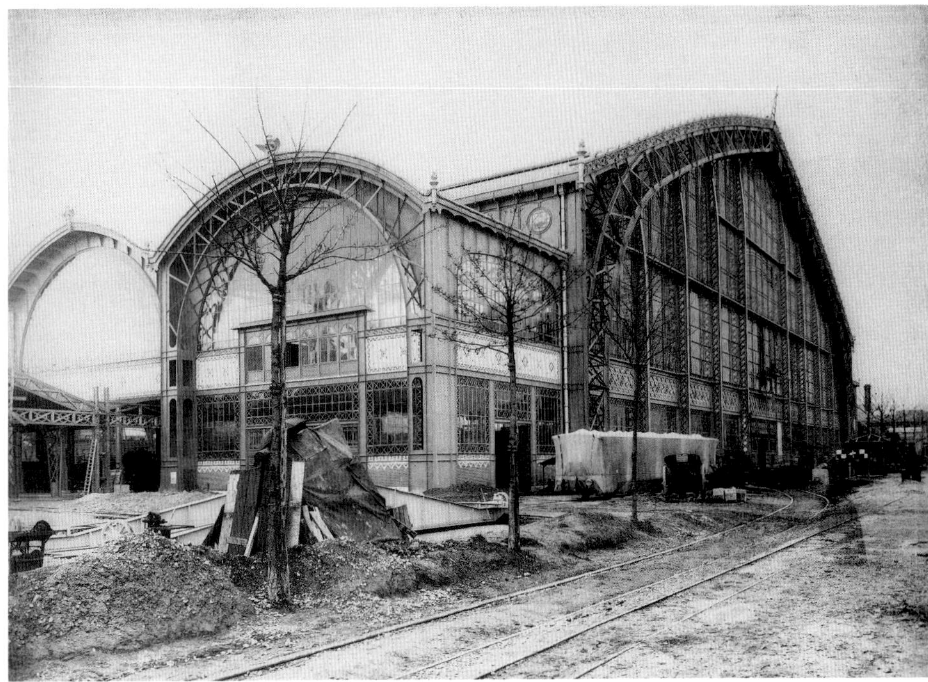

ticular, transcended purely architectural concerns and became an icon of modernity in painting and poetry.[48] Contemporary critics such as the modernist-oriented Frantz Jourdain, who admired the iron architecture, held that the Art Nouveau movement really began at the Exposition; more recently scholars have pointed out that the interplay between structural iron and colored materials, as in Formigé's Palace of Fine Arts (fig. 46), was also a predecessor. Indeed the

46.
Palais des Beaux-Arts, Exposition Universelle de Paris, 1889
Jean-Camille Formigé (1845–1927), architect
The Library of Congress, lot 6634

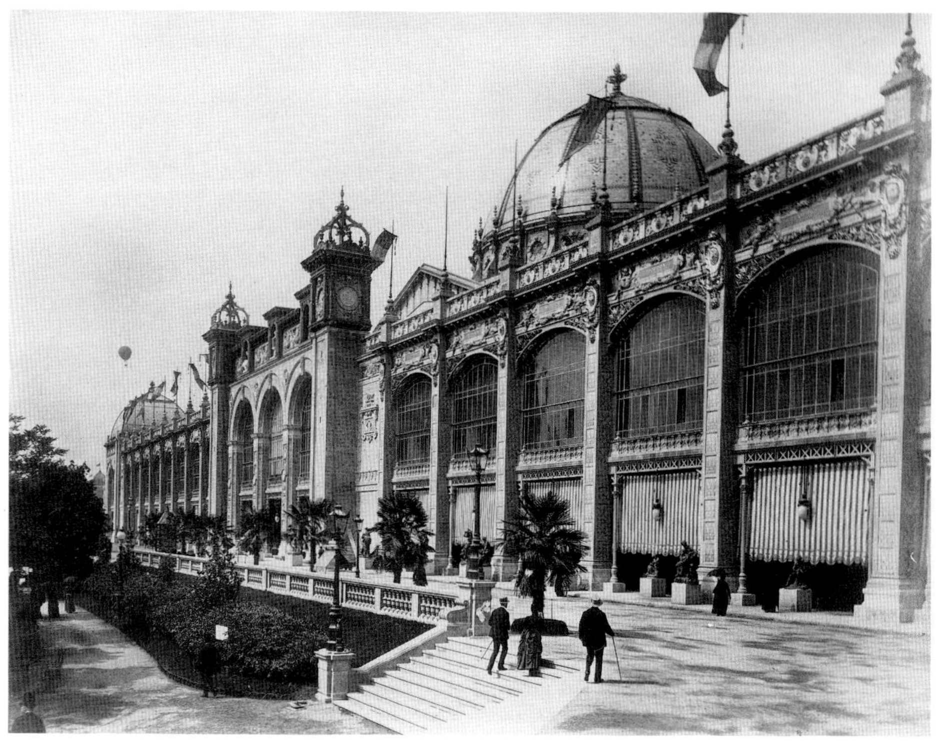

swirling forms of the statuary (see fig. 47) and the ornamental ironwork of the Tower and the Machinery Palace contain prototypes of Art Nouveau.[49] In the abstract patterns in the windows of the latter can be detected a similarity to the patterns of Frank Lloyd Wright and the Viennese Secessionists.

Neither the Tower nor the Palais des Machines had many successors; projects were announced for structures even taller or larger, but for the most part they came to naught. The Tower and the Machinery Palace were not the beginning of a tradition but the end of one: a conclusion to the nineteenth century's age of iron, with its huge train sheds and bridges.[50] Iron as a building material was already outmoded; steel and reinforced concrete would be the way of the future. Both structures were dinosaurs when built, and they were only obliquely influential on later exhibits and buildings in France, elsewhere in Europe, and in the United States.

Americans knew the 1889 Universal Exposition well. A few boosters claimed American superiority, but most Americans were overwhelmed by what they perceived as France's clear supremacy. The United States Commissioners reported that France was far ahead in the arts, and they harshly criticized the level of American culture and art, asserting that in America the only architecture worthy of note was Trinity Church in Boston and the new Public Library under construction across from it.[51] This feeling of inferiority was crucial, since it was during mid-1889, while the Paris fair was uppermost in the American mind, that the idea of a great international exposition to honor Columbus's discovery of the New World gained momentum. The idea had been discussed for years, but not until the summer of 1889, after the Paris fair had opened, did businessmen, architects, and politicians in rivalrous Chicago, New York, Washington, and St. Louis form committees and try to secure the fair for their own city. The decision in favor of Chicago did not become law until April 25, 1890.[52]

47.
Rotunda, Palais des Beaux-Arts, Exposition Universelle de Paris, 1889
The Library of Congress, lot 6001

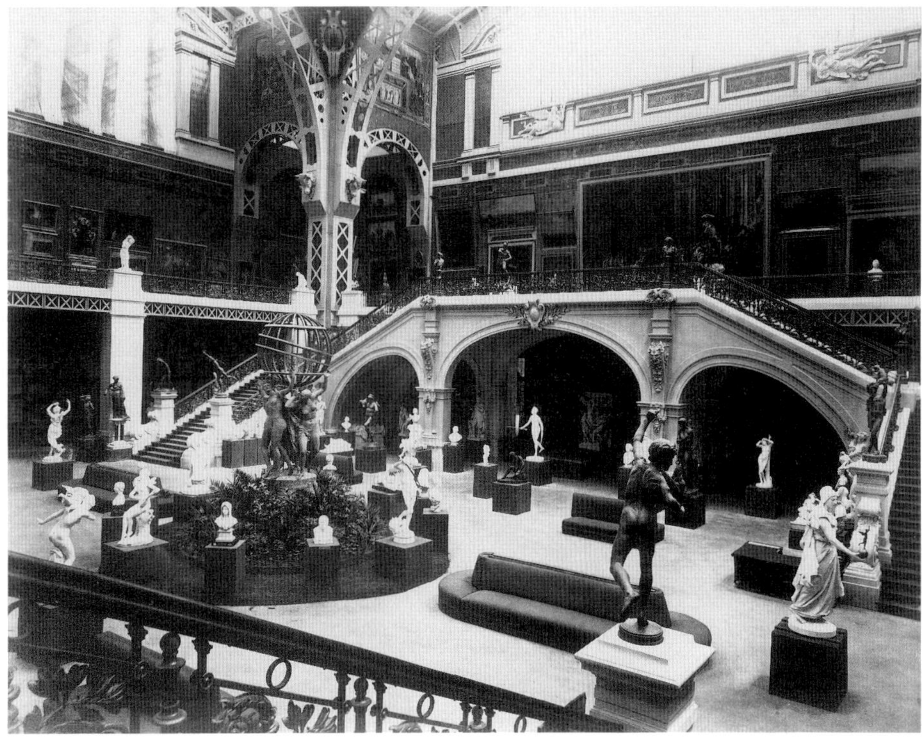

Many Americans approached with qualms the idea that the United States would compete on the international stage of world's fairs. At the Philadelphia Centennial in 1876 the country had tried to put its best foot forward, and while the America First-ers claimed a triumph, most of the cultural and intellectual establishment felt humbled. William Dean Howells wrote, "It is still in these things of iron and steel that the national genius most freely speaks," and a newspaper critic was of the same mind: "In science, in art, and particularly in taste we are far behind the Old World."[53] The American observers in Paris in 1889 worried about how America would present itself back home. The critic William Cary Brownell expressed concern about "corn-palaces and butter women. . . [and] our reproduction of the Venus of Milo in chocolate." Could the American exhibition, he asked, have the same unity and excellence as the French Exposition?[54] The *Century Magazine* hired Georges Berger, Director-General of the Paris exhibit, to write an article giving suggestions for the American show. Berger questioned whether it was prudent even to make the effort but concluded that while the Americans "possess neither an art of their own nor a history," still their energy might carry it through. He acknowledged that novelty was important but stressed that the architect should not design as if the buildings were temporary or of limited duration. "Otherwise, he will build nothing intellectually satisfying, and will fall short of the beauty which every type of edifice ought to possess."[55]

The planning of the World's Columbian Exposition (see fig. 48)—especially the architectural decisions made for the Court of Honor, in which East Coast–based architects trained at the Ecole des Beaux-Arts, such as Richard Morris Hunt and Charles F. McKim, dominated, imposing a classical image—has been an extremely controversial subject. The decisions made for Chicago become more understandable in the context of the Paris 1889 Exposition. The

48.
Bird's-eye view, World's Columbian Exposition, Chicago, 1893
Lithograph from Bancroft, *Book of the Fair,* 1893
The Library of Congress

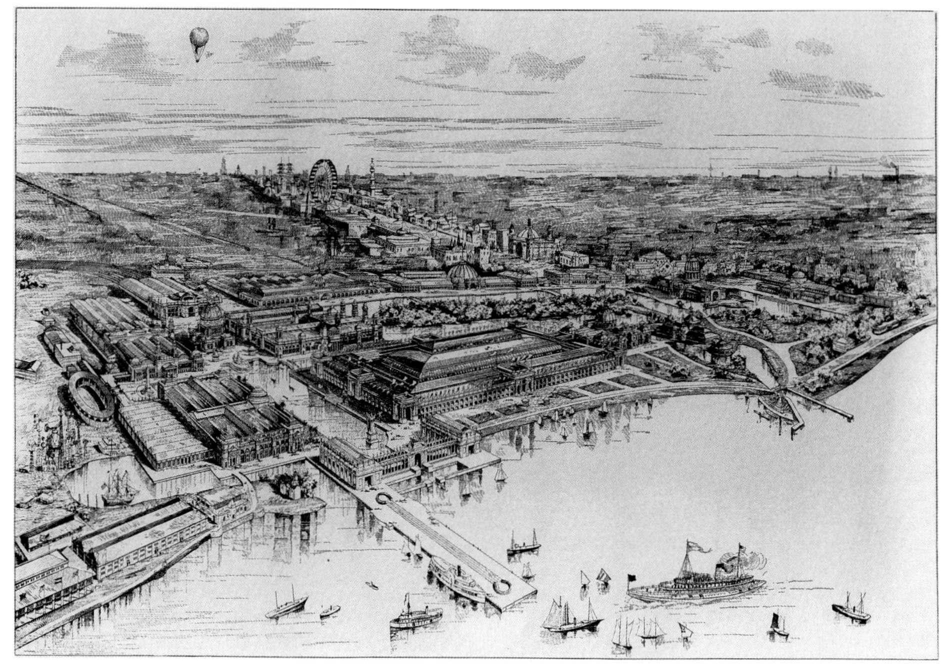

Americans were very familiar with the Eiffel Tower and the Palace of Machines and rejected them as architectural models. It is an irony of sorts that the French had characterized the Eiffel Tower as particularly American in inspiration; the protest of 1887 and other commentary linked the Tower to America, with the implication that only in a country with so brief a history and so little culture could such a monstrosity be erected.[56] A biting criticism of the iron structures at the Paris fair by the writer J.-K. Huysmans labeled them a "pylon of gratings" and assigned them to "an art of the Americans and the Kanakas [South Sea islanders]."[57] As a consequence, while proposals were made for gigantic—and fantastic—glass and steel tents by E. S. Jenison and by Harvey Ellis (working for Leroy Buffington) to be erected at the World's Columbian Exposition, they never stood a chance of being approved.[58] For Americans concerned about their cultural image, industrial forms as central motifs were to be avoided.

What Americans needed to demonstrate was a connection with the great cultural traditions of the past and not with the new, technologically advanced concepts. The only American building entered in the Paris Exposition's international survey of architecture was a rendering of the large Bates Hall in the Boston Public Library then under construction.[59] Modeled on the Italian Renaissance palazzo and intended to be richly decorated, the Boston Library, by McKim, Mead & White, indicates the major shift taking place by 1889 in the perception by many Americans of their culture and heritage. "The spirit of the Renaissance," as critic/historian Bernard Berenson maintained, "was the most appropriate model for American culture." And it led directly to the emergence of the American Renaissance.[60]

The Chicago businessmen, politicians, and architects instrumental in obtaining the World's Columbian Exposition for the city knew well the architectural character of the Exposition in Paris.[61] They had commissioned Edward T. Jeffery, Chairman of the Illinois Central Railroad, to visit Paris in mid-1889 and write a report. Jeffery analyzed the Exposition from a business

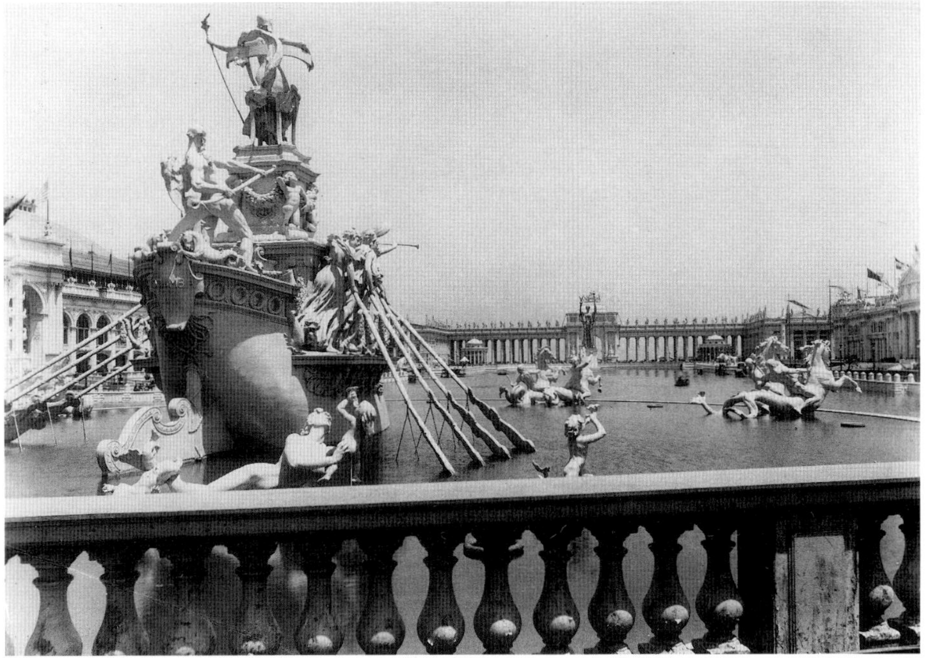

49.
Court of Honor, World's Columbian Exposition, Chicago, 1893: peristyle, Charles B. Atwood (1845–1898), architect; *Columbian Fountain and Barge of Columbia* by Frederick McMonnies (1863–1937); *Statue of the Republic* by Daniel Chester French (1850–1931)
The Library of Congress

point of view and, while expressing admiration for the Eiffel Tower and the Palace of Machines, indicated that Chicago would have to find a different motif. Octave Chanute, an engineer who accompanied Jeffery, conveyed praise for the Tower and the Machinery Palace but voiced concern: "One great difficulty that faces any future exposition will be to find some equally popular attraction without copying M. Eiffel." Chanute questioned whether American architects had the talent to design a comparable fair and suggested that French architects might be hired "to supervise" the American endeavor.[62]

Jeffery became the head of the Committee on Grounds and Buildings for the World's Columbian Exposition and appointed the Chicago architects Daniel Burnham and John Root to their central positions as planners and architects.[63] The decision to hire as the main designers of the Court of Honor a group of East Coast architects known for their commitment to classicism has always been a subject of contention, since the result, a white classical city, seemed to be at odds with the industrial-technological nature of Chicago and indeed of America. Louis Sullivan's well-known lament that the White City of the fair not only failed to represent America and Chicago but additionally set American architecture back fifty years implies that Burnham and his cohorts sold out a native American architecture. But Burnham and Root and the members of the Board of Directors such as Jeffery knew what they wanted: a classical image. In hiring Hunt, McKim, and the others they made sure they got it.[64] Hunt, who had visited Paris during the 1889 Exposition, explicitly condemned the iron-building approach; he regarded the Paris fair as a failure, commenting that the buildings lacked "the monumental look about them that they should have had."[65]

The surface image of white classicism on the Court of Honor appears as the opposite—the negative—of the highly colorful and technological Paris Exposition. But in many features the Chicago Fair owes a great debt to Paris. The Cour d'Honneur on the Champ-de-Mars was echoed in the enclosure of the Court of Honor, and the role of the Eiffel Tower as the keystone of the French scheme was taken in Chicago by Hunt's high-domed Administration Building. Even Hunt's ground plan, with its large foursquare corners, shows the footprints of the Eiffel Tower.[66] The great central fountain by Coutan in the Cour d'Honneur in Paris became the model for Frederick MacMonnies's *Columbian Fountain and Barge of Columbia* (fig. 49) at one end of the great basin in Chicago. And Daniel Chester French's *Statue of the Republic* in Chicago was clearly modeled on French statues at the 1889 Exposition. The profusion of statuary, the decorative mural paintings in the buildings, and the use of staff as a material were all inspired by the Paris show. Behind the classical facade of George B. Post's Manufactures and Liberal Arts Building, engineers under Daniel Burnham outdid the Palais des Machines' great trusses and clear span, creating a span of 368 feet, surpassing the French 364.2 feet, and a height of 211 feet, surpassing the French 147.5 feet.[67] The colorful character of the French Exposition obviously found no place on the Court of Honor. However, behind it stood the many-hued Transporation Building by Adler and Sullivan; this was the one American building the French critics liked.[68]

The overall scheme of the Chicago fair had three areas not dissimilar to features of the fair in Paris: the formal Court of Honor, the more informal parklike wooded isle and state pavilions, and finally the Midway. And the Chicago Fair organizers and architects did consider erecting a tower similar to Eiffel's—a Columbian Tower 1,500 feet in height. However it was to be placed not in a central position but at the head of the Midway Plaisance.[69] The concept hung on as a serious possibility until early 1892, when Burnham accepted the proposal of young George Washington Gale Ferris, Jr., to erect a 250-foot-diameter revolving wheel. The Ferris Wheel was intended to be in direct competition with the Eiffel Tower. Standing twenty-six stories in height and carrying 2,160 passengers when fully loaded, the Ferris Wheel did not match the height of the Tower, but it offered an equally dislocating and perhaps more stomach-churning sensation.[70]

The differing images of the 1889 Paris and 1893 Chicago expositions were directly related and afford insights into the respective cultures that produced them. Perhaps only a nation culturally so supremely self-confident could have produced an iron tower and palace. For the American architects the situation in Chicago was in a sense a repeat of the lessons American painters had put into practice when they exhibited at the Paris Exposition. There the American artists had compared favorably with the French by meeting them on their own ground and not appearing with a "barbaric yawp." They strove to be part of the European tradition of art and culture. For Chicago the architects created an image that they believed would connect them with the great traditions of high civilization: the American inferiority complex vis-à-vis European culture won out. Spinning away in the distance in the honky-tonk of the Midway might be the Ferris Wheel, but up close, classicism would dominate. The Ferris Wheel has of course attained a certain universality, but it is not tied to the Chicago Fair as is the Court of Honor, nor did it dominate the scene as did the Eiffel Tower. The Eiffel Tower is tied to Paris but it has far transcended its original intention: how many visitors remember it as the central landmark of the 1889 Exposition? The Tower and the White City represent twin and conflicting poles of architectural aspiration—images and symbols of cultural identity tied to the same concerns but destined for vastly different life spans.

NOTE. *I would like to thank Meredith Clausen, Richard Chafee, and Tony Wrenn for suggestions and help with aspects of this article.*

Notes

1. Umberto Eco, "A Theory of Expositions," in his *Travels in Hyperreality* (San Diego, 1986), pp. 289–307.
2. Theodore Stanton, "Open Letter: The International Exposition of 1900," *Century*, 51 (Dec. 1895), p. 317.
3. The figure 150,000 comes from H. Trueman Wood, "The Paris Exhibition," *Journal of the Society of Arts* (London), 38 (Dec. 13, 1889), p. 47.
4. Roland Barthes, *The Eiffel Tower and Other Mythologies* (New York, 1979), pp. 3–17.
5. Congrès international des architects, *Troisième Session, 17–22 Juin 1889. Organization compte rendu et notices* (Paris, Imprimerie et Librarie Centrales des Chemins de Fer, 1896), pp. xiii, 7–8, 386–88. The other U.S. members in 1889 were T. M. Clark of the Technical Institute, Boston, and William R. Ware of the Columbia University School of Architecture, New York; there is no evidence they ever attended. The Congress was well known; see *American Architect and Building News*, 25 (March 2 and April 6, 1889), pp. 98, 158. See also Paul R. Baker, *Richard Morris Hunt* (Cambridge, Mass., 1980), p. 333.
6. Russell Lewis, "Everything Under One Roof: World's Fairs and Department Stores in Paris and Chicago," *Chicago History*, 12 (1983), pp. 28–47.
7. "Under the Eiffel Tower," *New York Herald* (Paris ed.), June 13, 1889, p. 2; "Eve of the Big Show," "France's Great Jubilee," "Opening the Exposition," "Showing American Work," and "American Skill Shown," *New York Times*, May 5, 6, 7, 8, and 27, 1889, respectively (all on p. 1, except the first article, on p. 16). The *Times* articles were all "filed" the day before in Paris.
8. "The Paris Exhibition," *Boston Daily Evening Transcript*, May 9, 1889, p. 6.
9. "The Exhibition and Party," *Boston Daily Evening Transcript*, March 13, 1889, p. 6.
10. "Paris Illuminated," *Boston Daily Evening Transcript*, May 22, 1889, p. 5. Many of the accounts mention the night illumination; see *American Architect and Building News*, 21 (March 12, 1887), p. 122.
11. *American Architect and Building News*, 26 (Sept. 28, 1889), p. 142.
12. "Paris," *American Architect and Building News*, 27 (Feb. 15, 1890), pp. 105–6; [Sarah Butler Wister], "Loitering Through the Paris Exposition," *Atlantic*, 65 (March 1890), pp. 360–61.
13. William Walton, *Chefs-d'oeuvre de l'Exposition Universelle de Paris, 1889* (Philadelphia, ca. 1890), p. xv.
14. E. T. Jeffery, *Paris Universal Exposition 1889* (Chicago: Citizens' Executive Committee, 1889), p. 7.
15. "At the Paris World's Fair," *New York Times*, June 23, 1889, p. 16.
16. *Report of the United States Commissioners to the Universal Exposition of 1889 at Paris*, 5 vols. (Washington, D.C., 1891); Jeffery, op. cit., pp. 48–49.
17. *Report of the United States Commissioners*, vol. 1, pp. 20, 32.
18. Merle Curti, "America at the World's Fairs, 1851–1893," in his *Probing Our Past* (Gloucester, Mass., 1962), p. 267, citing French reports.
19. M. G. van Rensselaer, "Open Letters: Impressions of the International Exposition of 1889," *Century*, 17 (Dec. 1889), pp. 316, 318.
20. Quoted in Stanton, op. cit., p. 317.
21. Depending on how one defines world's fairs, they can be traced back to a Roman or an even earlier origin. Although large expositions were held in Paris in the 1790s, the London 1851 Great Exhibition of the Works of Industry of All Nations is normally regarded as the first of the great nineteenth-century fairs. For background see: John Allwood, *The Great Exhibitions* (London, 1977); *Le Livre des expositions universelles 1851–1989* (Paris, 1983); and Robert Rydell, *All the World's a Fair* (Chicago, 1984).
22. Jeffery, op. cit., p. 21.
23. In addition to the other sources cited, I have relied for background on *Catalogue officiel de l'Exposition Universelle de 1889* (Lille, 1889) and *L'Exposition de Paris 1889* (Paris, 1889), vols. 1–4. More recent works of value are Debora L. Silverman, "The 1889 Exhibition: The Crisis of Bourgeois Individualism," *Oppositions* 8 (Spring 1977), pp. 71–91, and Pascal Ory, *Les Expositions Universelles de Paris* (Paris, 1982).
24. W. C. Brownell, "The Paris Exposition," *Scribner's*, 7 (Jan. 1890), pp. 18–20.
25. Stanton, op. cit., p. 316.
26. M. Brincourt, "Paris Exhibition," *American Architect and Building News*, 25 (June 29, 1889), p. 307; "Eve of the Big Show," "France's Great Jubilee," and "Opening the Exposition," *New York Times*, May 5, 6, 7, 1889, pp. 16, 1, 1, respectively.
27. *Report of the United States Commissioners*, vol. 3, p. 830. A fuller statement of Eiffel's purpose is quoted in *L'Exposition de 1889: Guide illustré* (Paris, 1899), p. 91: "My goal was to show the world that, despite her undeserved misfortunes, France is still capable of succeeding where other nations failed, by her audacity and science. I wished to raise to the glory of modern science and to the honor of French industry a triumphal arch as striking as those that preceding nations raised to conquerors."
28. Frantz Jourdain, "L'Architecture à L'Exposition Universelle de 1889," *Construction Moderne*, 4 (July 13, 1889), p. 470. (This article originally appeared in *Le Figaro*.) "Opening the Exposition," *New York Times*, May 7, 1889, p. 1, compared the dome to St. Paul's.
29. Jeffery, op. cit., p. 10.
30. Frank I. Jenkins, "Harbingers of Eiffel's Tower," *Journal of the Society of Architectural Historians*, 16 (Dec. 1957), pp. 22–29.
31. There are many studies of Eiffel and the Tower. I have relied on Joseph Harris, *The Tallest Tower: Eiffel and the "Belle Epoque"* (Boston, 1975) and Henri Loyrette, *Gustave Eiffel* (New York, 1985).
32. "A One Thousand Foot Tower," *American Architect and Building News*, 17 (Feb. 21, 1885), pp. 90–91 and plate.
33. Quoted in Silverman, op. cit., p. 77.
34. Hilde de Hann and Ids Haagsma, *Architects in Competition* (London, 1988), pp. 64–71.
35. The protest and the replies were printed in "Eiffel Tower," *American Architect and Building News*, 21 (March 19, 1887), pp. 141–42, and *Report of the United States Commissioners*, vol. 3, pp. 831–32. Other significant American accounts of the Eiffel Tower appeared in William A. Eddy, "The Highest Structure in the World," *Atlantic*, 63 (June 1889), pp. 721–29; *American Architect and Building News*, 21 (Feb. 19, 1887), pp. 85–86, 24 (Nov. 24, 1888), p. 238, 25 (Feb. 23, 1889), p. 95, and 26 (July 6, 1889), p. 12.
36. Frantz Jourdain, *Exposition Universelle de 1889. Constructions élevées au Champ-de-Mars par M. Charles Garnier, architect . . . pour servir à l'histoire de l'habitation humaine* (Paris, 1889). See also an untitled editorial, *American Architect and Building News*, 25 (May 25, 1889), pp. 241–42, and H. Mereu, "History of Human Habitations," *American Architect and Building News*, 27 (March 8 and 15, 1890), pp. 149–51, 168–70.
37. Brincourt, op. cit., p. 307.
38. "L'Architecture à L'Exposition Universelle de 1889," *Construction Moderne*, 4 (May 25, 1889), p. 389, lists the architects of the *portes*.
39. Brownell, op. cit., p. 22.
40. A colorplate showing Formigé's elevation is in Claude Mignot, *Architecture of the Nineteenth Century in Europe* (New York, 1984), p. 209. See also Mardges Bacon, *Ernest Flagg: Beaux-Arts Architect and Urban Reformer* (New York and Cambridge, Mass., 1986), pp. 30–32.
41. *Report of the United States Commissioners*, vol. 3, p. 832.
42. [Wister], op. cit., p. 372.
43. Octave Chanute, quoted in "Paris Exposition of '89," *Chicago Tribune*, Sept. 27, 1890, p. 11. *Boston Daily Evening Transcript*, May 27, 1889, p. 7, reported, "A remarkable feature of the building is that the roof has no interior support."
44. The problem of determining the exact dimensions of the Palace des Machines is summarized in Donald Hoffmann, "Clear Span Rivalry: The World's Fairs of 1889–1893," *Journal of the Society of Architectural Historians*, 29 (March 1970), pp. 48–50. The generally accepted figures (on which I have relied) are those from "The Paris Exhibition," *Engineering* (London), 57 (May 3, 1889), pp. 452–62. Some writers, both at the time and recently, have stated that the Palais was constructed of steel; however, the primary structural material was iron. For other commentary, see Arthur Drexler, ed., *The Architecture of the Ecole des Beaux-Arts* (New York, 1977), pp. 450–53 (notes by Ann Van Zanten) and *American Architect and Building News*, 22, 26, 29 (Dec. 3, 1887, Oct. 19, 1889, Sept. 6, 1890), pp. 144, 187, 156, respectively.
45. William Watson, "Reports of Commissioners and Experts: William Watson, Civil Engineering, Public Works, and Architecture," *Report of the United States Commissioners*, vol. 3, p. 834.
46. Walton, op. cit., p. xii, and Meredith L. Clausen, *Frantz Jourdain and the Samaritaine* (Leiden, 1987), pp. 176–77.

47. Reyner Banham, *Age of the Masters* (New York, 1975), pp. 56–58; Sigfried Giedion, *Space, Time and Architecture*, 3rd ed. (Cambridge, Mass., 1959), pp. 275–88; Nikolaus Pevsner, *Pioneers of Modern Design* (Harmondsworth, 1960 [1936]), pp. 138–40.

48. The subject of the Eiffel Tower and modern art is worth a book; see Loyrette, op. cit., pp. 169–89.

49. Clausen, op. cit., pp. xviii, 84–86, 176–67; Mignot, op. cit., p. 208. Henry-Russell Hitchcock, *Architecture: Nineteenth and Twentieth Centuries* (Harmondsworth, 1971), p. 385.

50. Frances H. Steiner, *French Iron Architecture* (Ann Arbor, 1984); Robert Jay, "Taller than Eiffel's Tower: The London and Chicago Tower Projects, 1889–1894," *Journal of the Society of Architectural Historians*, 46 (June 1987), pp. 145–56.

51. Rush C. Hawkins, "Report on the Fine Arts," in *Report of the United States Commissioners*, vol. 2, p. 6; Hawkins characterized most American architecture as "white painted, peaked-roofed, enlarged dry-goods box with green blinds" (p. 13), asserted that American sculpture "constitutes one of the most discouraging chapters in our national history," and described Washington, D.C., as "a chamber of horrors" (p. 3). In Hawkins's opinion, "In the world of art the French have reached a higher standard of true excellence in many respects than any of the other nations" (p. 10).

52. The history of the decision for Chicago as the host city is long and extremely complicated. The determining factor was the House of Representatives' vote on February 24, 1890; however, President Harrison did not sign the bill, making it a law, until April 25, 1890. See Reid Badger, *The Great American Fair* (Chicago, 1979), chap. 6; see also David F. Burg, *Chicago's White City of 1893* (Lexington, 1976), pp. 42–43.

53. William Dean Howells, "A Seminight at the Centennial," *Atlantic*, 38 (July 1876), p. 96, and *Philadelphia Inquirer*, May 11, 1876 (quoted in Christine Hunter Donaldson, "The Centennial of 1876: The Exposition and Culture for America" [Ph.D. dissertation, Yale University, 1948], p. 108). All shades of opinion can be found among American reactions to the Centennial; for others, see: "Centennial Architecture, *American Architect and Building News*, 1 (June 3, 1876), p. 178; "American Art," *Scribner's*, 13 (Nov. 1876), pp. 126–27; and "From Humility to Excellence," *Scribner's*, 12 (July 1876), p. 431. See also John Maass, *The Glorious Enterprize: The Centennial Exposition of 1876* . . . (Watkins Glen: American Life Foundation, 1973); William Peirce Randel, *Centennial* (Philadelphia, 1969).

54. Brownell, op. cit., p. 23.

55. Georges Berger, "Suggestions for the Next World's Fair," *Century*, 39 (April 1890), pp. 845–51. An English reply is found in H. Trueman Wood, "M. Berger on the Chicago Exhibition," *American Architect and Building News*, 28 (June 7, 1890), pp. 148–50, reprinted from *Engineering* (London).

56. Sources on the protest are cited in note 35, above. See also E. Rumler, "La Tour de 300 Metres," *Construction Moderne*, 4 (April 20, 1889), pp. 325–27, which noted that America did not have a "monopole des phénomènes."

57. J.-K. Huysmans, "Iron" ("Le Fer" [1889]), in Elizabeth Gilmore Holt, ed., *The Expanding World of Art, 1874–1902* (New Haven, 1988), vol. 1, p. 77.

58. The Jenison proposal was published in the *Chicago Tribune*, March 9, 1890, p. 11, and is reprinted in Titus M. Karlowicz, "D. H. Burnham's Role in the Selection of Architects for the World's Columbian Exposition," *Journal of the Society of Architectural Historians*, 29 (Oct. 1970), pp. 247–54. The Ellis-Buffington proposal can be found in Jean France et al., *A Rediscovery—Harvey Ellis: Artist, Architect* (exhib. cat., Memorial Art Gallery of the University of Rochester, 1973), fig. 9.

59. *Report of the United States Commissioners*, vol. 1, p. 272. The rendering probably shown in Paris is reproduced in Richard Guy Wilson, *McKim, Mead & White, Architects* (New York, 1983), p. 142.

60. Bernard Berenson, *The Venetian Painters* (1894), reprinted in *The Italian Painters of the Renaissance* (Cleveland, 1957), p. iii. See also *The American Renaissance, 1876–1917*, with essays by Richard Guy Wilson, Dianne Pilgrim, and Richard Murray (Brooklyn and New York, 1979); and Richard Guy Wilson, "Architecture and the Reinterpretation of the Past in the American Renaissance," *Winterthur Portfolio*, 18 (Spring 1983), pp. 69–87.

61. The publication in the Chicago magazine *Building Budget* in 1887 and 1889 of views of the Paris Exposition is noted in Donald Hoffmann, *The Architecture of John Wellborn Root* (Baltimore, 1973), p. 222, and fig. 163. Hoffmann, p. 226, notes that one of the Burnham and Root draftsmen had visited the Paris Exposition, as had several men from Olmsted's office, including Henry S. Codman, who worked on the layout of the Chicago fair.

62. "Paris Exposition of 89," *Chicago Tribune*, Sept. 27, 1890, p. 11; Jeffery op. cit., pp. 71–72. According to Titus Karlowicz, "The Architecture of the World's Columbian Exposition" (Ph.D. dissertation, Northwestern University, 1965), pp. 23, 232, Jeffery and Chanute were asked to inquire about purchasing the French buildings and bringing them to Chicago for reuse. Apparently the idea was quickly dropped.

63. Burg, op. cit., p. 76. Jeffery's role is also discussed in Hoffmann, op. cit., p. 223, and D. H. Burnham et al., "Final Official Report of the Director of Works of the World's Columbian Exposition," 8 vols., mss. (ca. 1894) in the Burnham Library, Art Institute of Chicago.

64. Karlowicz, "D. H. Burnham's Role . . . ," *Journal of the Society of Architectural Historians*, 29 (Oct. 1970), pp. 247–54, and Louis H. Sullivan, *The Autobiography of an Idea* (New York, 1956 [1924]), pp. 323–25.

65. "Royal Institute of British Architects. Presentation of the Royal Gold Medal," *American Architect and Building News*, 41 (July 15, 1893), p. 41. Hunt expressed the same sentiments in his presidential address, *Proceedings of the 25th Annual Convention of the A.I.A.* (Boston, 1891), p. 14: "The last two French expositions showed great merit in the adaption of iron to architectural effects, but much yet remains to be accomplished before the artistic minds will be satisfied; and certainly, if Paris, with her multitude of artists and artisans of the highest grade, and having plenty of time for the study and execution of this problem, could not satisfactorily solve it, it would have been foolhardiness to attempt it on this occasion."

66. This observation is made in Hoffmann, op. cit., p. 229.

67. Titus M. Karlowicz, "Notes on the Columbian Exposition's Manufacturers and Liberal Arts Building," *Journal of the Society of Architectural Historians*, 33 (Oct. 1974), pp 214–18; and Hoffmann, op. cit.

68. Officially Sullivan received an award from the French Union Centrale des Arts Décoratifs for donating casts of the "Golden Door" of the Transportation Building and other materials for display; see Robert Twombly, *Louis Sullivan: His Life and Work* (New York, 1986), pp. 267-68, and Hugh Morrison, *Louis Sullivan: Prophet of Modern Architecture* (New York, 1935), pp. 138, 188–89. Of interest is the fact that Sullivan's work became identified in America as French and Art Nouveau, as Twombly points out (p. 385). Color also figured significantly in Root's initial schemes for the fair, which came to naught. He may have been influenced by the French use of color; see Hoffmann, op. cit., pp. 233, 238, and Harriet Monroe, *John Wellborn Root, Architect* (Boston, 1896), p. 243. Monroe, p. 245, claims that the colorful Fisheries Building by Henry Ives Cobb came the closest to Root's ideas on color. Monroe (p. 251–52) indicates that Root also considered presenting a History of Human Habitations exhibit similar to the one in Paris.

69. Illustrated in Gerald R. Larson, "The Iron Skeleton Frame: Interactions Between Europe and the United States," in John Zukowsky, ed., *Chicago Architecture, 1872–1922* (Munich, 1987), p. 53; Larson also argues that Eiffel's system of iron framing had an impact on American commercial architecture.

70. In advertising brochures, quoted in Burg, op. cit., p. 224, the Ferris Wheel Company compared the wheel to the Eiffel Tower. See also John A. Kouwenhoven, "The Eiffel Tower and the Ferris Wheel," in his *Half a Truth Is Better Than None* (Chicago, 1982), pp. 107–24, and Jack Fincher, "George Ferris Jr. and the Great Wheel of Fortune," *Smithsonian*, 14 (July 1983), pp. 109–18. There is some conflict as to the actual number of passengers the Ferris Wheel could carry; Burg (p. 224) puts the figure at 1,440, while Kouwenhoven (p. 121), Fincher (p. 110), and Badger (*The Great American Fair*, p. 108) put it at 2,160.

Catalogue of the American Paintings

AB	Annette Blaugrund
HPC	Holly Pyne Connor
JH	Judith Hayward
SJ-G	Susan James-Gadzinski
MCOB	Maureen C. O'Brien
KZ	Karen Zukowski

The catalogue is organized alphabetically, and catalogue numbers correspond to those of the original 1889 catalogue of American paintings, which is reproduced, with annotations, on pages 267–97. Of the two picture titles given in each caption, the first (in roman *type) is the 1889 title and the second (in italic type) is the current title.* *For notes, see pp. 252–65.*

OTTO HENRY BACHER (1856–1909)

Otto Bacher was born in Cleveland and studied there with DeScott Evans and Willis S. Adams. In 1878 he made his first trip abroad, with Adams and another Ohio painter, Sion Wenban, and enrolled in the Royal Academy of Munich.[1] After a sketching tour along the Danube in the summer of 1879,[2] Bacher joined a group of his Munich friends in Florence and resumed study under the American Frank Duveneck. In the summer of 1880, he traveled with this group to Venice, where he met Whistler. Already strongly interested in etching, Bacher improved his graphic skills under Whistler's guidance, as he recorded in his book *With Whistler in Venice*, published in New York in 1908.

Bacher remained abroad until 1883, when he returned to America to teach painting. In 1884 he conducted an art school in Cleveland with Joseph DeCamp, a friend from Duveneck's classes. Among his students were two members of the family of a Dr. Ewing, who is portrayed here driving a horse and buckboard along the dusty main street of Richfield, Ohio.[3] A slice of rural American life in the 1880s, the subject is reminiscent of mid-century genre painting. But the casually scattered organization suggests the use of photography, and the figures, frozen in bright sunlight and casting knife-sharp shadows, indicate Bacher's awareness of the "glare aesthetic" of the Italian Macchiaioli painters.[4] In its acute description of natural light, the painting differs significantly from Bacher's later works, in which academic Impressionism, diffused light, and a palette of softer, close-hued contrasts were applied to figures out of doors. Bacher's paint handling changed markedly after he returned to Europe, in 1885, to study in Paris with Carolus-Duran and with Gustave Boulanger and Jules-Joseph Lefebvre at the Académie Julian, but he selected this striking example of his earlier style for the 1889 Exposition.[5] MCOB

JAMES CARROLL BECKWITH (1852–1917)

James Carroll Beckwith studied painting in Chicago and New York[1] before he went to Paris, in 1873, and entered Carolus-Duran's atelier.[2] Along with the young Sargent, who joined the studio the following year, Beckwith flourished under the guidance of that master, a noted portraitist who preached the gospel of Velázquez, stressing the instinctive placement of lights and darks and the importance of seizing the subject *à premier coup*. While in Paris, Beckwith also studied at the Ecole des Beaux-Arts and at the atelier of Léon Bonnat. By 1877, the year in which he was invited to assist Carolus-Duran with ceiling decorations for the Louvre, he had made his first successful submission to the Salon, establishing himself at the age of twenty-five as a rising American artist.[3]

After exhibiting at the 1878 International Exposition, Beckwith returned to New York to teach at the Art Students League, quickly becoming a leader of the corps of young Americans imbued with the ideals of modern European painting. Among his close friends were the artists William Merritt Chase[4] and William Walton, who was also a translator and art critic. Walton's paintings, which reflected his wide reading and vivid imagination, were frequently of mythological and dreamlike subjects and "failed to be understood by those who were not acquainted with the sources of his researches and his knowledge of ancient legend."[5] He was better known for his elaborate volumes on the 1889

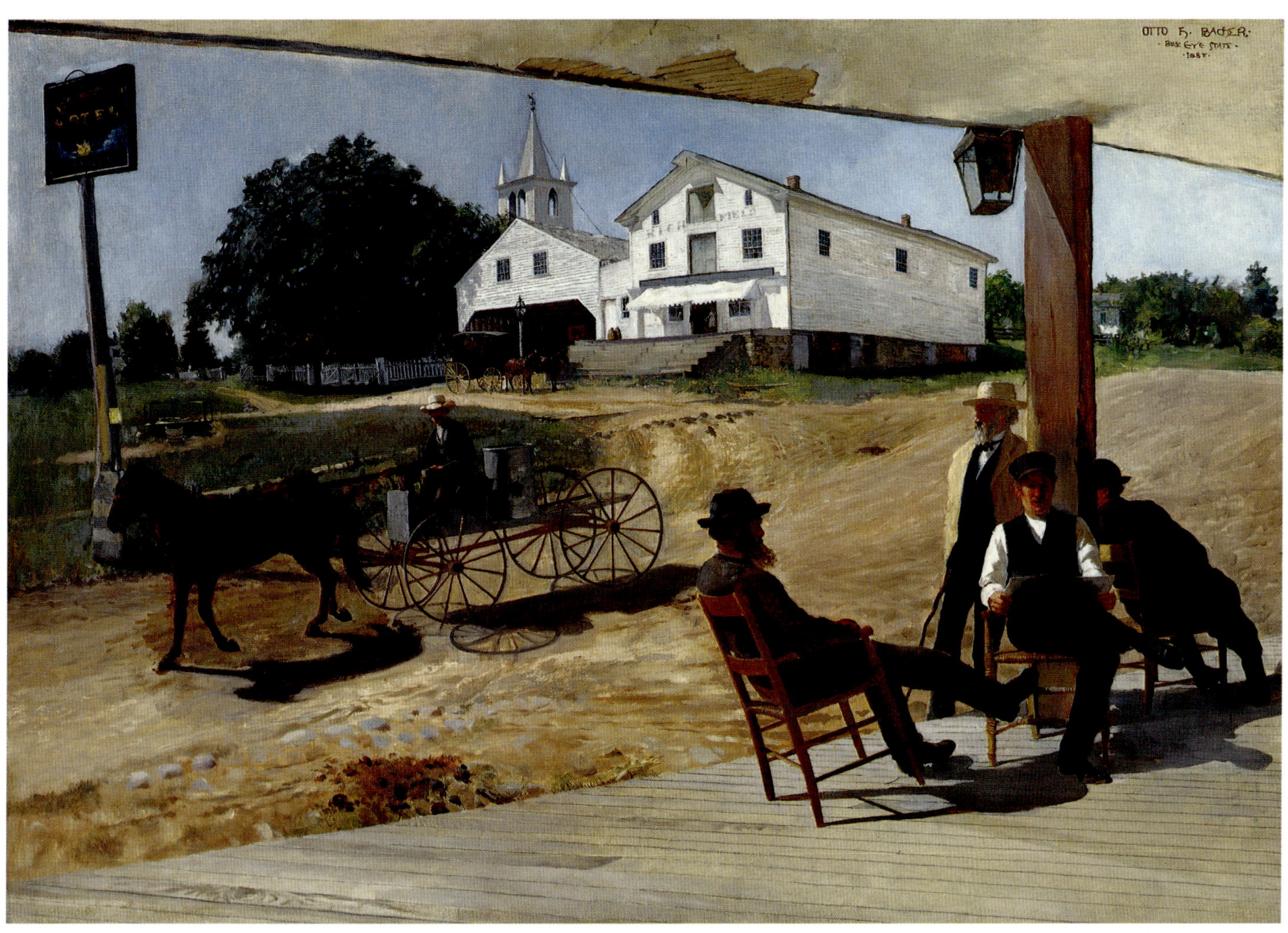

4.
Otto Henry Bacher
Richfield Center, Ohio
Ella's Hotel, Richfield Center, Ohio, 1885
Oil on canvas, 31 x 42½" (78.7 x 107.2 cm)
Manoogian Collection

Exposition and the 1893 World's Columbian Exposition, his translations of Balzac, Victor Hugo, and Flaubert, and his contributions to *Scribner's* magazine.

Beckwith painted the elegant, intense Walton in 1886, posed in front of a Pompeiian red wall on which hung Beckwith's own impressionistic watercolor and oil sketches, as well as his fencing mask.[6] Against the striking foil of the background, Walton's dark, slender figure is alert but relaxed; he holds a lighted cigarette in a gesture recalling Sargent's contemporary portrait of Robert Louis Stevenson,[7] but the figure's more static treatment and forthright pose reflect Beckwith's training with Léon Bonnat.

The portrait was exhibited in Beckwith's New York studio in March 1886 during an open house that, coinciding with an important sale of the art collection of Mrs. Mary Jane Morgan, drew many visitors.[8] Following this preliminary showing, it was sent to the 1887 Salon, where Carolus-Duran declared that it was "the best portrait that ever came from America,"[9] and the American critic Theodore Child called it "the strongest portrait I have ever seen issuing from a New York studio."[10] It was among the three paintings Beckwith submitted to the 1889 Exposition and helped him an win honorable mention. Presented in 1916 to the Century Association, the portrait remains a brilliant characterization of the artist and critic by his "old friend and atelier companion."[11] MCOB

EDWARD AUGUST BELL (1862–1953)

Born in New York, Edward Bell first studied art with his father, Edward A. Bell. In the early 1880s he took classes under William Merritt Chase and Walter Shirlaw at the Art Students League and also attended the National Academy of Design. Bell's first trip abroad, in 1883, saw him enrolled at the Royal Academy, Munich, as a student of Ludwig von Loefftz, a realist painter who stressed the importance of the Dutch and Spanish masters.[1] In Munich, Bell exhibited at the Royal Academy. He also sent paintings to the National Academy of Design in New York from 1886 to 1890,[2] but he had not shown in Paris prior to 1889.

Lady in Gray, which was exhibited in 1889 at the Royal Academy in Munich as well as at the Exposition in Paris, was the first painting to bring Bell international attention. Recalling Whistler's *The White Girl* (National Gallery of Art, Washington, D.C.) in pose and composition, *The Lady in Gray* portrays a flaxen-haired girl (a student at Munich's Conservatory of Music) wearing a simple dress and wide-brimmed hat and standing on a bearskin rug.[3] Bell incorporated as background a softly patterned skrim, a decorative device he would use in many later paintings of women. Although *Lady in Gray* won a silver medal at the Royal Academy in Munich, it was caricatured in the German review *Spottvogel*, and, according to the artist, it was considered "a very radical departure at the time."[4] Approval came from younger artists such as the Symbolist painter Franz von Stuck, who praised the painting for its loveliness and recalled it in his illustration entitled *A Dream of the Passing of the Exhibition*.[5]

At the 1889 Exposition, Bell's painting won a bronze medal, comparing favorably with the works of his former teacher, Chase. It was also shown at the 1893 World's Columbian Exposition, Chicago,[6] and at the 1897 Tennessee Centennial, Nashville, and won a silver medal at the 1901 Pan-American Exposition, Buffalo. Bell continued to achieve recognition in the 1890s following his return to New York, and after the turn of the century his delicately hued paintings of women brought him further renown. Drawing inspiration from both Whistler and Chase, he frequently incorporated Japanese decorative objects into his small idealized portraits.[7] *Lady in Gray*, a prototype of his later work, remained in his own collection until 1933, when Bell's colleague Irving Wiles prevailed upon him to present it to an American museum.[8] More naive, and larger in scale, than the easel paintings in which Bell refined his talent, it has an appealing naturalness and exuberance of technique. MCOB

EDWIN HOWLAND BLASHFIELD (1848–1936)

Edwin Howland Blashfield, who studied in Boston briefly in the mid-1860s with Thomas Johnston and William Rimmer, became the dean of American mural painting.[1] He trained in Paris from 1867 to 1870 and from 1874 to 1880 in the private atelier of Léon Bonnat, receiving supplemental criticism from Jean-Léon Gérôme. He lived in the Sherwood Studio Building in New York from 1881 to 1887 and traveled in Europe from 1887 to 1893, painting in oil and producing illustrations for magazines. During this period he exhibited at the Paris Salon, London's Royal Academy, and the National Academy of Design.

Blashfield returned to America to execute murals for the World's Columbian Exposition of 1893 and thereafter devoted himself to mural work. He developed a distinctive format that put real and allegorical figures together in pictures with historical and moral themes. His writings, including *Mural Painting in America*,[2] and his murals—among them those in the dome of the Library of Congress and in the Minnesota State Capitol—were integral to the American Renaissance revival of decoration in public buildings.[3] He was a long-time member of the Architectural League of New York and the National Society of Mural Painters, and was president from 1920 to 1926 of the National Academy of Design, which honored him in 1934 with a special gold medal.

In both his easel paintings and his murals Blashfield proceeded from careful black-and-white studies to finished oils on canvas. In most of his work he used the frieze-like format for his classically beautiful women depicted with elegant line and rich, inventive color. Although he recognized decorative qualities in great oil paintings, citing Rembrandt's chiaroscuro,[4] he saw the mural as very different from the easel painting. The mural, he wrote, "developed into beauty applied to utility, and it culminated as a supreme teacher, through the arts, of patriotism, morals and history. . . ."[5] The easel painting was incapable of conveying such profound lessons.

Portrait of the Artist's Wife conveys the personal background of the sitter, Blashfield's first wife, Evangeline, daughter of Charles Wilbour, journalist, translator, and Egyptologist, and Charlotte Beebee Wilbour, writer and feminist.[6] Details in the picture allude to Evangeline's remarkable family: the sphinx on the sofa and the ancient-coin sleeve clasp to her father's profession, the loose gown to her mother's interest in dress reform, and the interior as a whole to Evangeline's own involvement with the arts. The Blashfields, with A.A. Hopkins, edited a version of Vasari's *Lives*.

Blashfield's earliest works included historical genre costume pieces that demonstrate his interest in dress and furnishings.[7] In contrast to the earlier, anecdotal works, this painting emphasizes the grace, femininity, and decorative qualities of the subject, and the devices of monumental scale and strong profile contours seen here are developed later in the murals. More significant, Blashfield suppressed the personal qualities of his sitter and, through her averted gaze, distanced her from the viewer; she forecasts the symbolic women in his later paintings.

Dated "Mai 1889," the painting was probably executed in France for the Wilbours, who owned it at the time of the Exposition. It may have been painted with the fair in mind; it won a bronze medal.[8] Its sumptuous brushwork compares with that of Sargent and its successful wedding of idealism and portraiture with Thayer's *Winged Figure* (see page 216). Blashfield's only other entry in the Exposition was an allegorical oil entitled *Inspiration* (unlocated). KZ

ROBERT FREDERICK BLUM (1857–1903)

Robert Blum is best known for his paintings of Venice and Japan.[1] From 1874 to 1876 he trained as a draftsman in a lithography firm and studied at the McMicken School of Design in his native Cincinnati.[2] In 1876 he went to Philadelphia for a year's study at the Pennsylvania Academy of the Fine Arts. But Blum advised a fellow artist, "You are bound to come finally to the point of fighting out things for yourself and by yourself. . . by looking and searching out the lessons that any good picture contains."[3] The "good" pictures included those

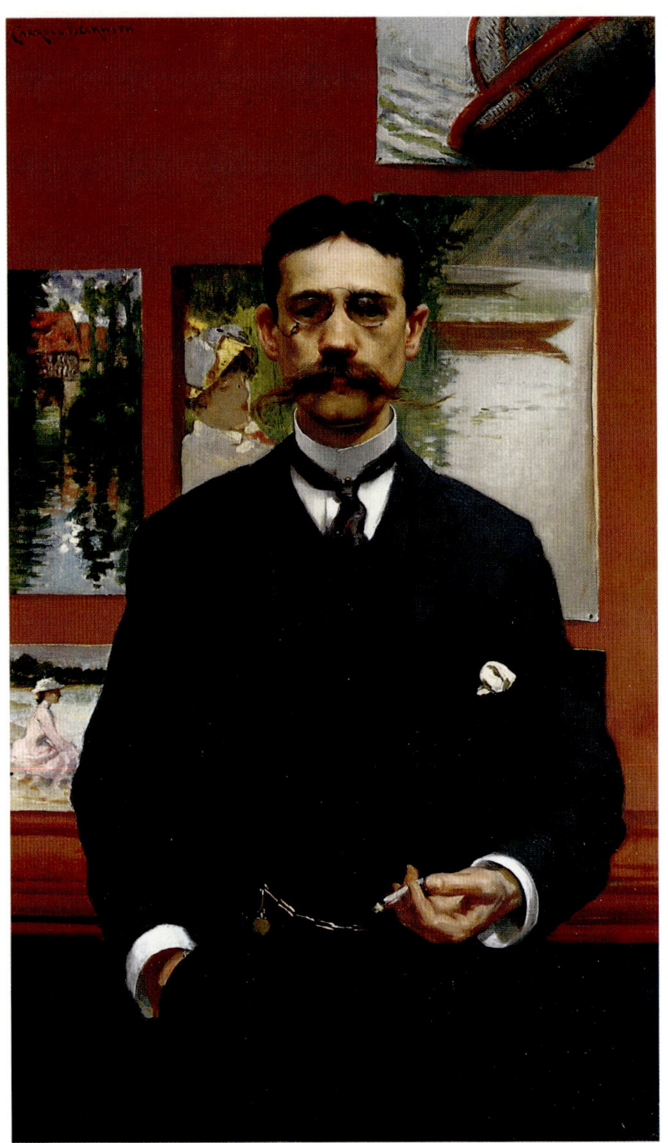

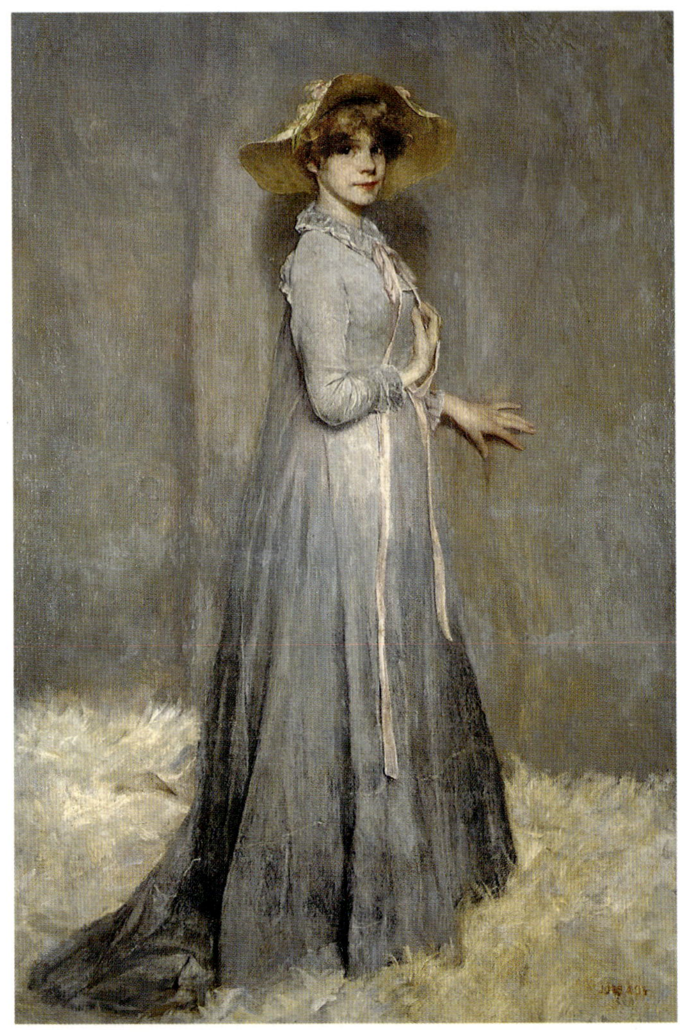

10.
James Carroll Beckwith
Portrait of William Walton
William Walton, 1886
Oil on canvas, 47⅞ x 28⅛" (120.3 x 71.5 cm)
The Century Association, New York,
Presented by Herbert Satterlee

12.
Edward August Bell
Portrait
Lady in Gray, 1887–88
Oil on canvas, 76⅛ x 49½" (193.2 x 125 cm)
Memphis Brooks Museum of Art,
Gift of the artist

of Velázquez and Ribera and of friends Chase, Whistler, and Duveneck. Blum was also inspired by the works of such contemporary European artists as Giovanni Boldini, Mariano Fortuny y Marsal, Degas, and the artists of The Hague School. He encountered Japanese art at the Philadelphia Centennial, and it fascinated him. Blum experimented in virtually all artistic mediums and was involved in the decorative arts and interior design. With Chase, Blum founded the Society of Painters in Pastel, in 1882, and he exhibited often with both the Society of American Artists and the National Academy of Design. As an illustrator for *Scribner's*, Blum traveled to Japan in 1890, and he produced memorable canvases inspired by that country. Among his last works were large-scale murals for two theaters in New York.

Venetian Lace Workers is one of Blum's masterpieces.[4] He spent much of the 1880s in Venice, etching and painting with other American and European artists, among them Duveneck and Whistler. Venice's lively women appear in many of his canvases, some engaged in lace-making, which was undergoing a

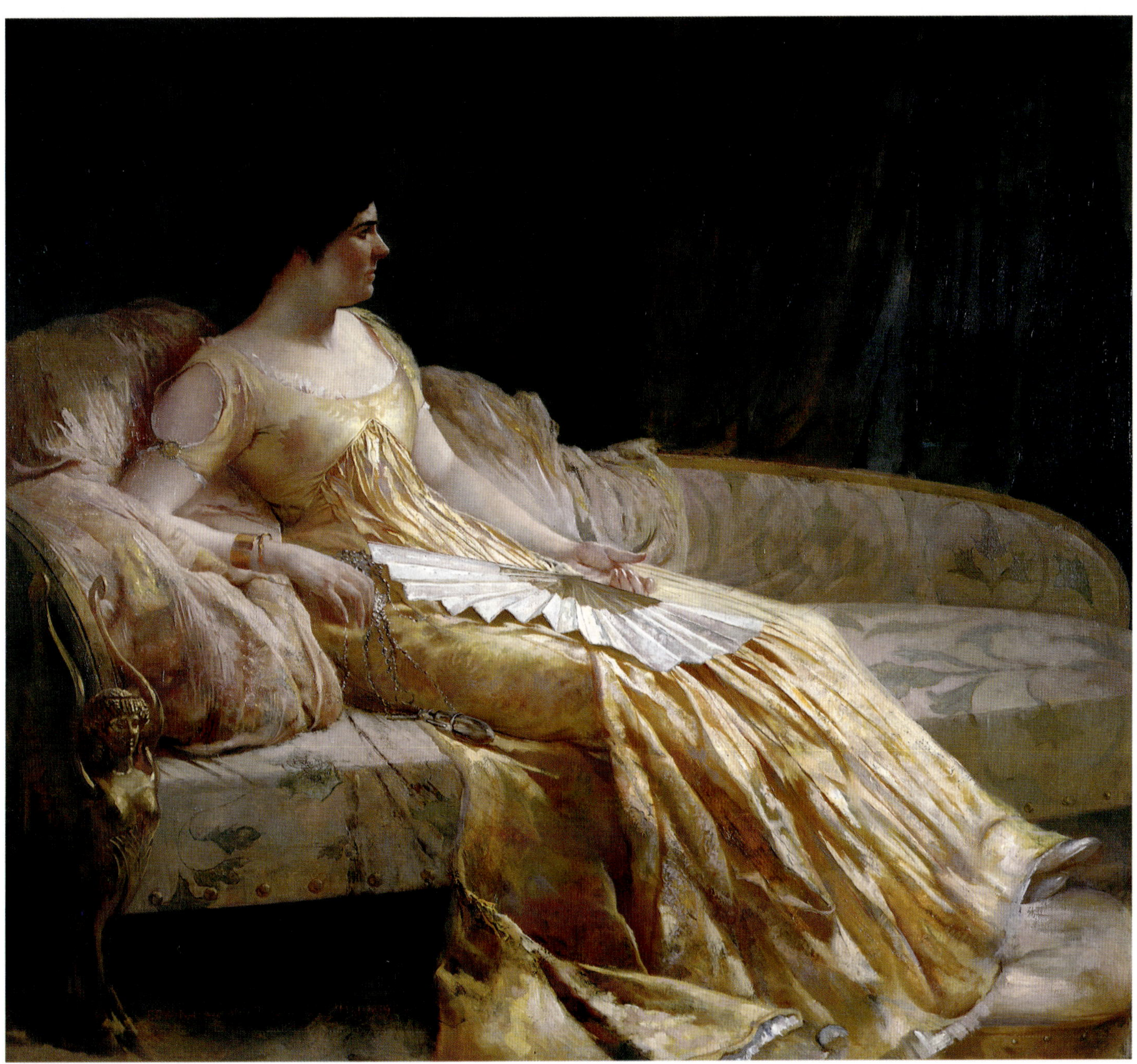

19.
Edwin Howland Blashfield
Portrait
Portrait of the Artist's Wife, 1889
Oil on canvas, 64½ x 69¼" (163.8 x 175.9 cm)
Owner in 1889 C.E. Wilbour
William Vareika Fine Arts, Newport, R.I.

revival. In the summer of 1886, Blum, his roommate, Otto Bacher, and Charles Ulrich all decided to attempt the subject, hiring models to pose. Blum, after laboring for months, finally completed his painting in New York in April 1887, in time for the Third Prize Fund Exhibition at the American Art Association. Critics immediately praised its "cleverness" and its figures, who were "not only really, but intensely alive," and pronounced it "much the best work he has ever exhibited."[5] The painting, also shown at the Royal Academy, London, in 1888, the Chicago Inter-State Industrial Exposition in 1890, and the St. Louis Universal Exposition of 1904, won Blum a bronze medal at the 1889 Exposition, establishing him in the front rank of American painters.

Venetian Lace Workers assimilates diverse strains. The innovative diagonal composition reflects Blum's observations of Degas's paintings, Japanese prints, and contemporary painting in Venice.[6] The startling contrast between the brilliant Venetian sun and the cool, dark interior shows familiarity with Velázquez's lighting effects and "the glare aesthetic" developed by landscapists to depict harsh sunlight.[7] The bold brushwork derives from Boldini, Chase, and, especially, Fortuny. As a collector and designer of fine decorative objects, Blum was interested in these Venetian lace-makers because of his respect for the craft and his preoccupation with the exotic. KZ

FRANK MYERS BOGGS (1855–1926)

Born in Ohio and raised in New York City, Frank Boggs spent most of his adult life abroad, ultimately becoming a French citizen. For a time he was better represented in private collections and museums in Europe than in the United States. By 1900, two of Boggs's pictures had been bought by the French government, and examples of his work were in museums in Le Havre, Nantes, and Dieppe.[1]

Initially an engraver for *Harper's Weekly*, Boggs became interested in scene painting, an activity which seems to anticipate the panoramic views that became the staples of his oeuvre. He went to France in 1876, seeking further training in scene painting, but ended up with Jean-Léon Gérôme, who steered him away from the studio toward plein-air work. While there may be no correlation between Boggs's limited academic exposure and the remarkable coherency of his style, it is interesting to note that other artists in the present exhibition with similarly restricted academic experience—for example, Walter Gay—showed a comparable stylistic unity. Once outdoors, Boggs quickly gravitated to the atmospheric harbor and city views that are his hallmark. His entries in the 1889 Exposition—*Place de la Bastille; La Place, St. Germain des Prés*; and *Old Canal at Dordrecht*—all in this vein, earned him a silver medal. These pictures had all been shown at Salons during the 1880s. In fact, the French government bought *Place de la Bastille* from the 1882 Salon for the Musée Vivinel at Compiègne.[2]

During the 1880s, two of Boggs's pictures were owned by the well-known American collector Thomas B. Clarke,[3] but in general his work was not popular in the United States at this time. Possibly his style, already termed Impressionist by 1884, was too advanced for American taste.[4] It is also possible that Americans were not interested in European views painted by an American artist. Perhaps sensitive to this attitude, Boggs included an American view, *Brooklyn Bridge* (unlocated), among his entries in the 1893 World's Columbian Exposition at Chicago. If Boggs's pictures were not well received in the United States during the 1880s, they were very popular abroad. Undoubtedly their market was that sector of a burgeoning Parisian population interested neither in the traditional subject matter of the Academy nor in the more modern city views offered by the Impressionists.[5] For although Boggs was termed "Impressionist," his work does not really accommodate such a definition; rather, his selection of quaint sites rendered in silvery tones aligned him with pre-Impressionists like Jongkind, whom he knew in the 1880s.[6]

In a sense, *Place de la Bastille* encapsulates Boggs's position. Its full Salon title, *Place de la Bastille, en 1882*, announces the artist's interest in contemporaneity, an assertion supported by rainy atmosphere and scurrying crowds. Yet the picture's great size, panoramic view, and low vantage point give it an old-fashioned monumentality that is underscored by the depiction of the central column, erected by Louis-Philippe to commemorate the revolutions of 1830 and 1848. While pictorially conservative, *Place de la Bastille* is symbolically appropriate to the 1889 Exposition, a commemoration of the French Revolution. JH

ROBERT BOLLING BRANDEGEE (1849–1922)

Robert Brandegee, who was born in Berlin, Connecticut, is best remembered as an American Pre-Raphaelite. It is believed that he studied with John Henry Hill and later had a winter of instruction with Thomas Charles Farrer.[1] Brandegee's early works were small-scale watercolors painted in the exacting technique and brilliant palette of the American Ruskinian circle.[2] On April 29, 1872, Brandegee left for Paris, where he worked in the small atelier of Louis-Marie-François Jacquesson de la Chevreuse and, on August 24, 1875, enrolled at the Ecole des Beaux-Arts.[3] Among the other American artists who studied with Jacquesson were J. Alden Weir, Dwight William Tryon, and Montague Flagg.[4] (Weir later became a member of the New York selection committee for the 1889 Exposition and was probably instrumental in having Brandegee's one entry accepted.) Once in Paris, Brandegee broadened his painting technique and abandoned his early interest in still-life and flower compositions to concentrate on portraiture and figure studies; his new concerns were a direct result of his instruction in Paris, which stressed drawing from the human figure.[5] By 1880 he returned to America, where until 1903 he channeled his energies more into his teaching at Miss Porter's School in Farmington, Connecticut, than into his painting. However, he exhibited his portraits at the Society of American Artists during the early 1880s and at the Pennsylvania Academy of the Fine Arts in 1901 (he had shown intermittently at the National Academy of Design from 1868 to 1880).

Portrait of Montague Flagg exemplifies the style Brandegee developed in Paris and practiced in America after 1880. The sitter is depicted frontally, close to the picture plane, and in a three-quarter-length view; attention is focused on the face. The influence of Frank Duveneck and the Munich School is apparent in the dramatic contrasts of light and dark and in the broad and direct painting technique. Although Brandegee may not have known Duveneck personally, he saw Duveneck's art at the Society of American Artists, where Brandegee, Duveneck, and Flagg all showed their portraits during the early 1880s. The *Portrait of Montague Flagg* also displays an appreciation of Titian, who was highly esteemed at the Ecole des Beaux-Arts, where the painstaking reproduction of old masters represented the core of the curriculum.[6]

Brandegee's personal affection for Montague Flagg is apparent in this sensitive portrayal. Although there is no direct reference to the sitter's profession, its alternative title, "The Wanderer," may allude indirectly to Flagg's European travels.[7] The bond between Brandegee and Flagg was strong. Brandegee painted Flagg's wife in 1878 (Collection Mr. and Mrs. Robert L. Brandegee, Salisbury, Conn.); he named his second son Paul Montague; and he worked with Flagg in both Paris and New York. According to Brandegee, "the *Portrait of Montague Flagg* was painted in one of the Holbeing [*sic*] Studios in 55th Street, New York City. Mr. Flagg and I worked in the same studio,

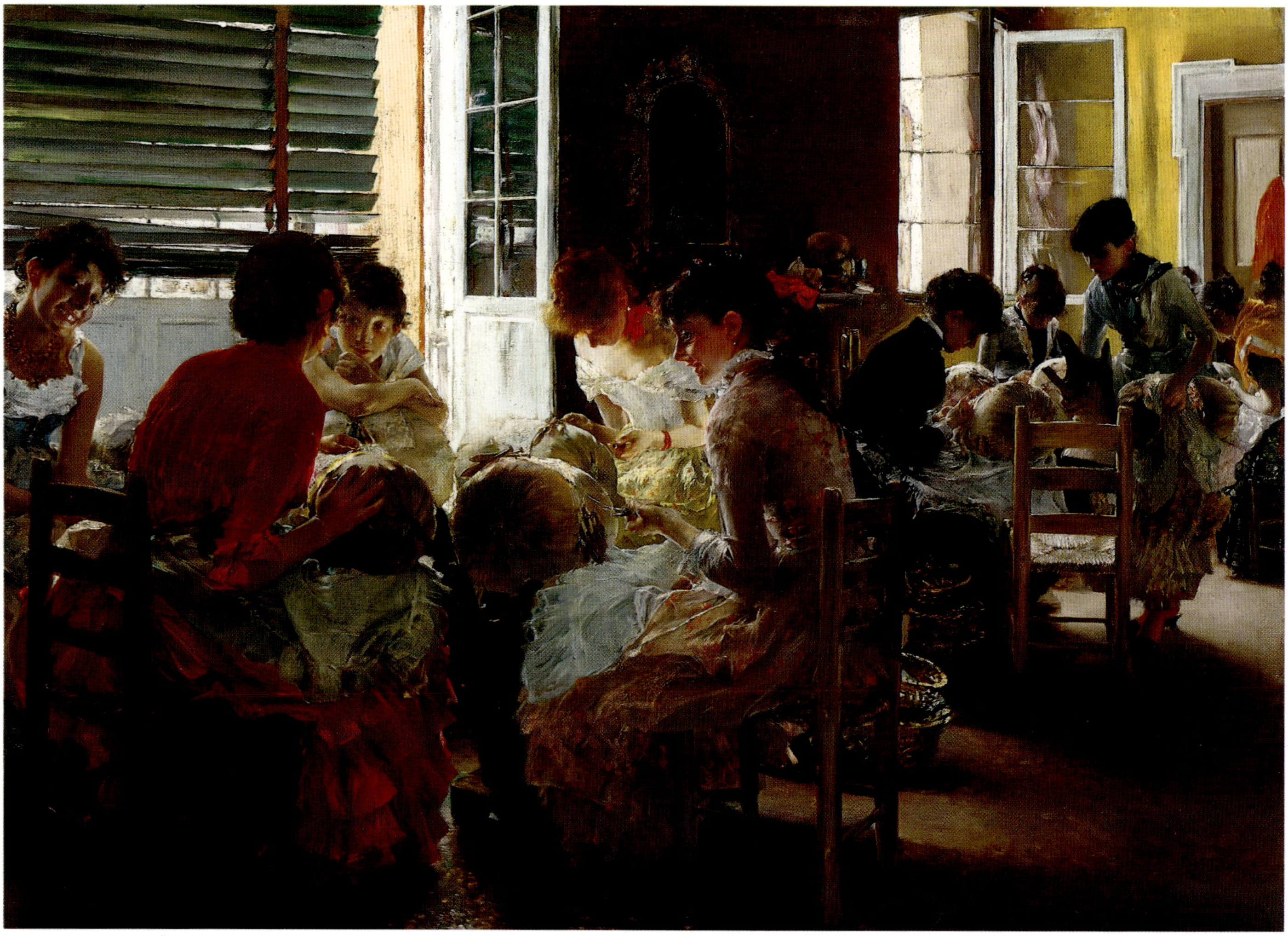

20.
Robert Frederick Blum
Venetian Lace Workers
Venetian Lace Makers, 1887
Oil on canvas, 30⅛ x 41¼″ (76.5 x 104.7 cm)
Cincinnati Art Museum,
Gift of Mrs. Elizabeth S. Potter

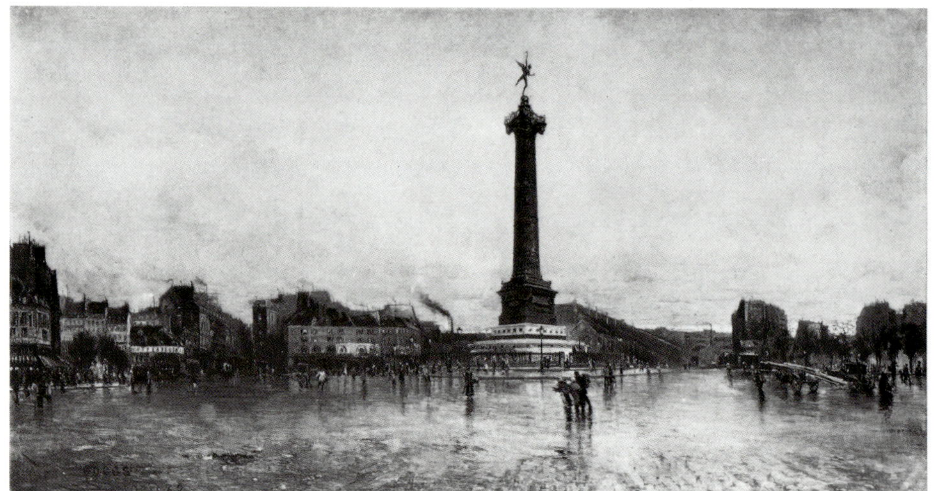

23.
Frank Myers Boggs
Place de la Bastille, Paris
Place de la Bastille, 1882
Oil on canvas, 55½ x 98⅛″ (140.2 x 249.2 cm)
Owner in 1889 the French government
Musée Vivinel, Compiègne

25.
Robert Bolling Brandegee
Portrait
Portrait of Montague Flagg (The Wanderer), 1887
Oil on panel, 24 x 20" (61. x 50.8 cm)
Collection Nelson Holbrook White

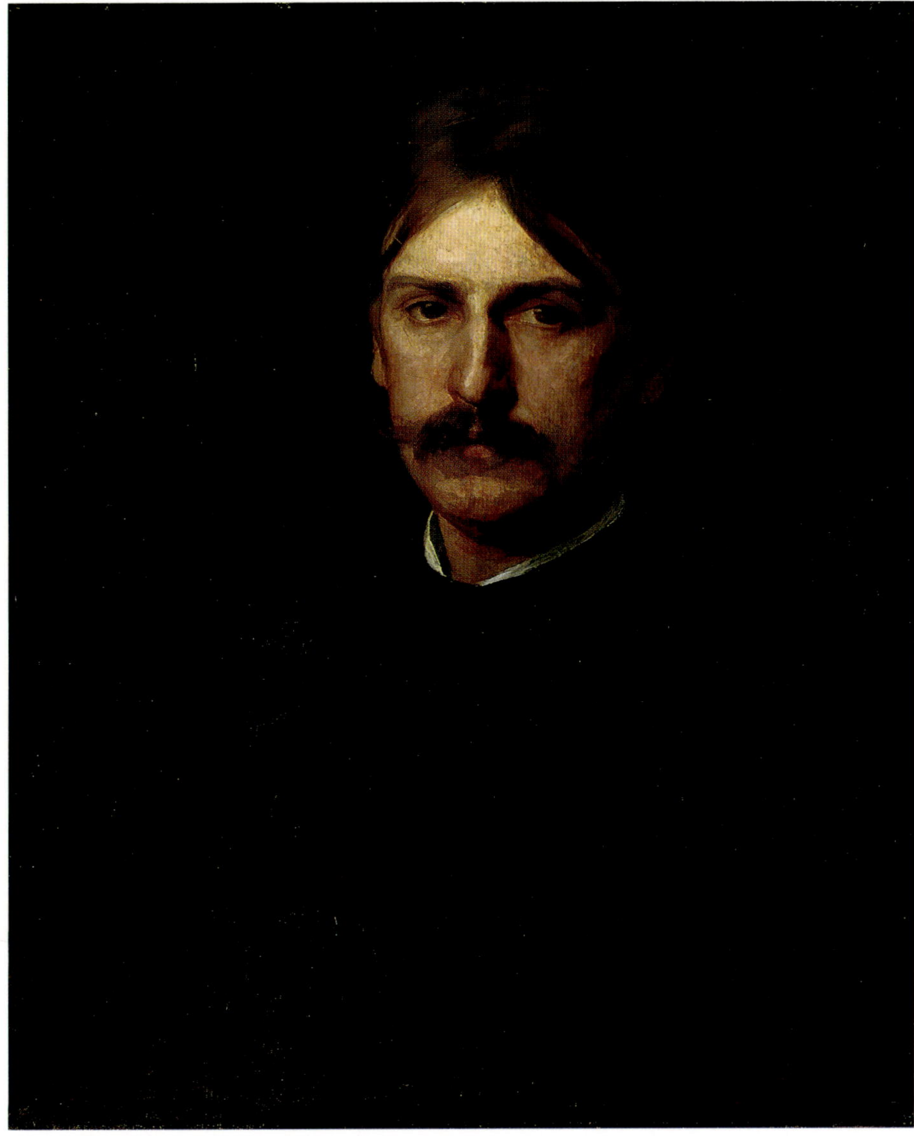

largely to reduce the rent."[8] Because he considered it one of his best works, Brandegee exhibited this portrait frequently during his lifetime. "There are parts of the head," Brandegee wrote in 1912, "that are better painted than anything I ever did before or since."[9] When the picture was shown in 1887 at the Society of American Artists, it received a favorable notice in *The Nation*: "It is an admirable head . . . and has a completeness about it that makes of this painting of the simplest of subjects a real work of art."[10] It was awarded a bronze medal at the 1889 Exposition, where a critic for the *New York Times* praised it as "about the best thing in the collection."[11] In 1911, *Portrait of Montague Flagg* was purchased from the artist by the Smith College Museum of Art, Northampton, Massachusetts; by 1947 it was in the collection of the Lyman Allyn Museum, New London, Connecticut.[12] HPC

FREDERICK ARTHUR BRIDGMAN (1847–1928)

American expatriate painter Frederick Bridgman was at the height of his career in 1889, when he was chosen to be chairman of the American artists' jury in Paris. He was born in Tuskegee, Alabama, and is said to have decided to be an artist at the age of five.[1] Before going to France, in 1866, Bridgman worked as an engraver at the American Bank-Note Company in New York and studied at the Brooklyn Art School and at the National Academy of Design. In Paris he enrolled in the Atelier Suisse, and he was an early member of the artists' colony in Pont-Aven, Brittany, where he painted peasant subjects sporadically for the next ten years.[2] On February 10, 1867, he began four years of study in the atelier of Jean-Léon Gérôme, where his American fellow students were Thomas Eakins and Harry Humphrey Moore.[3]

Bridgman thoroughly absorbed Gérôme's realism and his interest in exotic North African subject matter. With Charles Sprague Pearce, he made his only trip to Egypt in 1873.[4] This was part of a North African tour that lasted a year and included Algeria, one of Bridgman's favorite places, which he often visited in the 1870s and 1880s.[5] The costumes and props he collected were later used to decorate one of his Paris studios in the Egyptian style,[6] and the three hundred sketches[7] he made provided content for his paintings of the next several decades. When one of his early Egyptian paintings, *The Burial of a Mummy on the Nile* (unlocated), was awarded a medal at the 1877 Salon, a critic remarked that it could have been the work of Gérôme.[8]

Bridgman turned in the 1880s to a more painterly style—a brighter palette and looser brushwork. *Horse Market at Cairo*, an example of Bridgman's more Impressionistic approach, treats one of his favorite subjects—trading in bazaars. He used vivid colors for the robes of the central trio of figures, and his bravura brushwork caught the brilliant sunlight on the bare stucco wall. The painting was probably exhibited under that title at the 1889 Paris Exposition, along with five other works, which together won Bridgman a silver medal and which constitute a survey of his art of the previous decade.[9] A critic said his six entries were remarkable and that their "merits are well established."[10]

Since 1884, when *Horse Market at Cairo* was first exhibited at the Paris Salon as *Mon dernier Prix, marchand, au Caire*, there has been confusion about its title. It is known that Bridgman produced at least two paintings on the subject of horse trading, *Horse Market at Cairo* and *Hot Bargain, Cairo*, both shown at the International Exposition at Glasgow in 1888. The latter was priced higher, indicating that it was probably the larger canvas, and hence the one the artist most likely submitted to major expositions.[11] Since the painting in the present exhibition has been known by both titles, it may very well be the one that Bridgman sent to the 1889 Exposition. In 1886 an etching by James D. Smillie after *Hot Bargain, Cairo* appeared in a book on American art as its single example of orientalism.[12]

Hot Bargain, Cairo was shown in Bridgman's 1890 solo exhibition at the Art Institute of Chicago; probably it entered the collection of the Union League Club of Chicago at about that time.[13] In 1897 it was exhibited at the Tennessee Centennial in Nashville as owned by the Union League Club of Chicago.

Bridgman, who was elected an associate of the National Academy of Design in 1874 and an Academician in 1881 and became a member of the Society of American Artists in 1880, continued to live in France and to paint orientalist subjects. In 1898 he published *L'Anarchie dans l'art*, a thesis expounding his opposition to Impressionism, the movement that put his exotic and academic style out of favor. SJ-G

JOHN GEORGE BROWN (1831–1913)

In 1889, J. G. Brown was among the dwindling number of American artists who had not trained in Paris or Munich. In general, this group, whose pictures were installed in the gallery that had been set aside for artists residing in the United States, did not fare well at the 1889 Exposition. Theodore Child, the critic, stated bluntly that among them "there were but few exceptional achievements."[1] To Child, a proponent of the emerging Whistlerian aesthetic of "art for art's sake," Brown's pictures were too subject-oriented, too sentimental, and too finished—in short, old-fashioned. Despite this critical opinion, Brown won an honorable mention at the Exposition. Moreover, his status during this period is attested to by his position on the selection committee for the fair, as well as his long-term presidency of the American Watercolor Society. In fact, J. G. Brown was one of the most successful American artists of the late nineteenth century, and his old-fashioned pictures continued to sell.

Both Brown's story-telling subject matter and his highly detailed execution reflected the fact that he had trained in England. Born in Durham, Brown was apprenticed at an early age to a glass cutter in Newcastle-upon-Tyne. During this apprenticeship he studied art at the Newcastle School of Design. In 1852, after taking a job at the Holyrood Glass Works in Edinburgh, Brown entered the Royal Scottish Academy, then newly under the leadership of Robert Scott Lauder. In 1853, after a brief stay in London, he emigrated to the United States, where he found employment at the Brooklyn Flint Glass Company. Eventually Brown gravitated to the National Academy of Design and a full-time career in art.[2]

Brown established this career through his depiction of children—industrious waifs that the critics regarded as oversanitized but the public cherished as illustrations of the Horatio Alger myth.[3] Two of Brown's three entries in the 1889 Exposition portrayed the urban gamins who in the 1880s succeeded his earlier rural ones. Far from seeming deprived, street urchins such as those in *Morning Papers* conveyed to the viewer the ideals of the era: work, perseverance, and self-direction. At the fair the outcome of these virtues was everywhere conspicuous, not least in the accomplishments of Thomas Edison, the self-taught American hero whose incandescent light bulb helped make the 1889 Exposition the first to be illuminated at night.

The Longshoremen's Noon, Brown's third entry in the Exposition, was one of the artist's rare depictions of adult labor. Exhibited at the National Academy of Design in 1880, the picture had as its protagonists the urban counterparts of the Grand Menan fishermen that Brown painted around the same time but never expanded into compositions because such works were "received distrustfully by his old admirers."[4] Like his gamins, Brown's longshoremen were deemed too clean by the critics.[5] But he was credited for his depiction of laborers "with the different nationalities and characters well-observed and discriminated."[6] Neither writer nor painter alludes to the unstable working conditions of the period or to the tensions within a labor force in which new immigrants and blacks fared less well than Anglo-Saxon workers.[7] Rare in the real world of the New York docks was a contented circle enjoying a respite from labor such as Brown presents.

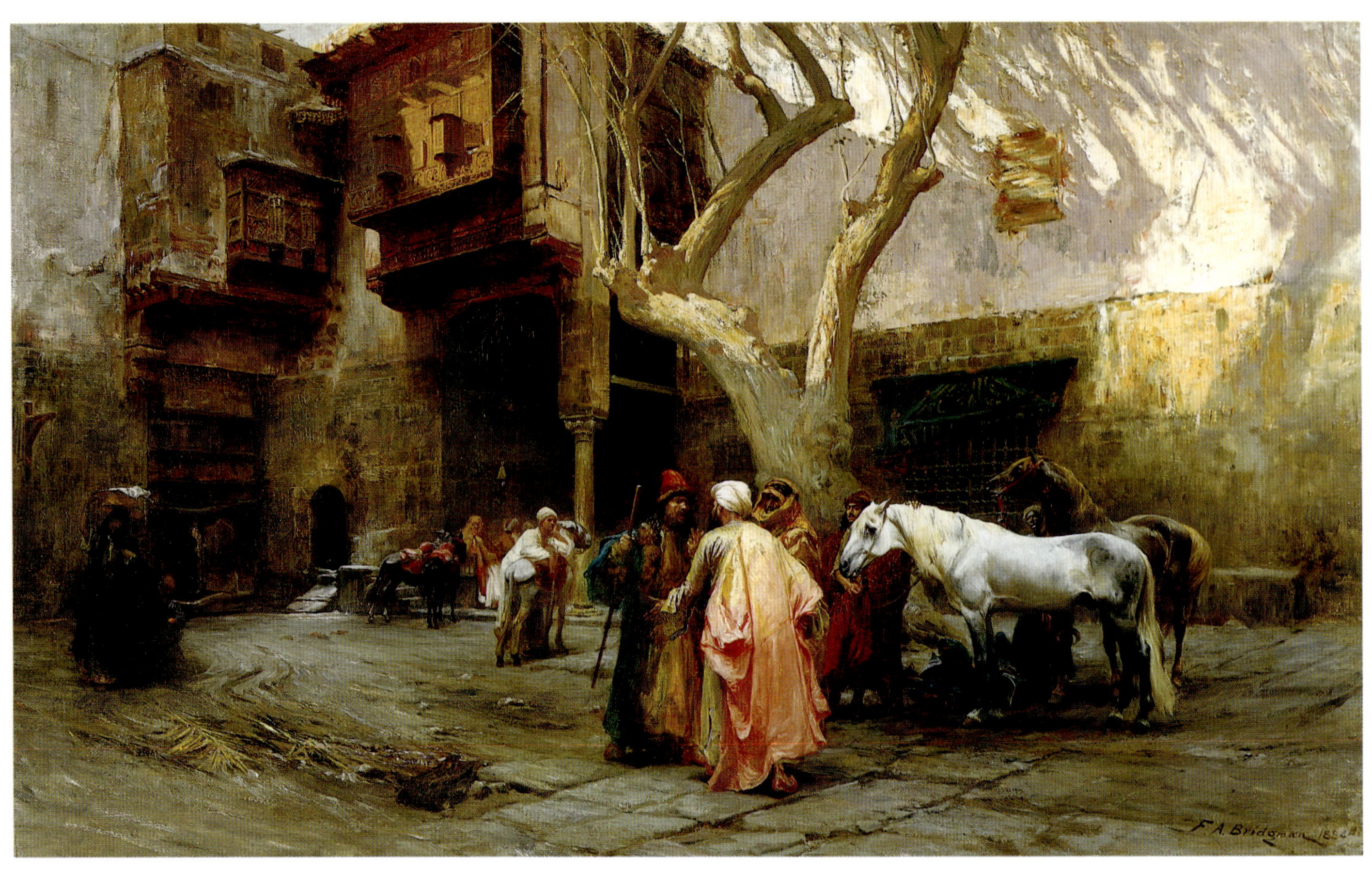

32.
Frederick Arthur Bridgman
Horse Market at Cairo
Hot Bargain, Cairo, 1884
Oil on canvas, 33 x 52" (83.8 x 132.1 cm)
Union League Club of Chicago

Like most of Brown's pictures, *Morning Papers* and *The Longshoremen's Noon* were affirmations of the "American way." In 1889, the latter picture was owned by self-made businessman William T. Evans, who lent at least seven other pictures to the Exposition.[8] For this gesture, the collector was cited by the press for his public-spiritedness and patriotism.[9] A year after the Exposition, Evans decided to sell off his European works in order to concentrate solely on pictures by Americans. Whether or not this decision was prompted by the response to his participation in the 1889 fair is unclear, but it was a further boon to American art at the end of the century. JH

HOWARD RUSSELL BUTLER (1856–1934)

Few artists were more aware of the uncertainties of earning a livelihood by painting than the landscapist Howard Russell Butler, who alluded to the financial limitations of a career in art several times in his unpublished autobiography. However, as the art historian Samuel Isham noted, Butler was an artist who "triumphantly refuted the idea that business capacity is incompatible with the practice of painting."[1] From the beginning, Butler placed art in the context of other pursuits. But whereas many American artists sought to expand

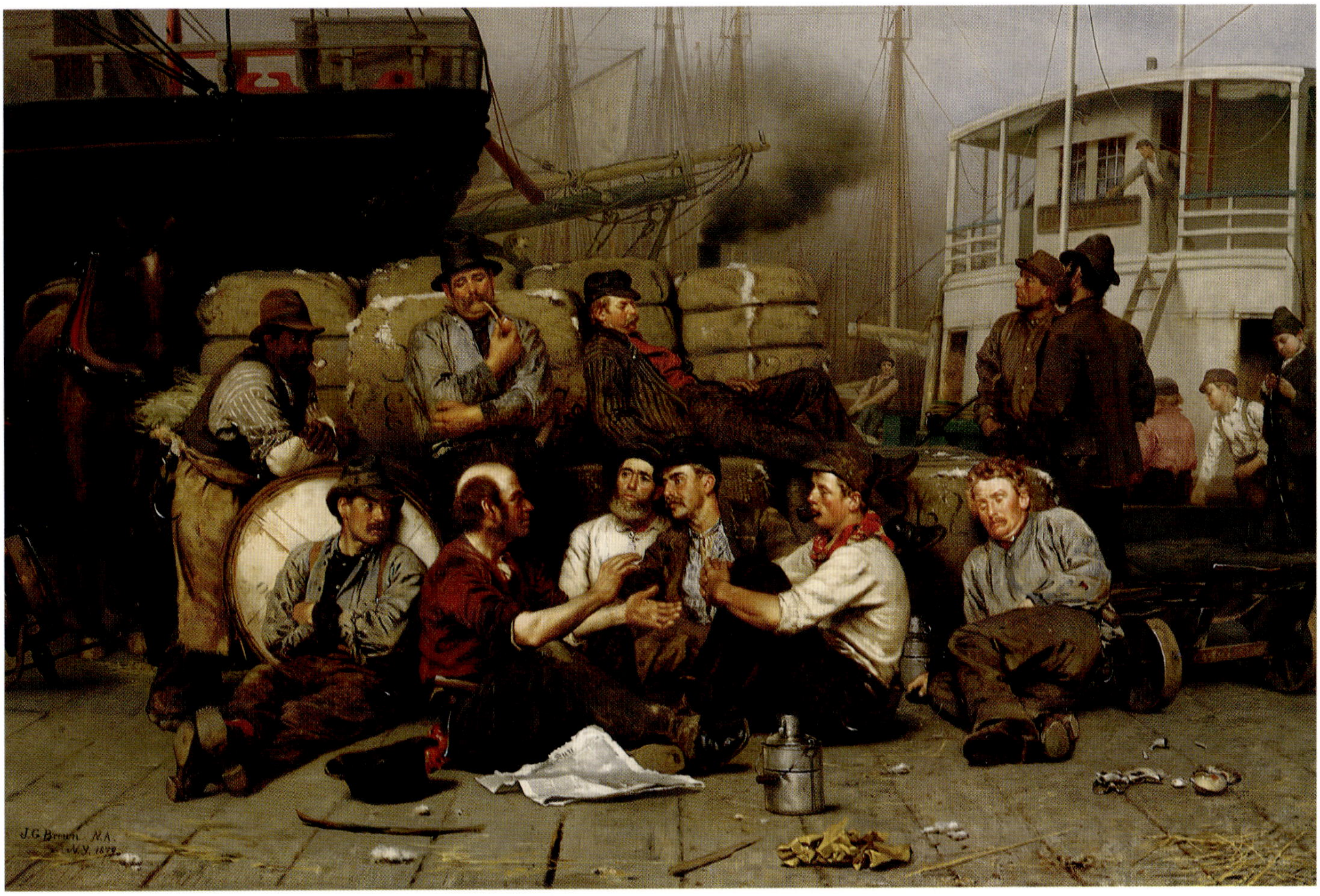

37.
John George Brown
The Longshoreman's Noon
The Longshoremen's Noon, 1879
Oil on canvas, 33¼ x 50¼″ (84.4 x 127.3 cm)
Owner in 1889 W.T. Evans
The Corcoran Gallery of Art, Washington, D.C.

39.
John George Brown
Morning Papers
Morning Papers, 1889
Oil on canvas, 39 x 36″ (97.5 x 90 cm), sight
Collection Dr. and Mrs. James E. Deitz

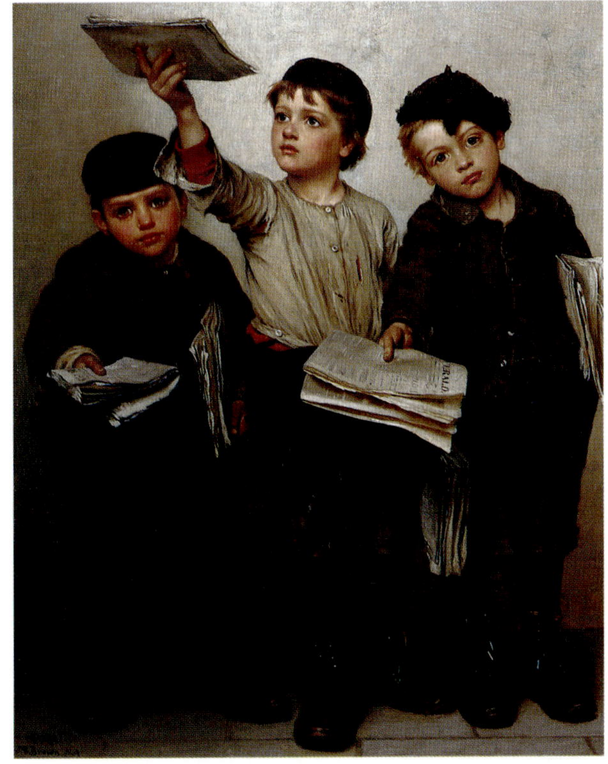

into tangential areas, he went farther afield, coupling his artistic talents with his scientific knowledge and managerial skills.

In 1876, soon after graduating from Princeton with a bachelor of science degree, Butler took part as a photographer in a geological expedition to the Rocky Mountains. In 1918, long after he was established as an artist, he would undertake a similar venture in order to paint a total eclipse of the sun. In the late 1870s and in the early 1880s, particularly after earning a law degree from Columbia University in 1882, Butler was involved in the legislating and marketing of American scientific inventions. A highly energetic individual, Butler immersed himself in diverse projects throughout his life; one closer to art was his involvement, in the late 1880s, in the organization of the American Fine Arts Society.[2] In the mid-1880s, art began to dominate Butler's focus. In 1884 he traveled to Mexico with Frederic E. Church, a rather unusual association in view of the fact that by this date the Hudson River School aesthetic was old-fashioned. Possibly aware of this, Butler then went to France, in 1885, staying for two years and sampling a variety of teachers, including Dagnan-Bouveret and Alfred-Philippe Roll.

An independent type, Butler was perhaps more in search of mentors than of teachers. Of his association with Church, Butler said years later, "He had taught me very little practically, but he had opened my eyes to possibilities in the development of my own future."[3] It was undoubtedly in this spirit that Butler sought out Alexander Harrison in Brittany. In the company of this expatriate American, Butler painted *The Seaweed Gatherers*, a large peasant scene. Harrison, known for his twilight pictures, may have influenced the soft coloring of Butler's panoramic canvas. In any case, Butler would go on to use his own scientific resources to expound color in a highly technical treatise, "Hints on a Method for Outdoor Painting."[4] Painted only two years after he had decided to become a professional artist, *The Seaweed Gatherers*, which received an honorable mention at the 1886 Salon and a Temple Silver Medal at the Pennsylvania Academy of the Fine Arts in 1888, was obviously a picture that Butler was proud of. In addition to submitting it to the 1889 Paris Exposition, where he also showed two other paintings, Butler exhibited the picture at Chicago in 1893.

The Seaweed Gatherers adheres to the popular European peasant motif in a fairly literal way. But in another of his 1889 entries, *Crossing the Yautepec*, the artist gave the genre a new twist by transferring it to a New World setting. The latter picture stemmed from sketches Butler drew on a second trip to Mexico, in 1887, made shortly after his return from Europe. The precise and colorful description of the picture's *vacheros*, or cowboys, in Butler's autobiography indicates that he saw these figures as picturesque subjects akin to those painted by American artists in Brittany and Normandy.[5] He replayed the theme a number of times; a large-scale *Rurales Crossing the Yautepec* (unlocated), which was exhibited at the Atlanta Exposition of 1894, Butler finally gave to that city because, in his own words, he "saw no chance of selling so large a painting."[6] An indefatigable traveler, Butler paid a visit to the 1889 Exposition. There, as scientist and artist, he must have felt encouraged both by the awards won by American science and by his own bronze medal in painting, which, he reported in his autobiography, "added to my happiness."[7] JH

William Merritt Chase showed eight pictures in the 1889 Exposition, more than any other American painter, and won a silver medal. The image of urbanity in his personal and his professional life, he had a fascinating studio in New York furnished with exotica from every era.[1] Chase's legacy as a teacher is perhaps unmatched in America: he first taught at the Art Students League, New York, in 1878, and he continued to teach there and later at many other institutions, including his own schools in New York and Shinnecock, Long Island. He was a frequent exhibitor at the National Academy and at the Society of American Artists, which he served as president, from 1880 to 1881 and from 1885 to 1895. As president, he helped choose the members of the 1889 Exposition's New York jury.

The bold brushwork and coloristic realism of the *Portrait of Mother and Child* reveal Chase's training at the Royal Academy in Munich with Karl von Piloty and the influence of Wilhelm Leibl.[2] In addition, Chase copied the old masters, especially Hals, Rembrandt, and Velázquez, on travels in Europe with Robert Blum and Frank Duveneck. By the time he returned to America, in 1878, Chase had made a name for himself with *Ready for a Ride* (Union League Club, New York), a startling black-on-black portrait. About 1888, Chase painted *Portrait of Mother and Child*, an updated application of his earlier black-on-black aesthetic; black is precisely but quietly measured against black and highlighted by a dash of white and red. The stridency of the earlier canvas has been mellowed here, in Chase's first portrait of his wife and their eldest child, Alice, which remained one of his most cherished pictures.[3] It was exhibited often, first in 1888 at the Society of American Artists, then in 1895 at the National Academy of Design, and in 1911 at the International Exposition in Rome.

At the 1889 Exposition, Chase showed two other portraits of women: *Portrait of Miss Gill* (unlocated), depicting a pupil of Chase's who also exhibited at the fair, and *Portrait of Mrs. C.*, a full-length portrait of Mrs. Marietta Benedict Cotton.[4] Mrs. Cotton is portrayed standing in a black dress against an ocher background, the composition enlivened with a pink rose on a walnut-brown table. Its tonal restriction and contrasting dashes of color are similar to those in *Portrait of Mother and Child*. Mrs. Cotton, who had come to him as a potential student, so inspired him that he begged her to model for him and painted the picture in one sitting that day. Chase believed that he had made "a vivid personality glow, speak, *live* upon the canvas."[5] The painting was shown at the National Academy (autumn 1888), and at the American Art Association (1890), before Chase gave it to the Metropolitan Museum of Art, in 1891.

Large-scale portraits with a limited palette were not uncommon at the Exposition; two by artists that Chase admired were Sargent's *Portrait of Mrs. White* and Whistler's *Arrangement in Black, # 7, Portrait of Lady Archibald Campbell* (see page 227). The three sitters are gracefully depicted—Chase's sweeter and more feminine than Sargent's and Whistler's, who are more socially and artistically sophisticated.

A City Park, painted virtually at the same time as *Portrait of Mother and Child* and *Portrait of Mrs. C.*, reveals another aspect of Chase's work. The model here may well be his wife and the setting a composite view of Central and Prospect parks.[6] With his new responsibilities as husband and father he curtailed his foreign travel, turning to Prospect Park in Brooklyn and Central Park in

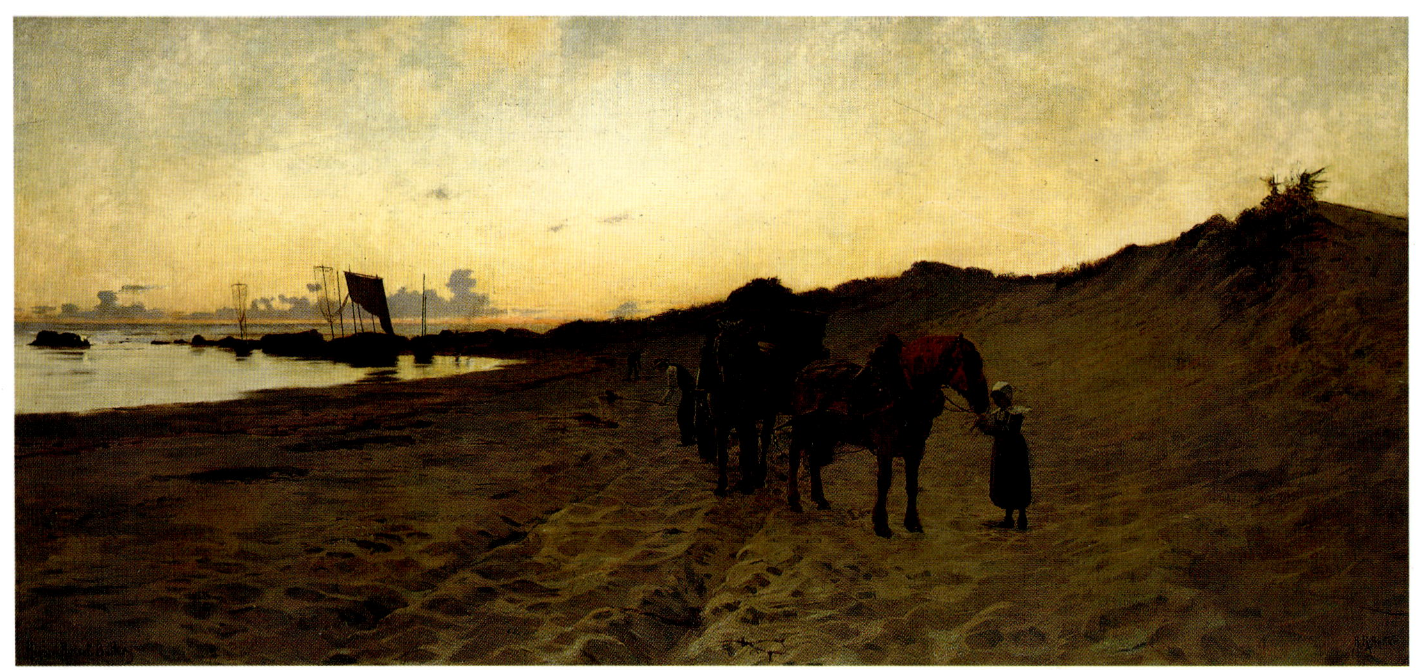

41.
Howard Russell Butler
Seaweed Gatherers
The Seaweed Gatherers, 1886
Oil on canvas, 46¾ x 96¼″ (118.7 x 244.4 cm)
National Museum of American Art,
Smithsonian Institution, Washington, D.C.,
Gift of Howard Russell Butler, Jr.

43.
Howard Russell Butler
Rurales Fording the Yantepec [*sic*]
Crossing the Yautepec, 1889
Oil on canvas, 21½ x 32″ (53.8 x 81.28 cm)
Private Collection

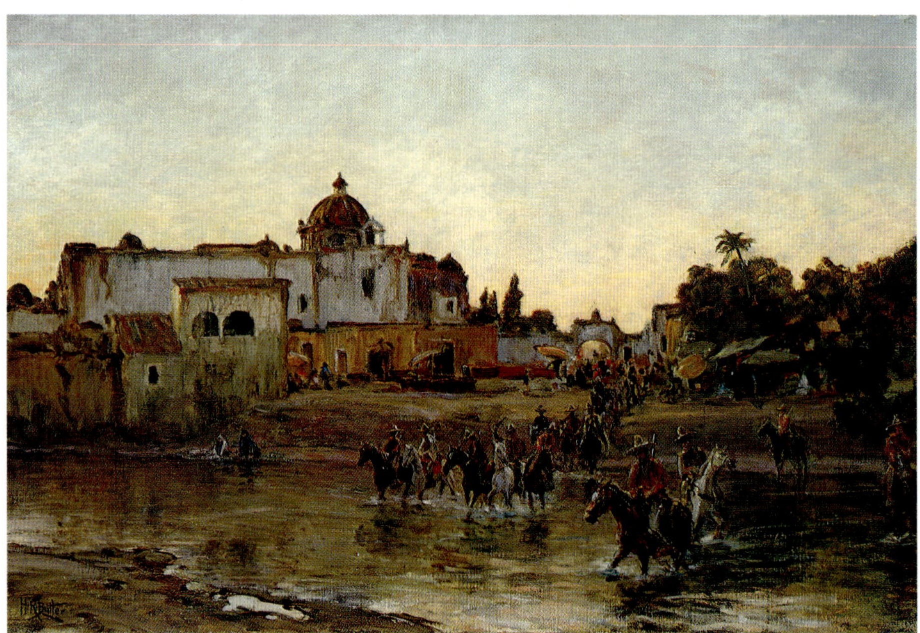

Manhattan for subjects. Between 1886 and the early 1890s he painted dozens of views of the leisure class enjoying these pleasure grounds. Critics hailed Chase for portraying ordinary city scenery and called his endeavor laudably American: other artists may "attempt to paint America through French spectacles [but Chase] has discovered Central Park."[7] Though he felt no need for foreign scenery, he realized his vision in the context of Renoir's and Degas's park views. *A City Park* appeared in 1888 at the Ninth Annual Exhibition of the Rochester Art Club.[8]

49.
William Merritt Chase
A City Park
The Park, c. 1888
Oil on canvas, 13⅝ x 19⅝" (34.6 x 49.8 cm)
© The Art Institute of Chicago,
Bequest of Dr. John J. Ireland, 1968.88

54.
William Merritt Chase
Portrait of Mother and Child
The First Portrait, c. 1888
Oil on canvas, 70⅛ x 40⅛" (178.1 x 102.0 cm)
The Museum of Fine Arts, Houston,
Gift of Ehrich Newhouse Gallery, New York

55.
William Merritt Chase
Portrait of Mrs. C.
Portrait of a Lady in Black
(Mrs. Leslie J. Cotton), 1888
Oil on canvas, 74¼ x 36$^{5}/_{16}$" (188.6 x 92.2 cm)
© The Metropolitan Museum of Art, New York,
Gift of William Merritt Chase. 91.11

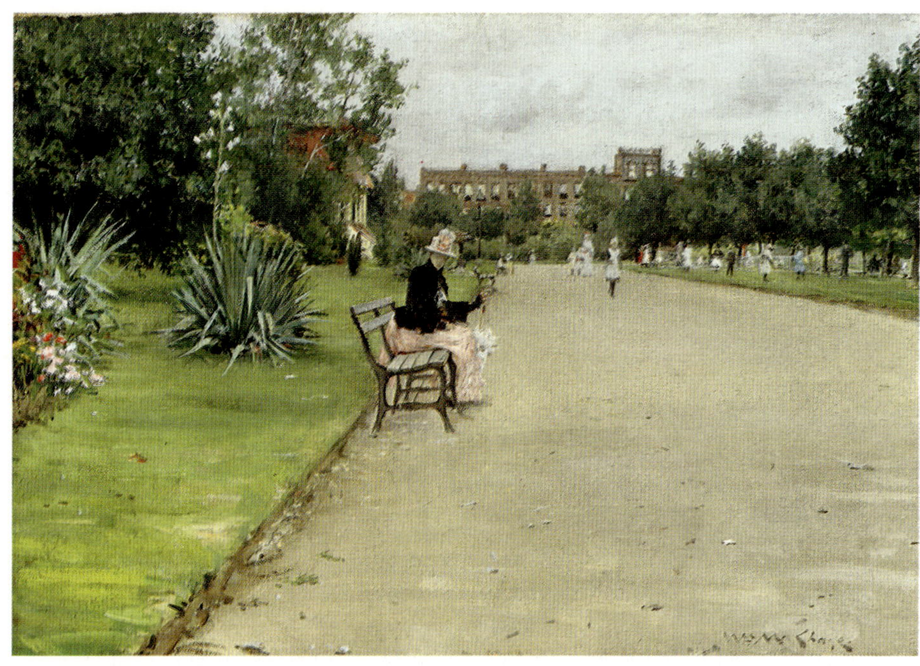

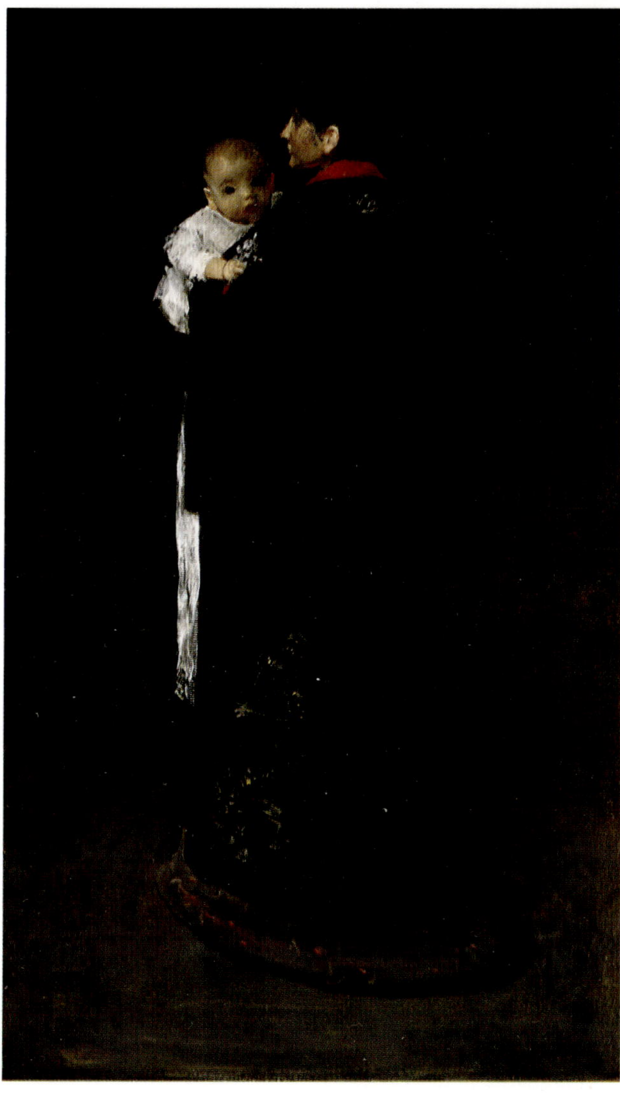

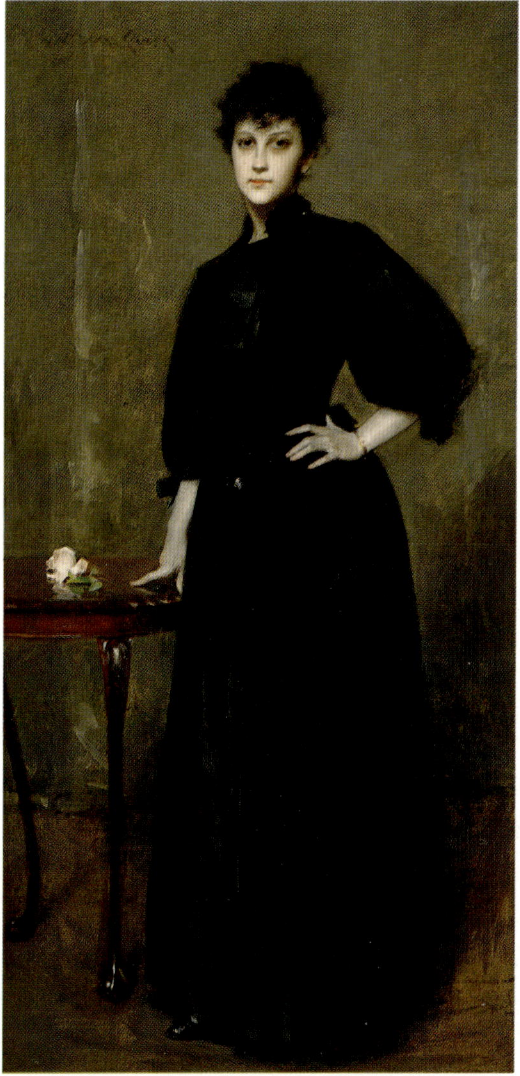

Chase's landscapes of the late 1880s and early 1890s were his first sustained attempts in a genre that would become part of his repertoire. These scenes were executed quickly, often *en plein air*. Kenyon Cox, calling them "veritable little jewels," said, "They are far and away the best things Mr. Chase has yet done. . . . they are perfection in their way and could not be improved upon."[9] Chase exhibited four other landscapes, all views in and around New York, at the 1889 Exposition: *Stoneyard*, *A Bit of Long Island*, and *Gowanus Bay* (all unlocated) and *Peace* (St. Louis Art Museum). Chase delighted in rendering the visual appeal of everyday sites, claiming: "If you want to know of good places to sketch in the vicinity of New York . . . I think I could easier tell you where they are not than where they are."[10] KZ

JOSEPH FOXCROFT COLE (1837–1892)

J. Foxcroft Cole was one of the leading landscape painters in the Boston area during the second half of the nineteenth century; he was also an important arbiter of taste instrumental in popularizing the French Barbizon style in America. Born in Jay, Maine, Cole began his career as a draftsman in two Boston lithographic firms: John Bufford's, where he and fellow employee Winslow Homer became friends, and Louis Prang's.[1] Even before he went to Paris, in 1860, Cole was familiar with French painting through his friend William Morris Hunt and through the Barbizon pictures exhibited at the Boston Athenaeum during the 1850s. Once in Paris, Cole came under the influence of Emile-Charles Lambinet, a landscapist who specialized in loosely painted rural subjects. He also studied the great European collections and copied a number of the seventeenth-century Dutch pictures in the Louvre.[2] From 1863 until his death he exhibited intermittently at the National Academy of Design. Cole returned to Boston in 1864 and established a studio in the Mercantile Library Building. During his second trip to Paris, in 1865, his mentor was Charles-Emile Jacque, an artist renowned for his farmyard scenes. In Jacque's studio, Cole had frequent contacts with Barbizon painters Corot, Charles-François Daubigny, and Constant Troyon.[3] For the next twelve years Cole divided his time between Boston and Paris, exhibiting at the Salon in 1866, 1867, and from 1873 to 1875; at the Society of American Artists, where he was made a member in 1880; and at the Royal Academy, London, in 1876 and 1877. By 1877 he had settled in Winchester, Massachusetts, where he remained for the rest of his life except for trips to California, France, and the Netherlands.

The Aberjona River, Winchester, painted near Cole's home on Mystic Lake, testifies in its poetic beauty to his appreciation of this picturesque area, as do the many other paintings of the region. As his friend and fellow artist Frederic Porter Vinton observed, "Through all his wanderings his love for the rugged hillsides of New England never grew cold."[4] In this work, the reflection of the delicate pinks of the sky in the waters of the river make the two elements appear as one, separated only by the horizon and the narrow bridge. Characteristically, Cole combines a New England locale with a style derived from French Barbizon art. When Henry James reviewed Cole's 1872 exhibition at Doll and Richards in Boston, he stressed Cole's European training. Referring to Cole's paintings, he wrote, "They are indeed themselves foreign works; and if we had not been otherwise informed, we should have taken them all for the produce of a French studio."[5] The luminous pinks and yellows in the sky of *The Aberjona River* indicate Cole's awareness of French Impressionism. As early as the 1870s his palette begins to lighten and by the 1890s the "influence of Claude Monet and the Impressionists is distinctly marked."[6] One of Cole's most renowned pictures, *The Aberjona River* has been frequently exhibited and reproduced. When it was shown in 1883 at the American Art Galleries, the *Art Amateur* described it as "a well and solidly painted work throughout."[7] Although Cole was revered in Boston art circles during the 1880s, he was represented only by this work at the 1889 Exposition. It is intriguing to speculate as to whether he limited himself to this one painting or whether the jury, composed almost entirely of New York artists, was not aware of Cole's standing in Boston.[8] *The Aberjona River* was shown at the St. Botolph Club in Boston in 1893 and the following year in the Cole memorial exhibition at the Boston Museum of Fine Arts. HPC

ALFRED BRYANT COPELAND (1839–1909)

American expatriate Alfred B. Copeland specialized in meticulous renderings of historic buildings in Antwerp and Paris. Born in 1839 into a socially prominent Boston family, he spent the early years of his career designing machinery for making artificial limbs for disabled Civil War veterans.[1] Copeland probably painted some New England landscapes in the early 1860s; his *Falling Leaves* (unlocated), a view of the Maine woods, was for sale at the Athenaeum Gallery (later the Boston Athenaeum) from 1867 to 1870.[2] In 1866 he went to Antwerp to study at the Royal Academy, where he may have met Frank Millet, who, along with Frederick Porter Vinton, was said to be among his friends. While in Antwerp, Copeland copied paintings by Rubens and made studies of the interiors of the Old Stein prison and several churches. Returning to Boston about 1872, he exhibited his copies and studies at the Boston Art Club (1873) and at the Massachusetts Charitable Mechanics Association (1874).[3] His copies after Gilbert Stuart's famous portraits of George and Martha Washington (unlocated) may date from this period.[4] From 1873 to 1874 Copeland was second professor of drawing in the department of polytechnics at Washington University in St. Louis.[5]

In 1875, Copeland went to Paris for further study, but it is not known where he studied or with whom.[6] His Antwerp interiors were seen at the Paris Salons of 1877, 1878, 1880, and 1881. The drawing *Outward Bound* (unlocated) was shown at the 1878 Paris Exposition.[7] Some scenes of Paris, among them detailed views of the Seine from his window, with the Pont Neuf, the Louvre, and Notre Dame, were well received when shown in Boston in 1879.[8] Copeland probably also worked from photographs, since there was a "chemical laboratory," or darkroom, in his Paris studio; an album of the artist's photographs contains pictures of his studio, showing his library, classical statues, picture gallery, and darkroom.[9] Copeland's *Corner of My Studio* (unlocated), shown at the Salon of 1884, exemplifies a genre that was popular with artists in Europe and America in the 1880s, among them William Merritt Chase.[10]

For the Pennsylvania Academy of the Fine Arts "Special Exhibition of Paintings by American Artists at Home and in Europe" in 1881, two of Copeland's paintings were chosen by a Paris jury that included Frederick A. Bridgman, Daniel Ridgway Knight, Charles Sprague Pearce, John Singer Sargent, and Edwin Lord Weeks, who were also active in the 1889 Exposition. In 1882 Copeland showed two paintings in the Pennsylvania Academy's 53rd

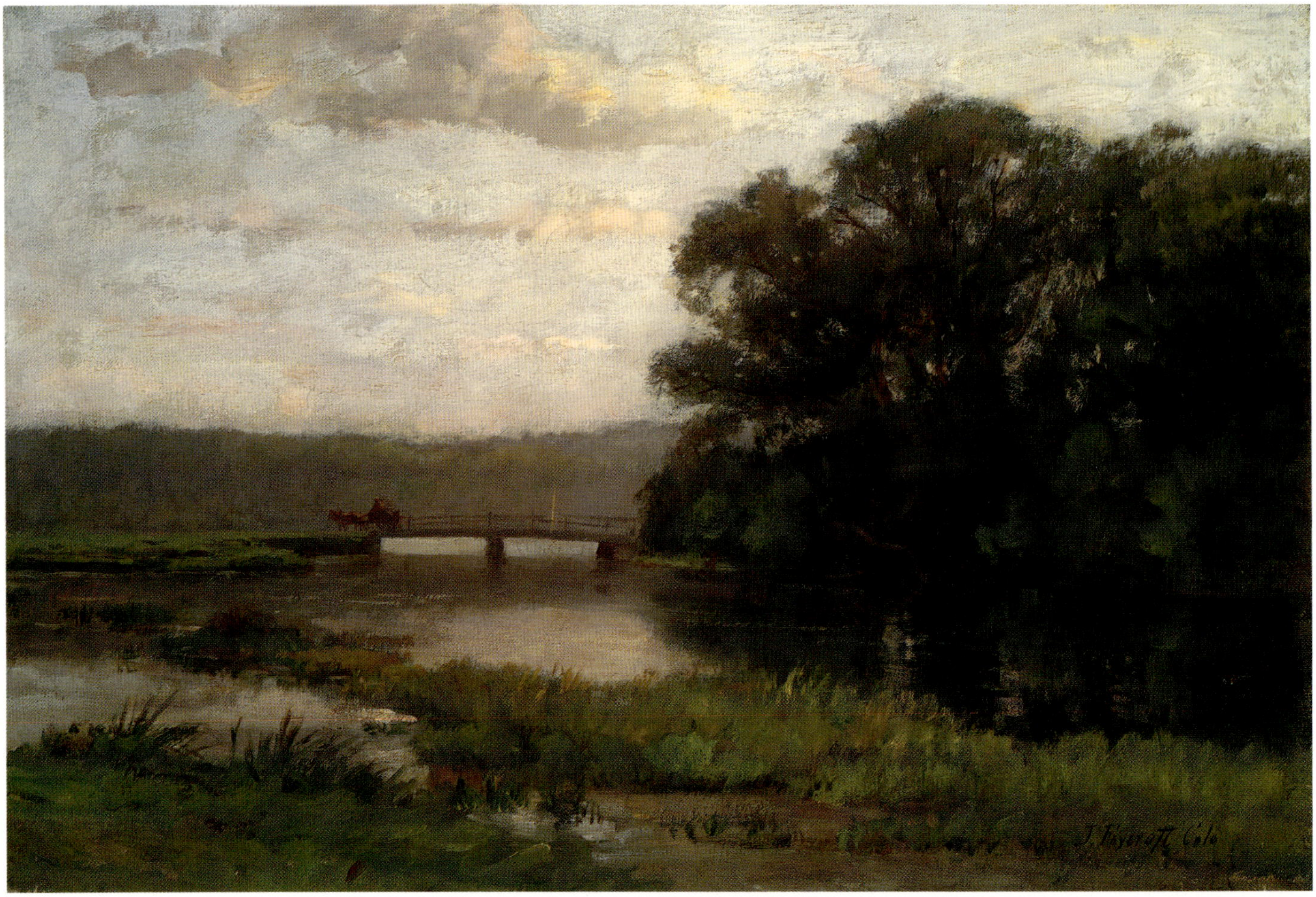

61.
Joseph Foxcroft Cole
Abbajona River, Mass.
The Aberjona River, Winchester, c. 1880
Oil on canvas, 18¼ x 26" (46 x 66 cm)
Museum of Fine Arts, Boston,
Gift of Alexander Cochrane

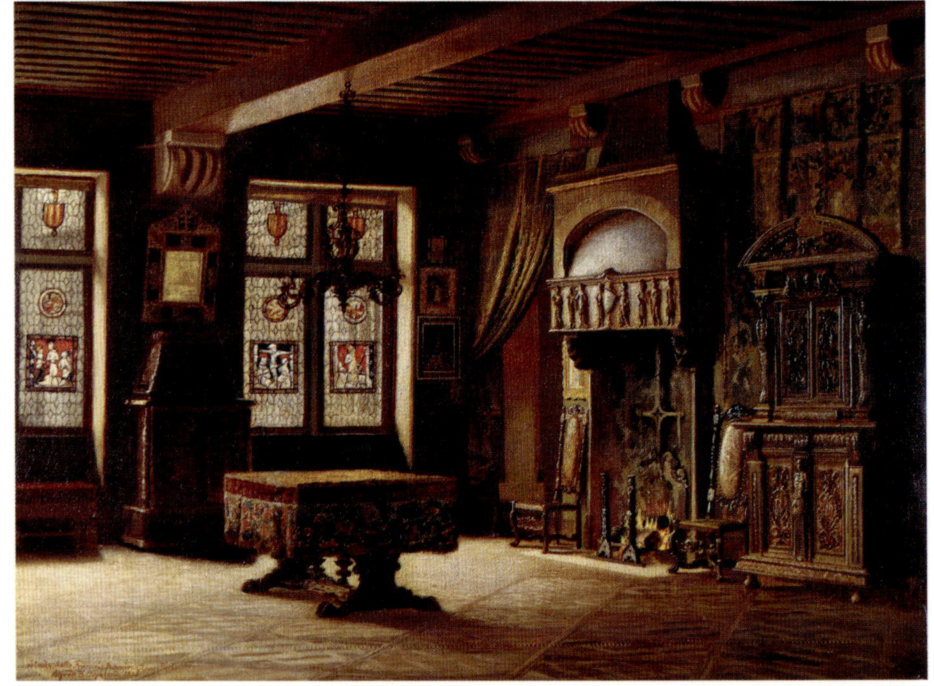

62.
Alfred Bryant Copeland
Salle François Ier, Cluny Museum
Study, Salle François Premier, Cluny, Paris, 1885
Oil on canvas, 16⅞ x 22¼" (41.2 x 56.1 cm)
Alexander R. Raydon, Raydon Gallery, New York

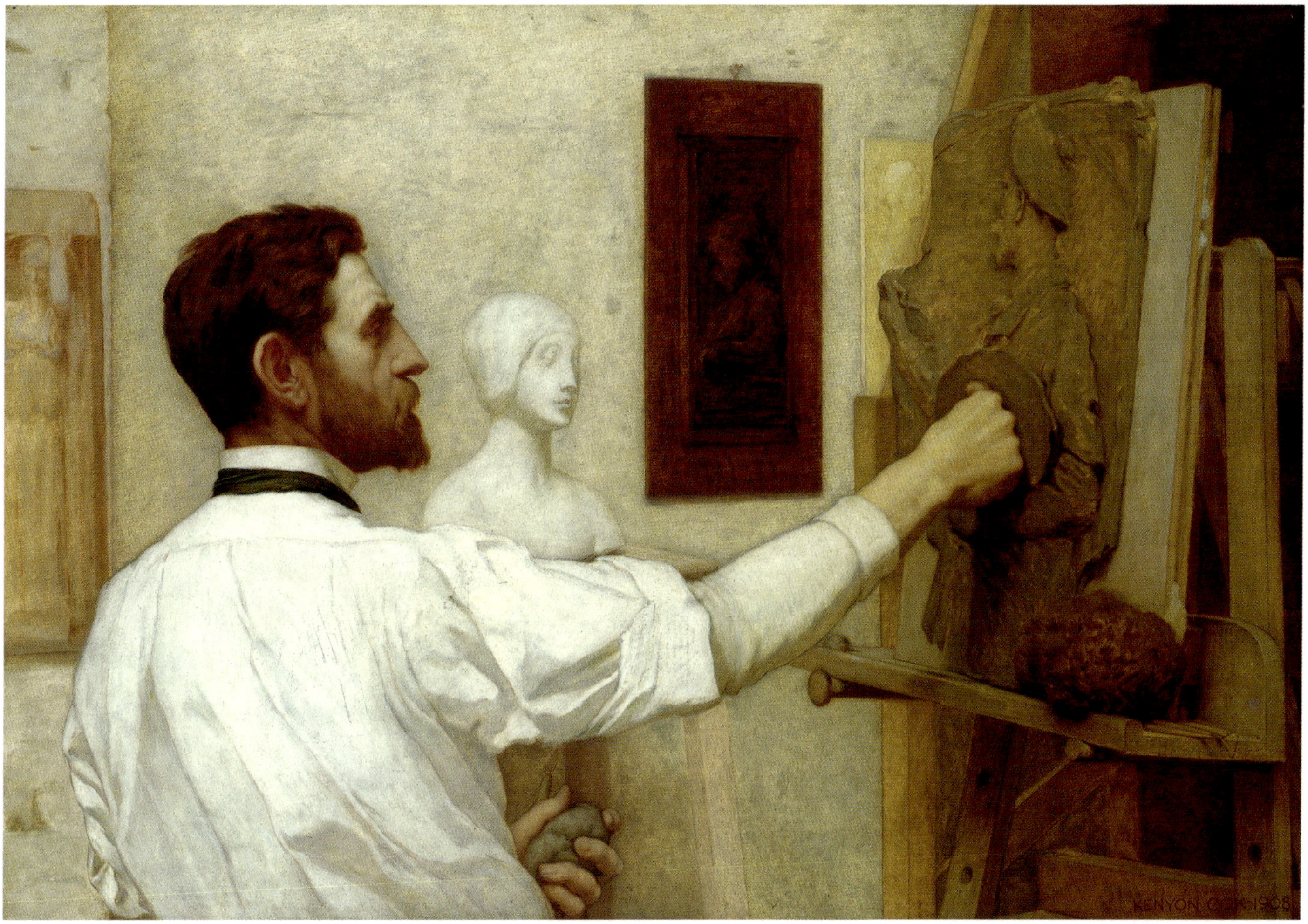

66.
Kenyon Cox
Portrait of Augustus Saint-Gaudens
Augustus Saint-Gaudens (original 1887, replica 1908)
Oil on canvas, 33½ x 46⅞″ (85.1 x 119.7 cm)
Owner in 1889 A. Saint-Gaudens
© The Metropolitan Museum of Art, New York, Gift of friends of the sculptor, through August F. Jaccaci. 08.130

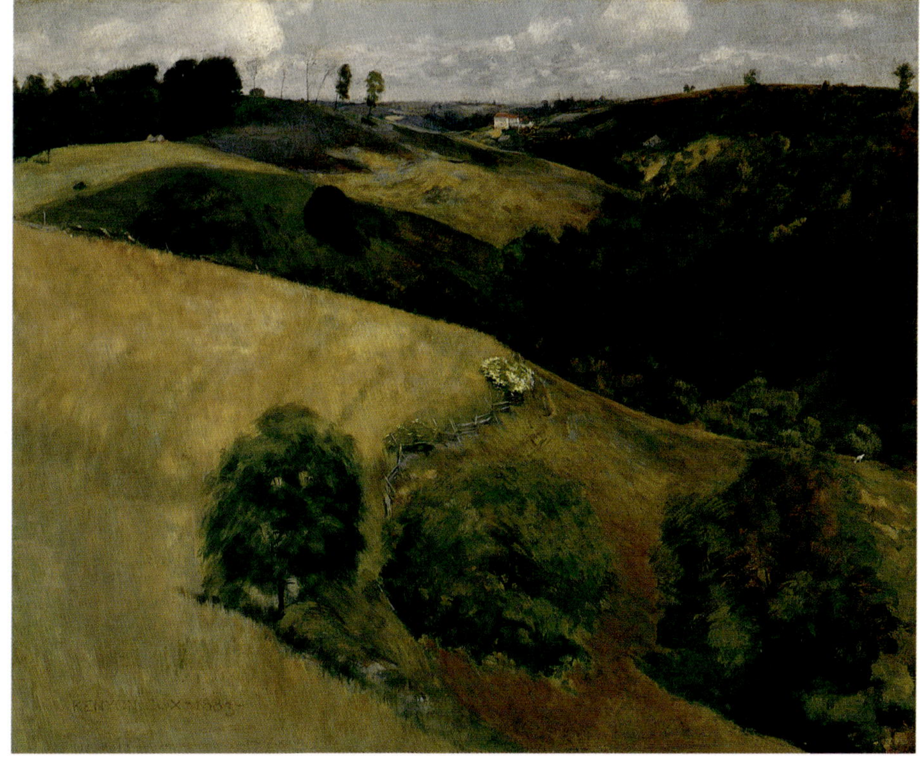

67.
Kenyon Cox
Flying Shadows
Flying Shadows, 1883
Oil on canvas, 30 x 36¼″ (76.2 x 91.7 cm)
The Corcoran Gallery of Art, Washington, D.C.

annual exhibition. While in Paris, Copeland made copies at the Louvre and the Luxembourg, including two of Alexandre Cabanel's *Birth of Venus*.[11] Forty-five copies were in his estate at his death. He apparently had a "remarkable capacity for reproducing the spirit and form of the originals."[12]

Study, Salle François Premier, Cluny, Paris is one of the two paintings of interiors that Copeland submitted to the 1889 Exposition. He made at least three studies, as he called his highly detailed renderings, of this room in the Cluny Museum.[13] He also painted a corridor and a garden, and copied some paintings in the Cluny. In this study, the only one from his Cluny series known to be extant, Copeland created one of his "marvels of close and studious application and observation."[14]

In 1896, Copeland returned to Boston, where he lived until his death, in 1909. An auction of his estate, presumably most of his life's work, included 178 original paintings—New England, French, and English landscapes, human and animal figures, and interiors—many copies, and 17 paintings by Europeans and Americans such as Mark Fisher and Antwerp-trained John Henry Dolph, both of whom were represented in the 1889 Exposition.[15] SJ-G

KENYON COX (1856–1919)

At the time of the 1889 Exposition, Kenyon Cox was one of the best-known figures in the American art world. In addition to producing works in several mediums, Cox addressed a broad range of artistic and philosophical subjects in his writings.

Cox grew up in an intellectual environment which apparently sustained him despite a childhood illness that disrupted his early education. He first studied art at the McMicken School of Design in Cincinnati. Leaving his home state in 1876, Cox spent a year at the Pennsylvania Academy of the Fine Arts before leaving for Paris, where he stayed for five years, between 1877 and 1882. Cox's French training was particularly diversified: a year in the studio of the portraitist Carolus-Duran; further training in drawing at the Ecole des Beaux-Arts under Cabanel; three years in the studio of Gérôme. Although he considered Gérôme the dominant influence on his development, he continued with other masters, studying also at the Académie Julian with Bouguereau, Lefebvre, Boulanger, and others.[1] Cox's experience highlights the fact that American artists went abroad for training, not for apprenticeship in a particular method.

While in France, Cox had exhibited at the Paris Salon. Upon his return to the United States, in 1882, he became a member of the Society of American Artists, and this organization was his main forum for exhibiting from the mid-1880s to the late 1890s. Nevertheless, he also showed work simultaneously at the National Academy of Design, which elected him an associate in 1900 and an Academician in 1903.

As a writer, Cox espoused artists as different as Veronese and Winslow Homer (on whom he wrote a monograph, one of the first on Homer). A similar catholicity marked Cox's painting, whose subject matter ranged from ideal themes to landscapes and portraits. Yet despite this broad span, it is simplistic to term Cox eclectic. Underlying his philosophy and practice of art were coherent ideas about meaning, form, and clarity of expression. Disenchanted with the literal transcription of the subject that characterized nineteenth-century naturalism, Cox sought certain underlying principles that linked all art, regardless of subject or century.[2]

The subjects that Cox sent to Paris were characteristically varied. *Painting and Poetry* and *Jacob Wrestling with the Angel* (both unlocated) were on ideal themes, anticipating his mural painting at the World's Columbian Exposition at Chicago in 1893. *Flying Shadows* and the *Portrait of Augustus Saint-Gaudens* were contemporary subjects not usually associated with Cox. All his 1889 entries had previously been exhibited at the Society of American Artists, and three would be exhibited again at Chicago in 1893. Cox was awarded prizes both in Paris (where he won two bronze medals, one for painting and one for his black-and-white drawings), and in Chicago.

Cox's homage to his friend Augustus Saint-Gaudens was among his most highly admired works, praised not only for its likeness as a portrait but also for its artful conception.[3] The original, owned by Saint-Gaudens, was destroyed in the fire in his studio in 1904; it was replaced by a replica that Cox painted in 1908. The picture's motif, the artist in his studio, was one of general interest to American painters during the 1880s, but most painters explored the subject's decorative aspect; Cox's rendition was more innovative, both in conception and in execution. Not only did he show Saint-Gaudens at work; he actually closed in on the sculptural process.

The artist depicted Saint-Gaudens close up, completing a relief of William Merritt Chase, and surrounded by other art works of direct significance to the sculptor.[4] One, a female bust in the background, makes a statement about the shared interests of Saint-Gaudens and Cox. Identified as a replica of a Renaissance bust in the Louvre, it alludes to Saint-Gaudens's muse, classical art.[5] Placed pregnantly between Saint-Gaudens and his work in progress, it connects the two while commenting on Cox's own conception of the artistic process as more than the direct transcription of subject.

Cox's ideas about art also pervade *Flying Shadows*, a landscape remarkably similar to J. Alden Weir's *Lengthening Shadows* (see page 226). In addition to having in common a high horizon and spare elements, both landscapes were painted at sites the artists knew well. *Flying Shadows*, painted in 1883, shortly after Cox returned from France, was painted along the banks of the Ohio River. According to a contemporary reviewer, the artist's familiarity with his subject infused the picture with a special feeling, absent from the usual American expatriate artist's transcription of French nature.[6] In addition, despite affinities with other contemporary landscapes, *Flying Shadows* has the compositional clarity and simplicity that Cox saw as attributes of good art and that are underlying features uniting all his works, regardless of subject matter. JH

RALPH WORMELEY CURTIS (1854–1922)

Ralph Wormeley Curtis, the son of Daniel Sargent Curtis and Ariana Wormeley Randolf Curtis, was born in Boston.[1] He was educated at Harvard College, where he was a cofounder, with classmates John T. and Edmund M. Wheelwright, of the *Lampoon*. In 1878, Curtis's parents rented, and later purchased, the Palazzo Barbaro on the Grand Canal, Venice, which soon became a gathering place for English and American artists and writers and was frequently visited by Bostonians Henry James and Isabella Stewart Gardner.[2]

After graduation from Harvard, in 1876, Curtis joined his family in Europe and took up residence in Paris, where he studied at the Académie Julian under Gustave Boulanger and Jules-Joseph Lefebvre.[3] He also entered the

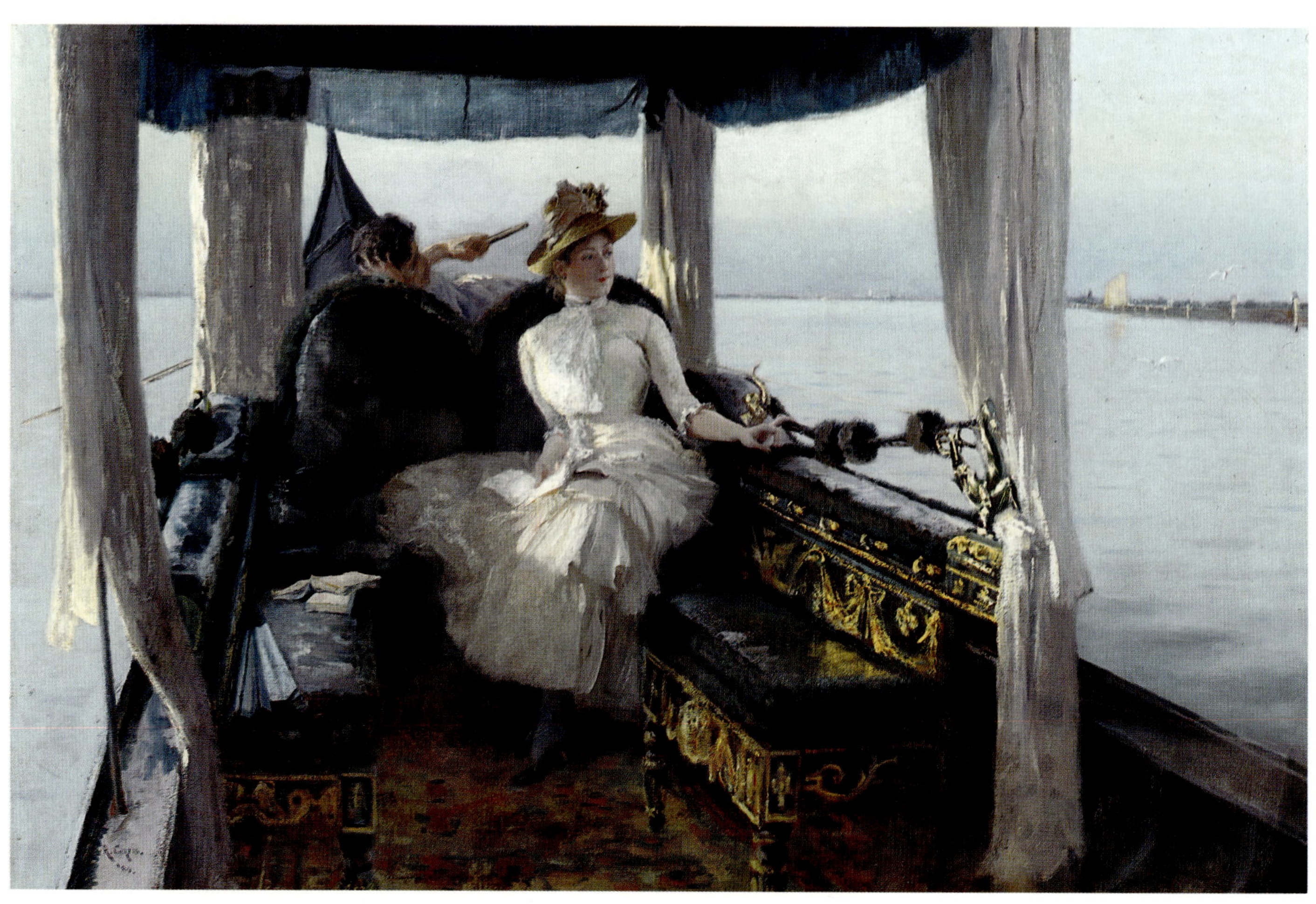

68.
Ralph Wormeley Curtis
View at Venice
Drifting on the Lagoon, 1884
Oil on canvas, 25½ x 37½" (64 x 94.5 cm)
Private Collection
Courtesy Richard York Gallery, New York

widening circle of Americans who studied under Carolus-Duran, and he became close friends with his distant cousin John Singer Sargent, who was a member of the circle. Curtis's first submission to the Salon was in 1881, when he sent a painting entitled *Venise*. During the following years he was often represented at the Salon by views of Venice and by contemporary genre scenes.[4]

In 1880, Curtis and Sargent made a sketching trip to Holland, and later they were reunited in Venice, where Curtis and his colleagues Charles Stuart Forbes, Julian Story, and Harper Pennington all attempted uncommissioned portraits of the poet Robert Browning.[5] Venice had become a mecca for American artists in 1880, attracting those on leave from ateliers in Paris as well as those from Florence and Munich. From Curtis's vantage point, the Palazzo Barbaro, Venice was a crossroads of art and society. It is thus not surprising that he remained abroad after completing his training in Paris, spending his summers in Venice.

Curtis spent the winter of 1884 in Paris and was on hand to commiserate with Sargent over the scandal caused by his *Portrait of Madame X* at the spring Salon. After he extracted a promise from Sargent to meet in Seville in November to sketch the Spanish "tobacco girls," he departed for Venice again to pass the summer months painting the sparkling waterways and their visitors.[6] *Drifting on the Lagoon* may have been the *Vue à Venise* that won Curtis an honorable mention

77.
William Turner Dannat
A study in red
La Femme en rouge, 1889
Oil on canvas, 83⅞ x 40″ (213 x 104 cm)

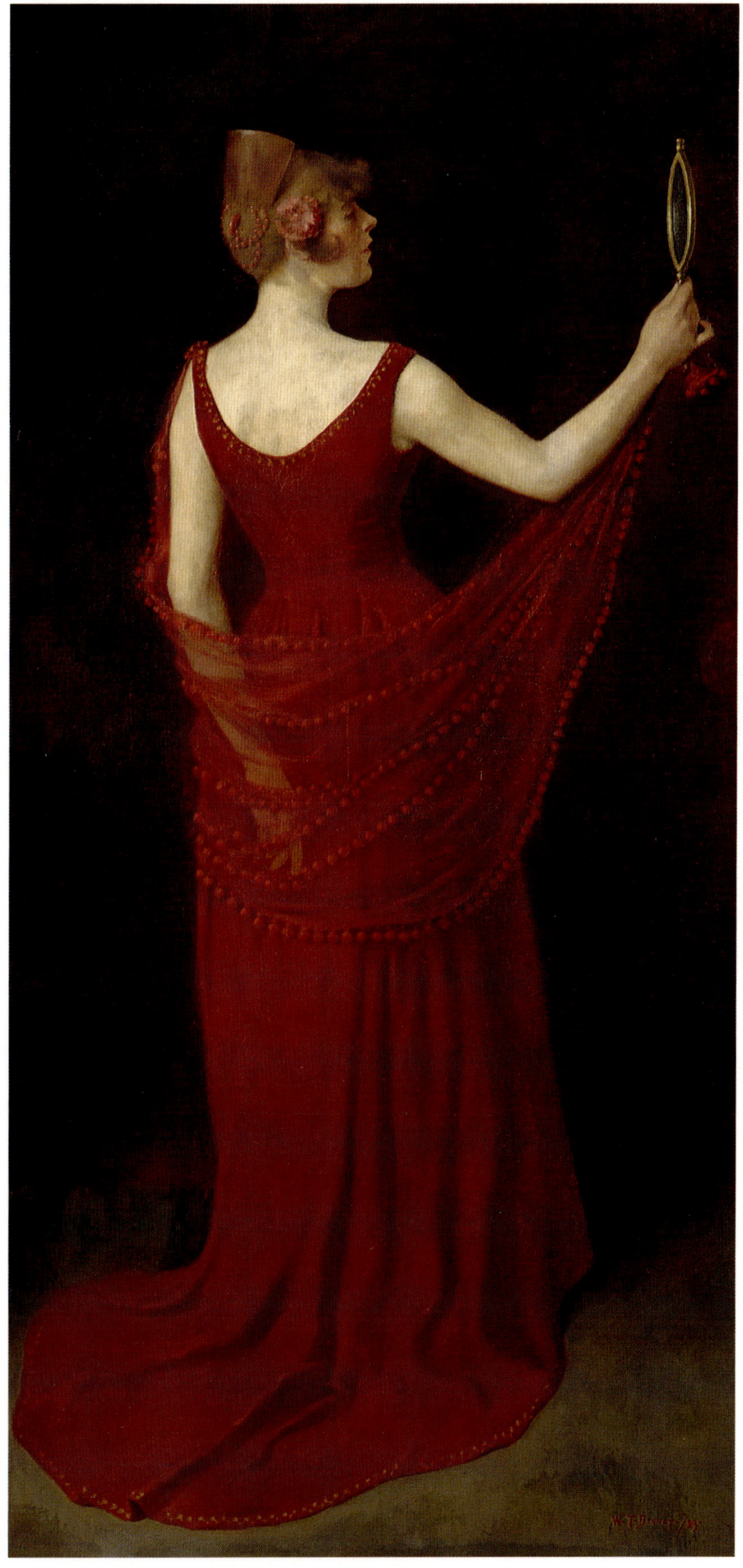

at the 1889 Exposition.[7] One of a series of Venetian scenes painted in the mid-1880s, it portrays a young woman seated in a handsomely appointed gondola, dreamily listening to a languorous gondolier. As contemporary genre the painting can be compared with the work of Giuseppe de Nittis and Giovanni Boldini, Italian artists who were much acclaimed in Paris in the 1870s and 1880s. There may also be a reference to the plein-air flirtation in Manet's *Chez Père Lathuille*.[8] Curtis made full use of his talent in documenting the attractive scenes of modern life that were always within reach in Venice. *Drifting on the Lagoon* shows a mastery of the effects of light on water, an internalization of French paint handling, and an illustrator's accurate draftsmanship, refined by Parisian training. MCOB

WILLIAM TURNER DANNAT (1853–1929)

William Turner Dannat, an American artist highly acclaimed during the last quarter of the nineteenth century, was born in New York to wealthy parents and taken abroad at the age of twelve. He studied architecture in Hanover and Stuttgart before enrolling in the art academies of Florence and Munich.[1] In the winter of 1877–78 Dannat returned briefly to New York, where he showed two works in the first exhibition of the Society of American Artists. In 1879 he went back to Paris and studied under Carolus-Duran and Mihály Munkácsy. Munkácsy's style, with its forceful realism and debt to Spanish painting, profoundly influenced Dannat's art during the early 1880s; it is noteworthy that in the official catalogue of the 1889 Exposition Dannat listed Munkácsy as his only master. In 1881, Dannat was elected to the Society of American Artists; he became one of its regular exhibitors. He showed at the National Academy of Design only in 1888 and 1904, revealing his preference for the more avant-garde group. Dannat received major recognition in 1883, when the French government purchased his *Le Contrebandier aragonais* (Musée d'Orsay, Paris) from the Salon.[2] From 1886 to 1889, Dannat did not exhibit at the Salon, apparently while working out a transitional stylistic phase, but he remained active in artistic circles, as evidenced by his appointment as secretary of the international art jury of the 1889 Exposition. A second major break in Dannat's exhibition schedule occurred in 1896, when he began an eight-year investigation into the painting techniques of the old masters, conducted with "the aid of rasping tools and of solvents."[3] Dannat, being independently wealthy, was free to paint for his own satisfaction and to experiment with a variety of pictorial styles. His late works were imaginary landscapes that recall rococo *fêtes galantes*.[4] In 1889 Dannat was named a Chevalier and in 1900 an Officier of the Legion of Honor. He was also president of the Paris Society of American Painters and taught at the Ecole des Beaux-Arts.[5] Dannat died in Monte Carlo.

Dannat demonstrated his versatility at the 1889 Exposition by exhibiting six paintings. *The Quartette*, to which Dannat referred as "my most notable picture,"[6] was singled out for high praise. "It occupied the place of honor in the United States section," wrote the well-known American art critic Theodore Child, who was also a close friend of Dannat's, "and [was] one of the most striking and . . . most completely successful works of the kind in the entire exhibition."[7] Together with *A Sacristy in Aragon* (unlocated; formerly at the Art Institute of Chicago) it represented Dannat's Spanish style of the early and middle 1880s. During this period, Dannat made several sketching tours of

Spain, inspired by the teachings of Carolus-Duran and Munkácsy, who helped to foster Dannat's profound appreciation of Spanish art. By 1889, the year *La Femme en rouge* was painted, Dannat's technique and subject matter had changed radically from his earlier Spanish style. The French art critic André Michel astutely differentiated between these two periods when he reviewed Dannat's entries in the Exposition: "'A Quartette' and 'A Sacristy in Aragon' are in his first manner, less self-contained, less subtle; but we admire in them at once a rare delicacy of eye, and his individuality is clearly written. The profile of the blonde in 'A Study in Red'... tone upon tone, reveals aspirations more and more refined, a great sureness of hand, and the most delicious talent."[8]

Clearly evidenced in *La Femme en rouge* is Dannat's new pictorial concern with dramatic color harmonies in a single hue. His preoccupation with feminine beauty, grace, and elegance, which began in the late 1880s, is also apparent. The erotic whiteness of the figure's arms and shoulders, her provocative décolletage, and her dramatic profile all recall Sargent's famous *Madame X* (Metropolitan Museum of Art, New York), which created a sensation at the Salon of 1884. Dannat, like Whistler, used the figure primarily as a vehicle to explore color harmonies. Although Dannat alluded to the transience of earthly beauty by including the *vanitas* emblem of a mirror, his primary interest was in pictorial relations. As Child observed, "Before we realize what the picture is, we already receive an impression of something rich, rare, and precious.... In the whole exhibition this picture stands out as something new, unlike all that we have seen—a thing of refined invention."[9] In 1890 *La Femme en rouge* was exhibited at the Royal Academy in London, and four years later it was purchased by the French government in exchange for the *Portrait of Eva Haviland*, acquired the year before. HPC

WILDER M. DARLING (1855–1933)

Wilder Darling's Dutch genre scenes are virtually unknown, and his biography can only be pieced together.[1] He was still in his teens in his native Sandusky, Ohio, when he chose an art career. He trained first in Cincinnati, perhaps at the McMicken School of Design under Henry Mosler. Sometime in the mid-1870s he went for further study to Munich, where he may have spent twelve years. It is possible that he attended the informal classes conducted by Frank Duveneck, a fellow Cincinnatian, in Munich and Polling from 1877 to 1878; he was enrolled at the Royal Academy of Munich at some time in the mid-1880s. He seems to have received training from Jean-Paul Laurens in Paris, probably at the Académie Julian. By 1887 he was at work with Henry Mosler, and a year later with Fernand Cormon, in Paris. He studied with William Merritt Chase, but it is uncertain where or when. By 1896 he had settled in Laren, a remote Dutch town popularized by The Hague School painters and adopted by many American artists as a place to live and to paint, and thereafter its villagers became Darling's primary subject. After 1902 he divided his time between Laren and Toledo, Ohio, giving up the Dutch studio only when America entered World War I. He painted in New York for two years, then settled in Toledo, where he found both patrons and pupils. Following the academic procedures he had learned in Munich and Paris, he emphasized correct draftsmanship over color and incorporated the few modern techniques he deemed worthwhile.

Darling's palette, limited to "rich monotones of red and gold and brown,"[2]

79.
Wilder M. Darling
Grandma's First Visit
Grandmother's First Visit, c. 1888
Oil on canvas, 36½ x 29¼" (92.7 x 75.6 cm)
The Toledo Club, Ohio

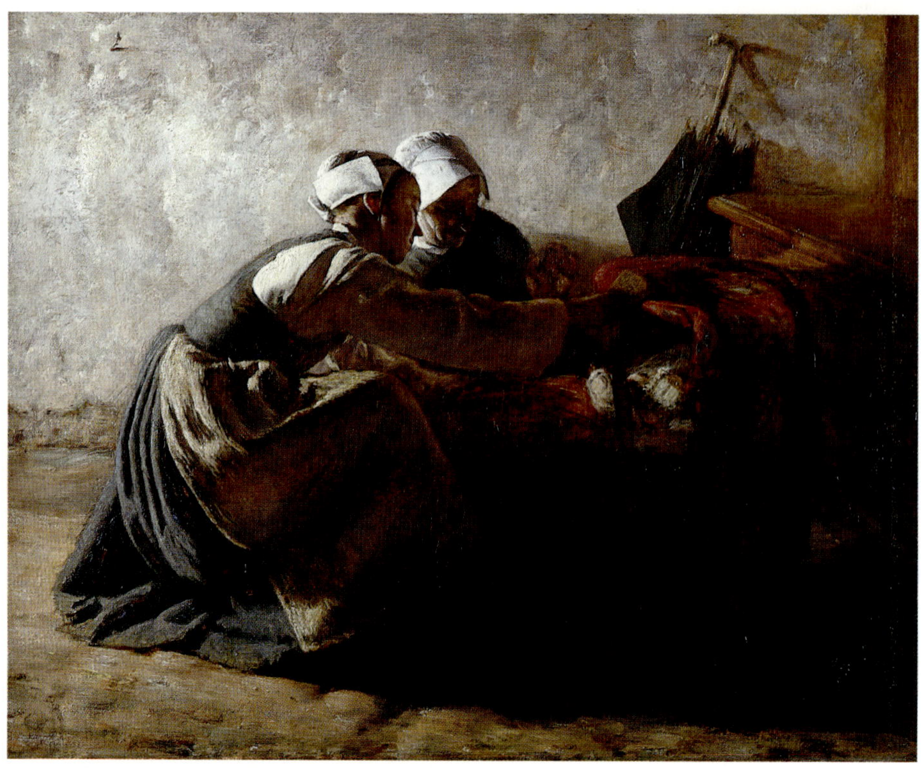

was a distillation of his diversified training. In his genre scenes of Dutch peasants, especially the household interiors of Laren, he sought to record a picturesque life-style that was fading even in villages like Laren. He maintained standards of "the inexorable old world variety,"[3] using a traditional technique to capture archetypical vignettes of a fleeting way of life.

A student of Mosler when he painted *Grandma's First Visit*, Darling may well have been influenced by Mosler's detailed Breton peasant scenes. But he used dim Rembrandtesque lighting, generalized peasant costume detail, and a limited palette of blues, buffs, and reds to simplify the scene. Darling was among many American painters who saw the peasant as a vestige of the past, unspoiled by modern civilization. He used the peasant motif to underscore the cyclical nature of life, in contrast to Daniel Ridgway Knight, whose *Hailing the Ferry* (see page 180) dwells on the peasant women's uncommon natural beauty, and to George Hitchcock, whose *Annonciation* (see page 171), like Charles Stanley Reinhart's *Awaiting the Absent* (see page 201), stresses the peasants' profound religious character. *Grandma's First Visit* premiered at the Salon of 1888 and was also seen at the National Academy of Design in 1891 before it entered the collection of the Toledo Club. KZ

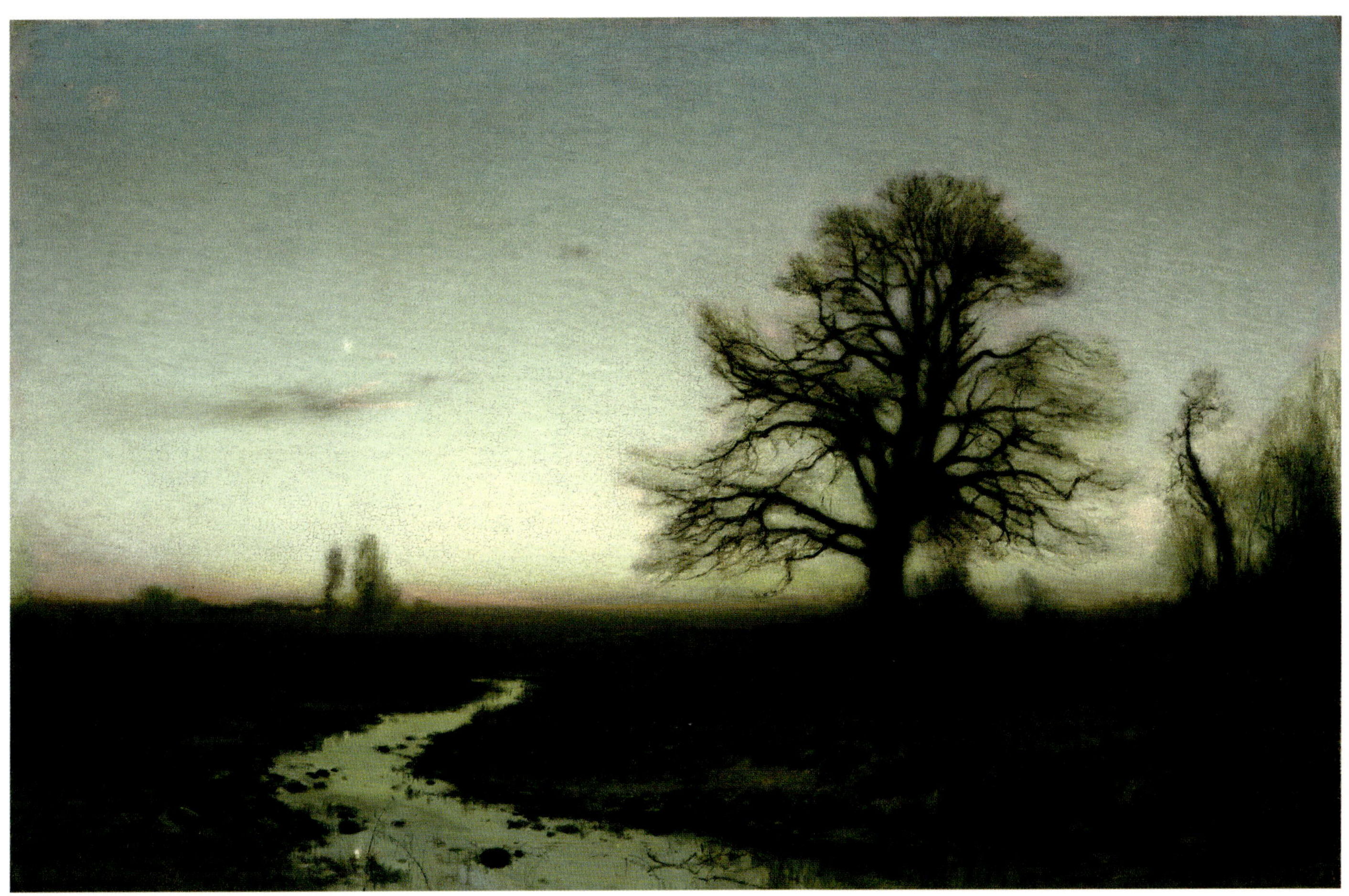

81.
Charles Harold Davis
The Valley (Evening)
Evening, 1886
Oil on canvas, 38⅛ x 57⅛" (96.7 x 147 cm)
Manoogian Collection

CHARLES HAROLD DAVIS (1856–1933)

Charles H. Davis is considered "one of the most talented American landscape painters."[1] Born in Amesbury, Massachusetts, Davis decided on an artistic career in 1874 after viewing an exhibition of Barbizon paintings at the Boston Athenaeum, which included works by Millet. Davis's early style reveals his strong debt to the Barbizon School. From 1877 to 1880, Davis studied at the School of the Museum of Fine Arts, Boston, under Emil Otto Grundmann. In September 1880, he left for Paris, where he briefly attended the classes of Boulanger and Lefebvre at the Académie Julian. By 1881 he had abandoned these formal studies, which stressed drawing from the figure, and had begun to paint outdoors. Inspired by his visits to the forests of Fontainebleau and St. Léger in Normandy, Davis decided to specialize in landscape painting. He settled in the village of Fleury, near Barbizon, and in 1881 started showing regularly at the Salon, winning an honorable mention in 1887. In America his paintings were exhibited frequently at the Pennsylvania Academy of the Fine Arts from 1882 to 1932 and at the National Academy of Design beginning in 1884. He was elected a member of the Society of American Artists in 1886 and of the National Academy of Design in 1903. Davis returned to America in 1890 and two years later settled in Mystic, Connecticut, where he lived for the rest of his life. In 1895 his style changed dramatically. Adopting a high-keyed Impressionist palette and a loaded brush, Davis painted landscapes in which the sky was often the dominant motif. These works, inspired by the cloud studies of the English artist John Constable, were the subject of the article Davis wrote for the September 1909 issue of *Palette and Bench*, entitled "A Study of Clouds." In 1913 he helped found the Mystic Art Association and exhibited at the Armory Show in New York.[2]

During the 1880s and early 1890s Davis was closely allied to the Tonalist movement through his reliance on a predominant color, his preference for flat, empty marshland scenes, and his poetic evocations of psychological states of mind. *Evening* is one of a series of paintings that includes *Evening II* (Collection Barbara B. Millhouse, New York), also of 1886, in which Davis captured the transient moment after sunset.[3] In each work a lone massive tree is silhouetted against the lighted sky while a glistening stream illuminates the darkened ground. Entitled *Le Soir* at the Salon of 1886, *Evening* was favorably reviewed by critic Theodore Child: "Charles H. Davis, who had one of the finest landscapes in last year's Salon, sends a charming evening effect—*Le Soir*. The moment represented is very late twilight."[4] Although *Evening* demonstrates a thorough knowledge of the French countryside, it is primarily an artificial composition in which the artist's own feelings are superimposed to create a heightened sense of mystery and revery. Davis stated, "I do not think that a piece of nature in a frame, though wonderfully well done, is very desirable as a picture effect;—*eloquent arrangement*, I may say, is for me the first thing to strive for."[5]

One of Davis's most frequently reproduced and exhibited paintings, *Evening* was given to the Metropolitan Museum of Art, New York, in 1887 by the well-known collector George I. Seney. Because it is not listed as being lent by the museum in the official catalogue of the 1889 Exposition, the possibility exists that this may not be one of the three twilight scenes Davis exhibited. Even Child's extensive discussion of Davis's four entries does not provide conclusive evidence. Davis's landscapes from this period are so similar, however, that this painting can stand for Davis's work in 1889. "Mr. Davis gives us refined and poetical visions of nature," Child wrote in 1889.[6] Davis was awarded a silver medal at the Exposition. HPC

SARAH PAXTON BALL DODSON (1847–1906)

Recognized as one of the leading American women artists in Paris during the 1880s, Sarah Paxton Ball Dodson was a versatile painter whose oeuvre included religious and mythological subjects as well as landscapes. Born in Philadelphia, Dodson was the daughter of the engraver, illustrator, and portraitist Richard Whatcoat Dodson, who did little to encourage her early interest in drawing and illustrating. In 1872, after her father's death, Dodson began a year's study at the Pennsylvania Academy of the Fine Arts under Christian Schussele.[1] By 1873 she was in Paris, where she received instruction from Evariste Vital Luminais until 1876 and later from Lefebvre and Louis-Maurice Boutet de Monvel. Dodson's early rococo style changed dramatically after a trip to Italy, probably between 1877 and 1879.[2] Inspired by the Renaissance masters, she infused her figures with classical monumentality. Although Dodson exhibited regularly at the Paris Salon from 1877, she showed at the Pennsylvania Academy of the Fine Arts only in 1883 and 1905, at the National Academy of Design during the 1880s and 1890s, and at the Society of American Artists in 1878. After 1884, Dodson started painting plein-air landscapes. By 1891 she had quit France and settled in Brighton, England, where she had previously spent her summers. Despite a chronic illness, which left her partially incapacitated in 1893, Dodson continued to paint until her death.

Dodson's artistic range was clearly demonstrated at the 1889 Exposition by her two entries: the symbolic *The Morning Stars* (unlocated) of about 1886 and the monumental *Meditation of the Holy Virgin*. The former displayed Dodson's talent for orchestrating large numbers of figures within a composition, an ability recognized by a critic in the *Art Amateur* as early as 1882: "Miss Dodson's figures were grouped," he wrote of *The Invocation of Moses* (St. Bartholomew's Church, Brighton), "and were vigorous in form even if somewhat spiritless in action; but she was the only one of our countrywomen who seemed to wrestle with other than the simplest forms of conventional, lady-like art."[3]

In contrast, *Meditation of the Holy Virgin* has only one life-size figure. The Virgin's static and hieratic pose and the picture's cool pale blues and greens, which bring to mind the palette of Puvis de Chavannes, reinforce the work's devotional theme. As the flower of the Virgin, the realistically painted foreground lilies symbolize purity; as the attribute of the archangel Gabriel, they evoke the Annunciation.[4] The outdoor setting reveals Dodson's growing interest in landscape and allies this painting to similar religious images by George Hitchcock such as *Annonciation* (see page 171). Unlike Hitchcock and the German artist Fritz von Uhde, however, Dodson has not clothed the Virgin in contemporary garb or attempted to disguise her halo. In this respect *Meditation of the Holy Virgin* relates more closely to the English Pre-Raphaelites, whose paintings clearly influenced Dodson during her late period, when her oeuvre becomes increasingly symbolic and mystical. Dodson's interest in portraying the Virgin paralleled the growing "fascination with her as a symbolic figure" at the end of the nineteenth century.[5] Other American expatriate artists, among them Hitchcock, Gari Melchers, and fellow Philadelphian Henry Ossawa Tanner, treated the Virgin pictorially, and Dodson, in the last three years of her life, portrayed the Virgin twice, in *Le Berceau* (Museum of Fine Arts, Boston) and *The Annunciation* (unlocated). HPC

(GAINES) RUGER DONOHO (1857–1916)

Ruger Donoho was born in Church Hill, Mississippi, in 1857, but fled to Washington, D.C., with his widowed mother during the Civil War. Following his schooling in Washington and Pennsylvania, he worked in the office of the United States Architect in Washington, where he developed his interest in painting. In 1878 he made a summer sketching trip to the Catskill Mountains, and that fall went to New York. There he attended the Art Students League and also worked with the landscape painter R. Swain Gifford, before leaving for Europe in 1879.[1]

Donoho's residence for the next eight years was Paris, where he entered the Académie Julian and studied under Lefebvre and Tony Robert-Fleury.[2] With his fellow students, during the summer months he indulged his passion for landscape painting, staying near the towns of Barbizon and Grez and sketching the countryside around the forest of Fontainebleau.

90.
Sarah Paxton Ball Dodson
Meditation of the Holy Virgin
Meditation of the Holy Virgin, 1889
Oil on canvas, 66⅞ x 45⅛" (166.5 x 113 cm)
Private Collection

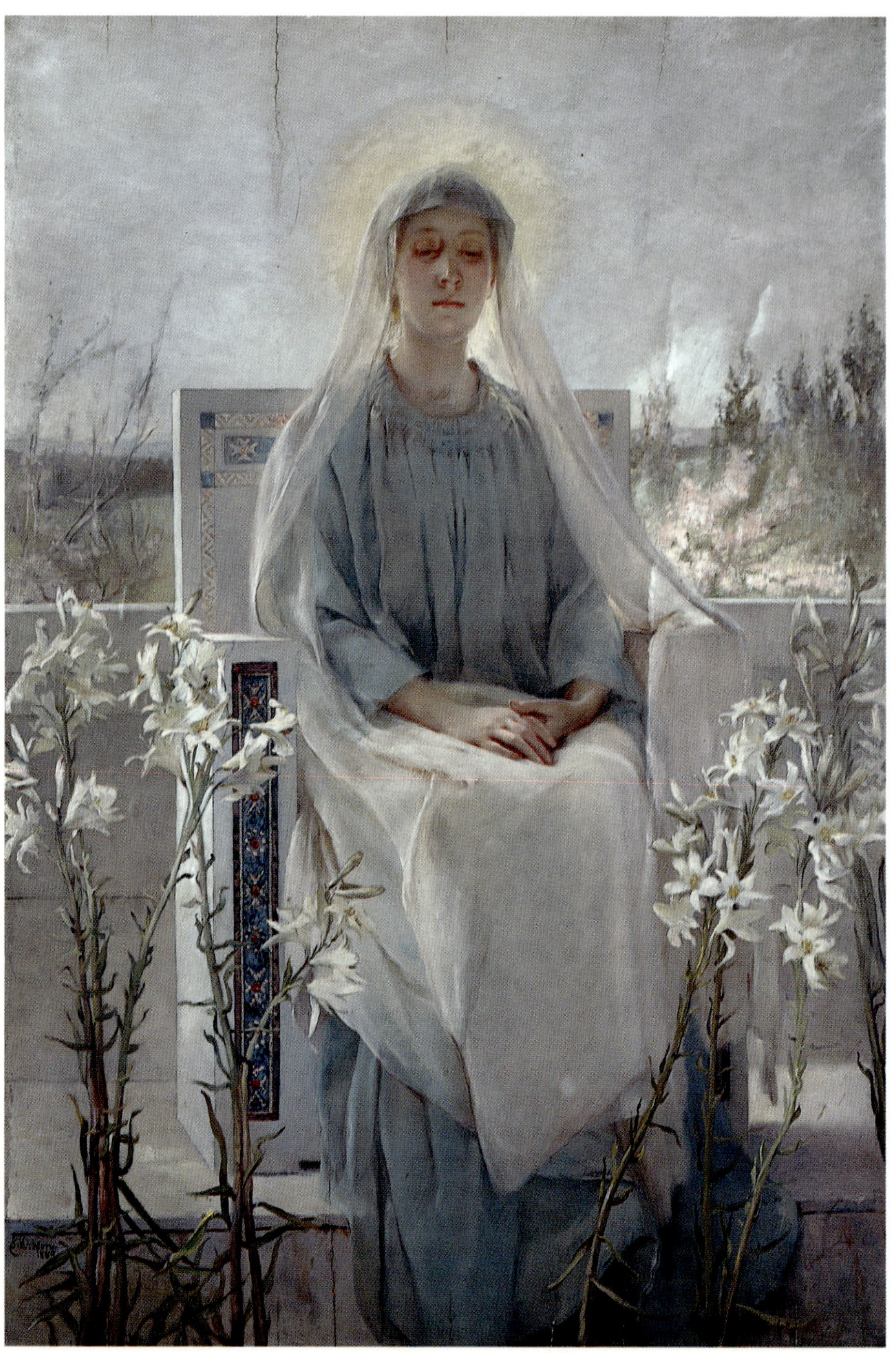

In Grez, Donoho found inspiration for one of his finest landscapes, *La Marcellerie*. It attracted attention first in the spring of 1882 at the Paris Salon and then in the fall of that year at the Pennsylvania Academy of the Fine Arts, where it was described as "a bit of luxuriant and carefully studied meadow" and complimented for a "feeling of freshness" and "successful rendering of atmospheric effects."[3] The painting drew praise in the spring of 1883 at the National Academy of Design as an "unusually excellent landscape study" and was

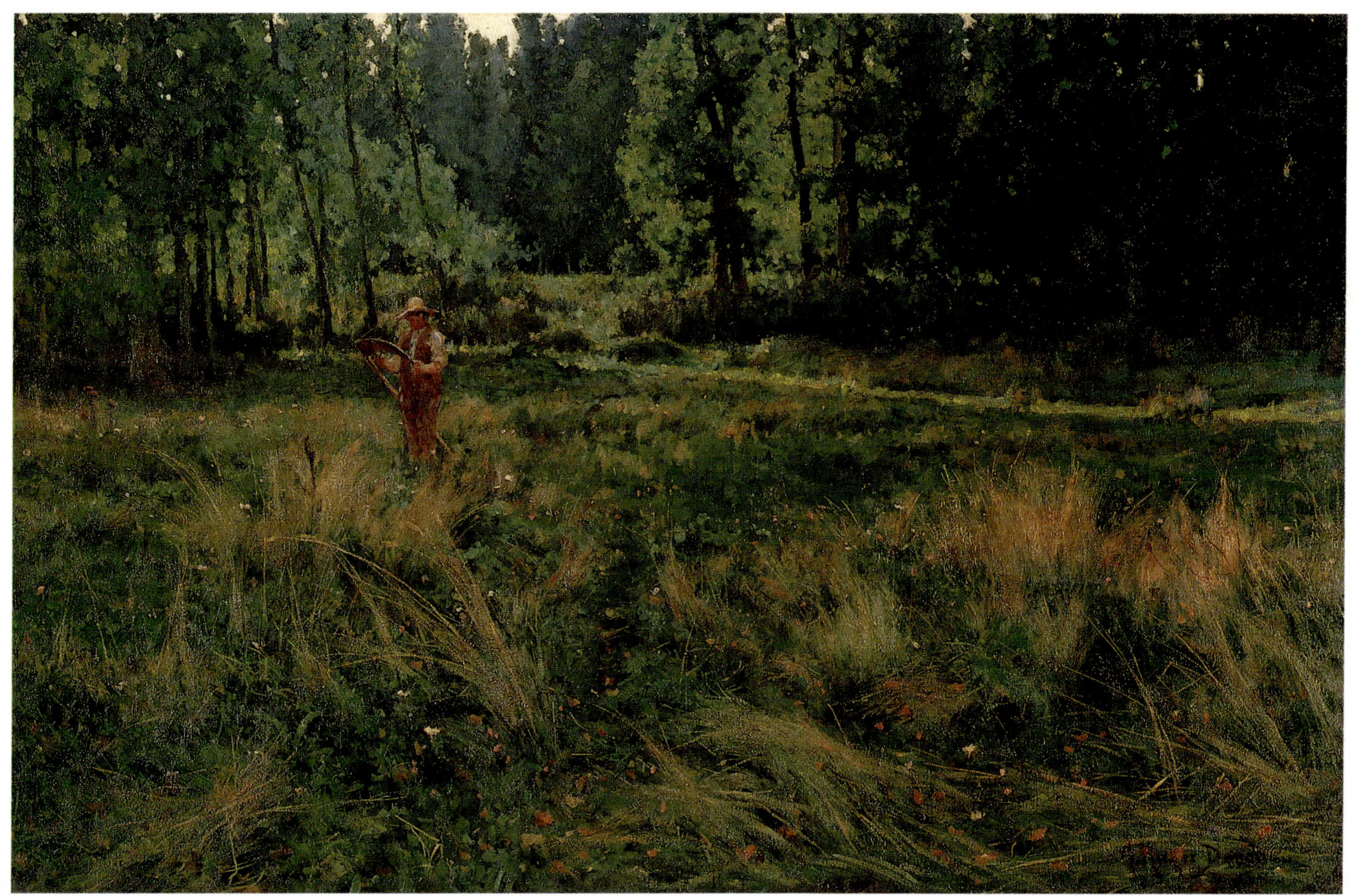

92.
(Gaines) Ruger Donoho
La Marcellerie
La Marcellerie, c. 1882
Oil on canvas, 51⅜ x 77⅛" (130.5 x 196 cm)
The Brooklyn Museum, New York,
Gift of George A. Hearn

illustrated by a line drawing by James D. Smillie in Charles M. Kurtz's publication on the show.[4] It appeared at the Society of American Artists' exhibition in Chicago in 1884[5] and was reproduced in the *Art Union* in the fall of 1885.[6] *La Marcellerie* won a silver medal at the 1889 Exposition and was also shown at the World's Columbian Exposition in Chicago in 1893.

Despite the inclusion of a figure, *La Marcellerie* is nonnarrative. Its broad paint handling, subdued palette, and quiet woodland view represent the ideals of Barbizon landscape adapted to an Impressionist format. Donoho had grasped the importance of attaining immediacy by eliminating the horizon and forcing the foreground up to dominate the picture. Like John Twachtman and Willard Metcalf, who also studied at the Académie Julian during the eighties, Donoho strove to fill the canvas with the close hues of the season, creating an overall surface richness.

After he returned to New York, in 1887, Donoho gradually withdrew from the competition of the art market and set up his home and studio in East Hampton, Long Island. Here sunlit garden scenes and tonal nocturnes replaced the French countryside of his young adulthood, reflecting the influence of his friend and neighbor Childe Hassam and a reciprocated admiration for Whistler. Although Donoho was reluctant to seek public recognition in later years, his work continued to be appreciated by his peers. It was warmly received at a memorial exhibition at the Macbeth Gallery, New York, in 1916.[7] MCOB

ARTHUR WESLEY DOW (1857–1922)

Arthur Wesley Dow, remembered as a writer on art education and teacher of a generation of abstractionists, was an aspiring landscapist in 1889.[1] He began his training in 1881 in Boston with the little-known artist James M. Stone, whose facile Munich manner he later repudiated. More important influences were William Morris Hunt and the French Barbizon paintings he imported to Boston. From 1884 to 1887 Dow worked under Boulanger at the Académie Julian. He spent the summer and fall of 1885 and of 1886 in Pont-Aven and its environs. Like many American artists, he came there to paint the picturesque peasants and the Breton landscape, emulating the pictures of Alexander Harrison and Jules Bastien-Lepage. After exhibiting the Breton scene *A Field at Kerloauen* (unlocated) in the Salon of 1887, Dow returned to New England to pursue his landscape work independently. In January 1888, at J. Eastman Chase's Gallery in Boston, he exhibited side by side his French and his American canvases, which showed many similarities in terrain and a predilection for a twilight setting. He returned to Brittany in May 1888.

At Evening is a synthesis of Dow's experiences as a landscapist. Painted in the fall of 1888 in Concarneau, it has a limited palette of related tones and a simple composition of bare tree limbs set against the sky. The twilight canvas melds the dark mood of the Barbizon landscape with the restricted, directly observed tonal harmonies of the Breton approach. Harrison, an adviser to Dow that fall, pronounced the painting "harmonious and charming."[2] As vice-president of the American jury in Paris for the 1889 Exposition (where Dow won an honorable mention), Harrison undoubtedly had much to do with the painting's acceptance. Among the many American twilight scenes at the Exposition, Dow's was less transcriptive than Harrison's *The Wave* and less elegiac than the Tonalist *Evening* of Charles H. Davis, with whom he shared a Boston heritage and Barbizon influence (see pages 141 and 163).[3]

Soon after he returned to America, in 1889, Dow's style changed. In 1891 he met Ernest Fenollosa, curator of Japanese art at the Museum of Fine Arts in Boston and became deeply interested in oriental art, eventually assuming Fenollosa's position. Dow's later oils and, especially, his woodcuts show Japanese principles of composition and a sophisticated sense of color. Concurrently, he developed a theory of art based on Japanese, Greek, and Italian quattrocento aesthetics, which he published in his *Compositions* (1899).[4] He spent much of his later life developing these theories into a curriculum of art instruction while teaching in his own summer school in Ipswich, Massachusetts, and at Teachers College of Columbia University, New York, counting Georgia O'Keeffe and Max Weber among his students.

In *At Evening* the planar composition and tightly controlled palette foretell Dow's interest in Japanese design principles of asymmetry, balance, and discipline, while the sinuous lines of trees prefigure his admiration for the linearity of Greek and Italian art. KZ

THOMAS EAKINS (1844–1916)

The 1889 Paris Exposition occurred only three years after Thomas Eakins chose to resign on principle as director of the Pennsylvania Academy of the Fine Arts rather than abandon his practice of using nude models in his life drawing class. This episode, well known in American art history, adversely affected Eakins's reputation—and his livelihood—for the remainder of the century. In view of his differences with conservative factions, it is surprising that Eakins participated in such establishment ventures as world's fairs. In 1889 this quintessentially American artist not only sent three pictures to the Exposition but also submitted three to the Paris Salon.[1] In fact, Eakins had been among the first Americans to go to Paris to study art. After a spell as a student at the Pennsylvania Academy, he left for Europe in 1866. Avoiding what would become the prerequisite pilgrimage to Barbizon, Eakins spent four years in the studio of Gérôme studying drawing. In 1869, seeking to gain more expertise in painting, he took classes with Bonnat, following these with a trip to Spain, where he acquainted himself with the Spanish masters, in particular Velázquez and Ribera. Returning home in 1870, Eakins taught at the Union League of Philadelphia (1874–1876) and at the Pennsylvania Academy (1876–1886).

At first glance, Eakins's contribution to the 1889 Exposition appears unprepossessing: a full-length portrait and two small pictures, one of which was a watercolor. The portrait, not included in the present exhibition, was of the artist's friend Professor George Barker (1886; Mitchell Museum, Mount Vernon, Ill.). His other entries were a bust-length portrait of student and colleague George Reynolds, *The Veteran* (1886), and a watercolor, *The Dancing Lesson* (1878). For a long time it was assumed that the latter picture must have been an oil. However, it has become possible to verify Lloyd Goodrich's statement that *The Dancing Lesson* is actually the watercolor known today as *Negro Boy Dancing* (1878).[2] A contemporary newspaper account states clearly that Eakins sent to the Exposition a "negro scene in watercolor."[3] As Goodrich conceded, Eakins's contribution was a "curious combination." In 1893, Eakins again made a curious combination when he included a watercolor among his entries to the Chicago world's fair.

Whatever Eakins's reasons for sending *The Dancing Lesson* to Paris may have been, records indicate that it was a work he valued highly, for in the 1880s it was his highest-priced watercolor.[4] Moreover, although the picture's narrative subject matter made it old-fashioned in terms of the latest dicta on the watercolor medium, *The Dancing Lesson* had been considered daringly sketchy when it was first exhibited at the American Watercolor Society, in 1878.[5] Despite the picture's genre subject, it incorporates a sense of movement eminently suited to a medium designed to capture transient effects. In this regard, *The Dancing Lesson* marks a considerable advance over watercolors like *John Biglin in a Single Scull* (1873–74), which Eakins's former master Gérôme, still alive in 1889, had critiqued as static.[6] *The Dancing Lesson* disperses a split second in time through a synapsis that connects the banjo player, leaning forward on a note, to the old man, who catches it with his tapping foot, to the figure of the child, "whose bare legs have absorbed all the liveliness from the face," as a contemporary reviewer perceptively noted.[7] The immediacy of *The Dancing Lesson* is countered by more enduring undertones. In the background of the picture is a miniature of Lincoln and his son—a minuscule touch that confines the background space while expanding the meaning of the picture. This oblique

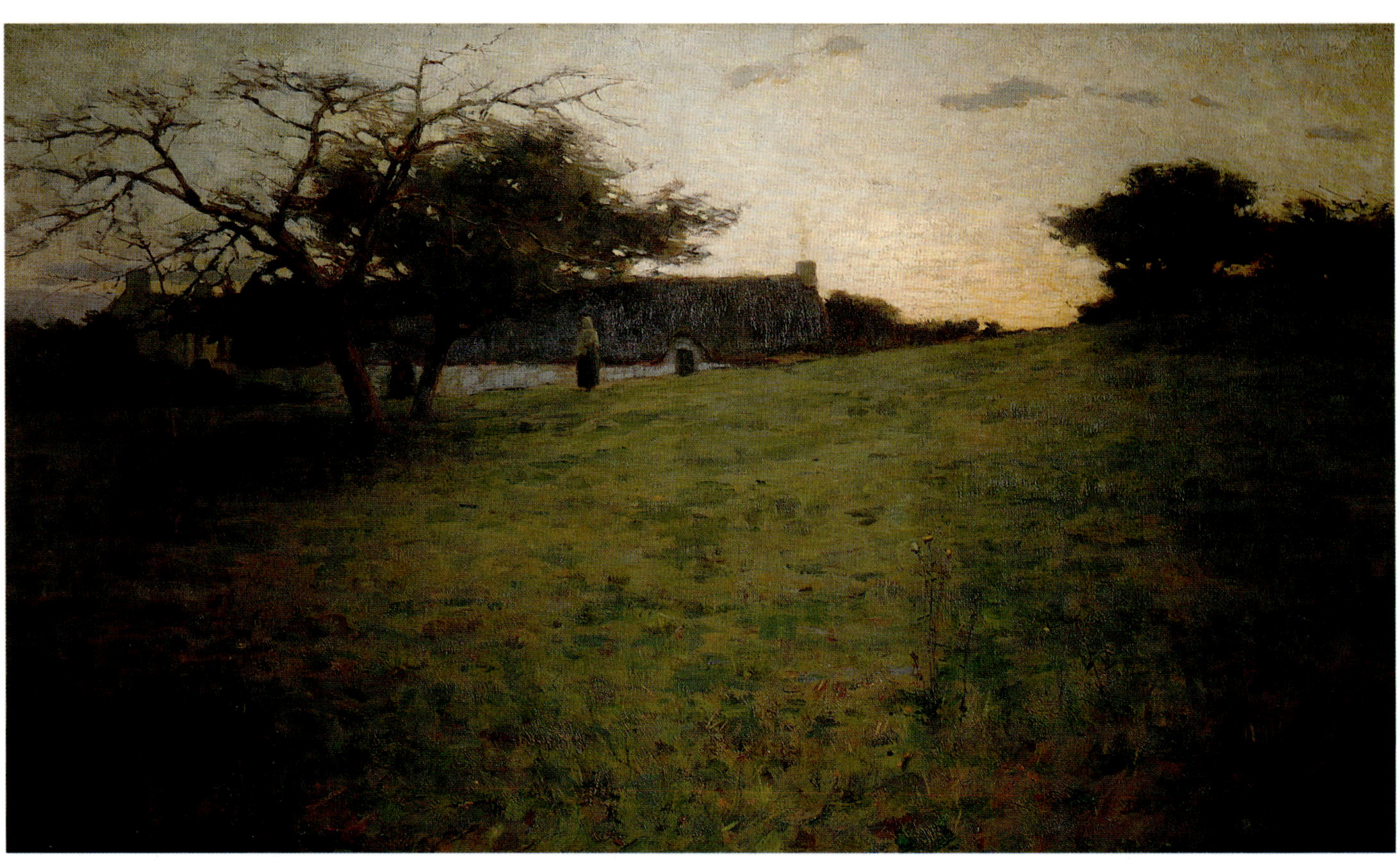

94.
Arthur Wesley Dow
At Evening
Au Soir, 1888
Oil on canvas, 32½ x 53½" (81.8 x 135.1 cm)
Ipswich Public Schools, Massachusetts

reference to the larger issue of the Civil War was perhaps secondary to Eakins himself but would surely have impressed Thomas Hovenden, who represented Philadelphia on the fair's selection committee.

Eakins made an even more indirect allusion to the Civil War in *The Veteran*, a portrayal of a man who, like Henry Fleming in Stephen Crane's *The Red Badge of Courage*, offers a counterpoint to the heroic images of generals that were appearing in these years on the pages of journals like *Century Magazine*. By obscuring the medal pinned to the sitter's lapel, Eakins reduced the decoration and the war itself to just one of the life experiences accumulated in the veteran's face. Significantly, it is the face and hands, not the medal, that are illuminated in the composition. During this period Eakins often used such small external references to focus the personality of his sitters, most of whom were not individuals he was commissioned to paint but persons he knew well. George Reynolds was among those who followed Eakins from the Pennsylvania Academy to the short-lived Art Students League of Philadelphia. Reynolds's portrait was one of a series in which Eakins used specific individuals to evoke types.[8] Nevertheless, *The Veteran* stands alone as a strong characterization of an individual. It was reputed to have been one of the artist's own favorites despite its neglect at the 1889 Exposition, where Eakins received no recognition. JH

98.
Thomas Eakins
The Dancing Lesson
Negro Boy Dancing, 1878
Watercolor, 18 1/18 x 22 5/8" (45.8 x 86.5 cm)
© The Metropolitan Museum of Art, New York,
Fletcher Fund. 25.97.1

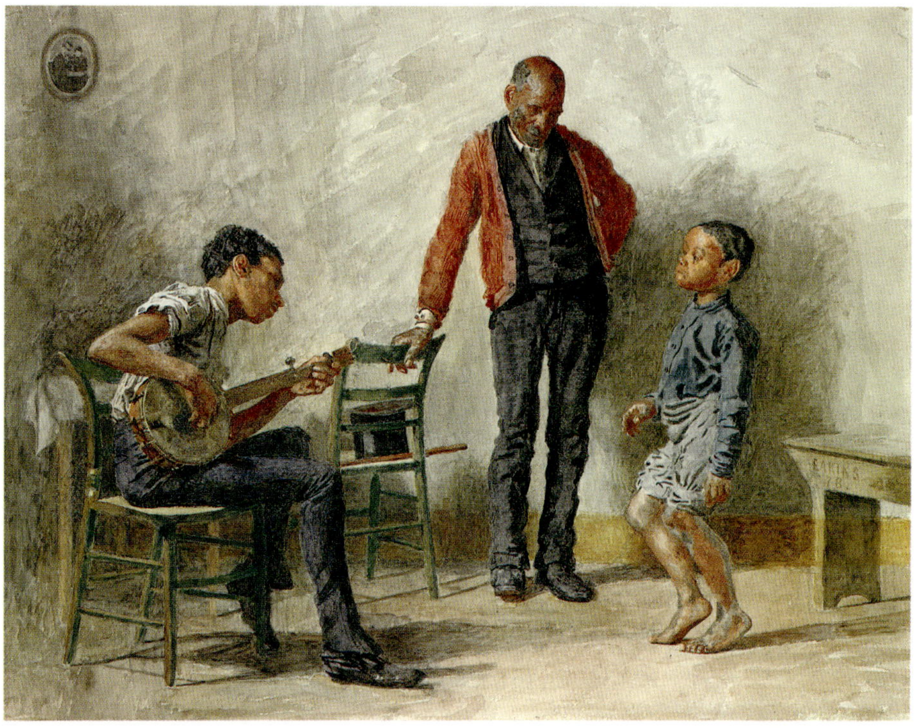

99.
Thomas Eakins
The Veteran (portrait of Geo. Reynolds)
The Veteran, c. 1886
Oil on canvas, 22 1/2 x 15" (56.4 x 37.5 cm)
Yale University Art Gallery,
Bequest of Stephen Carlton Clark, B.A. 1903

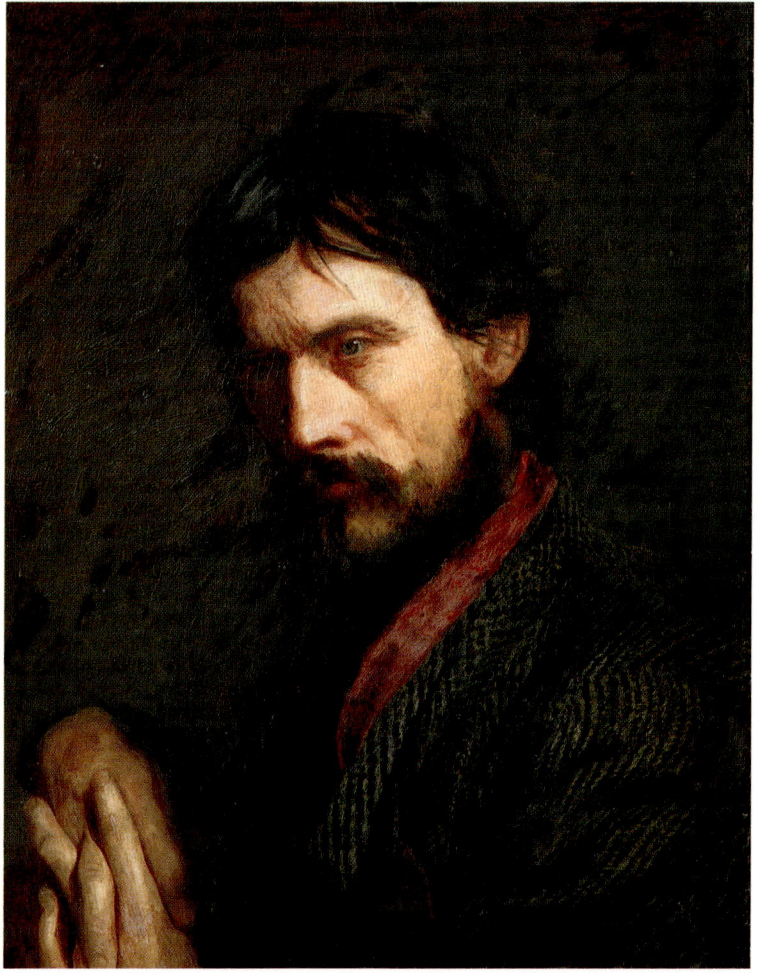

WYATT EATON (1849–1896)

Wyatt Eaton exhibited three portraits and a nude at the 1889 Exposition. While the number of his entries suggests Eaton's popularity in the nineteenth century, the imbalance in favor of portraiture suggests both the bread-and-butter basis of his art and the pragmatic eye with which many American artists viewed the expositions.

Like many American artists of the period, Eaton worked in different styles, depending on the subject he was depicting. In his case, this diversity was encouraged from early training onward. At the National Academy of Design, between 1867 and 1872, he studied under Samuel Colman, Daniel Huntington, and others while working in the studio of Joseph Oriel Eaton, a little-known artist (to whom he was not related).[1] Wyatt Eaton's was an environment in which, according to him, "every teacher contradicted every other teacher—a decided advantage to the pupils because it made them think for themselves and threw them upon their own resources."[2] Undoubtedly this heterogeneous background prepared Eaton for France, where, between 1872 and 1876, he drew technique from Jean-Léon Gérôme and inspiration from Jean-François Millet, whom he met through the Boston expatriate artist William Babcock.

Following his return from France, Eaton was among the young European-trained painters who, in 1877, formed the Society of American Artists in reaction to the discriminatory practices of the National Academy of Design. The founding group also included Helena de Kay, whose portrait was one of the three that Eaton exhibited at Paris in 1889. Eaton's friendship with de Kay and her husband, Richard Watson Gilder, editor of the *Century*, is reflected in the artist's close association with the magazine. In 1889, for example, it published Eaton's Barbizon memoir, "Recollections of Jean-François Millet."[3] Earlier, the magazine had published Eaton's portrait series of well-known Americans, among them William Cullen Bryant, Longfellow, Emerson, and Whittier. It is interesting to note that the engraver of the *Century* series, Timothy Cole, owned one of Eaton's 1889 entries, *Portrait of a Man with Violin*.

In addition to the portraits for which he was best known, Eaton painted pictures expressing what an early writer called his "poetic" side.[4] One of these, *Ariadne* (1888), then already owned by the well-known collector William T. Evans, was exhibited at the 1889 Paris Exposition. More than any other of Eaton's entries, this nude in a landscape—a classic studio motif with a setting that reflects the artist's direct observation of nature—exemplifies the way in which American artists synthesized their various European experiences.[5]

Although Eaton made a second trip to France in the 1880s, *Ariadne* appears to have been painted in this country. At the time, artists like Kenyon Cox were beginning to paint nudes, but the subject was still comparatively rare in American art. For that reason, writers of the period tended to compare Eaton's picture with John Vanderlyn's much earlier nude of the same name. But within the international context of the 1889 Exposition it becomes apparent that Eaton's *Ariadne* was very much a picture of the late nineteenth century, when images of sleeping and languishing women were popular throughout Europe.[6] Moreover, in this setting Eaton's conception of the nude seems less conservative than appears at first; it falls somewhere between the academicism of artists like Cabanel and the efforts of avant-garde artists unable to abandon this enduring artistic motif. JH

Born in 1822, George Fuller was a generation older than most of the artists who exhibited at the 1889 Paris Exposition; he had died five years prior to the fair and was the only artist shown posthumously. Fuller's inclusion in the Exposition is a measure of his importance within American art circles of the late nineteenth century.

In the years after his death, in 1884, a romantic aura surrounded Fuller. In part this stemmed from the fact that he had died at the peak of his popularity, which followed years of obscurity while he lived in isolation on his farm in Deerfield, Massachusetts.[1] After his emergence from Deerfield, in 1876, Fuller was welcomed by the young European-trained artists affiliated with the Society of American Artists, which elected him a member in 1880. Returning from Europe, these young artists saw parallels between Fuller's regionalism and that of Jean-François Millet.[2] More important to them was their idea of him as an artist who did not merely transcribe surface appearances but rather delved into the soul of his subjects. Further, Fuller expressed the essence of his subjects in the smoky tones and hazy forms that became characteristics of the Tonalist aesthetic, to which many of these younger artists would subscribe by the early 1890s. In short, for many European-trained artists attempting to reestablish their native roots, Fuller was a father figure who, not insignificantly, was also an American.[3]

There was some irony in the younger artists' espousal of Fuller. Not only did he lack European training; he was actually suspicious of it.[4] Nor did he paint outdoors or have much facility for the drawing that formed the core of the expatriate education. Indeed, to artists trained in the European academic tradition, Fuller's art background must have seemed unfocused. He had taken up sketching in the late 1830s during a trip to the West. In 1841, while traveling with his brother, an itinerant miniaturist, Fuller had begun to paint portraits. Subsequently he went to Albany, New York, where he took drawing lessons from the sculptor Henry Kirke Brown. Fuller was in Boston by the winter of 1842 and remained there for the next five years, becoming a member of the Boston Artists' Association and, for a period, taking evening art classes.

In 1847, Fuller moved to New York, where he lived for twelve years, painting portraits while both studying and exhibiting at the National Academy of Design. He was elected an associate member in 1857 but never became an Academician. From New York he made three protracted journeys to the South; in 1860 he spent six months in Europe, where he supplemented his early interest in Washington Allston with a new interest in Europe's old and modern masters. It was after this trip that Fuller retreated to Deerfield, where he spent the next fifteen years farming and developing his artistic style.

The Quadroon is typical of the mysterious and evocative pictures that appeared after Fuller emerged from Deerfield. Exhibited at the National Academy of Design in 1880, *The Quadroon* was owned in the 1880s by well-known Boston collector Samuel D. Warren. Its black heroine had her origins in the sketches Fuller had made on trips to the South many years earlier. But the selection of *The Quadroon* for the 1889 Paris Exposition probably had less to do with its subject matter than with the fact that it was widely regarded as one of Fuller's best works.[5] Unfortunately, the very qualities for which *The Quadroon* was prized in the nineteenth century make it unexhibitable in the twentieth. Like Albert Pinkham Ryder's, many of Fuller's surfaces have darkened and cracked

104.
Wyatt Eaton
Ariadne
Ariadne, 1888
Oil on canvas, 14⅛ x 18½″ (36.1 x 46.2 cm)
Owner in 1889 W. T. Evans
National Museum of American Art,
Smithsonian Institution, Washington, D.C.,
Gift of William T. Evans

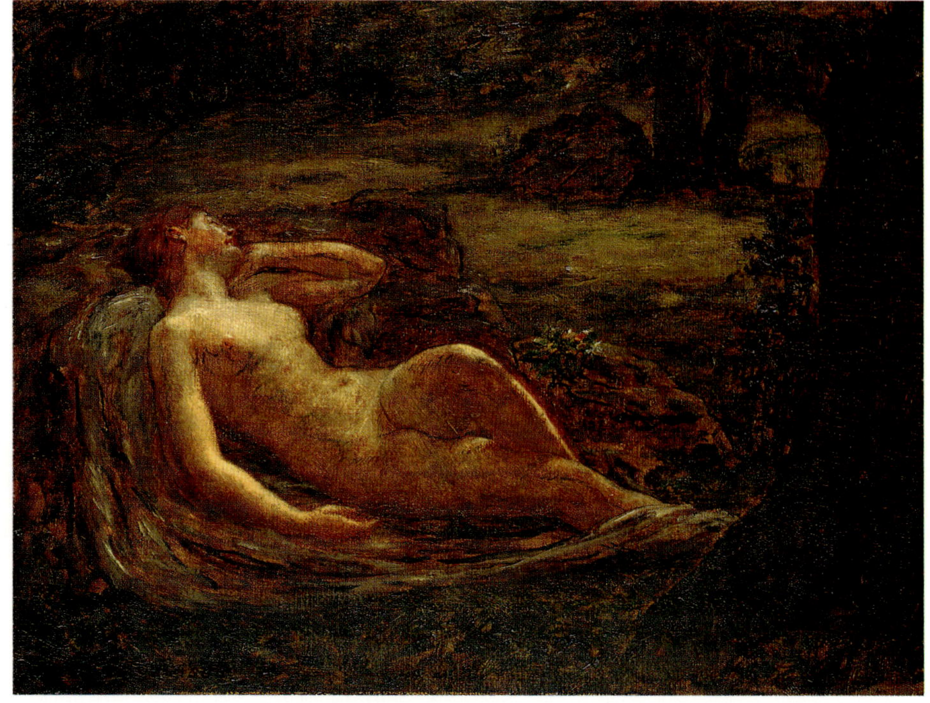

112.
George Fuller
The Quadroon
Study for The Quadroon, 1879
Oil on canvas, 30 x 25″ (76.2 x 63.5 cm)
Berry-Hill Galleries, New York
(Original, dated 1880, collection The Metropolitan
Museum of Art, New York)

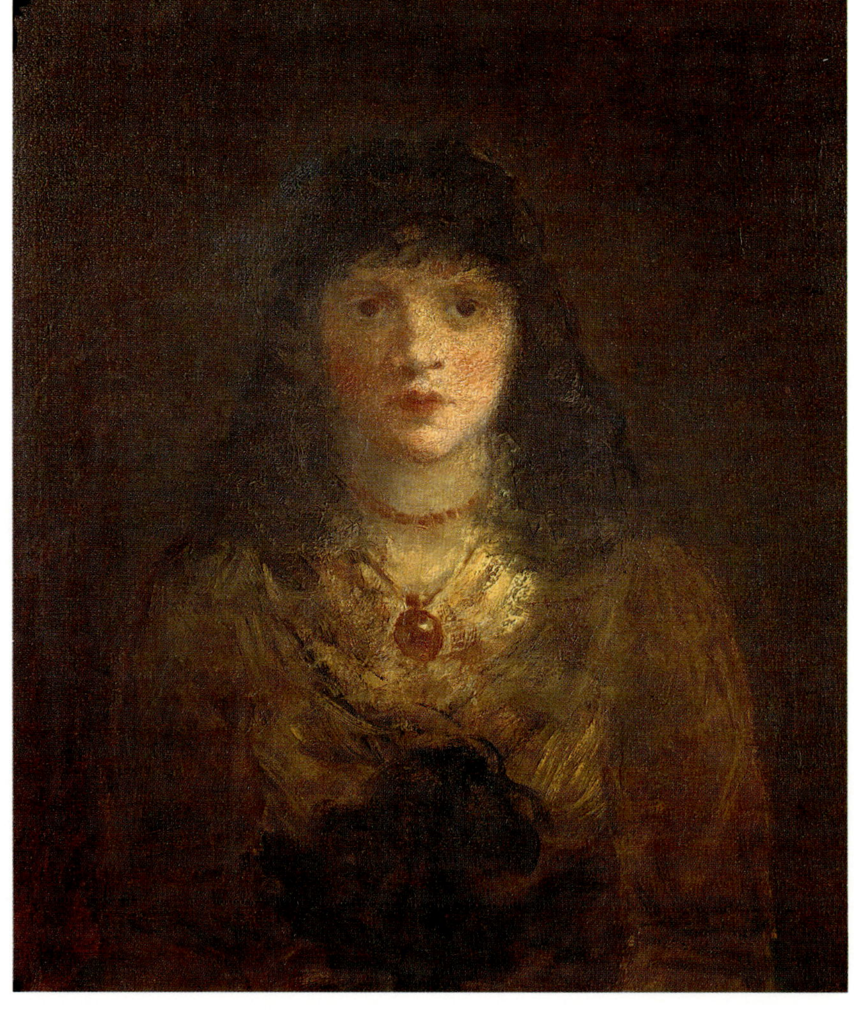

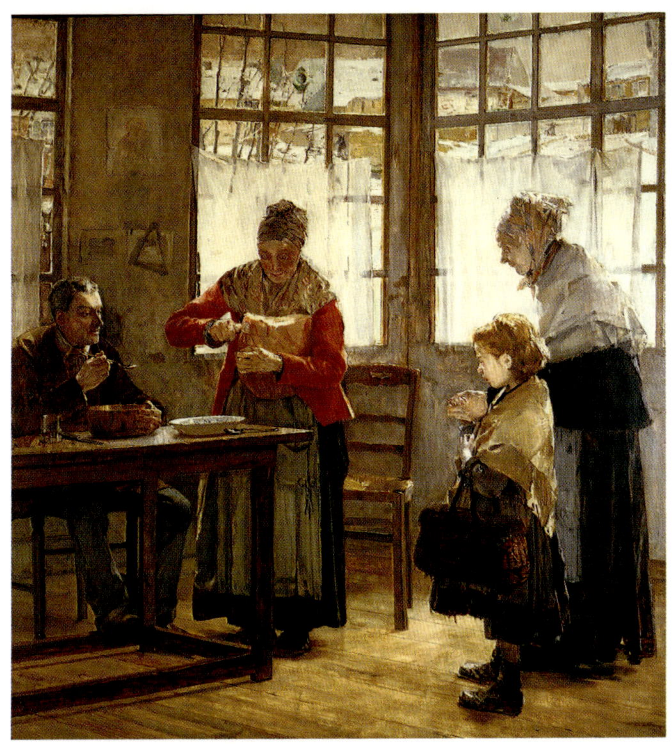

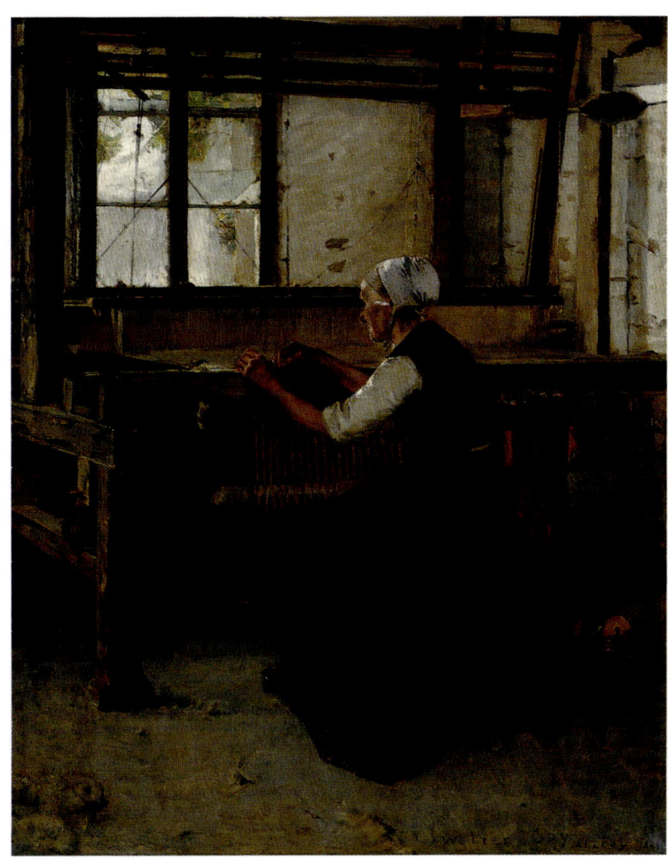

118.
Walter Gay
Charity
Charity, 1889
Oil on canvas, 102 x 88" (259.1 x 223.5 cm)
The Manney Collection, New York

120.
Walter Gay
The Weaver
The Weaver, 1886
Oil on canvas, 59¼ x 46¼" (151.8 x 117.4 cm)
Museum of Fine Arts, Boston,
Gift of Mrs. Walter Gay

as a result of extensive repainting and use of bitumen.[6] In the present exhibition, the final picture has been substituted for by its study, which bears a loose relationship to it because Fuller's method dictated organic evolution rather than direct transferral. *Study for The Quadroon* (1879), which isolates the single figure, nevertheless conveys the feeling of the final work. Characteristically, the figure fuses softly with the setting, and the olive tones of the face reveal traces of the wooden end of Fuller's brush. Fuller's studies were esteemed in their own right. The *Study for The Quadroon* was owned by the American Impressionist J.J. Enneking, a disciple of the artist, who probably bought it from Fuller's estate sale in 1884.[7]

JH

WALTER GAY (1856–1937)

When Walter Gay left the United States, in 1876, to study art, he moved to Europe for good, possibly because he was able to establish himself there both professionally and socially. As the nephew of the Boston painter Winckworth Alan Gay, the artist was well connected from the start. Through his uncle, the younger Gay met William Morris Hunt, with whom he studied in Boston between 1873 and 1876. Hunt then directed Gay toward Paris, where he entered the studio of Léon Bonnat, remaining there for three years.[1] While a student of

Bonnat, Gay became interested in the work of Mariano Fortuny. These combined influences, both stressing a painterliness derived from the Spanish School, provided an artistic training far less eclectic than that of most Americans abroad, which may have had a bearing on the overall cohesiveness of Gay's oeuvre.

An 1882 trip to Barbizon with his uncle supplied Gay with the theme that occupied him for the rest of the 1880s. During this period he painted the peasant scenes that dominated his contribution to the 1889 Exposition. Of the six pictures he showed, four were of this type: *The Spinners* (1885), *The Weaver* (1886), *Le Benedicité* (1888), and *Charity* (1889). At the time of the fair, *Le Benedicité* was already owned by the French government, which had bought it from the 1888 Salon for the Luxembourg Museum.[2] Gay borrowed the picture back in order to show it at the Exposition. Most of the pictures Gay showed at the 1889 Exposition had been exhibited at Salons throughout the 1880s. *The Weaver*, a peasant scene, had been submitted to the 1886 Salon. *Charity* was too recent to have been exhibited at a Salon—which undoubtedly accounted for Gay's insistence that it be included among his fair entries (see page 25). He would exhibit the picture again at the World's Columbian Exposition in Chicago in 1893. It is interesting that although Gay won a silver medal at the 1889 Paris Exposition and awards at other locations throughout Europe during these years, he won no prizes at the American fair in Chicago.

Sizable contributions like Gay's at the 1889 Exposition fueled complaints by resident American artists that the expatriate Americans favored themselves. Be that as it may, the number of Gay's entries enables us to focus on their remarkable stylistic coherency. For example, each of his peasant scenes depicts figures in a light-flooded interior. Despite the forceful characterization of the figures, the scenes differ from those of Gari Melchers, Charles Ulrich, and others in that their mood is largely derived from the setting itself.[3] Since Gay had begun his career as a flower painter, this infiltration of the decorative or pictorial does not seem surprising. Theodore Child sensed the essential character of Gay's peasant scenes, noting in *Le Benedicité* "a distinct charm in the picture considered as a symphony of greys of infinite delicacy as they pass from the depth of airy transparent shadow to the softness of demi-teinte and the complete intensity of full light."[4]

Such pictorial aspects, intimated at the 1889 Fair, would become explicit in the 1890s, when Gay dropped the figure altogether and concentrated on the setting. While his rococo interiors of later years do not constitute series in the sense of Monet's works during this period, their arrangements and repetitions address issues of artistic selection, taste, and style—that is, concerns of modernism—with which Gay has not usually been associated. JH

ROBERT SWAIN GIFFORD (1840–1905)

R. Swain Gifford was born on the Massachusetts island of Nonamesset, one of the Elizabeth Islands, and brought up in the fishing towns of New Bedford and Fairhaven.[1] *Near the Coast* was probably painted near Nonquitt, Massachusetts, where Gifford summered in the 1880s. Its quiet, sober subject and nonspecific site are characteristic of the style Gifford had devised by mid-career and typify his "desire to get into closer intimacy with Nature, by seeking her out in her most familiar aspects and least formal moods. . . ."[2]

Gifford's art education was inextricably entwined with the life, landscape, and atmospheric qualities of the New England coast. As a teenager he had received rudimentary training from the marine painter Albert Van Beest, and he assisted Van Beest and another New Bedford artist, William Bradford, in a commission to produce local scenes of whaling ships for a lithographic firm.[3] After Van Beest left New Bedford, Gifford shared a studio with the sculptor Walton Richetson,[4] but by 1864 he had established his own studio in Boston. During these formative years Gifford most likely studied the work of other American landscape painters, as well as Barbizon landscapes in Providence and Boston collections. When he arrived in New York, in 1866, his own style combined respect for nature with a tendency toward the romantic and picturesque. His talent was promptly acknowledged: he was made an associate in 1867 and a member in 1878 of the National Academy of Design. A commission to make sketches of Washington, Oregon, and California in 1869 for William Cullen Bryant's *Picturesque America* (New York, 1872–74), and a trip with Louis Comfort Tiffany to Europe and North Africa in 1870/71 afforded him opportunities to exercise his talents.

After Gifford's second trip to Europe, in 1874, when he saw a "fine collection of modern French paintings" in Marseilles,[5] he attained his mature landscape style, achieving greater economy of means and simplicity of subject matter. This development was concurrent with his involvement in the newly formed Society of American Artists and the New York Etching Club. *Near the Coast,* which was probably painted in 1884, after Gifford's second trip to Europe, is the epitome of his formula. The artist was so successful in distilling the elements of the composition that he made an etching of the scene for inclusion in Sylvester R. Koehler's *American Art* in 1886.[6]

Exhibited in both New York and Boston before being sent to Paris for the Universal Exposition, *Near the Coast* was acquired by the New York contributors to the 1885 Prize Fund Exhibition of the American Art Association and presented to the Metropolitan Museum of Art that year.[7] Gifford, who had also exhibited at the Paris Exposition of 1878, was represented by three paintings at the 1889 fair.[8] He was awarded a bronze medal, and was singled out by critic Theodore Child as one of the few American artists resident in the United States whose exceptional achievements were worthy of note.[9] MCOB

ROSALIE LORRAINE GILL (1867?–1898)

Little is known of the life and works of Rosalie Gill. She is thought to have been born in Elmira, New York.[1] In 1874 she moved from New York to Baltimore with her father, who probably encouraged her early interest in art, since he owned a painting collection and in 1888 helped found an art group in Baltimore called the Charcoal Club. Gill began her studies at the age of twelve at the Art Students League in New York. At the League she was instructed by William Merritt Chase, whose portrait of her (unlocated) was exhibited at the 1889 Exposition. Two of Gill's known pictures, *The New Model* (c. 1884) and *Lady with a Fan* (1884), both at the Baltimore Museum of Art, are stylistically and thematically related to Chase's oeuvre. In 1884, when Gill was painting these works, she listed her address as the Tenth Street Studio Building, where Chase's renowned studio was located. The year 1884 was an important one for Gill: she exhibited for the first time at both the National Academy of Design and the Society of American Artists. By 1888, when she began showing at the Paris

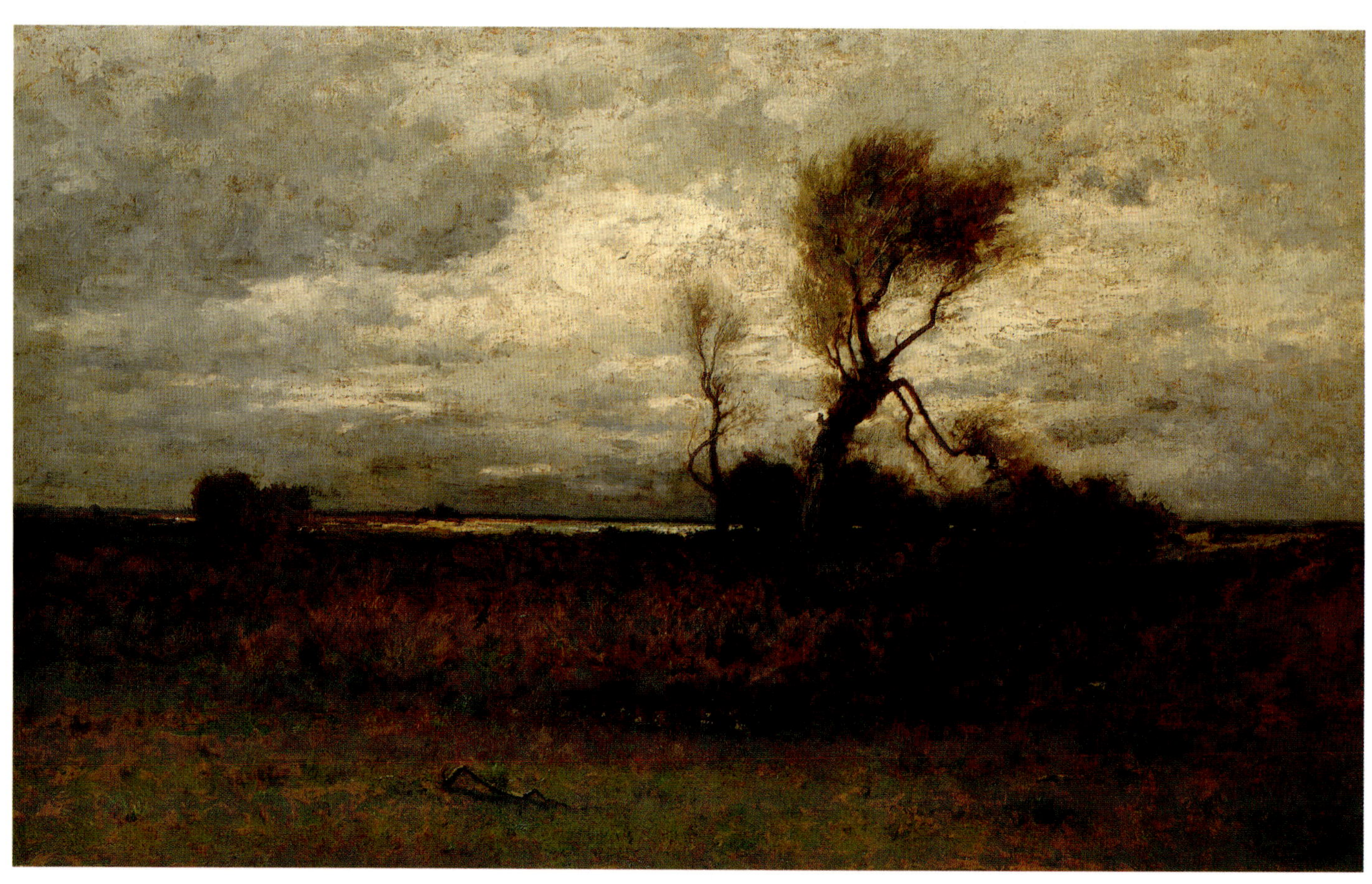

125.
Robert Swain Gifford
Near the Coast
Near the Coast, c. 1885
Oil on canvas, 32⅛ x 52¼" (335.6 x 130.2 cm)
© The Metropolitan Museum of Art, New York, Gift of an Association of Gentlemen, 1885. 85.7

Salon, she listed herself as a pupil of Alfred Stevens, the Belgian artist whose work Chase greatly admired. Gill married René Lara, compte de Chaban, in the mid-1890s and resided in Paris until her death.

The mother-and-child subject of *The Orchid*, which was painted during Gill's first years in Paris, enjoyed a tremendous vogue at the turn of the century. Many American artists, among them Mary Cassatt, Elizabeth Nourse, and George de Forest Brush, were drawn to it, perhaps because of its ability to convey "the memory of universal origins and protective love at a time when life—and art—was becoming increasingly fragmented and depersonalized."[2] At the 1889 Exposition, Enoch Wood Perry, George Hitchcock, Charles Frederic Ulrich, and Chase all exhibited paintings of a young mother with her infant.

Although Gill's interpretation is entirely secular, the figures' poses are related to the Standing Madonna and Christ Child motif in Christian iconography. The work reveals the stylistic influence of Gill's two masters, Chase and Stevens, in its painterly technique and its portrayal of an elegantly dressed woman against a dark background, a hallmark of the Munich School. When *The Orchid* was exhibited at the Philadelphia Art Club, a critic for the *Art Amateur* noted its similarity to a work by Chase: "Here again is the standing figure of a Mother and Child," he wrote; "there is again a dark dress, this time with the mauve of the orchid blossom."[3] Gill intentionally accentuated this flower in her painting, not only through the title but also through the colors. No doubt drawn

127.
Rosalie Lorraine Gill
The Orchid (detail)
The Orchid, 1889
Oil on canvas, 81 x 42″ (205.7 x 106.7 cm)
Peabody Institute of the Johns Hopkins University, Baltimore
Photograph by Harry Connolly

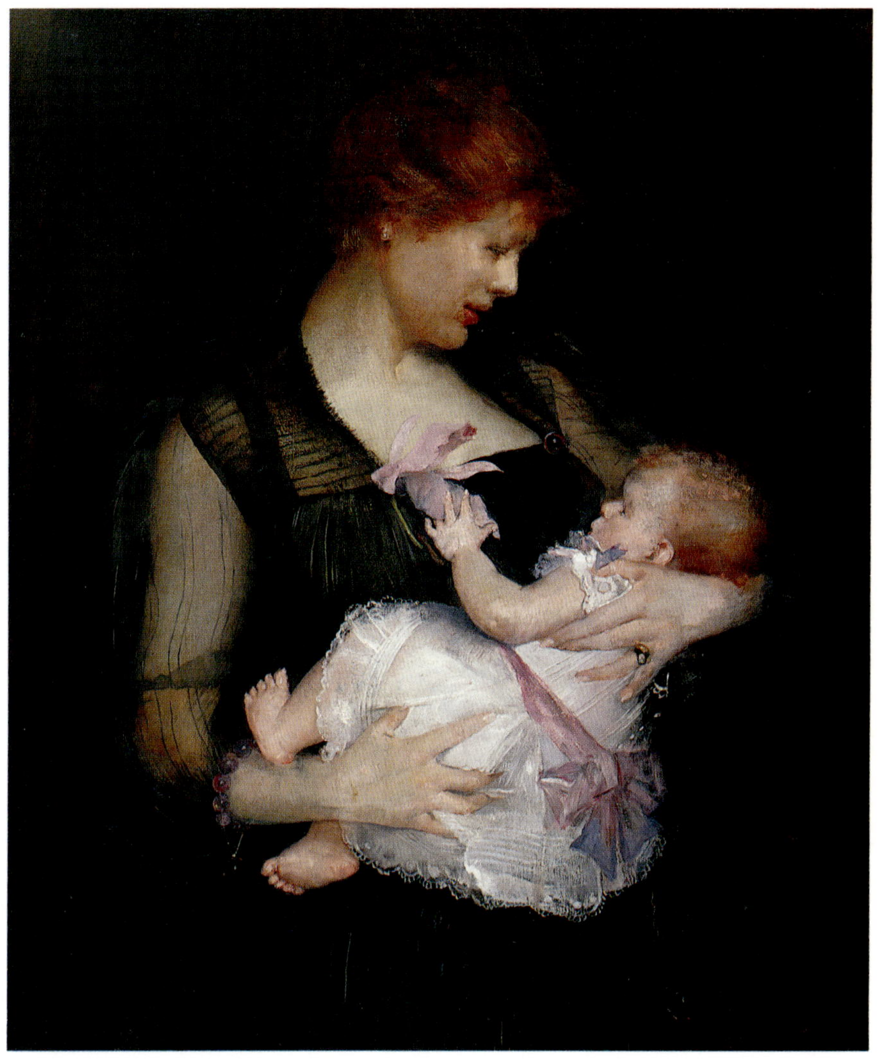

131.
Peter Alfred Gross
Road to the spring (Liverdun)
Road to the Spring, Liverdun, c. 1889
Oil on canvas, 28 x 40″ (71.1 x 101.8 cm)
Collection Mr. and Mrs. Benjamin L. Walbert

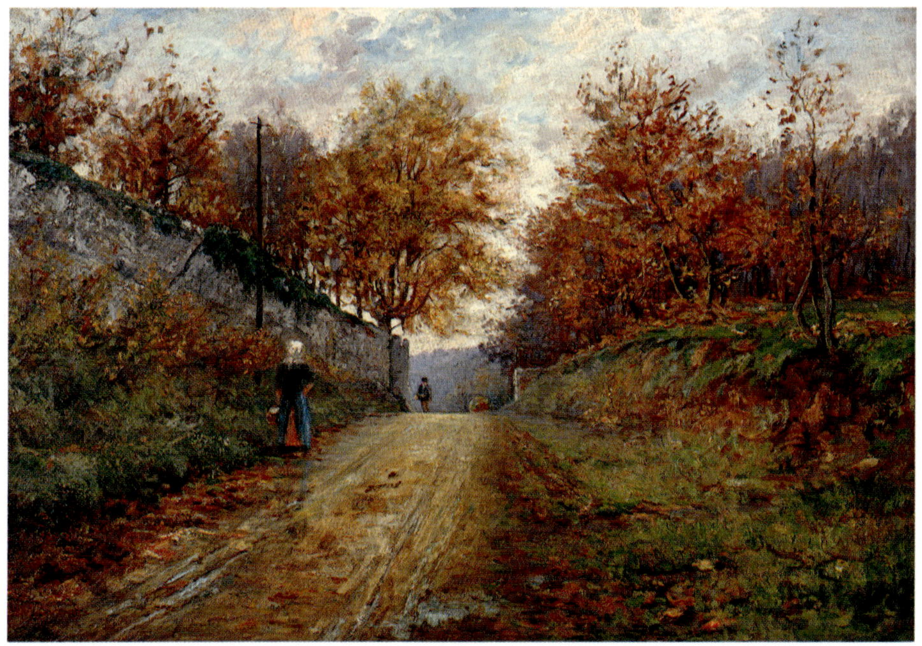

to the orchid for its decorative and exotic qualities, she may have been aware of its symbolic meaning as well. Orchids were strongly associated with sexuality and were thought to be an aphrodisiac.[4] In this context, the flower in Gill's painting perhaps subtly alludes to fertility and new life. *The Orchid* was exhibited frequently during Gill's lifetime. In 1890 it was shown at both the Philadelphia Art Club and the Society of American Artists. HPC

PETER ALFRED GROSS (1849–1914)

Peter Alfred Gross, who was born in Schnecksville, Pennsylvania, retained a deep affection for his native country despite his thirty-five-year residency in Europe. Encouraged by his mother, Gross began to draw at an early age.[1] By 1874 he was listed as a lithographer, artist, and portrait painter in the city directories of Toronto.[2] Two years later he published *Illustrated Toronto: Past and Present*, a guidebook containing approximately sixty of his topographical lithographs.[3] In 1878 Gross left for Paris, where he supported himself by his art and by teaching English at the Institute Rudy, a language school established by his uncle, Charles Rudy. His formal art instruction was provided by Edmond-Marie Petitjean and Edmond-Charles-Joseph Yon, two respected landscape artists. According to G.W. Sheldon, Gross began his studies with Yon in 1882 and with Petitjean about three years later.[4] In 1883 Gross exhibited for the first time at the Pennsylvania Academy of the Fine Arts and at the Paris Salon, where his master Yon was a member of the jury and was probably instrumental in having Gross's picture accepted. Gross contributed regularly to the Salon until 1913, the year he returned to America with his large art collection, intending to settle in his home state of Pennsylvania. Two months after his return he died, in Chicago.

Road to the Spring, Liverdun depicts a scene in the French countryside. Liverdun, a small village in the northeastern part of France, is about fifteen kilometers from Nancy, where Gross painted during the late 1880s and early 1890s. Concentrating on the rural landscape around Liverdun and nearby Essegney, Gross produced some of his largest and most fully realized compositions, including his masterpiece *Essegney* (Allentown Art Museum) of 1892, which was repeatedly exhibited, and his *Road to the Spring*, which was shown at the Berlin International Art Exhibition of 1891 and the Chicago World's Columbian Exposition of 1893.[5] Gross's two entries in the 1889 Exposition, for which he received an honorable mention, were both scenes of Liverdun. Gross painted throughout France, as evidenced by the locations inscribed on his canvases; Normandy and the places around Fontainebleau appear most frequently in his landscape titles. Like many of his fellow American expatriate artists, Gross spent the warm months sketching and painting outside Paris, but whether or not he was part of the informal art colonies that gathered around such individuals as Robert Wylie in Pont-Aven and Monet in Giverny has not been established.[6] His paintings, however, share many of their concerns: an interest in naturalism and in capturing atmospheric effects.

Road to the Spring's autumnal scene reveals a stylistic blend of Barbizon and Impressionist traits in its earthy browns and greens and the high-keyed blue of the sky. Gross repeatedly favored the compositional device found here of a central road or body of water leading the eye into the middle ground. A sense of depth is further established by the scale of the two figures and the wedge-shaped massive wall on the left that gives the illusion of receding into the picture. Although Gross's paintings are of uneven quality, he was well accepted by his contemporaries. Sheldon wrote that "his energy and talents are of a high order."[7]

HPC

CARL GUTHERZ (1844–1907)

Carl Gutherz was born in Schoeftland, Switzerland, in 1844 and was brought to America by his parents about 1851.[1] Raised near Cincinnati and later in Memphis, he practiced mechanical drawing to support himself after the death of his father.[2] About 1868, Gutherz returned to Europe and studied under Isadore Pils, whose military paintings he admired, at the Ecole des Beaux-Arts, Paris.[3] During the Franco-Prussian War he abandoned Paris to study in Brussels and Munich, then painted in Rome and traveled throughout Italy before returning to Memphis, in 1872.[4]

The twelve years following Gutherz's departure from Europe were occupied with portrait commissions, the designing of sets and costumes for the annual Memphis Mardi Gras celebration,[5] and the organization of the St. Louis School of Fine Arts.[6] In 1885, Gutherz returned to Paris, where he created his inspired religious pictures. Now a seasoned teacher, he became associated with Jules-Joseph Lefebvre and Gustave Boulanger and served as a critic at the Académie Julian.[7] In the mid-1880s his Salon entries included Civil War subjects as well as idealized interpretations of French country life, but in 1888 he completed a large visionary painting representing the birth of Christ.

Lux Incarnationis, a depiction of angels rejoicing over the light cast back at them from the village of Bethlehem, was described by Gutherz as "a picture for the end of the century 2000."[8] In a printed text prepared to accompany the painting on public exhibition, the artist wrote:

I took for my scheme the colour of the opal; the thought is this: up to the moment of the birth of Christ, the light of God came from heaven to earth—but, God here, the light glows back from earth to heaven, increasing in glory throughout the ages. Beholding this, the heavenly Host unite in rejoicing over the world redeemed.

The clouds upon which the angels are poised represent the incarnation of perfume. The angels are robed in symbolic dress, with emblematic flowers; incense, birds and butterflies symbolize the Christly creed, and the dark group of the picture is the foreshadowing of Christ. The crown of thorns is side by side with the crown of kingly rank. The motion of all the groups is cyclical.[9]

An ardent admirer of the art of Raphael, Gutherz studied and found inspiration in artists who preceded that master. Recalling the arrays of gilt haloes in paintings by Fra Angelico, Lorenzo Monaco, and Simone Martini, Gutherz also borrowed the Gothic arches of their frames, intensifying the religious import of his masterpiece. When the hanging committee at the Universal Exposition failed to recognize that this "large and unusual subject . . . one of the most original works in the entire exhibition" required a place on the line, the artist expressed his disappointment in a letter to the American Commissioner of Fine Arts.[10] First shown at the Paris Salon of 1888, *Lux Incarnationis* won a bronze medal in 1889, despite its being hung incongruously above William T. Dannat's *The Quartette*. In its elaborate iconography and execution it stood apart from the other American entries, reaching toward "a great stream of thought" that Gutherz found lacking in contemporary art.[11] He exhibited it again in 1893, along with two other paintings marked by the poetic rendering of religious symbolism, at the fair in Chicago.[12]

Gutherz's decorative power was also evident in *Memorialis*, the second painting he submitted to the 1889 Exposition. Here the gold-and-white costume of a winged recording angel is illumined by an inner source that sheds light on the tablet she inscribes. Gutherz's belief in the immortality of the soul is described on a gold ribbon proclaiming the eternal glory that will greet the departed. Preoccupied with the meaning of death, Gutherz wrote that it was "not necessarily less beautiful than any other creation of the Divine Intelligence."[13]

Gutherz's potential for painting on a large scale was realized in the mural commissions that followed his success in Paris. In 1895 he began a series of murals entitled *The Spectrum of Light* for the reading room of the Library of Congress in Washington, D.C. In these panels, and in murals for the People's Church in St. Paul, Minnesota, and the Fort Wayne Courthouse in Indiana, he gave free reign to the ideas that he had introduced in *Lux Incarnationis* and *Memorialis*.[14]

MCOB

(THOMAS) ALEXANDER HARRISON (1853–1930)

"At once a poet and a realist,"[1] Alexander Harrison was a leader of the American expatriate artists in France. He served as vice-president of the American jury in Paris and submitted to the Exposition six paintings that constituted a complete survey of his work to date.[2] He was named a Chevalier of the Legion of Honor in 1889.[3]

A native of Philadelphia, Harrison studied briefly at the Pennsylvania Academy of the Fine Arts. From 1872 to 1877 he worked for the United States Coast and Geodetic Survey, where he developed his drafting skills and a love of the coastline.[4] He then spent a year and a half at the Art School of San Francisco, following this by an equal stint at the Ecole des Beaux-Arts in Paris with Jean-Léon Gérôme. About 1881 he joined the American artists' colony in Pont-Aven (where his brother Birge was working).[5] Harrison's paintings in the Exposition can be compared with works by several of the American comrades in Brittany who looked to him for artistic advice, for example *Seaweed Gatherers* by Howard Russell Butler (see page 128) and *At Evening* by Arthur Wesley Dow (see page 148).

During the rest of his career, Harrison divided his time between Brittany and Paris, with short intervals in America. He exhibited internationally and participated in reformist artists' activities and organizations, among them the Society of American Artists, the Secessionists, and the Champ-de-Mars Salons of the 1890s in Paris. He also maintained his ties with mainstream institutions like the Pennsylvania Academy of the Fine Arts and the National Academy of Design. By the turn of the century his works were in many major museums and he had received high honors from several foreign governments.

Harrison's first successes were his paintings of youths "in the open air in sentimental and sympathetic accord with nature in her quiet moods."[6] *Castles in the Air*, exhibited in the Salon of 1882, established his reputation.[7] The work was sketched on the beach, then completed outside Harrison's Pont-Aven studio, where two cartloads of sand provided a beach for the model. Harrison intended his "color gamuts"—his calculated color systems—to convey not only surface texture but emotion. Here buff and blue convey a wistful atmosphere as well as the soft sea haze and the grainy sand. Harrison regarded as his master stroke the boy's eyes, expressing the dreams and visions of Longfellow's poem "Castles in Spain," from which the painting's title is taken. In *The Amateurs*, painted at Grez a year later, a boy and a girl in a dory fish with a single rod, flirting shyly. Using models, Harrison set the scene at twilight and attempted to sketch from a nearby raft. But the light faded, the raft rocked, and the scene was finished in his studio. Soon after its completion, the painting was purchased by public subscription for the Art Institute of Chicago, where it was exhibited in the Third Annual Exhibition (1885). It also appeared in the 1893 World's Columbian Exposition.

The showing of *Castles in the Air* in the 1882 Salon led Jules Bastien-Lepage to seek out Harrison. A major proponent of the plein-air movement and an inspiration to many Americans, Bastien-Lepage sensed similarities between his and Harrison's sympathetic, if at times unflattering, treatment of the figure and a bond in their idiosyncratic fidelity to nature. When Bastien-Lepage died, in 1884, his mantle was said to have been passed on to Harrison.[8] *Castles in the Air*, which was exhibited at the Pennsylvania Academy of the Fine Arts in 1882 and at the American Art Galleries in 1884 and 1894, became one of Harrison's best-known figural works.

Throughout his career Harrison painted the subject of gently breaking waves. Two of his most popular pictures with this theme appeared in the Exposition: *Crépuscule* (unlocated) and *The Wave*. Harrison sketched outdoors and developed his sketches in his studio into progressively larger canvases in a process he called "intuitive love selection and assimilation."[9] A walk along the shore with Bastien-Lepage in 1884, with the twilight gathering on the water, inspired two oils: *Crépuscule* and, a year later, based on sketches and memory, *The Wave*, which was exhibited at the Salon of 1885.[10] The critic Richard Muther wrote of *The Wave*: "The rendering of water . . . was so extraordinarily faithful that one was tempted to declare the water of the others was absolutely solid compared with this elemental essence of moisture."[11] In his later wave pictures Harrison used multiple transcriptive sketches and finished paintings to explore every nuance of sunlight and moonlight upon water. His serial paintings parallel those of the French Impressionist landscapists, especially Monet's, but while theirs stress neutral optical effects, his glorify the emotional tenor of light.

With *In Arcadia*, Harrison's single most famous work, he sought to show the French he could "beat them at their own game" by painting true plein-air nudes.[12] Only a few of Harrison's contemporaries had attempted the naturalistic nude, notably Renoir. Harrison found the work difficult: scandalized Bretons drove painter and model from the beach to the garden and, finally, to the woods. He would make twenty or thirty quick impressions outdoors, then work them into a large canvas in his studio. Plein-air nudes satisfied both academic interest in the subject and radical concerns with natural light effects. Critics took notice. One commented, "The nude bodies seemed to consist of nothing but colored patches of conflicting lights,"[13] and another said, "He has simply painted modern women nude in the open air, and reproduced, with the sincerity of contemporary analysis, the aspect of flesh that habitually wears clothes as it appears in the unusual condition of nudity."[14] Unlike the few other idealized American nudes at the Exposition, such as Walter Shirlaw's *Rufina* (see page 209) and Kenyon Cox's *Painting and Poetry* (unlocated), Harrison's were frank and literal. Some thought his treatment indecent; when *In Arcadia* was shown at

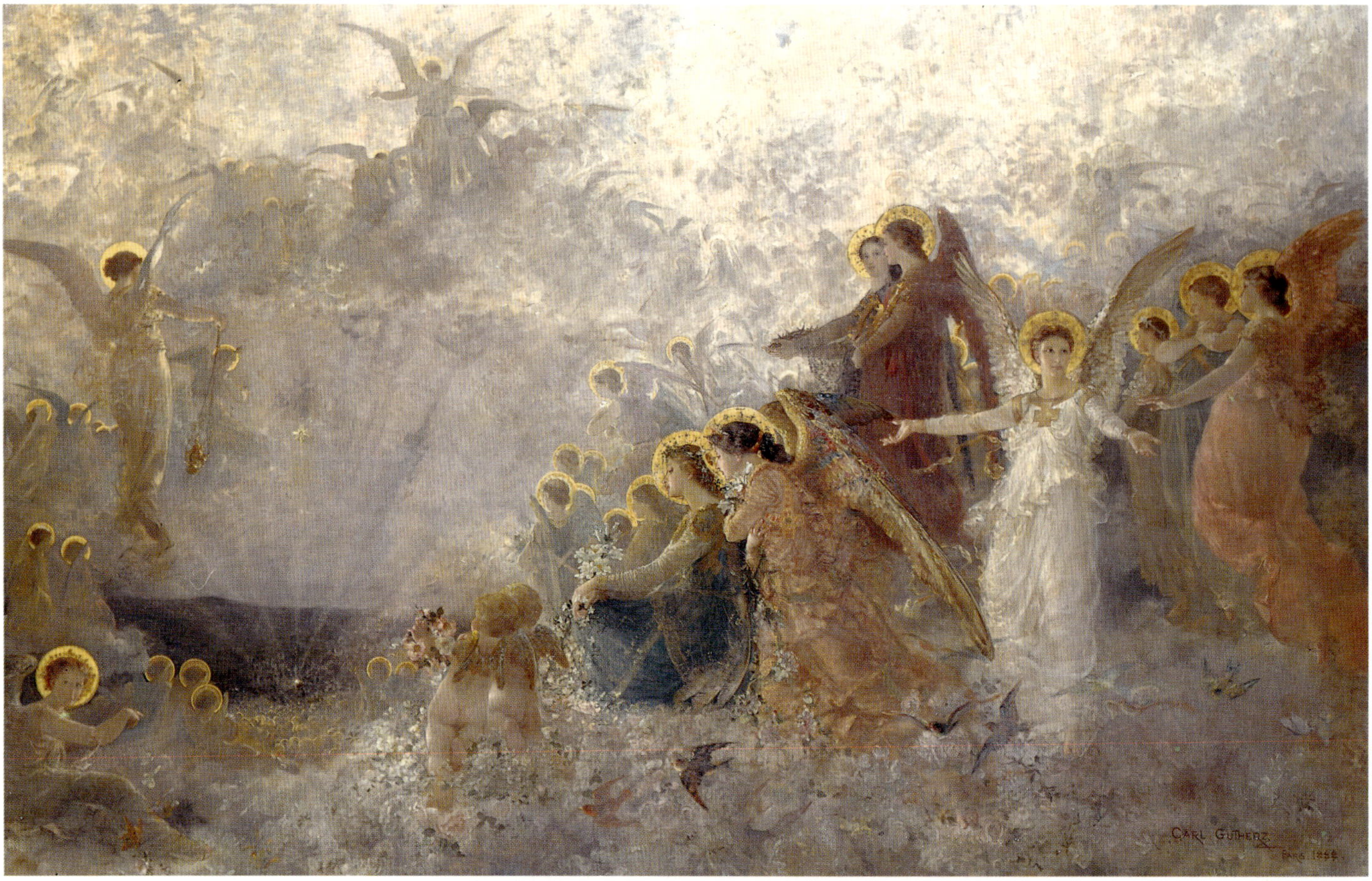

134.
Carl Gutherz
Lux incarnationis
The Light of the Incarnation, 1888
Oil on canvas, 114 x 77″ (289.6 x 195.6 cm)
Memphis Brooks Museum of Art,
Gift of Mr. and Mrs. Marshall F. Goodhart, 1968

135.
Carl Gutherz
Memorialis
Memorialis, 1880s
Oil on canvas, 38¾ x 24⅝″ (98.4 x 62.2 cm)
Private Collection

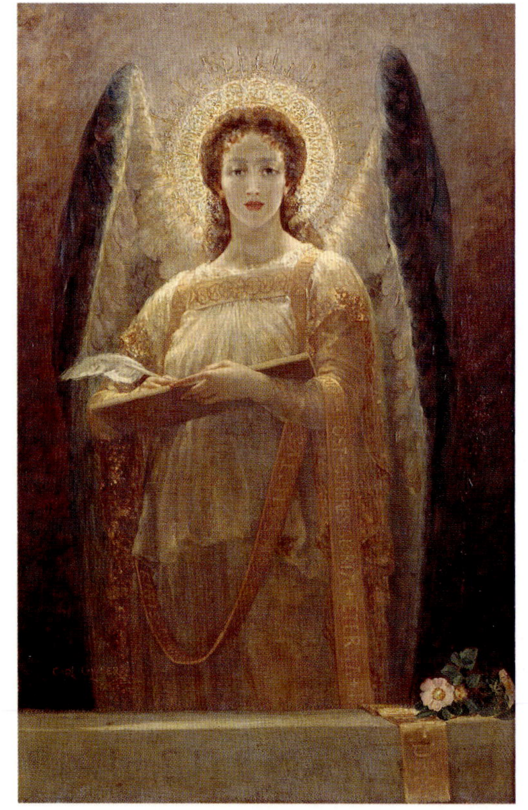

139.
(Thomas) Alexander Harrison
Castles in the air
Castles in Spain, c. 1882
Oil on canvas, 37⅜ x 73¾″ (94 x 187.3 cm)
Owner in 1889 John G. Johnson
© The Metropolitan Museum of Art, New York.
12.226

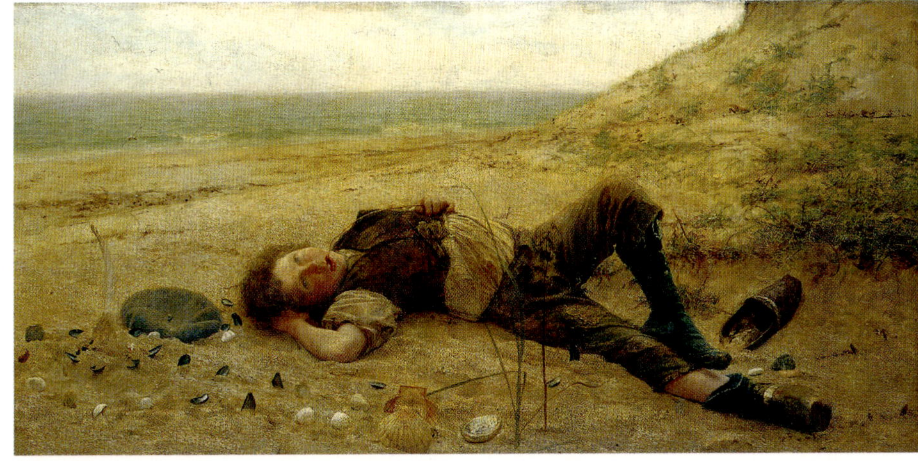

140.
(Thomas) Alexander Harrison
The Amateurs
The Amateurs, 1882–83
Oil on canvas, 57¼ x 89″ (144.8 x 222.5 cm)
Owner in 1889 Chicago Art Institute
Valparaiso University Museum of Art, Indiana,
Bequest of Percy H. Sloan

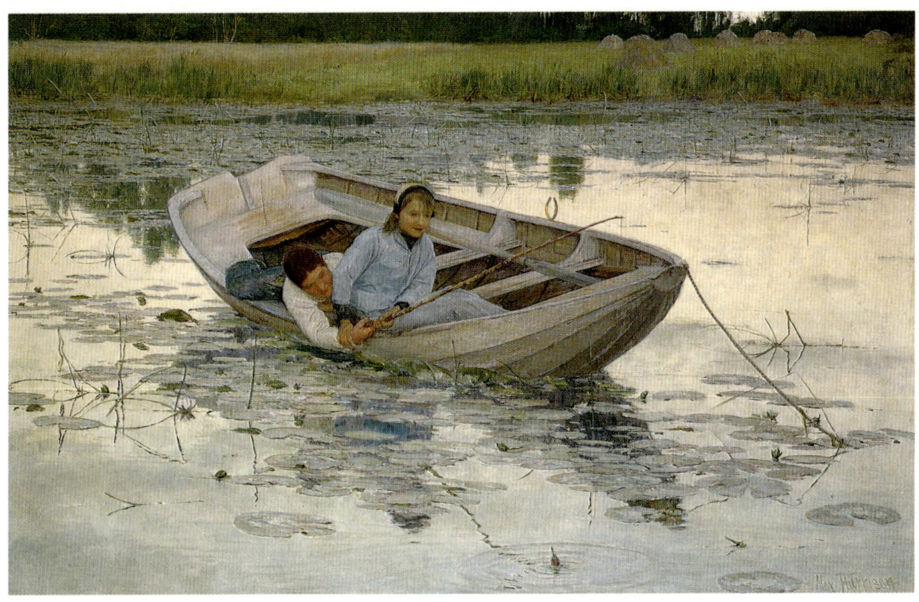

142.
(Thomas) Alexander Harrison
The Wave
The Wave, c. 1885
Oil on canvas, 39¼ x 118″ (99.7 x 229.7 cm)
Pennsylvania Academy of the Fine Arts,
Philadelphia, Joseph E. Temple Fund

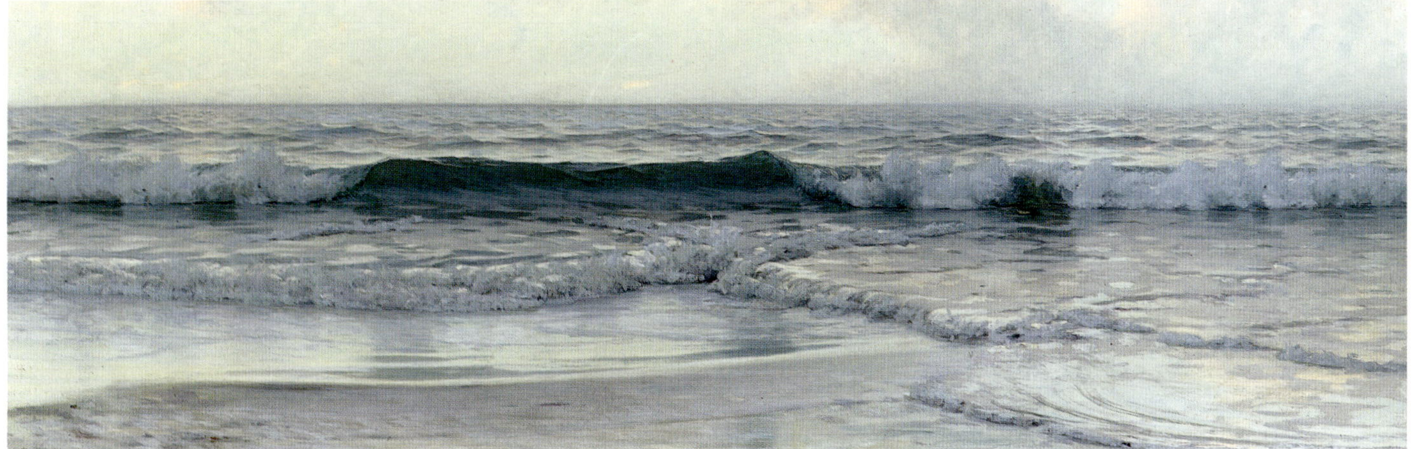

143.
(Thomas) Alexander Harrison
In Arcadia
In Arcadia, c. 1886
Oil on canvas, 77½ x 114¼" (1.97 x 2.9 m)
Musée d'Orsay, Paris

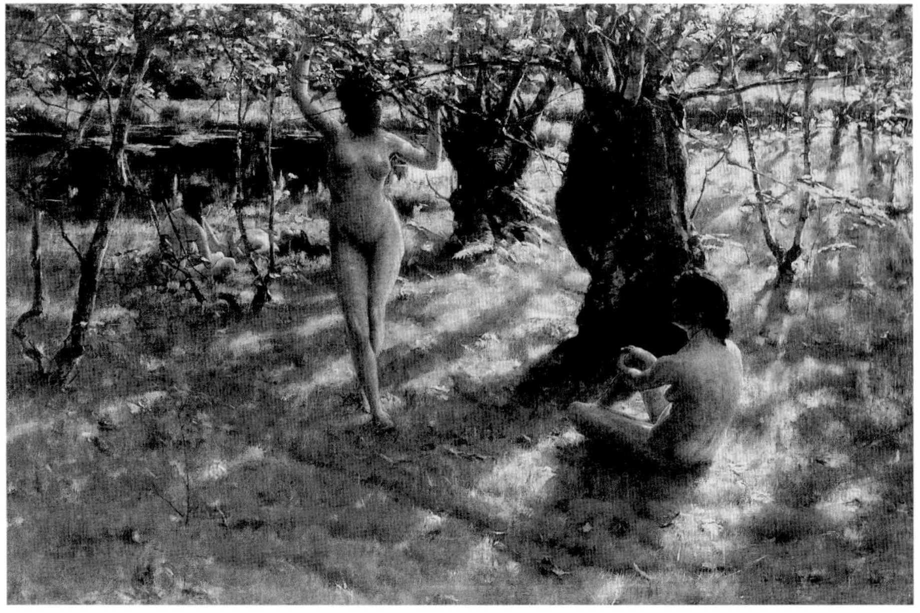

the Pennsylvania Academy of the Fine Arts in 1891, a petition was presented to the director objecting to the "indelicacy" of many of the exhibited pictures.[15] The picture had premiered in the 1886 Salon; by the time it was shown at the New English Art Club in London, a year later, it had inspired fellow exhibitors Philip Wilson Steer and Théodore Roussel to produce similar paintings.[16] By the 1890s, plein-air nudes were a popular and much less controversial theme. *In Arcadia* also appeared in the 1893 World's Columbian Exposition; its purchase in 1905 by the Luxembourg Museum accorded Harrison an honor won by only a few American artists. KZ

(LOWELL) BIRGE HARRISON (1854–1928)

Birge Harrison is best remembered, through his landscape paintings and his teaching, as a major exponent of the Tonalist style. Born in Philadelphia, Harrison received his early artistic instruction at the Pennsylvania Academy of the Fine Arts. In 1876 he met Sargent in Philadelphia at the Centennial Exposition and was advised by him to continue his studies under Sargent's own master, Carolus-Duran, Harrison left for Paris in 1876. He enrolled in Carolus-Duran's atelier in August 1877 and the following year attended Alexandre Cabanel's classes at the Ecole des Beaux-Arts.[1] In 1882, Harrison received official recognition when *Novembre* became one of the first paintings by an American to be purchased by the French government. At this time he spent his summers working both in Pont-Aven and Concarneau in Brittany and in Grez-sur-Loing and Giverny in Normandy.[2] Obliged by illness to stop painting temporarily, Harrison traveled extensively, visiting Australia, India, Asia, and Africa; during these sojourns he wrote and illustrated articles for such popular magazines as *Scribner's*, *Century Magazine*, and *Harper's New Monthly*. His paintings were exhibited regularly at the Society of American Artists during the early 1880s, at the National Academy of Design during the entire decade, and at the Pennsylvania Academy of the Fine Arts from 1889 until his death. Returning to the United States in 1897, he settled in New England, where he began to specialize in Tonalist landscapes and city scenes. In 1905 he helped found the Art Students League Summer School in Woodstock, New York, where from 1906 to 1911 he conducted experimental painting classes in which he expounded the tenets of Tonalism. These lectures were later incorporated into a book, *Landscape Painting*, which was published in 1909. Harrison was elected a member of the National Academy of Design in 1910.

Novembre is one of Harrison's masterworks from his French period. According to the artist, the scene depicted the "interior of a birchwood in autumn, with a single figure of a peasant girl raking up the dead leaves."[3] Harrison understated the narrative content in order to emphasize the landscape's decorative and emotive elements. While Millet, a generation earlier, had underscored the physical exertion of peasant labor, Harrison here depicted the effortlessness of the young woman's actions. The theme of transience is evoked by the fallen leaves and the barren trees of this time of year; November in Catholic countries is the month of All Souls.[4] *Novembre*'s melancholy mood is reinforced by the solitary figure, whose partially averted face appears pensive and withdrawn, and by the restricted palette of browns and grays.

By the early 1880s, Birge and his elder brother, Alexander, had come under the influence of Jules Bastien-Lepage, whose *Joan of Arc* (Metropolitan Museum of Art, New York) had created a sensation at the Paris Salon of 1880. Birge's and Alexander's adoption of a plein-air technique was the direct result of their personal contact with Bastien-Lepage; they "devoted themselves in the seclusion and quietude of Pont-Aven to a serious study of out-of-door nature."[5] Bastien-Lepage's impact is also reflected in the high horizon line, shallow space, and diffused gray light of *Novembre* and other paintings by Birge from this period.[6] In *Landscape Painting*, Harrison recalled the major stylistic breakthrough that he made in painting *Novembre*: "A Scandinavian painter," Harrison wrote, "had shown me the secret of atmospheric painting . . . [and] made clear to me . . . the importance of vibration and refraction in landscape painting."[7] *Novembre* was shown at the Paris Salon of 1882 and received a silver medal seven years later at the Universal Exposition, where it was Harrison's sole entry.

HPC

GEORGE PETER ALEXANDER HEALY (1813–1894)

G.P.A. Healy was the elder statesman among the American artists in Paris, and a member of the United States jury in Paris for the 1889 Exposition. Healy revered the work of the French painter Thomas Couture[1] and incorporated the teachings put forth in Couture's *Méthode et entretien d'atelier* into his own international portrait style.[2] The array of male portraits Healy exhibited in the 1889 Exposition bore traces of Couture's influence but were dominated by the straightforward presentation and care in draftsmanship that had become Healy's trademarks during a career of more than fifty years. Healy's paintings served as a counterpoint to the award-winning contemporary female portraits of his countryman Sargent, one of many younger artists he had advised and encouraged in the 1870s and 1880s. Known as "Pops" to artists like Gari Melchers, Kenyon

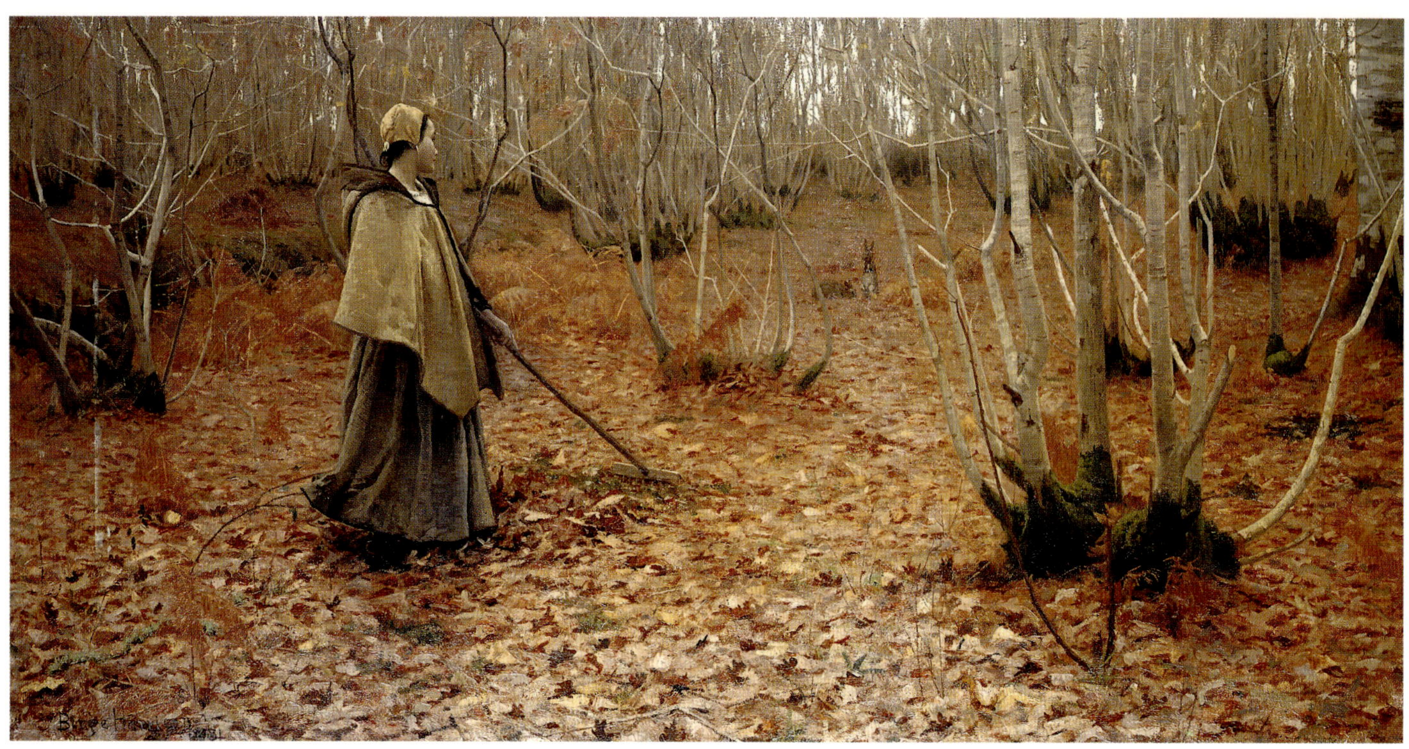

145.
(Lowell) Birge Harrison
Novembre
Novembre, 1881
Oil on canvas, 52 x 97⅝" (130 x 248. cm)
Owner in 1889 the French government
Musée des Beaux-Arts et d'Archéologie de Rennes

Cox, Childe Hassam, and Julian Alden Weir,[3] the distinguished portraitist had achieved a position in European and American social, political, literary, and aritistic circles to which few could aspire.

Healy, who was born in 1813 in Boston, was encouraged by the portrait painter Thomas Sully to open a studio in that city at the age of eighteen.[4] In 1834 he made his first trip abroad, entering the Paris studio of Baron Gros, where he made the acquaintance of Couture, then also a student there. While in Paris, Healy became attached to the court of Louis Philippe, who commissioned him to paint portraits of American statesmen for Versailles. He exhibited frequently at the Salon, winning a bronze medal in 1840, and was represented by fourteen paintings at the 1855 Universal Exposition.[5]

Healy's six paintings in the 1889 Exposition included *Study at the Harp* (unlocated) and five portraits: *Charles Bigot*, a portrait of his son-in-law, a French writer (unlocated); *King of Roumania* (1881; Newberry Library, Chicago); *Sir Henry Morton Stanley* (1888; Newberry Library); *Lord Edward Robert Bulwer-Lytton, 1st Earl of Lytton;* and *Orestes Brownson*, a portrait of the religious leader, social theorist, and noted author.[6] Healy had first met Brownson, whom he described as "only less than a miracle,"[7] while active, as a portraitist, in Chicago, from 1855 to 1867.[8] A devout Catholic, Healy credited Brownson's patriotic and spiritual eloquence with diminishing anti-Catholic sentiment in that city. He painted two three-quarter-length portraits of Brownson in 1863, posing him in a gilded Egyptian Revival chair and highlighting his intense, expressive head and powerful hands against a dark background.[9]

In contrast with the portrait of Brownson is Healy's portrait of Lord Lytton, a former viceroy of India and a poet (who wrote under the name of

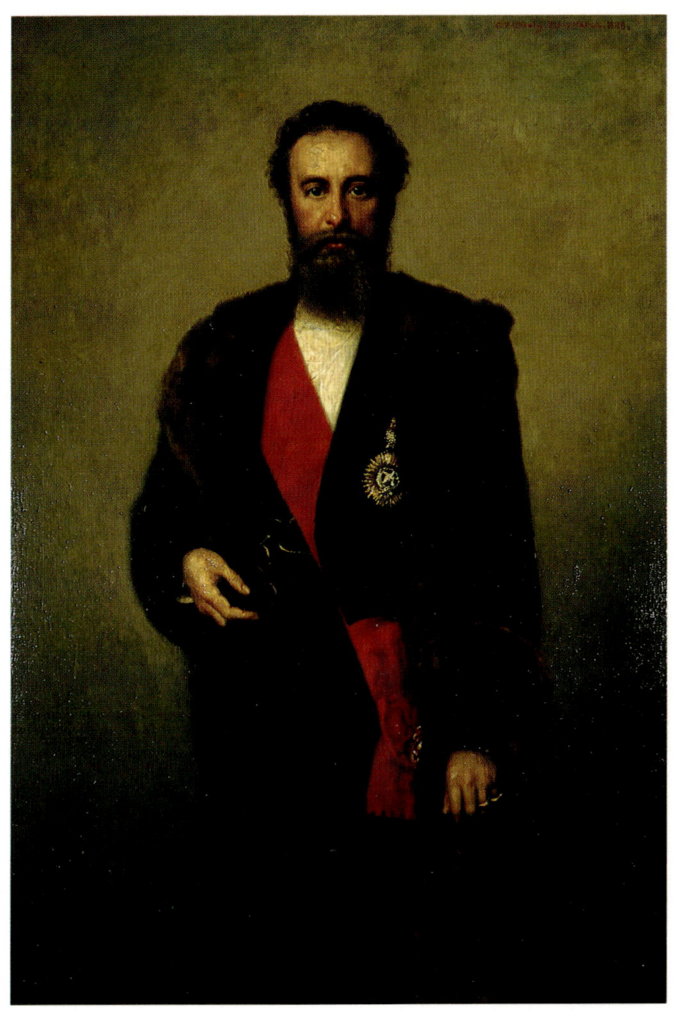

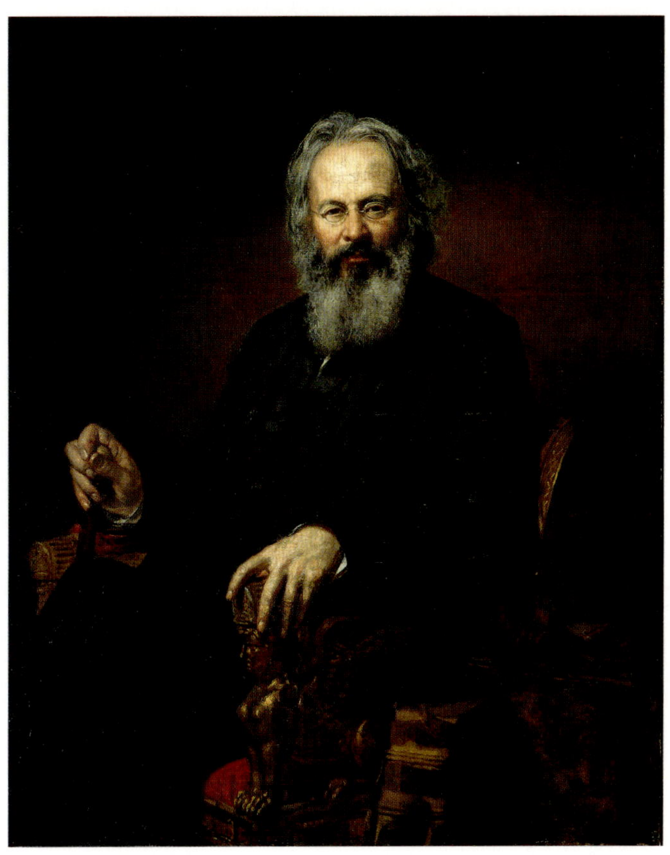

155.
George Peter Alexander Healy
Lord Lytton
Lord Edward Robert Bulwer-Lytton, 1888
Oil on canvas, 60⅝ x 40½" (154 x 102.9 cm)
The Newberry Library, Chicago,
Gift of the artist

159.
George Peter Alexander Healy
Portrait of M. Brownson
Orestes Augustus Brownson, 1863
Oil on canvas, 55¼ x 43½" (139.7 x 109.8 cm)
Museum of Fine Arts, Boston,
Gift of Mrs. Louisa Healy

Owen Meredith).[10] Completed in 1888, when Lytton was the English ambassador to France, the portrait luxuriates in the refined gold, silk, and fur textures of Lord Lytton's costume. Lytton's handsome head is clearly outlined, emerging from a light background that throws the entire figure into relief—a technique Healy had long since appropriated from Couture. Overall, the impression is of a formal, upper-class, nineteenth-century portrait, typical of conservative French studio style. The only American to have exhibited at the French world's fairs of 1855, 1867, 1878, and 1889, Healy set a standard in both technique and sophistication that his countrymen, almost to the end of the nineteenth century, strove to meet. MCOB

EDWARD LAMSON HENRY (1841–1919)

E.L. Henry's nostalgic and anecdotal genre paintings were a great popular success.[1] Born in Charleston, South Carolina, and raised in New York City and Connecticut, Henry may have begun to study drawing in the mid-1850s with Robert Weir, who was an art instructor at the United States Military Academy at West Point. In 1857 or 1858 he enrolled in the Pennsylvania Academy of the Fine Arts. He arrived in Paris in 1860 to spend two years in the atelier of Charles Gleyre, where instruction favored a tight painting technique. After traveling in Europe, he returned to the United States and enlisted in the Union army as a captain's clerk; in this post he was able to sketch scenes of the Civil War. He then settled in New York.

Henry was a meticulous realist with a flair for color and an innate sense of humor. He specialized in scenes of the recent past: buildings since torn down, outmoded means of transportation, antebellum estates. He cultivated a lifelong passion for antiques, collecting even carriages and salvaged building parts, and campaigned for the preservation of historic buildings. Throughout these years in New York he exhibited at the National Academy of Design. Henry and his wife, Frances Livingston Wells, an amateur artist, gathered New York's art world around them in their home in the Tenth Street Studio Building. Always more of a popular favorite than a critical success, Henry saw his work reproduced widely in engravings and chromolithographs; these remained in demand until the turn of the century.

Henry's two pictures in the Exposition, both of which show people in old-fashioned carriages conversing, won him an honorable mention. In *One Hundred Years Ago* (unlocated) the scene takes place in front of an elegant Federal town house as pleasantries are exchanged between the occupants of the carriage and a man standing beside it. In *The Latest Village Scandal* the scene is a country road on a mountaintop; the terrain identifies the setting as Cragsmoor in the Shawangunk Mountains, New York, where in 1883 the Henrys began to build a summer house.[2] They soon persuaded other artists to join them, thus creating an artists' outpost. The mountaintop provided spectacular views, picturesque neighbors who made their living in old-fashioned trades, and an absence of modern intrusions. In Cragsmoor, or working in New York from his Cragsmoor sketches, Henry painted many scenes of this vanishing rural life. The drivers of two buckboards meet on the road in *The Latest Village Scandal*, originally called *The Latest News*, and stop to gossip.[3] Henry used Oliver Evans and his wife, Nancy, as models for the lone man and the woman in this and in other scenes of rural life.[4] The new title encourages viewers to concoct their own versions of these country folks' conversation.[5]

Henry's brand of nostalgic humor, while distinctive, parallels that of many other French and American paintings in the Exposition. Counterparts to his scenes of American rural life can be found in the works of French painters like Jules Breton and P.A.J. Dagnan-Bouveret and American expatriates like Walter MacEwen, Walter Gay, and Frank Millet. Henry's pictures, though set in America, celebrate and freeze for all time, as theirs do, a slower pace of life. KZ

George Hitchcock has been called "the painter of sunlight," a sobriquet earned for him by his radiantly colorful canvases, many with religious overtones, depicting Dutch peasants set in a background of flowers.[1] Hitchcock was born in Providence and educated at Brown University and the Harvard Law School. Not until his late twenties did he decide upon a career in art. In 1880 he studied in Paris at the Académie Julian with Gustave Boulanger and Jules Lefebvre, and in 1881 he became an expatriate, settling in the town of Egmond, near Amsterdam, where he spent most of the year. During Hitchcock's first summers in Holland he worked in The Hague with Hendrik Mesdag. With the exhibition at the 1885 Salon of *Tulip Culture* (unlocated), which Gérôme cited as the best American picture shown that year, Hitchcock acquired an international reputation.[2] *Tulip Culture* was one of three paintings Hitchcock submitted to the 1889 Exposition, where he was very influential as secretary of the American art jury in Paris that made selections for the American fine arts section.[3]

Annonciation was another of the pictures Hitchcock showed at the Exposition. It belongs to a series dealing with religious themes presented in the guise of contemporary genre that Hitchcock began painting during the mid-1880s. Stylistically and thematically Hitchcock's paintings call to mind those of Jules Bastien-Lepage in France and Fritz von Uhde in Germany. Hitchcock's admiration of Botticelli links him also to the English Pre-Raphaelites.[4] His use of bright color parallels that of the Impressionists, although he did not share their interest in chromatic analysis. In Hitchcock's *Annonciation,* the Virgin is depicted as a Dutch peasant girl standing in a field of white lilies, symbolic of purity and the attribute of the message-bearing angel Gabriel. The Virgin's downcast eyes and gesture of humility were construed as her reaction to the divine message that she was to bear the Christ child.[5] At the 1889 Exposition the painting was admired by contemporary critics for its plein-air imagery and for its innovative interpretation.[6] Art critic Theodore Child singled it out as "one of the most refined and original pictures in the American section."[7] It had been exhibited in 1888 at the Royal Academy in Munich and the Paris Salon. The year after the Exposition, Hitchcock sold it to the Chicago collector Potter Palmer, who, in 1890, lent it to the Inter-State Industrial Exposition in Chicago (no. 145).[8]

Both the *Annonciation* and *Maternity* can be seen as part of a revival of interest in religious subjects. Religious genre such as Gustave Courbet's *A Funeral at Ornans* (1850; Musée d'Orsay), and Jean-François Millet's *The Angelus* (1856–59; Musée d'Orsay) began to become popular in the mid-nineteenth century.[9] By the time of the Exposition, even such avant-garde artists as Paul Gauguin had turned to painting religious customs, particularly among the Bretons. That two of Hitchcock's three entries blended the secular with the sacred highlights his emphasis in the eighties. Gari Melchers, who had followed Hitchcock to Egmond, was similarly focused, as is evidenced by his showing *The Sermon* and *Communion* (see page 185) in the Exposition.[10]

Maternity is set apart from Hitchcock's two other paintings by its silvery tonality and by the inclusion of three figures, a woman and two children, so that the group suggests the holy family. From Bouguereau to Puvis de Chavannes, the image of the mother and child, handled with a sense of its human as well as its divine import, was popular among French artists. Here the peasant mother's holiness is alluded to by the pastoral device of a winnowing basket appearing like

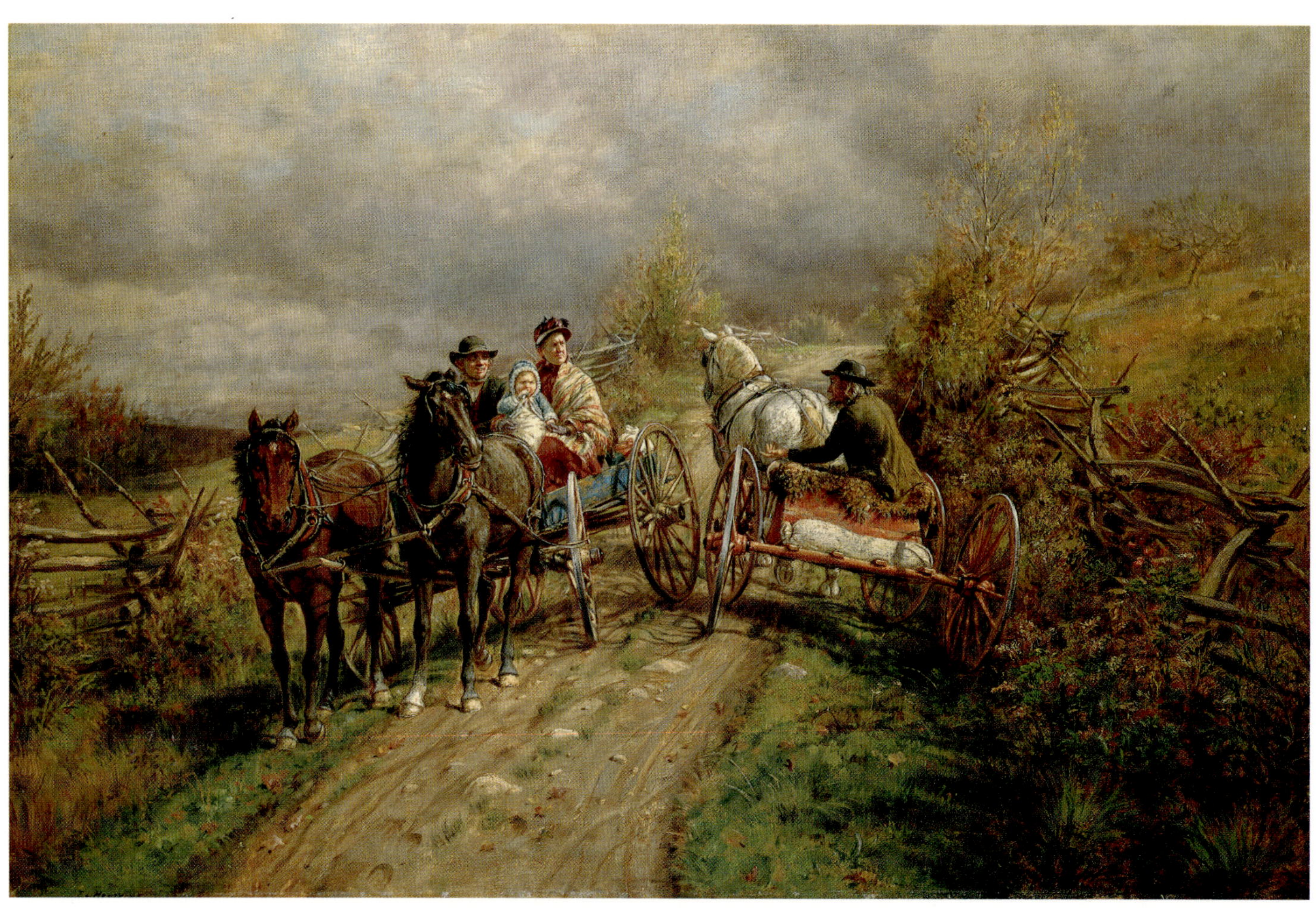

163.
Edward Lamson Henry
The Latest Village Scandal
The Latest Village Scandal, 1885
Oil on canvas, 17 x 25¼" (43.5 x 64 cm)
Collection Mr. and Mrs. Eddy G. Nicholson

a halo behind her head. This modern-day Virgin and Child with St. John, set frontally on a path in an open field rather than in a garden of tulips or lilies, is less decorative and more directly symbolic than Hitchcock's other two entries.[11] The almost monochromatic tonalities augment the mystical feeling and relate the painting to Symbolist works of the period. *Maternity*, which was probably painted expressly for the Exposition, was exhibited again, at the London Royal Academy, in 1891. It was owned by Mrs. George McCulloch before it was purchased, in 1913, by the Aberdeen Art Gallery and Museums. AB

THOMAS HOVENDEN (1840–1895)

In the 1880s and the early 1890s, Thomas Hovenden was an exponent of an anecdotal type of genre painting that by the time of his death, in 1895, was already in decline. Yet within Hovenden's oeuvre there were also a few pictures that established him as the period's foremost painter of American history. Among these was *The Last Moments of John Brown*, one of the most widely reproduced images of the late nineteenth century.

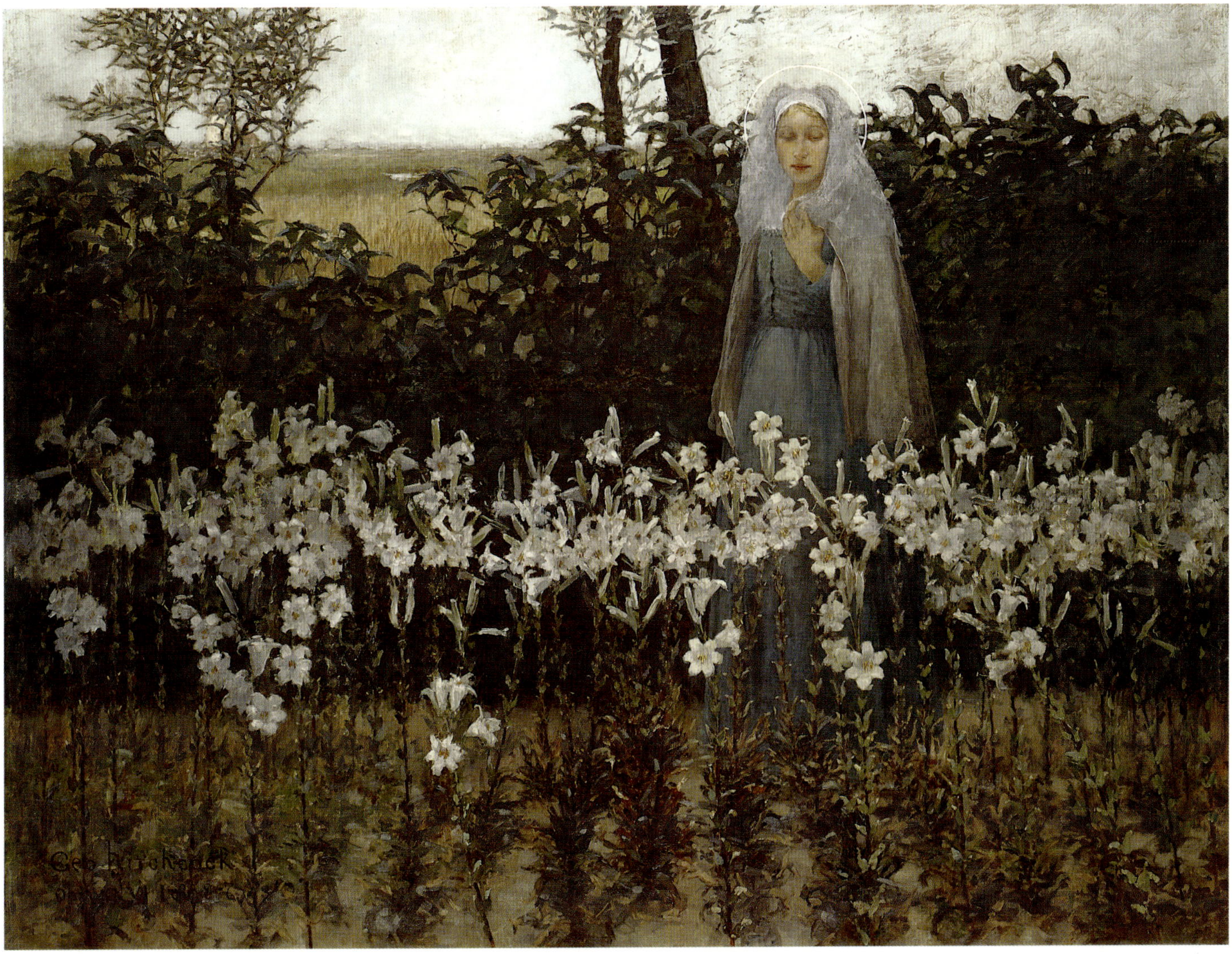

166.
George Hitchcock
Annonciation
Annunciation Lilies, 1887
Oil on canvas, 62½ x 80½″ (158.8 x 204.5 cm)
Owner in 1889 W. H. Tailer
© The Art Institute of Chicago,
Gift of Mr. and Mrs. Potter Palmer, 1930.1289

167.
George Hitchcock
Maternity
Maternité, 1889
Oil on canvas, 69½ x 98″ (176.5 x 248.9 cm)
Aberdeen Art Gallery and Museums, Scotland

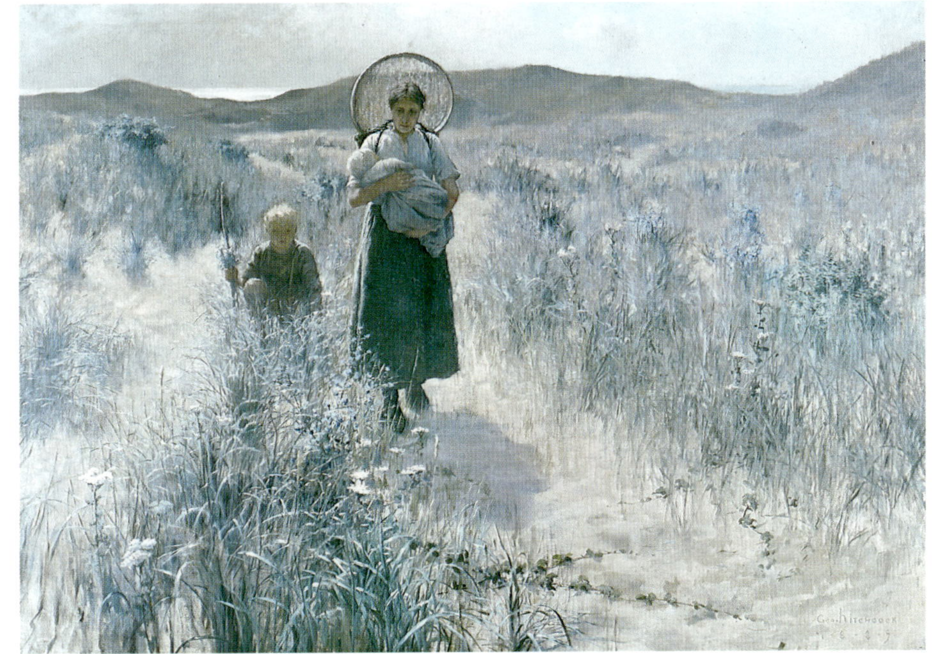

Hovenden's orientation toward sentimental genre and "story-telling" pictures doubtless stemmed from his British background and the fact that when he arrived in the United States he had already trained in his native Ireland, at the Cork School of Design. Hovenden continued his studies at the National Academy of Design before going to Paris, where, between 1874 and 1880, he studied with Cabanel. Certain pictures from these years indicate that, like many American artists, Hovenden broadened his horizon through Barbizon. In 1886, six years after his return from France, Hovenden succeeded Thomas Eakins as director of the Pennsylvania Academy of the Fine Arts.

The Last Moments of John Brown, painted between 1882 and 1884, combines Hovenden's recently acquired European technique with clearly American subject matter. The picture that was the original of the replica shown in the present exhibition was commissioned by Robbins Battell, a nineteenth-century collector who helped Hovenden formulate its conception. The picture's sources are well documented: a newspaper fabrication of a Civil War occurrence and its interpretation in a poem by Whittier. Both of these were given to Hovenden by Battell, who in return received a romanticization of a historical event.[1] Nevertheless, in the nineteenth century *The Last Moments of John Brown* was prized as much for its historical authenticity as for its pictorial qualities. Hovenden himself stated that he had eschewed narrative drama in the subject, hoping to forward instead the spirit of the man and his ideas.[2] In this vein the picture was described on at least one occasion as the pictorial analogue of "The Battle Hymn of the Republic."[3]

It was probably in this spirit that Hovenden, a member of the selection committee for the artists residing in the United States, exhibited *John Brown* at the 1889 Paris Exposition. It was his only entry despite the fact that he had another highly viable option in *In the Hands of the Enemy*, which had not only been a great success at the National Academy of Design earlier in the year but was also a Civil War subject.[4] It is possible that Hovenden chose to exhibit *John Brown* because its subject was already well known to the French through the writing of Victor Hugo. Indeed the image itself was known in France, since at least one engraving of *The Last Moments of John Brown* is known to have circulated in Paris in 1885. The American critic Earl Shinn wrote to Hovenden, "I saw some folks stopping to look at the picture yesterday before the window of a newspaper shop and such historical pictures do a great deal of good. The topic is apropros at the moment because of Victor Hugo's birthday. . . ."[5] The painting's appearance in Paris was surely even more felicitous in 1889, the anniversary of the French Republic. For if John Brown was seen as a symbol of the Civil War, as the century advanced the war itself was increasingly seen as the survival test of the American political system. This message was eminently appropriate at an exposition commemorating the centennial of the French Revolution.

The origin of the replica in the present exhibition remains obscure. It has been suggested that, since it is much smaller than the original, it was made for purposes of engraving by the artist himself.[6] Hovenden made at least one engraving of the picture, published in 1885 by George Gebbie and possibly based on this replica. At some point the replica was acquired by Albert Rosenthal, a Philadelphia artist who was also a collector of American art. The original of *The Last Moments of John Brown* was given to the Metropolitan Museum of Art in 1897 by Robbins Battell's heirs. JH

One of America's greatest nineteenth-century artists, George Inness was strongly influenced by French Barbizon art. After a two-year apprenticeship as an engraver, he studied painting about 1843 with the French expatriate landscapist Régis-François Gignoux in New York. His early works reveal his appreciation of Claude Lorrain and the seventeenth-century Dutch landscape masters, gained through studying prints. The first of Inness's four European visits occurred in 1850, when he spent fifteen months in Italy, stopping briefly in Paris, where he saw the works of Théodore Rousseau. But it was on his second trip abroad, in 1853–54, that Rousseau's and other Barbizon painters' influence took effect. They inspired the free brushwork, bright colors, and informal compositions of the late 1850s and 1860s. By 1863, Inness had moved to Perth Amboy, New Jersey, where fellow artist William Page introduced him to the theories of Emanuel Swedenborg. The Swedish philosopher's spiritualism made a deep and lasting impression and became a major force in his life. From 1870 to 1874, Inness lived in Italy, and before he returned to America, in 1875, he spent almost a year in Paris, where his son, George Inness, Jr., was studying with Léon Bonnat. In 1878, Inness gave public expression to his ideas about art, and that same year the prominent New York art dealer Thomas B. Clarke began to represent him.[1] A comprehensive exhibition of his works held in 1884 helped to establish Inness as the leading figure in American landscape painting, a status he enjoyed for the rest of his career. For this reason Rush C. Hawkins, the United States Commissioner of Fine Arts, insisted on including at least one of his paintings in the 1889 Exposition.[2]

Inness's only entry in the 1889 Exposition was the cause of a bitter controversy that divided the New York art community. When Hawkins asked Inness to submit one of his paintings, Inness refused. "I would have gladly exhibited," Inness said, "could all the phases of my work have been represented."[3] Ignoring Inness's wishes, Hawkins borrowed *A Short Cut, Watchung Station* from the American Art Association and submitted it to the New York jury, who approved it. Outraged, Inness attempted to thwart Hawkins's plans by having his wife petition members of the selection committee to sign a statement requesting that the painting be withdrawn.

Hawkins's desire "to get up the best art exhibition" was the cause of his insistence on including Inness.[4] Less easily explained is Inness's refusal. His criticism of *A Short Cut, Watchung Station* that it was "an unimportant, non-representative work" was not an opinion shared by contemporary reviewers, who continually praised the painting.[5] When Inness showed the work in the Sixth Annual Exhibition of the Society of American Artists, in 1883, *The Nation* gave it a long and favorable review, commenting, "The absolute justness of color relation in light and shades is rarely so admirably reached."[6] Furthermore, the work was unanimously accepted by the jury. "It is, in my opinion, one of Mr. Inness' best examples," wrote one reporter; "it is a work of large size and the jury hailed its appearance before it with pleasure."[7] The painting received international recognition when it was awarded a bronze medal at the 1889 Exposition. In 1895 it was purchased by the Philadelphia Museum of Art with funds from the Wilstach Estate. Inness's real reason for deciding not to submit a picture was probably that he had been promised a solo show in Paris. "Inness was induced not to send to the Universal Exposition," reported the *Art Amateur* in November 1889, "on the assurance of Messrs. Boussod, Valadon & Co. that they would

168.
Thomas Hovenden
Last Moments of John Brown, John Brown leaving the jail on the morning of his execution.
The Last Moments of John Brown (replica, 1884)
Oil on canvas, 46⅛ x 38⅛" (117.2 x 96.8 cm)
The Fine Arts Museums of San Francisco,
M. H. de Young Memorial Museum,
Gift of Mr. and Mrs. John D. Rockefeller, 3rd

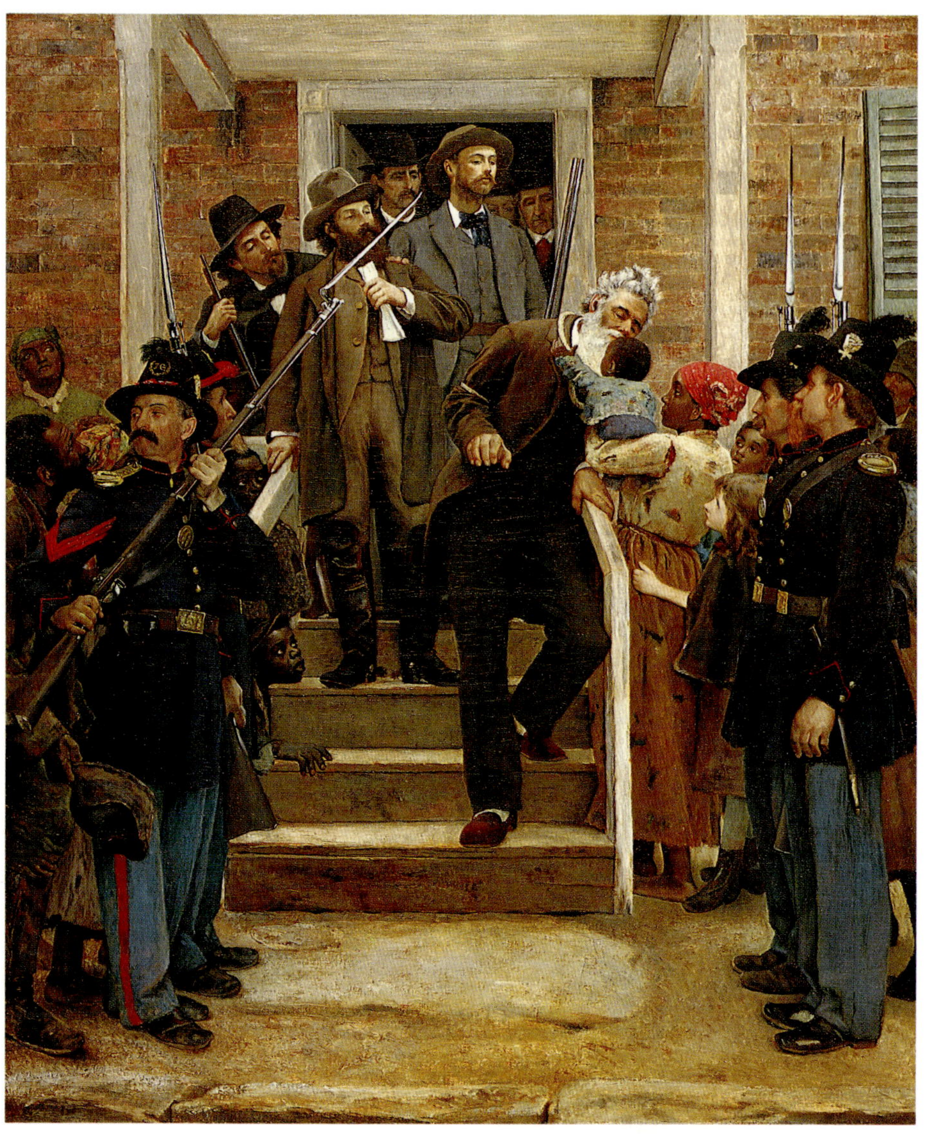

make a special exhibition of his works. But they left him in the lurch, and he was 'represented' . . . only by a single picture."[8]

A Short Cut, Watchung Station was painted near Inness's home in Montclair, New Jersey, where the artist had settled permanently in 1878. Perhaps the emphasis of the Society of American Artists on figure painting prompted Inness to incorporate larger and more prominent figures in his works of the early 1880s.[9] Inness may have reacted to this preference by attempting briefly to give greater importance and size to his depiction of the human form.[10] *A Short Cut, Watchung Station*, which was exhibited at the Society of American Artists in 1883, reveals this new, short-lived direction in Inness's art. Inness's criticism of this painting as a "non-representative work" is partially explained by the emphasis given the figure of the old man in the foreground and the vertical format of the composition, both unusual features in his oeuvre. They may also explain his vehement opposition to its being exhibited in Paris in 1889.

HPC

175.
George Inness
A shortcut to Wachung [*sic*] Station
A Short Cut, Watchung Station, N.J., 1883
Oil on canvas, 37¾ x 29″ (95.9 x 73.7 cm)
Owner in 1889 American Art Association
Philadelphia Museum of Art,
The W. P. Wilstach Collection. W95.1.5

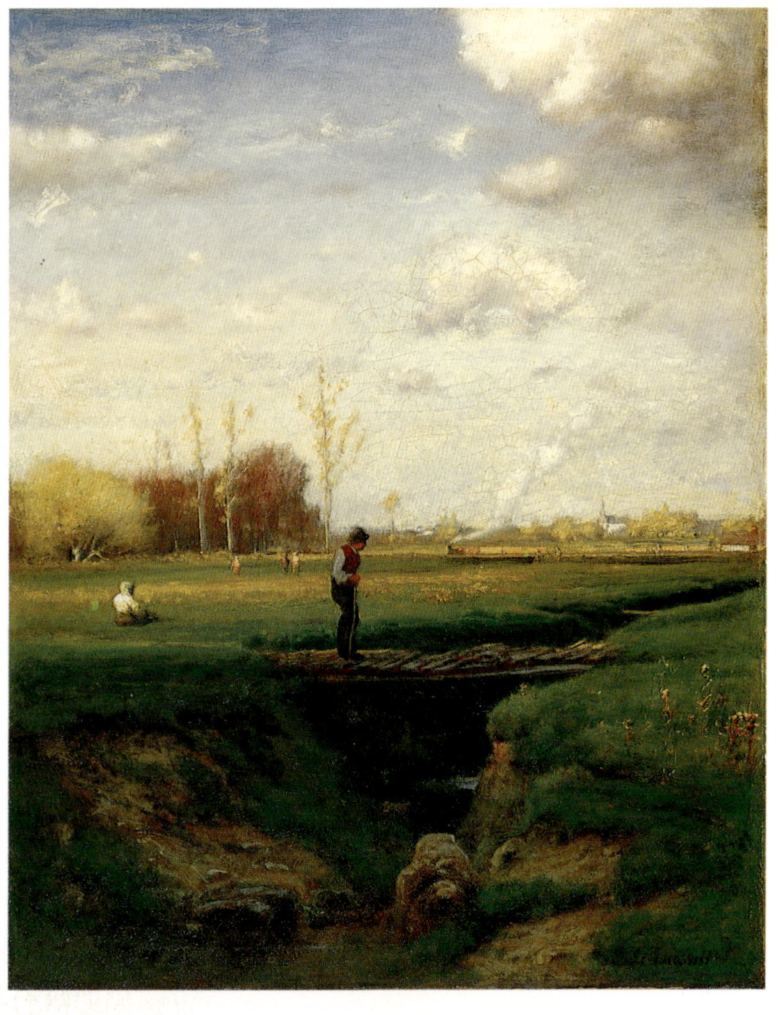

178.
Eastman Johnson
Two Men
The Funding Bill, 1881
Oil on canvas, 60½ x 78¼″ (153.7 x 198.8 cm)
© The Metropolitan Museum of Art, New York,
Gift of Robert Gordon, 98.14

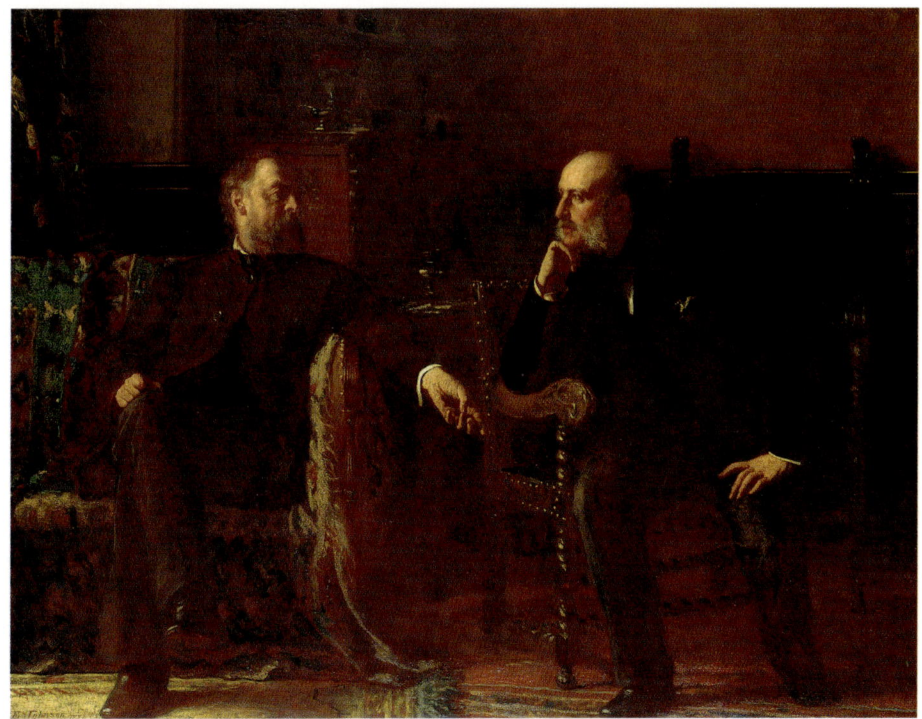

EASTMAN JOHNSON (1824–1906)

After an apprenticeship in a Boston lithography shop from 1840 to 1842, Eastman Johnson returned to his home town of Lovell, Maine, and worked as a portraitist, chiefly in pencil and crayon.[1] He studied oil painting in Düsseldorf at the Royal Academy from 1849 to 1850 and in Emanuel Leutze's studio in 1851. Johnson next went to The Hague, where for three years he devoted himself to examining seventeenth-century Dutch paintings and executing portraits. He traveled to Paris for two months' study under Thomas Couture in 1855. From this training Johnson acquired a precise linear style of controlled brushwork, rich color, and lighting contrasts. In the 1860s and 1870s Johnson established himself as one of America's ablest portraitists and genre painters. He produced scenes full of narrative details that were praised as typifying American life, and he painted portraits of American men and women of stature. In several highly regarded group portraits he merged the two genres; an example is *The Hatch Family* (Metropolitan Museum of Art, New York). As a member of the Union League Club, the Century Association, and the innovative Society of American Artists, he was prominent in the political, intellectual, and artistic life of New York.

In *Two Men* Johnson revealed a new painterly bravura in the familiar format of portraiture.[2] Originally titled *The Funding Bill*, it shows Robert Rutherfurd, the artist's brother-in-law, and Samuel Rowse, an artist, in Johnson's home discussing a congressional bill that would refund the national debt. The painting's free and visible brushwork and the speed of its execution (this large work was finished in three weeks in 1881) show Couture's influence.[3] The green, red, and yellow impasto of the couch throw and the sparkle of the upholstery nails seem to exist purely for their aesthetic appeal. In Johnson's earlier genre paintings objects are used to further the anecdote; here the rendering of the rich furnishings of an upper-middle-class parlor seems to be valued more for the visual delight it affords. The Düsseldorfian chiaroscuro is deepened with strong rusty-brown shadows cast on jet-black clothing in deference to Mihály Munkácsy, a contemporary Hungarian artist famous for his use of red-brown against black.[4] At the 1889 Exposition, Johnson's painting stood midway between the sober portraits of Healy and the vivacious works of Sargent, being aligned with the former in tone and with the latter in technique.

Johnson, who was at first reluctant to show in the Exposition, reportedly "did not at all approve of the way in which the business of the Commission was managed."[5] But when he realized that Commissioner Rush Hawkins would probably obtain one of his works whether or not he agreed, he capitulated and sent *The Funding Bill*, exhibiting it under the less specific title *Two Men*. While it was probably the best painting available, its choice by Johnson may have been somewhat ironic. Although Johnson's original title referred to a specific political issue of 1881 and not the politics of the Exposition, he may well have felt that its subject, two men in dispute, suited the occasion. *Two Men* repaid Johnson by winning him a bronze medal. It has had a distinguished exhibition history, including three appearances in 1881—at the National Academy of Design, the Pennsylvania Academy of the Fine Arts, and the Inter-State Industrial Exposition, Chicago—and an appearance in 1884 at the Southern Exposition, Louisville, Kentucky. KZ

183.
Alice De Wolf Kellogg
Portrait of Miss G. E. K.
Portrait of Gertrude E. Kellogg, 1888
Oil on canvas mounted on wood, 45 x 33⅛"
(114.3 x 84.1 cm)
Collection JoAnne W. Bowie

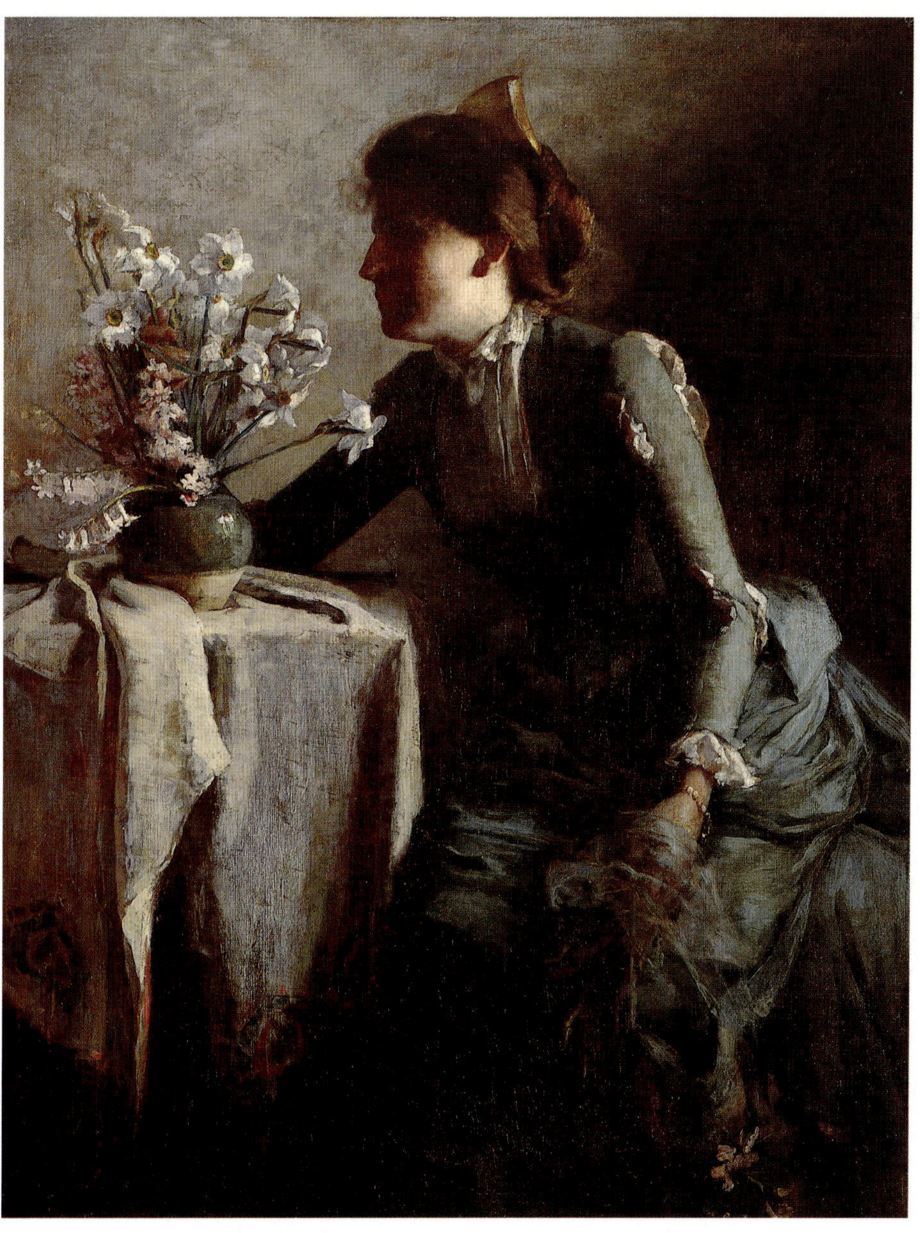

ALICE DE WOLF KELLOGG (1862–1900)

Little known today, Alice De Wolf Kellogg was a highly regarded teacher at the Art Institute of Chicago when she died, in 1900, at the age of thirty-seven.[1] One of six daughters of a Chicago doctor, Kellogg began her instruction in art in 1879 at the Chicago Academy of Fine Arts (which became the Art Institute of Chicago in 1882). She studied with H. F. Spread, L. C. Earle, and J. R. Robertson and graduated with honors.[2] In 1881 she started teaching at this institution, where she met the young Arthur B. Davies, who devotedly encouraged her and advised her about her work until their relationship ended, with his marriage, in 1892.

Kellogg left Chicago in the fall of 1887, in the company of her sister Gertrude, to begin two years of art study in Paris. Her frequent letters to her family document the life of a female art student at the Académie Julian and the Académie Colarassi and in the private atelier of Charles "Shorty" Lasar, an American expatriate who taught in Paris and at Concarneau.[3] At the Académie Julian, Kellogg singled out Boulanger as her favorite teacher. "His instruction was the simplest—most broad—most rousing . . . that I ever received," she wrote at the time of his death, in 1888.[4] One of the charcoal sketches she executed at the Académie was selected for the Salon of 1888. She was pleased, partly because as a participant she did not have to pay "to see the Salon thoroughly," which she felt was "a liberal education."[5] But she expressed disillusionment with the "influence and wire-pulling," and felt that she owed the selection of her picture to the fact that she was a pupil at Julian's. After Boulanger died, Kellogg moved and decided to try the more convenient and less expensive Colarossi's, which was "less rigidly organized" than Julian's.[6] At Colarossi's, where Dagnan-Bouveret was the honored professor who critiqued occasionally, Jean Rixens and Gustave Courtois were her masters.

Kellogg's talent and diligence won further recognition in 1889 with the selection of a pastel for the Salon and of the portrait of her sister Gertrude for the Exposition. Of the portrait she said, "It is pleasing and it is in many ways by far the best I ever did, but I could do better I believe now."[7] Upon seeing it in the American section she remarked that it was "badly hung" but that Gertrude looked quite good.[8] The free admission ticket that came with participation in the fair allowed her to savor the art of many nations. "I have come back from the Exposition in such a state of joy over the great works of Art there gathered together . . . . I am free—thanks to Gertrude's portrait—to go in and feast on the best pictures painted this century, by French, Belgian, Dutch, English, Austrian, Hungarian, Swedish, Norwegian, Swiss, Russian and American painters."[9]

Portrait of Miss G.E.K. is an informal portrait, reflective of her newly acquired training. Gertrude, seen in profile, shares the picture space with the vase of flowers on the draped table next to which she is seated. The picture was not mentioned in reviews, nor did it win a prize; nevertheless, it was a great compliment to this twenty-six-year-old neophyte to have been included in the American galleries with Sargent and in the same building as her teachers.

Kellogg returned to Chicago in 1889 and resumed teaching at the Art Institute. Her picture *The Mother* (1889), painted in Paris, was accepted for exhibition by the Society of American Artists in 1891, and she achieved the distinction of being made a member of that group. She also participated in the World's Columbian Exposition, where *Portrait of Miss G.E.K.* was again exhibited, as was *The Mother*. In these years she was actively involved with a women's art group called The Palette Club, of which she was president in 1891, 1892, and 1895. During an economic depression in 1892 the club wisely offered reasonably priced small pictures, which sold better than large ones[10]; this accounts for the small format of many of Kellogg's paintings of the 1890s, which reveal a broader brushstroke and a lighter palette than the more academic work executed in Paris. In 1894, Kellogg married Orno Tyler. She died six years later, cut off just as she had reached her prime. AB

DANIEL RIDGWAY KNIGHT (1839–1929)

The American expatriate Daniel Ridgway Knight began his studies in the late 1850s at the Pennsylvania Academy of the Fine Arts[1] and continued in Paris, from 1861 to early 1863, at the Ecole des Beaux-Arts and Charles Gleyre's atelier, and in Rome for eight months at the Accademia di San Luca.[2] He returned to America during the Civil War but was back in France by 1872. In 1875 he moved to Poissy to study informally with Ernest Meissonier, whose detailed historical genre scenes nourished Knight's narrative skills. Settling in the country, at Poissy and then at Seine-et-Oise, he chose the peasant as his theme. His reputation grew as critics compared his realism to that of Jules Bastien-Lepage; both painters depicted the everyday life of the peasant in a soft, even light.[3] By 1889, Knight was well established: he was a member of the American jury in Paris for the Exposition and showed three paintings of peasant subjects,[4] winning a silver medal. He remained active as a painter until the end of his life, exhibiting in the Salon until 1921. He served the French and American governments during World War I.

In *Hailing the Ferry*, Knight placed his classically posed and academically rendered peasant women in a realistic landscape. The linear precision of the figures owes much to Gleyre; their poses, especially the elegant contrapposto of the hailer, suggest Greek sculpture. In contrast, the landscape is broadly painted in mottled patches and streaks that show the influence of Bastien-Lepage. Knight augmented Bastien-Lepage's blue-green palette with brown and transformed his hazy atmosphere into silvery air. Figures and ground are united by the same tonal scheme, all suffused with pearly light.

Knight's modern pastorals were exceptionally popular. He painted peasants as natural beauties springing from a life uncontaminated by civilization. His viewpoint was favored by, among many others, Theodore Child: "His vision of rural life is that of a healthy, happy man, unperverted by pessimism or dilettantism or any other excess of mental refinement. . . . Mr. Knight selects what is beautiful and pretty in the peasant and avoids all that is hideous and unsightly. . . ."[5] Knight's themes parallel those of Corot, Millet, and Bastien-Lepage, whose painterly, poetic pictures of peasants, combining realism and idealism, at the Exposition were much praised, especially by American critics.[6]

Hailing the Ferry became Knight's best-known painting. It made his name at numerous exhibitions, including the 1888 Paris Salon, the 1888 Munich International Art Exhibition, the 1891 Pennsylvania Academy of the Fine Arts 61st annual exhibition, and the 1893 World's Columbian Exposition. Acquired by the Pennsylvania Academy in 1891, it was issued as a lithograph and became one of the most copied American paintings of the nineteenth century, appearing even on scarves and a tapestry. It remains a favorite. KZ

ROBERT KOEHLER (1850–1917)

In the aura of pride surrounding the American presence at the 1889 Paris Exposition, Robert Koehler's single and large-scale entry, *The Strike* (1886), must have made a dramatic impact, for it depicted a clash between America's two main sources of technological prowess: capital and labor. Koehler's picture would have stood out as the only one suggesting that there was a dark side to the late-

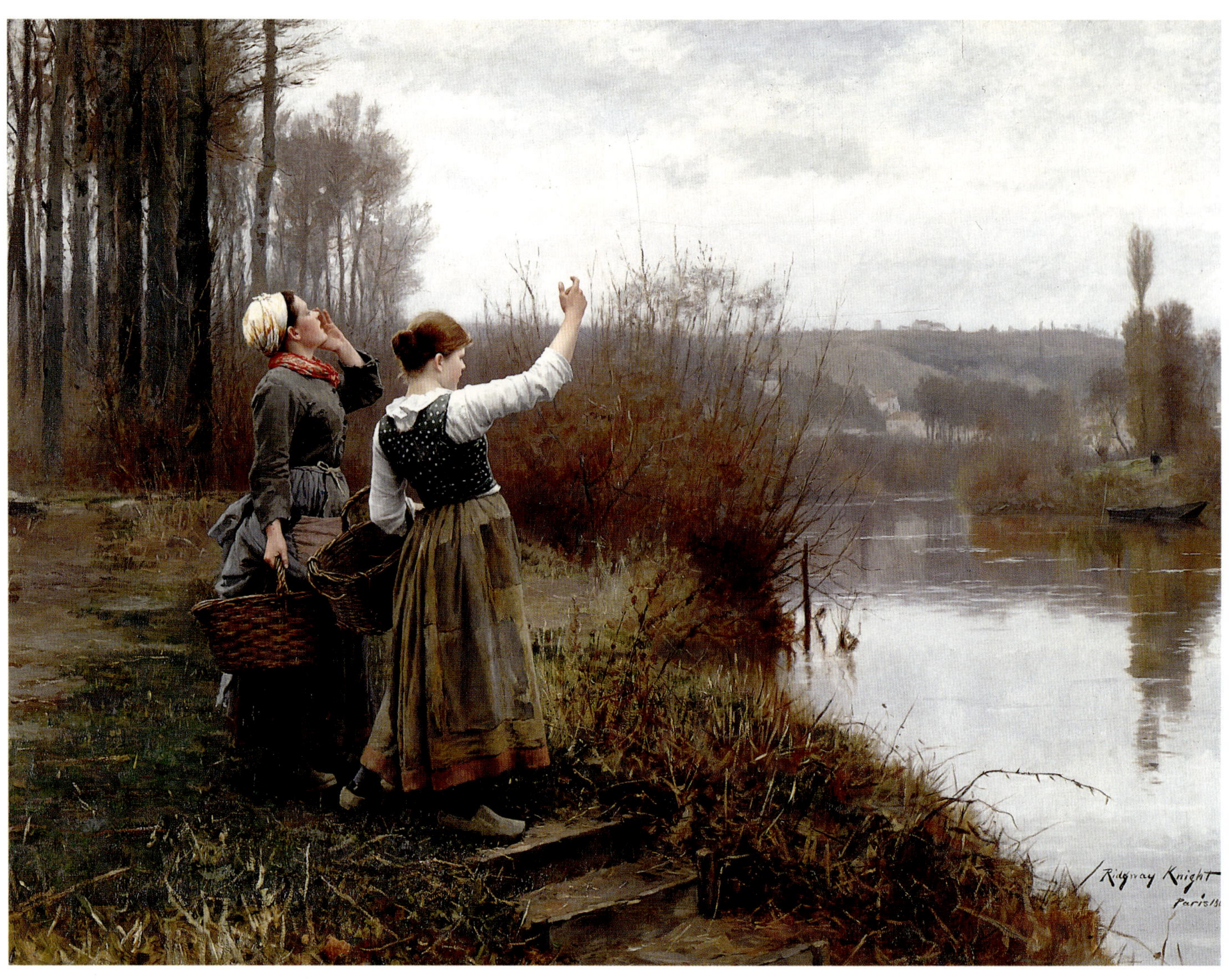

189.
(Daniel) Ridgway Knight
Hailing the Ferryman
Hailing the Ferry, 1888
Oil on canvas, 64½ x 83⅛" (163.8 x 211.1 cm)
Pennsylvania Academy of the Fine Arts, Philadelphia, Gift of John H. Converse

nineteenth-century American progress documented by one world's fair after another. (The only other picture in the exposition to address urban industrialization, J.G. Brown's *The Longshoremen's Noon* (see page 125), stressed leisure rather than labor.)

German-born and Munich-trained, Koehler developed a realism that was undoubtedly influenced by his background. Born in Hamburg in 1850, Koehler was brought to Milwaukee by his parents in 1854. He remained there until he moved to New York, in 1871. In New York he worked as a lithographer while studying at the National Academy of Design and at the Art Students League. Between 1873 and 1875 Koehler studied at the Royal Academy in Munich. He returned there in 1879 and remained for thirteen years, studying under Ludwig von Loefftz. In 1893, Koehler began a long association with the Minneapolis School of Art.[1]

The Strike was a well-known picture before it reached the 1889 Paris Exposition, where it won Koehler an honorable mention. It had already been

191.
Robert Koehler
The Strike
The Strike, 1886
Oil on canvas, 72⅝ x 110¾" (184.5 x 281.3 cm)
Manoogian Collection

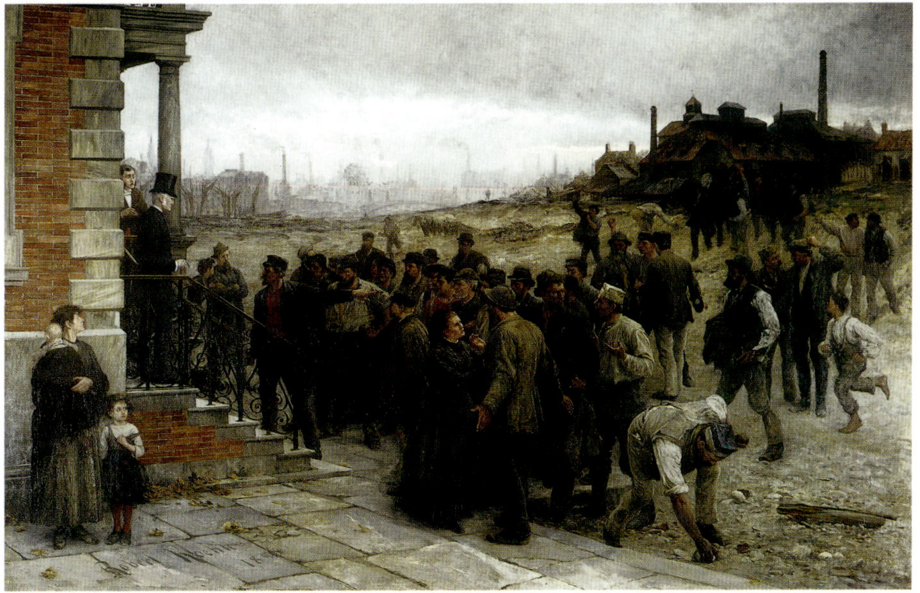

awarded a silver medal at the 1888 Exposition in Munich. Prior to that, the picture had been shown in 1886 at the National Academy of Design in New York, where it received considerable attention because its appearance virtually coincided with the Haymarket riot in Chicago.[2] Apparently suggested by the 1877 strike of Pittsburgh railroad workers, Koehler's picture was actually painted much later, in Munich, from studies of workers made in England.[3] Seemingly unaware of this, a *New York Times* critic praised the authenticity of its American workers of Irish and German background.[4] Overall, the realism of Koehler's account is restrained in comparison with newspaper reports of events in 1877, a year that saw some of the worst labor disputes in American history. In Pittsburgh a group of militia from Philadelphia fired into a crowd that included women and children.[5] This outburst precipitated rioting, arson, and the spread of unrest to other cities.[6]

Koehler's *The Strike* has a monochromatic palette that conveys an appropriate bleakness. But its subject matter is at odds with an academic treatment that turns a contemporary event into history painting. Any sense of action is slowed by the organization of the workers into a frieze that is halted by the strong verticality of the industrialist, noticeably aligned with the stable architectural column. Realism is further weakened by an abstract setting that evokes timelessness rather than immediacy. Even so, *The Strike* was controversial. In 1886 the *New York Times* reviewer had objected to Koehler's inclusion of the woman and child in the left foreground, arguing that "in trying to rouse us with a beggar woman, his moral gets heavy. American workmen are not beggars nor do their women become so through the fruit of capitalists."[7] The prevailing American taste for pictures by Jean-François Millet, Jules Breton, and others suggests that while Americans were sympathetic to the hardships of European peasants, they did not want misery brought too close to home. *The Strike*, which was exhibited again in 1893 at Chicago, remained in Koehler's hands for a number of years before being sold, in 1901, to the Minnesota Society of Fine Arts. JH

WALTER MACEWEN (1860–1943)

Walter MacEwen began his career in Chicago, where he briefly attended Northwestern University before setting off, in 1877, for Munich.[1] There he studied in the Royal Academy and in Frank Duveneck's informal classes. Sometime in the early 1880s he arrived in Paris to train with Tony Robert-Fleury at the Académie Julian and with Fernand Cormon in his private atelier. On his own by 1883, he eventually divided his time between Holland and France,[2] establishing his reputation with paintings of Dutch peasants and villagers. From the beginning, his work encompassed both complicated, precisely rendered compositions and simpler, sketchier schemes. Little documentation of later historical costume pieces survives, but MacEwen seems to have continued both modes, producing reprises of tightly painted seventeenth-century Dutch genre scenes and aestheticized single-figure works in bolder brushwork.[3] No matter which style he used, critics praised his coloring. Still young in 1889, when he won a silver medal at the Exposition, MacEwen went on to participate in dozens of international exhibitions and win honors from many European countries. He returned to America during World War II and died in New York.

MacEwen was part of a large contingent of American expatriates in Holland that included his friend Gari Melchers and also George Hitchcock and Wilder Darling. From about 1885 to 1905 he kept studios in Hattem and in Paris; he also painted in Volendam and other Dutch towns.[4] He returned often to Chicago, coming home especially to vote.[5] He believed that his Dutch subjects reflected American qualities: "The one thing a painter can't help doing . . . is to put himself into his pictures; and in the same way he can't help putting his nationality into them."[6] At the Exposition, MacEwen exhibited two of his Dutch scenes alongside his view of New York as a Dutch colony in 1650, perhaps implying a similarity.

MacEwen thought *A Ghost Story*, one of his three entries in the Exposition, was among his most important paintings and chose it for engraving.[7] Arriving in Volendam in 1887, MacEwen was one of the first Americans to paint the old-fashioned fishing town on the Zuyder Zee. The distinctive caps, called *boomhuls*, that the women wear in *A Ghost Story* identify them as Volendamers.[8] MacEwen excelled at a contemporary preoccupation—painting light-suffused white—yet also drew inspiration from the compositions and narratives of seventeenth-century Dutch genre scenes.

A Ghost Story is more than a charming, picturesque scene. According to one contemporary critic, by representing youth, maturity, and old age MacEwen alludes to the unchanging life cycle in rural cultures.[9] As MacEwen was also undoubtedly aware, the spinning wheel was a potent symbol in America.[10] Popularized in Longfellow's poetry and exhibited in numerous historical displays connected with the Centennial, the spinning wheel by the 1880s symbolized America's colonial past. Attributing many of America's cherished values and political systems to its Dutch heritage, American historians drew direct parallels between the Dutch and American peoples. Many artists composed pictures with the same message.[11] The Volendamers in *A Ghost Story*, unlike their industrialized American counterparts, still spin, maintaining the noble old ways. Born of a self-conscious nationalism, MacEwen's picture thus evokes not only vanishing Dutch customs but also American customs that had disappeared. *A Ghost Story* was exhibited at the Paris Salon in 1888; the Chicago Art

Institute in 1890; the World's Columbian Exposition, Chicago, in 1893; the Universal Exposition, Antwerp, in 1894; and the International Exhibition, Vienna, in 1902.

Another of MacEwen's entries, *Returning from Work*, shows the influence of The Hague School and reveals the artist at his least anecdotal and most painterly. The Hague School artists, like the French naturalists, favored spontaneous open-air painting and subjects taken from life rendered in loose brushwork.[12] Led by Josef Israels and Hendrik Mesdang, painters of The Hague School produced unsentimental views of the Dutch people and country, often emphasizing the landscape's horizontality and the rainy weather and earthy colors. Many Americans studied or worked with them, and MacEwen certainly knew their work.[13] Anton Mauve, one of the best-known artists of The Hague School, also painted peasants returning from the field. Mauve's landscapes often use the device of a path and a mid-canvas horizon line broken by figural groups that divides the canvas into quadrants unified by color. The device is used in *Returning from Work*, which also employs the bold brushwork of The Hague School; a Veluwe couple in Gelderland, recognizable by their clothes and the landscape,[14] exchange romantic glances at a crossroads. Here MacEwen, ignoring the religious or ethnographic viewpoints of other Americans in Holland, has, like Gari Melchers, invested his Dutch peasants with dignity and even a rugged beauty. *Returning from Work* was first exhibited at the Paris Salon in 1886, then, after the 1889 Exposition, at the Chicago Art Institute in 1890 and the Antwerp Universal Exposition in 1894. KZ

(JULIUS) GARI MELCHERS (1860–1932)

Gari Melchers impressed American and French critics alike with the four paintings he exhibited at the 1889 Exposition. *The Sermon* (1886; National Museum of American Art, Washington, D.C.), *The Pilots* (1887; Charles and Emma Frye Art Museum, Seattle), *Communion*, and *Shepherdess*, all scenes of Dutch life, contrasted dramatically with the fashionable portraits of Sargent, with whom Melchers shared the highest honors in the American section.[1] Unlike Sargent, Melchers had trained primarily in Germany, developing realist skills that he would later apply to genre painting.

Born in Detroit, Melchers was the son of Julius Theodore Melchers, a Westphalian who had studied sculpture at the Ecole des Beaux-Arts in Paris and worked as a modeler of decorations at the Crystal Palace Exposition in London before emigrating to America.[2] Melchers received his earliest instruction from his father but was sent to Europe in 1877 to pursue his studies at the Royal Academy in Düsseldorf. Working under the history painter Peter Janssens and the academic realist Eduard von Gebhardt, who specialized in religious subjects, Melchers became an expert draftsman and modeler of form. Four years after he arrived in Düsseldorf, he moved to Paris to continue his studies at the Académie Julian under Boulanger and Lefebvre, from whom he gained a heightened awareness of color and a loosening of paint handling.

Melchers' first Salon entry in 1882, *The Letter* (Corcoran Gallery of Art, Washington, D.C.), was strongly reminiscent of Vermeer. The painting set a standard for his important work of that decade, presenting a sober, precisely lit interior and apt characterizations of two Breton women, rendered in an appropriately guarded, low-key palette. This formula, set forth without senti-

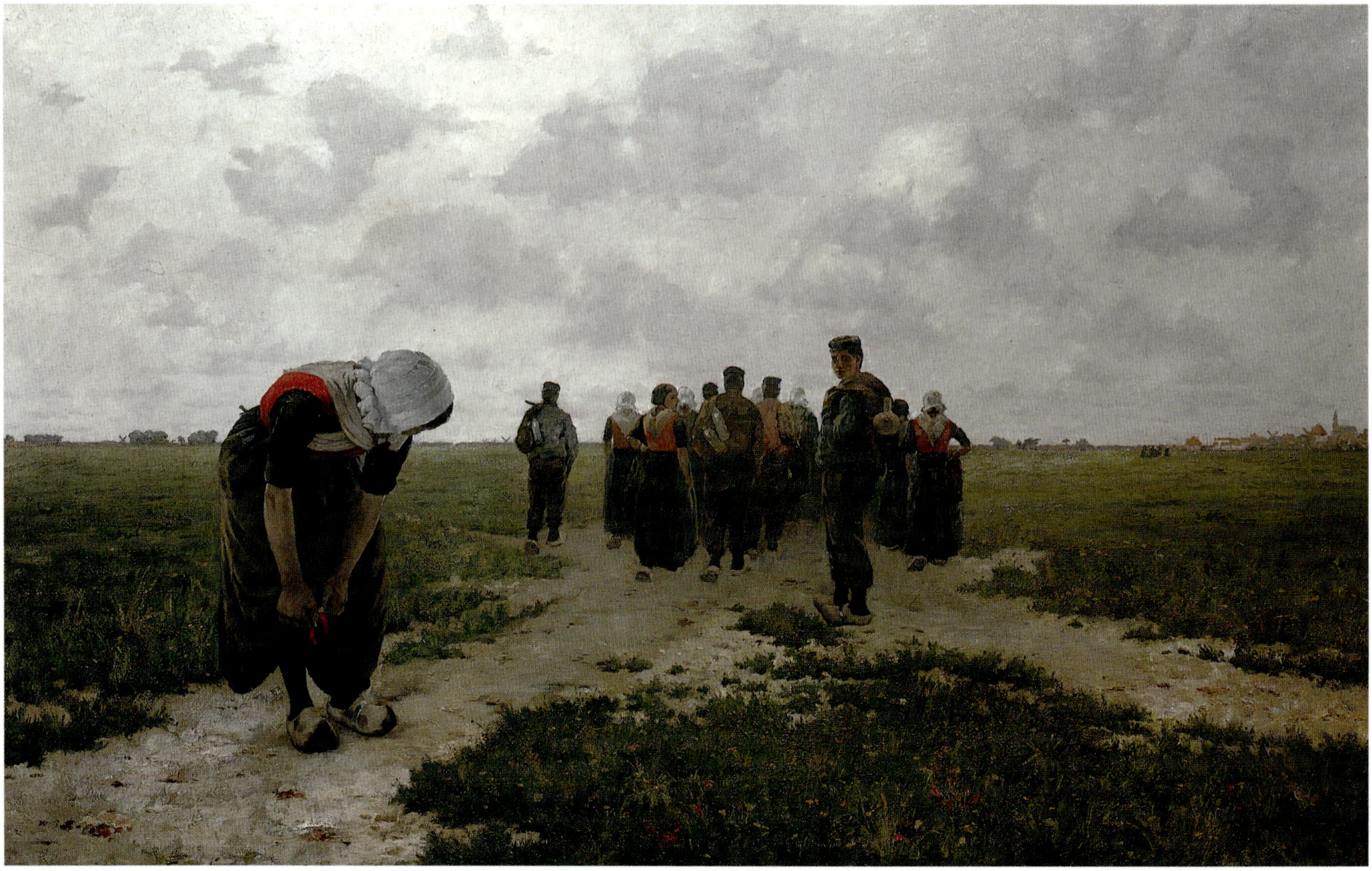

202.
Walter MacEwen
Returning from work
Returning from Work, c. 1885
Oil on canvas, 47½ x 75″ (120.7 x 190.5 cm)
Collection George Haigh

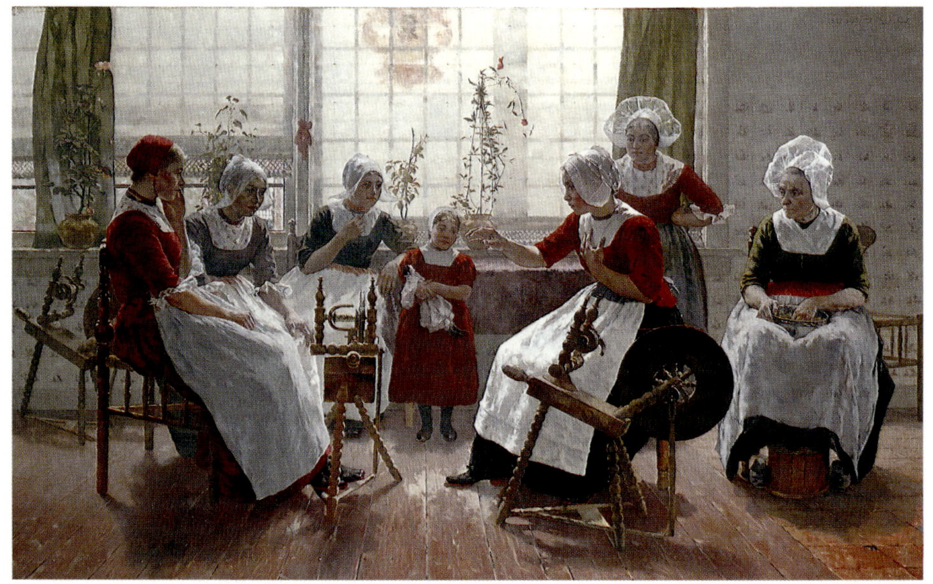

203.
Walter MacEwen
A Ghost story
A Ghost Story, 1887
Oil on canvas, 47¾ x 75¼″ (121.3 x 192.4 cm)
Cleveland Museum of Art,
Gift of Mrs. Edward S. Harkness

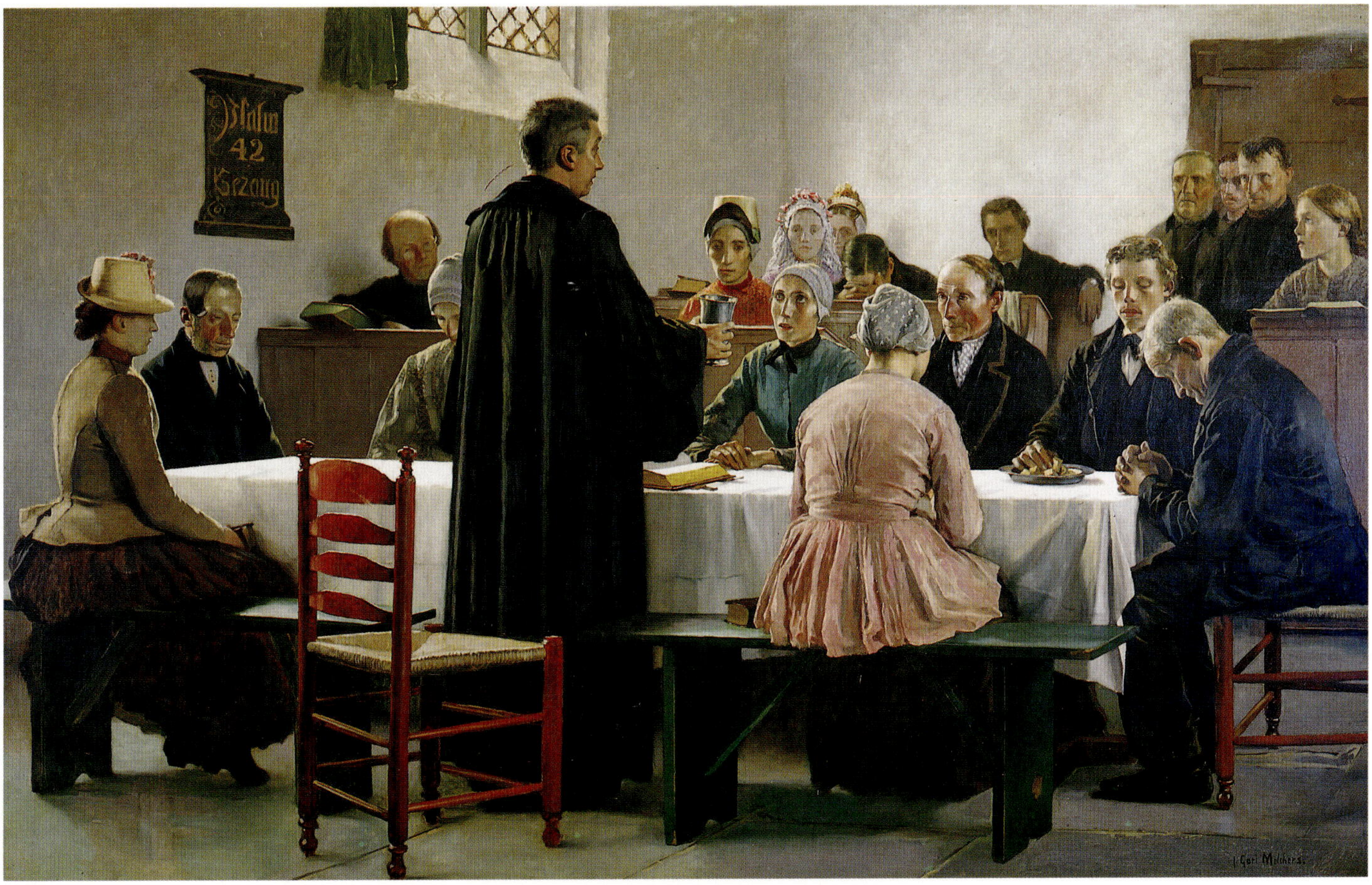

207.
(Julius) Gari Melchers
Communion
Communion Sunday in a Church in Holland, 1888
Oil on canvas, 86⅞ x 134¼″ (220.7 x 341 cm)
Cornell University, Ithaca, New York,
Gift of the artist and General Rush C. Hawkins

210.
(Julius) Gari Melchers
Shepherdess
Audrey the Shepherd Lass, 1886
Oil on canvas, 48 x 30″ (121.9 x 76.2 cm)
Watson Gallery, Wheaton College, Norton,
Massachusetts, Gift of Mrs. Thomas J. Watson

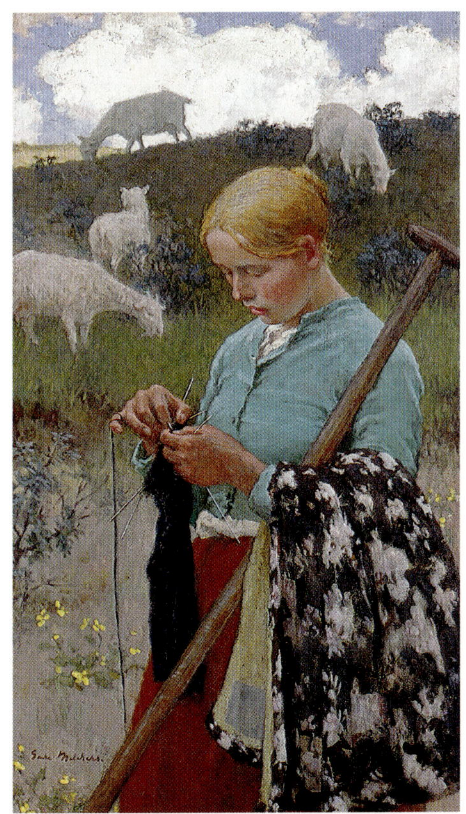

mentality in a larger and more complicated program, contributed to his success in 1889.

In 1884 Melchers joined his friend George Hitchcock in Holland and established a studio in Egmond, where he concerned himself with the lives and customs of Dutch peasantry. His first triumph at the Salon was in 1886 with *The Sermon*, a large painting of Dutch villagers at church.[3] Given an honorable mention at the Salon, and also exhibited in Brussels in 1887, *The Sermon* became the first painting by an American to be awarded a gold medal at the International Exhibition in Munich in 1888. To German critics, who weighed it against the realist aesthetic of Wilhelm Leibl and Fritz von Uhde, it struck an even deeper chord of appreciation than it had in France.[4]

Melchers sent another Dutch interior, *The Pilots*, to the 1888 Salon, winning a third-class medal and overwhelming critical support. The study of wizened old sailors examining a ship's model at their table in a local tavern confirmed Melchers' reputation as a superb chronicler of Dutch village life.[5] French reviewers signaled *The Pilots* "among the most noticed in this year's Salon,"[6] and Albert Wolff, writing in *Figaro-Salon*, declared it the best painting by a foreigner, exhibiting a "grand feeling for nature and a talent for staging and execution that must be credited to Melchers' exposure to French painting."[7] Of the many reviewers who discussed *The Pilots*, only one voiced serious objections, criticizing it for its overall blue tonality.[8]

Communion, a religious painting not shown previously at the Salon, enhanced the strong impression made by *The Sermon* and *The Pilots* in 1889.[9] In a view of a congregation from the front of a church, a standing minister offers communion to the devout seated at a simple altar table. Behind the communicants, other parishioners kneel in prayer or await their turn to come to the table. Although the churchgoers are clothed in appropriate Sunday attire, Melchers did not lavish attention on their dress but, avoiding decorative distractions, preserved the solemnity of the event. Reviewer Theodore Child described *Communion* as the artist's most ambitious painting but found it "positively and frankly ugly," an indication that Melchers was following in the footsteps of Courbet.[10] Nevertheless he found Melchers' paintings to be rich in color, technically and compositionally remarkable, and containing figures "full of character, studded with *esprit*, drawn faultlessly, and painted with simplicity and strength."[11] This opinion was shared by the French critic Thiébault-Sisson, who singled out Melchers' freshness of tones and irreproachable execution.[12]

Shepherdess, the smallest of the four paintings exhibited and the only single-figure subject, was overlooked by most critics. But this study of a peasant girl knitting intently as her flock grazes on the dune was the prototype of many of the outdoor subjects of Melchers' later career. Influenced by his colleague Hitchcock, Melchers devised a decorative standard whose components appear in the colorfully patterned cloak on the shepherdess's arm,[13] the delicate scattered wildflowers in the background, and the high horizon with a natural aureole of sheep and clouds. An indication of Melchers' future accomplishments, *Shepherdess* introduced the lightened palette of academic Impressionism, which, combined with careful drawing, constituted an international style hailed by contemporary critics.

MCOB

Born in Massachusetts of Pilgrim stock, Frank Millet graduated from Harvard in 1869. He worked as a newspaper correspondent and experimented with painting and lithography before going to Antwerp, in 1871, for two years' formal study at the Royal Academy.[1] He was soon expressing dissatisfaction with the Antwerp method, however: "Coarse models, coarse colors, coarse ideals—coarse but strong. There is virtue in strength, add refinement and you have the two elements of the most powerful art, the most perfect method."[2] Millet all but abandoned Antwerp's Rubensian emphasis on drawing with bold brushstrokes and found refinement in a precise realism. By the late 1870s he had developed a flair for historical domestic scenes. Based first in Boston, then in New York, he traveled frequently, and in 1884 he established dual residences, in America and England. He exhibited regularly at the National Academy of Design in New York and the Royal Academy in London. Millet was the catalyst for the formation of an informal artists' colony in the village of Broadway, Worcestershire, England, where, between 1885 and 1892, Edwin Howland Blashfield, John Singer Sargent, Edwin Austin Abbey, the writer Henry James, and others gathered. Beginning in the 1890s, Millet turned increasingly to mural painting for various civic buildings, which eventually led to extensive work at the Baltimore Custom House. He also held administrative posts with an astounding number of American art establishments, among them the Society of American Artists, the National Academy of Design, the American Federation of Arts, and the American Academy in Rome. Throughout his career he spent periods of time as a war correspondent or travel journalist. His death in 1912 in the sinking of the *Titanic* cut short an extraordinary career that was honored by numerous commemorative exhibitions.

Millet was an administrator and arbiter for many world's fairs, among them the 1873 Vienna Exposition, the 1878 Paris Exposition, and the 1893 World's Columbian Exposition, for which he was director of decorations and supervised all the interior murals. His role in the 1889 Exposition was limited to sitting on the New York jury for American paintings. Nevertheless he managed to exhibit in both the American and the English section of the fair, showing *The Piping Times of Peace* (unlocated) in the latter.

Millet's genre paintings reflect meticulous research but go beyond documentation to retrieve a lost world of pleasure and aesthetic refinement. In *A Difficult Duet* attention is lavished on the details of a late-eighteenth-century sitting room and its occupants.[3] Millet created authentic period interiors in his several studios, and *A Difficult Duet* was probably painted in Broadway.[4] Musical performances appear in several of Millet's canvases of the late 1880s: there were musicians in the Broadway group, including his wife.[5] Using a restrained palette, Millet called attention to the superb furnishings and costumes in the scene and suggested a flirtation carried on by the performers through their music. Soon after its completion, *A Difficult Duet* was purchased by Mrs. C.M. Raymond, who lent it to the 1889 Exposition and later to the World's Columbian Exposition.

From 1882 to 1888, Millet painted many genre scenes set in ancient Greece and Rome, *A Handmaiden* among them.[6] His first involvement with classical garments—designing the costumes for a production of *Oedipus Rex*—led to his becoming an authority on Roman clothing.[7] He gave public lectures on the topic in New York and Boston in 1882, draping the robes on a live model; the

212.
Frank (Francis Davis) Millet
A Handmaiden
A Handmaiden, 1886
Oil on canvas, 27⅛ x 16⅝" (68.9 x 42.2 cm)
Owner in 1889 George T. Seney
Private Collection
Courtesy Jordan Volpe Gallery, Inc., New York

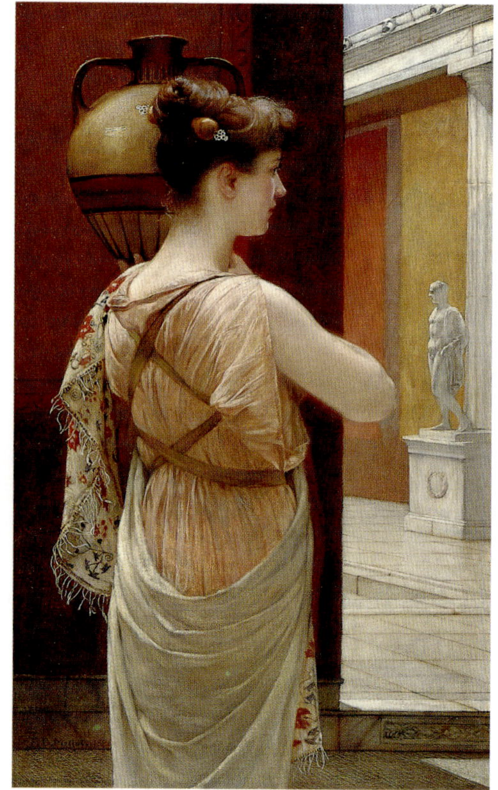

213.
Frank (Francis Davis) Millet
A difficult Duet
A Difficult Duet, 1886
Oil on canvas, 24¼ x 36¼" (61.6 x 92 cm)
Owner in 1886 Mrs. C. M. Raymond
Collection Mr. and Mrs. Richard M. Waitzer

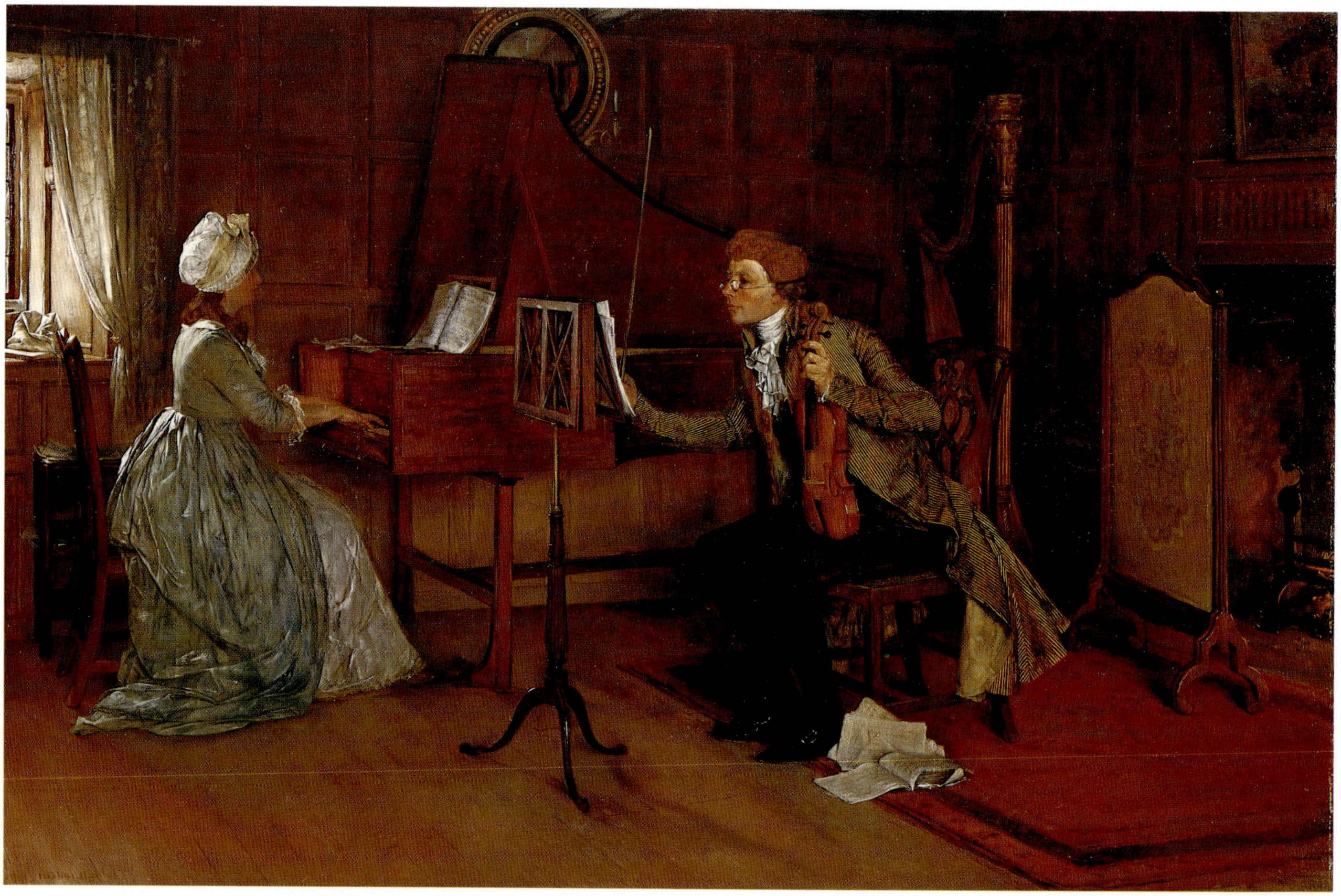

217.
Robert Hatton Monks
A Grey Day
A Gray Day, 1880s
Oil on canvas, 5½ x 9½″ (14 x 24.2 cm)
Collection Allen P. Crawford

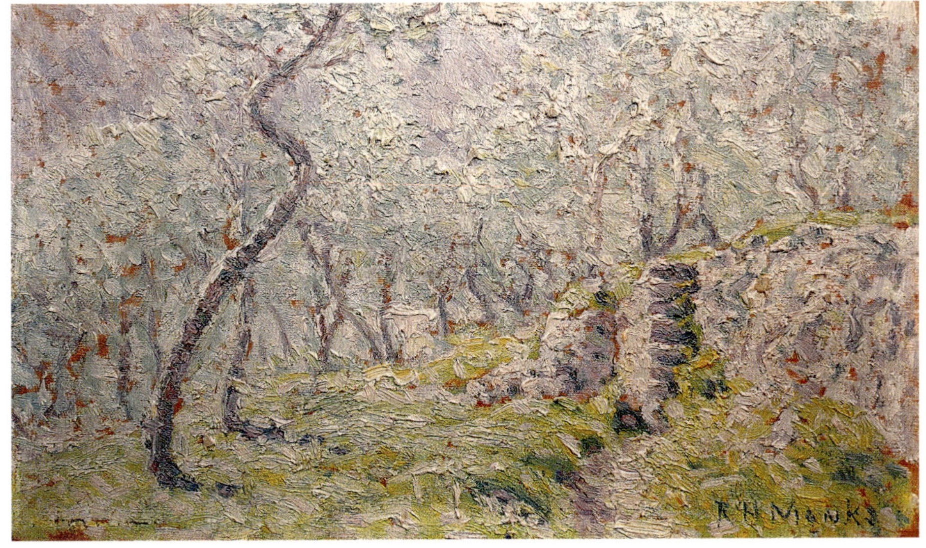

intricacy of the water carrier's garb in *A Handmaiden* gives evidence of his knowledge. Emphasis is placed on decorative rather than narrative qualities. *A Handmaiden*, one of the few paintings in the American section of the Exposition to evoke the classical past, is the classical ideal brought to life through historical research and artistic invention. Other works in this category—Kenyon Cox's *Painting and Poetry* and Edwin Howland Blashfield's *Inspiration* (both unlocated)—were allegorical. Millet's ancient settings tie him more closely to English artists, especially Lawrence Alma-Tadema, a friend and associate in Broadway and an exhibitor at the Exposition. *A Handmaiden* was exhibited infrequently, appearing only at the National Academy of Design in 1886 and in the exhibition of George I. Seney's collection at the Brooklyn Art Association in 1887. It achieved a degree of fame, however, after its publication in G.W. Sheldon's *Recent Ideals of American Art* of 1888.[8] KZ

ROBERT HATTON MONKS (1856–1923)

Robert Hatton Monks was born in Boston, where his father, an immigrant from Ireland, had settled in 1830.[1] His mother, the former Delia Smith Hatton, in her youth in Bangor, Maine, had painted still lifes and street scenes.[2] In 1877, at twenty-one, Monks began studying drawing and painting with German-born and Belgian-educated Emil Otto Grundmann and anatomy with sculptor and painter William Rimmer at the School of the Museum of Fine Arts, Boston. In 1881, he went to Paris, where he studied with William Adolphe Bouguereau and Tony Robert-Fleury at the Académie Julian. Upon arriving in Paris, instead of painting in the academic tradition of his teachers, he did plein-air subjects, like the Impressionists. One of his landscapes was shown at the Salons of 1884 and 1887.In 1883, Monks's *Environs de Fleury* (unlocated) was exhibited at the 54th annual exhibition of the Pennsylvania Academy of the Fine Arts.

Because of ill health, Monks returned to the United States; by 1891, he had settled in Waltham, Massachusetts. Twelve of his French landscapes had been shown in Boston in 1890, along with works by Edward H. Barnard and Charles Henry Hayden, fellow students at the Boston Museum of Fine Arts school and in Paris, who also exhibited at the 1889 Exposition. The titles of some of the paintings Monks showed in Boston indicate that he was interested in the ephemeral aspect lent by the time of day, the season, or the weather: *Marshes—Early Morning; Cottage and Fields—Late Afternoon; Early Spring; Ballancourt; First Snow;* and *Grain Fields—Misty Morning* (all unlocated).[3]

A Grey Day, which was given this title by its present owner, may be the painting that Monks showed in the 1889 Exposition.[4] It can probably be dated in the late 1880s because it is similar in subject matter to the paintings exhibited in Boston in 1890. The colors are the "cold blues and grays" that he used in other paintings of the period.[5] *A Grey Day* shows an Impressionistic landscape: bare trees in early spring, with a pathway leading to a stone wall. The artist's early interest in Impressionism is evident in his use of loose brushstrokes; although other artists, among them Theodore Robinson, were working in an Impressionist style, Monks was one of only a few artists at the Exposition to exhibit in this then avant-garde mode.

Monks returned to Europe in 1894, visiting Dresden, Munich, and Paris before going to Belgium to study with the Belgian Impressionist Emile Claus, whose only American pupil he was. Probably influenced by Claus, he began working in pastels, on still lifes and landscapes. In 1899, Monks's *Sunny Morning in October* (unlocated) was in the 68th annual exhibition at the Pennsylvania Academy, the second and final time he showed there. Monks was selected for membership in the Belgian Impressionist group Vie et Lumière in 1906. The paintings he showed in their exhibitions from then until 1914 were praised by Belgian critics.[6] Again for reasons of health, he returned in 1908 to the United States. He died in Wellesley, Massachusetts, in 1923.

In 1927 a group of Monks's paintings were given by Mrs. Robert H. Monks to the Fogg Art Museum, Harvard University. Two drawings, an oil portrait, and *Landscape: Winter Afternoon*, an undated Impressionist scene with farm buildings, were kept by the museum. The rest were returned in the 1930s to the artist's widow; their present whereabouts are unknown. SJ-G

HARRY HUMPHREY MOORE (1844–1926)

H. Humphrey Moore was one of the first American artists to travel to Japan. Born in New York, he was the son of a shipbuilder, and a descendant of the English painter Ozias Humphrey (1742–1810).[1] Moore showed an early interest in art. He studied art in Hartford, Connecticut, with Louis Bail, and also in New York and San Francisco before coming, about 1864, to Philadelphia, where he studied with the portraitist Samuel B. Waugh and drew from antique casts at the Pennsylvania Academy of the Fine Arts.[2] He traveled to Munich in 1865 and then to Paris. Moore was enrolled in Gérôme's atelier on October 29, 1866,[3] shortly after Thomas Eakins, who had been at the Pennsylvania Academy with him.[4] Eakins, a friend of Moore's family, learned sign language to communicate with Moore, who was deaf, and was his protector in the atelier, preventing him from being hazed as a new student.[5] On March 25, 1867, Moore began studying at the Ecole des Beaux-Arts,[6] probably with Adolphe Yvon, who taught drawing, and perhaps with Gustave Boulanger, who was then teaching at the Académie Julian.

In December 1869, Moore and Eakins traveled in Spain with the Philadelphia engraver William Sartain. In May 1870, they traveled to Madrid, where Moore met the Spanish painter Mariano Fortuny y Marsal. After a period of a few years in Morocco, Moore spent 1873–75 in Rome with Fortuny, learning watercolor technique; during this time he painted a picture of an exotic dancer, *Almeh, A Dream of the Alhambra* (unlocated), which was awarded a medal at the 1876 Centennial Exposition in Philadelphia.[7]

Moore apparently had the means to travel widely and in 1880–81 went to Japan.[8] Although the influence of Japanese art had been felt for some time, few artists had actually traveled to Japan. (Moore is said to have prompted Robert Blum's trip there in 1890.[9]) Moore painted about sixty small Japanese scenes, whose subjects included "Japanese temples, formal gardens, tombs, tradespeople, workmen and Geisha girls."[10] He won a bronze medal for the three *Japanese Views* he showed at the 1889 Exposition.[11] Although it is not certain that *Glimpse into the Pleasure Quarters, Yoshiwara* was one of these views, it is representative of his precise, richly colored Japanese works of this period.[12] Since it was painted about six years after his visit to Japan, Moore probably worked from studies and artifacts he collected there. The painting does not incorporate conventions of Japanese art; it is painted in the academic tradition of Gérôme. John Singer Sargent said that he "never saw such exquisite technique as that which distinguished these paintings," and Gérôme wrote to Moore saying, "I am proud of having been your professor."[13] Eakins praised Moore as "one of the greatest artists of his day."[14] Despite efforts by the influential Paris art dealer Goupil and various American collectors to purchase the entire series, most of the Japanese paintings remained in Moore's possession until his death.

In his later years Moore painted conventional portraits of children and of European royalty. He visited Philadelphia in 1916 and saw his ailing friend Thomas Eakins; several months later he was one of Eakins's six pallbearers.[15] After Moore's death, in 1926, his paintings remained in his Paris studio, owned by his second wife, Polish-born Maria Humphrey Moore. During World War II, just before she was deported to a concentration camp, the paintings were covered with ashes and hidden in garbage cans. Later they were retrieved, and in 1948 they were brought to the United States; they were exhibited in New York the next year.[16] SJ-G

EDWARD MORAN (1829–1901)

Edward Moran was the eldest in a large and well-known family of nineteenth-century American painters, each with a particular expertise. Moran earned his reputation as one of the best marine painters of his generation after overcoming considerable hardship early in life. Arriving in the United States from Lancashire, England, in 1844, he was obliged to contribute to the support of his father's large family, and he worked in various capacities in Maryland and then Philadelphia before he was able to begin to pursue his goal of becoming an artist. In contrast to most of the younger artists exhibiting at the 1889 Exposition, Moran had limited formal training. Whatever he learned he passed on to his younger brothers and, ultimately, to two sons, who also became painters.

By 1854, Moran was exhibiting at the Pennsylvania Academy of the Fine Arts, which named him an Academician in 1860. (He resigned in 1869 over a dispute about its hanging practices.) In 1857, Moran was successful enough to

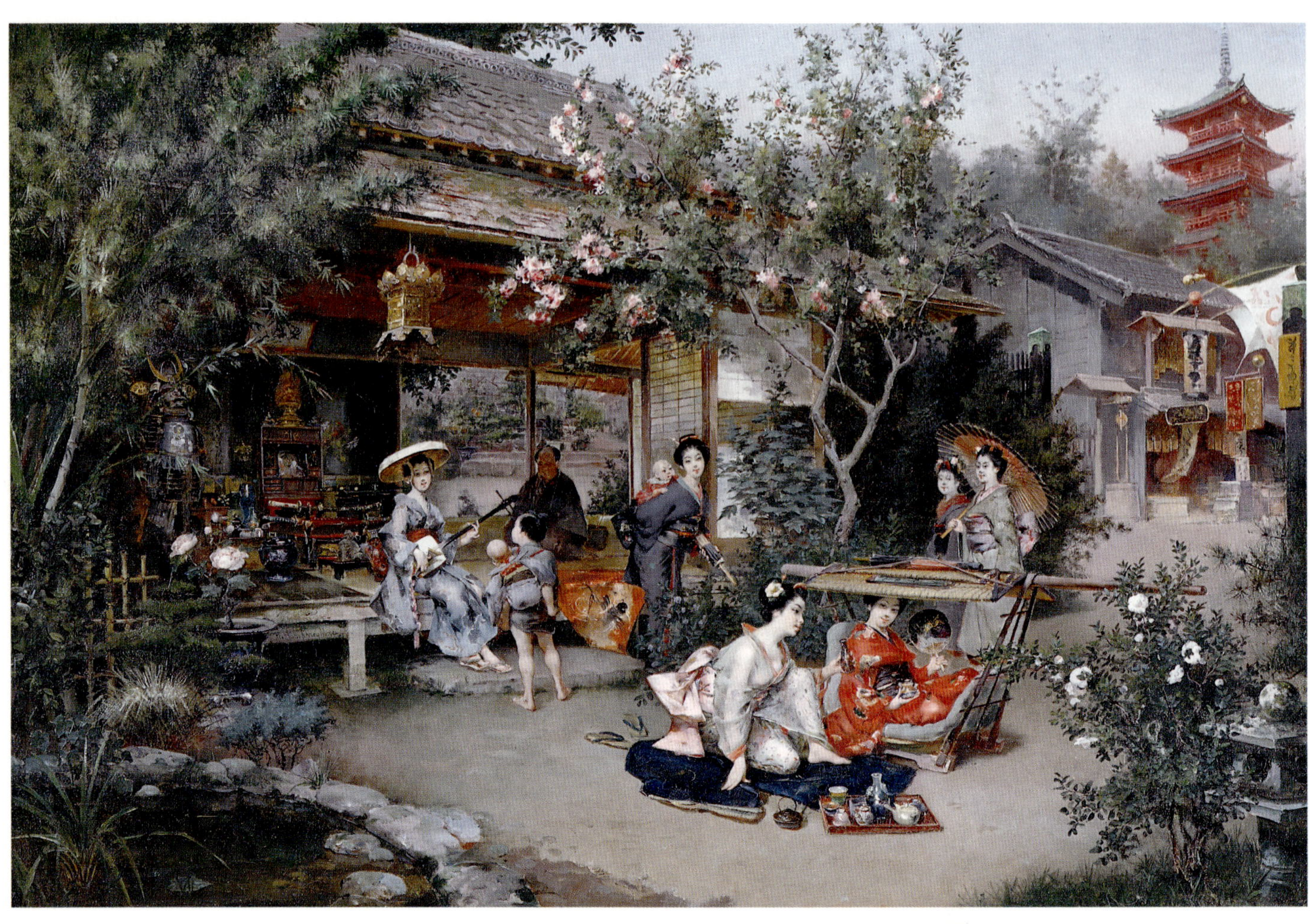

218.
Harry Humphrey Moore
Japanese Views
Glimpse into the Pleasure Quarters, Yoshiwara, 1887
Oil on canvas, 24 x 36″ (61 x 91.5 cm)
Rifkin-Young Fine Arts, Inc., New York

open a studio in Philadelphia, where he was joined by his brother Thomas. By 1861 they had earned enough money to make a six-month trip to England together. At some point early in his career, Moran studied in Philadelphia with the landscape painter Paul Weber and with the marine painter James Hamilton. The latter was undoubtedly the most important influence on Moran and surely whetted his taste for J.M.W. Turner, whose work Moran saw and admired while in England.

In 1872, Moran moved to New York; he exhibited at the National Academy of Design with unfailing regularity for the rest of the century. Although he was elected an associate of the Academy in 1874, he was never made an Academician—a fact that may reflect the subsidiary role ascribed to marine painting within the American landscape tradition.[1] But Moran was not a one-dimensional artist. Like his brother Thomas, he was also a prolific watercolorist, active in the American Water Color Society and a member of the London Water Color Society. Moreover, Moran also had some facility in figure painting, as is evidenced by the pictures of Brittany fisher girls that emerged from a rather mysterious stay in France between 1878 and 1880.[2]

In Moran's eyes, his magnum opus was a series of thirteen pictures representing the "Marine History of the United States," which occupied him for

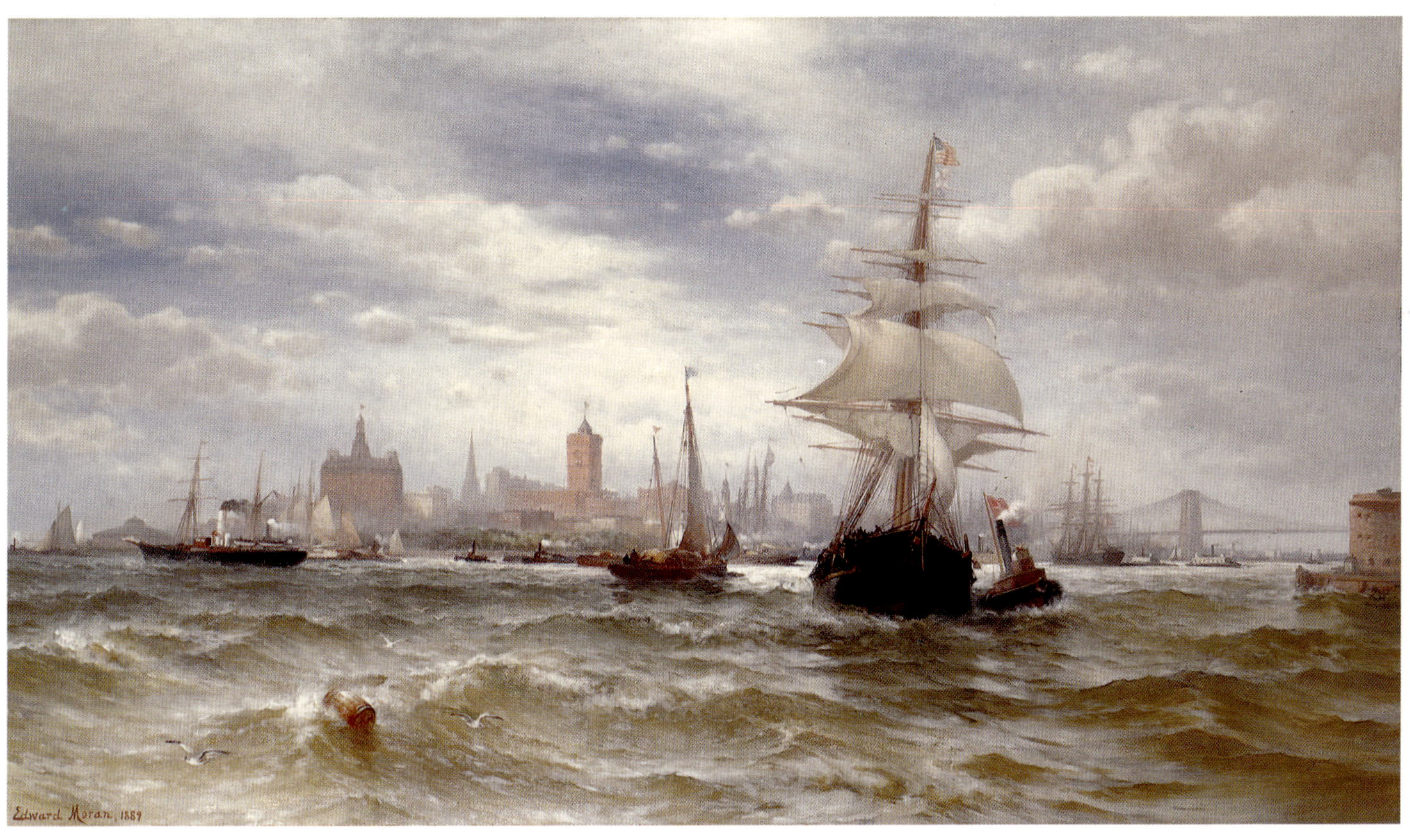

221.
Edward Moran
New York City from the Channel
City and Harbor of New York, 1889
Oil on canvas, 36½ x 68" (92.7 x 170 cm)
The Berkshire Museum, Pittsfield, Massachusetts, Bequest of Richard Lathers, Jr.

the last years of his life. During Moran's lifetime two of these pictures were exhibited, appropriately enough, at the World's Columbian Exposition in Chicago, in 1893, but as a group they were exhibited only once, in Washington, D.C., and Philadelphia in 1900.[3] Moran's popularity, however, rested not on history themes but on the more intimate harbor views that earned him a reputation for naturalism.[4] His inclusion of recognizable landmarks such as those apparent in *City and Harbor of New York* no doubt enhanced this reputation. In the case of this picture, which was Moran's sole entry in the 1889 Exposition, specificity might have been dictated by the fact that it was a commission from a collector engaged in marine activities in New York.

In the present exhibition, Moran's American vista provides an interesting counterpoint to the European one shown by Frank Boggs (see page 120), painted in the same year. Boggs's picture is contemporary in feeling, even if artistically conservative, whereas a slight shift in coloring, a distancing of the cityscape, and the edge given to sail over steam, all place Moran's picture firmly in the romantic tradition. Moreover, the pervasive atmospheric effects evoke British marine painting, in particular that of Turner, with whom Edward Moran was usually less closely associated than his brother Thomas. A handsome picture, *City and Harbor of New York* is in some ways the most traditional of all the American paintings sent to Paris in 1889. As such, it illuminates the way in which international expositions encompassed the past as much as the present. JH

HENRY MOSLER (1841–1920)

Henry Mosler was living abroad at the time of the 1889 Exposition, yet, as an early writer pointed out, he did not "denationalize himself as too many Americans have done."[1] Mosler was born in New York of German parents, who, while he was still a child, moved to Cincinnati. It was there that he took his first formal art lessons, between 1859 and 1861, studying with James Beard, a painter of portraits and genre. Between 1862 and 1863, Mosler worked as a Special Artist Correspondent for *Harper's Weekly*, a post in which he developed a lasting talent for factual accuracy. Mosler gave up this grueling occupation in 1863, when he had saved enough money to go to Düsseldorf to continue his art studies. Six months before returning to the United States, in 1866, Mosler left Düsseldorf, traveling to Paris, where he studied with Ernest Hébert.

Mosler began his long period of expatriation in 1874, when he returned to Europe, this time to Munich. In their rich tonality, all the pictures Mosler submitted to the 1889 Exposition show traces of the Munich School. Yet their subject matter was French, since in 1877 Mosler had moved to France, where he lived (in Brittany) until 1894, when he moved back to the United States for good. Living in New York, in 1895 Mosler was made an associate at the National Academy of Design, from which he resigned in 1906.

Despite a lukewarm endorsement by the Academy, Mosler's pictures found their way into a number of important collections in the United States. Possibly this was the result of a strong reputation in France, assured, shortly after his arrival there, when his *Le Retour (The Return of the Prodigal Son)*, shown at the 1879 Salon, was the first American painting bought by the French government and placed in the Luxembourg Museum in Paris. *Le Retour* was listed in the 1889 catalogue as an entry to be seen at the Luxembourg. However, five other pictures by Mosler were installed on the premises of the fair, all in the American expatriate section. They were: *The Last Sacraments*, in the present exhibition, *The Young Bag-Piper*, *The Last Moments*, *Harvest Festival*, and *New Year's Morning*.

As the titles of some of Mosler's entries imply, his reputation was based on genre pictures of a certain type—pictures that were not merely anecdotal but, to critics partial to the restrained poeticism of the Tonalists, overly emotional and dramatic.[2] These characteristics are absent, however, from *The Last Sacraments*, which is subdued in composition and narrative. The artist focuses on the religious rite rather than on the pathos of the situation.

In *The Last Sacraments* Mosler depicted a time-honored ritual whose authenticity was heightened by a realism derived from his painstaking attention to detail. Living in Brittany at the time, Mosler drew as well on his Munich training and perhaps even on his background in journalistic illustration. Whatever the source of Mosler's precision, he was known as a fastidious painter who composed his final pictures from a large number of preliminary sketches, which he kept carefully ordered.[3] Aside from their artistic merit, many of his pictures were of value as records of vanishing customs. Of the paintings Mosler sent to the Exposition, *The Last Sacraments* was the best-known, having won the Prize Fund award at the American Art Association in 1885.

In many ways Mosler's contribution to the 1889 Exposition focuses the dilemma posed by "nationalism" and "internationalism" in American art during the last quarter of the nineteenth century. Like other expatriate artists at the fair, Mosler depicted foreign themes, set in specific foreign locales, with figures wearing authentic regional costumes rendered in accurate detail. Such specificity distanced the expatriate American artists from those residing in the United States, even when the latter had had European training.

Interestingly, it was the American critics who touted the American expatriates' internationalism, while foreign writers commenting on the expositions were often in search of the national.[4] Nevertheless, international juries tended to be partial to expatriates like Mosler, who won a silver medal. Years later, Dorothy Weir Young echoed the resentment of resident artists in her comment that her father had managed to win both silver and bronze medals despite "the hold of the expatriates."[5] JH

JOHN DOUGLAS PATRICK (1863–1937)

The appearance of *Brutality* in the Exposition marked John Douglas Patrick's brief moment of fame. As a young child he moved with his family from Pennsylvania to a farm near Lenexa, Kansas.[1] In 1880 he went to St. Louis to study art with Halsey C. Ives, remaining there for five years. In 1885 he arrived in Paris and entered the Académie Julian; his teachers included Boulanger, Lefebvre, Théobald Chartran, and perhaps Gérôme.[2] A precocious student, Patrick soon showed two pictures in the Salon: in 1886 *Etude*, a study of a woman's head, which had earned Lefebvre's praise while Patrick was completing it in his class,[3] and in 1887 *Jerry*, a picture of a mule, supposedly painted in the early 1880s during his student days in St. Louis.

In the fall of 1887, Patrick witnessed a driver beating his horse and was moved by indignation to paint the scene. Unable to afford paints and canvas, he pledged his future work to a dealer to obtain them. To make studies of horses and carts he journeyed to England, and back in Paris he worked through the winter on the huge canvas.[4] He completed it in time for the 1888 Salon and later entered it in the Exposition.[5] For several months in 1889 Patrick traveled in Italy and England, after which he returned to the United States to take up a post as instructor in painting at the St. Louis School of Fine Arts. There he learned that he had won a bronze medal at the Exposition.

Patrick intended to return to Paris eventually but was prevented from doing so by adverse circumstances: he suffered a long illness, and then the death of two sisters obliged him to return home to care for his mother in Lenexa. For the next fifteen years he farmed, painting when he could. He produced scenes of the Kansas countryside and its people and some commissioned portraits. In 1904 he returned to the art world, showing at the Louisiana Purchase Exposition in St. Louis, and a year later he accepted a post as instructor at the Kansas City Fine Arts Institute. In 1908 Kansas City merchant J. Logan Jones sent an agent to Paris to buy *Brutality*. He gave the painting a triumphant homecoming and induced Patrick to mount a retrospective show in his store.[6] *Brutality* hung there until 1933.[7] Patrick continued to teach, moving to the Kansas City Art Institute in 1922,[8] but he rarely exhibited or sold his work.[9] After his death, on January 19, 1937, *Brutality* was shown only once, in 1961, in an exhibition of Patrick's work held in a shopping mall in Kansas City.[10]

Brutality was the cause of both social and artistic controversy when it was first shown. Contemporary newspapers document American outrage at the French treatment of horses.[11] Patrick must have hoped his canvas would activate social reformers, and it did apparently touch off the passage of a law prohibiting the mistreatment of animals.[12] One of the voices raised in the debate in art circles

222.
Henry Mosler
The Last Sacraments
The Last Sacraments, 1884
Oil on canvas, 62 x 46½" (157.4 x 118.1 cm)
Owner in 1889 Louisville Polytechnic Association
Private Collection

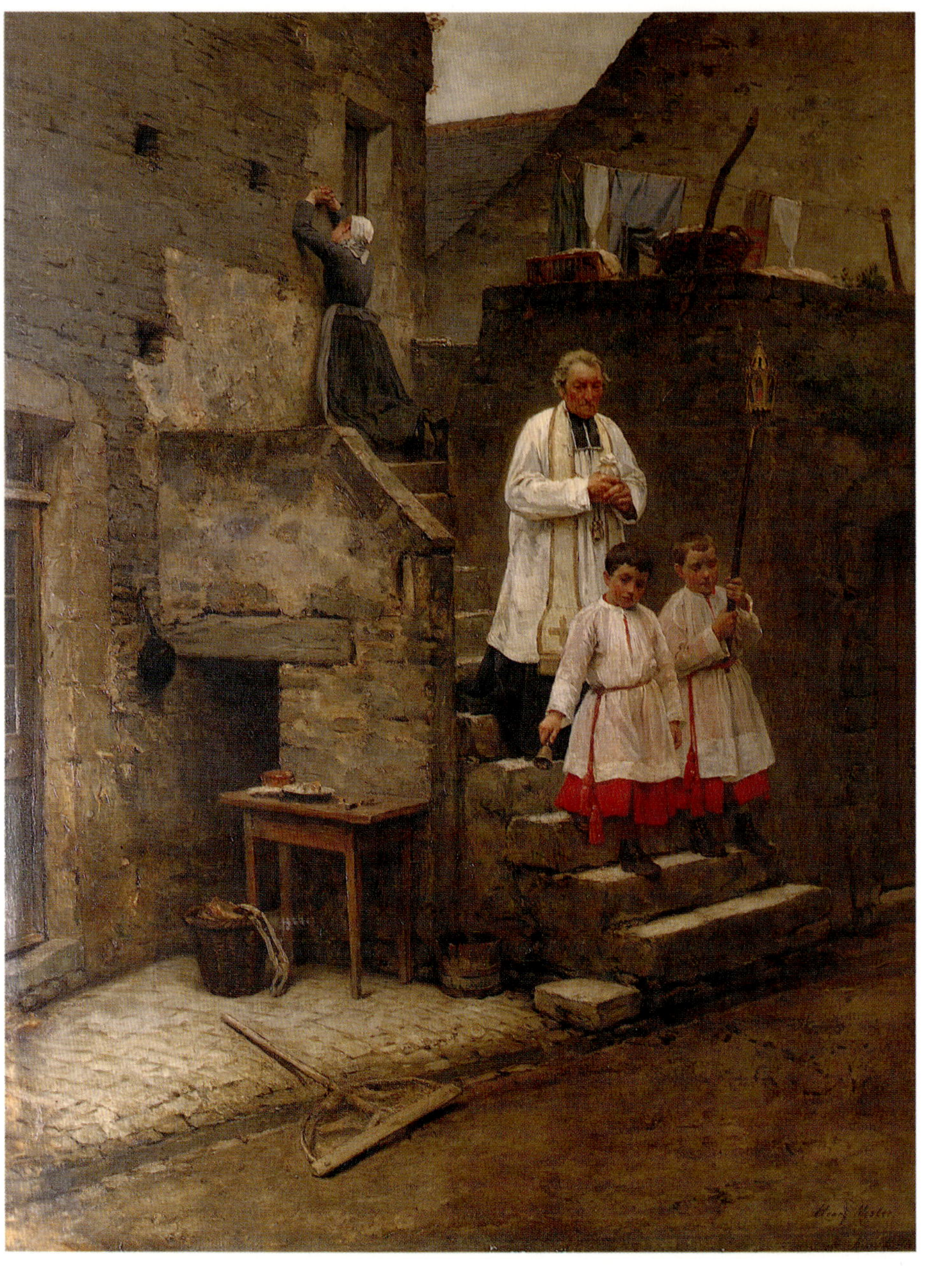

235. *Opposite*
John Douglas Patrick
Brutality
Brutality, 1888
Oil on canvas, 138 x 114" (350.5 x 289.7 cm)
Owner in 1889 Paul Foinet
Collection Grayce Patrick Wray and
Hazel Patrick Rickenbacher

was that of critic Theodore Child, who commented: "*Brutality* is a bold effort, it is a piece of real and cruel life closely observed and rendered with singular intensity. One would have preferred to see Mr. Patrick use his undeniable talent on a less repulsive subject."[13] Patrick's brutish urban peasant is in sharp contrast to the American expatriates' serene rural peasants. His painting was one of the few at the Exposition to make a social statement; Robert Koehler's *The Strike* (see page 181), which depicts the germination of violence between worker and employer, was another. The theme of urban reform found no further expression in Patrick's relatively limited oeuvre. KZ

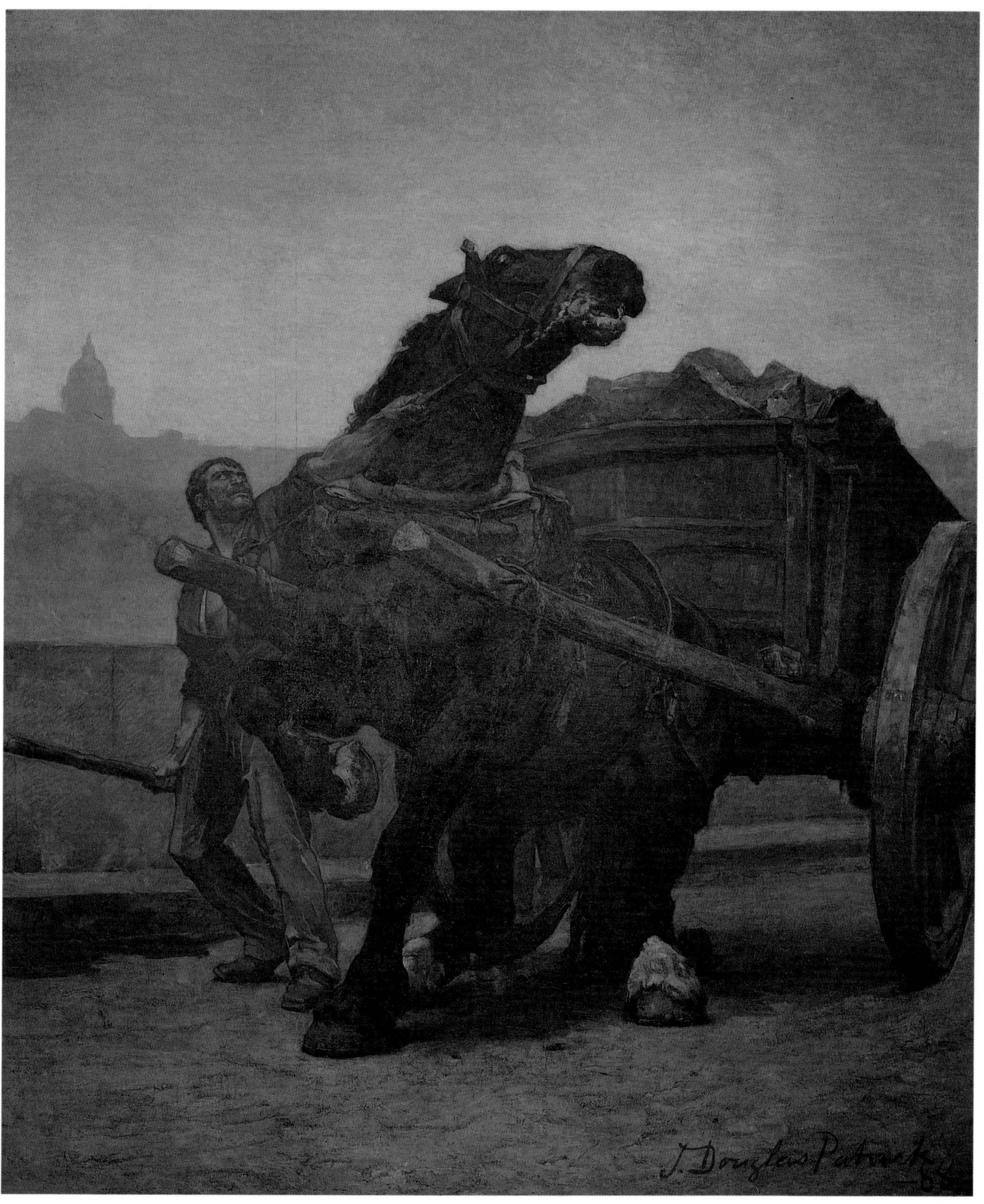
J. Douglas Patrick

CHARLES SPRAGUE PEARCE (1851–1914)

Born into a prominent Boston family, Pearce was the grandson and namesake of the poet Charles Sprague. Although he had initially intended to study in Munich, his friend William Morris Hunt persuaded him, in 1873, to go instead to Paris. He entered the studio of Léon Bonnat but was forced by ill health to interrupt his studies and go south for the winter. With the artist Frederick Bridgman, Pearce spent the winter of 1873 in Egypt, and he returned to Egypt in 1874. For the next several years Pearce traveled along the Mediterranean during the winters; during the summers, confined to his studio because of his health, he received individual instruction from Bonnat. In 1876 he exhibited at the Royal Academy, London, and also began showing regularly at the Paris Salon, where he was awarded an honorable mention in 1881. In America, Pearce's paintings were exhibited at the Society of American Artists in 1878, at the National Academy of Design beginning in 1883, and at the Pennsylvania Academy of the Fine Arts from 1883 to 1909. During the 1870s and the early 1880s Pearce specialized in portraits, religious subjects, and oriental genre.[1]

Settling permanently in the village of Auvers-sur-Oise, about twenty miles north of Paris, in 1885, Pearce, like other artists of the period, such as Monet and Daniel Ridgway Knight, had "a glass studio attached to his principal studio [where he was] able to paint summer landscapes in all weathers."[2] Pearce was particularly active in artistic circles. He served as a juror in Paris for the 1889 Exposition and organized the American fine arts section of the 1894 Antwerp world's fair, "the first large-scale exhibition of American art in Belgium."[3] He was also a founding member of the Paris Society of American Painters. In the late 1890s he painted a series of seven lunette murals for the Great Hall of the Jefferson Building of the Library of Congress in Washington, D.C. In 1894, Pearce was named a Chevalier of the Legion of Honor. He died in Paris.

About 1883, Pearce had begun to concentrate on portrayals of peasant life in northern France: *Evening* was painted in Auvers-sur-Oise. During the 1880s, Pearce's peasant subjects, like those of his countrymen Alexander and Birge Harrison, reveal the impact of Bastien-Lepage; *Evening*'s evenly diffused light and muted tonalities suggest that master's influence. As the art historian G.W. Sheldon noted in 1888, "Mr. Pearce has recently been painting his pictures in a grey tone."[4] The lone shepherd or shepherdess was a subject that Pearce painted repeatedly, and these works were influenced by Charles-Emile Jacque, who specialized in pictures of sheepherding. Pearce's penchant for the shepherd theme may have derived from its association with Christian pastoralism.[5] The artist's religious subject matter of the 1870s was transformed by the next decade into a more subtle spiritual iconography. In *Evening* the religious implications are conveyed by the mystical quality of the moonlight, which appears to have transfixed both man and dog. Pearce's peasants are thematically related to those of George Hitchcock (see page 171). Although many of the jurors of the 1889 fair exhibited six entries, Pearce displayed only four: two figure studies revealing the influence of Bonnat and two sheepherding scenes, which were favorably reviewed.[6] *Evening* was subsequently shown in 1890 at both the National Academy of Design and the Pennsylvania Academy of the Fine Arts.[7]

HPC

EDWARD HENRY POTTHAST (1857–1927)

Remembered chiefly as a painter of Impressionist beach scenes, Edward Potthast painted *Study: A Britany [sic] Girl*[1] at a pivotal point in his career.[2] At the age of sixteen Potthast took up commercial lithography, which was a means of support for most of his life. In his native Cincinnati, a center for both printing and art, from 1879 to 1882 and from 1885 to 1887 he worked during the day at the Strowbridge Lithography Company and attended night classes at the McMicken School of Design, where he had been intermittently enrolled since 1870. He studied in Europe from 1882 to 1885—first, briefly, in Antwerp, then in Munich. He resumed his painting studies in France about 1887, probably at various art colonies, including the one at Barbizon, and in the atelier of Fernand Cormon in Paris.[3]

Potthast met Robert Vonnoh in Grez in 1888, and the encounter proved a seminal experience.[4] Though Vonnoh showed a conservative portrait, *Studio Comrade* (see page 221), in the 1889 Exposition, he was moving in a new direction under the influence of the Irish artist Roderic O'Connor, whom he had met in Grez. O'Connor's plein-air landscapes pointed the way to Fauvism. Vonnoh adopted many of O'Connor's methods, and Potthast, inspired by Vonnoh's work, painted *A Britany Girl*. Using the high-keyed color and the broad, stubby brushwork of his mentors, Potthast in this picture drew not only on O'Connor's near abstraction but also on the Impressionists' fleeting effects of sunshine.

A Britany Girl was one of the few Impressionist works and one of the few portraits of children in the Exposition. Beckwith and Weir submitted more traditional portraits of children (see pages 116 and 226), and Sargent entered his dramatic *The Daughters of Edward Darley Boit*. In contrast to these, Potthast's Breton girl is painted in bright sun-dappled colors. Though by 1889 Impressionism was an established if vanguard aesthetic in France, it was not yet in the mainstream in America. *A Britany Girl* was stylistically innovative, and by labeling it a "study" in the Exposition, Potthast called attention to its experimental aspect.[5] At the Exposition, the relatively small picture received no critical attention, but when it was shown in 1892 at Barton's Art Store in Cincinnati reviewers noted its Impressionist manner and its "rankly hot" color.[6] The painting prefigured the direction of Potthast's work.

After his return to Cincinnati, in 1889, Potthast painted portraits and landscapes in a somber Munich palette and resumed working for the Strowbridge Lithography Company. Although he occasionally ventured the brighter colors and luminous lighting of *A Britany Girl*, he did not take up the Impressionist palette and stroke again until he moved to New York, in 1896. By 1910 he was painting the cheerful bathing scenes in the vibrant contrasting blocks of color that became his trademark. KZ

CHARLES STANLEY REINHART (1844–1896)

Charles Stanley Reinhart left his native Pittsburgh in 1867 to attend the Atelier Suisse in Paris, and by 1868 had entered the Munich Royal Academy.[1] On his return to America, in 1870, Reinhart found employment with Harper and Brothers, and through this connection he met Winslow Homer and Edwin

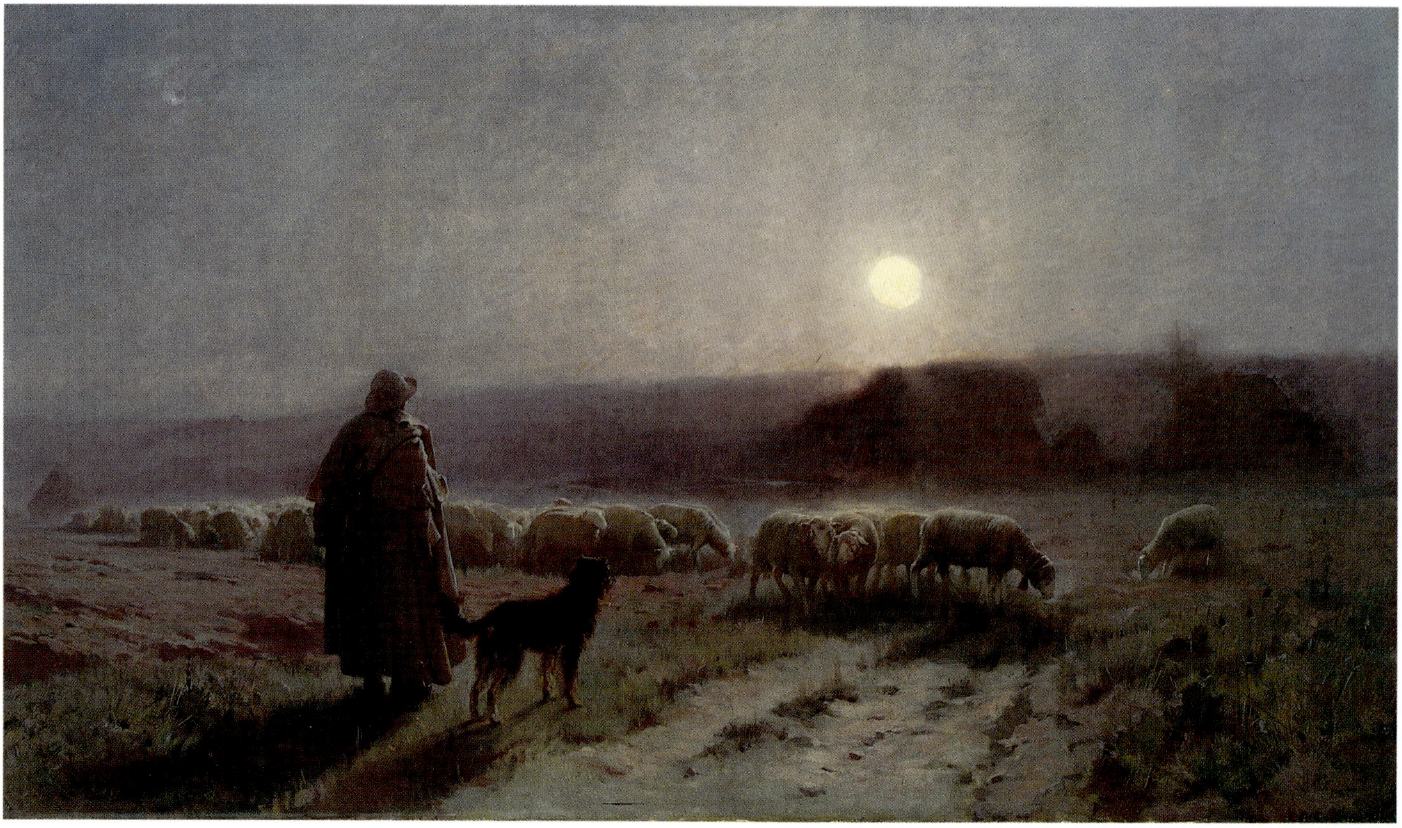

237.
Charles Sprague Pearce
Evening
Evening (Auvers-sur-Oise), 1880s
Oil on canvas, 40 x 70″ (101.6 x 177.8 cm)
Collection Jane and John D. Caruthers

245.
Edward Henry Potthast
Study: A young Britany [*sic*] Girl
Sunshine, 1889
Oil on canvas, 31 1/16 x 25 5/8″ (78.9 x 65.1 cm)
Cincinnati Art Museum,
Gift of Mrs. Larz Anderson

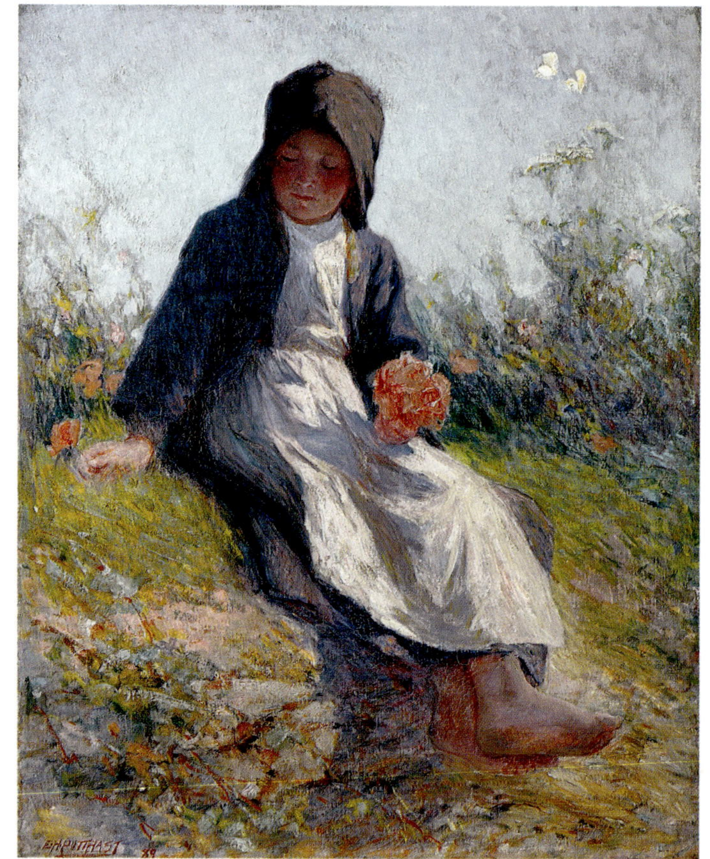

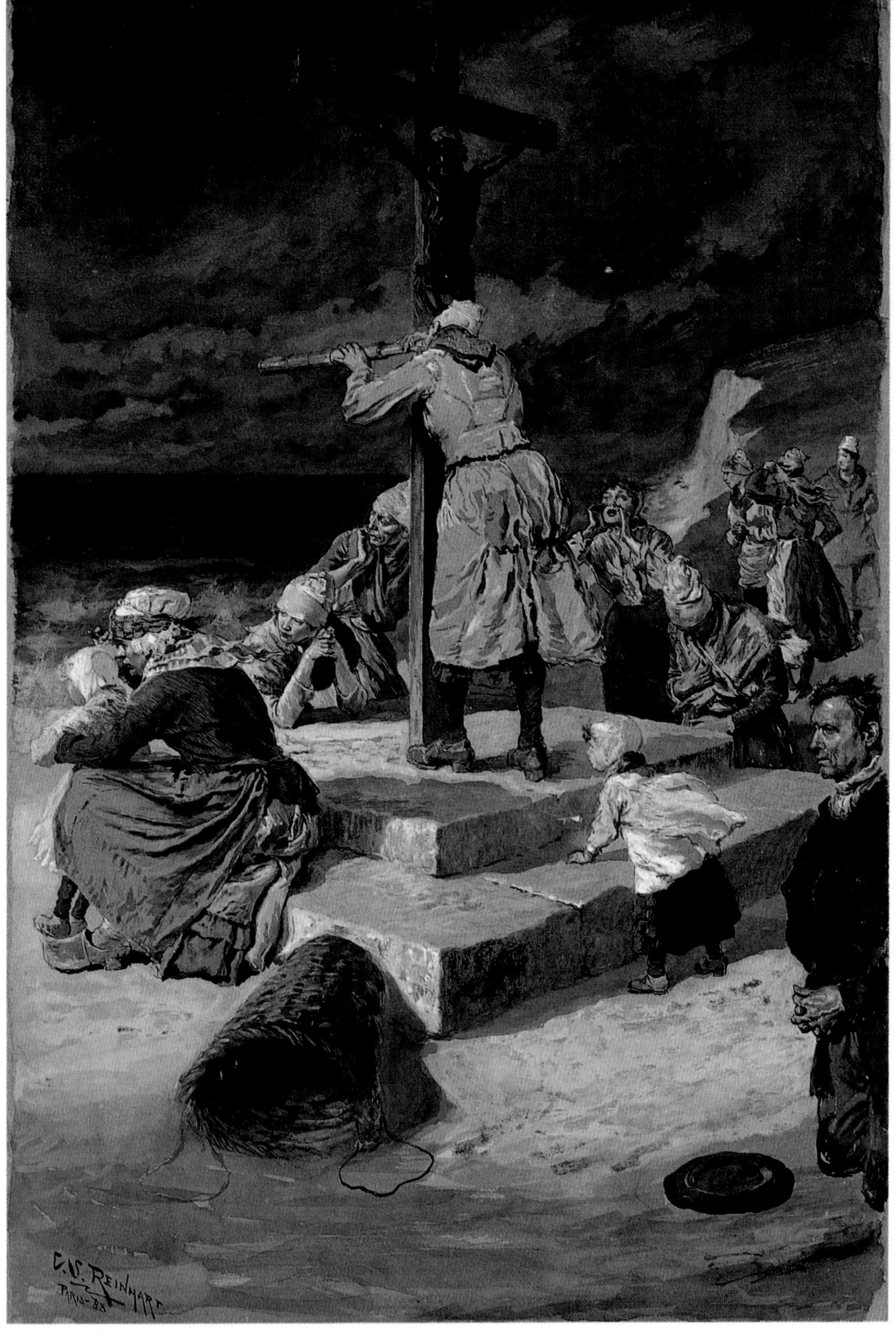

248.
Charles Stanley Reinhart
Awaiting the Absent
Study for Awaiting the Absent, 1888
Crayon and gouache on blue paper mounted on canvas, 28½ x 18¾" (72.4 x 47.6 cm)
The Carnegie Museum of Art, Pittsburgh, Gift of Charles Stanley Reinhart, Jr., Liliane Reinhart Bennet, and John Reinhart Bennet
Photograph by Richard Stoner

Austin Abbey. In 1880 he returned to Paris to take up painting full-time, beginning a period when he produced his best-known canvases. Six of his genre and marine paintings were shown at the Exposition, and they won Reinhart a silver medal. Two of them, *Awaiting the Absent* and *Washed Ashore* (both unlocated), appeared in exhibitions throughout Europe and America, the latter winning the 1888 Temple Gold Medal for best figure painting at the Pennsylvania Academy of the Fine Arts 59th annual exhibition. In 1890 Reinhart returned to New York to pursue a dual career, as painter and illustrator; he died prematurely six years later.

Reinhart's fame rests mainly on his work as an illustrator. From his student days in Paris, he maintained a connection with Harper and Brothers: hundreds of his images appeared in their publications. On assignment for them he traveled the world, drawing both domestic and foreign landscapes and peoples. Using a spare and deft line that gives the illusion of color, he specialized in figural sketches drawn rapidly from life, "brightened by a quick and ready humor."[2] He showed twenty-one illustrations at the Exposition and served on the American jury in Paris, judging entries in black-and-white. The critics unanimously ranked him among America's best illustrators, and he and Abbey won gold medals for drawing and watercolor.

With *Awaiting the Absent* Reinhart made the transition from illustrator to painter. Both the study and the large painting of 1888 depict the women of Villerville in Normandy awaiting their fishermen, coming home late from the sea.[3] The study's wide range of darks and lights and dynamic contour line, as well as the strong facial expressions of the women, reveal Reinhart's skills as a fresh and vibrant illustrator; its formal composition and the slightly stilted poses of the figures show the artist approaching the more static, studied medium of oils.[4] In the finished painting, Reinhart retained the study's overall composition but reduced the number of figures, altering some of their poses, and he substituted fog for the storm. While the critics praised the painting, they cited its coldness, which they attributed to Reinhart's relative inexperience in oils and, more serious, his detached illustrator's viewpoint.

In the study, the waiting peasant women, piously leaning on their faith in a time of trial, are treated as character types. Peasants in other American paintings at the Exposition—for example, Melchers' dignified worshipers and Hitchock's gentle madonnas—are also portrayed as profoundly religious. But while Melchers' and Hitchcock's peasants are appealing and sympathetic, Reinhart's have exaggerated facial expressions and gestures. Yet Reinhart the journalist-illustrator produced a painting charged with pictorial interest and ethnographic insight. KZ

THEODORE ROBINSON (1852–1896)

Theodore Robinson, one of the pioneers of American Impressionism, began his formal study of art in Chicago around 1870.[1] Suffering from asthma, which plagued him throughout his life and was the cause of his early death, Robinson interrupted his studies several times before settling in New York, in 1874. There he sought out Winslow Homer, whose figural naturalism was one of the first influences on his own development.[2] He enrolled in classes at the National Academy of Design and was among the artists involved in the founding of the Art Students League.

Robinson made his first trip to Europe in 1876 and immediately entered Carolus-Duran's popular atelier, where he met, among other American students, Will H. Low, J. Carroll Beckwith, and Sargent.[3] Like Low, who became a lifelong friend, he left Carolus-Duran's studio the following year to pursue a more academic course of study under Jean-Léon Gérôme at the Ecole des Beaux-Arts. During the summer of 1877, following the acceptance of his first submission to the Salon, he joined several of his new friends at Grez, near Fontainebleau. There he initiated a pattern of plein-air sketching and painting that would be the source of much of his later work.

After further study that included a visit to Italy, where he met and became an admirer of Whistler, Robinson returned to the United States in 1879.[4] He stayed with his family in Wisconsin for a brief time, then moved to New York to accept a teaching position. The next four years were spent working on decorative commissions under John La Farge and Prentice Treadwell in New York and Boston, interrupted by summer visits to Vermont, Wisconsin, and Nantucket. In 1884 he returned to France, and he spent much of the next eight years painting in and near Paris, Barbizon, and Giverny.

Robinson's work of the 1870s and 1880s is not well known, but his landscapes of the mid-1880s document his openly professed admiration for Charles Daubigny and Corot. His canvases remained relatively small, since he lacked the strength to carry heavy equipment to sites out of doors. He could rarely afford to employ studio models but used photography in composing figural works.

The Forge was painted in Paris in 1886. Its size indicates that it was done in the studio and probably with a photographic prototype. Its dark tonalities and unsentimentalized subject place it in the mainstream of contemporary French realism and outside the decorative influence of mural painting. Robinson clearly planned it as a Salon picture, combining the fresh, broad paint application of the most advanced ateliers and the sure modeling, solid draftsmanship, and attention to detail taught at the Ecole. It was not a subject that he repeated, although he attempted other interiors, both rustic and urban.

By 1888, the year in which *The Forge* was exhibited at the Salon, Robinson was a regular visitor to Giverny. His relation with Monet marks a shift to a lighter palette, less academic construction, and looser paint handling. It is noteworthy that he selected *The Forge* to represent him at the Exposition rather than *La Vachère* (1888; Baltimore Museum of Art), painted in his recently achieved Impressionist technique, which he sent to the 1889 Salon. MCOB

JOHN SINGER SARGENT (1856–1925)

Fifteen years after he arrived in France to study at the atelier of Carolus-Duran, John Singer Sargent was awarded a medal of honor for the six paintings he exhibited at the 1889 Exposition and named a Chevalier of the Legion of Honor.[1] At the age of thirty-three he was already an internationally recognized artist, and although he had been born and raised abroad he participated in the Exposition as an American and served as a member of the United States jury in Paris. His stature among his peers was based not only on the successful exposure of his work in Paris over the previous ten years but also on the position he held in the contemporary English art scene and on the acknowledgment given his painting in both Boston and New York.[2] The paintings he sent to France in 1889 represented his work in each of these arenas; that they were all portraits indicated his wish to enhance and confirm his reputation in that field. His entries were two French paintings, *The Daughters of Edward D. Boit* (see fig. 19) and *Mrs. Henry White* (1883; Corcoran Gallery of Art, Washington, D.C.); a triple portrait, *The Misses Vickers* (Sheffield City Art Galleries), painted in England in 1884; and three more current portraits of women, painted in America during the late fall and winter of 1887–88.

An eccentrically composed, square-format group portrait, the depiction of the four daughters of Sargent's friend the painter Edward Darley Boit remains

260.
Theodore Robinson
The Forge
The Forge, 1886
Oil on canvas, 60 x 50" (152 x 127 cm)
Berry-Hill Galleries, New York

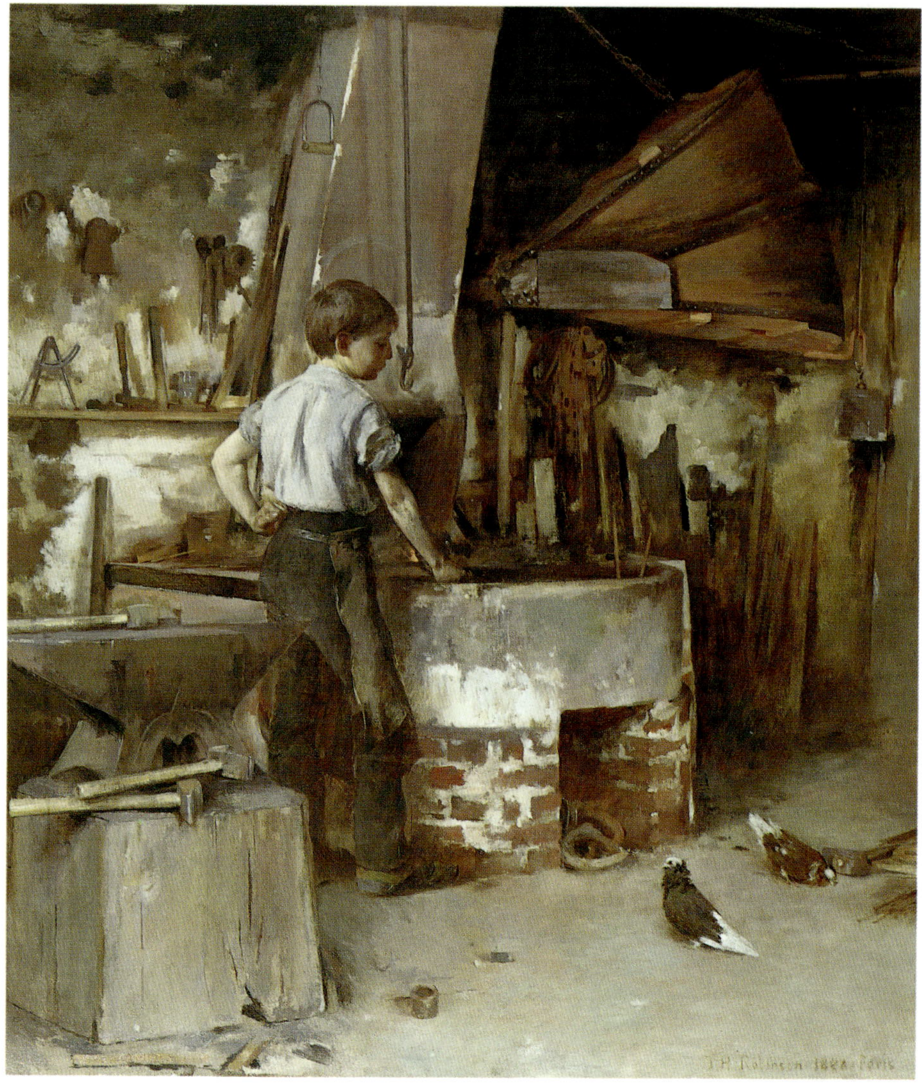

an icon of Sargent's originality. Sargent's other five entries at the Exposition upheld the impression of the critic Thiébault-Sisson that he was an artist who painted scarcely anything but women.[3] The formal full-length portrait of Mrs. Henry White had been commissioned to complement Léon Bonnat's painting of her diplomat husband, who became first secretary at the American Embassy in London in 1884. R.A.M. Stevenson, an English painter and writer who had studied with Sargent at Carolus-Duran's, praised its "eloquent workmanship" and found it exemplified "that large and noble disposition of figure that we admire so much in the old masters."[4] At the Universal Exposition, where it was hung beside *The Daughters of Edward Boit*, the critic for the *Art Amateur* selected it as the painting that showed Sargent to greatest advantage.[5]

In contrast to the stately portrait of Mrs. White was the more informal grouping of three young Englishwomen whom Sargent had met when they were studying art in Paris.[6] He painted *The Misses Vickers* in Sheffield during the summer following the hostile reception of his *Madame X* (Metropolitan Museum of Art, New York) at the 1884 Salon. In a brilliant reversal of the

264.
John Singer Sargent
Portrait of the Misses V.
The Misses Vickers, 1884
Oil on canvas, 52 x 72″ (137.8 x 182.9 cm)
Owner in 1889 Colonel Thomas Vickers
Sheffield City Art Galleries, England

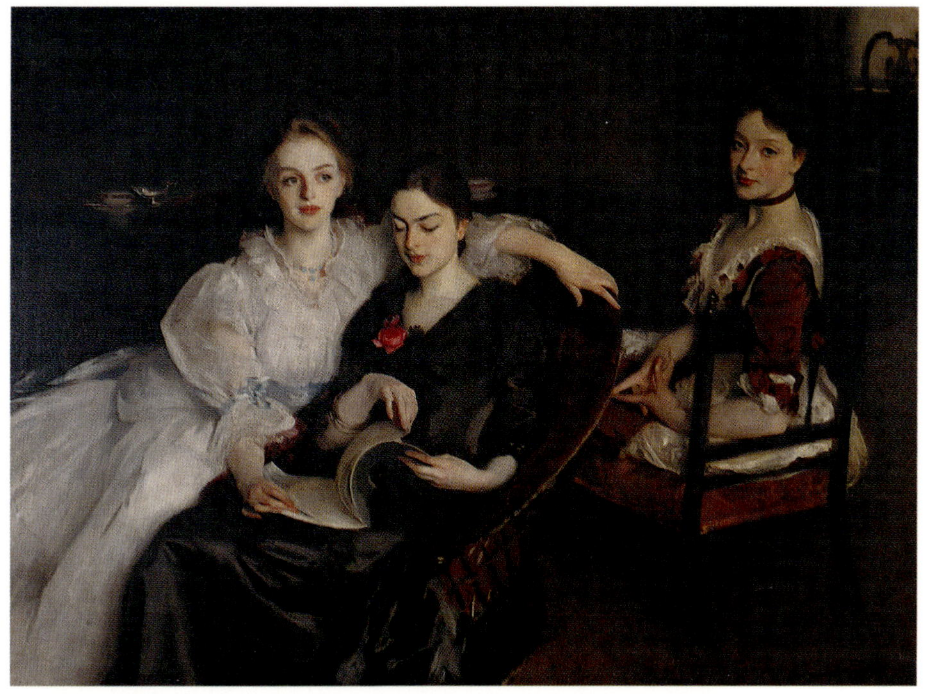

265.
John Singer Sargent
Portrait of Mrs. R. [*sic*]
Portrait of Mrs. Edward D. Boit, 1888
Oil on canvas, 60½ x 42″ (153 x 106.7 cm)
Owner in 1889 Mr. and Mrs. Edward D. Boit
Museum of Fine Arts, Boston,
Gift of Mrs. Julia Overing Boit

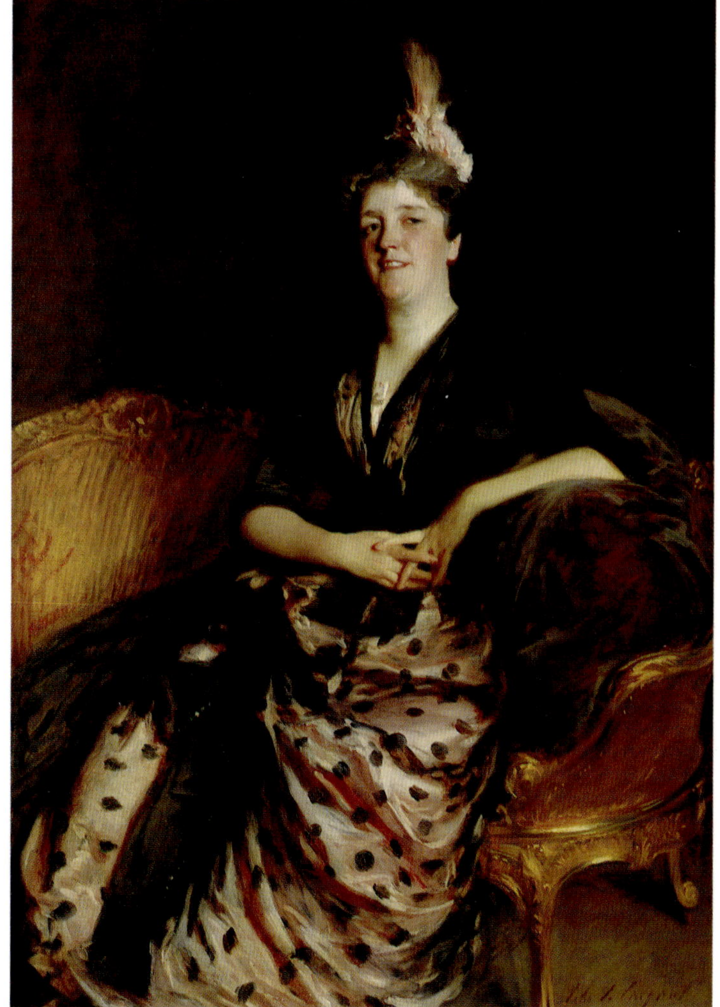

portrait of the Boit children, the figures are pushed out of a darkened interior onto the surface of the picture plane, their presence heightened by dramatic foreshortening, intricacy of pose, asymmetry of composition, and clever contrast of costumes. Initially a commission for which he had little enthusiasm, *The Misses Vickers* became a prototype for the increasingly complicated and elaborate group portraits of his later career.[7] It was shown first at the 1885 Salon, where it helped reestablish Sargent's reputation in Paris, but English critics who saw it at the Royal Academy exhibition in 1886 dismissed its technical skill and audacity as a mask for what was "essentially shallow, pretentious and untrue."[8] Once again coming to Sargent's defense, R.A.M. Stevenson recalled in 1888 that he had been spellbound by the painting's "fervid singleness of impression."[9]

Balancing these outstanding European subjects were three paintings executed during Sargent's first professional visit to America. The earliest of the three was a seated portrait of Mary Louisa Cushing Boit, the mother of the four little girls he had painted in 1882. After a month in Newport in the fall of 1887 and a brief visit to New York, Sargent had joined the Boit family in the house they were renting on Beacon Hill in Boston.[10] It was here that he painted the vivacious Mrs. Boit. Attired in a mauve dotted-silk gown with a black lace overdress, and sporting a feathery pink cockade in her upswept hair, she represented the antithesis of formal Boston portraiture. The painting was shown in Sargent's 1888 St. Botolph Club exhibition, and while it was admired for the rendering of the dress, it was thought to be one of the paintings lacking a true likeness.[11] In Paris, again, the "marvellous brushwork" of the gown was distinguished from the "coarsely rendered" features of the sitter.[12]

Sargent took a significant amount of artistic license in his paintings of the Boit family, which were not ordinary portrait commissions. His remaining two works in the Exposition were painted in New York for members of a socially prominent family, but these, too, were distinctive in color and technique, and one at least was controversial in pose. Mrs. Elliott Fitch Shepard, the eldest daughter of William H. Vanderbilt, was the mother of six children and an active contributor to New York charities.[13] Sargent's full-length standing portrait of Mrs. Shepard was described as that of a "handsome and graceful brunette in flowing red robes"[14] when shown in Paris in 1889; however, it did not please the sitter's husband, who recognized neither the gown nor the coiffure and sent the painting back to Sargent for alterations in 1890.[15] For the portrait of Mrs. Shepard's aunt, Mrs. Benjamin Kissam, Sargent invented an exuberant pose to show off a lavender satin dress trimmed with crimson flowers. Wrote one reviewer at the Exposition: "The loudness of the color is in keeping with the vulgarity of the pose, and, in fact, of the whole picture—the lady is holding up her train, clutching it with both hands, as if in celebration of 'washing day.'"[16]

While the six portraits sent to Paris might at first glance have appeared to be a conservative choice for Sargent, clearly each had challenged its first viewers and continued to astonish visitors to the Exposition. Sargent's highest accolades came not from more sophisticated Europeans but from American reviewers who took national pride in his accomplishments. The Paris edition of the *New York Herald* wrote that his paintings were unquestionably "the finest works in the gallery."[17] In retrospect it can be argued that Sargent's skill and confidence set the high tone of the American section. His contribution, as acknowledged by the awards jury, helped it achieve the distinction of being second only to the French display in its variety, technique, and originality. MCOB

WALTER SHIRLAW (1838–1909)

Renowned for his genre and figure paintings, Walter Shirlaw was also a respected teacher who pioneered efforts to establish good art instruction in New York and Chicago. He was born in Paisley, Scotland, but in 1841 his family moved to America, where at the age of fourteen he was apprenticed to a banknote engraving company in New York. In 1861 he began exhibiting at the National Academy of Design and the Pennsylvania Academy of the Fine Arts. By this year Shirlaw had also established his own studio. Financial problems forced him to resume his former profession, however, and in 1865 Shirlaw went to work at the Western Bank Note Company in Chicago, where he helped form the Chicago Academy of Design the following year.[1] Shirlaw traveled through the Rocky Mountains before he left for Europe in September 1870. He had initially planned to study in Paris, but when he found it under siege because of the Franco-Prussian War he went to Munich instead. During his seven years in Munich, Shirlaw studied at the Royal Academy with Johann Leonhard Raab, Alexander Wagner, Arthur von Ramberg, and Wilhelm von Lindenschmit. Returning to America in 1877, Shirlaw was elected an associate member of the National Academy of Design, and he became a founder and the first president of the Society of American Artists. At this time he also taught at the Art Students League in New York. During the 1880s and 1890s Shirlaw painted murals for the 1893 Chicago World's Columbian Exposition, the Library of Congress, and various private residences. In 1889 he was sent by the United States government to the Crow and Cheyenne reservations to record their ways of life.[2] Shirlaw died in Madrid while traveling through Spain.

Rufina is characteristic of the female nudes Shirlaw produced after his return from Munich, where with Frank Duveneck and William Merritt Chase he was among the first Americans to study at the Royal Academy. Indeed, *Rufina* relates to the figural style of both Duveneck and Chase in the way the model is placed against a dark background and in the dramatic use of a strong light that illumines only portions of her figure. Shirlaw's stay in Germany during the 1870s coincided with what the art historian Michael Quick has described as the First Munich Period, when the "training in the Academy was to a large extent the imitation of the style of the Old Masters."[3] *Rufina* displays an appreciation of the nudes of Titian, who was well represented in German public collections. But as William Gerdts has noted, "the American nude was closely associated with Titian and the Venetian school."[4] Although the nude had an enormous vogue in France, it never attained a similar popularity in America. Nevertheless, at the 1889 fair there were at least seven examples.[5]

One of his most important exhibition pieces, *Rufina* was Shirlaw's sole entry in the 1889 Universal Exposition, where it received an honorable mention. Shown again the following year, at the National Academy of Design, it was favorably reviewed in the *Art Amateur*; "Mr. Shirlaw is represented," a critic wrote, "by a study of a female figure called 'Rufina' which has already been commended in these columns as beautiful in color and quality of its warm flesh tones."[6] In 1892 *Rufina* was presented by A.W. Drake and other subscribers to the Century Association, New York, of which Shirlaw had been a member for seven years. Relegated to storage for many years owing to changing tastes, *Rufina* has been restored specially for the present exhibition. HPC

266.
John Singer Sargent
Portrait of Mrs. S.
Mrs. Elliott Fitch Shepard, 1888
Oil on canvas, 84¼ x 48¼″ (214 x 122.6 cm)
Owner in 1889 Mr. and Mrs. Elliott Fitch Shepard
San Antonio Museum of Art, Texas,
Cullen Fund

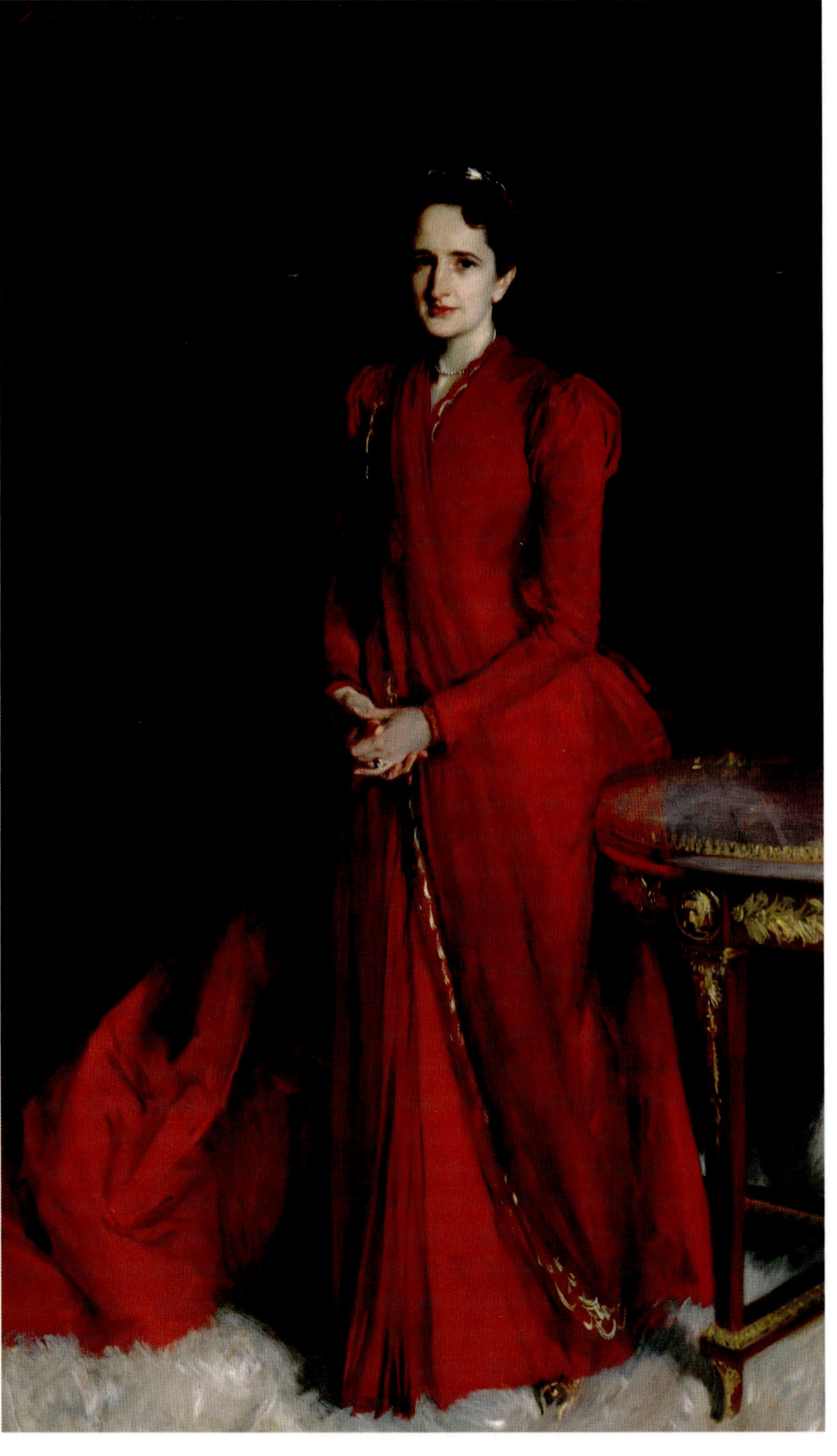

270.
Walter Shirlaw
Rufina
Rufina, c. 1887–88
Oil on canvas, 40⅝ x 27⅜" (103.2 x 69.5 cm)
The Century Association, New York,
Presented by Alexander Walter Drake and others

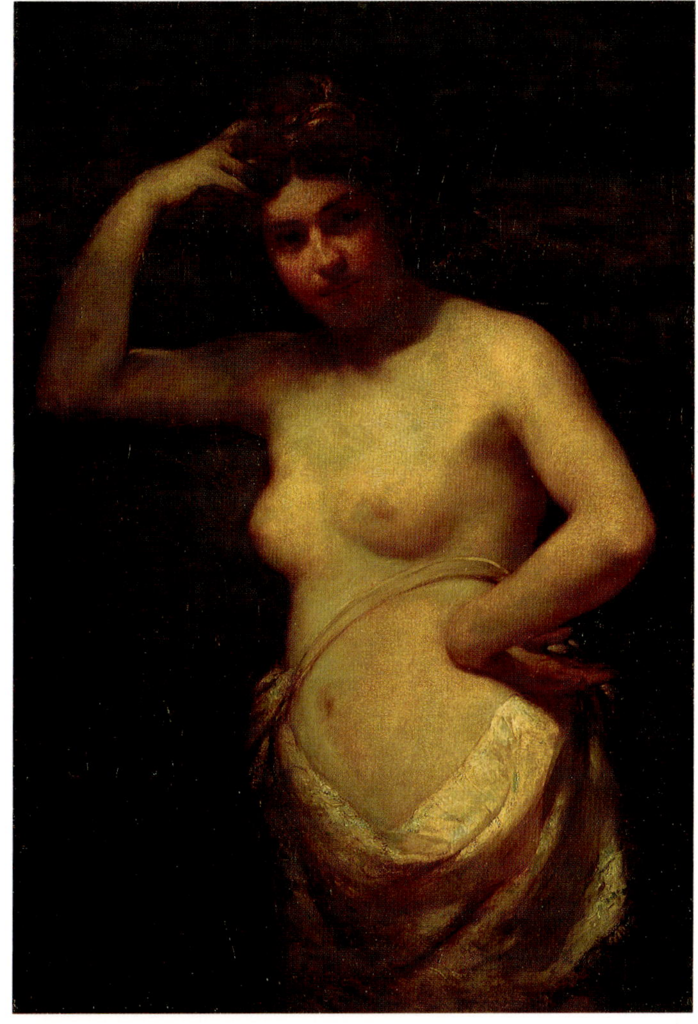

272.
Edward Emerson Simmons
Night
Night, St. Ives Bay, 1889
Oil on canvas, 50¼ x 66½" (127.6 x 168.9 cm)
Collection Hardwick Simmons

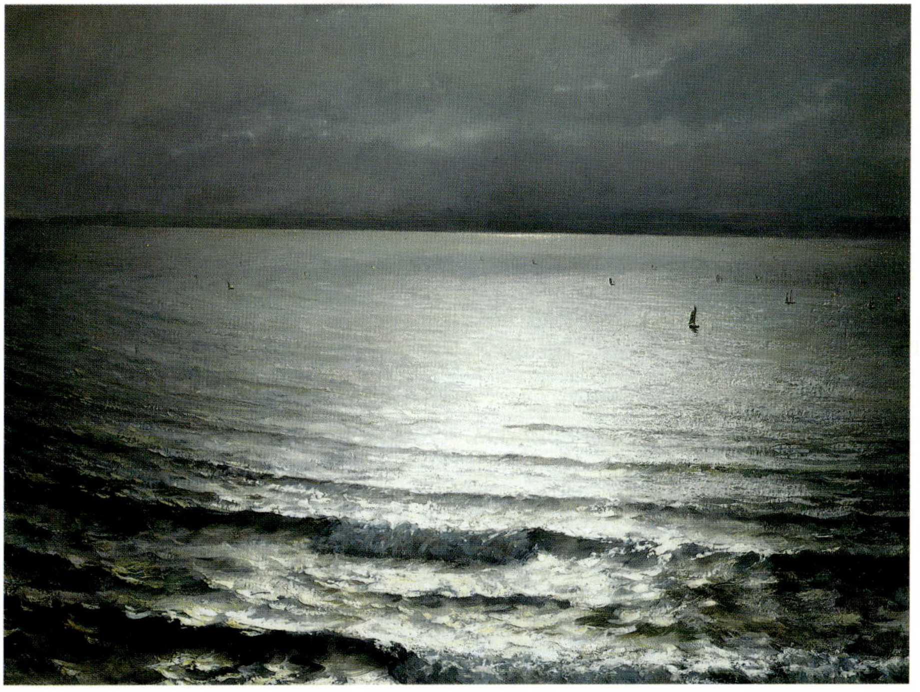

EDWARD EMERSON SIMMONS (1852–1931)

Edward Emerson Simmons, who was a cousin of Ralph Waldo Emerson's, grew up in Concord, Massachusetts.[1] After graduating from Harvard, in 1874, he spent a few adventurous years teaching on the California frontier, turning to art only in the late 1870s. He studied for about a year in Boston at the School of the Museum of Fine Arts under Frederick Crowninshield and William Rimmer. He went to Paris about 1879 and studied at the Académie Julian with Lefebvre and Boulanger; in 1880 he enrolled in the Ecole des Beaux-Arts. The year 1881 marked both his first acceptance at the Salon and his move to Concarneau, where he helped to establish the American art colony.[2]

By 1886 Simmons was living in St. Ives, Cornwall, the setting of his marine paintings.[3] He repatriated in 1891 for a stained-glass commission and became known as a muralist. Simmons showed in the 1880s with the Society of American Artists and about the turn of the century with The Ten; both groups were noted for their innovative aesthetics. He also showed at the more traditional Royal Academy in London and at the Paris Salon. In his autobiography, marked by a biting wit, Simmons offered insights both into his work and into the contemporary art world. As a member of the American jury in Paris that selected the paintings for the 1889 Exposition, he described its workings. He found all such duties thankless, writing that the jury was invariably "dominated by some bugbear of politics or obligation."[4] In addition to *Night*, Simmons showed *The Farmer* and a study (both unlocated), winning a bronze medal.

Simmons was one of a group of European and American artists who in the late nineteenth century developed a type of realistic marine painting attuned to the poetic aspect of nature. Concarneau was one of their laboratories. Toward the end of Simmons's stay in Concarneau, Alexander Harrison produced several large-scale paintings that captured the precise color and texture of breaking waves at sunset (see page 163). In the winter of 1883–84, Whistler executed a series of St. Ives beach scenes in single-color harmonies that Simmons may well have known. He may even have discussed St. Ives with Whistler, since the two were friendly by then.[5] Other artists, including the English painter Henry Moore, portrayed specific weather conditions; Moore's *The Clearness After the Rain* (unlocated), a large canvas of 1887, appeared in the 1889 Exposition.

Night, one of Simmons's many marines, is both a naturalistic portrayal of the St. Ives coast and an aesthetic conception in which paint handling predominates.[6] The effects here of fleeting weather conditions and the silvery gray color scheme relate this work to the landscapes of other Concarneau painters and to Whistler's. Simmons's large-scale format signals his ambition to make a mark at the Exposition, but also to create an environment that would envelop the viewer. Simmons painted a number of marines in St. Ives that won him acclaim.[7] The critic Clarence Cook called them "ethereal transcripts [where] as we seem to gaze upon a light that never was on sea or shore, we yet feel that, somewhere, it is real, and that were we blessed with the artist's power of vision, we too might see it as he has seen it."[8]

KZ

JULIUS LEBLANC STEWART (1855–1919)

Born in Philadelphia, the son of a wealthy sugar plantation owner, Julius Stewart belonged to the elite society he depicted in his portraiture and multifigured genre scenes.[1] He became an expatriate at the age of ten, when he moved with his family to Paris, where he lived for the rest of his life. In Paris his father collected contemporary art, and Stewart grew up in a circle that included Mariano Fortuny y Marsal, Giovanni Boldini, Ernest Meissonier, Léon Bonnat, Jean-Léon Gérôme, and a group of Spanish painters, among them Raimundo de Madrazo y Garreta and Eduardo Zamacois y Zabala. Success came to Stewart early with the acceptance of a painting by the 1878 Salon. While exhibiting at numerous international exhibitions through the 1880s and 1890s, including that of the prestigious Société Internationale des Peintres et Sculpteurs in 1880, he maintained his ties with America by showing at the Pennsylvania Academy of the Fine Arts. Rush Hawkins, United States Commissioner of Fine Arts to the Exposition, summed up Stewart's work: "He is a painter of thoroughly chic portraits of women, and . . . always produces genteel results. He never paints a woman who appears to be of lower rank than that of baroness, and all his young girls look like daughters of duchesses."[2] In the mid-1890s he expanded his repertoire to include more landscapes and cityscapes and nudes painted in the open air. By the turn of the century, Stewart's reputation was in decline, and though, after a religious conversion, he took a new direction, painting moralistic genre scenes of modern life, the trend was never reversed.

Stewart's art training was unusual. In 1870 he studied for a few months with his first teacher, Zamacois, whose humorous genre scenes, with their jewellike colors, brightened Stewart's palette. In 1873 he entered Gérôme's atelier at the Ecole des Beaux-Arts. Sometime in the mid-1870s he moved into his own studio, adjacent to that of Madrazo, his third and perhaps most influential teacher. The paintings in his father's collection must also have been an influence, especially those of Fortuny and Boldini, with their bold and individualistic brushwork.

Stewart developed a distinctive format that combined portraiture and genre on an ambitious scale. His paintings of the leisured aristocracy parallel works by the European artists James Tissot, Jean Béraud, and Auguste Toulmouche, who also exhibited at the fair. He set his parties, ceremonies, and strolls in wellknown locales and incorporated portraits of socialites. Viewers delighted in identifying the people and places portrayed, but critics were divided in their opinions. Proponents cited his technical dexterity and acute observation of elegant manners.[3] Detractors pointed out the shallowness of his characterizations and the triviality of documenting a group whose chief virtue was wealth.[4] Nonetheless, Stewart's paintings served then, as they do now, as a type of historical genre.

Stewart showed six paintings in the Exposition: three genre scenes of high society, two portraits of baronesses, and a Cairo street scene. He served on the American jury in Paris and on the international jury for wood engraving. His failure to win a medal at the Exposition was interpreted by some as a critical slight, but in fact his jury service made him ineligible for awards.

A Hunt Ball and *A Hunt Supper* were touchstones of Stewart's career as well as highlights of the Exposition.[5] *A Hunt Ball*'s appearance at the 1885 Paris Salon had confirmed Stewart's mastery of the multifigured genre scene of high society. Its success prompted Stewart to paint *A Hunt Supper* in 1889 as a com-

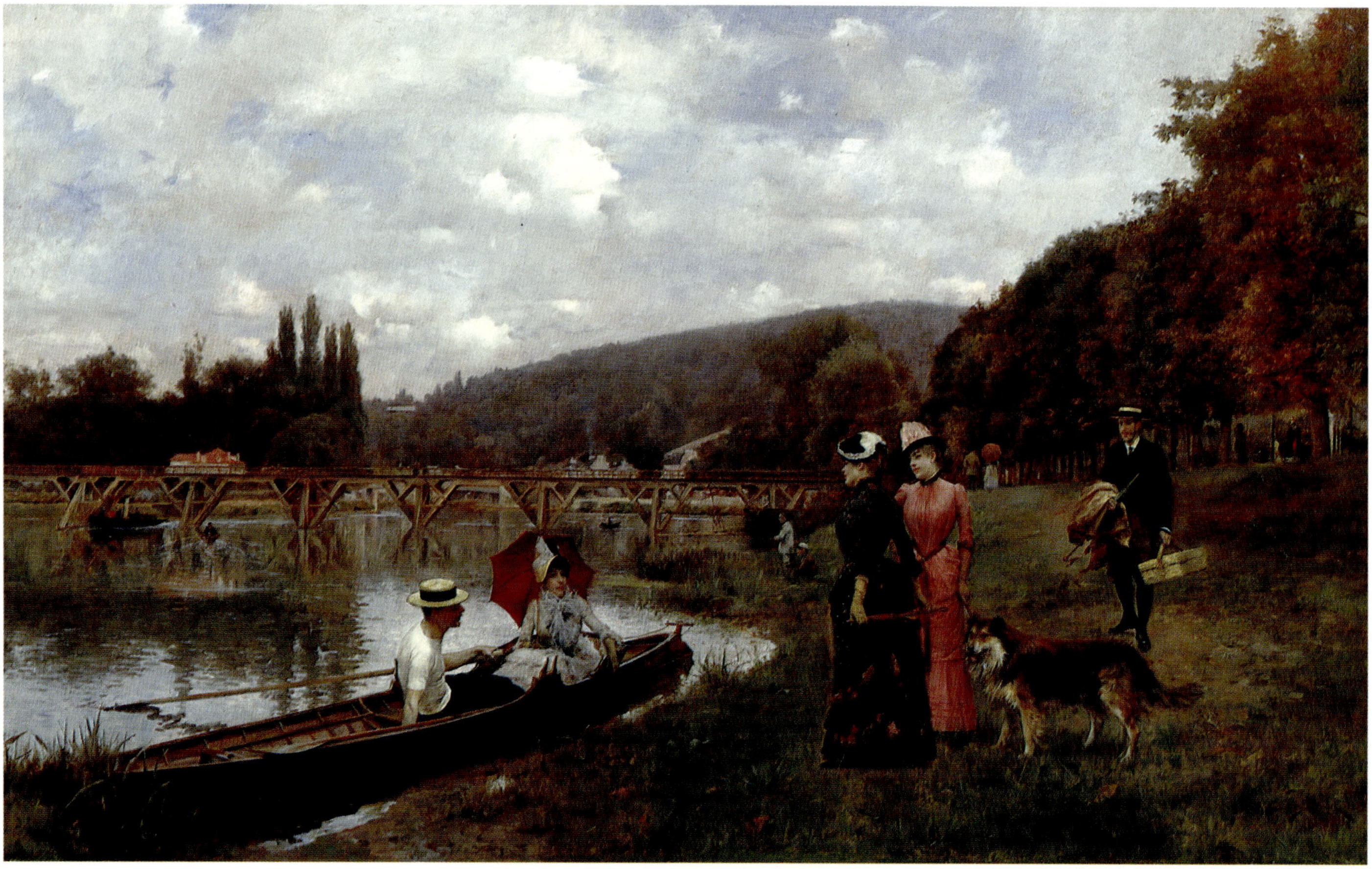

277.
Julius LeBlanc Stewart
The Seine at Bougival
On the Banks of the Seine at Bougival, 1885
Oil on canvas, 29½ x 48″ (74.9 x 121.9 cm)
Manoogian Collection

278.
Julius LeBlanc Stewart
A Hunt Ball
The Hunt Ball, 1885
Oil on canvas, 49 x 79″ (124.5 x 200.7 cm)
Essex Club, Newark

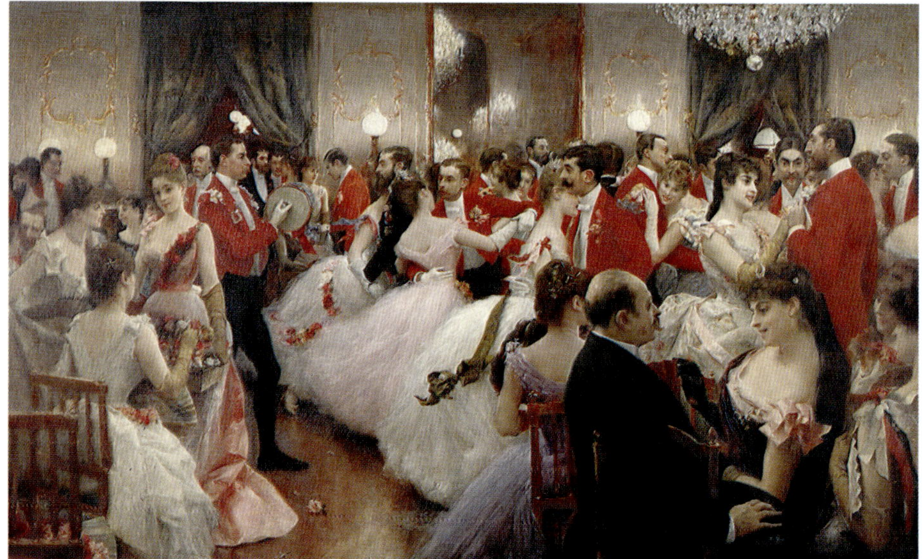

panion piece specifically for the Exposition. Together they show two moments in a cotillion: the supper served on the terrace at twilight and the later dance in the ballroom. *A Hunt Ball* reputedly contains portraits of the Vicomte de Jange, the Duc de Morny, Baron Rothschild, and Lily Langtry, as well as Stewart's self-portrait, visible above the tambourine.

288.
Edmund Charles Tarbell
Portrait of Mme. T.
Portrait of Madame Tarbell, 1888
Oil on canvas, 76 x 44" (193 x 111.8 cm)
Owner in 1889 Mme Tarbell
Private Collection
Photograph by Alexander Studio

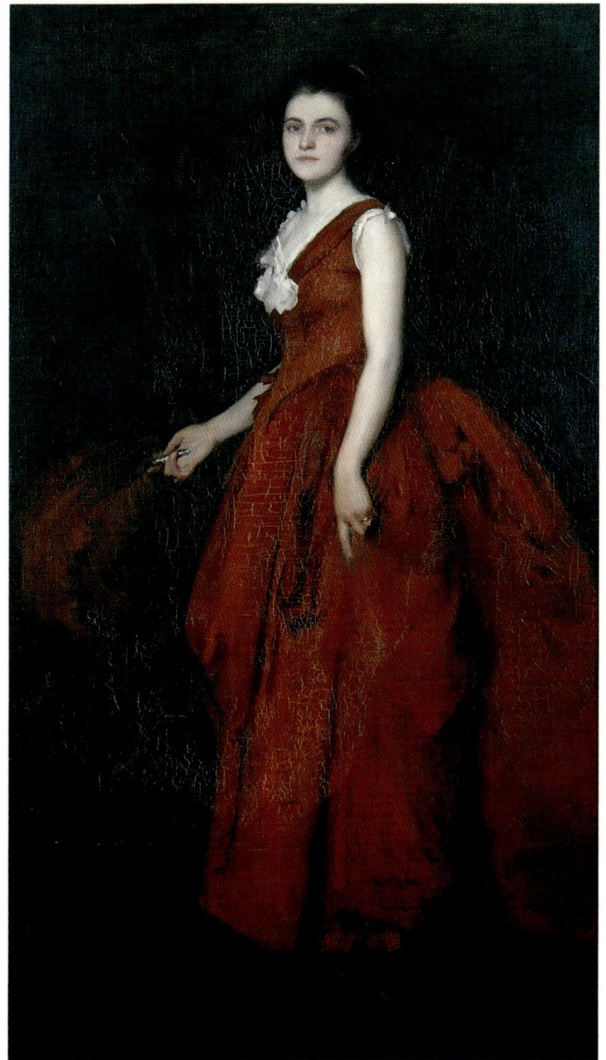

A Hunt Ball, the more famous of the two, was purchased by George I. Seney after the Salon of 1885 and exhibited with his well-known collection of American expatriate and European art at the Brooklyn Art Association in 1887. It was also shown at the World's Columbian Exposition of 1893.

In *The Seine at Bougival*, Stewart moved high society outdoors. The figure at the right with the basket is Stewart's friend and patron James Gordon Bennett, owner of the *New York Herald* and founder of its Paris edition. In the 1890s Stewart painted several scenes set aboard the *Namouna*, Bennett's luxurious yacht. Bennett lent Stewart his house in Bougival during the summer, and here the artist returned to painting landscapes, last undertaken in his 1880 *L'Eté*. Stewart's picnickers in *The Seine at Bougival* form an interesting parallel to such other plein-air subjects as the attractive peasants of Daniel Ridgway Knight and the rugged fisher folk of Charles Stanley Reinhart. *The Seine at Bougival* was first exhibited at the 1887 Salon. After being shown at the Exposition, it appeared at the 1891 Berlin International Art Exhibition and the 1894 Exposition Internationale at Antwerp. KZ

EDMUND CHARLES TARBELL (1862–1938)

A leading Boston figure painter and portraitist, Edmund Charles Tarbell was a founding member of The Ten, a group of American Impressionist painters. He was born in West Groton, Massachusetts, but grew up in Boston, where he studied at the School of the Museum of Fine Arts with Emil Otto Grundmann and Frederick Crowninshield. With his friend and fellow artist Frank W. Benson, whose *In Summer*, a picture of a woman in a landscape, was also exhibited at the 1889 Exposition, he went to Paris in 1883.[1] There he enrolled in the Académie Julian and studied with Boulanger and Lefebvre. While in Europe, Tarbell traveled to England, Italy, and Germany.

In 1886, Tarbell returned to Boston, where he became part of an artistic community that included Dennis Miller Bunker, Frederic Porter Vinton, and, at times, John Singer Sargent. From 1889 to 1913, Tarbell taught at the School of the Museum of Fine Arts. So strong was his influence that one critic named his numerous followers the "Tarbellites."[2] He experienced early success, beginning, in 1890, with the Thomas B. Clarke figure painting prize at the National Academy of Design. Later prizes included a medal at the World's Columbian Exposition in 1893, as well as awards from the Pennsylvania Academy of the Fine Arts annual exhibitions, among them the Temple Gold Medal and the Walter Lippincott Prize in 1895 for the best figure paintings.

In 1888, Tarbell married Emeline Arnold Souther, a former student of his at the Boston Museum school, and painted her portrait, which he proudly submitted to the Exposition the following year.[3] Portraits of artists' wives (their identities masked by the use of noncommittal titles) were a common feature of the Exposition; Tarbell's *Portrait of Mme. T.*, William Merritt Chase's *Portrait of Mother and Child*, and Edwin Howland Blashfield's *Portrait* are examples (see pages 127, 114). Tarbell's only entry, a full-length figure in a red dress, dramatically silhouetted against a dark background, parallels one of Sargent's entries, the *Portrait of Mrs. Elliott Fitch Shepard* (see page 208), and represents the height of French academic influence.[4]

Tarbell was elected a member of the Society of American Artists in 1887, and this portrait was shown in their 1890 exhibition.[5] His change to the Impressionist-like pictures he produced during the 1890s was announced by the Salon-size outdoor subject, *In the Orchard*, that he painted in 1891. This picture, so different from his 1889 entry, was entered at the World's Columbian Exposition and illustrates the new aesthetic that pervaded the Chicago fair.[6] By the end of the decade, Tarbell turned to painting decorative images of women in interiors. Tarbell resigned from the Society of American Artists in 1897, the year he joined in the founding of The Ten. Of the ten artists in the group, eight had exhibited at the 1889 Exposition. Tarbell became an Academician of the National Academy of Design in 1906 and head of the Corcoran Art School in Washington, D.C., in 1918. In 1925 he resigned from teaching and moved to New Castle, New Hampshire, where he spent the rest of his life. SJ-G

ABBOTT HANDERSON THAYER (1849–1921)

Abbott Handerson Thayer began his art training in Boston in 1865 with the animal painter Henry Morse.[1] From 1868 to 1874 he attended first the Brooklyn Art School, then the National Academy of Design. In 1875 he went to Paris and studied for three years with Henri Lehmann and Jean-Léon Gérôme at the Ecole des Beaux-Arts. In 1879 he returned to New York; he exhibited with the progressive Society of American Artists and continued to show at the National Academy of Design and the Paris Salon. Thayer made his name initially as a portraitist of women, formulating a style that combined realism and an aura of spirituality. In the 1890s he turned increasingly to painting idealized women, and landscapes as well, spending more time in the country. After delivering a public lecture on protective coloration in 1896, Thayer went on to develop and publish his book *Concealing Coloration in the Animal Kingdom* (1909); his theories of camouflage proved controversial at the time, and he did not succeed in having them adopted by the military in World War I. Thayer continued to promote his camouflage theories and continued to paint until his death, in 1921.

Winged Figure was probably Thayer's first portrayal of a woman as angelic, a theme that helped establish his reputation.[2] It is a portrait of his eldest daughter, Mary, at the age of eleven, on the brink of womanhood, posed against a pair of wings in the bright sunlight, her hair and gown wind-swept. Visible brushwork preserves the spontaneity of the moment, yet classical culture is invoked by the Renaissance-style frame and by the allusion in Mary's pose and dress to the Hellenistic sculpture *Nike of Samothrace* (Musée du Louvre, Paris). These signals and the figure's isolation against the blue sky remove it from this world. As Thayer wrote: "I have put on wings . . . to symbolize an exalted atmosphere (above the realm of genre painting) where one need not explain the action of [one's] figures."[3] Thayer trod carefully the line between the real and the ideal.

Critics recognized this dichotomy as a strength. Theodore Child called the figure a "white winged body on a blue ground, with a face of singular intensity of expression, a beautiful and fascinating vision."[4] A critic for *The Nation* was even more precise: "It is not characterized by any intentional idealization of face with a religious motive, just as it is not treated, either, as a piece of realistic figure painting with a conventional addition of wings. . . . "[5] Idealized women were seen as religious symbols or allegories in paintings at the fair by Sarah Paxton Ball Dodson, Kenyon Cox, and Edwin Howland Blashfield, and a peasant is portrayed as the Virgin Mary in George Hitchcock's *Annonciation* (see page 171). Thayer's conflation of realism and reverence is most closely paralleled in the work of his friend George de Forest Brush (not represented at the fair), whose depictions of motherhood endow it with sanctity. *Winged Figure* premiered at the 1888 exhibition of the Society of American Artists and won a bronze medal at the 1889 Exposition. It has remained one of Thayer's most highly regarded works.[6] KZ

289.
Abbott Handerson Thayer
Winged Figure
Angel, 1888
Oil on canvas, 36¼ x 28⅛" (92.0 x 66.4 cm)
Owner in 1889 Arthur A. Carey
National Museum of American Art,
Smithsonian Institution, Washington, D.C.,
Gift of John Gellatly

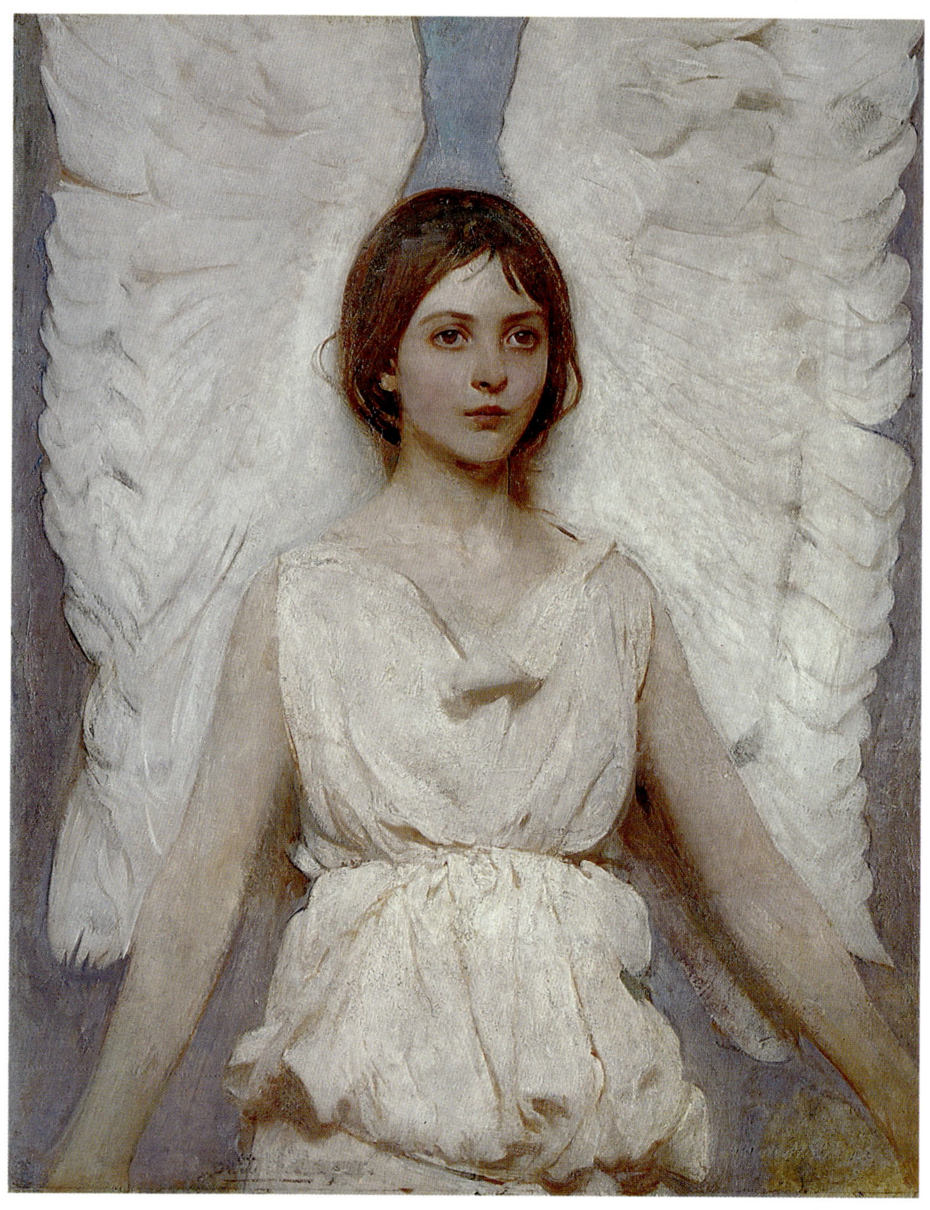

EUGENE LAWRENCE VAIL (1857–1934)

Eugene Lawrence Vail was born in the Brittany town of Saint-Servan, the son of a French mother and an American father. Educated in Paris and New York, he studied mechanical engineering at the Stevens Institute of Technology in Hoboken, New Jersey, and after graduating joined a geographical expedition to the American West as a member of the National Guard. On returning to New York, Vail studied at the Art Students League with James Carroll Beckwith and William Merritt Chase, then in 1882 departed for France to enter the Ecole des Beaux-Arts. In Paris he studied with Alexandre Cabanel and also with Raphael Collin and P.A.J. Dagnan-Bouveret.[1]

301.
Eugene Lawrence Vail
Fishing harbour
Le Port de peche, Concarneau, c. 1884
Oil on canvas, 52 x 74 13/16" (132 x 190 cm)
Musée Municipal de Brest
Photograph by Jacques Bocoyram

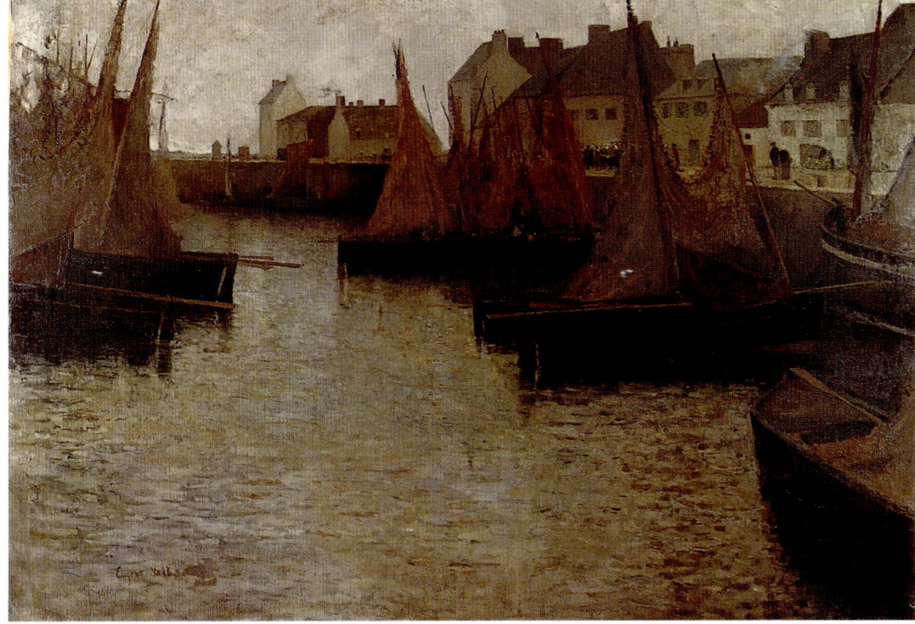

303.
Eugene Lawrence Vail
On the Thames
Marine, On the Thames, 1886
Oil on canvas, 82 1/4 x 69 1/4" (208.9 x 175.9 cm)
Collection Chris Whittle
Photograph courtesy Richard York Gallery

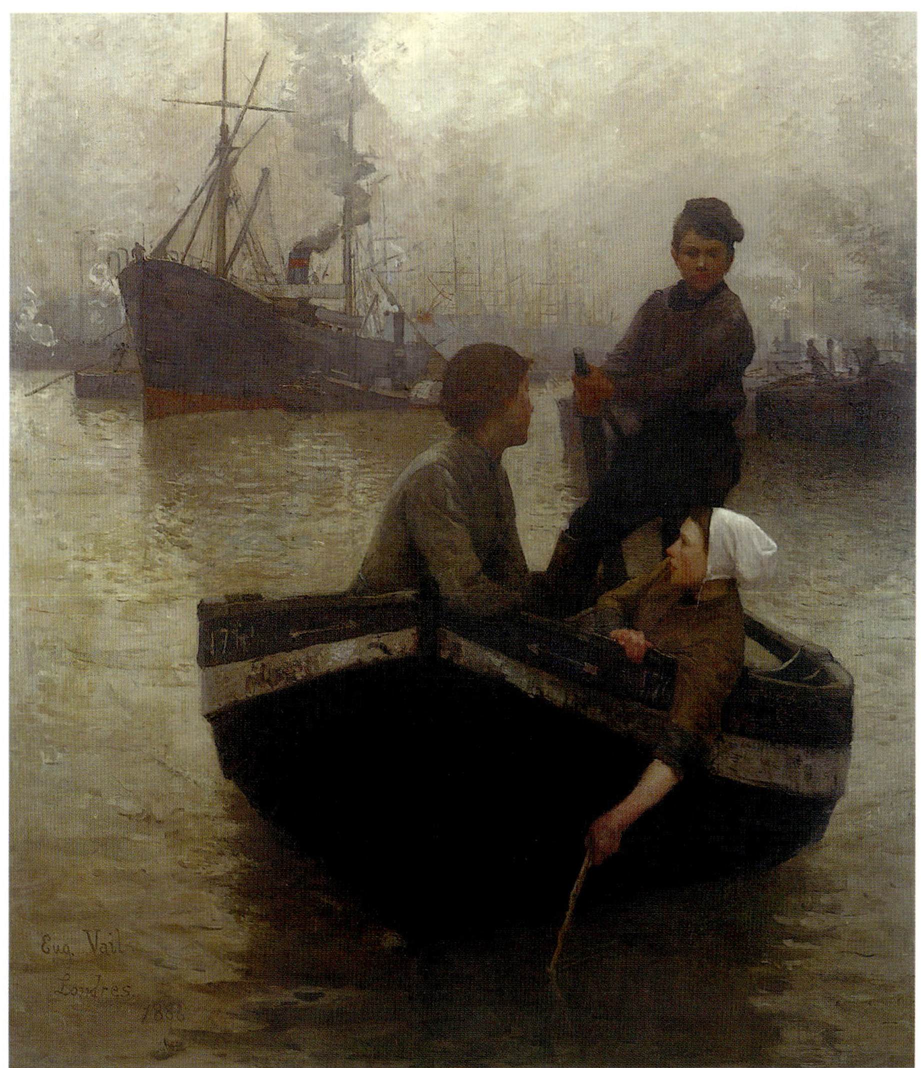

Vail made his first Salon entry in 1883, and the following year exhibited *Fishing Harbour*, a view of the fishing village Concarneau, where he painted after leaving the Ecole.[2] Admired by French critics, it was eventually purchased for the Musée du Luxembourg. Another maritime subject, *Marine, On the Thames*, Vail's Salon entry of 1886, was called "un des plus distingués cadres du Salon"[3] and was illustrated in the catalogue of the Salon.[4] This great atmospheric rendering of a dory being steered among the ships on the busy Thames waterfront won Vail a diploma of honor at the International Art Exhibition at Berlin in 1891. Both in this work and in *The Widow* (unlocated),[5] a painting of a young Breton fisherwoman and her child that was shown at the Salon of 1887, Vail's strong figural concern reflects the influence of Dagnan-Bouveret, an outstanding contemporary realist who often painted Breton peasant life.[6]

All three of these works and *Ready About* (unlocated),[7] a large, dramatic painting of fishermen bringing their boat about in stormy seas, were exhibited at the 1889 Exposition and were described by the American critic Theodore Child as "very beautiful in color, and amongst the very strongest and best pictures of this kind in the Exhibition."[8] *Ready About*, shown at the Salon of 1888, won Vail a first-class gold medal, as well as renewed praise for his capture of movement and intense involvement with his subject.

With the exhibition of this group of paintings in 1889, Vail, a member of the international jury for the Exposition, was established as an important painter with a "grand cachet de verité à ses scènes de la vie des marins."[9] According to his biographer, Louise Gebhard Cann, his knowledge of the sea was drawn from firsthand experience: he delighted in "cruising with the fishermen and making studies directly from nature."[10] So convincing was his familiarity with the French coast that the critic Thiébault-Sisson claimed him as a Frenchman and declared that no American marine painter could touch his skill.[11] Honors from France continued to accrue to Vail; he was named a Chevalier of the Legion of Honor in 1894. After his death, a retrospective of Vail's work was held at the Société Nationale des Beaux-Arts. MCOB

ELIHU VEDDER (1836–1923)

Elihu Vedder, an expatriate who spent over sixty years of his career in Italy, is best known for his imaginative paintings and his mystical illustrations. He began his studies in the Parisian atelier of François-Edouard Picot in 1857, but he became disillusioned with academic training and traveled to Florence in 1858. There he was exposed not only to classical and Renaissance painting and sculpture but also to the work of the Macchiaioli, a group of Italian artists inspired by French plein-air painting. His later decorative work was influenced by the writings and drawings of William Blake and by Edward FitzGerald's translation of the *Rubáiyát of Omar Khayyám*.

From May 1883 to March 1884, Vedder completed fifty-six illustrations for a deluxe edition of FitzGerald's translation published by Houghton Mifflin in 1884 to critical acclaim.[1] Vedder, who supervised every facet of this publication, considered it his major achievement. He subsequently developed several of the drawings into paintings, four of which were lent to the 1889 Exposition.[2] *The Cup of Death* was an elaboration of quatrain 49 of the *Rubáiyát:*

So when the Angel of the darker Drink
At last shall find you by the river-brink,
And, offering his Cup, invite your Soul
Forth to your lips to quaff—you shall not shrink.

Vedder painted two versions of *The Cup of Death* in 1885, each with a full-length winged male figure leading a young woman to the edge of the riverbank as he holds a cup to her lips. The first of these, painted in somber tints, was initially disappointing to Vedder, who kept it in his studio and left it unfinished until 1911.[3] According to his daughter, he "laid out another and repainted it entirely with another coloring more rich and brilliant."[4] The second painting also differed from the first in the extensive use of river grasses to extend the angel's wing and in the alteration of his drapery. This was the version, later sold to Susan Minns of Boston, "whose fad is to have the greatest collection of *dances of death* going,"[5] that he exhibited at the 1889 Exposition.

Like *The Cup of Death*, *The Fates Gathering In the Stars* interprets verses from the *Rubáiyát*. The three Fates, Clotho, Lachesis, and Atropos, preside over human destiny and, respectively, spin the thread of life, fix its length, and cut it at the appointed time. In June 1883, Vedder had written to Joseph B. Millet of the publishing house of Houghton Mifflin, commenting that the "drawing of the Fates Gathering in the Stars is particularly my own invention, and I intend to make a picture of it someday."[6] His painting followed the illustration for quatrains 72 through 74:

We are no other than a moving row
Of Magic Shadow-shapes that come and go
Round with this Sun-illumin'd Lantern held
In Midnight by the Master of the Show;

Impotent Pieces of the Game He plays
Upon this Chequer-board of Night and Days;
Hither and thither moves, and checks, and slays,
And one by one back in the Closet lays.

The Ball no question makes of Ayes and Noes,
But Right or Left as strikes the Player goes;
And He that toss'd you down into the Field,
He knows about it all—He knows—HE Knows!

The final version of *The Fates Gathering In the Stars* was first exhibited in Boston at the Doll and Richards Gallery in March 1887, and the following month at H. Wunderlich and Company in New York. Although the publication of the *Rubáiyát* had met with great success in America, Vedder's paintings were not well received in New York. His calligraphic, mannerist line, the peculiarity of his color, and the dryness of his handling were appreciated, however, by devoted admirers and by a growing circle of American muralists and architects. During the 1890s, Vedder's classically draped figures found permanent homes on the walls and ceilings of the Walker Art Gallery, Bowdoin College Museum of Fine Arts, Brunswick, Maine; the Huntington mansion, New York; and the Library of Congress; and his work was highly regarded by those who valued individuality and imagination. MCOB

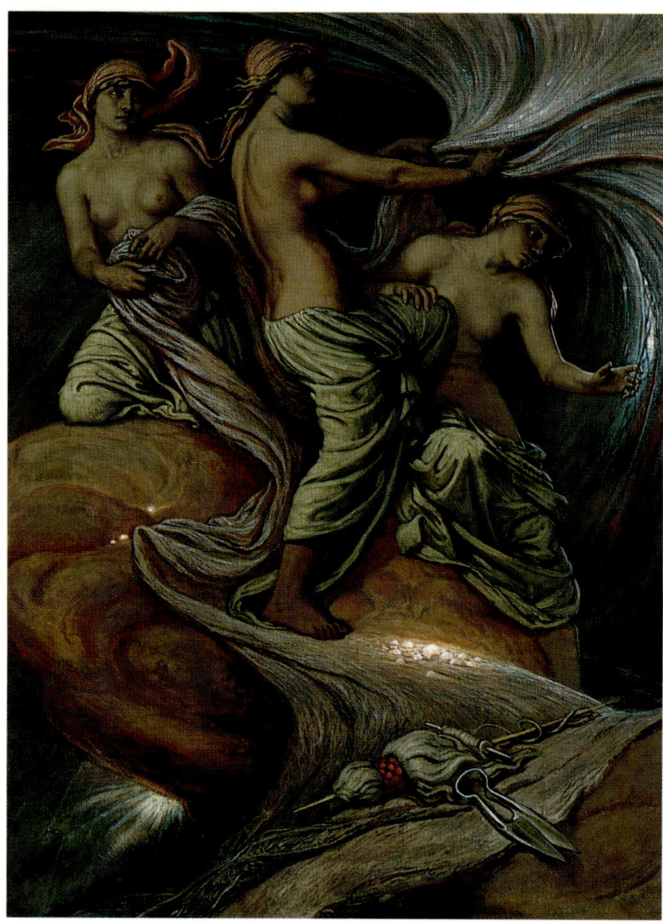

305.
Elihu Vedder
The Fates gathering in the Stars
The Fates Gathering In the Stars, 1887
Oil on canvas, 44½ x 32½" (114 x 82.6 cm)
© The Art Institute of Chicago,
Friends of American Art Collection. 1919.1

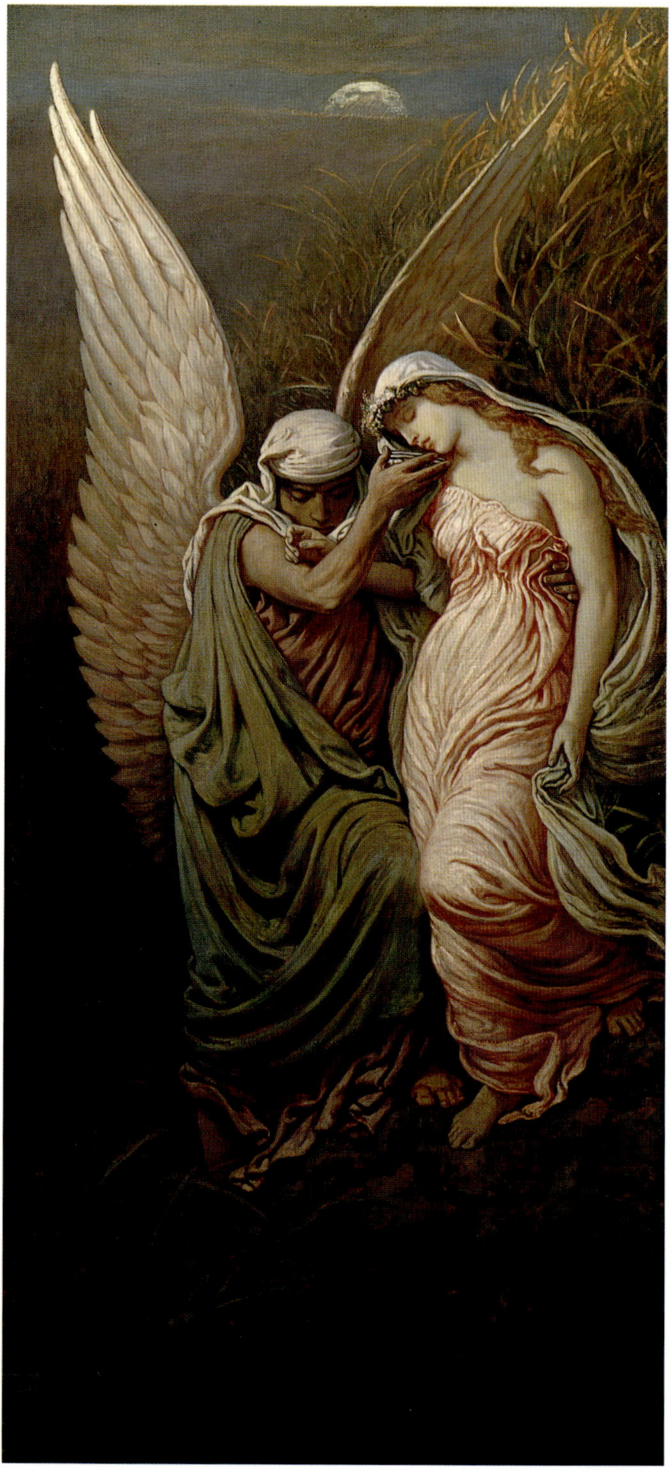

307.
Elihu Vedder
The Death Cup
The Cup of Death, 1885
Oil on canvas, 44⅛ x 20¾" (112.7 x 52.7 cm)
Virginia Museum of Fine Arts, Richmond,
The Williams Fund

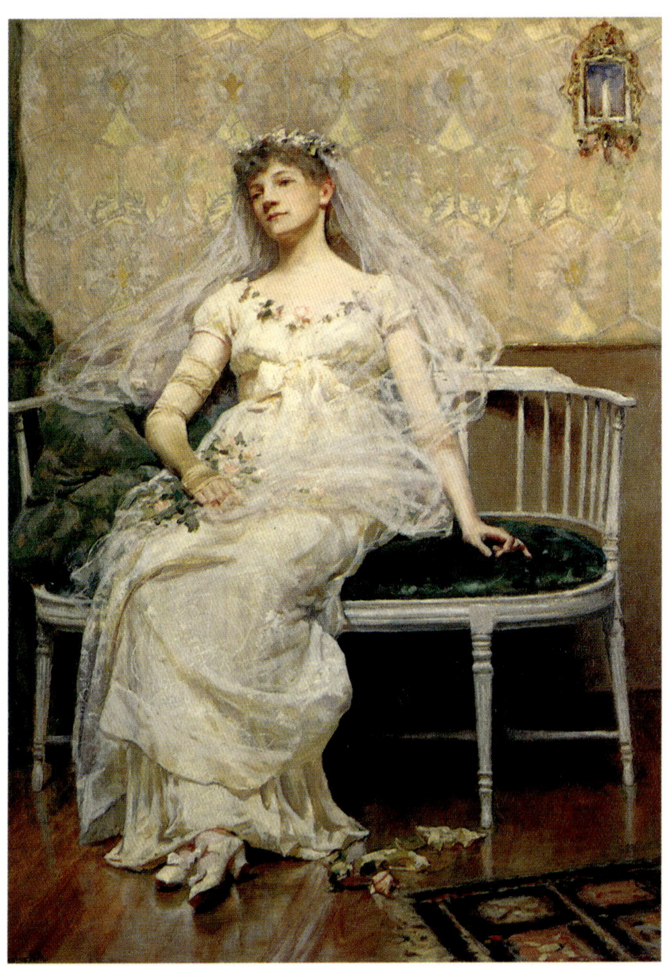

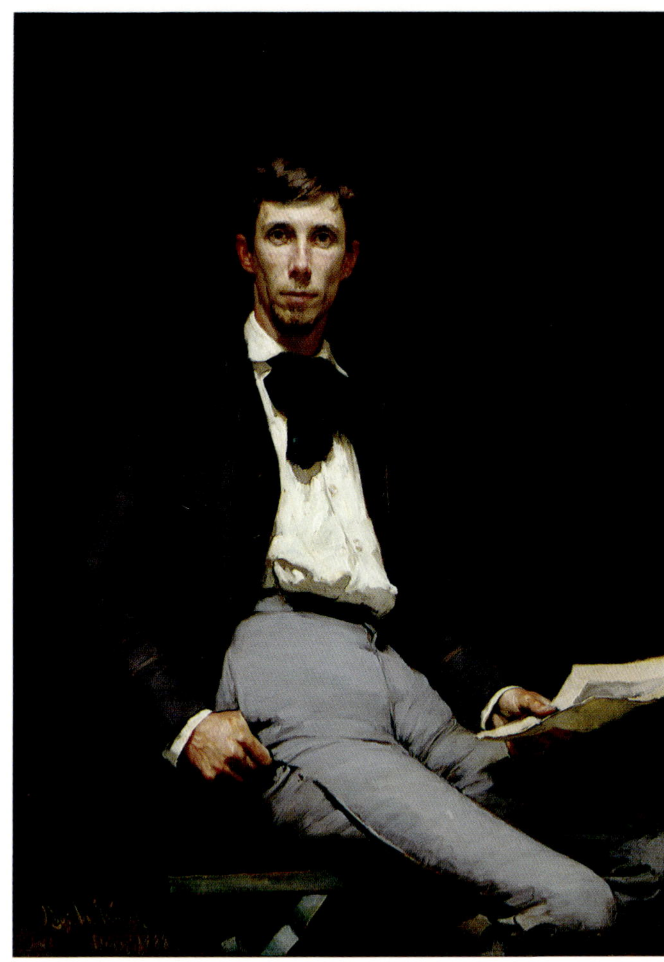

310.
(Stephen) Douglas Volk
After the Reception
After the Reception, 1887
Oil on canvas, 34¼ x 25½ (87 x 64 cm)
The Minneapolis Institute of Arts,
Gift of Mr. and Mrs. E.J. Phelps

311.
Robert William Vonnoh
Studio Comrade
Companion of the Studio, 1888
Oil on canvas, 51¼ x 36¼" (129.89 x 91.7 cm)
Pennsylvania Academy of the Fine Arts,
Philadelphia, Joseph E. Temple Fund

(STEPHEN) DOUGLAS VOLK (1856–1935)

Douglas Volk, the son of Leonard Wells Volk, the noted sculptor of Abraham Lincoln, and Emily Clarissa Barlow Volk,[1] was encouraged to develop his talents in his father's Chicago studio. Volk traveled to Italy with his parents in 1870, where he remained to study painting when they returned home the following year. In Rome he enrolled in the Accademia di San Luca and also enjoyed the guidance of George Inness and other artists in the American circle.[2] In 1873, Volk went to Paris, where he became a student of Jean-Léon Gérôme at the Ecole des Beaux-Arts. Gérôme's insistence on perfection of drawing, unity of design, and pursuit of individuality formed the basis of Volk's skill as a painter.

Volk's initial public recognition came with the acceptance of a painting by the 1875 Paris Salon and of another by the Centennial Exhibition in Philadelphia the following year, making him one of the youngest American painters to be so honored. In 1879, having already exhibited with the fledgling Society of American Artists in New York, he returned to the United States and taught at the Cooper Union. During the next few years he produced a number of the Puritan subjects that had signaled his early success and began to establish the principles of art education that would inform his teaching at the Minneapolis School of Fine Arts, which he founded in 1886, and later at the Art Students League and the National Academy of Design.[3]

After the Reception was one of two paintings sent by Volk to the 1889 Exposition.[4] Painted in 1887, it demonstrated his mastery of French technique, his appreciation of English aestheticism, and his assimilation of both in a genre subject that had sophistication and wide appeal. The model was a young Minneapolis woman, Caroline Keith Thompson, who appeared as a pilgrim maid in another of Volk's paintings and whose parents were friends of Volk and his wife.[5] Volk portrayed Miss Thompson as a happy bride caught in a moment of weariness and reflection at the conclusion of her wedding celebration. Her face and gown are warmed by a golden light that enhances the mood of reverie and unifies the complementary hues of the room's interior.

The contemplative moment was a recurring theme of the 1880s and 1890s in Volk's costume pictures and in his studies of women in contemporary dress. Although the subject and its treatment in *After the Reception* bear comparison with Whistler's tonal harmonies and with Thomas Dewing's ethereal women, the narrative content relates to Alfred Stevens's paintings of elegant Parisian women, which were admired by Americans and Europeans alike. Given Volk's interest in anecdote, it is likely that he would have looked past the nonnarrative arrangements of Whistler to the attitudes of feminine anticipation, thoughtful preoccupation, and repose that were the keys to the success of more fashionable narrators of modern life.

MCOB

ROBERT WILLIAM VONNOH (1858–1933)

Robert Vonnoh, a highly successful Boston portraitist, was one of the first Americans to paint in an Impressionist mode, adopting it as early as the late 1880s.[1] A similar precociousness inaugurated his artistic career. Deciding at the age of fourteen to become an artist, Vonnoh apprenticed himself to a lithographer; his next move was to the Massachusetts Normal Art School, from which he graduated in 1879. (He would later, in an article titled "The Relationship of Art to Existence," advocate this kind of early and directed vocational training.[2]) Making his first trip to France in 1881, Vonnoh spent two years at the popular Académie Julian under the tutelage of Boulanger and Lefebvre. Returning to Boston in 1883, he became principal of the Boston Evening Drawing School, remaining there until 1885. During these years he taught simultaneously at the Cowles Art School. From 1885 to 1887 he taught at the Boston Museum of Fine Arts school, and subsequently, from 1891 to 1894 and from 1918 to 1920, he was an instructor at the Pennsylvania Academy of the Fine Arts, where his students included Robert Henri and John Sloan.

In 1886, Vonnoh made a second trip to France, remaining there until 1891. After a brief return to the Académie Julian, he abandoned Paris, moving to Grez-sur-Loing, a small town near the forest of Fontainebleau. Here for the next five years he "made nature his sole mistress."[3] It was during this time, and in this locale, that Vonnoh painted his poppy fields, brilliantly colored landscapes that predated American Impressionism by a number of years. Interestingly, Vonnoh chose not to be represented by such adventurous work at the Exposition of 1889. Taking a more conservative course, he entered a figure piece titled *Reverie* (unlocated) and the soberly toned *Studio Comrade*.

Studio Comrade is an academic portrait for which a fellow art student, John Pinhey, posed. Painted during Vonnoh's Grez period, it suggests, in its loose handling, as well as its date of 1888, some contact with Paris, possibly with Bonnat. *Studio Comrade* also recalls a portrait Vonnoh painted of another artist friend in 1883, during his first Paris stay, that of John Severinus Conway. The two portraits share a frontal directness that contrasts noticeably with the oblique complexity manifested in Eakins's portrait of his studio companion, George Reynolds (see page 149). Neither the Pinhey nor the Conway portrait really anticipates Vonnoh's ultimate reputation for psychological portrayals of men.

The fact that Vonnoh's portrait of Conway had earned him a gold medal at the Massachusetts Charitable Mechanics Association Exhibition of 1884 may have affected the artist's decision to exhibit the similar *Studio Comrade* at Paris in 1889.[4] Indeed the painting won Vonnoh a bronze medal at the Paris Exposition, and it was undoubtedly on the basis of this success that he showed it once again at the World's Columbian Exposition of 1893. In the light of Vonnoh's plein-air work, his conservatism here was particularly ironic, for Chicago was the forum that launched Impressionism in America. JH

EDWIN LORD WEEKS (1849–1903)

Edwin Lord Weeks set off on his first voyage when he was twenty, and the urge to travel never left him.[1] Though he was not formally registered as a student of either Jean-Léon Gérôme or Léon Bonnat in Paris, he seems to have studied in both their ateliers at some time in the mid-1870s. Weeks's painting style reflects these two teachers' stylistic polarities, the linear and the painterly modes.

During the 1870s, Weeks traveled in the Near East, North Africa, and Spain. He exhibited scenes of the Islamic world as well as of the New England countryside at the Boston Art Club, the Royal Academy, London, the Paris Salon, and the Pennsylvania Academy of the Fine Arts. He also showed at the Centennial Exhibition in Philadelphia. By 1880 he had established a remarkable studio filled with travel souvenirs in Paris, where he exhibited almost annually in the Salon. An active participant in the expatriate community, he served on the American jury in Paris for the 1889 Exposition. In the 1880s he adopted India as his primary subject, recognizing it as a theme virtually unexplored by Western artists.[2] By the 1890s his interest had shifted to Persia. He wrote numerous articles charting his travels; these were published in 1895 as *From the Black Sea Through Persia and India*.[3]

Weeks's status as a leading orientalist was confirmed by the inclusion of his five paintings of India in the Exposition and by his winning of a gold medal. One of Weeks's showpieces at the Exposition was *The Rajah of Jodhpare* (Nationalgalerie, West Berlin),[4] depicting a rajah and his retinue of courtiers and elephants in front of an intricately decorated red sandstone palace. It is typical of Weeks's Indian works in its emphasis on the visual richness of a procession. Compared with his fellow orientalists, among them Frederick Arthur Bridgman and Harry Humphrey Moore, Weeks was cool and detached in his view of India.[5] Evidently he often used photography to document the Indian scenery he painted, a practice that distanced him from his subject.

With the exhibition of *The Last Journey, Souvenir of the Ganges*, Weeks publicly measured himself against his teacher Gérôme and his peer Bridgman.[6] He had exhibited his first picture of India in 1883, and, soon after, he painted

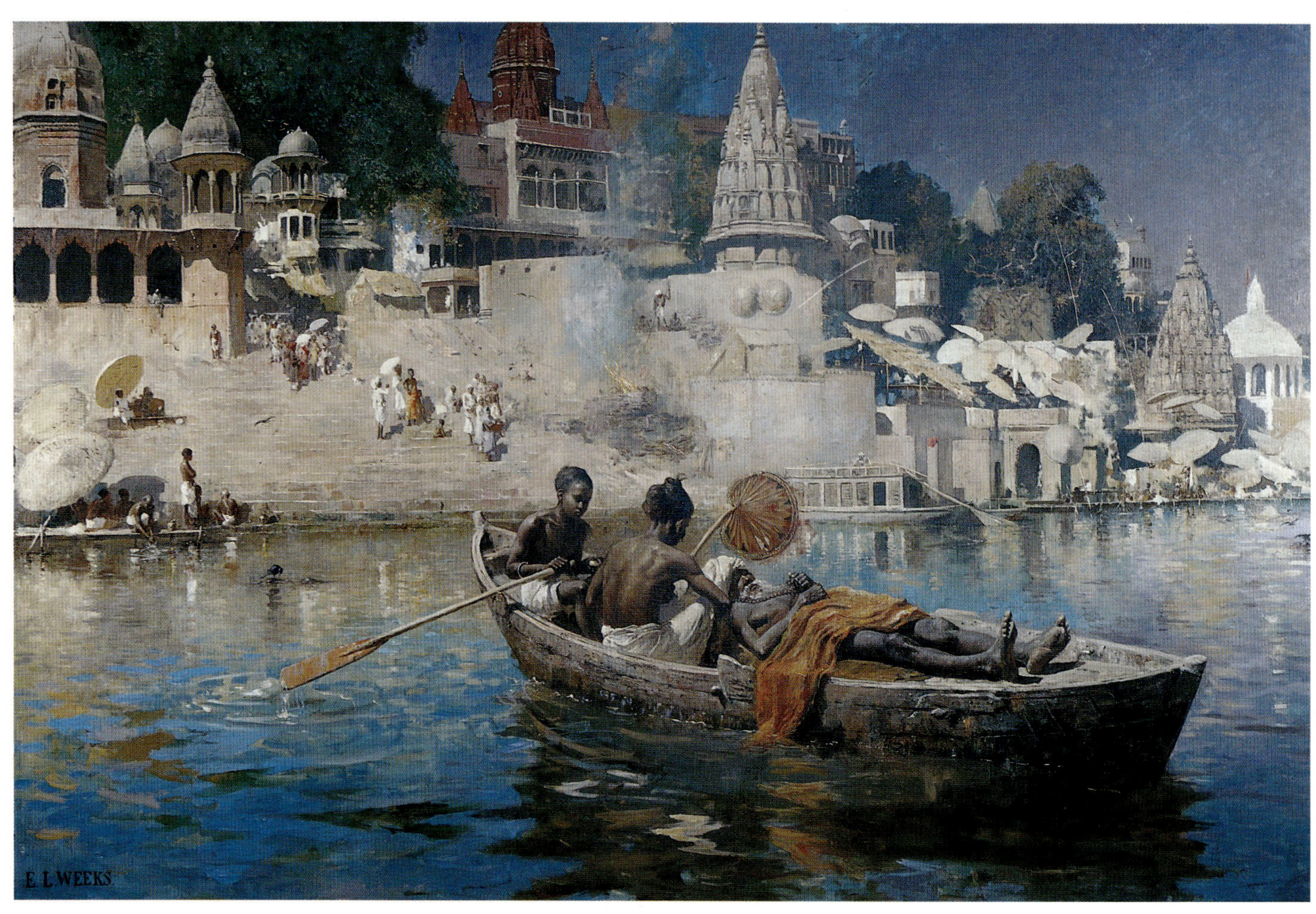

319.
Edwin Lord Weeks
The last Journey; Souvenir of the Ganges
The Last Voyage: A Souvenir of the Ganges, c. 1884
Oil on canvas, 83½ x 121¼" (211.3 x 307.6 cm)
Collection Stuart Pivar, N.Y.; on extended loan to the Bayly Art Museum, University of Virginia, Charlottesville
Photograph by Joseph E. Garland

The Last Journey.[7] Here a fakir near death is being rowed across the Ganges to die in the sacred city of Benares. Compositionally the picture is modeled on one of Gérôme's most famous paintings, *The Prisoner* (1861; Musée des Beaux-Arts, Nantes), which depicts a bound Nubian in a boat on the Nile; it also borrows from Bridgman's 1877 *The Burial of a Mummy on the Nile* (unlocated), which shows the royal barges bearing mourners. Weeks exhibited *The Last Journey* in the Salon of 1885, inviting comparison with these two precedents.

All three paintings share a concern with costumes and boating equipage, solemnity of circumstance, and nuances of reflections of light on water. Weeks changed the locale to India, and he detached himself from the emotional content by focusing on the brilliant play of color and light. Critics praised this new, drier orientalism; *The Last Journey* became an icon of Weeks's oeuvre, appearing in the 1888 International Art Exhibition in Munich, the 1893 World's Columbian Exposition in Chicago, and the 1894 Exposition in Antwerp. The painting was the only one donated by Weeks's widow to a museum. The artist's reputation, then on the rise, later declined dramatically, and the painting passed into private hands.[8] KZ

JULIAN ALDEN WEIR (1852–1919)

J. Alden Weir, who became a leading American Impressionist and a founding member of the secessionist group The Ten, had one of the most thorough academic art educations of the period. Weir's career encapsulates the paradoxical rapprochement between "advanced" and "conservative" American art at the end of the century that is embodied in the 1889 Exposition.

As the son of Robert Walter Weir and the younger brother of John Ferguson Weir, the painter grew up in an artistic family. His early instruction from his father was supplemented by formal training at the National Academy of Design, where he studied between 1870 and 1872, principally under Lemuel Wilmarth. From 1873 to 1877, Weir was in Paris, where he worked for four years with Gérôme, spending the inevitable summer sojourns in Barbizon. In contrast to most Americans, Weir was also a matriculated student at the Ecole des Beaux-Arts. While in Paris, Weir won awards and honors that were to be the earliest of many. A teacher at the Cooper Union and the Art Students League, a member of the Society of American Artists and the National Academy of Design as well as the Tile Club, the American Water Color Society, the New York Etching Club, and others, Weir was an insider all his life.

Directly after his return from Paris, and only months after the group's inception, in 1877, Weir had joined the Society of American Artists, remaining an active member until his defection to The Ten in 1897. Composed largely of young artists returning from Europe, and conceived out of differences with the conservative National Academy of Design, the new organization stood for progressive ideals in art. At first glimpse, then, it appears ironic that these two rival groups exhibited together at the 1889 Exposition, in the gallery reserved for stateside artists, where they were reviewed by the critics as a single entity.

Interestingly, Weir's own exhibiting record illuminates the paradox of the two groups' joint appearance at the Exposition. For despite Weir's allegiance to the progressive Society of American Artists, he had been exhibiting simultaneously at the National Academy of Design since 1878. Moreover, in 1885 the older institution had made him an associate, electing him an Academician the following year. In Weir's stated opinion, by the mid-1880s distinctions between the progressive and the conservative organization had begun to evaporate.[1] Yet Weir's own contributions to the 1889 Exposition refute the idea that the two main exhibiting forums in New York had interchangeable personalities. A very different sensibility distinguishes Weir's *Portrait of Artist's Child* (a portrait of Caroline Weir) from the children painted by National Academy stalwart J.G. Brown (see page 125). Auguring a period characterized by artistic subjectivity and individualism, the three pictures Weir submitted to the painting section of the fair were all of subjects very personal to him—his daughter and the countryside near his farm in Branchville, Connecticut.

Portrait of Artist's Child, shown in the present exhibition, was noticed at the fair by *Harper's* critic Theodore Child, who conceded, "It is a refined composition, but its excellence is in intention rather than achievement."[2] It is possible that Child, despite his own progressiveness, found the picture too informally modern. For although its overall palette is conservative, the bold foreground placement of the figure and the witty fillip of local color provided by the orange held against the child's white dress reflect the interest in Manet that Weir developed in the early 1880s.[3]

325.
J. Alden Weir
Lengthening Shadows
Lengthening Shadows, 1887
Oil on canvas, 20¾ x 25″ (53 x 63.5 cm)
Owner in 1889 W. T. Evans
Collection Dr. and Mrs. Demosthenes Dasco

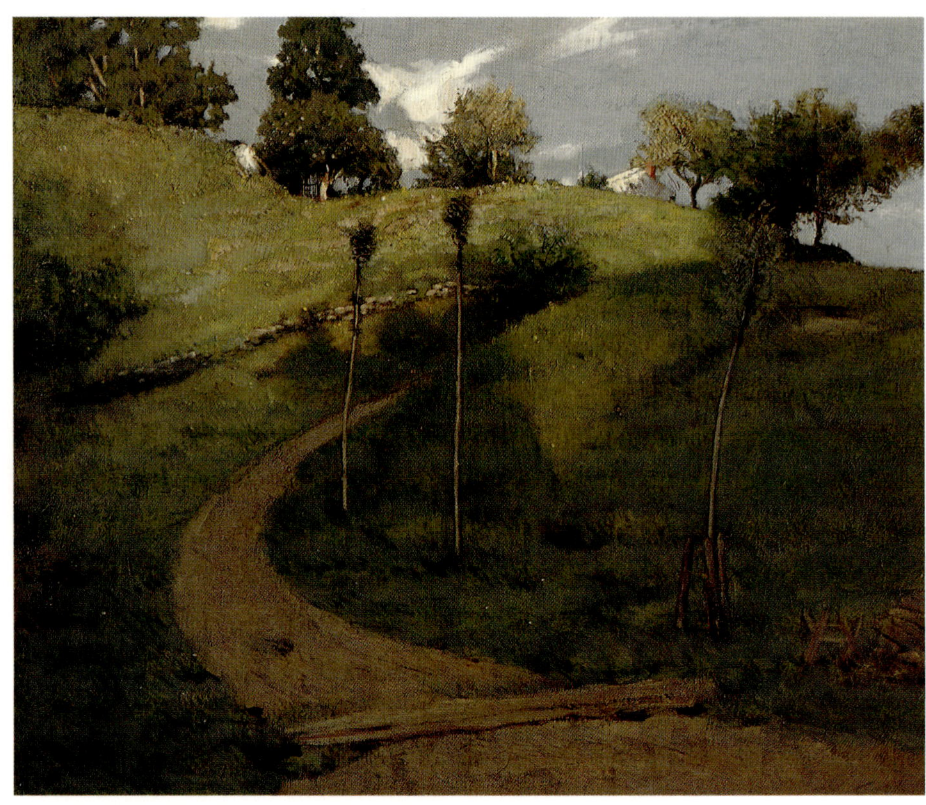

326.
J. Alden Weir
Portrait of Artist's Child
Portrait of Caro, 1887
Oil on canvas, 49⅛ x 36″ (124.6 x 91.4 cm)
Private Collection
Photograph courtesy Doreen Bolger

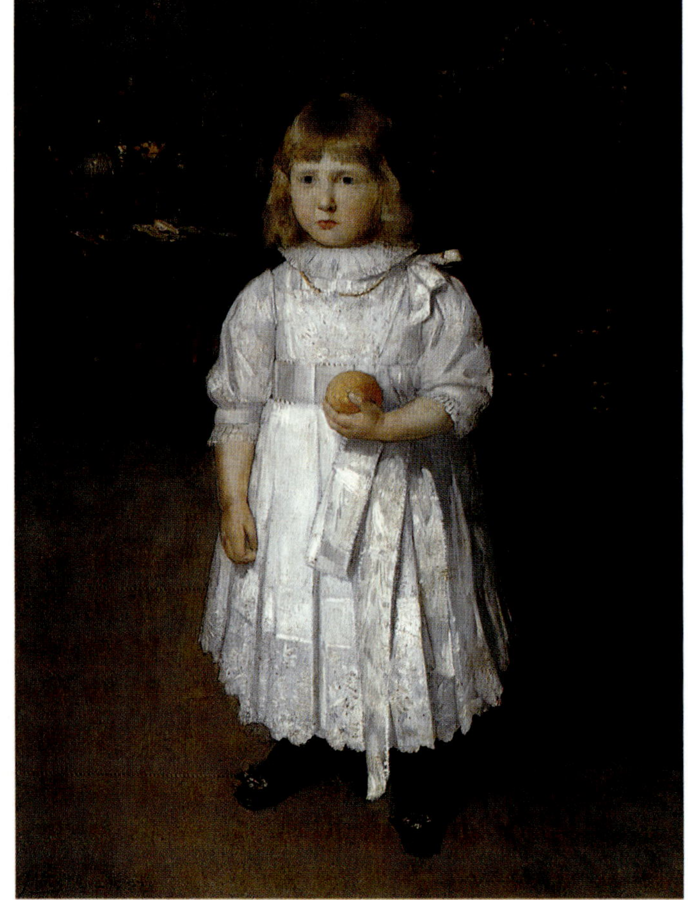

165. British section
James Abbott McNeill Whistler
Arrangement in Black, #7, Portrait of Lady Archibald Campbell
Arrangement in Black: The Lady in the Yellow Buskin (Lady Archibald Campbell), c. 1883
Oil on canvas, 86 x 43½″ (215. x 109.7 cm)
Philadelphia Museum of Art,
W. P. Wilstach Collection

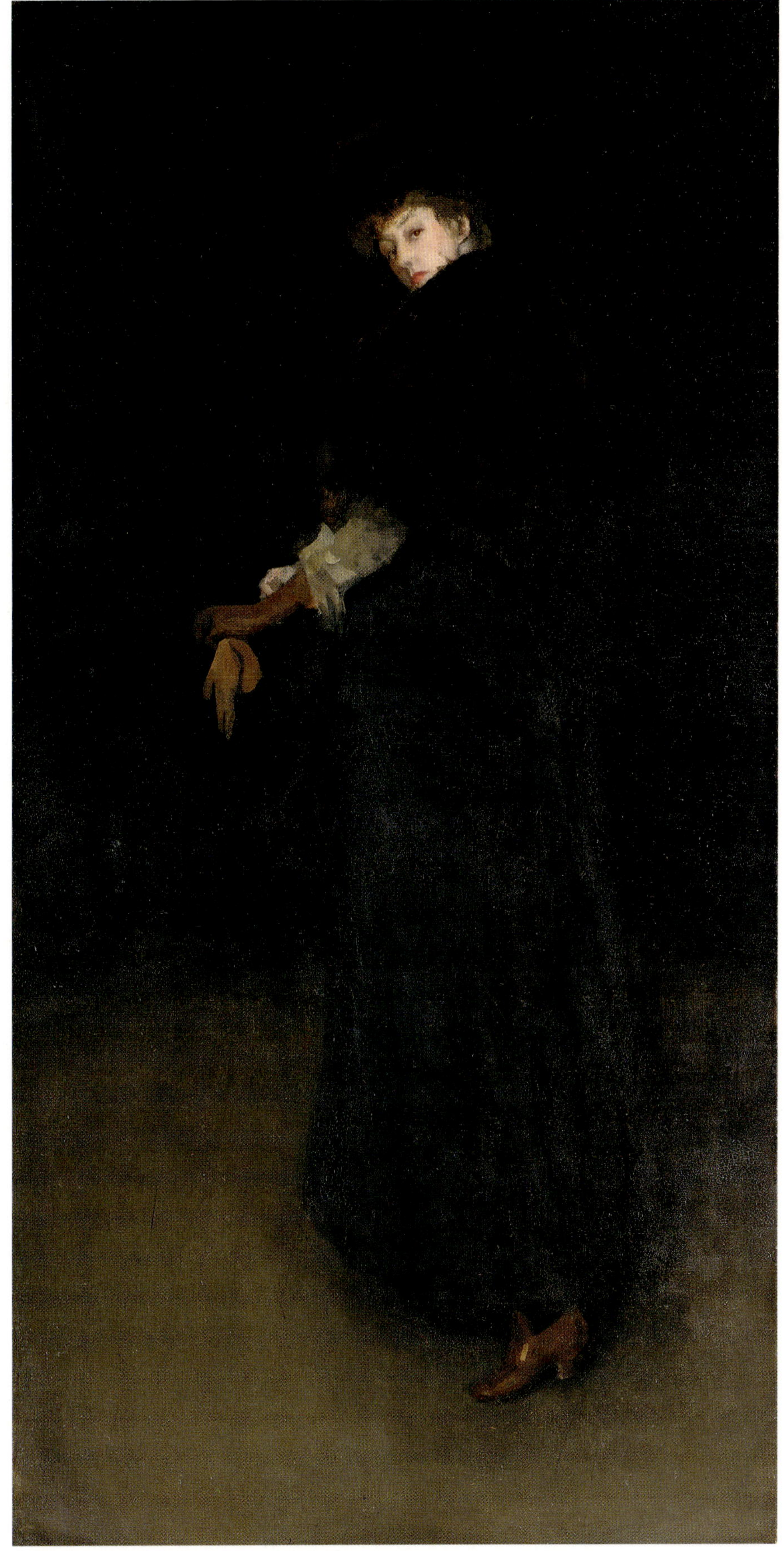

Lengthening Shadows (1887), another 1889 entry in the present exhibition, was an even more adventurous work. Here subject matter is virtually subsumed in an abstract composition: landscape elements become verticals and curving diagonals, and descriptive color becomes a play of tones over the surface of the canvas. The picture's light palette, a new departure for Weir, suggests that it was painted outdoors. Its high horizon and cropping indicate the probable influence of John Twachtman, a lifelong friend with whom Weir was in close contact in the late 1880s.[4]

Lengthening Shadows was yet another of the pictures lent to the Exposition by William T. Evans. It was auctioned at the collector's sale of 1900, where it was described as "one of Mr. Weir's most celebrated landscapes."[5] Undoubtedly some of its prestige stemmed from its exhibition at the 1889 Exposition, where Weir won a silver medal for painting and a bronze medal for work in other mediums.

JH

JAMES ABBOTT McNEILL WHISTLER (1834–1903)

One of the most lauded American artists at the 1889 Exposition, James Abbott McNeill Whistler showed not with the Americans but with the British. Born in Massachusetts, raised partly in Russia, active in the art worlds of London and Paris, Whistler considered himself an American.[1] Drawing was stressed in his early art training, which included classes from 1851 to 1854 with Robert W. Weir, the drawing master at the United States Military Academy at West Point, New York. In Paris he studied with Charles Gleyre in 1885. Later influences were his friends the French artists Courbet, Fantin-Latour, and Monet and the English Pre-Raphaelite artist Dante Gabriel Rossetti. They introduced him to new artistic approaches and encouraged his own originality. Whistler's personality was as complex as his art. Publicly he assumed the role of "the fop, the cynic, the brilliant, flippant, vain and careless idler,"[2] as if to protect himself against all who made no effort to comprehend his art.

Invited by both the British and the Americans to exhibit at the 1889 Exposition, Whistler submitted one painting and twenty-seven etchings to the American jury. Because of space limitations—and possibly because of antagonism within the jury—ten etchings were rejected.[3] Upon receiving a form letter from Commissioner Rush Hawkins requesting him to remove the rejected works, Whistler took away all his entries. In letters and interviews published in English and American newspapers, Whistler and Hawkins aired their views.[4] Whistler naively expressed surprise that the Americans were limited in space and hinted that the jury was unqualified, but mainly he objected to the "military" manner of his notification. Hawkins responded that he had nothing to do with the selection, commenting that Whistler ended with even less space in the British section and that the artist "detect[ed] a snub where none exists."[5] Whistler sent nine etchings and two paintings to the British section, and received a gold medal.

Neither the conception nor the completion of *Arrangement in Black, #7* came easily to Whistler. *Arrangement in Black, #7* is the only one of the three portraits for which Lady Archibald Campbell sat in 1883 to survive. Whistler worked and reworked all of them, ultimately destroying the other two. Lady Campbell, a patron of the arts and of Whistler, had agreed to sit for the three separate uncommissioned portraits, but her patience was tried by the laborious creative process to the point where she was ready to abandon the project; she was persuaded to continue by the critic Théodore Duret, who was sitting at the same time for his portrait. *Arrangement in Black, #7*, which Whistler was unable to sell for nearly ten years, became one of his best-known works. It was exhibited at numerous times and places: the Grosvenor Gallery, London, 1884; the 1885 Paris Salon; the Munich International Art Exhibition, 1888; Goupil Brothers, London, 1892[6]; the World's Columbian Exhibition, Chicago, 1893; and the Pennsylvania Academy of the Fine Arts, 1894. At the Pennsylvania Academy it won the Temple Gold Medal for figure painting. Purchased the same year by the W.P. Wilstach Collection for the Philadelphia Museum of Art, it was Whistler's first work to enter an American public collection.

The second painting Whistler sent to the British section provides a context for other American work with limited tonal range seen at the Exposition. His 1865 multifigured *Variations in Flesh Color and Green: The Balcony* (Freer Gallery of Art, Washington, D.C.) depicts women in Japanese costumes painted in a pale green and pink palette. By the time he painted *Arrangement in Black, #7*, he restricted his palette and composition further to achieve even more subtle effects. His portraits of the 1880s and 1890s continue the black-on-black scheme. In *Arrangement in Black, #7*, Whistler caught the elusive harmonies of the static blacks and browns of the dress, offsetting them by the motion of the yellow boot, or buskin, as he called it. Although Whistler's painting was not shown with the American works, its influence on them can be seen in such single-tone, single-figure portraits as William Merritt Chase's *Portrait of Mrs. C.* and Edward Bell's *Lady in Gray* (see pages 129, 116). KZ

(THOMAS) WORTHINGTON WHITTREDGE (1820–1910)

A leader of the second generation of the Hudson River School, Worthington Whittredge was still a highly respected figure in 1889, though interest in his paintings was declining.[1] He had obtained his training in Düsseldorf with Emanuel Leutze and the German landscapists associated with the Royal Academy. After he returned to New York, in 1859, Whittredge established his reputation with panoramic views of the Hudson River Valley, Rhode Island coast, and Western plains, as well as forest interiors. He exhibited regularly at the National Academy of Design, serving as its president from 1874 to 1877. Whittredge was a member of the selection committees for the 1876 Philadelphia Centennial Exhibition and the 1878 Paris Exposition and was named president of the New York jury for the 1889 Exposition.[2]

Between the Centennial and the mid-1880s, Whittredge turned to the French Barbizon painters, whose pictures by then were widely circulated in New York.[3] Without abandoning the Hudson River School's classically balanced compositions, he adopted the Barbizon School's sparer compositional format and some of its techniques. Whittredge was awarded an honorable mention for the two paintings he submitted to the Exposition, a trifling honor for an artist of his stature. His paintings were eclipsed by newer approaches to landscape such as those of Alexander Harrison and Arthur Wesley Dow, and he received virtually no critical attention.

In the mid-1880s, Whittredge produced some plein-air sketches near Tiverton, Rhode Island, that seem to show, in color and execution, the influence of the Barbizonists Théodore Rousseau and Charles-François Daubigny.[4] These

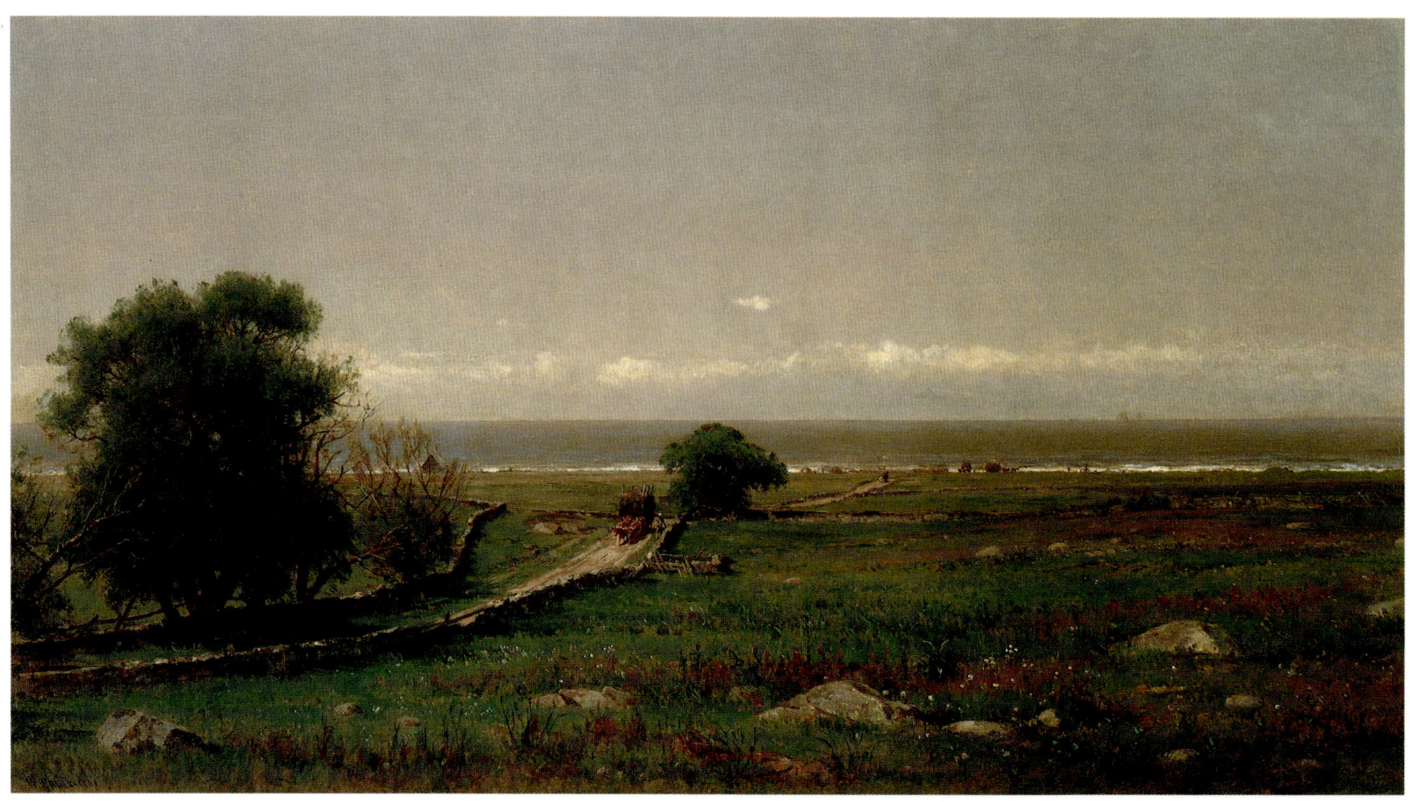

328.
(Thomas) Worthington Whittredge
The Old Road to the Sea
Harvest of Seaweed, c. 1884
Oil on canvas, 31 x 51″ (77.5 x 127.5 cm)
Owners in 1889 Messrs. Pettus & Curtis
Private Collection
Courtesy Spanierman Gallery, New York

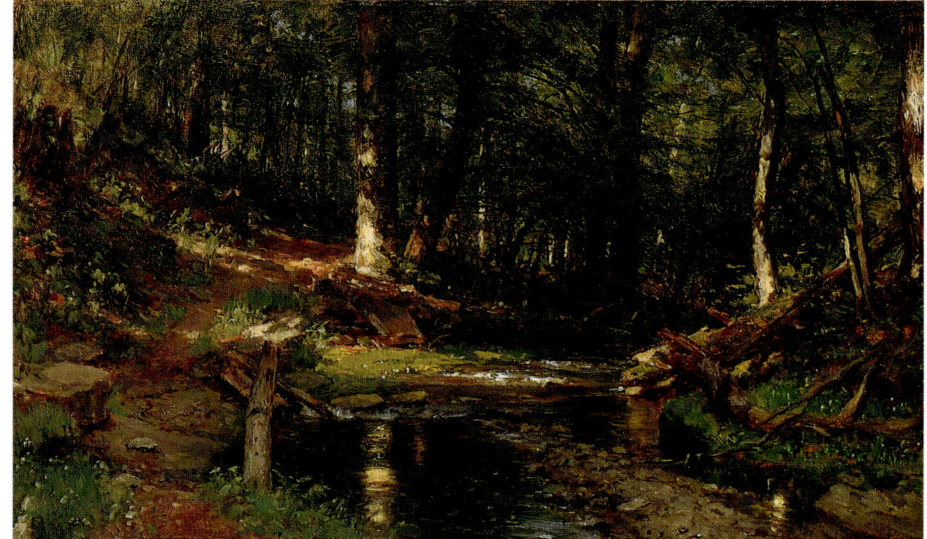

329.
(Thomas) Worthington Whittredge
A Brook in the Woods
I come from Haunts of Coot and Hearn (replica, c. 1889)
Oil on canvas, 12⅛ x 20⅞″ (30.6 x 51.7 cm)
Trinity College, Hartford,
George F. McMurray Collection

sketches led to the large canvas *The Old Road to the Sea*, which Whittredge sent to the National Academy of Design in 1884[5] and subsequently to the 1889 Exposition. Whittredge had often painted views of the Rhode Island coast from an elevated point but had never rendered this particular topography. The forceful brushwork in the foreground, which leaves the shrubbery relatively undefined, relates this canvas to the Barbizon technique. With its simplified composition dividing it into sky and pasture, its restricted green-and-gray color

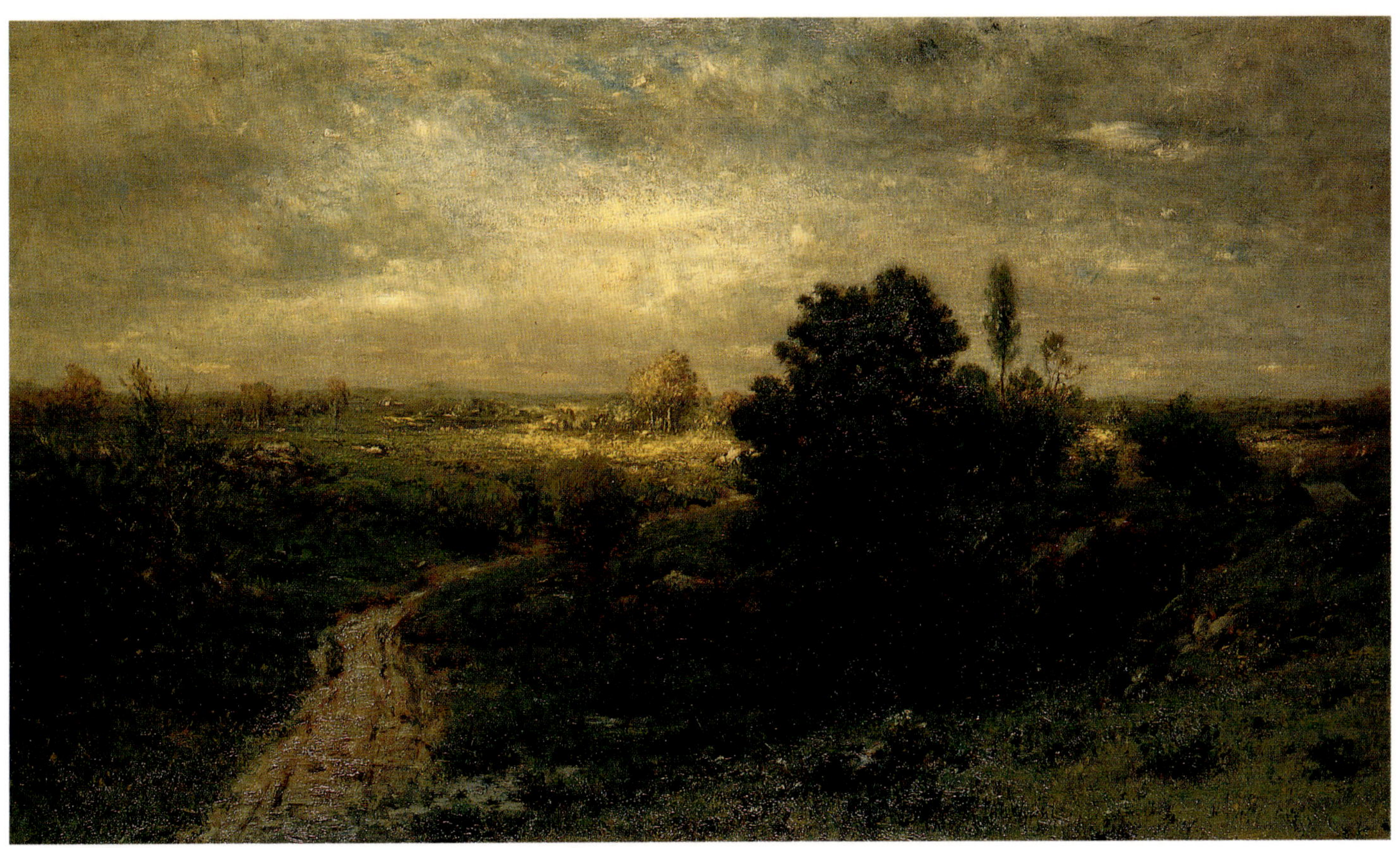

336.
Alexander Helwig Wyant
Landscape
Keene Valley, c. 1880s
Oil on canvas, 18⅛ x 30" (46 x 76.2 cm)
Owner in 1889 Carll H. De Silver
The Brooklyn Museum, New York,
Gift of Mrs. Carll H. De Silver
in memory of her husband

scheme, and its hazy light, Whittredge's painting parallels the works of the younger generation of American landscapists, including Alexander Wyant and R. Swain Gifford. In contrast to their moody canvases, however, Whittredge's picture has the optimistic tone of his earlier paintings of the coast.

In 1884, Whittredge placed an ambitious price tag of twelve hundred dollars on *The Old Road to the Sea*. The next year, at the Brooklyn Art Association Annual, he reduced the price to eight hundred dollars. In 1887, at an auction of his work at Ortgies' Art Galleries, Whittredge finally sold the painting, perhaps for as little as four hundred dollars.[6] This sequence of events was solid evidence of the waning interest in his work.

In *A Brook in the Woods* Whittredge redefined his most pervasive theme, the forest interior. An admirer of Asher B. Durand's woodland scenes, Whittredge often painted this subject, and over the course of his career he exhibited many pictures with the title *A Brook in the Woods* at the National Academy of Design. In mid-1886 he painted a small painting of a shallow brook winding through a wilderness forest, and a year or so later produced a large version of the same composition.[7] The small painting is in a private collection; the large painting (unlocated) was exhibited as *A Brook in the Woods* in 1888 at the Academy,[8] then submitted a year later to the 1889 Exposition. In late 1889 or 1890, perhaps on commission, Whittredge made a smaller replica, which is shown in the present exhibition.[9] Although the viewpoint resembles his earlier treatments of the theme, it differs in its visible paint texture, especially in the loose brushwork rendering the brilliant flecks of sunlight. Here Whittredge brought foreign stylistic influences to bear on a particularly native subject—the wild American woodland interior—producing a truly contemporary version of his perennial subject.[10] KZ

ALEXANDER HELWIG WYANT (1836–1892)

When he was twenty-one years old and working as a sign painter in Port Washington, Ohio, Alexander Wyant, on a trip to Cincinnati, saw George Inness's early work. He was so moved by the experience that he decided to become an artist.[1] In 1859, Wyant met Inness and was introduced by him to the philanthropist Nicholas Longworth, who financed Wyant's visits to New York in 1860 and to Cincinnati from 1861 to 1863. Wyant presumably received art training in these cities. He moved to New York in 1863 and the next year exhibited for the first time at the National Academy of Design, where he showed throughout his life. Seeing the landscapes of the Norwegian painter Hans Gude in 1863 inspired Wyant to go to Karlsruhe, Germany, in 1865 to study with Gude. On a visit to London he reportedly saw paintings by Constable and Turner in the National Gallery. He returned to New York in 1866.

Wyant's life was dramatically changed in 1873, when he suffered a stroke that paralyzed his right side. He learned to paint with his left hand, using a freer brushstroke and confining himself to smaller canvases. He participated in many of New York's art organizations, including the Society of American Artists and the American Watercolor Society. Summers were spent in the company of landscapists at Keene Valley in the Adirondacks, and later at Arkville in the Catskills.[2]

Eventually various stylistic influences coalesced in Wyant's paintings.[3] His early work shows the effects of the pictures by Inness that Wyant saw in Cincinnati and of Gude's similarly linear and precise manner. But by some time in the late 1860s Wyant's paintings express Constable's vision, the Barbizon School's naturalism, and Inness's later pensiveness. Physically limited by his stroke, Wyant developed an introspective, reflective view of nature. His later landscapes often retain the elevated viewpoint and traditional balance between foreground and background of his early work but are soft in focus, mellow in color, and tranquil in tone; they have been described as both Barbizonist and Tonalist.[4] His paintings embody the Barbizon reverence for nature and the Tonalist emphasis on mood through the use of a limited palette. In *Landscape*, a Keene Valley scene, Wyant captures the precise moment when the sun's rays break through lowering clouds to spotlight a patch of pastureland.

The careers of Inness and Wyant intersected again at the Exposition. Neither artist wanted to be represented in the fair, so Commissioner Rush Hawkins had to borrow examples of their work from private collections.[5] *Landscape* won Wyant a bronze medal at the Exposition. By 1889, Wyant and Inness, and, to a lesser degree, Worthington Whittredge, had left the most obvious aspects of the Hudson River School behind them, abandoning spectacular scenery for more intimate landscape views. Through looser paint handling, more evocative of emotion, they kept pace with the younger generation of landscapists at the fair, among them Charles Davis and Robert Minor, who went on to develop the Tonalist aesthetic. KZ

MAUREEN C. O'BRIEN

French Paintings

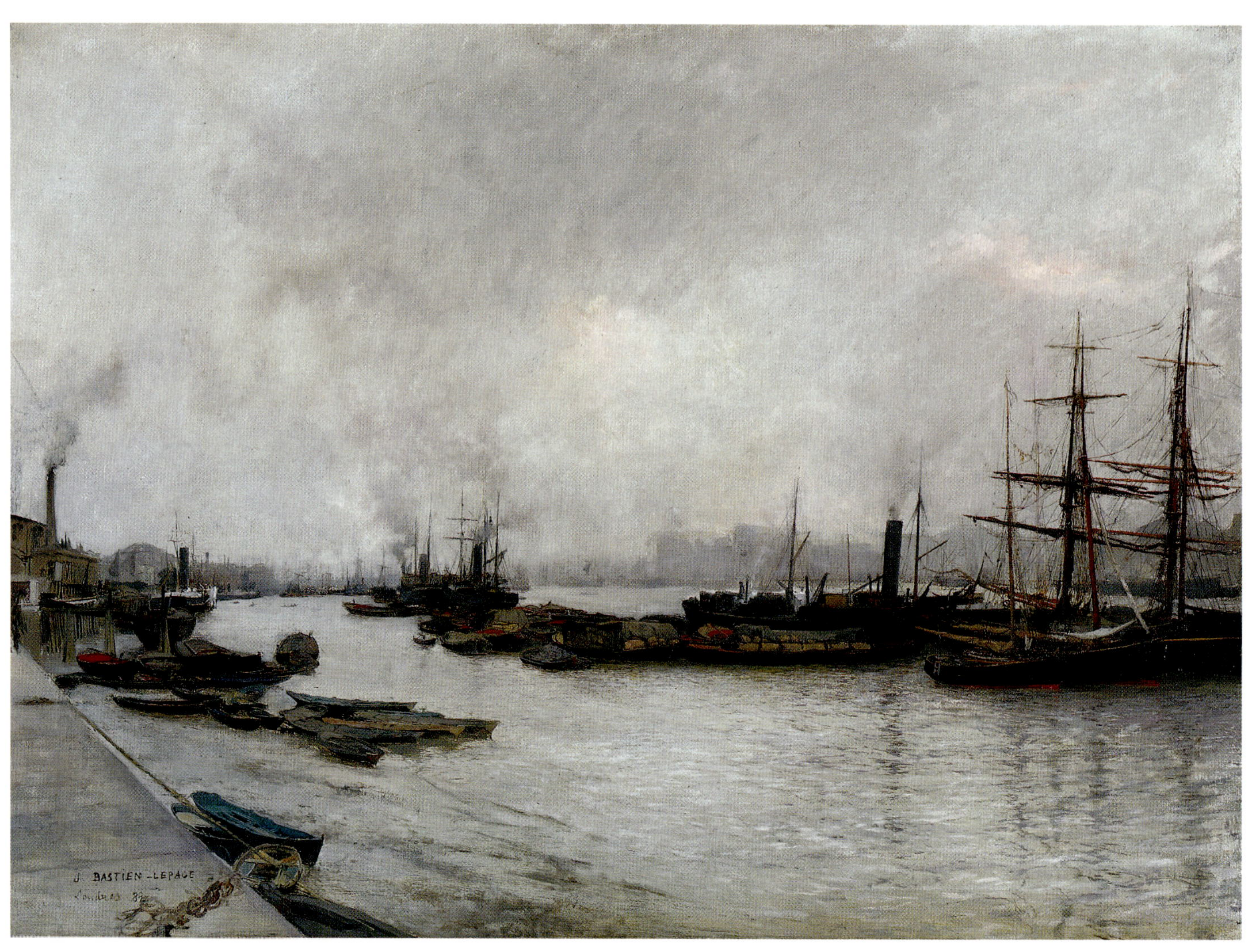

Jules Bastien-Lepage
Thames, London, 1882
Oil on canvas, 21¾ x 29¾" (54.1 x 92.9 cm)
Philadelphia Museum of Art,
John G. Johnson Collection

JULES BASTIEN-LEPAGE (1848–1884)

Jules Bastien-Lepage, an artist whose naturalist paintings of the 1870s and early 1880s were admired for linking the realism of Courbet and Millet with the light and technique of the Impressionists, had a significant influence on the art of his peers both in France and abroad.[1] A native of the town of Damvillers, he had worked briefly as a postal clerk in Paris while studying part-time at the Ecole des Beaux-Arts before he entered the studio of Alexandre Cabanel as a full-time student, in 1868.[2] His skill as a portraitist was evident in early Salon entries in which his precise draftsmanship evoked comparison with the styles of Clouet and Holbein. Through close observation of nature and confident paint handling, he eventually created plein-air paintings of peculiarly original impact: acute characterizations of rural and urban working people against fluently brushed and copiously detailed backgrounds.

The outstanding example of Bastien-Lepage's mastery of technical effect, *Joan of Arc* (1879; Metropolitan Museum of Art, New York), was not fully appreciated when exhibited at the 1880 Salon. On the advice of the artist's American colleague and admirer Julian Alden Weir, the painting was purchased

Joseph-Florentin-Léon Bonnat
The Barber of Suez, 1876
Oil on canvas, 31½ x 23″ (78.7 x 58.4 cm)
The FORBES Collection, New York
Photograph by Otto. E. Nelson

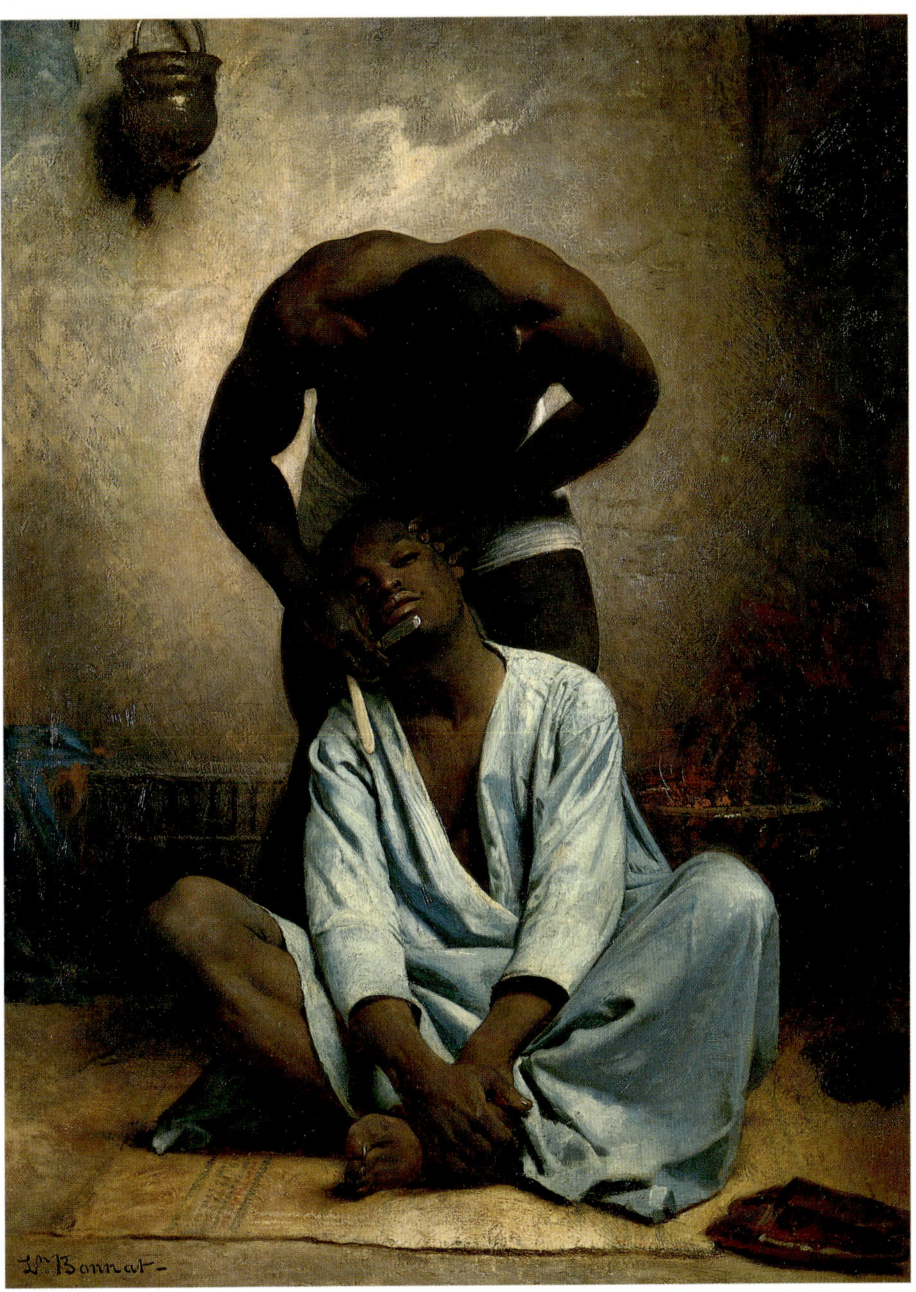

in 1881 by New York collector Erwin Davis, who lent it to France for the 1889 Exposition's centennial exhibition of French painting.[3] *Le Père Jacques* (1881; Milwaukee Art Museum), another work that entered an American collection in the 1880s, was comparable with *Joan of Arc* in its dense overall effect and the disconcerting "airless" perspective of its background.[4]

Bastien-Lepage made four trips to London between 1879 and 1882, exhibiting his paintings on several occasions and familiarizing himself with the work of English artists. *The Thames, London*, painted on his final trip, in 1882, was one of a group of unpopulated river views that demonstrate the effect of Whistler's *Nocturnes* on the development of Bastien-Lepage's pictorial sense. However, its recording of waterfront activity and industry reflect an artist whose mission as a realist painter was rooted in close attention to the life around him.

Bastien-Lepage's premature death from cancer, in 1884, cut short a career of signal importance to his contemporaries. And at the 1889 fair it placed his works in the Exposition Centennale of French painting rather than in the section devoted to the art of the past decade.[5] In a review of his accomplishments by the French critic Paul Mantz, in 1889, Bastien-Lepage was remembered as an artist who clung most fervently to the ideal of moral verisimilitude and one whose loss was most persistently felt by his colleagues.[6]

LEON-JOSEPH-FLORENTIN BONNAT (1833–1922)

Born in Bayonne, in southwestern France, Léon Bonnat perhaps enjoyed more direct contact with the works of the Spanish masters than any other painter of the French realist school. He received his earliest training in Madrid, after moving there with his parents at the age of thirteen.[1] Following studies with José and Federigo Madrazo in Madrid, he was sent to Paris with a grant from his native city, and entered the studio of Léon Cogniet in 1854. His achievements were acknowledged by a second prize in the Prix de Rome competition in 1857, and with private support and a continuing pension from Bayonne he embarked on a three-year period of study at the Villa Medici.[2] In Rome he made copies after Michelangelo, Giulio Romano, and others, and he painted academic subjects that he submitted to the Paris Salon.

His competence as a draftsman, combined with an intense commitment to the observation of nature, contributed to Bonnat's development as an important realist painter and portraitist after his return to Paris. By the mid-1860s he had established an atelier for students who wanted to study painting apart from the Ecole des Beaux-Arts. It was frequented by artists of all nationalities, including the American Edwin Howland Blashfield, who wrote of Bonnat's passion for the work of Rembrandt, Ribera, and Velázquez and his admiration for the drawings of the Renaissance masters.[3] Bonnat preached a forceful realism expressed through strong lights and dark shadows, local color, and vigorous paint application with a loaded brush.

For a period after 1869, when he concluded a trip to the Near East with Jean-Léon Gérôme, Bonnat painted a number of subjects that were orientalist in inspiration.[4] Among these was a study of two black men entitled *The Barber of Suez*, which he submitted to the 1876 Salon. Here Bonnat eschewed the exotic ambience and ethnographic detail that filled the paintings of other orientalists and treated the two figures as a single column in a simplified setting, contrasting the angles of their limbs in a pose that reflected his study of Italian Mannerist painting and sculpture. A tour de force of lights and darks, this impressive study shows Bonnat's strong aptitude for composition, an aspect of his talent that is sometimes obscured by his enduring reputation as one of the leading portraitists of the Third Empire.

WILLIAM ADOLPHE BOUGUEREAU (1825–1905)

William Adolphe Bouguereau, the son of a wine merchant from La Rochelle, studied drawing at the Collège de Pons (Saintes) before enrolling in the Ecole des Beaux-Arts of Bordeaux in 1842. Armed with skills as a portraitist and history painter, he moved to Paris in 1846 and entered the studio of François Picot.[1] Under Picot's guidance, Bouguereau competed for the Ecole des Beaux-Art's prestigious Prix de Rome, which, in 1850, both he and another Picot student, Paul Baudry, were awarded.[2] The next four years in Italy afforded Bouguereau an opportunity to study and make copies after Giotto and Raphael, and many of his later compositions were infused with the imagery and humanism of the Renaissance masters.

Both secular and religious subjects were included in the body of Bouguereau's work after his return from Rome. When they were combined in themes of maternal affection, as in *Mother and Children* (which was owned by Ohio collector Hinman Hurlbut at the time of the 1889 Exposition[3]), Bouguereau's precise drawing, careful modeling, and invisible brushstroke were tempered by greater naturalism. He occasionally used his first wife, Marie Nelly Montchablon, as a model but more often employed women from the Italian quarter of Paris, encouraging them to bring their own children or siblings to pose with them.[4] Whether a young peasant woman tending her sleepy children on a hillside overlooking Rome, or a Michelangelesque allegory of the Holy Family, Bouguereau's convincing portrayals of maternity reflected the "knowledge, taste and refinement"[5] that were the qualities prized by American collectors. By the 1880s, dozens of his works were owned by Americans, and owing to the proliferation of engravings and photogravures one critic was able to report that "hardly any modern French painter can be named who is more widely popular in America than Bouguereau."[6]

The winner of numerous official awards at Salons and international exhibitions, Bouguereau was also a teacher at the Académie Julian and a professor at the Ecole des Beaux-Arts. He exhibited a total of fourteen paintings at the 1889 Exposition; he also served on its international jury.[7] Although his cool, seamless *pompier* style had been eclipsed by the bravura techniques of younger artists, his peers acknowledged his unmatched achievements as a fluent and conscientious draftsman of the human form.[8]

GUSTAVE RUDOLPH BOULANGER (1824–1888)

Gustave Boulanger, a native Parisian, studied with history painters Pierre-Jules Jollivet and Paul Delaroche before entering the Ecole des Beaux-Arts, in 1840. His first Salon entries, in 1848—*Indians Playing with Panthers* and *A Moorish Café*—reflected a taste for exotic subjects that he had acquired during an eight-month visit to Algeria a few years earlier.[1] In 1849 Boulanger won the coveted Prix de Rome with his *Ulysses Recognized by Euryclea*, a painting, in the neo-grec style, in which E.J. Delecluze found "something asiatic, oriental and quite peculiar."[2] Another critic thought it heralded a true painter, "a heretic at the *Académie*, but a man of talent elsewhere."[3] Boulanger confirmed this expectation as a teacher at the Académie Julian, where he worked closely with Jules-Joseph Lefebvre in an atmosphere in which independent stylistic development was encouraged.

Hercules at the Feet of Omphale, which was shown at the Salon of 1861, demonstrated Boulanger's continuing interest in orientalist subjects. It tells the story of Hercules after he has been sold by Apollo as a slave to the Lydian queen Omphale, in order to be purified after his murder of Iphitus. In Boulanger's painting, Hercules' dark, contorted body forms a baroque counterpoint to the

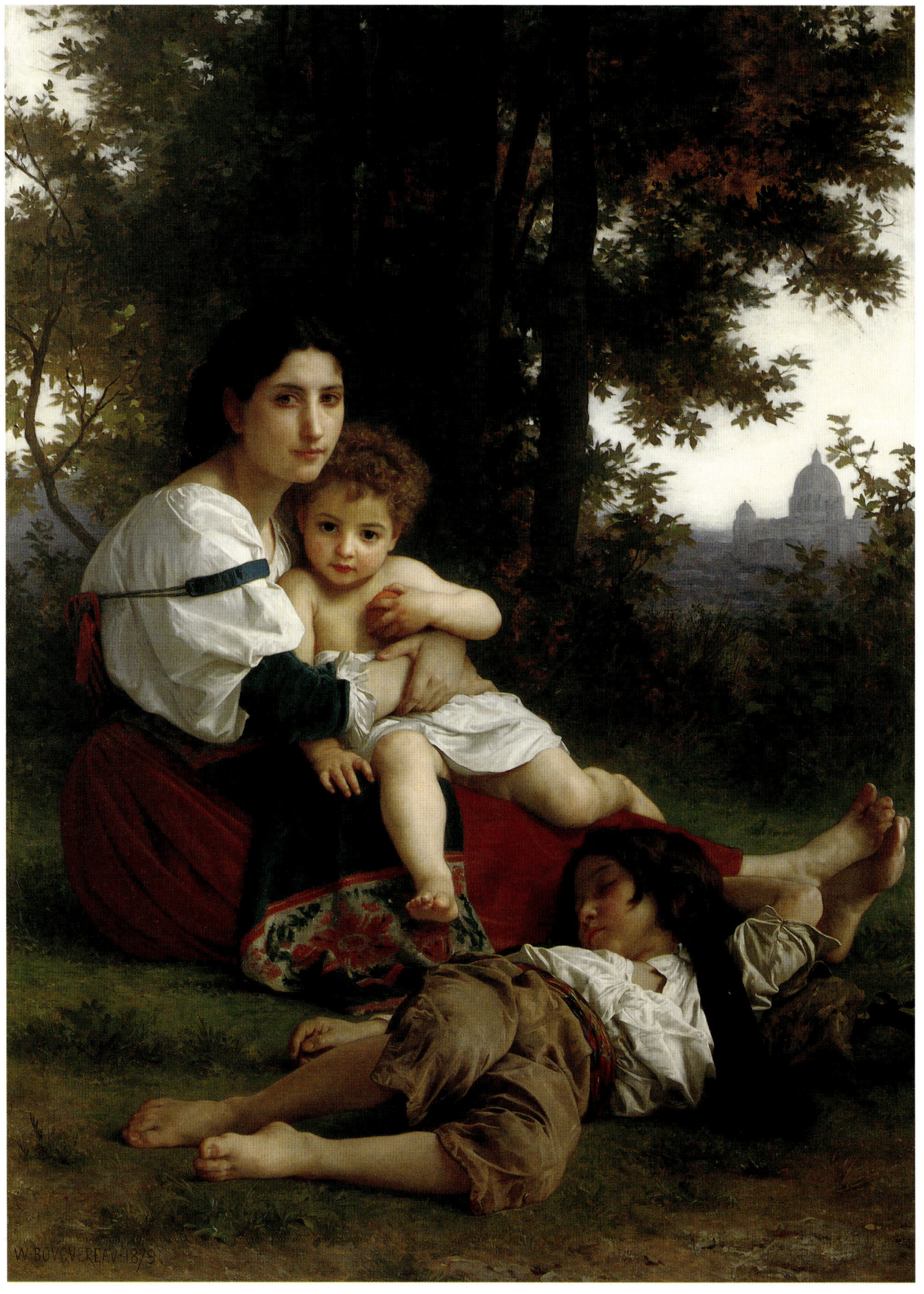
W-BOVGVEREAV-1879

Gustave Boulanger
Hercules at the Feet of Omphale, 1861
Oil on canvas, 93 x 68″ (236.2 x 172.7 cm)
The FORBES Collection, New York

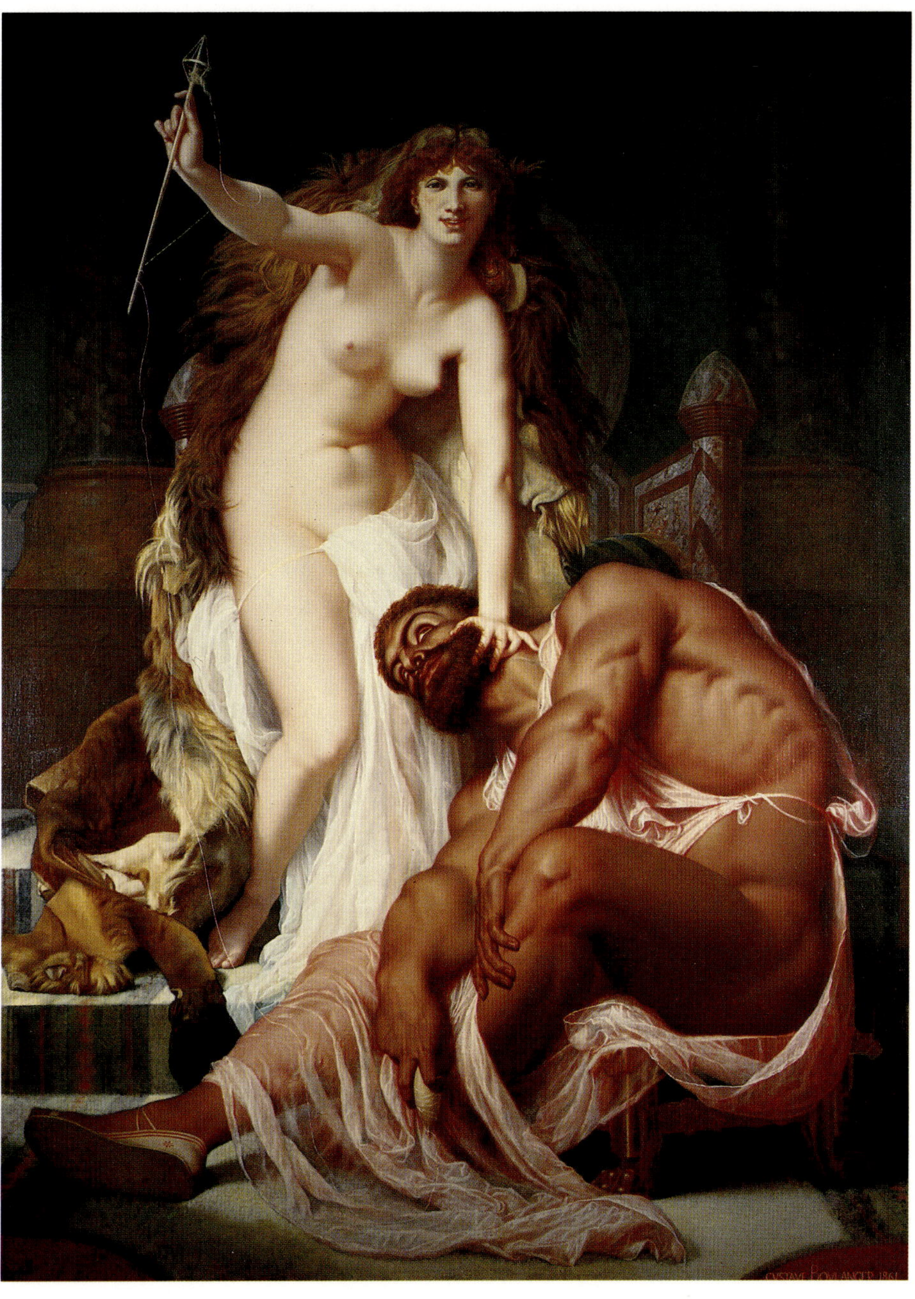

extenuated limbs of a triumphant Omphale. The painting was criticized for making Hercules appear glossy and inflated and for an execution that suggested equal smoothness on every surface.[4] Edward Strahan, describing a painting by this title in the collection of W.W. Kenyon of Brooklyn, New York, in the early 1880s was equally disturbed by the interpretation of the male figure: "We seem to see the Farnese Hercules broken up on the ground with its joints snapped, and with the power accompanying the statue's connected posture wholly dissipated and irretrievably lost."[5] More appealing to American collectors were Boulanger's orientalist and classical genre scenes; at least seven were in American collections in the early 1880s.

Opposite
William Adolphe Bouguereau
Mother and Children, 1879
Oil on canvas, 64¾ x 46¼″ (164.5 x 117.1 cm)
The Cleveland Museum of Art,
Hinman B. Hurlbut Collection. 432.15

JULES-ADOLPHE-AIME-LOUIS BRETON (1827–1906)

Jules Breton was born into a leading family in Courrières, a village in the coal-mining region of northern France. He was tutored as a child by his uncle Boniface Breton and received a classical education at the Collège St. Bertin in St. Omer. At the age of sixteen he began three years of work with the Belgian painter Félix de Vigne at the Royal Academy of Ghent, and later he spent six weeks as a student of Gustave Wappers in Antwerp. In 1847 he went to Paris to complete his studies, working at the Ecole des Beaux-Arts under Michel-Martin Drolling. He marked his Salon debut in 1849 with *Misère et désespoir*, a painting that expressed his horror at the violent events of the 1848 revolution.[1]

By the early 1850s, Breton had begun painting scenes around Courrières, developing skills in rendering landscapes that would show his enduring sympathy with the Barbizon painters. His own deep sentiment for the work and the traditions of his native region was one of the sources of a long and successful career as a painter of French peasant life, marked by excellence in both landscape and figure painting and in the harmonious union of the two. By 1867, when Breton exhibited ten paintings at the Universal Exposition in Paris, his fame had spread to America, where, after the conclusion of the Civil War, his reassuring rural subjects, "far removed from Parisian wickedness,"[2] began to arouse the interest of major collectors in New York, Baltimore, and Philadelphia.[3] Even more than Jean-François Millet, an artist with whom he was frequently compared, Breton was credited with having introduced to the public a taste for peasant subjects. His influence on other artists became visible in both French and foreign sections of Salons and international exhibitions to such an extent that by 1889 the integrity of his own imagery had been undermined by its pervasive influence on the works of others.

The Song of the Lark (1884) was typical of Breton's later works in its depiction of a solitary peasant girl. Exhibited at the Salon of 1885, and acquired shortly afterward by Chicago businessman Henry Field, it was praised by critics for its treatment of early morning light, but challenged for imposing too great an aesthetic awareness on its subject.[4] The girl's spiritual awakening to the music of the lark as she walks to the fields at daybreak reflected Breton's own appreciation of this particular moment "when dawn was set on fire, becoming redder all the time, and more beautiful. . . ."[5]

The Song of the Lark was reproduced as an etching in 1887.[6] It was not one of the fifteen paintings shown by Breton at the 1889 Exposition, but it was widely admired by the American public when shown at the World's Columbian Exposition in Chicago in 1893. Its strong appeal, lasting well into the twentieth century, lay not only in the sentiment it expressed but also in the authenticity of its subject and in Breton's skillful and convincing realist style.[7]

ALEXANDRE CABANEL (1823–1889)

Alexandre Cabanel, an academic painter who entered the Ecole des Beaux-Arts in 1840 and studied under François Edouard Picot, won the Prix de Rome in 1845.[1] After five years in Italy studying the Renaissance masters, he returned to Paris to resume a Salon career dominated by paintings of mythological and religious subjects that were received with great favor in official circles and won the artist numerous private and public mural commissions. Although trained as a precise draftsman in the tradition of Ingres, Cabanel tempered his academicism with sentiment and became known for softly colored pictures of female nudes—works attuned to Second Empire taste.

Cabanel's Salon painting of 1863, *The Birth of Venus* (Musée du Louvre), was purchased by Napoleon III, and was later lent to the 1867 Universal Exposition. Despite the fact that Emile Zola called the figure "a goddess of pink and white almond paste in a river of milk,"[2] *The Birth of Venus* became one of the most admired paintings of the nineteenth century.[3] In 1889, the year of Cabanel's death, it was remembered as representing the return of a calm and elevated sense of plastic beauty that had seemed on the verge of disappearing, and was viewed as one of the most characteristic and exemplary works of contemporary painting.[4]

For American collectors, few French artists rivaled Cabanel's importance or the importance of the academic tradition he represented. John Wolfe, a New Yorker who sold his collection of German paintings in the 1860s in order to buy French works, commissioned a version of *The Birth of Venus* (Metropolitan Museum of Art, New York) in 1875. The slightly smaller version in the present exhibition was owned by Philadelphia businessman Henry C. Gibson, who hung it in one of the chapel-like galleries he had built for his collection. An American viewer who saw it there in the 1880s described it as installed in "a little bower of drapery, in the innermost room of all, the folds of which drapery flow away from her figure in every direction—altogether centrifugally, and with a slight air of sarcasm."[5]

CAROLUS-DURAN (1838–1917)

Born in the northwestern city of Lille, Charles-Emile-Auguste Durand, known as Carolus-Duran, received training there in the early 1850s under François Souchon, a former student of Jacques-Louis David.[1] His family moved to Paris in 1853, but financial difficulties, illness, and the death of his father hindered his progress as an artist, and he eventually returned to Lille and sought out portrait commissions there. A stipend awarded in a local competition in 1859 enabled Carolus-Duran to return to Paris and to enroll in the Académie Suisse. During the next four years he developed friendships with other young realist painters and became a supporter of the work of Edouard Manet, with whom he shared an admiration for the paintings of Velázquez.

After an extended trip to Italy, a return to Lille, and a visit to Spain in the 1860s, Carolus-Duran established himself in Paris, and he won Salon acclaim in 1869 with his *Portrait de Mme XXX* (*La Dame aux gants*), a work that was purchased by the French government for the Luxembourg Museum. In 1872, the year when two of his portraits of fashionably dressed women were favorably received at the Salon, he opened a studio for young artists on the Boulevard Montparnasse. This atelier, in which instruction was offered without charge, embraced the techniques of its master, rejecting preparation through preliminary drawing. Julian Alden Weir, who studied there briefly before going on to Gérôme in 1874, wrote, "He puts them [his pupils] in front of the living model and with the brushes in their hands [encourages them] to represent the model as well as possible, making them draw and paint at the same time."[2] Although Weir found Carolus-Duran's antiacademic approach too undisciplined for a

Jules Breton
The Song of the Lark, 1884
Oil on canvas, 43½ x 33¾" (110.6 x 85.8 cm)

Henry Field Memorial Collection, 1894.1033

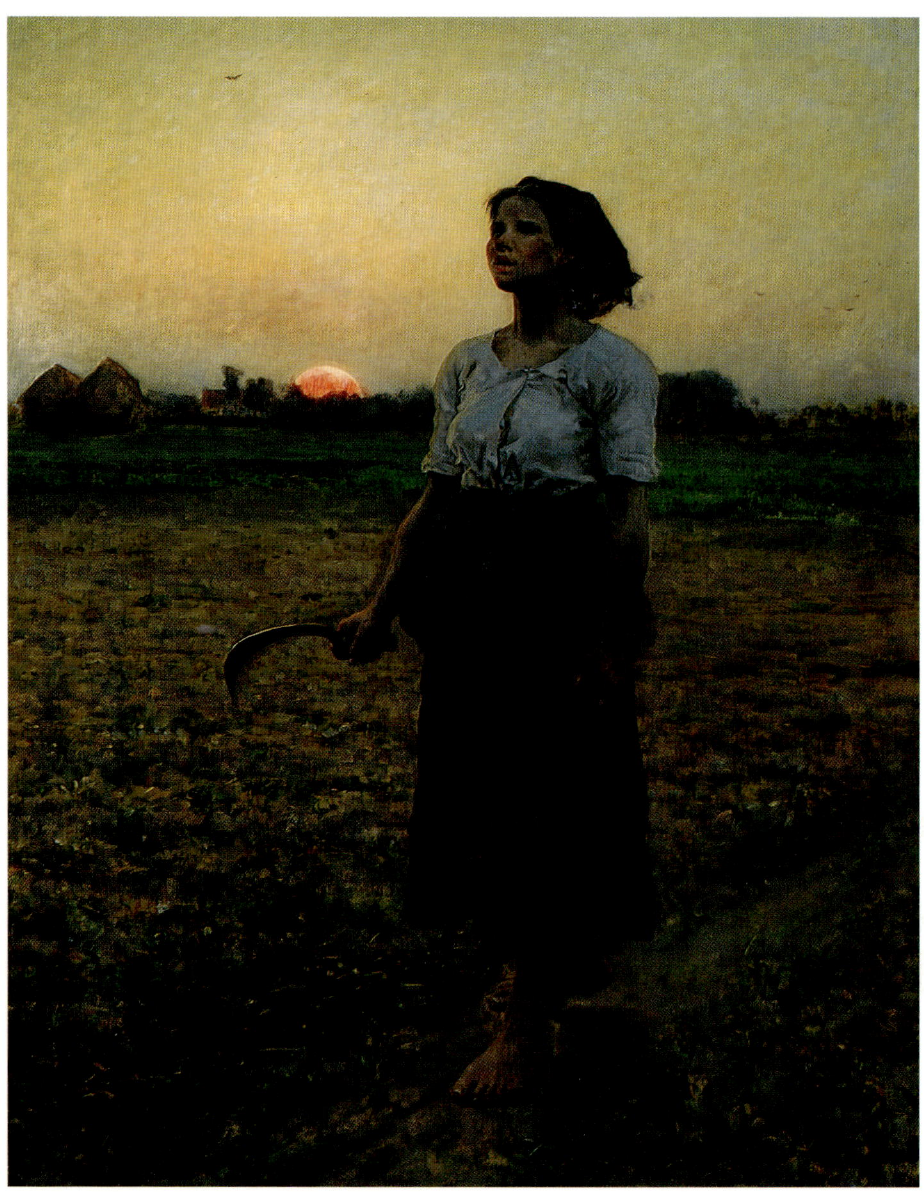

young artist, his colleague John Singer Sargent, who entered the studio in 1874, thrived in this atmosphere and developed a technical proficiency that owed much to his teacher's liberating methods.

Dominated by foreign students, including many Americans, Carolus-Duran's studio was popular with women, who were excluded from the Ecole des Beaux-Arts.[3] One of his American students, Lucy Lee Robbins of New York, posed for Carolus-Duran in an 1884 portrait that was shown at the Salon the following year. A classic example of the artist's style, it depicts a vivacious, attractive young woman holding a single rose in her lap. *Portrait of Lucy Lee Robbins* was one of twelve paintings Carolus-Duran exhibited at the 1889 Exposition.[4] Critics noted his preoccupation with color and praised his use of the brush, "at the same time very knowledgable and very free . . . an instrument that is wielded with a happy and triumphant ease."[5]

Alexandre Cabanel
The Birth of Venus, 1863
Oil on canvas, 31½ x 53" (80 x 134.6 cm)
Pennsylvania Academy of the Fine Arts,
Philadelphia, Bequest of Henry C. Gibson

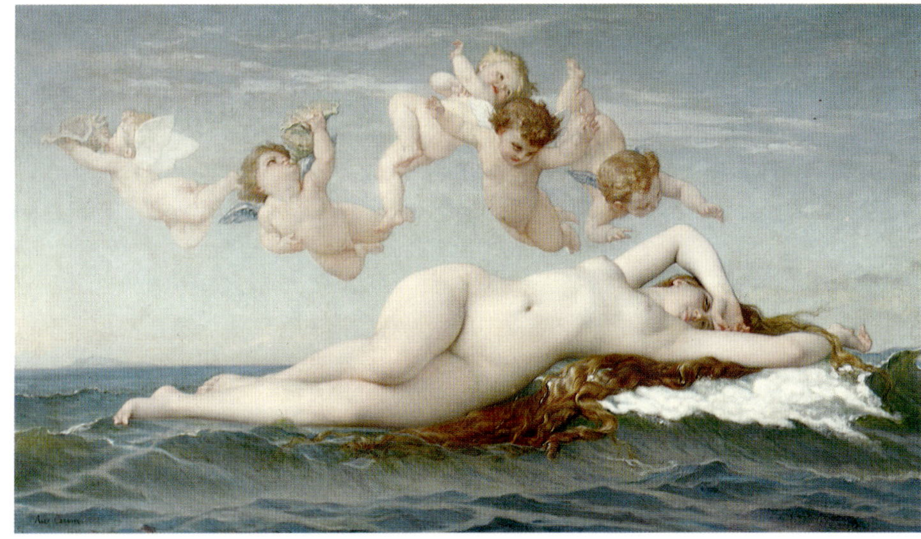

Carolus-Duran
Portrait of Lucy Lee Robbins, 1884
Oil on canvas, 67¼ x 50¼" (170.8 x 127.6 cm)
The Chrysler Museum, Norfolk,
Gift of Walter P. Chrysler, Jr.

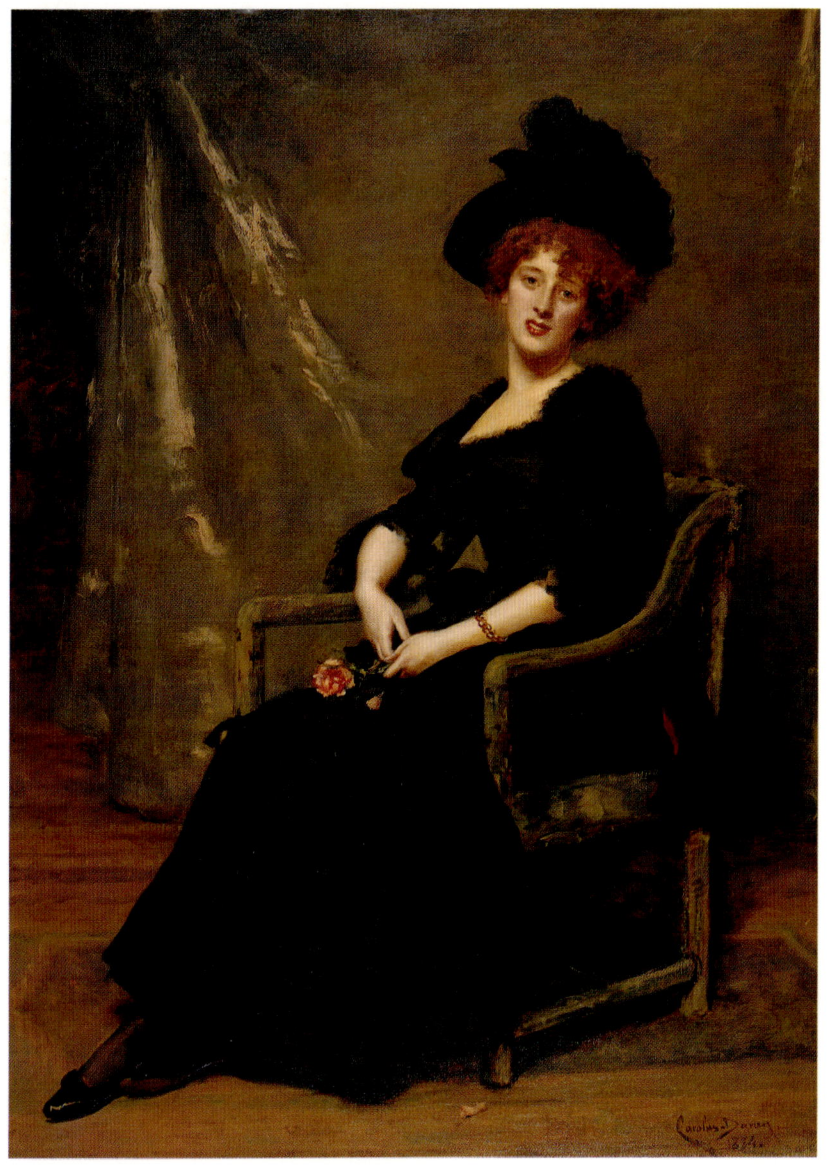

PASCAL-ADOLPHE-JEAN DAGNAN-BOUVERET (1852–1929)

Pascal-Adolphe-Jean Dagnan-Bouveret studied briefly with Alexandre Cabanel before entering the studio of Jean-Léon Gérôme, in 1869.[1] The confident draftsmanship he developed under Gérôme led to success in his academic studies, including the winning of second prize in the Prix de Rome competition of 1875. After frequent visits to the Franche-Comté with his friend the painter Gustave Courtois, Dagnan-Bouveret shifted his interest from the mythological subjects he favored under Gérôme to observations of regional life.

During the early 1880s, Dagnan-Bouveret shared the laurels of the realist school with Jules Bastien-Lepage, assuming its leadership after the latter's death, in 1884. *Horses at the Watering Trough* (Musée des Beaux-Arts, Chambéry) Dagnan's triumph of the 1885 Salon,[2] confirmed his importance and secured his reputation not only in Europe but also in the United States.[3] Among Dagnan-Bouveret's nine entries in the 1889 Exposition were paintings owned by the French government, the Munich Pinakothek, and collectors or dealers in London, Moscow, and Baltimore.[4]

The Pardon in Brittany, which had been shown at the 1887 Salon, was among the works that won Dagnan-Bouveret a medal of honor in 1889. The painting, later purchased by New York collector George F. Baker,[5] may represent the pardon of St. Jean-du-Doigt, the anniversary of which is observed in the Finistère region during the month of June.[6] It depicts a segment of the austere annual pilgrimage in an arresting composition that features a cross section of the solemn procession of the faithful carrying lighted tapers. The starched headdresses and collars of the women provide a decorative foil for the stark characterizations of the pilgrims and of the poor who beg alms of them. But the serious religious nature of the pardon and its place in Breton tradition clearly serve as the basis of Dagnan-Bouveret's imagery.

CHARLES-FRANÇOIS DAUBIGNY (1817–1878)

In the context of the present exhibition, the art of Charles-François Daubigny represents the enduring influence of the Barbizon School on the American landscape painters who exhibited in Paris in 1889.[1] The youngest of the loosely associated band of French artists who worked in and near the forest of Fontainebleau before 1850, Daubigny was widely appreciated in America by the 1880s and was known to have been generous and encouraging to students who sought his advice.[2] To a generation whose teachers espoused the clarity and specificity of the Hudson River School, Daubigny's confirmed plein-air style offered a liberating alternative in which accuracy of detail was less important than unity of impression.

The son of an artist, Daubigny studied first with his father, Edmé-François Daubigny, then with Corot's master, Victor Bertin. He made his Salon debut in 1838, showing both paintings and etchings, and in 1840 prepared for the Prix de Rome competition as a student of the history painter Paul Delaroche.[3] Discouraged after his first attempt at the prize, he turned from academic art to his original passion, landscape, and after 1846 he exhibited regularly at the Salon.

Solitude is one of a number of landscapes related to *L'Etang de Gylieu près d'Optevoz (Isère)*, one of the paintings for which Daubigny was awarded a first-class medal at the Salon of 1853. A view of the pond at Gylieu, in which a brilliant sky is reflected and cranes fish undisturbed, it is typical of the Daubignys that were owned by American collectors in the 1880s.[4] In their simplicity and breadth of treatment, these paintings influenced American artists who were unable to study abroad as well as 1889 medalists such as Charles Davis, Ruger Donoho, and R. Swain Gifford. *Solitude*, not only in its execution but also as an example of Barbizon subject matter, clearly represents the interest in light, atmosphere, and time of day and the sentiment experienced in the private contemplation of nature, that produced a stylistic revolution in landscape painting during the last half of the nineteenth century.

JEAN-LEON GEROME (1824–1904)

Jean-Léon Gérôme, a leading painter of historical and ethnographic subjects and the recipient of numerous official honors in France, trained in the studio of Paul Delaroche in the early 1840s and was briefly enrolled as a student of Charles Gleyre in 1843. He gained recognition with the exhibition of *The Cock Fight* (*Jeunes Grecs faisant battre les coqs*, Musée du Louvre) at the Salon of 1847, and through his involvement in the neo-grec movement of classical genre painting. After 1854, when he made his first trip to Greece and Turkey, much of his inspiration came from Egypt, North Africa, and the Near East.[1]

In 1863 Gérôme was appointed a professor at the Ecole des Beaux-Arts, a position that gave him considerable influence with academically trained painters over the next four decades. French students of Gérôme ranged from P.A.J. Dagnan-Bouveret to Pierre Bonnard and Odilon Redon; among the Americans who recognized the value of his instruction and gained admission to his studio were Thomas Eakins, Julian Alden Weir, and Theodore Robinson.[2] Polled in 1889 by *Century Magazine*, Gérôme's former American students wrote in praise of his fidelity to truth and his insistence on "perfection in drawing and complete harmony and unity of design."[3] By the end of the century, dozens of his paintings had entered American collections, so great was the appeal of his classical and exotic subjects and meticulously finished canvases.

The Death of Caesar, painted in 1859 and exhibited at the Universal Exposition of 1867, was one of the most refined examples of Gérôme's skill in historical narrative. In the collection of John Taylor Johnston of New York by the early 1870s, it was among the best known and most widely admired of the paintings by Gérôme owned by Americans at the time of the 1889 Exposition.[4] The scene, which was painstakingly described by the critic Edward Strahan after the painting was acquired by John Jacob Astor in 1876,[5] depicted the theater of Pompey, in Rome, with the dead Caesar's body, exquisitely foreshortened, lying in the shadows of the foreground. The event, captured at its denouement, is recorded in the departure of Caesar's assassins from the center of the impeccably, if imaginatively, constructed interior, while a lone senator, frozen by the horror of the deed, sits motionless at the right. When it was exhibited at Yale University in the early 1870s, the artist John Ferguson Weir, Yale's first professor of art, in a letter to his brother, Julian, described *The Death of Caesar* as "one of the greatest works of modern Art."[6] In its scholarly interest, forthright color, and skillful organization, the painting represented values that appealed to American collectors and students long after they had been overshadowed in France by the precepts of naturalism.

Pascal-Adolphe-Jean Dagnan-Bouveret
The Pardon in Brittany, 1886
Oil on canvas, 45⅛ x 33⅜" (114.6 x 84.8 cm)
© The Metropolitan Museum of Art, New York, Gift of George F. Baker. 31.132.34

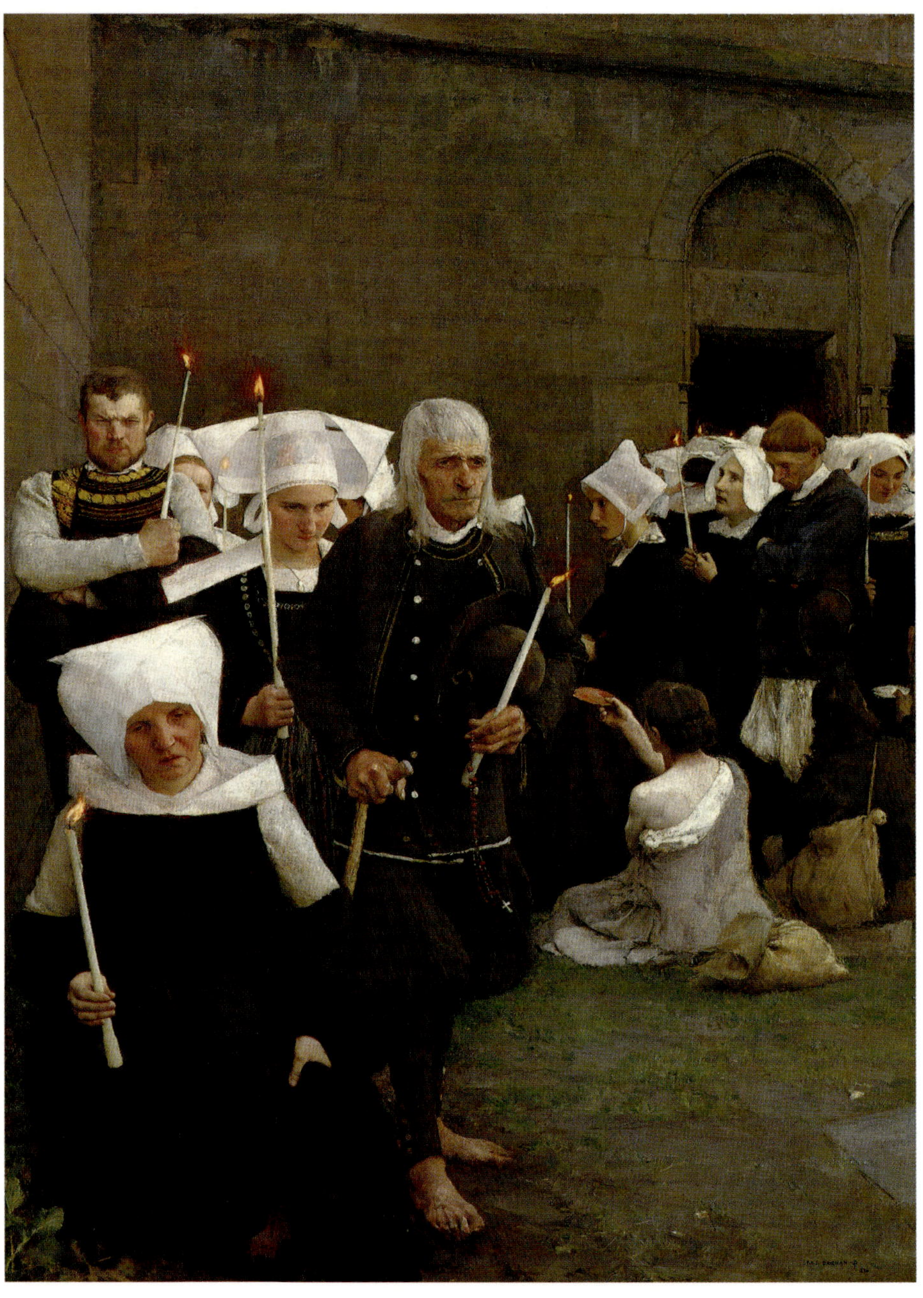

Opposite top
Charles François Daubigny
Solitude, 1869
Oil on canvas, 19¾ x 36½" (50.2 x 92.7 cm)
Philadelphia Museum of Art, George W. Elkins Collection

Opposite bottom
Jean-Léon Gérôme,
The Death of Caesar, 1859
Oil on canvas; 33¹¹⁄₁₆ x 57½" (85.5 x 145.5 cm)
The Walters Art Gallery, Baltimore

MARC GABRIEL CHARLES GLEYRE (1806–1874)

Charles Gleyre, who was born in Switzerland and trained in the applied arts in his uncle's textile factory in Lyons, entered the Paris studio of Louis Hersent in 1825.[1] Within a year he had left Hersent and had established a program of study that accommodated morning classes at the Ecole des Beaux-Arts, afternoons in the studio of English watercolorist R.P. Bonington, and evenings drawing from the live model at the Académie Suisse. In the fall of 1828 he departed for Italy,

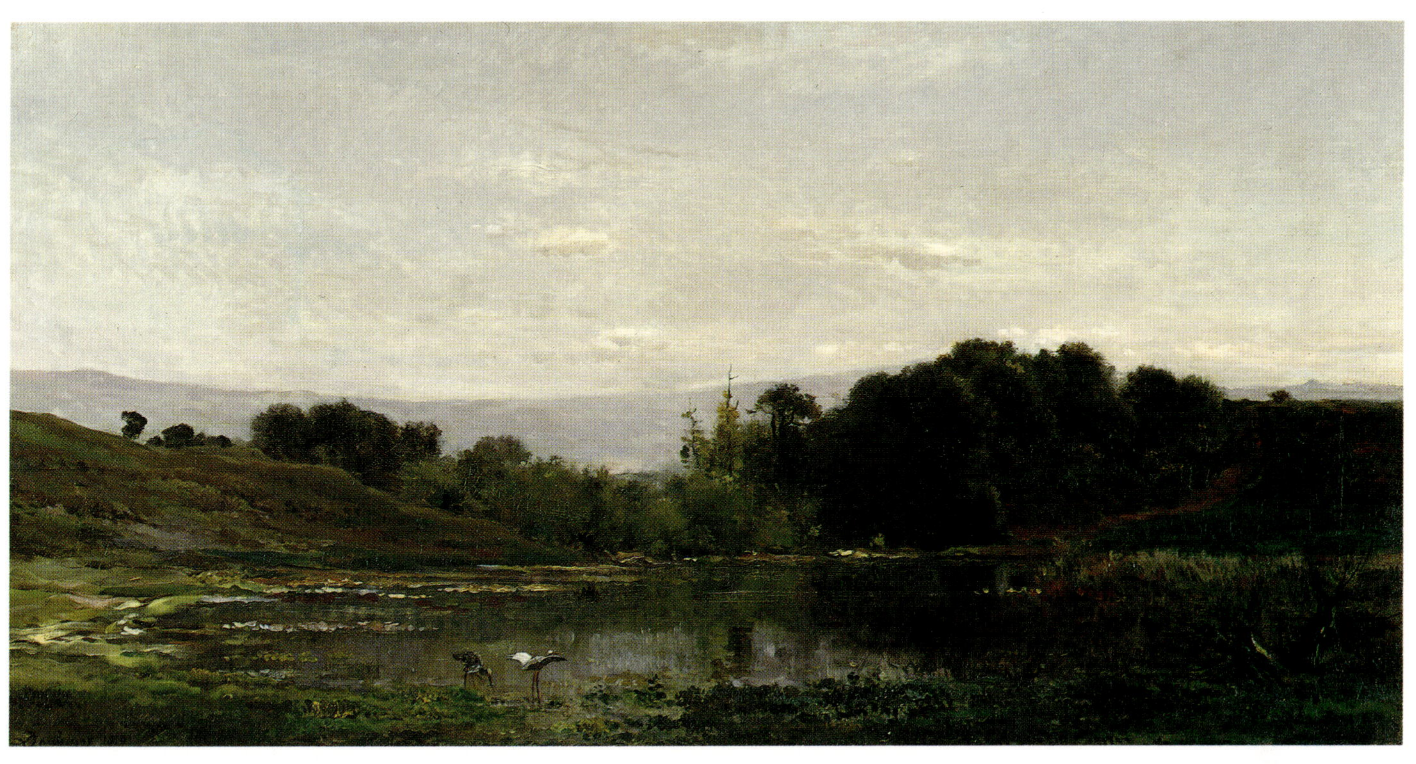

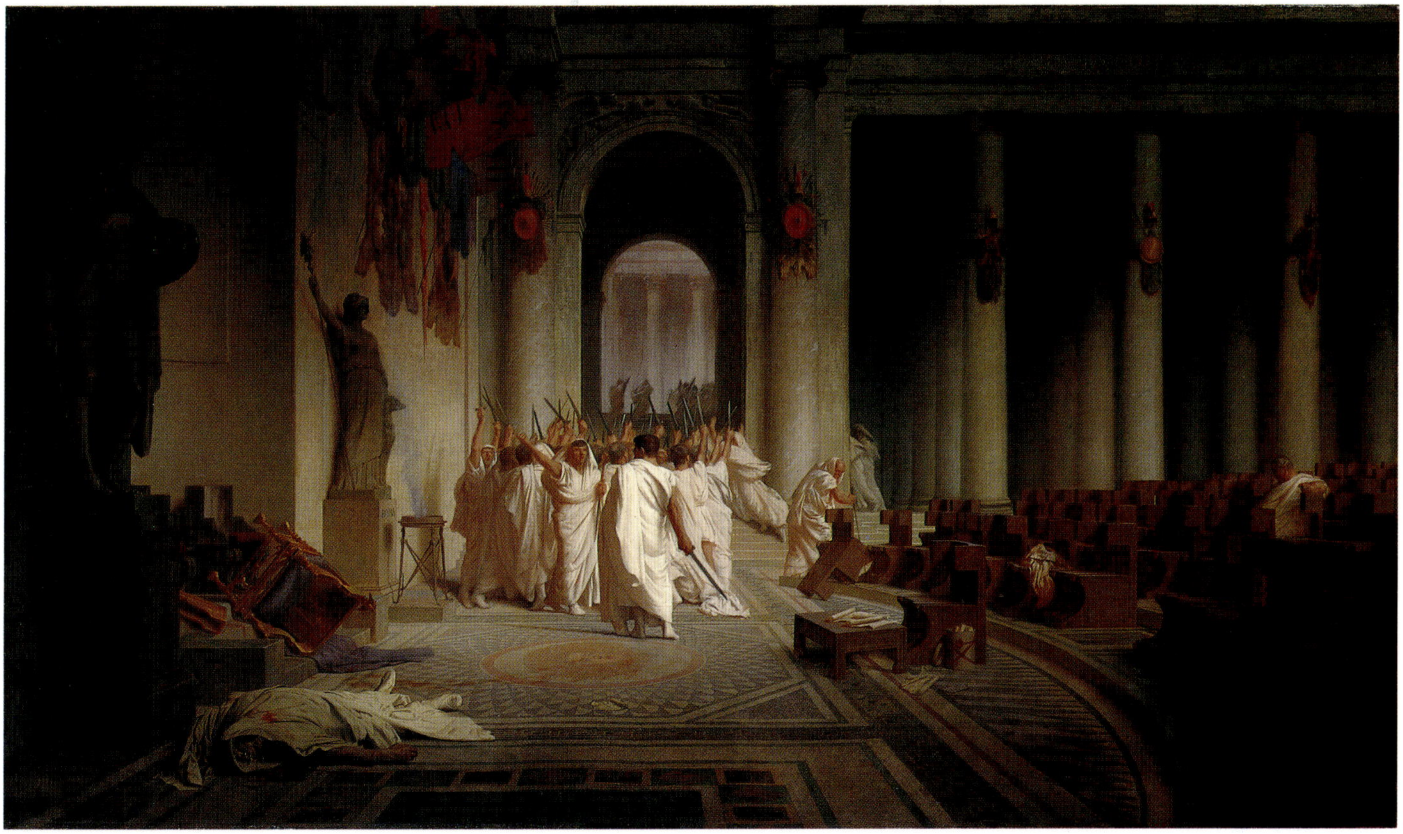

settling in Rome, where he took a studio in the Via Condotti and made acquaintances among the German artists at the Caffe Greco and the French *boursiers* at the Villa Medici. On the recommendation of Horace Vernet, he embarked on an extended trip to Greece, Turkey, and Egypt in 1834 as the artist-companion of an American, John Lowell, Jr., but while traveling suffered bouts of illness that plagued him until his return to France, in 1837.[2]

During the next few years, Gleyre executed a number of works that recalled his eastern trip, and in 1840 he won an important, but ill-fated, commission from the Duc de Luynes for the decoration of his chateau at Dampierre.[3] He finally achieved Salon success in 1843 with a painting entitled *Le Soir (Lost Illusions)*, an artist's vision in which an aged poet, seated on the bank of the Nile, watches as his illusions pass by on a bark filled with youthful female musicians. The painting, now in the Louvre, was so well received that it was copied by the artist in several versions, including one commissioned by the American collector William T. Walters, which was completed in 1867.[4]

In 1843, Gleyre had also taken over the directorship of the studio of his friend Paul Delaroche, a position he would maintain for more than twenty years. Among the students he inherited were a group who, under his influence, developed the style known as neo-grec. Practiced by Jean-Léon Gérôme, Jean-Louis Hamon, and others, it lent itself to the portrayal in antique settings of themes from everyday life. An example from Gleyre's later career is *The Bath*, of 1868, a painting in which two graceful Roman women prepare to bathe a reluctant child. Set in an outdoor pavilion, through whose columns can be glimpsed the surrounding landscape, the scene exemplifies Gleyre's skill as a draftsman, his close observation of nature, and his use of natural light as the key to both illumination and modeling.

Owned by New York collector Charles S. Smith in the 1880s, *The Bath* was described as "one of the most remarkable paintings in the country."[5] Its qualities were accessible not only to connoisseurs of the neo-grec style but also to a range of students that included the Impressionist painters Claude Monet, Pierre-Auguste Renoir, Alfred Sisley, and Frédéric Bazille, as well as the English artists Val Prinsep and Edward Poynter and the American artist James A.M. Whistler. Although Gleyre was not represented in the 1889 Universal Exposition, his contribution to the art of the period, more clearly perceived in recent years, was present on many levels in the work of others.[6]

JULES-JOSEPH LEFEBVRE (1834–1911)

Born in Tournan and raised in Amiens, Jules-Joseph Lefebvre was sent to Paris in 1852 to pursue a career as an artist. A student of Léon Cogniet, he entered the Ecole des Beaux-Arts that year, and in 1861 won the Prix de Rome for his painting *The Death of Priam*. A greater interest in drawing from nature was evident after his return from Rome, and academic subjects were of concern only insofar as they were premises for his sculptural female nudes.[1] He became known as a consummate painter of women, and his allegorical interpretations won awards at the Universal Expositions of 1878 and 1889.

By the early 1880s, important paintings by this "wonderfully severe and accurate limner of feminine purity in its nude perfection"[2] were in the collections of prominent Americans, including William Astor, William H. Vanderbilt, and Catherine Lorillard Wolfe.[3] Another aspect of Lefebvre's talent could be seen in his paintings of women in folkloric costume or exotic dress. *The Language of the Fan (Une Japonaise)*, whose model is dressed in a fashionably draped and fancifully patterned robe, reflects the interest in things Japanese that was having currency in the paintings of the Impressionists. Unlike Lefebvre's cool, seamless female nudes, this decorative model flirts openly with the viewer, using her fan seductively. Lefebvre's openness to combining academic drawing with contemporary themes must have appealed to the many American students who studied under him at the Académie Julian in the 1870s and 1880s. Despite his reputation as a painting master who rarely praised,[4] they sought his instruction and advice; more than thirty of the American artists exhibiting at the 1889 Universal Exposition, among them Thomas Dewing, George Hitchcock, Gari Melchers, and Robert Vonnoh, acknowledged Lefebvre as their teacher.

ALFRED-PHILIPPE ROLL (1846–1919)

Alfred-Philippe Roll, a realist painter who created grand historical compositions during the Third Republic, studied with Henri Harpignies and at the Ecole des Beaux-Arts under Jean-Léon Gérôme and Léon Bonnat. Influenced by the writings of Emile Zola and by the antiacademic plein-air paintings of the Impressionists, Roll emerged in the 1880s as a painter of social history whose canvases were distinguished by free but confident facture and by his determination to capture the movement and sensation of modern life.

A capable portraitist and painter of urban and rural landscapes, Roll combined his skills on several occasions in large works that documented events in the life of the Republic. *The Miners' Strike*, of 1880 (formerly Musée de Valenciennes; destroyed in World War II; see fig. 29), an early essay at naturalist subject matter, was the prototype of a mural of men at labor that he was commissioned to paint for the Hôtel de Ville of the city of Paris. *The Festival of July 14, 1880* (Salon of 1882),[1] an immense and lively commemoration of one of the "grandes journées républicaines et populaires"[2] of the Third Republic, served as the forerunner of another quasi-panoramic painting that he conceived in 1889.

The Festival of the Centennial of the Revolution Celebrated at Versailles in 1889, completed in 1893, took Roll nearly four years to paint. This enormous canvas chronicled the arrival of the cortege of dignitaries at the Bassin de Neptune in Versailles, and showed the officials amid throngs of spectators, whose animation is repeated in the dancing waters of the pool. The product of an artist who had invested it with "all his conviction, all his civic and artistic faith,"[3] the painting was acclaimed as the greatest of all Roll's investigations into the events of his time.[4]

The scene comprised numerous portraits, including that of Sadi Carnot, president of the Republic, who inaugurated the festival of the Centennial on May 4, 1889—an event followed two days later by the opening of the galleries of art and industry at the Champ-de-Mars. Surrounding Carnot in the painting were Pierre-Emmanuel Tirard, his council president and minister of commerce; Charles-Louis de Freycinet, minister of war; Eugene Spuller, minister of foreign affairs; and journalist Yves Guyot, minister of public works. Mingling with the crowd of men, women, and children, who have knocked down barricades to be closer to the popular officials, are generals, judges, and magistrates, along with artists Léon Bourgeois and Claude-Albert Waltner, as well as Emile

Marc Gabriel Charles Gleyre
The Bath, 1868
Oil on canvas, 35 x 25" (88.9 x 63.5 cm)
The Chrysler Museum, Norfolk,
Gift of Walter P. Chrysler, Jr.

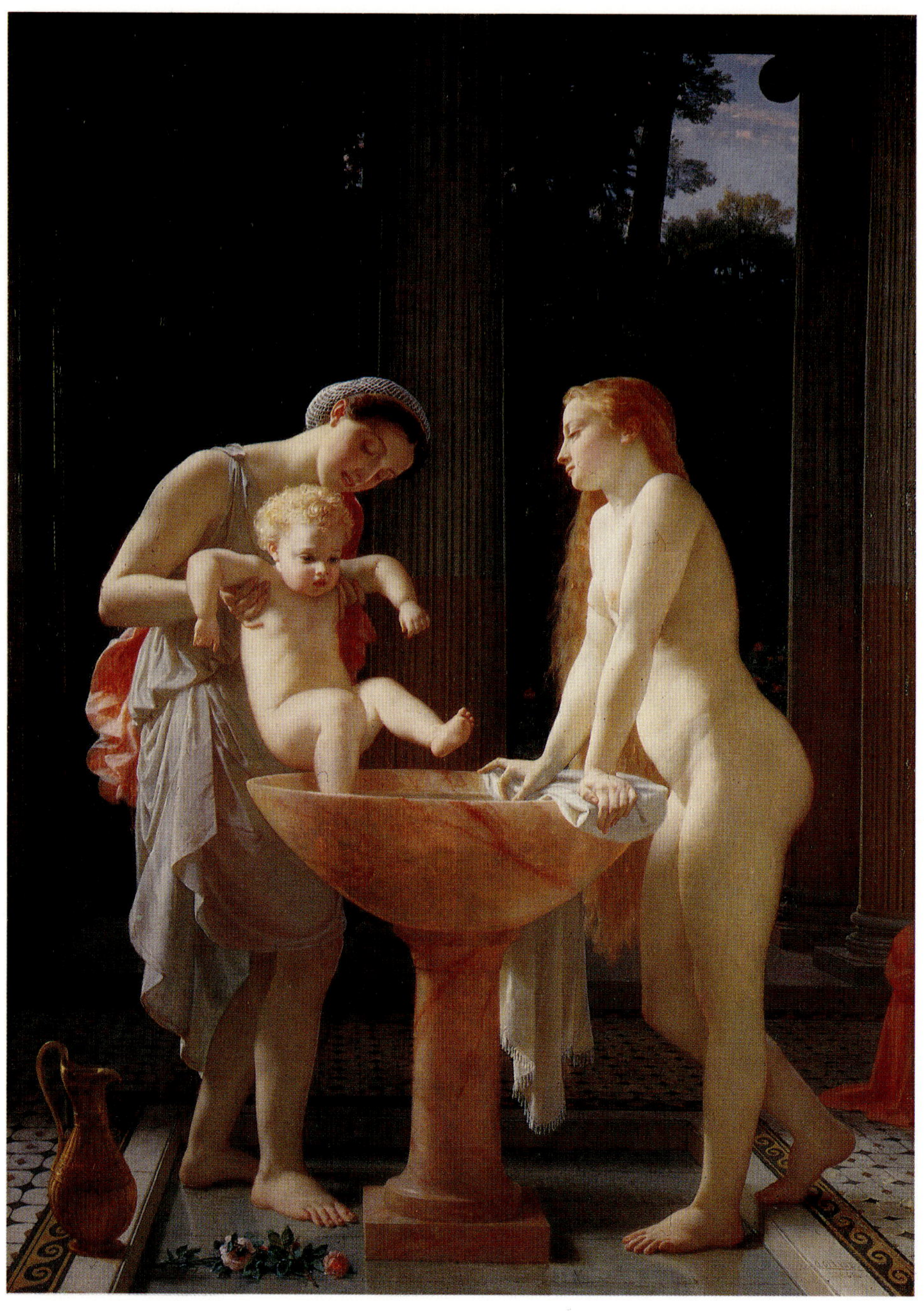

Zola and Roll himself.[5] When exhibited in 1893 at the Salon of the Société Nationale des Beaux-Arts, the vast blue-gray canvas was received as an audaciously successful page out of contemporary history,[6] one that represented a magnificent temperament, an artist with "guts."[7] Roll's truth to nature and unwillingness to yield to an official or premeditated program of organization were acknowledged by critics as the qualities of an artist who was a man of his time and who painted things exactly as he saw them.[8]

Jules-Joseph Lefebvre
The Language of the Fan (Une Japonaise), 1882
Oil on canvas, 51½ x 35½″ (130.8 x 90.2 cm)
The Chrysler Museum, Norfolk,
Gift of Walter P. Chrysler, Jr.

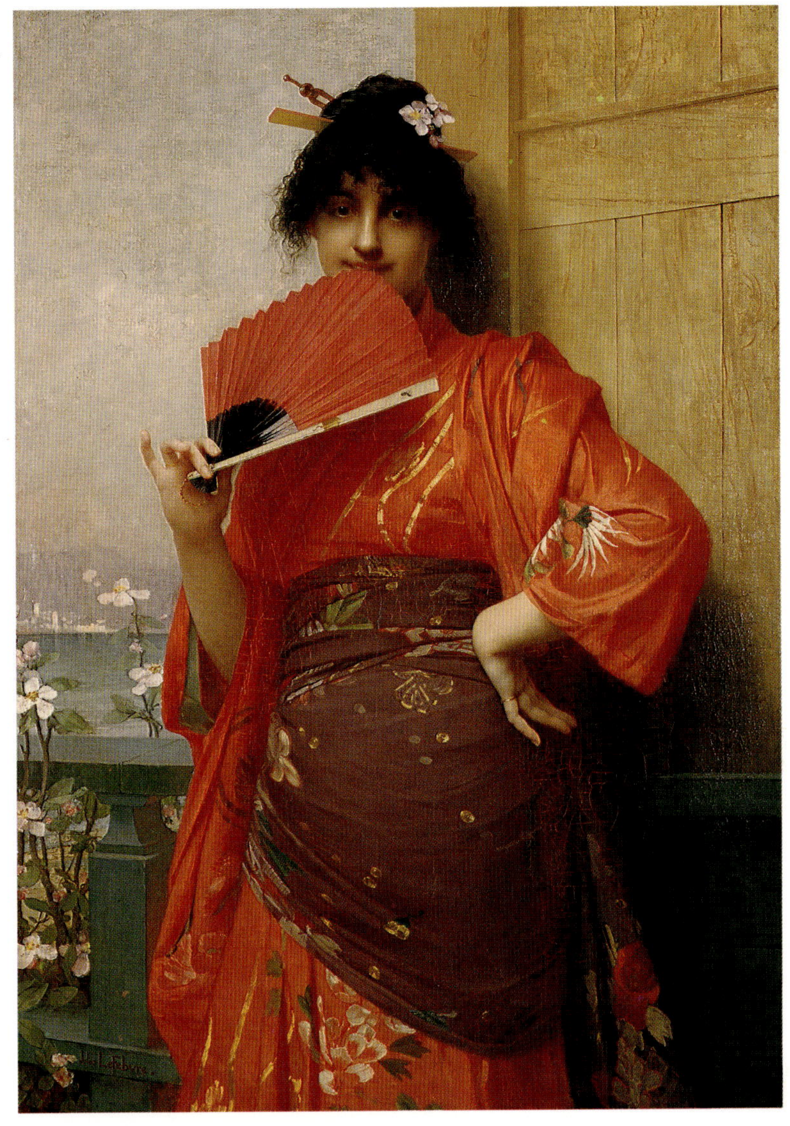

Alfred-Philippe Roll
Study for *The Festival of the Centennial of the Revolution Celebrated at Versailles in 1889*, 1893
Oil on canvas, 55½ x 88½″ (1.40 x 2.22 m)
Musée National du Château de Versailles

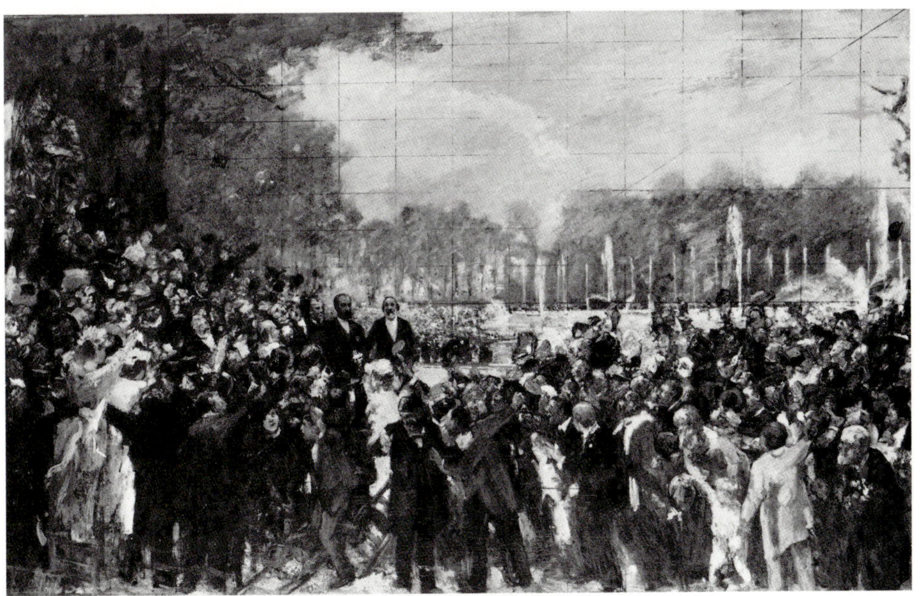

Notes

American Paintings

BACHER

1. Wilfred H. Alburn and Miriam Russell Alburn, *This Cleveland of Ours* (Chicago, 1933), vol. 2, p. 1055. I am grateful to Mary Sayre Haverstock, Ohio Artists Project, Oberlin College Library, for providing this and other references on Bacher. See also William H. Gerdts, *American Impressionism* (exhib. cat., University of Washington, Henry Art Gallery, 1980), p. 25, and Judith A. Barter and Lynn E. Springer, *Currents of Expansion: Painting in the Midwest, 1820–1940* (exhib. cat., St. Louis Art Museum, 1977).
2. Bacher produced a series of etchings from his outings around Munich and along the Danube. See Sylvester R. Koehler, "Works of American Etchers. XVI. Otto H. Bacher," *American Art Review*, 2, part 1 (1881), pp. 51–52. For Bacher's Venetian etchings, see Koehler, "Mr. Bacher's Venetian Etchings," *American Art Review*, 2, part 2 (1881), pp. 231–32; for the relation between Bacher's etchings and Whistler's etchings, see Robert A. Getscher, *The Stamp of Whistler* (Oberlin, 1977), pp. 176-78. For Bacher's graphic work, see William W. Andrew, *Otto Bacher* (Madison, Wis., 1977). See also Margaretta M. Lovell, *Venice: The American View 1860–1920* (exhib. cat., Fine Arts Museums of San Francisco, 1985), pp. 22–23. Bacher's graphic works are in the Library of Congress and the Prints Division, New York Public Library.
3. This information is cited in Sotheby's, New York, sale cat., Nov. 17, 1980, cat. no. 140.
4. Since Bacher returned to Europe in March 1885 and remained there until 1886, there is additional reason to believe that he worked in his studio from a photograph in order to complete the painting and date it 1885.
5. Bacher submitted one painting to the Salon in 1886, no. 82, *Palazzo Cadora—Venise*. Although he exhibited paintings at the National Academy of Design, New York, in the 1880s and early 1890s, he showed only drawings and black-and-white illustrations at the 1893 World's Columbian Exposition in Chicago. A related picture, *Country Store, Richmond, Ohio*, 1892, was shown by D. Wigmore Fine Art, New York, in 1988 (ill. in *Antiques*, 133 [May 1988]), p. 1032. In general, Bacher's paintings remain less well known than his graphic work.

BECKWITH

1. Beckwith trained with Walter Shirlaw in Chicago and under Lemuel Wilmarth at the National Academy of Design in New York.
2. Beckwith became *massier*, or superintendent, of the Carolus-Duran atelier. Fellow student Will H. Low described the routine of the atelier in *A Chronicle of Friendships* (New York, 1908). Beckwith himself later wrote of his teacher in an article for *Century Magazine* later republished as a chapter entitled "Carolus-Duran" in John Van Dyke, *Modern French Masters: A Series of Biographical and Critical Reviews by American Artists* (New York, 1896), pp. 75–80.
3. Paris Salon of 1877, no. 151, *Portrait de M.****.
4. See Maureen C. O'Brien et al., *In Support of Liberty: European Paintings at the 1883 Pedestal Fund Art Loan Exhibition* (Southampton, New York, 1986), for Beckwith's association with Chase in organizing the Pedestal Fund show.
5. Bertha Beckwith, "William Walton," *American Magazine of Art*, 7, no. 6 (April 1916), p. 244. A manuscript catalogue and price list of Walton's 1916 memorial exhibition at the Century Association, New York, names over 100 oil paintings and 50 watercolors. *Thessalian Plain*, an oil of a female centaur in a verdant landscape, was acquired by the Century Association at that time and remains in its collection. For this information I am grateful to Jonathan Harding, Curator, The Century Association. Not surprisingly, Walton admired Elihu Vedder and praised the paintings he exhibited at the 1893 World's Columbian Exposition. (William Walton, *World's Columbian Exposition, Art and Architecture* [Philadelphia, 1893], vol. 1, p. 24.)
6. Beckwith's diaries (Collection National Academy of Design, New York) make frequent references to Walton in early 1886. Beckwith served at one time as president of the New York Fencing Club, as noted in *Paris—New York* (exhib. cat., Wildenstein & Co. New York, 1977), p. 54. The portrait is cat. no. 55, fig. 82.
7. John Singer Sargent, *Portrait of Robert Louis Stevenson*, 1884(?), oil on canvas, 20 x 24" (Taft Museum, Cincinnati). See Trevor J. Fairbrother, *John Singer Sargent and America* (New York, 1986), p. 133, n. 15, on the dating of this painting.
8. In his diaries Beckwith discusses the many visitors to his open house, held on March 5, and implies that the activity surrounding the Morgan sale, which attracted 2,000 visitors on the evening of March 4, heightened public interest.
9. Montezuma, "My Notebook," *Art Amateur*, 17, no. 4 (Sept. 1887), p. 72. Courtesy Beverly Rood.
10. Theodore Child, "The Paris Salon of 1887," *Art Amateur*, 17, no. 1 (June 1887), p. 4. Courtesy Beverly Rood.
11. Bertha Beckwith, op. cit. Walton committed suicide in 1915, as did Beckwith in 1917.

BELL

1. According to Michael Quick, *Munich and American Realism* (exhib. cat., E. B. Crocker Museum of Art, Sacramento, 1978), p. 25, Loefftz, a friend and former classmate of Frank Duveneck, took over the Academy classes of Wilhelm von Dietz in 1877 and inherited Dietz's American students.
2. A New York address is listed in the National Academy of Design catalogue of 1892. Bell became an associate of the Academy in 1901 and a member in 1906.
3. The model and her reaction to the painting were described by Bell in a letter to Louise B. Clark, Brooks Memorial Art Gallery, Memphis, July 19, 1933. Courtesy William Heidrich, Memphis Brooks Museum of Art.
4. Ibid.
5. Ibid.
6. Illustrated in Charles M. Kurtz, ed., *Illustrations from the Art Gallery of the World's Columbian Exposition* (Philadelphia, 1893), p. 87.
7. See Robert Preato, "Whistler's Aesthetics and Japanese Design: Their Combined Influence on American Painting 1880–1917" (cat. nos. 30–32) in *La Femme: The Influence of Whistler and Japanese Prints on American Art 1880–1917* (exhib. cat., Grand Central Art Galleries, New York, 1983).
8. Wiles and Bell both had studios in northeastern Long Island in the 1930s. Wiles's encouragement of the gift to Memphis was reported in an undated clipping, c. July 1933, from *The Commercial Appeal* (Memphis). Courtesy William Heidrich, Memphis Brooks Museum of Art.

BLASHFIELD

1. For Blashfield's mural painting, see Royal Cortissoz, *The Works of Edwin Howland Blashfield* (New York, 1937); Leonard N. Amico, *The Mural Decorations of Edwin Howland Blashfield 1848–1936* (exhib. cat., Sterling and Francine Clark Art Institute, Williamstown, Mass., 1978); *A Catalogue of an Exhibition of the Works of Edwin Howland Blashfield* (exhib. cat., American Academy and Institute of Arts and Letters, New York, 1927); "Edwin Blashfield, Noted Artist, Dies," *New York Times*, Oct. 13, 1936. For his easel painting, see Homer Saint-Gaudens, "Edwin Howland Blashfield," *International Studio*, 35 (Sept. 1908), pp. LXIX–LXXVIII, and Grace Whitworth, "The Work and Workshop of Edwin Howland Blashfield," *Fine Arts Journal*, 23 (Nov. 1910), pp. 284–90.
2. Edwin Howland Blashfield, *Mural Painting in America* (New York, 1913).
3. See *The American Renaissance 1876–1917* (exhib. cat., Brooklyn Museum, New York, 1979).
4. Blashfield, op. cit., p. 29.
5. Ibid., p. 27.
6. *Appleton's Cyclopaedia of American Biography*, s.v. "Charles Edwin Wilbour."
7. See *New York Evening Post*, Dec. 2, 1876, p. 1.
8. The painting by Blashfield shown in the National Academy of Design in 1891 as *Portrait of a Lady* was possibly this work.

BLUM

1. See Bruce Weber, "Robert Frederick Blum (1857–1903) and His Milieu" (Ph.D. dissertation, City University of New York, 1985); Doreen Bolger Burke, *American Paintings in the Metropolitan Museum of Art* (New York, 1980), vol. 3, pp. 301–5; Margaretta M. Lovell, *Venice: The American View 1860–1920* (exhib. cat., Fine Arts Museums of San Francisco, 1984), pp. 23–28; and *Robert F. Blum* (exhib. cat., Cincinnati Art Museum, 1966).
2. In 1871 the McMicken School of Design was incorporated into the McMicken University of Cincinnati; in 1884 it was transferred to the Cincinnati Museum Association and became the Art School of Cincinnati; and in 1887 it was renamed the Art Academy of Cincinnati.
3. Quoted in Burke, op. cit., p. 301.
4. See Weber, op. cit., pp. 278–307. See also *The Golden Age—Cincinnati Painters of the 19th Century*

in the Cincinnati Art Museum (exhib. cat., Cincinnati Art Museum, 1979), pp. 39–40.
5. See Marianna Griswold van Rensselaer, "The Third Prize Fund—Exhibition 1," *Independent* (New York), 2 (June, 1887), p. 582, and "Fine Arts. The American Art Association," *The Nation*, 44 (May 26, 1887), p. 457. Both articles are quoted in Weber, op. cit., pp. 290ff.
6. Weber, op. cit., pp. 285–86.
7. Weber, op. cit., pp. 180–81, discusses Blum's knowledge of the "glare aesthetic."

BOGGS

1. *Who's Who in America* (New York, 1901), vol. 2, p. 109.
2. Susan Grant, "American Paintings Acquired by the French Government, 1879–1900" (master's thesis, George Washington University, 1983), p. 36.
3. See H. Barbara Weinberg, "Thomas B. Clarke: Foremost Patron of American Art from 1872 to 1899," *American Art Journal*, 3 (May 1976), p. 72.
4. Theodore Child, "Frank Myers Boggs," *Art Amateur*, 11 (August 1884), p. 53.
5. See Theodore Reff, *Manet and Modern Paris* (exhib. cat., National Gallery of Art, Washington, D.C., 1982), p. 33.
6. Doreen Bolger Burke, *American Paintings in the Metropolitan Museum of Art* (New York, 1980), vol. 3, p. 181.

BRANDEGEE

1. H. W. French, *Art and Artists in Connecticut* (Boston and New York. 1879), p. 158.
2. Linda S. Ferber and William H. Gerdts, *The New Path: Ruskin and the American Pre-Raphaelites* (exhib. cat., Brooklyn Museum, New York, 1985), p. 235.
3. H. Barbara Weinberg, "Nineteenth-Century American Painters at the Ecole des Beaux-Arts," *American Art Journal*, 13 (Autumn 1981), p. 72.
4. See Doreen Bolger Burke, *J. Alden Weir: An American Impressionist* (New York and London, 1983), pp. 60, 63.
5. Ibid.
6. Albert Boime, *The Academy and French Painting in the Nineteenth Century* (New York and London, 1971), p. 123. Nelson White noted that this portrait reminded him of Titian's *Man with a Glove* (Musée du Louvre, Paris) in *An Exhibition of the Work of Robert Bolling Brandegee, A.N.A., 1849–1922* (exhib. cat., New Britain Museum of American Art, New Britain, Conn., 1971), p. 16.
7. According to the Brandegee family the portrait was called "The Wanderer" because Flagg had traveled so frequently; see undated letter by Robert Brandegee in the archives of Smith College Museum of Art, Northampton, Mass. Artists often gave alternative titles to their portraits.
8. Robert Brandegee, letter to Mr. Churchill, Farmington, Conn. March 1, 1912 (archives of Smith College Museum of Art, Northampton, Mass.).
9. Ibid.
10. "Review of the Exhibition of the Society of American Artists," *The Nation*, 44 (May 12, 1887), p. 415.
11. Harold Frederic, "American Art in Paris," *New York Times*, June 16, 1889, p. 11.
12. *80 Eminent Painters of Connecticut* (exhib. cat., Lyman Allyn Museum, New London, Conn., 1947), cat. no. 112.

BRIDGMAN

1. *Appleton's Cyclopaedia of American Biography* (New York, 1888), vol. 1, p. 373. A chronology of Bridgman's life appears in *The Drawings of Frederick A. Bridgman* (New York, 1983), with introduction and chronology by Ilene Susan Fort, based on her forthcoming Ph.D. dissertation, "Frederick Arthur Bridgman and the American Fascination with the Exotic Near East" (City University of New York, 1989). See also Michael Quick, *American Expatriate Painters of the Late Nineteenth Century* (exhib. cat., Dayton Art Institute, 1976), pp. 20–21, 44, 88–89, 148; Lynne Thornton, *The Orientalists: Painter-Travellers 1828–1908* (Paris, 1983), pp. 172–77; *The Quest for Unity: American Art Between the World's Fairs 1876–1893* (exhib. cat., Detroit Institute of Arts, 1983), pp. 90–91.
2. See David Sellin, *Americans in Brittany and Normandy 1860–1910* (exhib. cat., Phoenix Art Museum, 1982), pp. 16, 23, 28–30, 112, 138–40. Bridgman's first public recognition came in 1870 with the purchase of *American Circus in Brittany* (collection Nelson Holbrook White).
3. H. Barbara Weinberg, *The American Pupils of Jean-Léon Gérôme* (Fort Worth, Tex., 1984), pp. 48–51.
4. Despite published statements to the contrary, Bridgman went to Egypt only once, according to Ilene Susan Fort, in conversation, November 28, 1988.
5. Bridgman used his paintings as illustrations for his book *Winters in Algeria* (New York, 1890).
6. Thornton, op. cit., p. 172.
7. G. W. Sheldon, *American Painters* (New York, 1879), p. 153.
8. Weinberg, op. cit., p. 49, footnote 42. The same painting was shown at the Paris Exposition of 1878, where it was selected as one of the two best paintings in the American section by Theodore Child, "American Artists at the Paris Exhibition," *Harper's New Monthly Magazine*, 79 (Sept. 1889), p. 489. Bridgman won the silver medal and was named a Chevalier of the Legion of Honor in 1878.
9. Of the five other paintings Bridgman showed at the 1889 Exposition, two are now in private collections in France and three are unlocated. I am grateful to Ilene Susan Fort for sharing with me this information from her dissertation, cited in n. 1.
10. Child, op. cit., p. 518.
11. A letter of Dec. 5, 1988, from Ilene Susan Fort includes a list of the eleven exhibitions between 1884 and 1891 in which the horse-trading paintings were shown. *My Last Price* is listed twice, *Hot Bargain, Cairo* appears four times, and *Horse Market at Cairo* appears six times. The listings for *My Last Price* are thought to refer to *Hot Bargain, Cairo*.
12. S. R. Koehler, *American Art* (New York, London, Paris, and Melbourne, 1886), illus. facing p. 6, pp. 52–53.
13. *Hot Bargain, Cairo* is first mentioned in the Union League Club of Chicago acquisitions book in 1895. However, it has been published in William B. Mundie, "Oriental Scene Theme of Popular Painting," *Union League Club Bulletin*, 4 (April 1927), p. 5, as having come via the Illinois Club in Chicago, which, according to the *Bulletin*, had purchased the painting in 1887 (accession no. 1887.1) from Bridgman's solo exhibition in New York. But Bridgman had New York exhibitions in 1881 and 1890, not in 1887, and the painting was shown in a group exhibition there in 1885. It may have been shown in a group exhibition in Brooklyn in January 1886. *Hot Bargain, Cairo* was shown in 1887 in London, where it may have been purchased, although two versions were listed as for sale the next year in Glasgow.

BROWN

1. Theodore Child, "American Artists at the Paris Exhibition," *Harper's New Monthly Magazine*, 79 (Sept. 1889), p. 519.
2. See Natalie Spassky, *American Paintings in the Metropolitan Museum of Art* (New York, 1985), vol. 2, pp. 337–42; see also *National Cyclopaedia of American Biography*, vol. 10, pp. 373–74.
3. See Patricia Hills, *The Painter's America* (New York, 1974), pp. 646–47.
4. Samuel Isham, *The History of American Painting* (New York, 1927), p. 344.
5. *Art Journal*, 6 (1880), p. 265.
6. Isham, op. cit., p. 344.
7. See Alan Trachtenberg, *The Incorporation of America: Culture and Society in the Gilded Age* (New York, 1982), pp. 90–95.
8. Evans lent Brown's *The Longshoremen's Noon*, C. Harry Eaton's *A Normandy Landscape*, Wyatt Eaton's *Ariadne*, Gilbert Gaul's *Charging the Battery*, Robert Minor's *Close of Day*, Platt Powell Ryder's *A Game of Marbles*, Charles Ulrich's *In the Land of Promise*, and J. Alden Weir's *Lengthening Shadows*. Evans's possible loan of Louis Moeller's *A Doubtful Investment* and Elihu Vedder's *The Cup of Death* cannot be verified.
9. "Our Artistic Show at Paris," *New York Herald*, March 8, 1889, p. 6.

BUTLER

1. Samuel Isham, *The History of American Painting* (New York, 1927 [1905]), p. 395.
2. See Doreen Bolger Burke, *American Paintings in the Metropolitan Museum of Art* (New York, 1980), vol. 3, pp. 283–85.
3. Howard Russell Butler, "Biographical Notes," Howard Russell Butler Papers, Archives of American Art, Roll 93, frame 125.
4. Butler, op. cit., Roll 349, frames 1059–1064.
5. Butler, op. cit., Roll 93, frame 197.
6. Butler, op. cit., Roll 93, frame 221.
7. Butler, op. cit., Roll 93, frame 229.

CHASE

1. See Ronald G. Pisano, *A Leading Spirit in American Art: William Merritt Chase* (Seattle, 1983), the

standard monograph on the artist, and Doreen Bolger Burke, *American Paintings in the Metropolitan Museum of Art* (New York, 1980), vol. 3, pp. 80–81, for a concise summary of his life.

2. See Kenyon Cox, "William M. Chase, Painter," *Harper's New Monthly Magazine*, 78 (March 1889), pp. 549–57; Marianna Griswold van Rensselaer, "William Merritt Chase," *American Art and American Art Collections* (Boston, 1889), vol. 1, pp. 209–30; and Pisano, op. cit., passim.
3. Chase kept the painting, hanging it in his house or studio. Katherine Metcalf Roof, *The Life and Art of William Merritt Chase* (New York, 1975 [1917]), p. 154, records it in the studio, and an inscription by Mrs. Chase on the back of a photograph of the work (Museum of Fine Arts, Houston, departmental files) notes that the painting hung in their house.
4. Identified only as *Portrait of Mrs. C.* at the Exposition. W. A. Cooper in "Artists in Their Studios," *Godey's Magazine*, 130 (March 1895), p. 295, identifies this picture as the one in the fair. Burke, op. cit., pp. 86–87, catalogues the work.
5. W. M. Chase, "How I Painted My Greatest Picture," article (n.d.) in the clipping file, Corcoran Gallery of Art, Washington, D.C.; cited in Burke, op. cit., p. 87.
6. Extensive research on file at the Art Institute of Chicago has not located the painting's site. I am grateful to Milo M. Naeve, Field-McCormick Curator of American Art, Art Institute of Chicago, for giving me access to the file on this work.
7. "Mr. Chase and Central Park," *Harper's Weekly*, May 2, 1891, p. 327.
8. Chase painted at least two pictures he called *A City Park* or *City Park*. See *Catalogue of Paintings by William Merritt Chase . . . to be sold at Auction, March 6, 1891* (Fifth Avenue Art Galleries, Ortgies & Co., New York, 1891), nos. 31, 39. This picture is illustrated in *Ninth Annual Exhibition of the Rochester Art Club* (exhib. cat., Rochester Art Club, New York, 1888), n.p.
9. Cox, op. cit., p. 556.
10. "Suburban Sketching Grounds," *Art Amateur*, 25 (Sept. 1891), p. 80.

COLE

1. Trevor J. Fairbrother, *The Bostonians: Painters of an Elegant Age, 1870–1930* (exhib. cat., Museum of Fine Arts, Boston, 1986), p. 204.
2. Wayne Craven, "J. Foxcroft Cole (1837–1892): His Art and the Introduction of French Painting to America," *American Art Journal*, 13 (Spring 1981), p. 57.
3. Peter Bermingham, *American Art in the Barbizon Mood* (exhib. cat., National Collection of Fine Arts, Washington, D.C., 1975), p. 129.
4. *Memorial Exhibition of the Works of J. Foxcroft Cole* (exhib. cat., Museum of Fine Arts, Boston, 1893), p. 9.
5. Henry James, "Art, Boston," *Atlantic Monthly*, 29 (March 1872), p. 372.
6. *Memorial Exhibition*, Museum of Fine Arts, Boston, p. 9.
7. "Boston Art in New York," *Art Amateur*, 8 (Feb. 1883), p. 56.
8. Cole was a mentor for many of the younger Boston artists. See "Foxcroft Cole and His School," *Art Amateur*, 11 (Oct. 1884), p. 96.

COPELAND

1. Most of the biographical information in this entry—including Copeland's year of birth, which has been variously cited—comes from his obituary, "Recent Deaths: Prominent American Artist," *Boston Daily Evening Transcript*, Feb. 1, 1909, p. 12. The Copeland family was one of the few to have a tomb on Boston Common, but Alfred's sister would not allow the tomb to be opened for his burial.
2. *Falling Leaves* is not in the collection of the Boston Athenaeum as was reported in Copeland's obituary, which cites it as Copeland's first painting of importance. Henry T. Tuckerman, *Book of the Artists* (New York, 1966 [1870]), p. 491, describes it as a "strong picture . . . treated with simplicity, and has vigor of touch, and is good in color." *Falling Leaves, Maine Woods* is listed for sale in Leonard & Co., *Special Auction Sale of Paintings by the late Alfred Bryant Copeland* (sale cat., Bromfield Art Galleries, Boston, March 16–20, 1909), cat. no. 79, p. 10.
3. Clara Erskine Clement and Laurence Hutton, *Artists of the Nineteenth Century and Their Works* (Boston, 1879), vol. 1, p. 155, state that the works by Copeland brought good prices at the Art Club exhibition. According to Copeland's obituary, art connoisseur Thomas Gold Appleton bought several paintings. See also James L. Yarnall and William H. Gerdts, compilers, *The National Museum of American Art's Index to American Art Exhibition Catalogues* (Boston, 1986), pp. 817–18.
4. Leonard & Co., op. cit., cat. nos. 45, 46, p. 8. Gilbert Stuart's originals were then in the Boston Athenaeum, and are now jointly owned by the Museum of Fine Arts, Boston, and the National Portrait Gallery, Washington, D.C. Leonard & Co., op. cit., states that Copeland owned two original Gilbert Stuart paintings: a portrait of General Knox (cat. no. 123, p. 13), now at the Museum of Fine Arts, Boston, and a self-portrait (unlocated; cat. no. 107, p. 12, ill. p. 5) which was obtained through a friend of Stuart's, a Mr. Bass.
5. I am grateful to Dorothy Claybourne, research librarian at St. Louis University, for this information.
6. Copeland's obituary states that he spent twenty-one years in Paris, returning to Boston in 1896. He may have gone to Paris with Boston portrait and landscape painter Frederick Dickinson Williams.
7. Clement and Hutton, op. cit., vol. 1, p. 155.
8. Copeland's *Pont Neuf and Louvre from the Quai des Grandes Augustins*, a small oil on panel dated 1877, is illustrated in color in *New Acquisitions in American Paintings* (exhib. cat., Kenneth Lux Gallery, New York, Nov. 22–Dec. 17, 1988), cat. no. 8. I am grateful to William H. Gerdts for making his files available, and to him and Karen Zukowski for bringing this catalogue to my attention.
9. Albert Bryant Copeland [Album of Photographs of His Life and Work], William Morris Hunt Memorial Library, Museum of Fine Arts, Boston. I am grateful to Judith Hayward, who took notes on the album for me.
10. J. Louis Webb, a student of William Merritt Chase, showed *A Studio Corner* (unlocated) at the 1889 Exposition.
11. According to Copeland's obituary, he was commissioned to paint copies of Cabanel's *Birth of Venus* for Frank Carey of Oswego, New York, and for Henry Miller of Boston (both copies are unlocated).
12. Leonard & Co., op. cit., p. 2.
13. Copeland's title, which is inscribed on the painting at the lower left, is not the one used in the 1889 catalogue of the American paintings. Three studies of this room are listed in Leonard & Co., op. cit., cat. nos. 37, 39, 96 (pp. 7, 12), and are illustrated in the album of photographs. The room was dedicated to Francis I, king of France from 1515 to 1547, a great Renaissance patron of the arts. Nancy Allen, chief librarian, William Morris Hunt Memorial Library, Museum of Fine Arts, Boston, assisted me by telephone with descriptions of Copeland's studies.
14. Leonard & Co., op. cit., p. 2.
15. Four copies and a landscape by Copeland are extant, according to the Inventory of American Paintings, National Museum of American Art, Smithsonian Institution, Washington, D.C.

COX

1. See William A. Coffin, "Kenyon Cox," *Century Magazine*, 41 (Jan. 1891), pp. 333–37.
2. See Pierce Rice and Henry Hope Reed's introduction in Kenyon Cox, *The Classic Point of View* (New York, 1980 [1911]).
3. Minna C. Smith, "The Work of Kenyon Cox," *International Studio*, 32 (July 1907), p. xi.
4. See Doreen Bolger Burke, *American Paintings in the Metropolitan Museum of Art* (New York, 1980), vol. 3, pp. 215–16.
5. Suggested by Burke, op. cit., p. 215.
6. Coffin, op. cit., p. 337.

CURTIS

1. Mrs. Curtis, the daughter of an English admiral, was painted by Sargent in 1882 (*Portrait of Mrs. Daniel Curtis*, Helen Foresman Spencer Museum of Art, Lawrence, Kans.) and with her family in his 1899 diploma painting, *An Interior in Venice*, for the Royal Academy of Arts, London.
2. Two paintings by Curtis are in the Isabella Stewart Gardner Museum, Boston: *The Gondola*, 1884, and *A Japanese Teahouse*, a watercolor. A third picture, *The Garden*, was also owned by Mrs. Gardner but was "left at her house Green Hill in Brookline" (Philip Hendy, *European and American Paintings in the Isabella Stewart Gardner Museum* [Boston, 1974], p. 68).
3. Curtis's 1881 Salon entry lists him as a student of Boulanger and Lefebvre, and also of Carolus-Duran. After 1881 only Carolus-Duran is listed.
4. Curtis's Salon entries during the 1880s in addition to *Venise* (1881) included *Flirtation* (1882), *Retour de la campagne* (1883), *Une Fainéante vénitienne* (1884).
5. Stanley Olsen, Chronology, in Patricia Hills et al., *John Singer Sargent* (New York, 1986), p. 277, puts Sargent in Holland with Curtis and Francis Brooks

Chadwick in August 1880. Sargent's *Ralph Curtis on the Beach at Scheveningen* (High Museum of Art, Atlanta, Ga.) dates from that trip. The Browning portraits are noted by Charles Merrill Mount, *John Singer Sargent: A Biography* (New York, 1955), p. 408. Both Forbes and Story also exhibited paintings at the 1889 Exposition.

6. Curtis, who used Sargent's Boulevard Berthier address in the Salon catalogue of 1884, wrote to his parents to describe the critical reaction to Sargent's *Portrait of Madame X* and mentioned the proposed trip to Seville (Evan Charteris, *John Sargent* [New York, 1927], pp. 61–62).
7. *The Gondola* (Isabella Stewart Gardner Museum, Boston) is also representative of Curtis's important work of that period.
8. *Chez Père Lathuille* (1879; Musée des Beaux-Arts, Tournai) was shown in Paris during the winter of 1884 at the posthumous exhibition of Manet's work. Curtis's admiration for Manet, which was shared by Sargent, is noted by Hendy, op. cit.

DANNAT

1. According to Theodore Child, "American Artists in Paris," *Art Amateur*, 10 (March 1884), p. 86, he studied with Frank Duveneck while he was in Munich.
2. Susan Grant, "American Paintings Acquired by the French Government, 1879–1900" (master's thesis, George Washington University, 1983), p. 42.
3. Armand Dayot, "William T. Dannat," *Craftsman*, 6 (May 1904), p. 161.
4. Doreen Bolger Burke, *American Paintings in the Metropolitan Museum of Art* (New York, 1980), vol. 3, p. 156.
5. Richard Muther, *The History of Modern Painting* (New York, 1907), vol. 4, p. 300.
6. William T. Dannat, letter to J. Seligmann, Dec. 3, 1919 (curatorial files of the Metropolitan Museum of Art, New York).
7. Theodore Child, "American Artists at the Paris Exhibition," *Harper's New Monthly Magazine*, 79 (Sept. 1889), p. 502.
8. André Michel, *Journal des Débats* (Sept. 22, 1889); reprinted in *Reports of the United States Commissioners to the Universal Exposition of 1889 at Paris* [Washington, D.C., 1891], vol. 3, p. 110.
9. Child, "American Artists at the Paris Exhibition," pp. 500, 502.

DARLING

1. Biographical sources include: *Toledo Blade* of Nov. 26, 1903; June 5, 1929; and May 17, 1933; *Toledo Times* of June 6, 1929, and Nov. 13, 1932; Annette Stott, "American Painters Who Worked in the Netherlands" (Ph.D. dissertation, Boston University, 1986), pp. 194–95 and chap. 5, passim; Susan E. Strickler, *The Toledo Museum of Art: American Paintings* (Toledo, 1979). I am indebted to Mary Haverstock and the Ohio Artists Project for corroborating my information.
2. *Toledo Times*, June 5, 1929.
3. Ibid.

DAVIS

1. William H. Gerdts, *Tonalism: An American Experience* (exhib. cat., Grand Central Art Galleries, New York, 1982), p. 80.
2. See Thomas L. Colville, *Charles Harold Davis N.A. 1856–1933* (exhib. cat., Mystic Art Association, Mystic, Conn., 1982).
3. See *The Quest for Unity: American Art Between World's Fairs 1876–1893*, essay by David Huntington (exhib. cat., Detroit Institute of Arts, 1983), pp. 219–20.
4. Theodore Child, "American Pictures at the Salon," *Art Amateur*, 14 (May 1886), p. 124.
5. Louis Bliss Gillet, "Charles H. Davis," *American Magazine of Art*, 27 (March 1934), p. 108.
7. Theodore Child, "American Artists at the Paris Exhibition," *Harper's New Monthly Magazine*, 79 (Sept. 1889), p. 508.

DODSON

1. William H. Gerdts, *Revealed Masters* (exhib. cat., American Federation of Arts, New York, 1974), p. 72.
2. Barbara Gallati, "The Paintings of Sarah Paxton Ball Dodson (1847–1906)," *American Art Journal*, 15 (Winter 1983), p. 70.
3. "American Women in the Paris Salon," *Art Amateur*, 7, no. 4 (Sept. 1882), p. 68.
4. George Ferguson, *Signs and Symbols in Christian Art* (London, Oxford, New York, 1961), p. 33.
5. Charles C. Eldredge, *American Imagination and Symbolist Painting* (exhib. cat., Grey Art Gallery, New York, 1979), p. 68.

DONOHO

1. See Childe Hassam, Foreword, in *Memorial Exhibition, Paintings of the Late Ruger Donoho* (exhib. cat., Macbeth Gallery, New York, Nov. 14–27, 1916), n.p.; Ronald G. Pisano in *G. Ruger Donoho (1857–1916): A Retrospective Exhibition* (exhib. cat., Hirschl & Adler Galleries, New York, 1977); and Doreen Bolger Burke, *American Paintings in the Metropolitan Museum of Art* (New York, 1980), vol. 3, pp. 305–7. See also Archives of American Art, Charles Feinberg Autograph Papers, D30:425–26, for a letter from Donoho's mother to landscape painter Jervis McEntee dated Sept. 21, 1878, asking him to take her son as a student. Donoho apparently studied with R. Swain Gifford, at the Cooper Union, not with McEntee.
2. Burke, op. cit., p. 306. Pisano, op. cit. n. 7, states that Donoho received criticism from Boulanger and was listed as a student of Bouguereau, as well.
3. "Art in Philadelphia. The Galleries of the Pennsylvania Academy," *Boston Daily Advertiser*, Nov. 18, 1882, Roll P53, frame 311, Archives of American Art, Smithsonian Institution.
4. Charles M. Kurtz, ed. *Illustrated Art Notes upon the Fifty-Eighth Annual Exhibition of the National Academy of Design, New York* (New York, 1883), p. 47, illus. p. 46.
5. In 1883 a painting entitled *La Marcelline*, possibly another work, was exhibited at the Society of American Artists, New York. Contemporary criticism of this work ("Fine arts. The Sixth Annual Exhibition of the Society of American Artists," *The Nation*, 36, no. 928 [April 12, 1883], p. 328) discusses a painting that does not appear to fit the description of *La Marcellerie*. Courtesy Jennifer M. Bienenstock.
6. *Art Union, A Monthly Magazine of Art*, 2, no. 4 (Oct. 1885), p. 83.
7. See Artist's File, Brooklyn Museum of Art, Department of Paintings and Sculpture, for reviews and clippings.

DOW

1. See Frederick Campbell Moffat, "The Breton Years of Arthur Wesley Dow," *Archives of American Art Journal*, 15 (1975), pp. 2–8, and *Arthur Wesley Dow* (Washington, D.C., 1977), especially chap. 2; "Paris and Brittany," pp. 24-39; David Sellin, *Americans in Brittany and Normandy 1860–1910* (exhib. cat., Phoenix Art Museum, 1982), pp. 53–54 and passim; and *The Quest for Unity: American Art Between the World's Fairs 1876–1893*, essay by David Huntington (exhib. cat., Detroit Institute of Arts, 1983), pp. 224–26.
2. Moffat, op. cit. (1975), p. 6.
3. Dow painted two smaller versions of this picture in 1888 and 1889; several of his twilight scenes have similar titles.
4. Arthur Wesley Dow, *Compositions* (New York, 1899). The book had gone through thirteen editions by 1931.

EAKINS

1. Lloyd Goodrich, *Thomas Eakins* (Cambridge, Mass., 1982), vol. 2, pp. 161–62, notes that Eakins submitted *The Crucifixion*, *The Writing Master*, and a watercolor, *Mending the Net*, to the 1889 Salon. All were rejected, but *The Writing Master* was accepted at the 1890 Salon.
2. Goodrich, op. cit., p. 161.
3. *New York Herald*, March 8, 1889, p. 6. This source, discovered by Annette Blaugrund, also verifies that J. Alden Weir's *Preparing for Christmas* was a watercolor.
4. Goodrich, op. cit., p. 165.
5. See *The Nation*, 61 (Feb. 1878), p. 157.
6. See Donelson Hoopes, *Eakins Watercolors* (New York, 1971), p. 22.
7. *The Nation*, 61 (Feb. 1878), p. 157.
8. See Kate Keman Rubin, "*The Veteran*," *Yale University Art Gallery Bulletin*, vol. 30 (Winter 1984), p. 24.

EATON

1. See Frederick Fairchild Sherman, *American Painters of Yesterday and Today* (New York, 1919), pp. 39–44.
2. Quoted in Laura L. Meixner, *An International Episode: Millet, Monet and Their North American Counterparts* (exhib. cat., Dixon Gallery and Gardens, Memphis, 1982), p. 45.
3. Wyatt Eaton, "Recollections of Jean-François Millet," *Century*, 38, n.s.16 (Oct. 1889), pp. 90–104.

4. See George Hellman, "Wyatt Eaton," *Art World*, 3 (Dec. 1917), pp. 204–9.
5. See William Gerdts, *The Great American Nude*, (New York, 1974), p. 105.
6. See, e.g., Bram Dijkstra, *Idols of Perversity: Fantasies of Feminine Evil in Fin-de-siecle Culture* (New York, 1986).

FULLER

1. Sarah Burns, "A Study of the Life and Poetic Vision of George Fuller (1822–1884)," *American Art Journal*, 13 (Autumn 1981), p. 20, notes that Fuller exhibited several times while at Deerfield and also kept abreast of developments in art.
2. William Dean Howells, in Josiah B. Millet, ed., *George Fuller, His Life and Works* (Boston, 1886), p. 40, implies that Fuller might actually have been emulating artists like Millet by taking a studio away from the city.
3. Burns, op. cit., p. 11, sees Fuller as a link between older American romantic painting and that of later American Tonalists.
4. See also Millet, op. cit., p. 4.
5. For example, Walter Montgomery, *American Art and American Art Collections* (Boston, 1889), vol. 2, p. 951, states that *The Quadroon* "for pathos and expression, must be reckoned Fuller's greatest work."
6. See Natalie Spassky, *American Paintings in the Metropolitan Museum of Art* (New York, 1985), vol. 2, pp. 151–53.
7. William H. Downes, "George Fuller's Pictures," *International Studio*, 75 (July 1922), p. 268, notes that Enneking bought a picture from Fuller's estate.

GAY

1. See Gary Reynolds, *Walter Gay: A Retrospective* (exhib. cat., Grey Art Gallery, New York, 1980).
2. Susan Grant, "American Paintings Acquired by the French Government, 1879–1900" (master's thesis, George Washington University, 1983), p. 48.
3. See Michael Quick, *American Expatriate Painters of the Late Nineteenth Century* (exhib. cat., Dayton Art Institute, 1976), p. 100.
4. Theodore Child, "American Artists at the Paris Exhibition," *Harper's New Monthly Magazine*, 79 (Sept. 1889), p. 11.

GIFFORD

1. Natalie Spassky, *American Paintings in the Metropolitan Museum of Art: Catalogue of Works by Artists Born Between 1816 and 1845* (New York, 1985), vol. 2, p. 549; *Near the Coast* is discussed on pp. 550–51.
2. Sylvester R. Koehler, "R. Swain Gifford, N.A.," *American Art Review*, 2, no. 2 (1880); reprinted in Walter Montgomery, ed., *American Art and American Art Collections* (Boston, 1889), vol. 1, p. 242.
3. Spassky et al., op. cit., note that the commission was for the lithographic firm of Charles Taber and Company.
4. Peter Bermingham, *American Art in the Barbizon Mood* (exhib. cat., National Collection of Fine Arts, Washington, D.C., 1975), p. 141.
5. From a letter written by Gifford's wife, Frances Eliot Gifford, quoted in *R. Swain Gifford, 1850–1905* (exhib. cat., Whaling Museum, Old Dartmouth Historical Museum, New Bedford, Mass., and Hudson River Museum, Yonkers, N.Y., 1974), text by Elton W. Hall, p. 2. Hall dates *Near the Coast* c. 1883.
6. Sylvester R. Koehler, *American Art* (New York, 1886), p. 24, fig. 24, facing p. 52. See Patricia C. F. Mandel in *The American Painter-Etcher Movement* (exhib. cat., Parrish Art Museum, Southampton, N.Y., 1984), catalogue by Maureen C. O'Brien and Patricia C. F. Mandel, p. 28, for a discussion of the etching.
7. Mandel, op. cit., cites *Illustrated Catalogue of Paintings by American Artists Contributing to the Prize Fund Exhibition of the American Art Association of New York 1885* (exhib. cat., Museum of Fine Arts, Boston, 1886 [no. 106, p. 12, illus. p. 19]), which notes that *Near the Coast* was "awarded a prize of $2500 in the First Competitive Prize Fund Exhibition of the American Art Gallery, New York, April 1885." The exhibition, which opened in New York in April 1885, was shown in Boston in February and March 1886.
8. The others were *Early Summer*, lent by Jerome B. Wheeler, and *A Kansas Ranch*.
9. Theodore Child, "American Artists at the Paris Exhibition," *Harper's New Monthly Magazine*, 79, no. 472 (Sept. 1889); pp. 518–20.

GILL

1. See Sona K. Johnston, *American Paintings 1750–1900 from the Collection of The Baltimore Museum of Art* (Baltimore, 1983), pp. 68–70.
2. Lois Marie Fink, "Elizabeth Nourse: Painting the Motif of Humanity," in *Elizabeth Nourse, 1859–1938: A Salon Career* (exhib. cat., National Museum of American Art, Washington, D.C., 1983), p. 118.
3. "The Philadelphia Art Club Exhibition," *Art Amateur*, 24 (Dec. 1890), p. 4.
4. See Theodore E. Stebbins, Jr., *The Life and Works of Martin Johnson Heade* (New Haven and London, 1975), pp. 138–49.

GROSS

1. Joseph P. Deibert, *Shining Lights of Schnecksville 1840–1940* (New Tripoli, Penn., n.d.), p. 77.
2. *Peter Alfred Gross (1849–1914): Pennsylvania Expatriate* (exhib. cat., Allentown Art Museum, Pa., 1979), p. 5.
3. Peter Alfred Gross, *Illustrated Toronto: Past and Present* (Toronto, 1876); see also Sally Lorensen Gross, "Peter Alfred Gross (1849–1914)," unpublished paper in the curatorial files of the Allentown Art Museum, Pennsylvania.
4. George William Sheldon, *Recent Ideals of American Art* (New York and London, 1977), p. 140.
5. *Peter Alfred Gross* (Allentown Art Museum), pp. 11, 14.
6. Gross is reported to have had a summer house in Brittany, but it is not mentioned in David Sellin, *Americans in Brittany and Normandy 1860–1910* (exhib. cat., Phoenix Art Museum, Ariz., 1982).
7. Sheldon, op. cit., p. 140.

GUTHERZ

1. See Warren P. Brown, *Carl Gutherz 1844–1907* (exhib. cat., Brooks Memorial Art Gallery, Memphis, 1968); William Heidrich, "Carl Gutherz," *West Tennessee Historical Society Papers*, 40 (Dec. 1986), pp. 1–5; and Douglas K. Hyland, "Carl Gutherz and His Utopian Vision," *Interpretations: A Journal of Ideas, Analysis and Criticism* (Memphis State University, Department of English), 13 (Spring 1982), pp. 45–71.
2. Heidrich, op. cit., p. 1, quotes Gutherz's "Green Book," an unpublished notebook in the collection of his son, Marshall Goodheart, which explains that both of Gutherz's parents had artistic talent (his father was an accomplished draftsman and a potter) and that the artist had supported himself as a young man by making election transparencies in Cincinnati during the John Charles Frémont campaign in 1856 and "patruns *[sic]* for Guns and Machinery for Gun boats" in Memphis.
3. Clara Erskine Clement and Laurence Hutton, *Artists of the Nineteenth Century and Their Works* (Boston, 1879), vol. 1, p. 321, note that Gutherz was also a student of Cabasson in Paris.
4. Clement and Hutton, op. cit., state that Gutherz studied with Joseph Stallaert and A.N.N. Robert in Belgium and Antwerp after leaving Paris. Hyland, op. cit., p. 48, notes that Gutherz copied works by Rubens in Belgium, and that his study of seventeenth-century Flemish and Dutch painters impelled him to seek instruction in Munich, where he became a student of Wilhelm von Kaulbach at the Royal Academy in 1871.
5. Gutherz's Mardi Gras designs, which he continued to do through 1881, are discussed in Joseph S. Czestochowski, Jr., *Carl Gutherz 1844–1907: Designs for Memphis Celebrations 1873–1881* (exhib. cat., Brooks Memorial Art Gallery, Memphis, 1974). Hyland, op. cit., p. 55, notes that Gutherz did similar work for the annual St. Louis Veiled Prophet celebration.
6. According to Hyland, op. cit., Gutherz founded the St. Louis School of Fine Arts with Halsey G. Ives and served on the school's faculty for nine years.
7. The 1889 catalogue does not cite Gutherz's studies under Pils and Cabasson in the early 1870s; by the time he returned to Paris, in the mid-1880s, he was in all likelihood a colleague rather than a student. Michael Quick, *American Expatriate Painters of the Late Nineteenth Century* (exhib. cat., Dayton Art Institute, 1976), p. 102, notes that Gutherz served as a critic at the Académie Julian.
8. Gutherz, "Greenbk2," p. 4, from typescript. Courtesy William Heidrich, Memphis Brooks Museum of Art.
9. Gutherz, "Lux-Incarnationis (Light of the Incarnation)." Courtesy William Heidrich, Memphis Brooks Museum of Art.
10. Letter from Gutherz to Rush Hawkins, May 14, 1889, Scrapbook, no. 14, p. 5 (Annmary Brown Memorial Library, Brown University, Providence, R.I.).
11. Gutherz, "Thoughts and Ideas" (unpublished notebook), p. 37, cited in Hyland, op. cit., p. 52.
12. The two other paintings were *Arcessita ab Angelis* and *Temptation of St. Anthony*.
13. Gutherz, "The Blue Book" (unpublished notebook), pp. 120 ff., cited in Hyland, op. cit., p. 64.
14. See Hyland, op. cit.

HARRISON, A.

1. Ishmael, "Through the New York Studios–I. Alexander Harrison," *Illustrated American*, 5 (Jan. 3, 1891), pp. 238–39.
2. See his letter to the editor, *New York Herald* (Paris ed.), May 28, 1889, p. 2, for more on his role as vice-president.
3. See page 28.
4. See Doreen Bolger Burke, *American Paintings in the Metropolitan Museum of Art* (New York, 1980), vol. 3, pp. 159–61; Charles Louis Borgmeyer, "Alexander Harrison," *Fine Arts Journal*, 29 (July–Dec. 1913), pp. 514–42; "Harrison, Painter, Dies in Paris Studio," *New York Times*, Oct. 14, 1930; and William A. Coffin, "Alexander Harrison," *Century Magazine*, 42 n.s., 20 (May–Oct. 1891), p. 637.
5. See David Sellin, *Americans in Brittany and Normandy 1860–1910* (exhib. cat., Phoenix Art Museum, 1982), pp. 39–40, 45–47, and passim.
6. Borgmeyer, op. cit., p. 530.
7. In the Salon it was entitled "*Châteaux en Espagne*." See Burke, op. cit., pp. 160–61.
8. Michael Quick, *American Expatriate Painters of the Late Nineteenth Century* (exhib. cat., Dayton Art Institute, 1976), p. 103.
9. Borgmeyer, op. cit., p. 523. Borgmeyer and Cecilia Beaux (in Sellin, op. cit., pp. 46–47), a fellow painter in Concarneau, give detailed explanations of Harrison's working procedures and theoretical concerns.
10. See Sellin, op. cit., pp. 118–19; Quick, op. cit., p. 103; and *Post Impressionism: Cross Currents in European Painting* (exhib. cat., Royal Academy of Arts, London, 1979), p. 195.
11. Quoted in: *Catalogue of Two Exhibitions of Paintings by Alexander and Birge Harrison* (exhib. cat., Chicago Art Institute, 1913), n.p.
12. Ishmael, op. cit., p. 238.
13. Sadakichi Hartmann, *A History of American Art* (Boston, 1902), vol. 2, p. 178.
14. Theodore Child, "American Artists at the Paris Exhibition," *Harper's New Monthly Magazine*, 79 (Sept. 1889), p. 508.
15. The petition and other manuscript materials documenting the issue are in the archives of the Pennsylvania Academy of the Fine Arts. I am indebted to Cheryl Leibold, archivist at the Pennsylvania Academy, for the discovery of this material.
16. *Post Impressionism* (exhib. cat., Royal Academy of Arts, London, 1979), pp. 205–6, 345–46.

HARRISON, B.

1. H. Barbara Weinberg, "Nineteenth-Century American Painters at the École des Beaux-Arts," *American Art Journal*, 13 (Autumn 1981), p. 73.
2. For Harrison's activities in France, see David Sellin, *Americans in Brittany and Normandy 1860–1910* (exhib. cat., Phoenix Art Museum, Ariz., 1982).
3. Birge Harrison, *Landscape Painting* (New York, 1909), p. 137.
4. Susan Grant, "American Paintings Acquired by the French Government, 1879–1900" (master's thesis, George Washington University, 1983), pp. 40–42. Grant further notes that Walter Gay in 1885 and Robert William Vonnoh in 1890 executed large Salon paintings entitled *November*, each of which had a theme similar to Harrison's.
5. George William Sheldon, *Recent Ideals of American Art* (New York and London, 1888), vol. 6, p. 106.
6. See Jennifer A. Martin Bienenstock, *The Forgotten Episode: Nineteenth Century American Art in Belgian Public Collections* (exhib. cat., American Cultural Center, Brussels, 1987), pp. 40–41.
7. Harrison, op. cit., pp. 138–39.

HEALY

1. See Healy's *Reminiscences of a Portrait Painter* (Chicago, 1894), pp. 77–106, and Albert Boime, *Thomas Couture and the Eclectic Vision* (New Haven, 1980), pp. 574–78.
2. Healy also incorporated them into his own *Talks on Art*, 2 vols. (Boston, 1894–95).
3. Boime, op. cit., p. 577.
4. Healy, *Reminiscences*, p. 25. Healy was brought to Sully's attention by Jane Stuart, the daughter of the portrait painter Gilbert Stuart, who had painted a portrait of Healy's father.
5. One was a history painting and thirteen were portraits.
6. Healy presented the Newberry Library, Chicago, with a large number of his portraits in 1887. The portrait of Lord Lytton was among those delivered in a second shipment from Paris in 1892.
7. Marie de Mare, *G.P.A. Healy, American Artist: An Intimate Chronicle of the Nineteenth Century* (New York, 1954), pp. 209–10. See Carol Troyen, *The Boston Tradition: American Paintings from the Museum of Fine Arts, Boston* (New York, 1980), p. 132, for a discussion of Healy's portrait of Brownson. See also *Dictionary of American Biography* (New York, 1929), vol. 3, pp. 178–79; Henry F. Brownson, "Orestes Brownson," *Catholic Encyclopedia* (New York, 1908), vol. 3, pp. 1–3.
8. Healy was invited to come to Chicago by the city's first mayor, William B. Ogden. He painted about 500 portraits during the twelve years he lived there, many of which were lost in the Chicago fire.
9. De Mare, op. cit., p. 209, notes that Healy painted a third portrait of Brownson later in Paris.
10. Lytton (1831–1891), the son of the English novelist Edward Bulwer-Lytton, was educated at Harrow and privately in Bonn. A career diplomat, he was viceroy of India from 1876 to 1880 and ambassador to France from 1887 until his death, in 1891.

HENRY

1. See Elizabeth McCausland, *The Life and Work of Edward Lamson Henry, N.A. (1841–1919)* (Albany, 1945) and *The Works of E.L. Henry: Recollections of a Time Gone By* (exhib. cat., R.W. Norton Art Gallery, Shreveport, La., 1987).
2. See Maureen Radl and Jan Christman, *E.L. Henry's Country Life* (Cragsmoor, New York, 1981); Barbara Buff, "Cragsmoor: An Early American Art Colony," *Antiques*, 114 (Nov. 1978), pp. 1056–65; Margaret Hakam and Susan Houghtaling, *Cragsmoor—An Historical Sketch* (Cragsmoor, New York, 1983).
3. Two versions of the painting exist; the other (unlocated) is dated 1884 and though identical in composition is slightly bigger. The New York State Museum in Albany owns a photograph of the 1884 version, which is also documented in McCausland, op. cit., p. 181. Henry was known to paint similar versions of popular works, as well as many variations on a favorite theme. One of these versions was exhibited at the National Academy of Design in 1886.
4. For information pertaining to this painting and to Henry's life in Cragsmoor I am indebted to Kaycee Benton Para, who is conducting research on the Cragsmoor artists and plans a biography of Henry. She identified the models in a letter dated August 17, 1988.
5. Para owns a photograph of the 1884 painting signed by Henry, titled *The Latest News*. However for the Exposition he labeled it *The Latest Village Scandal*.

HITCHCOCK

1. Christian Brinton, "George Hitchcock—Painter of Sunlight," *International Studio*, 26 (July 1905), pp. i–vi.
2. Lionel G. Robinson, "Mr. George Hitchcock and American Art," *Art Journal*, 43 (Oct. 1891), pp. 289–95.
3. Hitchcock's influence benefited one of his students, Agnes O'Halloran of St. Paul, Minn., with whom he had an affair. According to an article entitled "Hitchcock Elopes," *New York Herald*, June 25, 1889, p. 1, "Miss O'Halloran attempted to paint some Dutch sketches, one of which, after the 'master' had completed it and sufficiently used his influence with the jury, was placed on the top line in the American gallery in the Exhibition."
4. Richard Muther, *The History of Modern Painting* (London, 1907), vol. 4, pp. 303–4.
5. Theodore Child, "American Artists at the Paris Exhibition," *Harper's New Monthly*, 79 (Sept. 1889), p. 508. The halo that originally appeared about the Virgin's head, and is seen in the *Illustrated Salon Catalogue 1888*, Hitchcock apparently painted out after the 1888 Salon exhibition, changing the headdress so that it merely suggested a halo.
6. "George Hitchcock," *Art Amateur*, 22 (Feb. 1890), pp. 54–56. This article states that in America the large white lilies are referred to as "Annunciation lilies," which perhaps accounts for the current title. It also records praise for the painting in French periodicals.
7. Child, op. cit., p. 508.
8. I am grateful to Milo Naeve, Field McCormick Curator of American Art at the Art Institute of Chicago, for supplying the exhibition history and documentation of this painting from the departmental files. Biographical information on Hitchcock is found in Doreen Bolger Burke, *American Paintings in the Metropolitan Museum of Art* (New York, 1980), vol. 3, pp. 113–15.
9. See also Richard R. and Caroline B. Brettell, *Painters and Peasants in the Nineteenth Century* (Geneva, 1983).
10. Walter MacEwen, who also worked in Holland, settled in Haarlem, not Egmond. I am grateful to Dr. Annette Stott, who has written extensively about American artists in the Netherlands, for sharing the results of her research with me.
11. Child, op. cit., p. 508, criticized the figures.

HOVENDEN

1. See Natalie Spassky, *American Paintings in the Metropolitan Museum of Art* (New York, 1985), vol. 2, pp. 541–42.
2. *New York Herald*, May 16, 1884, p. 4.
3. George Gebbie, *The Battle Hymn of the Republic*, p. 7, reproduced in Scrapbooks of Thomas Hovenden, Archives of American Art, Roll P13, frame 11.
4. A newspaper clipping in Hovenden's Scrapbooks (Archives of American Art, Roll P13) records that Battell also bought the later Civil War picture and was considering establishing a gallery of American historical art.
5. Letter in Hovenden Scrapbooks, Archives of American Art, Roll P13.
6. See E. P. Richardson, *American Art: An Exhibition from the Collection of Mr. and Mrs. John D. Rockefeller, 3rd* (Fine Arts Museums of San Francisco, 1976), p. 180.

INNESS

1. George Inness, "A Painter on Painting," *Harper's New Monthly Magazine*, 56 (Feb. 1878).
2. See Nicolai Cikovsky, Jr., *The Life and Works of George Inness* (New York, 1977); Leroy Ireland, *The Works of George Inness: An Illustrated Catalogue Raisonné* (Austin, 1965); and Metropolitan Museum of Art, *American Paradise: The World of the Hudson River School*, introduction by John K. Howat (New York, 1987), p. 232.
3. *New York Herald*, March 9, 1889. Quoted in Cikovsky, *The Life and Works of George Inness*, p. 95.
4. Cikovsky, op. cit.
5. *New York Herald*, March 8, 1889.
6. "Fine Arts: The Sixth Annual Exhibition of The Society of American Artists," *The Nation*, April 12, 1883, p. 327.
7. *New York Herald*, March 9, 1889.
8. *Art Amateur*, 21 (Nov. 1889), p. 115.
9. Jennifer A. Martin Bienenstock, "The Formation and Early Years of the Society of American Artists: 1877–1884" (Ph.D. dissertation, City University of New York, 1983), p. 140.
10. See Nicolai Cikovsky, Jr., and Michael Quick, *George Inness* (exhib. cat., Los Angeles County Museum of Art, 1985), p. 162.

JOHNSON

1. See Patricia Hills, "The Genre Paintings of Eastman Johnson" (Ph.D. dissertation, New York University, 1973), especially pp. 125–26. See also her *Eastman Johnson* (New York, 1972).
2. The painting is thoroughly catalogued in Natalie Spassky, *American Paintings in the Metropolitan Museum of Art* (New York, 1985), vol. 2, pp. 233–36.
3. See Albert Boime, *Thomas Couture and the Eclectic Vision* (New Haven and London, 1980), pp. 595–602.
4. See Hills, op. cit. (1973), pp. 126, 158–59, and "American Studio Talk," *International Studio* 5 (1898), suppl., pp. ii–iii. About 1875, Johnson painted two similar cabinet-sized versions of *Milton Dictating to His Daughters* and exhibited one at the Philadelphia Centennial of 1876. Munkácsy's well-known painting on the same theme dates from 1878 and resembles Johnson's in composition but is much larger, with nearly life-sized figures. Johnson, in turn, copied the Munkácsy painting as a sketch sometime around 1879.
5. *Art Amateur*, 20 (April 1889), p. 98.

KELLOGG

1. There has been some question about the year of Kellogg's birth; the latest research, by JoAnne Bowie, great-great-niece of the artist, has established 1862 as correct.
2. Chris Pettys, *Dictionary of Women Artists* (Boston, 1985), p. 385.
3. Much of the biographical material about Kellogg was supplied by JoAnne Bowie, who kindly gave me her transcripts of Kellogg's letters in the Archives of American Art. Two small catalogues written by Melissa Pierce Williams of Williams & McCormick to accompany their circulating exhibition of some of Kellogg's paintings have also been helpful.
4. Letter to her sister Mary, Sept. 24, 1888. Archives of American Art.
5. Letter to her sister Kate, Feb. 19, 1888. Archives of American Art.
6. Letter to her sister Gertrude, Sept. 1888. Archives of American Art.
7. Letter numbered 440, Archives of American Art. An oil study (16 x 12") for the finished painting is included in the present exhibition (Collection JoAnne Bowie).
8. Letter to her mother, May 23, 1888. Archives of American Art.
9. Letter numbered 510, Archives of American Art.
10. "Art and Artists," *The Graphic* (May 28, 1892), pp. 398–99.

KNIGHT

1. Sources on Knight, centering on *Hailing the Ferry* and a drawing for it, include: Jennifer A. Martin Bienenstock, *The Forgotten Episode: Nineteenth-Century American Art in Belgian Public Collections* (exhib. cat., American Cultural Center, Brussels, 1987), pp. 46–47; *The Quest for Unity: American Art Between the World's Fairs 1876–1893*, essay by David Huntington (exhib. cat., Detroit Institute of Arts, 1983), pp. 234–35; David Sellin, *Americans in Brittany and Normandy 1860–1910* (exhib. cat., Phoenix Art Museum, 1982), pp. 191–92 and passim; Michael Quick, *American Expatriate Painters of the Late Nineteenth Century* (exhib. cat., Dayton Art Institute, 1976), pp. 107–8.
2. See Albert Boime, "The Instruction of Charles Gleyre and the Evolution of Painting in the Nineteenth Century," *Charles Gleyre ou les illusions perdues* (exhib. cat., Kunstmuseum, Winterthur; 1974), pp. 102–25.
3. See William Steven Feldman, "The Life and Work of Jules Bastien-Lepage 1848–1884" (Ph.D. dissertation, New York University, 1973), especially chaps. 4, 5, and 8. I am indebted to Dr. Feldman for a conversation about Bastien-Lepage and Knight that further clarified my thinking.
4. The other two (both unlocated) were *The Meeting*, a rustic courtship scene, and *Mourning*, described as an early work. See "American Painters," *New York Herald* (Paris ed.), July 7, 1889.
5. Theodore Child, "American Artists at the Paris Exhibition," *Harper's New Monthly Magazine*, 79 (Sept. 1889), p. 512.
6. See especially M[arianna] G[riswold] van Rensselaer, "Impressions of the International Exhibition of 1889," *Century Magazine*, 17 (Dec. 1889), p. 317.

KOEHLER

1. See Rena Coen, *Painting and Sculpture in Minnesota: 1820–1914* (exhib. cat., University Gallery, University of Minnesota, Minneapolis, 1976).
2. See Elizabeth Broun, "American Paintings and Sculpture in the Fine Arts Building of the World's Columbian Exposition . . ." (Ph.D. dissertation, University of Kansas, 1976), p. 184.
3. See Patricia Hills, *The Painter's America: Rural and Urban Life, 1810–1910* (New York, 1974), p. 123.
4. *New York Times*, April 4, 1886, p. 4. In "Friedrich Pecht on the American Section in the Art Exposition at Munich," *Studio* (Aug. 1888), p. 136, the author defends this aspect of the picture against European critics who do not accept the idea that Koehler's picture is "American."
5. *New York Times*, July 21, 1877, front page.
6. See Philip Foner, *The Great Labor Uprising of 1877* (New York, 1977), pp. 55–77.
7. *New York Times*, April 4, 1886, p. 4.

MacEWEN

1. See Jennifer A. Martin Bienenstock, *The Forgotten Episode: Nineteenth Century American Art in Belgian Public Collections* (exhib. cat., American Cultural Center, Brussels, 1987), pp. 50–52; Annette Stott, "American Painters Who Worked in the Netherlands, 1880–1914" (Ph.D. dissertation, Boston University, 1986), pp. 262–65, 337–38, and passim; *The Quest for Unity: American Art Between the World's Fairs 1876–1893* (exhib. cat., Detroit Institute of Arts, 1983), pp. 236–37; list of awards and principal works compiled by Walter MacEwen on file at the American Academy and Institute of Arts and Letters, New York.
2. In his early years MacEwen seems to have been especially peripatetic. When he exhibited in the 1883 Munich International Art Exhibition, he listed his residence as Munich, and Bienenstock, op. cit., notes he opened a studio in Egmond aan Zee, Holland, in 1883.
3. The former are documented in *The Quest for Unity* (cited in n.1), p. 236, the latter in a series of indexed scrapbooks of newspaper and magazine articles chronicling the careers of Chicago artists in The Ryerson and Burnham Libraries, Art Institute of Chicago (hereinafter cited as AIC scrapbooks), especially *Chicago Record Herald*, Oct. 22, 1905 (AIC scrapbook, vol. 21, p. 93), and an unlabeled clipping illustrating *The Yellow Robe*, c. 1905 (AIC scrapbook, vol. 21, p. 95). I am indebted to Woodman Taylor, Art Institute of Chicago, for providing me with copies of these clippings.
4. A letter from MacEwen dated March 7, 1938, in the curatorial files of the Cleveland Museum of Art notes that he kept a studio in Hattem for "a large

part of twenty years." Other sources record him in Volendam, Egmond, and Haarlem, but Stott, op. cit., p. 286, notes she has found no evidence of studios in those towns. MacEwen undoubtedly did extensive sketching all over Holland, painting his final works in Hattem and Paris.

5. *Philadelphia Evening Post*, Jan. 12, 1901 (AIC scrapbook, vol. 13, p. 113).
6. *Chicago American*, Nov. 25, 1905 (AIC scrapbook, vol. 21, p. 107).
7. *Philadelphia Evening Post*, Jan. 12, 1901 (AIC scrapbook, vol. 13, p. 113) and American Academy list (see n. 1).
8. While it portrays Volendamers, MacEwen stated he painted *A Ghost Story* in Hattem (see n. 4).
9. Quoted in *The Quest for Unity* (cited in n. 1), p. 237.
10. See Christopher Monkhouse, "The Spinning Wheel as Artifact, Symbol, and Source of Design," in *Victorian Furniture: Essays from a Victorian Society Autumn Symposium*, ed. by Kenneth L. Ames (*Nineteenth Century*, 8, nos. 3–4 [1982], pp. 153–73).
11. Stott, op. cit., chap. 3, pp. 73–116, makes this point.
12. Ronald de Leeuw, John Sillevis, and Charles Dumas, eds., *The Hague School—Dutch Masters of the 19th Century* (exhib. cat., Royal Academy of Arts, Musée du Louvre, and Haags Gemeentemuseum, 1983).
13. Mary Ann Goley, *The Hague School and Its American Legacy* (exhib. cat., Board of Governors of the Federal Reserve System, Washington, D.C., 1982). MacEwen's ties with The Hague School artists have yet to be defined.
14. Stott, op. cit., p. 344, n. 19.

MELCHERS

1. Melchers and Sargent each received the medal of honor.
2. Joseph G. Dreiss, in *Gari Melchers: His Works in the Belmont Collection* (Charlottesville, Va., 1984), p. 1. Belmont (the Gari Melchers Memorial Gallery, Fredericksburg, Virginia) was the home of Gari Melchers from 1916 to 1932. A major retrospective exhibition of Melchers' work is scheduled for 1990. I am grateful to Joanna D. Catron, assistant director, Belmont, for providing copies of critical reviews of Melchers' paintings from Belmont's extensive archive.
3. The subject of this painting has generally been interpreted as a peasant girl, wearied by her week's labor, asleep in church.
4. Thiébault-Sisson, "L'Art des États-Unis," *L'Exposition de Paris*, 3, no. 58 (Dec. 4, 1889), p. 143, expresses sentiments that typified the French reaction to Melchers in 1889. Describing *The Sermon*, which he called *Femmes de Hollande à l'église*, he wrote: "Et je ne sais ce qu'il faut le plus admirer dans cette toile, ou la merveilleuse fermeté du dessin, ou le charme exquis de la couleur. Toutes ces têtes sont autant de portraits, d'une conscience et d'un scrupule infinis, et le ton lilas des corsages marié au bleu clair du banc d'oeuvre est d'une fraîcheur de tons délicieuse."
5. Although the majority of French critics described this scene as old sailors admiring a toy ship, greater gravity is attributed to the subject by at least two sources—M.G., *Le Nord* (Lille, May 28, 1888), and *L'Avenir de Calvados* (Caen, May 1, 1888), which interpreted the ship's model as part of a votive tablet commemorating a rescue at sea.
6. E. Cardon, *Moniteur des arts* (Paris), June 19, 1888.
7. Albert Wolff, *Figaro–Salon* (Paris), May 1888.
8. P. Vernon, *Le Charivari* (Paris), May 3, 1888, wrote that "this infuriating and abusive *indigotage* should be suppressed."
9. *Communion*, which was later acquired by Rush C. Hawkins, the United States Commissioner to the 1889 Exposition, was given to Cornell University in 1910. According to Joanna D. Catron (letter to MCOB, Oct. 24, 1988), two figures, a bonneted girl in the upper center and a standing man second from top right, were added by Melchers to the painting after the 1891 Berlin International Exposition and probably before the 1893 World's Columbian Exposition, Chicago, where it was again exhibited.
10. Theodore Child, "American Artists at the Paris Exhibition," *Harper's New Monthly Magazine*, 79, no. 472 (Sept. 1889), p. 510.
11. Ibid.
12. Thiébault-Sisson, op. cit.
13. Annette Stott, "American Painters Who Worked in the Netherlands, 1880–1914" (Ph.D. dissertation, Boston University, 1986), discusses the collections of Dutch costumes owned and shared by Melchers and Hitchcock and notes the reappearance of items of clothing in various paintings.

MILLET

1. See H. Barbara Weinberg, "The Career of Francis Davis Millet," *Archives of American Art Journal*, 17 (1977), pp. 2–18. See also Millet's papers at the Archives of American Art, especially Hilda Millet Booth and John Alfred Parsons Millet, "Frank Millet: A Versatile American" (c. 1938), John A. Millet papers, Roll 1100; Francis Millet Rogers, "Frank D. Millet, American of Americans" (c. 1945), Francis Millet Rogers papers, Roll 1096; the Frank Millet scrapbooks at the American Academy and Institute of Arts and Letters, New York; and *The American Renaissance 1876–1917* (exhib. cat., Brooklyn Museum, 1979), pp. 41, 57, 131, 171, and passim.
2. Quoted in Weinberg, op. cit., p. 4.
3. Sometime in the late 1870s, Millet constructed a colonial kitchen in his East Bridgewater, Massachusetts, studio, and in Broadway he rented first a Cotswolds cottage and then a priory called Abbot's Grange. In the 1880s in his New York studio he incorporated a wainscoted room taken from an English house of the Elizabethan period.
4. This is documented by Rogers, op. cit., chap. 8, p. 6.
5. Roll 1100, frame 702–5, Archives of American Art.
6. He used the theme intermittently until 1897.
7. Millet's involvement with classical dress is documented in Weinberg, op. cit., pp. 7–8, and Millet scrapbook 2 (various clippings from 1881–82, including *New York Daily Tribune*, May 16, 1881, and *Freund's Daily* [New York], c. 1881).
8. It was also published in the *Francis Davis Millet Memorial Meeting*, a commemorative book of 1912 issued by the American Federation of Arts. Millet may have painted more than one version of the work, which was known sometimes as *A Water Carrier*.

MONKS

1. Most of the biographical information on Monks is from Jennifer A. Martin Bienenstock, *The Forgotten Episode: Nineteenth Century American Art in Belgian Public Collections* (exhib. cat., American Cultural Center, Brussels, 1987), pp. 23, 25, 64–65.
2. Conversation on Jan. 25, 1989, with Robert A.G. Monks, a great-nephew of Robert Hatton Monks.
3. *Exhibition of Pictures by Edward H. Barnard, Charles H. Hayden, and R. H. Monks* (J. Eastman Chase's Gallery, Boston, Jan. 30–Feb. 13, 1890; Archives of American Art, Smithsonian Institution, Washington, D.C., Roll MB507).
4. *A Grey Day* is referred to as *Landscape—Spring* in the Inventory of American Paintings, National Museum of American Art, Smithsonian Institution, Washington, D.C. The only other listings for Monks in the inventory are the paintings at the Fogg Art Museum, Harvard University, Cambridge, Mass.
5. Monks's painting *Marshes near Ballancourt*, which was shown at J. Eastman Chase's Gallery, Boston, in 1890, was described on the annotated checklist as: "cold blues & grays, mist, grasses, naked willows."
6. Bienenstock, op. cit., pp. 23, 25.

MOORE

1. Maria Humphrey Moore, letter to the director of the Pennsylvania Academy of the Fine Arts (Joseph T. Fraser, Jr.), April 22, 1955, Pennsylvania Academy of the Fine Arts Archives.
2. Pennsylvania Academy of the Fine Arts Student Register, Nov. 2, 1864, no. 453, Pennsylvania Academy Archives, gives the date when Harry H. Moore registered for the class.
3. H. Barbara Weinberg, *The American Pupils of Jean-Léon Gérôme* (Fort Worth, Tex., 1984), p. 102.
4. Letter from Thomas Eakins to Benjamin Eakins, Nov. 1, 1866 (Charles Bregler's Thomas Eakins Collection; purchased with the partial support of the Pew Memorial Trust, Pennsylvania Academy of the Fine Arts Archives). I am grateful to Cheryl Leibold, archivist of the Pennsylvania Academy, for bringing the Eakins letters to my attention.
5. Lloyd Goodrich, *Thomas Eakins* (Cambridge, Mass., and London, 1982), vol. 1, pp. 20–21, 54–59. Goodrich also mentions Moore and Eakins in Spain.
6. Weinberg, op. cit., p. 102, lists Moore as also matriculating on October 21, 1867.
7. Clara Erskine Clement and Laurence Hutton, *Artists of the Nineteenth Century and Their Works* (Boston, 1879), vol. 2, p. 127. Moore also showed *The Moorish Merchant* (unlocated) at the Centennial Exposition. His paintings were shown in four annual exhibitions at the Pennsylvania Academy between 1876 and 1896.
8. *Appleton's Cyclopaedia of American Biography* (New York, 1888), vol. 4, p. 380.
9. "Paintings of Japan by H. H. Moore," *New York Sun*, Nov. 14, 1919, quoted in Eugene A. Hajdel, *Harry H. Moore* (Jersey City, 1950), p. 24.

10. "Oils by Humphrey Moore," unidentified clipping, [Jan.] 1920, clipping file, Pennsylvania Academy of the Fine Arts Library. *L'Equilibriste japonais* was shown in 1891 at the Royal Academy of Arts, London, and at the Pennsylvania Academy the following year. *Japanese Musicians* was exhibited at the World's Columbian Exposition in 1893. Exhibitions of Moore's work that included many of his Japanese scenes were held in November 1919 at the Union League Club in New York and in January 1920 at the Architectural League of New York.
11. They were described as "exquisite Japanese studies" in Theodore Child, "American Artists at the Paris Exhibition," *Harper's New Monthly Magazine*, 79 (Sept. 1889,) p. 518.
12. The present title was given to the work several years ago by the oriental expert at the Butterfield & Butterfield auction house in San Francisco. Yoshiwara Licensed Quarters was the "red-light" district of Tokyo in the seventeenth century.
13. "Exhibition of Paintings of Japanese at the Union League Club in New York," *New York Times* [Nov.] 1919, excerpted in Hajdel, op. cit., pp. 19–20.
14. Clipping from the magazine of the *Philadelphia Press*, 1916, excerpted in Hajdel, op. cit., p. 15.
15. Goodrich, op. cit. vol. 2, p. 272.
16. Hajdel, op. cit., pp. 9–10. The location of the September 1949 New York exhibition is unknown. Hajdel's book, published in 1950, was a follow-up to the exhibition; it includes excerpts from Moore's scrapbook and illustrations of his work and is the only known publication about the artist. The Inventory of American Paintings at the National Museum of American Art, Smithsonian Institution, Washington, D.C., lists seven extant paintings by Moore.

MORAN

1. See John Wilmerding, *American Marine Painting* (Boston, 1968), intro.
2. See Natalie Spassky, *American Paintings in the Metropolitan Museum* (New York, 1985), vol. 2, pp. 308–10; *National Cyclopaedia of American Biography* (New York, 1897), vol. 11, p. 302; Hugh Coleman, "The Passing of a Famous Artist," *Brush and Pencil*, 8 (July 1901), pp. 188–92.
3. See Theodore Sutro, *Thirteen Chapters in American History* (New York, 1905).
4. G.W. Sheldon, "American Painters—Edward Moran," *Art Journal*, 6 (1880), p. 259.

MOSLER

1. *Art Amateur*, 13 (1885), p. 114.
2. *Chicago Tribune*, Feb. 22, 1890, p. 9.
3. *Art Amateur*, 13 (1885), p. 115.
4. See "Friedrich Pecht on the American Section in the Art Exposition at Munich," *The Studio*, 3 (1888), pp. 135–36.
5. Dorothy Weir Young, ed., *The Life and Letters of J. Alden Weir* (New Haven, 1960), p. 170.

PATRICK

1. Kansas newspapers are virtually the only sources of information on Patrick. See *Kansas City Star*, Sept. 4, 1904; *Kansas City Post*, Mar. 1, 1908; *Kansas City Times*, Jan. 20, 1937. "The Home Coming of the Famous Painting *Brutality*," a pamphlet issued by the Jones Dry Goods Store in 1908, recounts the story of the painting. I am indebted to Cherie Wray Smith, Patrick's granddaughter, for making her research available to me.
2. The tie with Chartran is recorded in the *Kansas City Journal Post*, Dec. 3, 1936; Gérôme (spelled Jerome) is mentioned as teaching Patrick animal studies in the *Kansas City Star*, Aug. 3, 1929.
3. Patrick also titled this picture *Psyche* (see *Kansas City Star*, Sept. 4, 1904).
4. Several surviving preparatory studies for the painting are in the family's collection, including an oil on canvas (30 1/2 x 25") of the finished composition.
5. *Brutality* is not listed in the catalogue of the 1888 Salon, but clippings and exhibition reviews indicate it was shown there.
6. *Kansas City Journal*, Mar. 1, 1908; *Kansas City Post*, March 1, 1908.
7. *Kansas City Star*, Dec. 3, 1936.
8. *Art Digest*, Dec. 15, 1936, p. 12.
9. *Kansas City Star*, Dec. 3, 1936. Exhibitions are recorded in 1914, 1915, and 1936. (the year he retired).
10. "Art Exhibit Contains Prominent Persons," *Broadway Valentine Shopper*, May 24, 1961.
11. "Paris Drivers," *New York Herald* (Paris ed.), June 5, 1888.
12. "The Home Coming" records this.
13. Theodore Child, "The Paris Salon," *Harper's Weekly*, 33 (April 21, 1888), p. 287.

PEARCE

1. Doreen Bolger Burke, *American Paintings in the Metropolitan Museum of Art* (New York, 1980), vol. 3, pp. 117–18.
2. George William Sheldon, *Recent Ideals of American Art* (New York and London, 1888), vol. 1, p. 9.
3. Jennifer A. Martin Bienenstock, *The Forgotten Episode: Nineteenth Century Art in Belgian Public Collections* (exhib. cat., American Cultural Center, Brussels, 1987), pp. 15, 16; idem, "From Yankee Ingenuity to Yankee Artistry: American Artists at the Antwerp World's Fair of 1894," *Museum Magazine*, 7 (1987), pp. 36–48.
4. Sheldon, op. cit., p. 10.
5. See Richard R. Brettell and Caroline B. Brettell, *Painters and Peasants in the Nineteenth Century* (Geneva, 1983), pp. 88–89.
6. Theodore Child, "American Artists at the Paris Exhibition," *Harper's New Monthly Magazine*, 79 (Sept. 1889), p. 514.
7. *Evening* is mentioned in Ernest Knaufft, "Pennsylvania Academy Exhibition," *Art Amateur*, 22 (March 1890), p. 75.

POTTHAST

1. The work is known now as *Sunshine*, a title probably assigned to it after it left Potthast's hands.
2. See Arlene Jacobowitz, "Edward Henry Potthast," *Brooklyn Museum Annual*, 9 (1967/68), pp. 113–28.
3. In the catalogue for the Salon of 1889, Potthast lists himself as a student of Cormon.
4. See William H. Gerdts, *American Impressionism* (New York, 1984), p. 244.
5. The Mary Leonhard Ran Gallery in Cincinnati, in a projected catalogue raisonné of Potthast's oeuvre, documents another, slightly more finished, version of this painting in a Cincinnati private collection. This was almost certainly the painting exhibited as *Une Bretonne* in the 1889 Salon, concurrent with the Exposition.
6. "Some Notable Pictures by Cincinnati Artists," *Cincinnati Commercial Gazette*, June 19, 1892, p. 17; quoted in *The Golden Age: Cincinnati Painters of the Nineteenth Century Represented in the Cincinnati Art Museum* (exhib. cat., Cincinnati Art Museum, 1979), p. 93.

REINHART

1. See Ishmael, "Through the New York Studios—II. Charles Stanley Reinhart," *Illustrated American*, 5 (Jan. 10, 1891), pp. 277–81; *American Drawings and Watercolors* (exhib. cat., Carnegie Institute, Pittsburgh, 1985), pp. 79–80, 294, which catalogues the sketch; and John O'Conner, Jr., "From Our Permanent Collection—*Awaiting the Absent*," *Carnegie Magazine*, 25 (June 1951), pp. 204–7.
2. Ishmael, op. cit., p. 278.
3. The painting *Awaiting the Absent* was exhibited at the 1888 Paris Salon; the 1888 Munich International Art Exhibition; the National Academy of Design and the Pennsylvania Academy of the Fine Arts in 1891; and the 1893 Chicago World's Columbian Exposition. It was donated by Andrew Carnegie in 1897 to the Carnegie Institute, which sold it in 1966.
4. A 36-page sketchbook records Reinhart's further studies for the figures in *Awaiting the Absent*. Some of these are illustrated in O'Conner, op. cit., p. 206.

ROBINSON

1. Robinson did not belong to The Ten, he counted among his friends several of its members, including Julian A. Weir, John Twachtman, and Childe Hassam. His interest in French Impressionist techniques, which paralleled theirs, began to evidence itself only in the late 1880s, but his close association with Monet in Giverny confirms that he was a leader in the understanding and promotion of the Impressionist aesthetic.
2. Robinson recalls this visit in an entry of Feb. 11, 1893, in his diary (Frick Art Reference Library, New York).
3. Low discusses the Carolus-Duran atelier and his friendship with Robinson in his *A Chronicle of Friendships* (New York, 1908).

4. See Eliot Clark, *Theodore Robinson: His Life and Art* (Chicago, 1979), p. 5, and Sona Johnston, *Theodore Robinson 1852–1896* (Baltimore Museum of Art, 1973), p. xix. Johnston illustrates an oil sketch by Whistler that was owned by Robinson.

SARGENT

1. Born in Florence of American parents, Sargent studied at the Accademia delle Belli Arti there before he moved to Paris with his family in 1874. After entering the studio of Carolus-Duran, he also began studies at the Ecole des Beaux-Arts. He apparently attended classes at the atelier of Léon Bonnat and at the Académie Julian as well. Major studies of Sargent's life and work are William H. Downes, *John S. Sargent: His Life and Work* (Boston, 1925); Evan Charteris, *John Sargent* (New York, 1927); Charles M. Mount, *John Singer Sargent: A Biography* (New York, 1955); Richard Ormond, *John Singer Sargent: Paintings, Drawings and Watercolors* (New York, 1970); Patricia Hills et al., *John Singer Sargent* (New York, 1986).
2. Stanley Olson, Chronology, in Hills et al., op. cit., pp. 276-83, notes the exhibitions of Sargent's work in Europe and America.
3. Thiébault-Sisson, *"L'Art des Etats-Unis," L'Art de Exposition*, 3, no. 58 (Dec. 4, 1889), p. 143.
4. R.A.M. Stevenson, "J. S. Sargent," *Art Journal*, 50 (1888), p. 68.
5. Montezuma, "My Note Book," *Art Amateur*, 21 (August 1889), p. 46.
6. James Lomax and Richard Ormond, *John Singer Sargent and the Edwardian Age* (Leeds, London, and Detroit, 1979), p. 35. The three sisters were Florence, Mabel, and Clara Vickers, daughters of Colonel Thomas Vickers, the head of a Sheffield engineering firm.
7. In January 1884 Sargent wrote to his friend Violet Paget: "Will you be in England next summer? If so I shall see you there for I am to paint several portraits in the country and three ugly young women at Sheffield. . . ." (letter in collection, Colby College, Waterville, Me.; cited in Lomax and Ormond, op. cit.). Subsequent paintings on this theme include *Mrs. Carl Meyer and Her Children* (1896; Sir Anthony Meyer, Bt), *The Wyndham Sisters* (1899; Metropolitan Museum of Art), and *The Acheson Sisters* (1902; Trustees of the Chatsworth Settlement).
8. Harry Quilter, *Spectator*, May 1, 1886, p. 35.
9. Stevenson, op. cit., p. 68.
10. Trevor Fairbrother, *John Singer Sargent in America* (New York and London, 1986), p. 94. Fairbrother extensively documents the portrait of Mrs. Boit, which he believes may have been painted as a gift to Sargent's hosts rather than as a commissioned portrait.
11. *Boston Morning Journal*, Feb. 4, 1888, supplement; cited in Fairbrother, op. cit., p. 103.
12. Montezuma, op. cit.
13. San Antonio Museum of Art, curatorial records, note that Mrs. Shepard, the former Margaret Louisa Vanderbilt (1845–1924), was a supporter of the Young Women's Christian Association, for which she built the Margaret Louisa Home at 14 East Sixteenth Street, New York. Courtesy John A. Mahey.
14. Montezuma, op. cit.
15. Fairbrother, op. cit., p. 115. The controversy seems to indicate the extent of Sargent's involvement in the selection of his sitters' costumes.
16. Montezuma, op. cit. An English reviewer for the London *Telegraph* in 1890 took even greater offense, asking if the pose were "a study for the higher development of the kangaroo dance." (Quoted in *The Artist*, June 1, 1890, pp. 186–87; cited in Fairbrother, op. cit., p. 117.)
17. "American Painters," *New York Herald* (Paris ed.), July 7, 1889.

SHIRLAW

1. *American Landscape and Genre Paintings in the New-York Historical Society*, compiled by Richard J. Koke (New York, 1982), vol. 3, p. 138.
2. Dorothea A. Dreier, "Walter Shirlaw," *Art in America*, 7 (1919), p. 210.
3. Michael Quick and Eberhard Ruhmer, *Munich and American Realism in the 19th Century* (exhib. cat., E.B. Crocker Art Gallery, Sacramento, Calif., 1978), p. 27. Duveneck, Chase, and Shirlaw were such close friends in Munich that the "trio was christened 'the Father, Son, and Holy Ghost' by the other American artists." Ibid., p. 38.
4. William H. Gerdts, *The Great American Nude: A History in Art* (New York and Washington, D.C., 1974), p. 77.
5. Besides Shirlaw, Kenyon Cox, Sarah Dodson, Wyatt Eaton, Frederick W. Freer, Alexander Harrison, and Elihu Vedder all showed pictures that included the female nude.
6. "The Academy Exhibition," *Art Amateur*, 22 (May 1890), p. 113. *Rufina* is an intriguing and unusual title. Shirlaw may be referring here to Pomponia Rufina, "a vestal virgin in the reign of Caracalla, put to death for violation of her vow of chastity." See William Smith, ed., *Dictionary of Greek and Roman Biography and Mythology* (Boston, 1849), vol. 3, p. 493.

SIMMONS

1. *Dictionary of American Biography*, s.v. "Edward Emerson Simmons"; Arthur Hoeber, "Edward Emerson Simmons," *Brush and Pencil*, 5 (March 1900), pp. 241–48; Edward Emerson Simmons, *From Seven to Seventy—Memoirs of a Painter and a Yankee* (New York and London, 1922); and Kathleen Walsh Rosetti, "Edward Emerson Simmons: Gilded Age Artist," unpublished paper, 1984. I am indebted to Kathleen Walsh Rosetti for sharing her research with me.
2. See David Sellin, *Americans in Brittany and Normandy, 1860–1910* (exhib. cat., Phoenix Art Museum, 1982), especially pp. 43–45.
3. Michael Jacobs, *The Good and Simple Life: Artist Colonies in Europe and America* (Oxford, 1985), pp. 143–66, describes life in St. Ives.
4. Simmons, op. cit., p. 222.
5. Peter Davies, *The St. Ives Years* (London, 1984), pp. 6–8.
6. See Bruce Weber and William H. Gerdts, *In Nature's Ways: American Landscape Painting of the Late Nineteenth Century* (exhib. cat., Norton Gallery of Art, West Palm Beach, Fla., 1987), p. 12.
7. Many of them seem to have been nocturnes. He exhibited at the Society of American Artists in 1888 a painting (called *Bay of St. Ives at Evening*) that, judging from a contemporary description, must have greatly resembled *Night*; see "Fine Arts—Society of American Artists—II," *The Nation*, 46 (May 3, 1888), p. 374. Simmons may have repainted and redated the Society of American Artists canvas, transforming it into *Night* for the 1889 Exposition. The *Early Moonlight, Bay of St. Ives* exhibited in the World's Columbian Exposition of 1893 may have been *Night*.
8. Clarence Cook, *Art and Artists of Our Time* (New York, 1888), vol. 3, p. 299; quoted in Weber and Gerdts, op. cit., p. 12.

STEWART

1. See Sue Carson Joyner, "Julius L. Stewart: Life and Work" (master's thesis, Hunter College, New York, 1982); D. Dodge Thompson, "Julius L. Stewart: A 'Parisian from Philadelphia,'" *Antiques*, 130 (Nov. 1986), pp. 1046-58.
2. Thompson, op. cit., p. 1047.
3. George W. Sheldon, cited in Thompson, op. cit., p. 1052, praised his "patrician air."
4. Clarence Cook held this view. See Joyner, op. cit., p. 4.
5. For more on *A Hunt Supper*, see Michael Quick, *American Expatriate Painters of the Late Nineteenth Century* (exhib. cat., Dayton Art Institute, 1976), p. 135.

TARBELL

1. Patricia Jobe Pierce, *Edmund C. Tarbell and the Boston School of Painting 1889–1980* (Hingham, Mass., 1980), p. 18. Later sources include: Carol Troyen, *The Boston Tradition: American Paintings from the Museum of Fine Arts, Boston* (New York, 1980), pp. 186–89; William H. Gerdts, *American Impressionism* (New York, 1984), pp. 114–18, 201-2; Trevor J. Fairbrother, *The Bostonians: Painters of an Elegant Age, 1870–1930* (Boston, 1986), pp. 56–58, 69, 71–72, 226–27.
2. See Sadakichi Hartmann, "The 'Tarbellites,'" *Art News*, 1 (March 1897), pp. 3–4, and *A History of American Art* (Boston, 1902), vol. 2, pp. 237, 247–48.
3. This was Tarbell's second portrait of Emeline. In 1883, before he left to study in Europe, he drew her in charcoal; see Pierce, op. cit., p. 219.
4. William T. Dannat also exhibited a portrait of a woman in a red dress, *La Femme en rouge*.
5. Pierce, op. cit., pp. 89, 219, mistakenly lists the painting's date as 1886 and states that it earned Tarbell membership in the Society of American Artists.
6. Pierce, op. cit., p. 23, compares *In the Orchard* to Renoir's *Luncheon of the Boating Party* (1881; The Phillips Collection, Washington, D.C.). Tarbell had met Renoir in about 1890 and been captivated by his work.

THAYER

1. See Ross Anderson, *Abbott Handerson Thayer* (Syracuse, N.Y., 1982). This is the best monograph to date on Thayer.

2. See unpublished typescript catalogue entry written by Susan Hobbs in the files of the National Museum of American Art, Smithsonian Institution, Washington, D.C.
3. Abbott Thayer, letter of 1912 to the director of the Hillyer Art Gallery, in *Bulletin of the Smith College Hillyer Art Gallery* (March 10, 1937), quoted in *The American Renaissance, 1876–1917* (exhib. cat., Brooklyn Museum of Art, 1979), p. 30.
4. Theodore Child, "American Artists at the Paris Exhibition," *Harper's New Monthly Magazine*, 79 (Sept. 1889), p. 519.
5. "Fine Arts—Society of American Artists—1," *The Nation*, 46 (April 26, 1888), p. 352.
6. The painting was owned in turn by two of Thayer's most important patrons, Arthur Carey and John Gellatly. It was shown in 1922 in the *Memorial Exhibition of the Works of Abbott Handerson Thayer* at the Metropolitan Museum of Art, New York, and in 1949 in the *Centennial Exhibition of Paintings by Abbott Handerson Thayer* at the Smithsonian Institution, Washington, D.C.

VAIL

1. See essay by Louise Gebhard Cann in *Eugene Lawrence Vail: Exposition rétrospective* (exhib. cat., Galerie Jean Charpentier, Paris, 1937), n.p., with an introduction by Henri Le Sidaner. See also David Sellin, *Americans in Brittany and Normandy, 1860–1910* (exhib. cat., Phoenix Art Museum, 1982), p. 159.
2. *Le Port de pêche—Concarneau*, no. 2331, Salon of 1884.
3. *L'Intransigeant* (Paris, c. 1883), quoted in printed text of critical comments on the work of Eugene Vail, curatorial file, Museum of Art, Rhode Island School of Design, Providence.
4. *Sur la Tamise*, no. 2334; illustrated in *Catalogue illustré du Salon* (Paris, 1886), p. 54.
5. *Veuve*, no. 2343, Salon of 1887; illustrated in *Eugene Lawrence Vail: Exposition rétrospective.*
6. See William A. Coffin, "P.A.J. Dagnan-Bouveret," in John C. Van Dyke, ed., *Modern French Masters: A Series of Biographical and Critical Reviews by American Artists* (New York, 1896), pp. 239–48.
7. *Pare à virer*, no. 2422, Salon of 1888; detail of man in center illustrated in *Catalogue illustré du Salon* (Paris, 1888), p. 223.
8. Theodore Child, "American Artists at the Paris Exhibition," *Harper's New Monthly Magazine*, 79 (Sept. 1889), p. 518.
9. Albert Wolff, *Le Figaro*, c. 1889; quoted in Child, op. cit.
10. In *Eugene Lawrence Vail: Exposition rétrospective.*
11. Thiébault-Sisson, "L'Art des États-Unis," *L'Exposition de Paris*, 3 (Dec. 7, 1889), p. 150.

VEDDER

1. *Rubáiyát of Omar Khayyám—The Astronomer Poet of Persia, Rendered into English Verse by Edward FitzGerald with an Accompaniment of Drawings by Elihu Vedder* (Boston, 1884). The original drawings for the book, on which the verses were inscribed, were sold to Vedder's patron Agnes E. Tracy in 1888. They are now in the collection of the National Museum of American Art, Smithsonian Institution, Washington, D.C.
2. *The Last Man* (c. 1886–87, unlocated) and *Love Always Present* (1887; Collection James Ricau, on loan to the Brooklyn Museum, New York) were the two paintings shown in addition to the two in the present exhibition.
3. The first painting, which was exhibited in Rome in 1911 under the title *Angelo della morte* (*Catalogue of the Rome International Exhibition*, Istituto Italiano d'Arti Grafiche, Bergamo, 1911, p. 58), was purchased by the American collector William T. Evans and in 1912 given to the Smithsonian; it is now at the National Museum of American Art.
4. Anita Vedder, letter to Mr. Rathbun, May 21, 1912, Rome; cited in Regina Soria, *Elihu Vedder: American Visionary Artist in Rome* (Cranbury, N.J., 1970), p. 333. See also Vedder's autobiography, *Digressions of V.* (Boston, 1910), and *Perceptions and Evocations: The Art of Elihu Vedder* with an introduction by Regina Soria and essays by Joshua C. Taylor, Jane Dillenberger, and Richard Murray (National Collection of Fine Arts, Washington, D.C., 1979).
5. Vedder, letter of Jan. 23, 1900; cited in Soria, op. cit., p. 226.
6. Vedder, letter to J. Millet, June 28, 1883 (Papers of the Houghton Mifflin Company, Houghton Library, Harvard University, Cambridge, Mass.). I am grateful to Milo M. Naeve, Field-McCormick Curator of American Art, Art Institute of Chicago, and his research staff, for this information.

VOLK

1. *National Cyclopaedia of American Biography* (New York, 1930), vol. 100, p. 138. Volk was named after Stephen Arnold Douglas, a cousin of his mother, but he used only the forename Douglas.
2. Volk traveled to Venice during the summers of 1871 and 1872 with another of Inness's American students, William Lamb Picknell (see Doreen Bolger Burke, *American Paintings in the Metropolitan Museum of Art* (New York, 1980), vol. 3, p. 287.
3. Volk went to Minneapolis in 1886 to organize an art school under the auspices of the Minneapolis Fine Art Society and was director of the school until 1893. He then returned to New York to teach at the Art Students League until 1898, the Cooper Union from 1906 to 1912, and the National Academy of Design from 1910 to 1917 (*The Quest for Unity: American Art Between World's Fairs 1876–1893*, essay by David Huntington [exhib. cat., Detroit Institute of Arts, 1983], p. 138). Volk's theory of art instruction as a part of public education was put forth in a pamphlet entitled *Art Education in the Public Schools.*
4. The other painting was *The Puritan Captives* (unlocated), which was also sent to the 1893 World's Columbian Exposition, Chicago.
5. According to a letter from Miss Thompson's daughter, Charlotte Crockett Young, to Samuel Sachs, Minneapolis Institute of Arts, Feb. 22, 1966, Caroline Keith Thompson and her sister, Abbie Gail Thompson, were referred to in the Minneapolis newspapers as "the beautiful Thompson sisters." Courtesy Jane Immler Satkowski.

VONNOH

1. See William H. Gerdts, *American Impressionism* (New York, 1984), and May Brawley Hill, *Grez Days: Robert Vonnoh in France* (exhib. cat., Berry-Hill Galleries, New York, 1987).
2. "The Relationship of Art to Existence," *Arts and Decoration*, 17 (Sept. 1922), pp. 328–29.
3. *National Cyclopaedia of American Biography* (New York, 1897), vol. 7, p. 462.
4. See "Robert Vonnoh, Painter of Men," *Arts and Decoration*, 2 (Sept. 1912), p. 381.

WEEKS

1. See *The Art of Edwin Lord Weeks (1849–1903)* (exhib. cat., University Art Galleries, University of New Hampshire, Durham, 1976) and D. Dodge Thompson, "Edwin Lord Weeks: American Painter of India," *Antiques* 128 (Aug. 1985), pp. 246–58.
2. Thompson, op. cit. (1985), p. 252, notes that an 1875 painting by the Russian Vasily Vereshchagin of a procession in India was a model for Weeks's work.
3. Edwin Lord Weeks, *From the Black Sea Through Persia and India* (New York, 1895).
4. *The Rajah of Jodhpare* was exhibited in the 1888 Salon and the 1891 International Art Exhibition in Berlin before it entered the collection of Kaiser Wilhelm.
5. For discussions of the orientalists, see D. Dodge Thompson, "American Artists in North Africa and the Middle East, 1797–1914," *Antiques* 126 (Aug. 1984), pp. 303–12, and Lynne Thornton, *The Orientalists: Painter-Travellers, 1828–1908* (Paris, 1983).
6. H. Barbara Weinberg advances this argument in *The American Pupils of Jean-Léon Gérôme* (Fort Worth, Tex., 1984), pp. 49–55. *The Last Journey* is also catalogued in *The Quest for Unity: American Art Between World's Fairs 1876–1893*, essay by David Huntington (exhib. cat., Detroit Institute of Arts, 1983), pp. 139–40.
7. Records of the Pennsylvania Academy of the Fine Arts indicate that Weeks exhibited *A Maharajah's Boat on the Ganges* and *A Street in Ahmedabad* in its 54th annual exhibition, in 1883.
8. Michael Quick, *American Expatriate Painters of the Late Nineteenth Century* (exhib. cat., Dayton Art Institute, 1976), p. 88, notes this shift in taste.

WEIR

1. See Dorothy Weir Young, ed., *The Life and Letters of J. Alden Weir* (New Haven, 1960), p. 163.
2. Theodore Child, "American Artists at the Paris Exhibition," *Harper's New Monthly Magazine*, 79 (Sept. 1889), p. 520.
3. See Doreen Bolger Burke, *J. Alden Weir: An American Impressionist* (Newark, Del., 1983), pp. 114–18.
4. See Burke, op. cit., p. 149.
5. American Art Association, Catalogue of American Paintings Belonging to William T. Evans (New York, 1900), no. 163.

WHISTLER

1. Elizabeth and Joseph Pennell, *The Life of James McNeill Whistler* (London, 1908), especially vol. 1, pp. 222, 305–6, and vol. 2, pp. 88–92; Andrew McLaren Young et al., *The Paintings of James McNeill Whistler* (New Haven and London, 1980), especially vol. 1, pp. 133–35, 155–56; Elisabeth Luther Cary, *The Works of James McNeill Whistler* (New York, 1907), pp. 87–88.
2. William Merritt Chase, "The Two Whistlers—Recollections of a Summer with the Great Etcher," *Century Magazine*, n.s. 58 (June 1910), p. 222.
3. In his 1922 autobiography, *From Seven to Seventy* (New York and London), pp. 223–24, Edward Emerson Simmons recounted what he considered the farcical deliberations of the jury, led by one unnamed member. When questioned by Simmons, the juror declared that he disliked Whistler so much he would never vote for his work.
4. James McNeill Whistler, *The Gentle Art of Making Enemies* (London, 1892), pp. 264–76.
5. Whistler, op. cit., p. 270.
6. Whistler added the phrase *La Dame au Brodequin Jaune* (Lady with the Yellow Buskin) to the title for the exhibition of his work in 1892 at Goupil Brothers, London.

WHITTREDGE

1. See Cheryl A. Cibulka, *Quiet Places: The American Landscapes of Worthington Whittredge* (exhib. cat., Adams Davidson Gallery, Washington, D.C., 1982) and *American Paradise: The World of the Hudson River School* (exhib. cat., Metropolitan Museum of Art, New York, 1987), pp. 179–93 and passim. See also Anthony Janson, "The Paintings of Worthington Whittredge" (Ph.D. dissertation, Harvard University, 1979).
2. Cibulka, op. cit., pp. 26–27, documents Whittredge's experience at the Centennial; the Gifford Pinchot Papers, Library of Congress, note Whittredge's duties on the 1878 Exposition commission. I am indebted to Anthony Janson for this information.
3. See Janson, op. cit., pp. 112–25, and Cibulka, op. cit., pp. 26–28.
4. Cibulka, op. cit., p. 28 (where the painting is entitled *Harvest of Seaweed*); and, in conversation on Oct. 20, 1988, with Anthony Janson.
5. Illustrated in Charles M. Kurtz, ed., *National Academy Notes . . . of the Fifty-Ninth Spring Exhibition* (New York, 1884), p. 30.
6. Cibulka, op. cit., p. 29.
7. Information on these mid-1880s versions of *A Brook in the Woods* is from Anthony Janson, in the conversation cited in n. 4.
8. Illustrated in Charles M. Kurtz, ed., *National Academy Notes and Complete Illustrated Catalog, 1888* (New York, 1888), p. 69.
9. Since this painting does not seem to have appeared at the Academy, it may have been a commission resulting from the exhibiting of the large picture in the Exposition. See Kenneth Myers, *The Catskills: Painters, Writers and Tourists in the Mountains, 1820–1895* (exhib. cat., Hudson River Museum, Yonkers, New York, 1987), pp. 191–92.
10. John I.H. Baur, ed., *The Autobiography of Worthington Whittredge 1820–1910* (New York, 1969 [1942]), p. 42.

WYANT

1. See *Alexander Helwig Wyant 1836–1892* (exhib. cat., Utah Museum of Fine Arts, University of Utah, Salt Lake City, 1968); and Natalie Spassky, *American Paintings in the Metropolitan Museum of Art* (New York, 1985), vol. 2, pp. 411–20.
2. See Lizzie W. Champney, "The Summer Haunts of American Artists," *Century Magazine*, 30 (May–Oct. 1885), p. 858; and Sandra S. Phillips and Linda Weintraub, eds., *Charmed Places: Hudson River Artists and Their Houses, Studios and Vistas* (exhib. cat., Edith C. Blum Institute, Bard College and Vassar College Art Gallery, 1988), pp. 75–76; 95–96.
3. For a stylistic analysis and reproductions, see Eliot Clark, *Alexander Wyant* (New York, 1916) and *Sixty Paintings by Alexander Wyant* (New York, 1920).
4. See Peter Bermingham, *American Art in the Barbizon Mood* (exhib. cat., National Collection of Fine Arts, Washington, D.C., 1975), and *Tonalism, an American Experience* (exhib. cat., Grand Central Art Galleries, New York, 1982).
5. See *Art Amateur*, 20 (April 1889), p. 98, and "Our Artistic Show at Paris," *New York Herald*, March 8, 1889.

French Paintings

BASTIEN-LEPAGE

1. See Henri Houssaye, *L'Art francais depuis dix ans* (Paris, 1883), p. 36. Julian Alden Weir, in "Jules Bastien-Lepage," in John C. Van Dyke, ed., *Modern French Masters: A Series of Biographical and Critical Reviews by American Artists* (New York, 1896), pp. 227–34, recounts the impact of Bastien-Lepage's art on American contemporaries. Kenneth McConkey, in "The Bouguereau of the Naturalists: Bastien-Lepage and British Art," *Art History*, 3 (Sept. 1978), pp. 371–82, discusses Bastien-Lepage's influence on English and Scottish artists.
2. See K[enneth] McC[onkey], "Jules Bastien-Lepage," in Gabriel P. Weisberg, *The Realist Tradition: French Painting and Drawing 1830–1900* (Cleveland, 1980), pp. 267–69; Marie-Madeleine Aubrun, *Jules Bastien-Lepage 1848–1884, Catalogue raisonné de l'oeuvre* (Paris, 1984); Walter S. Feldman, "The Life and Work of Jules Bastien-Lepage, 1848–1884" (Ph.D. dissertation, New York University, 1973); Louis de Fourcaud, *Bastien-Lepage: Sa Vie et ses oeuvres* (Paris, 1885); Ada Cartwright, *Jules Bastien-Lepage* (London, 1894).
3. See Frances Weitzenhoffer, "First Manet Paintings to Enter an American Collection," *Gazette des Beaux-Arts*, 6 (March 1981), pp. 125–29.
4. The curatorial files of the Milwaukee Art Museum note that E.P. Allis of Milwaukee acquired the painting by 1888, possibly through the firm of Arthur Tooth and Son, London, which had exhibited the painting in November of 1882 (see McConkey, op. cit., p. 375), or through the firm's Milwaukee agent, Bressler Gallery.
5. Nineteen paintings by Jules Bastien-Lepage were shown in the Exposition Centennale of the 1889 world's fair. *The Thames, London* was not among them.
6. Paul Mantz, "La Peinture française," *Gazette des Beaux-Arts*, 31 (Oct. 1889), p. 365.

BONNAT

1. See William R. Johnston, *The Nineteenth Century Paintings in the Walters Art Gallery* (Baltimore, 1982), pp. 123–26, and A.C.J. [Anne Clark James], "Léon Bonnat," in Gabriel P. Weisberg, *The Realist Tradition: French Painting and Drawing 1830–1900* (Cleveland, 1980), pp. 271–73.
2. Weisberg, op. cit., p. 272.
3. Edwin H. Blashfield, "Léon Bonnat," in John C. Van Dyke, ed., *Modern French Masters: A Series of Biographical and Critical Reviews by American Artists* (New York, 1896), pp. 47–56. Blashfield and Thomas Eakins were among the first of many Americans to study at Bonnat's atelier. Bonnat's collection of old master drawings, which is mentioned by Blashfield, op. cit., p. 55, is now housed in the Musée Bonnat, Bayonne.
4. Bonnat's orientalist paintings are noted in Donald A. Rosenthal, *Orientalism: The Near East in French Painting, 1800–1880* (Rochester, 1982); *The Barber of Suez* is illustrated, p. 96. Other orientalist subjects by Bonnat, noted by Johnston, op. cit., pp. 123–24, include *An Arab Sheik* (Walters Art Gallery), *A Fellah Woman and Her Child* (1870), *Sheiks of Akkabah* (1872), and *Turkish Barber* (1873).

BOUGUEREAU

1. For discussions of Bouguereau's life and work and a current bibliography, see *William Bouguereau, 1825–1905* (exhib. cat., Montreal Museum of Fine Arts, 1984).
2. Ibid., p. 61: Mark Steven Walker notes that Paul Baudry won the Grand Prix de Rome in the 1850 competition, but a vacancy at the Villa Medici led the jury to award a second Grand Prix, which went to Bouguereau.
3. Edward Strahan, ed., *The Art Treasures of America* (Philadelphia, 1879–82), vol. 1, p. 67.

4. Mark Steven Walker, "Bouguereau at Work," in *William Bouguereau, 1825–1905*, p. 73.
5. Clarence Cook, *Art and Artists of Our Time* (New York, 1888), vol. 1, p. 86.
6. Ibid. Strahan, op. cit., vol. 3, p. 132, lists over seventy paintings by Bouguereau in American collections, exclusive of portrait commissions. Robert Isaacson, "Collecting Bouguereau in England and America," in *William Bouguereau, 1825–1905*, pp. 104–13, also discusses the wide sale of printed reproductions of Bouguereau's paintings.
7. Four of Bouguereau's paintings were shown in the Exposition Centennale, the other ten in the Exposition Décennale.
8. Exposition Universelle de 1889 à Paris, *Rapports du jury international*, "Peintures à l'huile—Peintures diverses et dessins" (Paris, 1890), p. 39.

BOULANGER

1. Judith Landrigen, "The Forbes Magazine Collection at the Palais Mendoub, Tangier," *Antiques*, 121 (June 1982), caption, pl. IV, p. 1386.
2. *Journal des Débats*, Sept. 28, 1849, p. 3; cited in Philippe Grunchec, *The Grand Prix de Rome: Paintings from the Ecole des Beaux-Arts 1797–1863* (exhib. cat., International Exhibitions Foundation, Washington, D.C., 1984–85), p. 104.
3. Lord Pilgrim, *L'Artiste* (Oct. 1849), pp. 207–8; cited in Grunchec, op. cit.
4. Léon Lagrange, "Salon de 1861," *Gazette des Beaux-Arts*, 10 (June 1861), p. 266.
5. Edward Strahan, ed., *The Art Treasures of America* (Philadelphia, 1879–82), vol. 3, p. 124.

BRETON

1. See Hollister Sturges et al., *Jules Breton and the Rural French Tradition* (exhib. cat., Joslyn Art Museum, Omaha, Neb., 1982), and Gabriel P. Weisberg, *The Realist Tradition: French Painting and Drawing 1830–1900* (Cleveland, 1980).
2. William J. Hoppin, chairman of the Advisory Committee on American Art for the 1867 Universal Exposition, in "A Glimpse of Contemporary Art in Europe, Part 2," *Atlantic Monthly*, 22 (Sept. 1873), p. 259. Hoppin is cited in Madeleine Fidell-Beaufort, "Jules Breton in America," in Sturges et al., op. cit., p. 51.
3. Fidell-Beaufort, op. cit., pp. 51–61, discusses Breton's American collectors and notes the market for Breton's paintings, and for prints and photographs after his works, in Belgium and England as well.
4. André Michel, "Le Salon de 1885," *Gazette des Beaux-Arts*, 31 (May 1885), p. 490, praised Breton's expression of the religious solemnity of the hour but found the peasant girl too self-conscious for a person of her station. Clarence Cook, *Art and Artists of Our Time* (New York, 1888), vol. 2, p. 235, thought the work a piece of pure sentimentality.
5. See Jules Breton, *La Vie d'un artiste: Art et nature* (Paris, 1890), pp. 56–57.
6. Fidell-Beaufort, op. cit., p. 57, and p. 61, n. 68, cites George A. Lucas, *The Diary of George A. Lucas, An American Art Agent in Paris, 1857–1909*, ed. Lilian M.C. Randall, 2 vols. (Princeton, 1979), as recording the arrangements for the etching.
7. See catalogue entry no. 39, *The Song of the Lark*, in Sturges, op. cit., p. 95, for discussion of a 1934 *Chicago Daily News* poll that named this work America's most popular painting.

CABANEL

1. The Grand Prix de Rome was awarded to Léon Bénouville, another student of Picot, in the 1845 competition; Cabanel won second prize but it was elevated to a Grand Prix by the government, which awarded him a pension at the Villa Medici that same year. For a discussion of this painting, see Philippe Grunchec, *The Grand Prix de Rome: Paintings from the Ecole des Beaux-Arts 1797–1863* (exhib. cat., International Exhibitions Foundation, Washington, D.C., 1984–85), pp. 99–102.
2. Emile Zola, *La Situation*, July 1, 1867, reprinted in F.W.J. Hemmings and R.J. Niess, eds., *Emile Zola, Salons* (Geneva, 1959), p. 111.
3. Joseph C. Sloane, *French Painting Between the Past and the Present: Artists, Critics, and Traditions, from 1848 to 1870* (Princeton, 1973 [1951]), p. 122.
4. Georges Lafenestre, "Alexandre Cabanel," *Gazette des Beaux-Arts*, 31 (1889), p. 276.
5. Edward Strahan, ed., *The Art Treasures of America* (Philadelphia, 1879–1882), vol. 1, p. 67. Strahan also notes that Gibson acquired his version of *The Birth of Venus* in 1870.

CAROLUS-DURAN

1. See Gabriel P. Weisberg, *The Realist Tradition: French Painting and Drawing 1830–1900* (Cleveland, 1980), pp. 279–80, for a biography of Carolus-Duran.
2. Letter from Julian Alden Weir to John Henry Niemeyer, Paris, Jan. 11, 1874, quoted in Dorothy Weir Young, ed., *The Life and Letters of Julian Alden Weir* (New York, 1960), p. 28. See also J. Carroll Beckwith, "Carolus-Duran," in John C. Van Dyke, ed., *Modern French Masters: A Series of Biographical and Critical Reviews by American Artists* (New York, 1896), pp. 73–80; Will H. Low, *A Chronicle of Friendships, 1873–1900* (New York, 1908), p. 23; R.A.M. Stevenson, *Velásquez* (London, 1908), pp. 107–8; and a transcription of the artist's own writings in "A French Painter and His Pupils," *Century Magazine*, 31 (1885), pp. 372–76.
3. Lois Marie Fink, "Elizabeth Nourse: Painting the Motif of Humanity," in Mary Alice Heekin Burke, *Elizabeth Nourse (1859–1938), A Salon Career* (exhib. cat., National Museum of American Art, Smithsonian Institution, Washington, D.C., and Cincinnati Art Museum, 1983), p. 11, notes that, largely through the efforts of the Union des Femmes peintres et sculpteurs, the Ecole des Beaux-Arts was officially opened to women in 1897.
4. Carolus-Duran exhibited two paintings in the Exposition Centennale and ten in the Exposition Décennale at the 1889 fair. At least six were portraits of women.
5. Paul Mantz, "La Peinture francaise," *Gazette des Beaux-Arts*, 31 (Nov. 1889), p. 522.

DAGNAN-BOUVERET

1. See Gabriel P. Weisberg, *The Realist Tradition: French Painting and Drawing 1830–1900* (Cleveland, 1980), pp. 238–84. Earlier sources include William A. Coffin, "Dagnan-Bouveret," *Century Magazine* (May 1894), pp. 4–15; P. Dampt, "P.A.J. Dagnan-Bouveret, 1852–1929," in *Catalogue des oeuvres de M. Dagnan-Bouveret (Peintures)* (Paris, 1930).
2. *Horses at the Watering Trough (Chevaux à l'abreuvoir)* was purchased by the French government after it was exhibited at the 1885 Salon. It entered the collection of the Luxembourg Museum and was assigned in 1892 to the Musée des Beaux-Arts, Chambéry. See Gabriel P. Weisberg in "P.A.J. Dagnan-Bouveret, Jules Bastien-Lepage and the Naturalist Instinct," *Arts*, 56 (April 1982), pp. 25ff.
3. Both William A. Coffin (op. cit.) and Julian Alden Weir (Dorothy Weir Young, ed., *The Life and Letters of Julian Alden Weir* [New York, 1960]) attested to Dagnan-Bouveret's importance to young American artists in France. The accounts of the art dealer George A. Lucas (Lilian M.C. Randall, ed., *The Diary of George A. Lucas, An American Art Agent in Paris, 1857–1909* [2 vols., Princeton, 1979]) show that he visited Dagnan-Bouveret's studio several times in the autumn of 1879 and wrote to Walters about the artist's 1879 Salon painting *The Accident* (Walters Art Gallery, Baltimore) in November of that year. Edward Strahan, ed., *The Art Treasures of America* (Philadelphia, 1879–82), notes that Dagnan-Bouveret's *The Lovers' Quarrel* and *Burial of Manon Lescaut* were also in American collections by the early 1880s. By 1894 (see Coffin, op. cit.) American collectors also owned *La Bernoise*, *Young Breton Peasant*, *Madonna*, and *The Blessed Bread*.
4. These were, respectively, *Horses at the Watering Trough* (Luxembourg Museum, Paris), *Madonna* (Munich Pinakothek), *Vaccination* (Turner Collection, London), *The Pardon* (Messrs. Tooth, London), *The Benediction* (Tretiakoff Collection, Moscow), and *The Accident* (William T. Walters, Baltimore).
5. The painting was owned by the London dealers Arthur Tooth and Son, in 1889, but Coffin in 1894 (op. cit., p. 5) illustrates *The Pardon in Brittany*, noting that it was in the collection of George F. Baker.
6. See Charles Sterling and Margaretta M. Salinger, *French Paintings: A Catalogue of the Collection of The Metropolitan Museum of Art, XIX Century* (New York, 1960), vol. 2, pp. 220–21; Gabriel P. Weisberg, "Vestiges of the Past: The Brittany Pardons of Late Nineteenth Century French Painters," *Arts*, 55 (Nov. 1980), pp. 134–38.

DAUBIGNY

1. See Peter Bermingham, *American Art in the Barbizon Mood* (exhib. cat., National Collection of Fine Arts, Washington, D.C., 1975).
2. The American landscape painter Dwight W. Tryon, who sought Daubigny's advice in Paris in the 1870s, wrote of the older artist's encouragement in "Charles-François Daubigny," in John C. Van

Dyke, ed., *Modern French Masters: Biographical and Critical Essays by American Artists* (New York, 1896), pp. 155–66.

3. For biographical and critical appreciations of Daubigny, see: Etienne Moreau-Nelaton, *Daubigny raconté par lui-même* (Paris, 1925); Madeleine Fidell-Beaufort and Janine Bailly-Herzberg, *Daubigny, La Vie et l'oeuvre*, 1, Paris, 1975; Robert Hellebranth, *Charles-François Daubigny* (Morgues, 1976).
4. Another version of this painting, dated 1877, in the collection of Robert Graves of Brooklyn, was sold at the American Art Association, New York, Feb. 9–11, 1887, ill., cat. no. 187. Related works are in the collections of the Metropolitan Museum of Art, New York, and the Cincinnati Art Museum.

GEROME

1. See Gerald M. Ackerman, *The Life and Work of Jean-Léon Gérôme: With a Catalogue Raisonné* (London and New York, 1986), and *Jean-Léon Gérôme (1824–1904)* (exhib. cat., Dayton Art Institute, 1972; text by Gerald M. Ackerman). *The Death of Caesar* is discussed at length by William R. Johnston in *The Nineteenth Century Paintings in the Walters Art Gallery* (Baltimore, 1982), pp. 101ff.
2. See H. Barbara Weinberg, *The American Pupils of Jean-Léon Gérôme* (Fort Worth, 1984).
3. George de Forest Brush in "Open Letters. American Artists on Gérôme," *Century Magazine* (Feb. 1889), p. 635. Also included were letters from Edwin Howland Blashfield, Julian Alden Weir, Kenyon Cox, Will H. Low, Wyatt Eaton, Abbott Thayer and others.
4. Edward Strahan, ed., *The Art Treasures of America*, 3 vols. (Philadelphia, 1879–82) lists over fifty works by Gérôme in American private collections. For an indication of America's enthusiasm for Gérôme, see also Edward Strahan, ed., *Gérôme: A Collection of the works of J.L. Gérôme in one hundred photogravures* (New York, 1881–83). Edward Strahan was the pseudonym of Earl Shinn, an American who had studied under Gérôme in Paris.
5. Strahan, op. cit., vol. 2, pp. 3ff.
6. Dorothy Weir Young, ed., *The Life and Letters of J. Alden Weir* (New York, 1960), p. 45. Johnston, op. cit., p. 101, cites the Yale exhibition as taking place in 1872.

GLEYRE

1. See Paul Mantz, "Charles Gleyre," *Gazette des Beaux-Arts*, 11 (1875), March 1, pp. 233–44, and May 1, pp. 404–14; Charles Clément, *Gleyre, étude biographique et critique* (Paris, 1878); *Charles Gleyre ou les illusions perdues* (exhib. cat., Kunstmuseum, Winterthur, 1974); and *Charles Gleyre, 1806–1874* (exhib. cat., Grey Art Gallery, New York, 1980).
2. The drawings and watercolors made by Gleyre on this trip were brought back to Boston by Lowell, who died soon afterward, and are now the property of the Lowell Institute, Boston. See Nancy Scott Newhouse, "From Rome to Khartoum: Gleyre, Lowell, and the Evidence of the Boston Watercolors and Drawings," in *Charles Gleyre, 1806–1874* (Grey Art Gallery, New York, 1980), pp. 79–117.
3. The Duc de Luynes later had Gleyre's paintings effaced and hired Jean-Auguste-Dominique Ingres to decorate the space with his celebrated *Age d'or*.
4. According to William R. Johnston, *The Nineteenth Century Paintings in the Walters Art Gallery* (Baltimore, 1982), p. 96, this painting, *Lost Illusions*, was commissioned by Walters through the firm of Goupil in 1865. Other oil replicas are in the Walker Art Gallery, Liverpool, and the Kunstmuseum, Winterthur.
5. Edward Strahan, ed., *The Art Treasures of America* (Philadelphia, 1879–82), vol. 2, p. 88, with full-page illus., entitled *Young Roman at the Bath*, opp. p. 88. *The Bath* was first in the collection of John Taylor Johnston of New York, but was sold in 1876. When the painting was described by Strahan, it was already in Smith's collection. Contemporary sources that discuss *The Bath* include *The Second Empire, 1852–1870: Art in France under Napoleon III* (exhib. cat., Philadelphia Museum of Art, 1978), p. 311, and Jefferson C. Harrison, *French Paintings from The Chrysler Collection* (exhib. cat., Chrysler Museum, Norfolk, Va., 1986), pp. 42–44.
6. See Albert Boime, "The Instruction of Charles Gleyre and the Evolution of Painting in the Nineteenth Century," *Charles Gleyre ou les illusions perdues* (Kunstmuseum, Winterthur, 1974), pp. 102–24.

LEFEBVRE

1. Eric Zafran, *French Salon Paintings from Southern Collections* (Atlanta, 1982), p. 138, notes that Pandora, Sappho, Diana, Ondine, and Mary Magdalene were in the series of female nudes painted by Lefebvre. Zafran also discusses the dating of *The Death of Priam*, which he places in 1882.
2. Edward Strahan, ed., *The Art Treasures of America* (Philadelphia, 1879–82), vol. 1, p. 69.
3. Each of these collectors owned several major paintings by Lefebvre. Strahan, op. cit., vol. 3, p. 137, lists sixteen works by Lefebvre that were in important collections by the early 1880s.
4. Lois Marie Fink, "Elizabeth Nourse: Painting the Motif of Humanity," in Mary Alice Heekin Burke, *Elizabeth Nourse, 1859–1938: A Salon Career* (Washington, D.C., 1983), p. 92.

ROLL

1. Collection Musée des Beaux-Arts de la Ville de Paris. Illustrated in André Michel, "Alfred Roll (1846–1919)," *Gazette des Beaux-Arts*, Feb. 1920, pp. 106–26, ill. p. 117.
2. Ibid., p. 116.
3. Ibid., p. 118.
4. According to Michel, op. cit., p. 120, Roll used the word *recherchés* to describe these paintings.
5. Michel, op. cit., pp. 120–22, identifies many of the figures in Roll's painting. I am grateful to Véronique Wiesinger, curator of graphic arts, Centre Georges Pompidou, Paris, and curator at the Museé de Blérancourt, for providing information about the artist.
6. Henri Bouchot, "Les Salons de 1893," *Gazette des Beaux-Arts*, 35 (June 1893), p. 468.
7. Ibid., p. 470; Bouchot described Roll's temperament as "ce que nous nommons un estomac dans nos langages de décadences."
8. Ibid.: "Il est de son temps, il fait ce qu'on lui montre."

Allwood, John. *The Great Exhibitions.* London: Studio Vista, 1977.

———. *Le Livre des expositions universelles 1851–1889.* Paris: Union Centrale des Arts Décoratifs, 1983.

The American Renaissance (exhib. cat., with essays by Richard Guy Wilson, Dianne H. Pilgrim, and Richard N. Murray). Brooklyn Museum, New York, 1979.

Badger, Rodney Reid. *The Great American Fair: The World's Columbian Exposition and American Culture.* Chicago: Nelson Hall, 1979.

Barthes, Roland. *The Eiffel Tower and Other Mythologies.* New York: Hill and Wang, 1979.

Bermingham, Peter. *American Art in the Barbizon Mood* (exhib. cat.). National Collection of Fine Arts, Smithsonian Institution Press, Washington, D.C., 1975.

Bienenstock, Jennifer A. Martin. *The Forgotten Episode: Nineteenth Century American Art in Belgian Public Collections* (exhib. cat.). American Cultural Center, Brussels, 1987.

Boime, Albert. *The Academy and French Painting in the Nineteenth Century.* London: Phaidon Press, 1971.

Brettell, Richard R., and Caroline B. Brettell. Painters and Peasants in the Nineteenth Century. Geneva: Editions d'Art Albert Skira S.A., 1983.

Brincourt, Maurice. *L'Exposition universelle de 1889.* Paris: Frimin-Didot, 1890.

Brownell, W. C. "The Paris Exposition." *Scribner's,* 7 (Jan. 1890), pp. 18–35.

Catalogue officiel de l'Exposition Universelle de 1889. Lille: Imprimerie L. Danel, 1889.

Child, Theodore. "American Artists at the Paris Exhibition." *Harper's New Monthly Magazine,* 79 (Sept. 1889), pp. 489–521.

Complete Official Catalogue of the Paris Universal Exhibition 1867. London and Paris: J. M. Johnson & Sons, 1867.

Curti, Merle. "America at the World's Fairs, 1851–1893." *American Historical Review,* 55 (July 1950), pp. 833–856.

Davis, Julia Finette. "International Expositions, 1851–1900." In *The American Association of Architectural Bibliographers Papers,* edited by William B. O'Neal, vol. 4. Charlottesville: University of Virginia Press, 1967.

Demy, Adolphe. *Essai historique sur les expositions universelles de Paris.* Paris: Alphonse Picard et fils, 1907.

Dumas, F. G., and L. de Fourcaud. *Revue de l'Exposition Universelle de 1889,* 2 vols. Paris: L. Baschet, 1889.

L'Exposition de Paris 1889, 4 vols. Paris: La Librairie Illustrée, 1889.

Figaro–Exposition 1889. Paris, 1889.

Fink, Lois Marie. "The Role of France in American Art, 1850–1870." Ph.D. dissertation, University of Chicago, 1970.

———. "American Participation in the Paris Salons, 1870–1900." In *Saloni, Gallerie, Musei e loro influenza sullo sviluppo dell'arte dei Secoli xix et xx atti del xxiv Congresso Internazionale di Storia dell'Arte,* edited by Francis Haskell, pp. 89–93. Bologna, 1981.

Gerdts, William H. *American Impressionism.* New York: Abbeville Press, 1984.

Gerdts, William H., Diana D. Sweet, and Robert R. Preato. *Tonalism: An American Experience* (exhib. cat., Grand Central Art Galleries). New York: Art Education Association, 1982.

Grant, Susan. "American Paintings Acquired by the French Government 1879–1900." Master's thesis, George Washington University, Washington, D.C., 1983.

Harris, Joseph. *The Tallest Tower: Eiffel and the "Belle Epoque."* Boston: Houghton Mifflin, 1975.

Holt, Elizabeth Gilmore, ed. *The Expanding World of Art, 1874–1902.* Vol. 1, *Universal Expositions and State-sponsored Fine Arts Exhibitions.* New Haven and London: Yale University Press, 1988.

Isaac, Maurice. *Les Expositions en France et dans le régime international.* Paris: Dorbon ainé, 1928.

Jeffery, Edward T. *Paris Universal Exposition 1889.* Chicago: Citizens' Executive Committee, 1889.

Jourdain, Frantz. *Exposition Universelle de 1889. Constructions élevées au Champ-de-Mars par M. Charles Garnier, architect... pour servir à l'histoire de l'habitation humaine.* Paris: Librarie Centrale des Beaux-Arts, 1889.

Kurtz, Charles M., ed. *Official Illustrations from the Art Gallery of the World's Columbian Exposition.* Philadelphia: George Barrie, 1893.

Loyrette, Henri. *Gustave Eiffel.* New York: Rizzoli, 1985.

Mainardi, Patricia. *Art and Politics of the Second Empire: The Universal Expositions of 1855 and 1867.* New Haven: Yale University Press, 1987.

Monod, Emile. *L'Exposition universelle de 1889; grand ouvrage illustré historique, encyclopédique, descriptif publié sous le patronage de M. le Ministre du Commerce, de l'Industrie et des Colonies.* 3 vols. and album. Paris: E. Denton, 1889.

Ory, Pascal. *Les Expositions Universelles de Paris.* Paris: Editions Ramsay, 1982.

Plum, Werner. *World Exhibitions in the Nineteenth Century: Pageants of Social and Cultural Change.* Bonn–Bad Godesberg, 1977.

The Quest for Unity: American Art Between World's Fairs 1876–1893 (exhib. cat.). Essay by David Huntington. Detroit Institute of Arts, 1983.

Quick, Michael. *American Expatriate Painters of the Late Nineteenth Century* (exhib. cat.). Dayton Art Institute, Ohio, 1976.

Reed, J. Eugene. *Selected Paintings from the Paris Exhibition, 1889.* Philadelphia: Gebbie & Co., 1889.

Rensselaer, Mariana Griswold van. "Open Letters: Impressions of the International Exhibition of 1889." *Century Magazine,* 39 (Dec. 1889), pp. 316–18.

Rousselet, Louis. *Exposition Universelle de 1889.* Paris: Librairie Hachette et Cie., 1890.

Reports of the United States Commissioners to the Paris Universal Exposition, 1867. Washington, D.C.: Government Printing Office, 1870.

Reports of the United States Commissioners to the Paris Universal Exposition, 1878. Washington, D.C.: Government Printing Office, 1879.

Reports of the United States Commissioners to the Universal Exposition of 1889 at Paris. 5 vols. Washington, D.C.: Government Printing Office, 1890–91.

Rogers, Joseph. "Lessons from International Exhibitions." *Forum,* 32 (Nov. 1901), pp. 500–510.

Rydell, Robert W. *All the World's a Fair: Visions of Empire at American International Expositions, 1876–1916.* Chicago and London: University of Chicago Press, 1984.

Sellin, David. *Americans in Brittany and Normandy 1860–1910* (exhib. cat.). Phoenix Art Museum, Arizona, 1982.

Sheldon, George William. *Recent Ideals of American Art.* New York and London: D. Appleton & Co., 1890.

Silverman, Debora L. "The 1889 Exhibition: The Crisis of Bourgeois Individualism." *Oppositions,* 8 (Spring 1977), pp. 71–91.

Stanton, Theodore. "America at the Paris Exhibition." *Boston Daily Evening Transcript,* June 29, 1889.

———. "Open Letter: The International Exposition of 1900." *Century Magazine,* 51 (Dec. 1905), p. 317.

Troyen, Carol. "Innocents Abroad: American Painters at the 1867 Exposition Universelle, Paris." *American Art Journal,* 16 (Autumn 1984), pp. 3–29.

Varigny, C. de. "L'Exposition des Etats-Unis." *L'Exposition de Paris (1889).* Vol. 2, pp. 90–91. Paris, 1889.

Walton, William. *Chefs-d'oeuvre de l'Exposition Universelle de Paris, 1889.* 10 vols. Philadelphia: George Barrie, 1889.

Weimann, Jeanne Madeline. *The Fair Women: The Story of The Woman's Building, World's Columbian Exposition.* Chicago: Academy of Chicago, 1981.

Weinberg, H. Barbara. "Nineteenth-Century American Painters at the Ecole des Beaux-Arts." *American Art Journal,* 13 (Autumn 1981), pp. 66–71.

———. *The American Pupils of Jean-Léon Gérôme.* Fort Worth, Tex.: Amon Carter Museum of Western Art, 1984.

[Wister, Sarah Butler]. "Loitering Through the Paris Exposition." *Atlantic Monthly,* 65 (March 1890), pp. 360–74.

Wood, H. T. "Exposition of 1889." *Journal of the Society of Arts,* 38 (Dec. 13, 1889), pp. 45–62.

Paris Universal Exposition 1889

OFFICIAL CATALOGUE OF THE UNITED STATES

Class I—Oil Paintings

Annotated by Annette Blaugrund and Judith Hayward

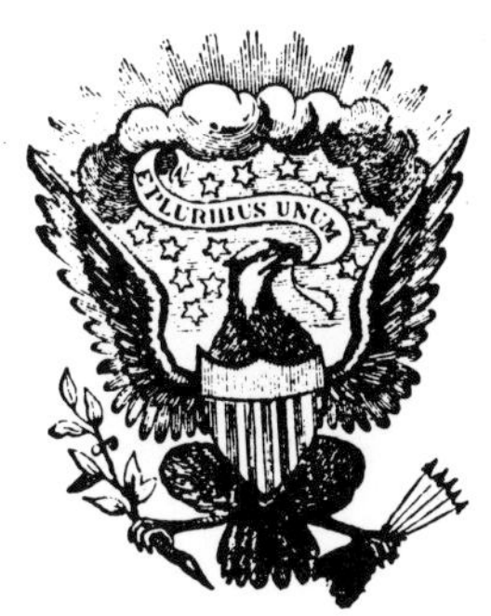

The text of the original catalogue of paintings is set in roman type. Annotations (additions and corrections) are set in italics. For paintings included in the present exhibition, a page reference directs the reader to the illustrated entry in the catalogue section of this book. Short titles are used for books listed in the bibliography. Abbreviations include:

ASL	*Art Students League*
E.U.	*Exposition Universelle*
PAFA	*Pennsylvania Academy of the Fine Arts*
NAD	*National Academy of Design*

ALLEN, Thomas *1849–1924*
Born at Saint-Louis, Mo.; *died Worcester, Mass. Masters: Andreas and Carl Muller, Eugène Drucker*
1. Cattle *(unlocated)*

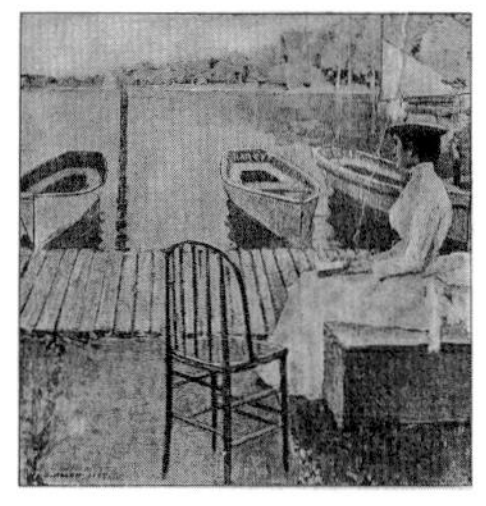
2.

ALLEN, William S*ullivant*
Born at New York, N.Y. Masters: Lefebvre, Claude Monet, Bouguereau. *Recompense: Bronze medal 1889*
2. Evening by the Lake, *1887 (unlocated). Engraving after the painting, from William Walton,* Chefs-d'oeuvre, *vol. 10, p. 109. Photograph courtesy The Library of Congress*

ANDERSON, A*braham* Archibald *1847–1940*
Born at New York. Masters: Bonnat, Cormon and Collin; *Cabanel, Rodin*
3. Portrait of the Right Rev'd A.C. Coxe, bishop of Western New York *(unlocated)*

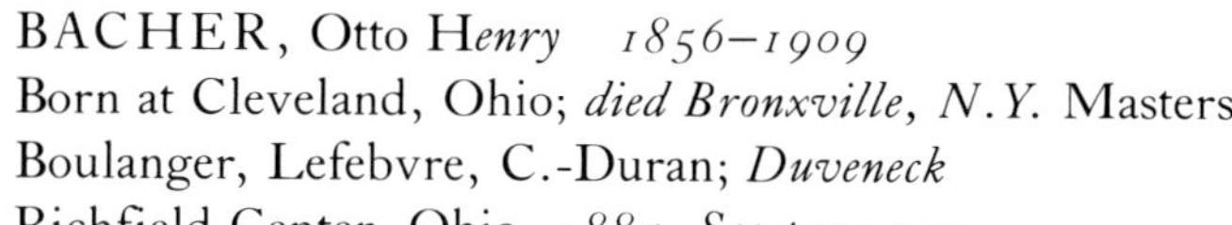

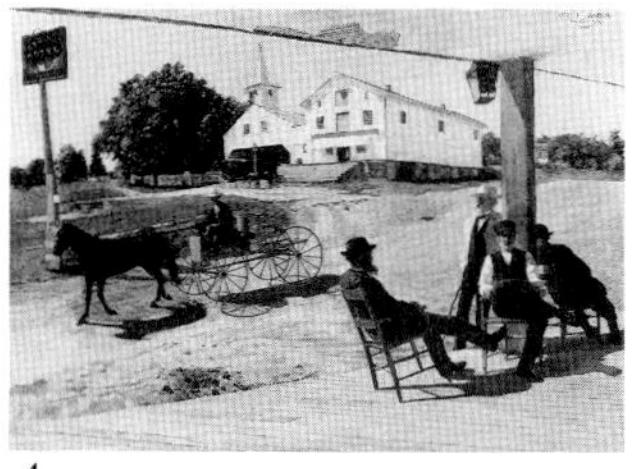
4.

BACHER, Otto H*enry* *1856–1909*
Born at Cleveland, Ohio; *died Bronxville, N.Y.* Masters: Boulanger, Lefebvre, C.-Duran; *Duveneck*
4. Richfield Center, Ohio, *1885.* *See page 112.*

BACON, Henry *1837–1912*
Born at Boston, Mass.; *died Cairo, Egypt.* Master*s*: Cabanel, *Edouard Frère*
5. Astray *(unlocated)*

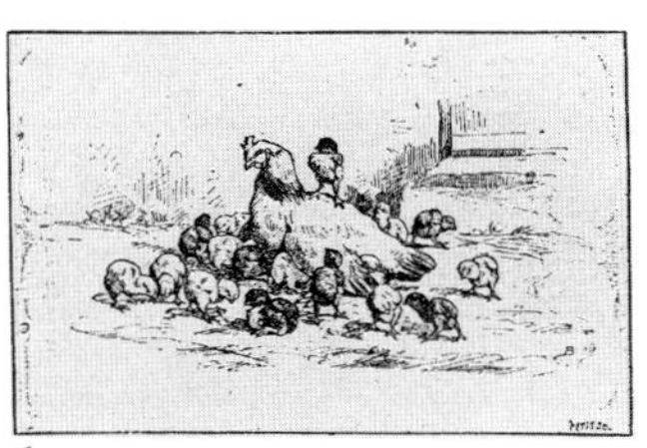
6.

BAIRD, William *Baptiste* *1846–after 1899*
6. En famille *(unlocated). Engraving after the painting, from E. Bernard,* Salon de 1882 *(Paris), p. 218*

BARNARD, Edward H*erbert* *1859–1909*
Born at Belmont, Mass.; *died Belmont, Mass.* Masters: Lefebvre, Collin, and Otto Grundman*n*
7. Pastime in the Middle age *(unlocated)*

BEAUX, Miss *Cecilia* *1855–1942*
Born at Philadelphia, Pa.; died Gloucester, Mass. Masters: Bouguereau, T. Robert-Fleury, Constant
8. Portrait *Mrs. Katherine S. Conant, 1888 (unlocated)*

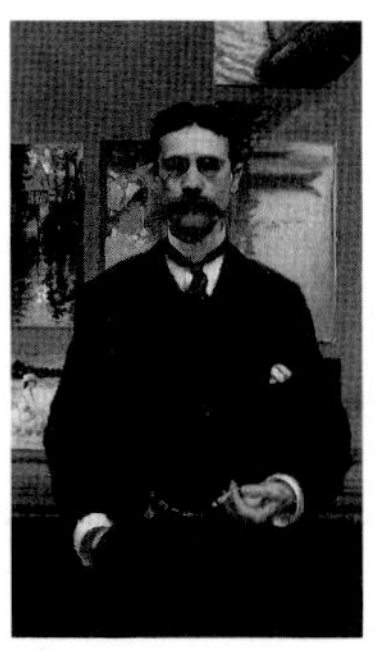
10.

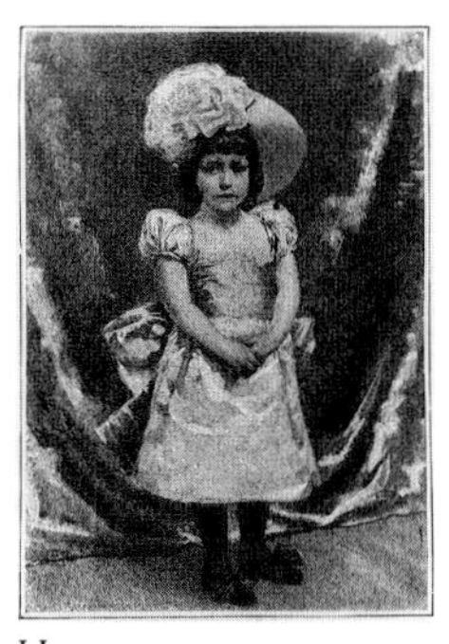
11.

BECKWITH, J*ames* Carroll *1852–1917*
Born at Hannibal, Mo.; *died New York, N.Y.* Masters: Carolus-Duran; *Bonnat, Wilmarth.* Recompense: Honorable mention, Salon of 1887; *bronze medal 1889*
9. A Lady of California *(unlocated)*
10. Portrait of William Walton, *1886.* *See page 112.*
11. Portrait of a Child (Owner, H.W. Poor, New York). *Ill. from G.W. Sheldon,* Recent Ideals, *p. 21. Photograph courtesy The New-York Historical Society*

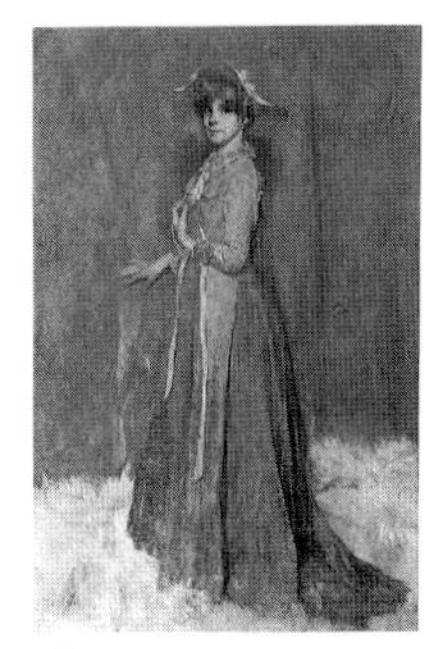
12.

BELL, Edward A*ugust* *1862–1953*
Born at New York, N.Y. Masters: Edward A. Bell; *von Loefftz, Chase, Shirlaw. Recompense: Bronze medal 1889*
12. Portrait. *Lady in Gray, 1887–88.* *See page 114.*

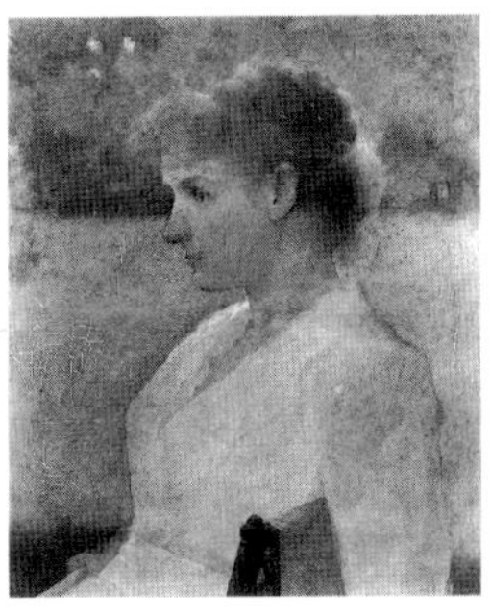
13.

BENSON, Frank W*eston* *1862–1951*
Born at Salem, Mass.; *died Salem, Mass.* Masters: Jules Lefebvre and Gustave Boulanger
13. In Summer. *Private collection, cut down.*

BIRNEY, William Verplanck *1858–1909*
Born at Cincinnati, Ohio. Masters: Julius Benzur and Wilhelm Lindenschurst, of Munich.
14. Dolce far Niente, representing a southern colored waiter boy taking his ease during working hours *(unlocated)*
15. The Labor Question in the South, representing a colored boy cleaning silverware on a terrace *(unlocated)*

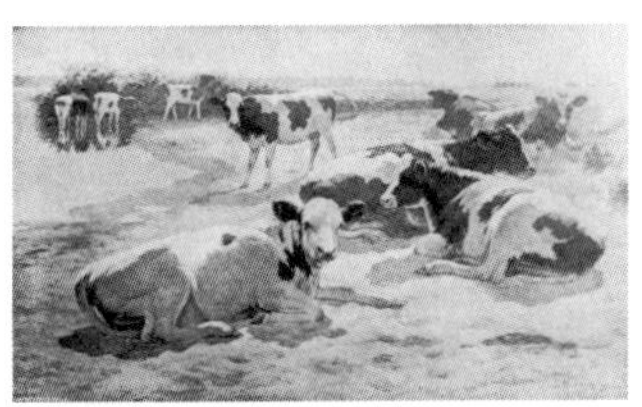
16.

BISBING, Henry S*inglewood* *1849–1933*
Born at Philadelphia, Pa. Master: M.F. de Vuillefroy
16. The Siesta on the Beach *(unlocated)*

BLACKSTONE, Mrs. Sadie
Born at Halifax, Nova Scotia; *died Norwich, Conn.?* Masters: Simabildi and de Montaland
17. Senlisse; Valley of Chevreuse *(unlocated)*

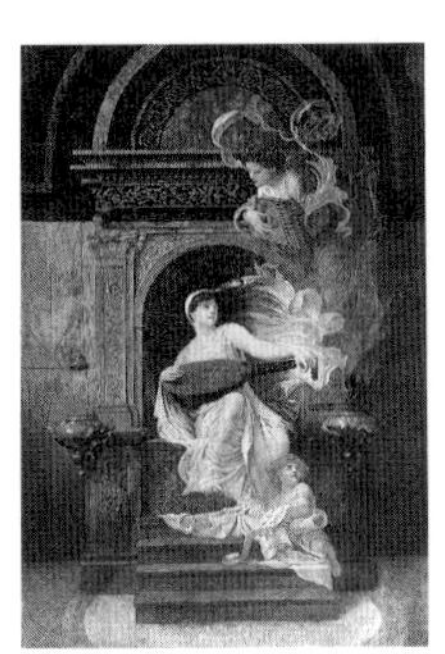
18.

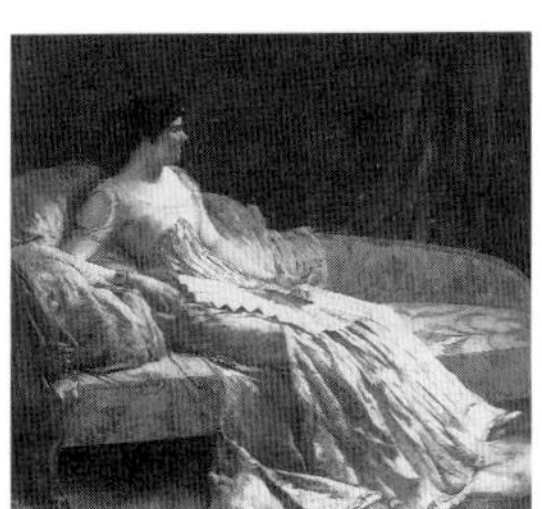
19.

BLASHFIELD, Edwin Howland *1848–1936*
Born at New York, N.Y. *(Brooklyn); died South Dennis, Mass.* Masters: Léon Bonnat; *Gérôme, Thomas Johnston, William Rimmer. Recompense: Bronze medal 1889*
18. Inspiration (Owner, Col. H. M. Boies) *(unlocated). Engraving after the painting, from G.W. Sheldon,* Recent Ideals, *p. 68. Photograph courtesy The New-York Historical Society.*
19. Portrait (Owner, C.E. Wilbur [*sic*]). *Portrait of the Artist's Wife, 1889.* *See page 114.*

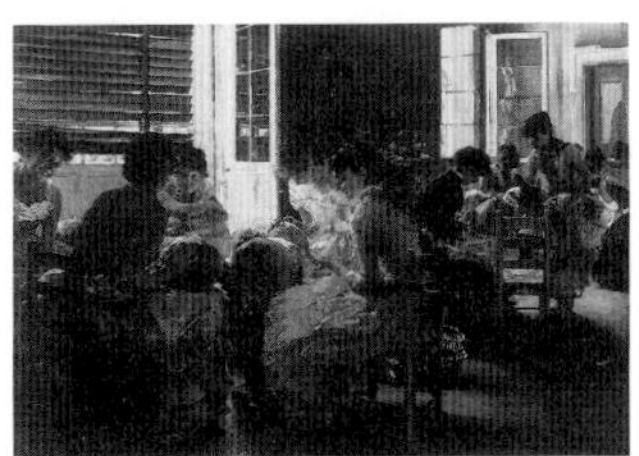
20.

BLUM, Robert F*rederick* *1857–1903*
Born at Cincinnati, Ohio; *died New York, N.Y. Student at McMicken School of Design, Cincinnati; PAFA.* Recompense: Gold medal Am. Art Assn.; *bronze medal 1889*
20. Venetian Lace Workers, *1887.* *See page 115.*

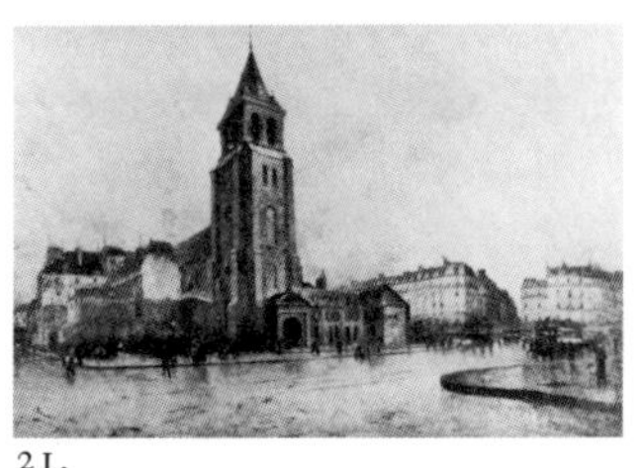
21.

BOGGS, Frank M*yers* *1855–1926*
Born at New York, N.Y. *[Springfield, Ohio]; died Meudon, France.* Master: Gérôme. *Recompense: Silver medal 1889*
21. Saint-Germain des Près, *1883* (Owner, Mons. Diot) *(unlocated). Ill. from Arsène Alexandre,* Frank Boggs *(Paris, 1929).*

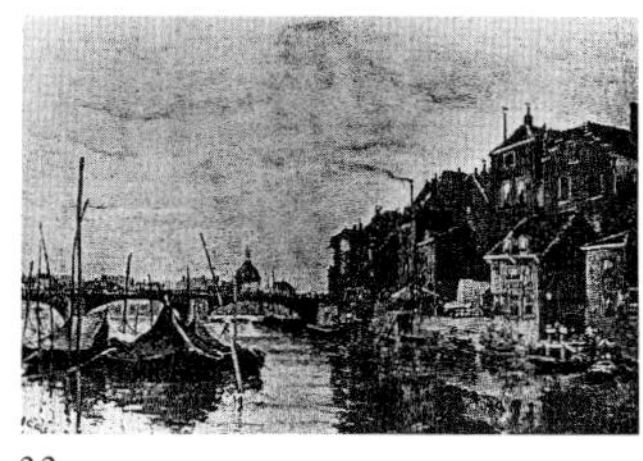

22.

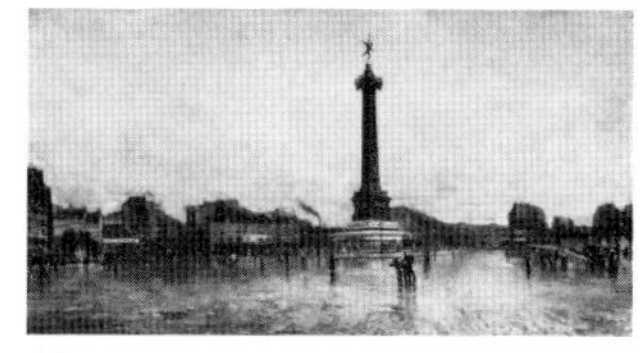

23.

22. View of Dordrecht (Owner, Mons. Diot). Old Canal at Dordrecht, *1884 (unlocated). Ill. from Clarence Cook,* Art and Artists of Our Time *(New York, 1888), vol. 3, p. 296.*

23. Place de la Bastille, Paris, *1882* (Owner, French Gov't). *See page 118.*

BOYDEN, Frederick D*wight* *1860–?*
Born at Boston, Mass. Masters: Boulanger and M.J. Lefebvre

24. Pastures at Cape Ann, Massachusetts *(unlocated)*

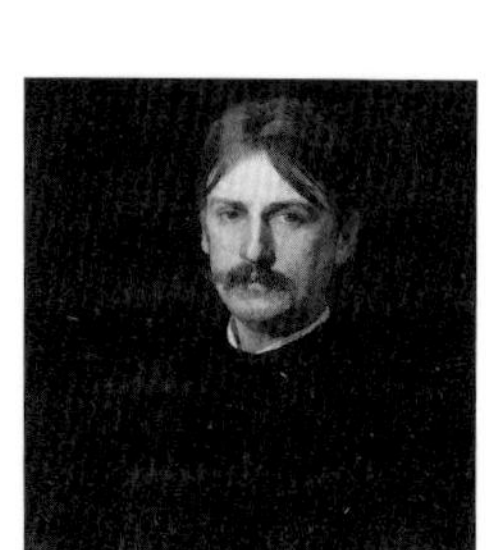

25.

BRANDEGEE, Robert B*olling* *1849–1922*
Born at Berlin, Conn.; *died Farmington, Conn.* Master: M. Jacquesson de la Chevreuse; *Ecole des Beaux-Arts Recompense: Bronze medal 1889*

25. Portrait. *Portrait of Montague Flagg, 1887. See page 119.*

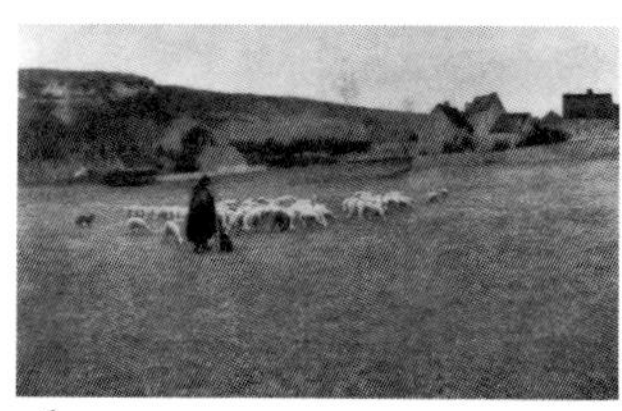

26.

BRECK, John L*eslie* *1860–1899*
Born at sea; died Boston, Mass. Masters: Straehuber (Munich); Verlat (Antwerp); Académie Julian. Recompense: Honorable mention 1889

26. Autumn. *Autumn, Giverny or The New Moon. Oil on canvas, 51 x 85". Terra Museum of American Art, Chicago*

27. The First Born *(unlocated)*

BRICHER, Alfred T*hompson* *1837–1908*
Born at Portsmouth, N.H.; *died New York*

28. On the Rockbound Coast of Massachusetts *(unlocated)*

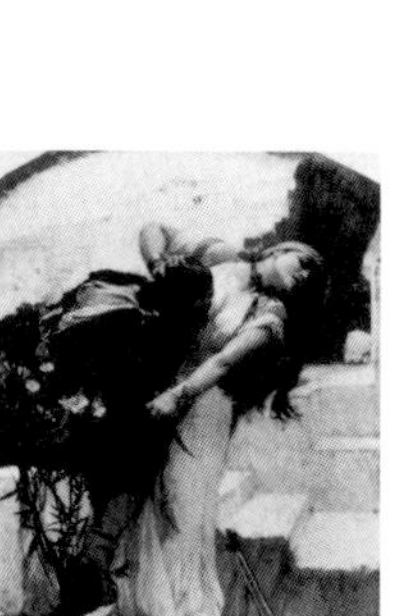

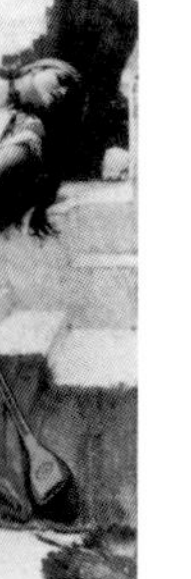

29.

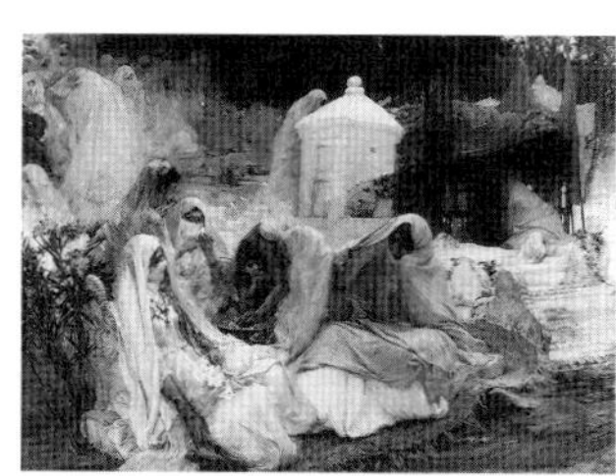

30.

BRIDGMAN, Frederick Arthur *1847–1928*
Born at Tuskagee *[sic]*, Alabama; *died Rouen, France.* Master*s*: J.L. Gérôme; *Atelier Suisse; Brooklyn Art School; NAD. Recompenses:* Medal 3rd class 1887 and 2nd class 1878 (E.U.). Chevalier of Legion of Honor 1878; *silver medal 1889*

29. The Pirate of Love, *1889. Ill. from Lynn Thornton,* La Femme dans la peinture orientaliste, *p. 186.*

30. Fête of the Prophet at Oued-el-Kebir (Blidah), *1889. Oil on canvas, 59 1/16 x 66 3/4". Private collection, France. Photograph courtesy Lynn Thornton.*

31. Negro Fête at Blidah, *c. 1889 (unlocated)*

32. Horse Market at Cairo, *1884. See page 122.*

33. Portrait of Mme. B., *1877 (unlocated). Photograph from Bridgman Family Collection, courtesy Ilene S. Fort*

34. On the House-tops, Algiers, *1887. Engraving after the painting, from William Walton,* Chefs-d'oeuvre, *vol. 2, p. 12. Photograph courtesy The Library of Congress*

32.

33.

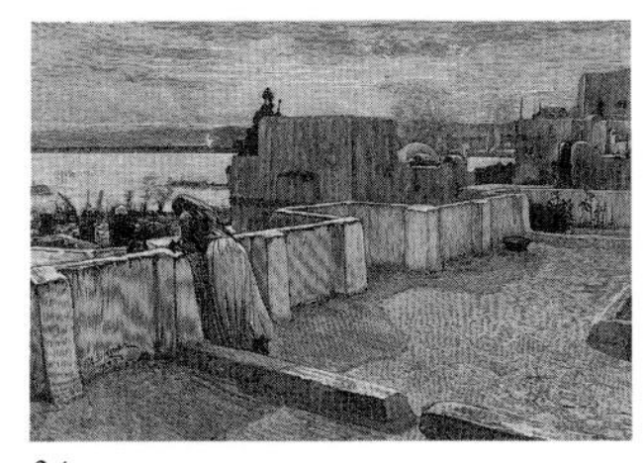
34.

BRISTOL, John Bunyan *1826–1909*
Born at Hillsdale, N.Y. Master: Henry Ary, Hudson, N.Y. Recompenses: Medal, Centennial Exposition of 1876; *honorable mention 1889*

35. Haying Time, near Middlebury, Vt. *(unlocated)*

BROOKS, Maria *1845?–1913*
Born in England *(Middlesex); died New York.* Student of South Kensington School of Art, and Schools of the Royal Academy, London, England. Recompenses: 2 gold, 1 silver, 3 bronze medals; Crystal Palace, London 1878; Dipl, 3rd order of Merit, Melbourne, etc.

36. Ready for a Bowl *(unlocated)*

BROWN, J*ohn George* *1831–1913*
Born in Scotland *[Durham, England]; died New York. Masters: William Bell Scott, Robert Scott Lauder, Thomas Seir Cummings. Recompense: Honorable mention 1889*

37. The Longshoreman's Noon (Owner, W.T. Evans).
The Longshoremen's Noon, 1879. *See page 123.*

38. New York Street Band *(unlocated)*

39. Morning Papers, *1889.* *See page 123.*

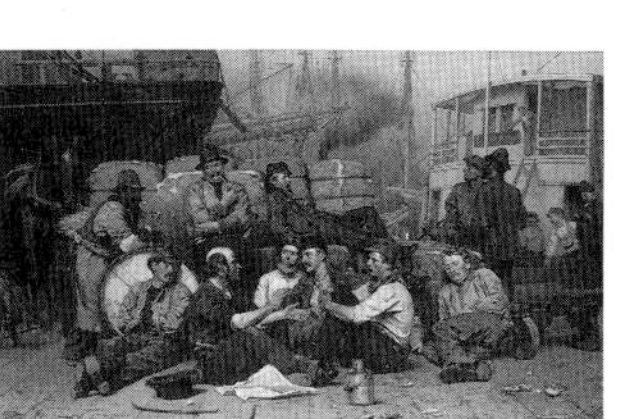
37.

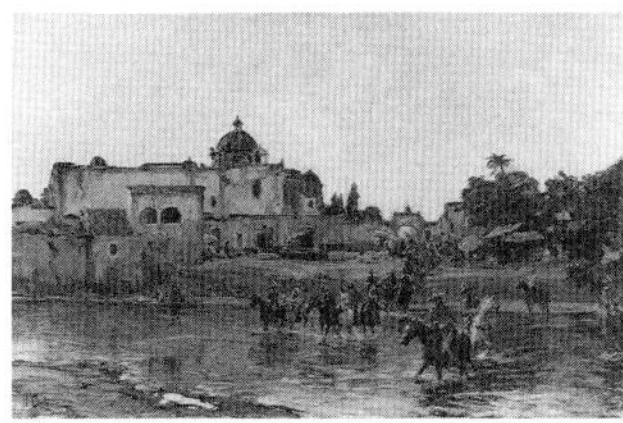
39.

BROWN*E*, Charles Francis *1859–1920*
Born at Waltham, Mass.; *died Waltham, Mass.* Masters: Boulanger, Lefebvre, Gérôme; *Schenck*

40. Landscape *(unlocated)*

BUTLER, Howard Russell *1856–1934*
Born at New York, N.Y.; *died Princeton, N.J.* Masters: Dagnan-Bouveret, Roll, Gervex, Beckwith. Recompenses: Honorable Mention, Paris Salon, 1886; "Temple" Marine and Landscape Medal, Philadelphia, 1888; *bronze medal 1889*

41. Seaweed Gatherers, *1886.* *See page 124.*

42. Low Tide, St. Ives, Cornwall, England *(unlocated)*

43. Rurales Fording the Yantepec [*sic*], *1889.* *See page 124.*

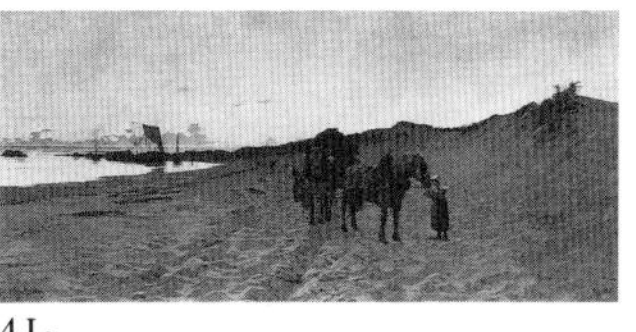
41.

43.

BUTLER, George B*ernard* *1838–1907*
Born at New York, N.Y.; *died Croton Falls, N.Y. Masters: Hicks, Couture. Recompense: Honorable mention 1889*

44. Portrait of Mrs. Stimson *(unlocated)*

45. Tambourine Players *(unlocated)*

CARR, Lyell *1857–1912*
Born at Chicago, Ill.; died New York. Masters: Boulanger, Lefebvre

46. Good Luck *(unlocated)*

CAULDWELL, Leslie Giffin *1864–1941*
Born at New York. Masters: Boulanger, Lefebvre, Carolus-Duran

47. Portrait of my Fencing-master, M. Rougé *(unlocated)*

CHAPMAN, Carlton T*heodore* *1860–1925*
Born at New London, O*hio*. Student at National Academy of Design and Art Students' League, New York. *Masters: Lefebvre, Boulanger*

48. Early Morning in a Harbor *(unlocated)*

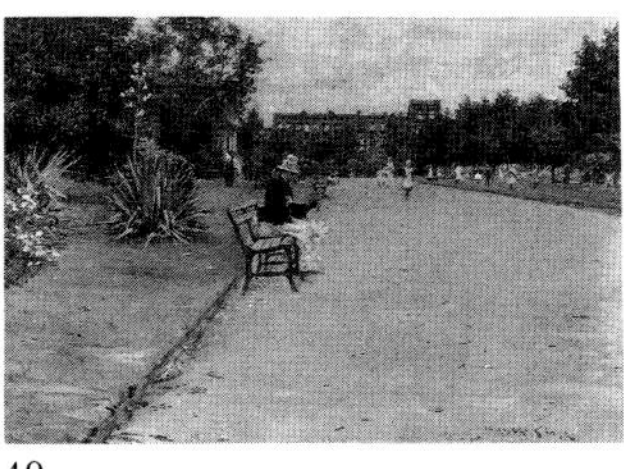
49.

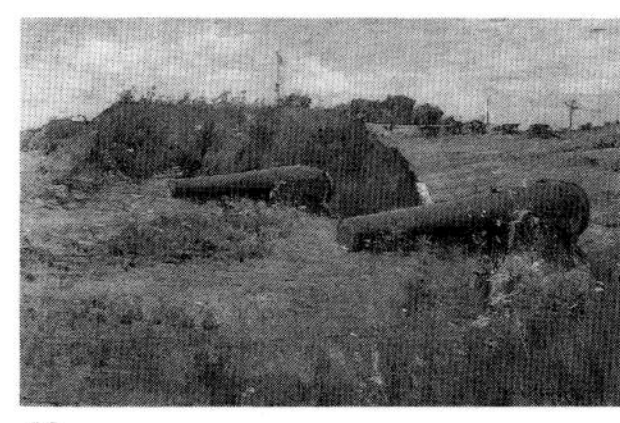
50.

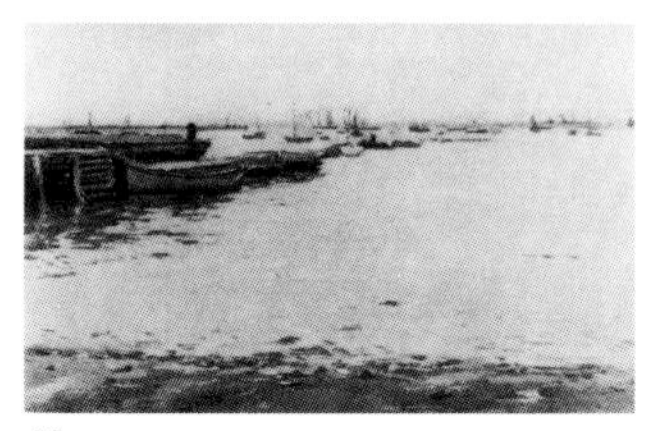
53.

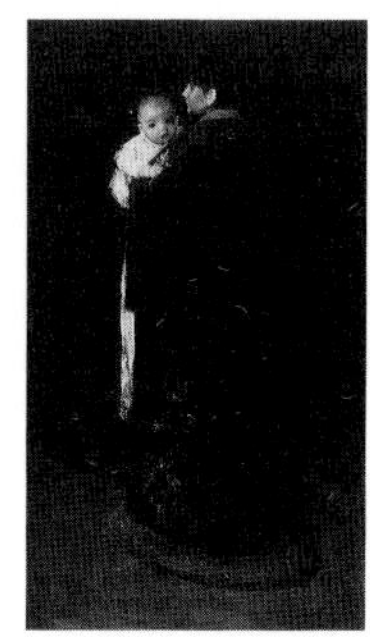
54.

CHASE, William M*erritt* *1849–1916*
Born at Williamsburg (now Nineveh), Indiana; died New York. Masters: Wilmarth, von Piloty; influenced by Leibl. Recompense: Silver medal 1889

49. A City Park, *c. 1888. See page 127.*
50. Peace. *Peace, Fort Hamilton. Oil on panel; 10 3/16 x 15 7/8". The St. Louis Art Museum*
51. A Bit of Long Island. *Oil on canvas, 14 x 18" (unlocated)*
52. Stoneyard *(unlocated)*
53. Gowanus Bay, *c. 1887. Oil on panel, 10 x 15 1/2". Ill. from Sotheby's N.Y. catalogue, April 20, 1979, no. 45*
54. Portrait of Mother and Child. *The First Portrait, 1888. See page 127.*
55. Portrait of Mrs. C. *Portrait of a Lady in Black, 1888. See page 127.*
56. Portrait of Miss Gill *(unlocated)*

55.

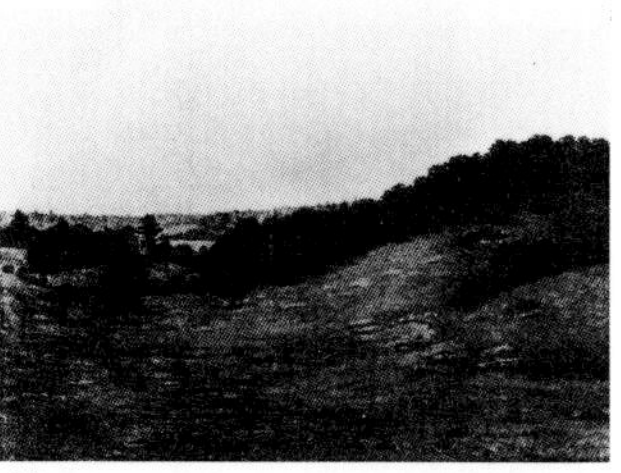

59.

COFFIN, William Anderson *1855–1925*
Born at Allegheny City, Pa.; *died New York.* Master: Léon Bonnat. Recompense: 2nd Hallgarten Prize, National Academy of Design, N.Y. 1886; *bronze medal 1889*

57. Moonlight in Harvest *(unlocated)*
58. September *(unlocated)*
59. Early Moonrise. *Oil on canvas, 30 x 40". Ill. source unknown*
60. After the Storm *(unlocated)*

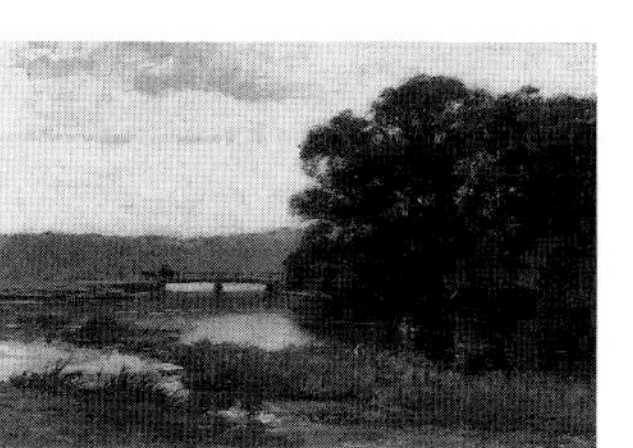
61.

COLE, J*oseph* Foxcroft *1837–1892*
Born at Jay, Maine; *died Boston, Mass.* Master: Charles Jacques *[sic]; Lambinet.* Recompense: Medal. Centennial Exposition of 1876

61. Abbajona River, Mass., *c. 1880. See page 130.*

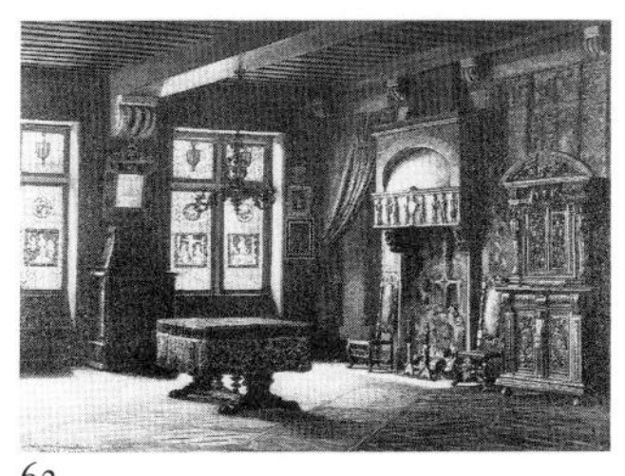

62.

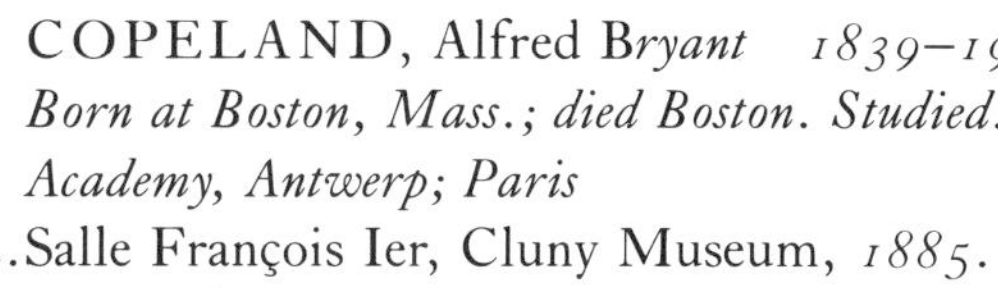

COPELAND, Alfred *Bryant* *1839–1909*
Born at Boston, Mass.; died Boston. Studied: Royal Academy, Antwerp; Paris

62. Salle François Ier, Cluny Museum, *1885. See page 131.*
63. Study of Interior *(unlocated)*

COX, Kenyon *1856–1919*
Born at Warren, Ohio; *died New York.* Masters: J. L.

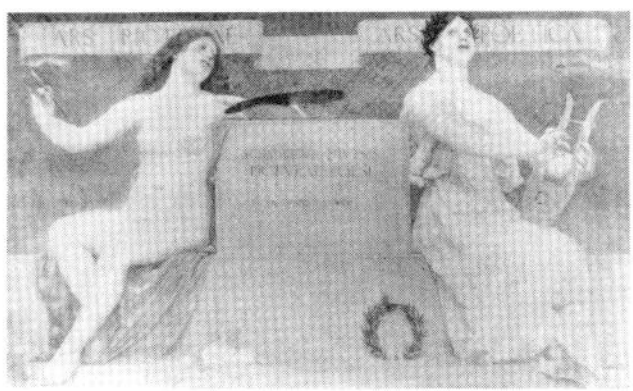

64.

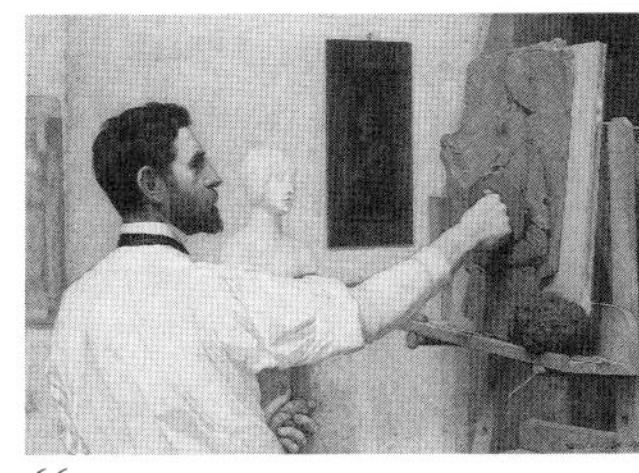

66.

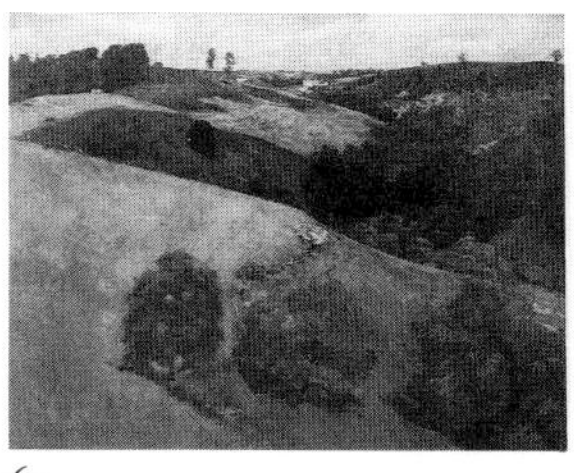

67.

Gérôme and Carolus-Duran; *Cabanel, Bouguereau, Lefebvre, Boulanger. Recompense: Bronze medal 1889.*

64. Painting and Poetry, *c. 1887 (unlocated). Ill. from* Official Illustrations from the Art Gallery of the World's Columbian Exposition *(1893), p. 289.*
65. Jacob wrestling with the Angel, *c. 1888 (unlocated)*
66. Portrait of Augustus Saint-Gaudens, *1887* (Owner, A. Saint-Gaudens). *See page 134.*
67. Flying Shadows, *1883. See page 134.*

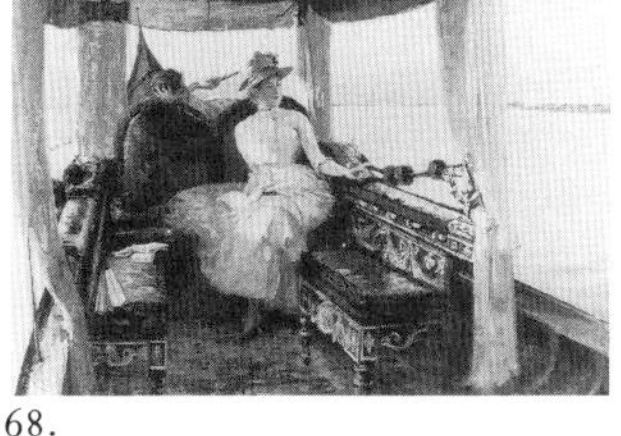

68.

CURTIS, Ralph *Wormeley* *1854–1922*
Born at Boston, Mass.; died Beaulieu, Alpes-Maritimes, France. Masters: Boulanger, Lefebvre, Carolus-Duran. Recompense: Honorable mention 1889

68. View at Venice, *1884. See page 135.*

DANA, *William Parsons Winchester* *1833–1927*
Born at Boston, Mass.; *died in England.* Masters: Eugène Le Poittevin; *Picot. Recompenses:* Med. 3rd cl. 1878, Exp. Univ.; *bronze medal 1889*

69. Christ walking on the Sea *(unlocated)*
70. Hay Barges on the Thames *(unlocated)*
71. Calm Evening on the Thames *(unlocated)*
72. A Good Breeze, moonlight effect *(unlocated)*

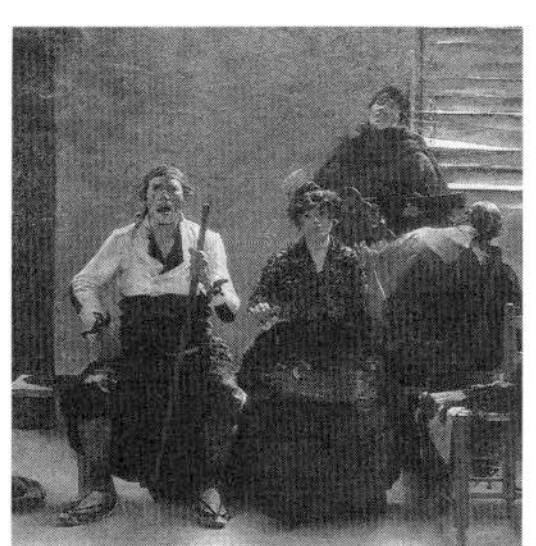

73.

DANNAT, William *Turner* *1853–1929*
Born at New York; died Monte Carlo, Monaco. Masters: M. Munkácsy; *Royal Academy, Munich; Carolus-Duran, Paris. Recompenses:* Medal 3rd class, 1883; *Chevalier of the Legion of Honor 1889*

73. A Quartette. *The Quartette, 1884. Oil on canvas, $94\frac{3}{4}$ x $91\frac{3}{4}$". See fig. 24.*
74. A Sacristy in Aragon, *1884. Oil on canvas, $53\frac{1}{4}$ x $56\frac{1}{4}$". Formerly at Art Institute of Chicago. (Sold at Parke Bernet, New York, May 5, 1944, lot 78)*

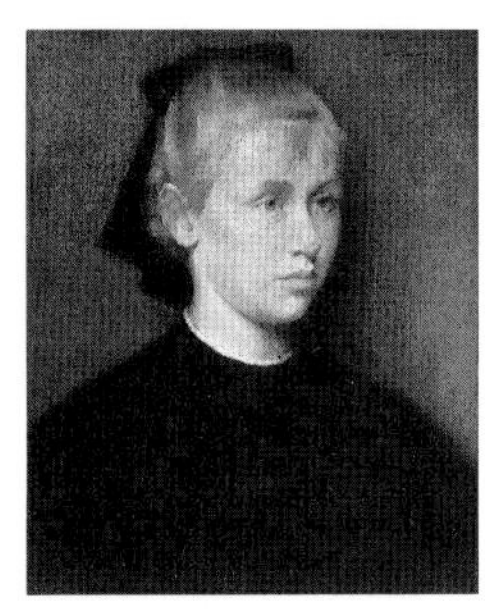
75.

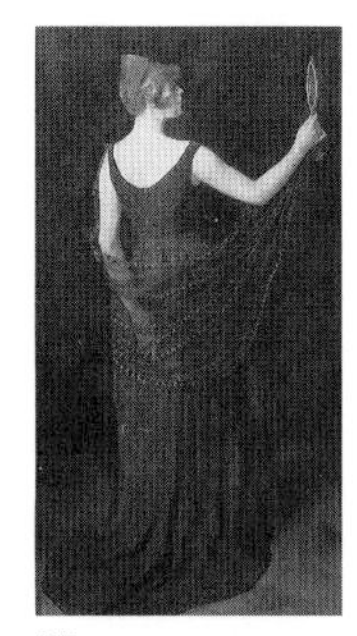
77.

75. Portrait of Miss H. *Portrait of Eva Haviland, 1886. Oil on canvas, 21¼ x 17". Museum of Fine Arts, Boston*
76. Mariposa *(unlocated)*
77. A study in red. *La Femme en rouge, 1889. See page 138.*
78. Une Saducéenne *(unlocated)*

DARLING, Wilder M. *1855–1933*
Born at Sandusky, Ohio; *died Toledo, Ohio*
Masters: Cormon and H. Mosler; *Laurens, Duveneck, Chase*

79. Grandma's First Visit, *c. 1888. See page 139.*

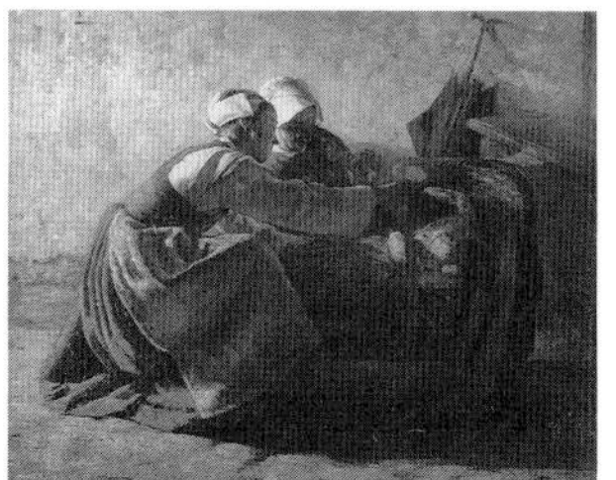
79.

DAVIS, Charles H*arold* *1856–1933*
Born at Amesbury, Mass.; *died Mystic, Conn.* Masters: Boulanger and Lefebvre; *Grundmann. Recompense: Silver medal 1889*

80. A Winter Evening *(unlocated)*
81. The Valley (Evening), *1886. See page 141.*
82. The Hillside *(unlocated)*
83. Evening after the storm *(unlocated)*

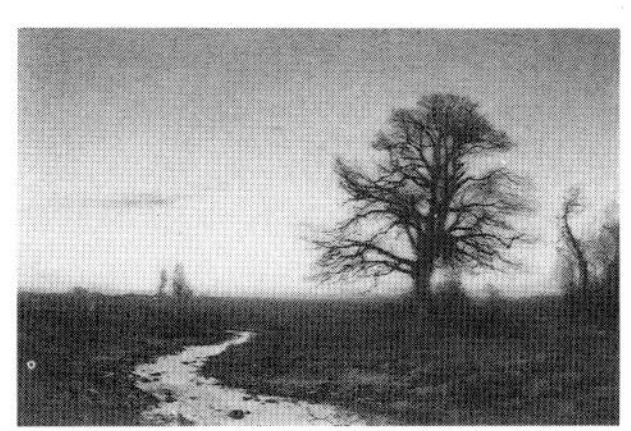
81.

DELACHAUX, Leon D. *1854–1919*
Masters: Duez, Dagnan-Bouveret. Recompense: Bronze medal 1889

84. Portrait of Mlle H. *(unlocated)*
85. Engaging Servants in the Olden Times *(unlocated)*

DENMAN, H*erbert* *1855–1903*
Born at Brooklyn, N.Y. Master: Carolus-Duran. *Recompenses:* Honorable mention, Paris Salon, 1886; *honorable mention 1889*

86. Offering to Aphrodite (Owner, Mrs. Wallace) *(unlocated)*

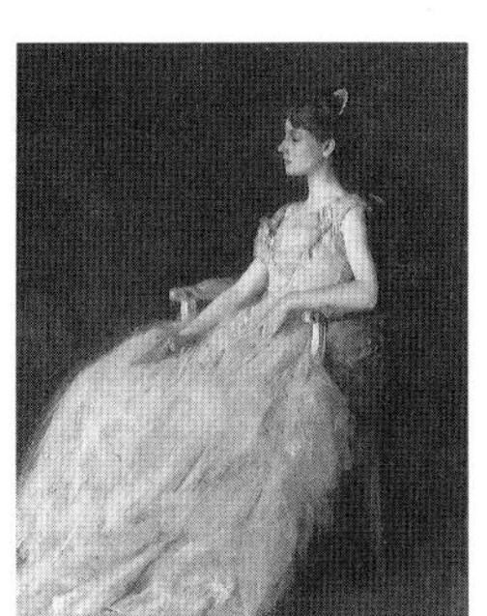
87.

DEWING, Thos. W*ilmer* *1851–1938*
Born at Boston, Mass.; *died New York.* Masters: Lefebvre and Boulanger. *Recompense: Silver medal 1889*

87. Lady in Yellow. (Owner, Mrs. J. Gardner) *Oil on canvas, 19¾ x 15¾". Isabella Stewart Gardner Museum, Boston*

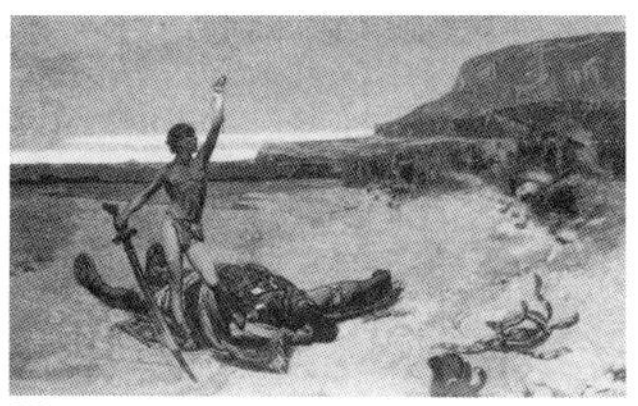
88.

DODGE, W*illiam de* L*eftwich* *1867–1935*
Born in Virginia; *died New York.* Masters: Gérôme, Collin, Courtois. *Recompense: Bronze medal 1889*

88. David. *David and Goliath, 1887 (destroyed in fire). Engraving after the painting by H. Wolf, from* Century Magazine. *(May–Oct., 1891), p. 664. Photograph courtesy The Library of Congress*

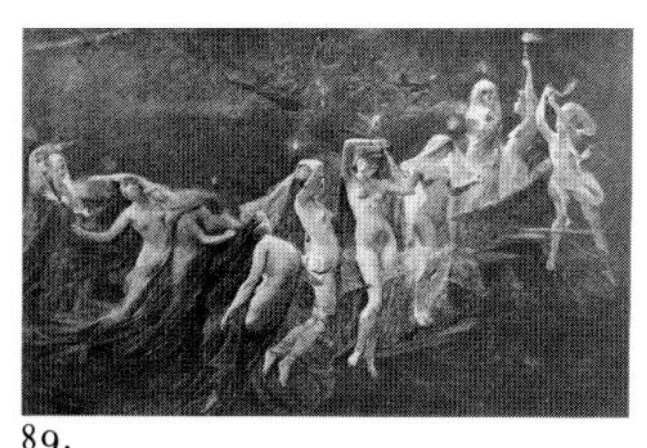
89.

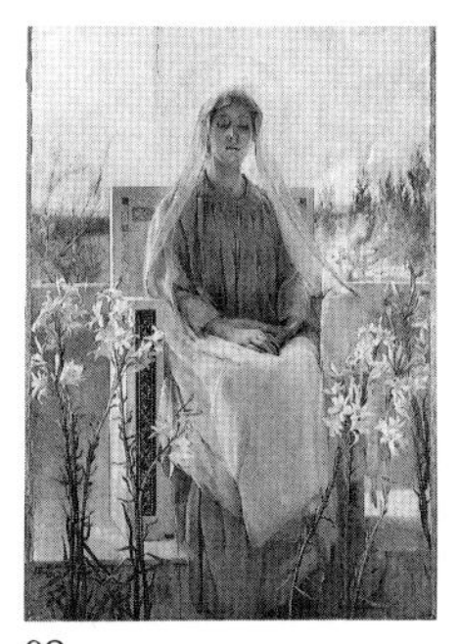
90.

DODSON, Sarah *Paxton* Ball *1847–1906*
Born at Philadelphia; died Brighton, England. Masters: Luminais, Lefebvre, de Monvel, Schussele

89. Morning Stars, *1886. Oil on canvas, 23 x 30". Ill. from* American Art Journal *(Winter 1983), p. 77.*

90. Meditation of the Holy Virgin, *1889. See page 142.*

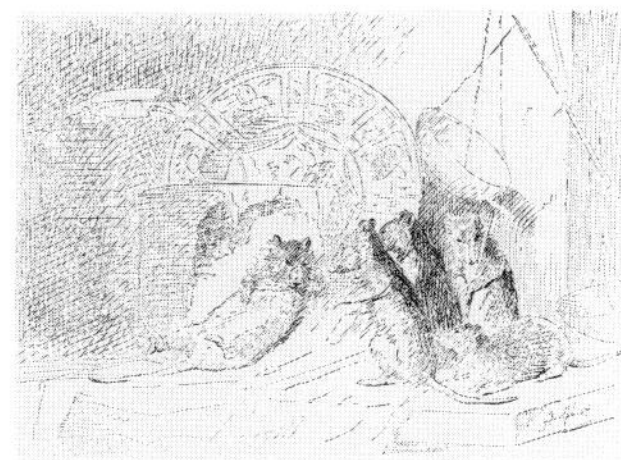
91.

DOLPH, John *Henry* *1835–1903*
Born at Fort Ann, New York. Master: Louis Van Kuyck of Antwerp. *Recompense: Silver medal 1889*

91. The Rat retired from the world. *Oil on canvas, 22 x 30" (unlocated). Engraving after the painting, from* National Academy Notes *(1884), p. 96. Photograph courtesy The New-York Historical Society*

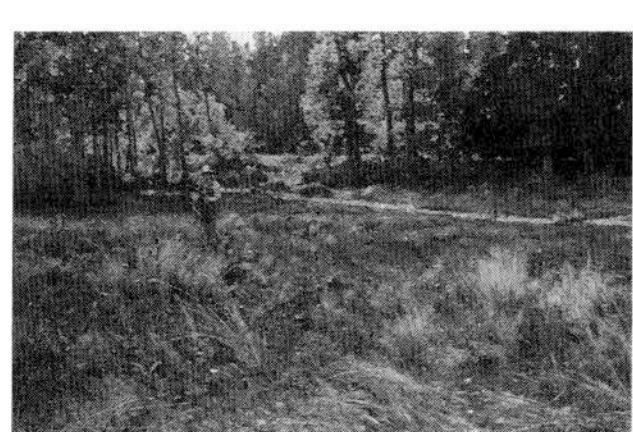
92.

DONOHO, *Gaines* Ruger *1857–1916*
Born at Churchill, Miss.; *died New York*. Masters: Boulanger, Lefebvre, Bouguereau and Fleury; *R.S. Gifford. Recompense: Silver medal 1889*

92. La Marcellerie, c. *1882. See page 143.*

93. The edge of a forest *(unlocated)*

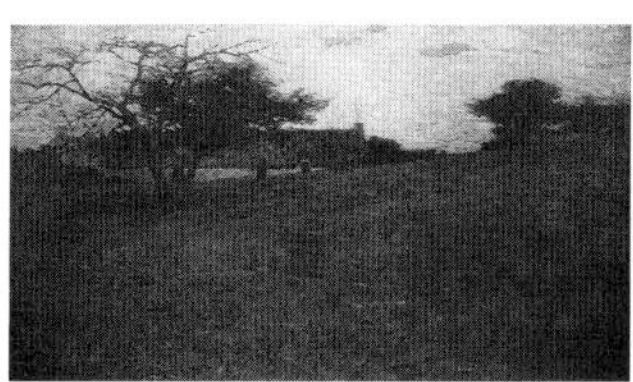
94.

DOW, Arthur *Wesley* *1857–1922*
Born at Ipswich, Mass; *died New York*. Masters: Boulanger, Lefebvre, Doucet and Paul Delance. *Recompense: Honorable mention 1889*

94. At Evening, *1888 See page 146.*

DYER, Charles Gifford *1846–1912*
Born at Chicago, Ill.; died Munich, Germany. Master: Jacquesson de la Chevreuse; Royal Academy, Munich

95. On the Riva; Venice *(unlocated)*

96. San Giorgio, seen from the Giudecca; Venice *(unlocated)*

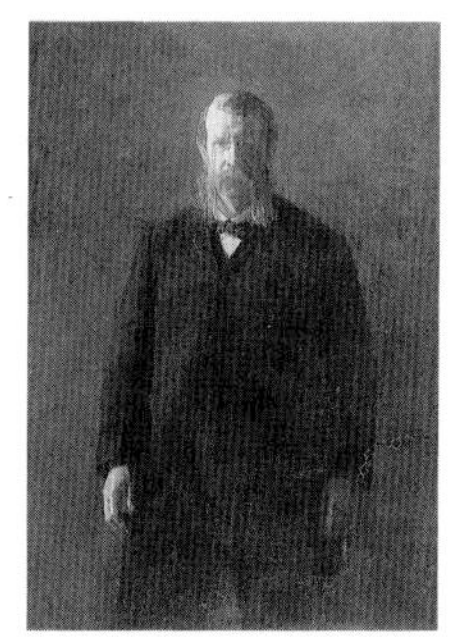
97.

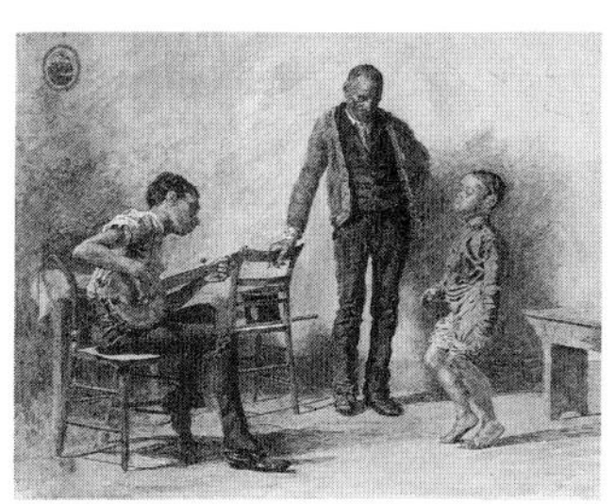
98.

EAKINS, Thomas *1844–1916*
Born at Philadelphia; died Philadelphia. Master: Gérôme

97. Portrait, Professor Geo. H. Barber *[sic]. Professor George H. Barker, 1886. Oil on canvas, originally 60 x 40" (subsequently cut down). Mitchell Museum, Mount Vernon, Ill. John R. and Eleanor Mitchell Foundation*

98. The Dancing Lesson. *Negro Boy Dancing*, 1878. *See page 147.*

99. The Veteran (portrait of Geo. Reynolds), *c. 1886. See page 147.*

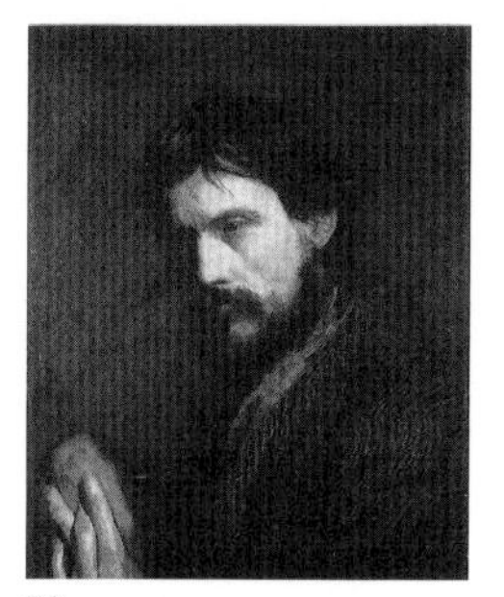
99.

EATON, *Charles* Harry *1850–1901*
Born near Akron, Ohio; *died Leonia, N.J.*

100. Landscape (Owner, W. T. Evans). A *Normandy Landscape, 1885 (unlocated). Oil on canvas, 24 x 36"*

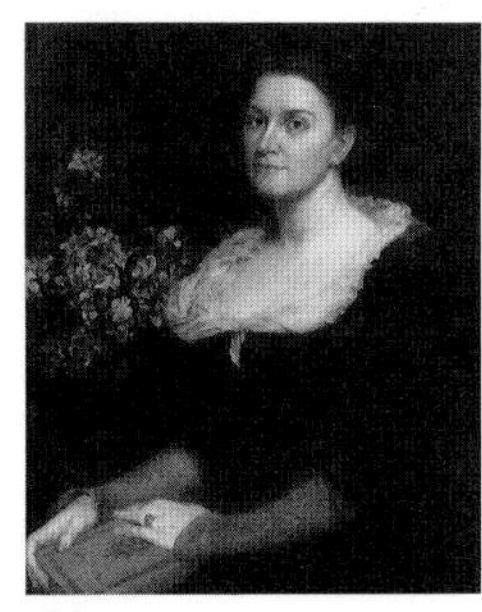

102.

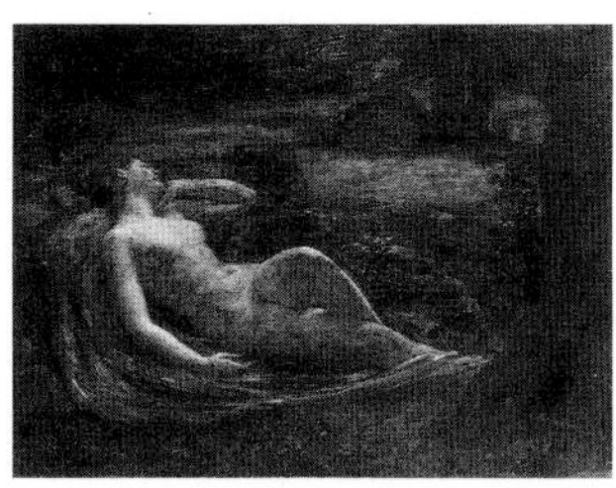

104.

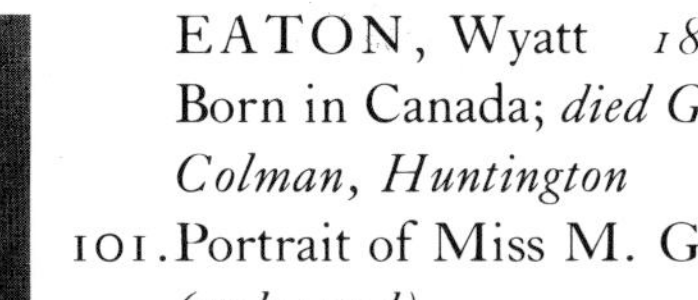

EATON, Wyatt *1849–1896*
Born in Canada; *died Glen Ridge, N.J.* Masters: Gérôme; *Colman, Huntington*

101. Portrait of Miss M. G. R. (Owner, Mrs. S. Reed) *(unlocated).*
102. Portrait of Mrs. R. W. G. (Owner R.W. Gilder). *Portrait of Mrs. Richard Watson Gilder (Helena de Kay). Oil on canvas, 36½ x 28½". The Palmer Gilder Collection*
103. Portrait of man with violin (Owner, T. Cole). *Portrait of Timothy Cole, 1885 (unlocated)*
104. Ariadne, *1888* (Owner W.T. Evans). *See page 150.*

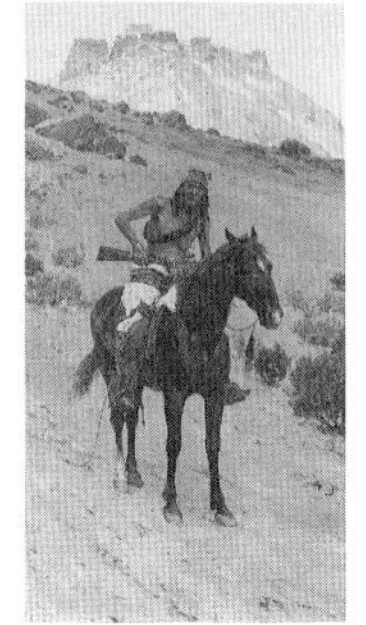

105.

FARNY, Henry F. *1847–1916*
Born at Cincinnati, Ohio *[Ribeauville, Alsace]; died Cincinnati, Ohio. Recompense: Bronze medal 1889*

105. Danger, *1888* (Owner A. Howard Hinkle). *Oil on canvas, 40⅜ x 22¼". Private collection. Photograph courtesy Spanierman Gallery, New York*

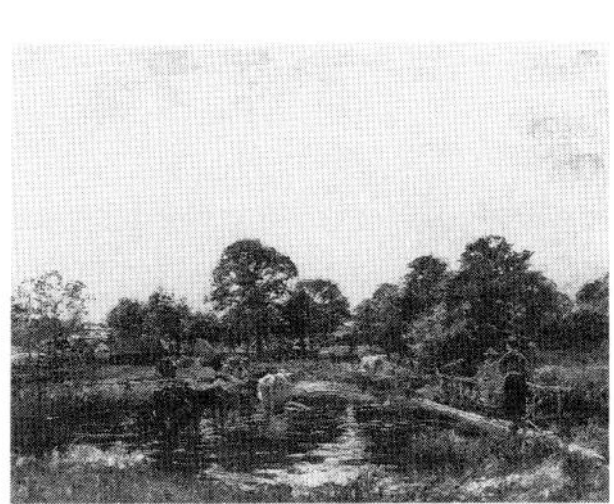

107.

FISHER, *William* Mark *1841–1923*
Born at Boston, Mass.; died London, England. Master: Gleyre

106. Winter Fare *(unlocated)*
107. A Ford; Valley of the Test *(unlocated). Formerly Carnegie Institute, Pittsburgh. Sold at Sotheby's, New York, Feb. 24 1987, lot no. 342*

FORBES, Charles F. *[sic] Stuart* *1856–1926*
Born in Geneva, Switzerland. Recompense: Bronze medal 1889

108. Portrait *(unlocated)*
109. Portrait of Mlle F. F. *(unlocated)*

FOWLER, Frank *1852–1910*
Born at Brooklyn, N.Y.; *died New Canaan, Conn.* Masters: Carolus-Duran and Cabanel. *Recompense: Bronze medal 1889*

110. At the Piano *(unlocated)*

FREER, Frederick W*arren* *1849–1908*
Born at Chicago, Ill. *[Kennicott's Grove, Ill.]; died Chicago.* Student at Royal Academy of Fine Arts, Munich

111. Nude Study *(unlocated)*

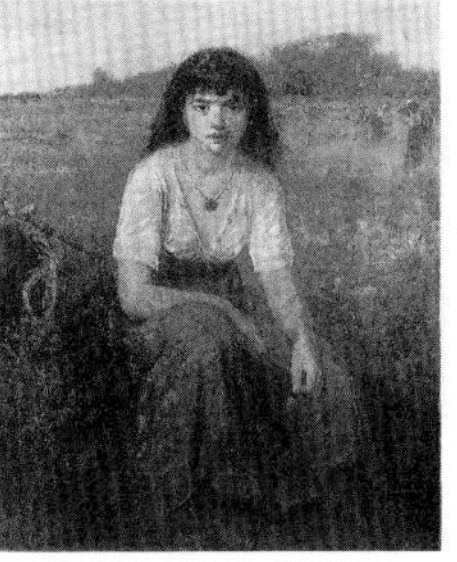

112.

FULLER, Geo., born 1822, died 1884
Born at Springfield, Mass.; died Brookline, Mass. Masters: Henry Kirke Brown; NAD

112. The Quadroon, *1880* (Owner, Mrs. S.D. Warren). *Oil on canvas, 50½ x 40½". © The Metropolitan Museum of Art, New York, Gift of George A. Hearn. 10.64.3 See page 151.*

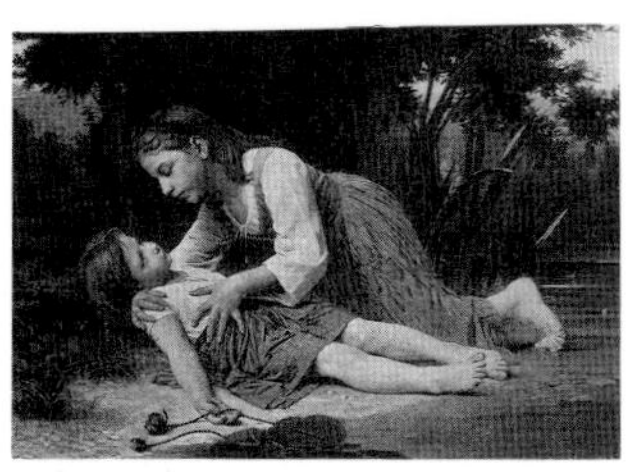
113.

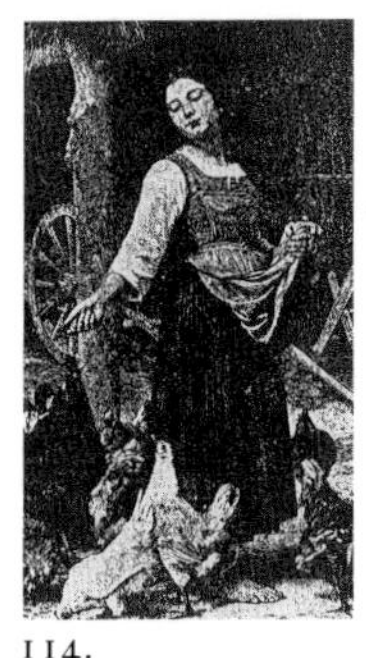
114.

GARDNER, Miss Elizabeth Jane *1837–1922*
Born at Exeter, N.H.; *died St. Cloud, France.* Masters: Bouguereau and J. Lefebvre. *Recompenses:* Medal, 3rd class. 1886; *bronze medal 1889*

113. Too imprudent, *c. 1886 (unlocated) Ill. from G. W. Sheldon,* Recent Ideals, *p. 136. Photograph courtesy The Library of Congress.*

114. The Farmer's Daughter *(unlocated). Engraving after the painting, from William Walton,* Chefs d'oeuvre, *vol. 1, p. 8.*

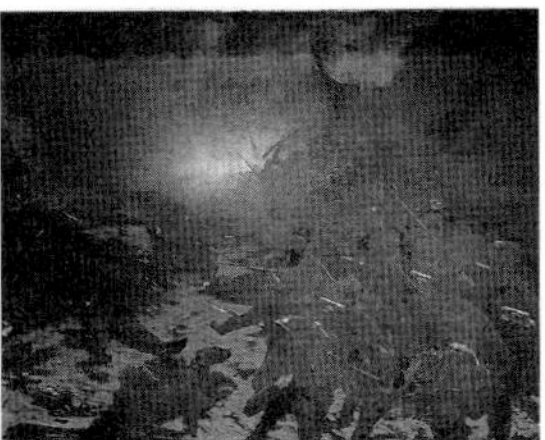
115.

GAUL, *William* Gilbert *1855–1919*
Born at Jersey City, N.J.; *died New York. Recompense: Bronze medal 1889. Masters: Wilmarth, J.G. Brown*

115. Charging the Battery (Owner, W.T. Evans). *The Charging of the Battery (Night Attack—Civil War),* c. 1882. *Oil on canvas, 36 x 44". Photography courtesy The New-York Historical Society*

116. The Wounded Officer *(unlocated)*

GAY, Edward *1837–1928*
Born in Ireland; *died Mt. Vernon, N.Y.* Masters: Jas. M. Hart and Geo. H. Baughton; *Lessing, Schirmer, Düsseldorf.* Recompense: Prize of 2,000 dollars American Art Association, New York

117. The Old Boundary Line *(unlocated)*

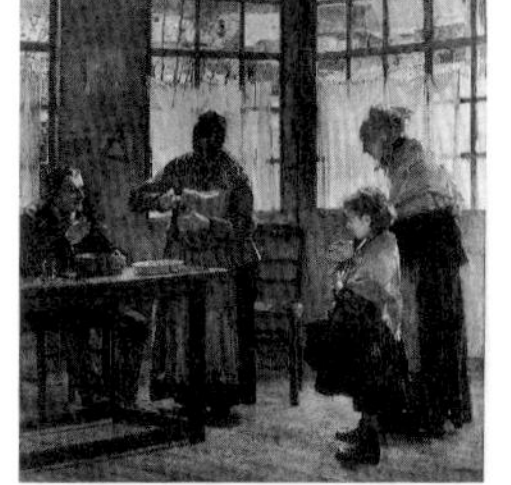
118.

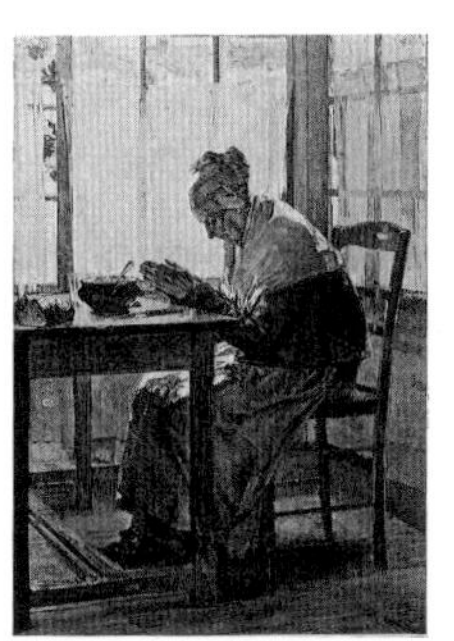
119.

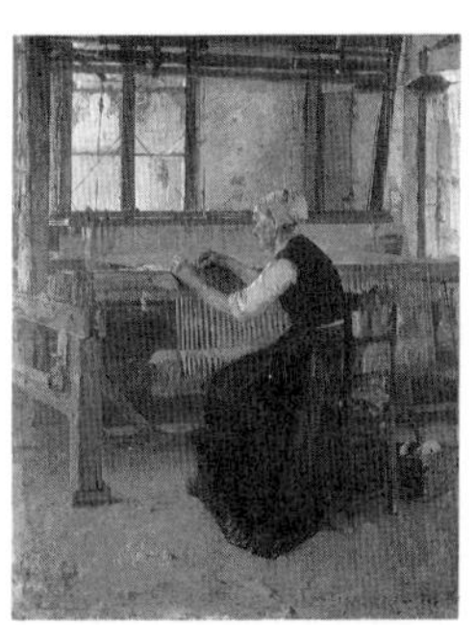
120.

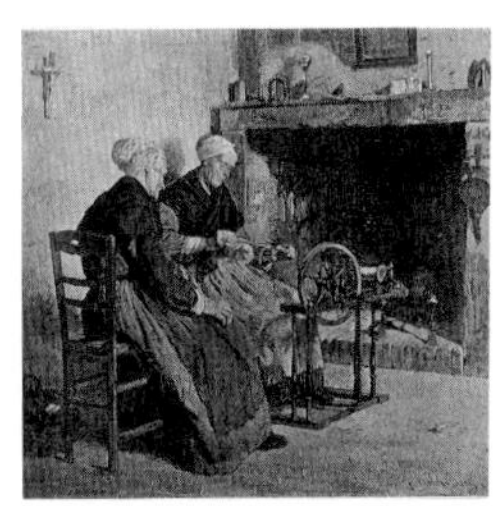
121.

GAY, Walter *1856–1937*
Born at Boston, Mass.; *died Château Breau, near Fontainebleau, France.* Masters: Bonnat; *Wm. Morris Hunt. Recompenses:* Medal, 3rd class, 1888; *silver medal 1889*

118. Charity, *1889. See page 153.*

119. Le Benedicité, *1888* (M.I.P. & B.-A.) *Oil on canvas, 72 x 48". Musée de Picardie, Amiens. Ill. from G.W. Sheldon,* Recent Ideals, *p. 85. Photograph courtesy The Library of Congress*

120. The Weaver, *1886. See page 153.*

121. The Spinners, *1885 (unlocated). Oil on canvas, 16⅜ x 19½". Ill. from G. W. Sheldon,* Recent Ideals, *p. 91. Photograph courtesy The Library of Congress*

122. The Book-worm *(unlocated)*

123. A Dominican *(unlocated)*

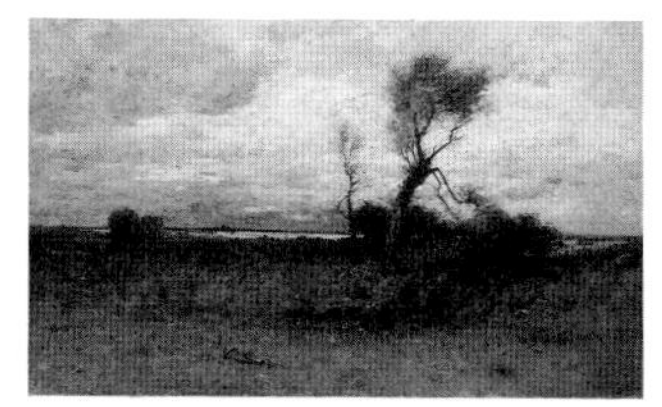
125.

GIFFORD, Robert Swain *1840–1905*
Born at Naushon Island, Mass.; *died New York.* Master: Albert Van Beest. Recompenses: Centennial Medal; and American Art Association Prize of 2,500 dollars; *bronze medal 1889*

124. Early Summer (Owner, Jerome B. Wheeler) *(unlocated)*
125. Near the Coast, *c. 1885* (Owner, New York Metropolitan Museum). *See page 154.*
126. A Kansas Ranch *(unlocated)*

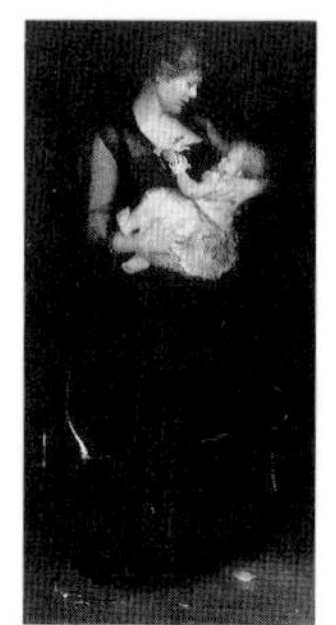
127.

GILL, Miss R*osalie* Lorraine *1867?–1898*
Born at Baltimore, Md. *(probably Elmira, N.Y.); died Paris, France.* Masters: Wm. M. Chase and Alfred Stevens

127. The Orchid, *1889. See page 155. Photograph by Harry Connolly, Baltimore*

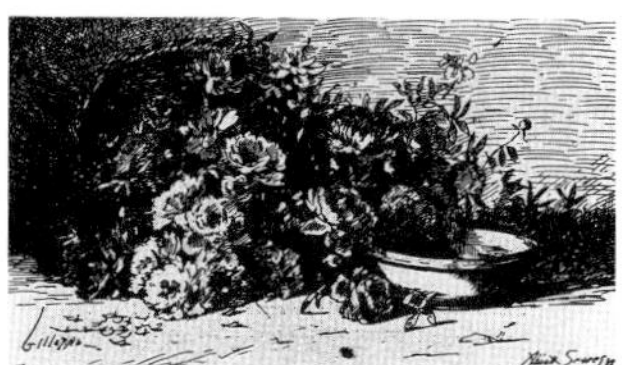
128.

GRAVES, Abbott *1859–1936*
Born at Weymouth, Mass.; *died Kennebunkport, Maine.* Masters: M. Cormon; *Georges Jeannin*

128. Peonies, *c. 1888 (unlocated). Formerly collection Boston Art Club. Engraving by Gillat after the painting, from* Salon de 1888 *(Paris), p. 195.*
129. Basket of Flowers *(unlocated)*

GREATOREX, Miss Eleanor Elizabeth *1854–1897*
Born at New York, N.Y. *[Hoboken, N.J.]; died New York.* Master*s*: M. Henner; *Lambinet, Toussaint*

130. Tea Roses *(unlocated)*

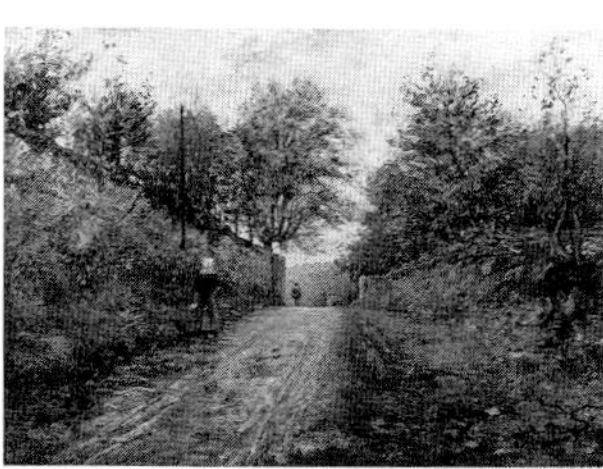
131.

GROSS, Peter Alfred *1849–1914*
Born at Allentown, Pa. *[Schnecksville]; died Chicago.* Masters: Yon and Petitjean. *Recompense: Honorable mention 1889*

131. Road to the spring (Liverdun). *See page 158.*
132. View of the Moselle (Liverdun) *(unlocated)*

GUISE *(Newcomb)*, Marie *1865–1895?* Born at New York, N.Y. *[Newark, N.J.]*. Master: Schenck

133. Haying Time in Ecouen, France *(unlocated)*

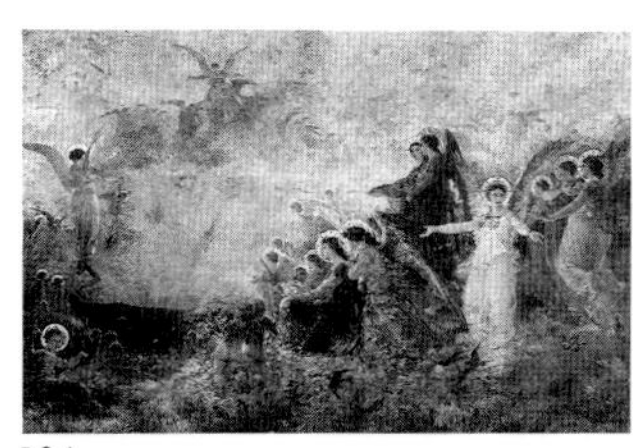
134.

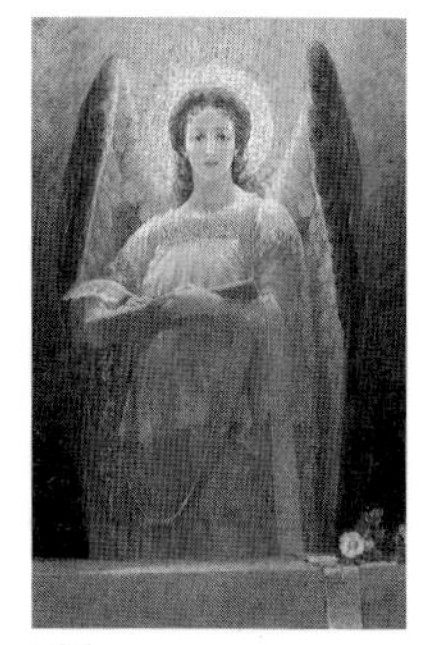
135.

GUTHERZ, Carl *1844–1907*
Born in Switzerland *(Schoeftland); died Washington, D.C.* Masters: Boulanger, Lefebvre; *Pils, Cabasson, Stollaert, A.N.N. Robert. Recompense: Bronze medal 1889*

134. Lux incarnationis, *1888. See page 159.*
135. Memorialis. *See page 159.*

HAAS, Maurits *Frederick* Hendrick *De* *1832–1895*
Born at Rotterdam, Holland; *died New York*. Masters: Louis Meyer; *Albert van Beest*. Recompenses: Medal Centennial Exposition of 1876 and medals from Boston, Cincinnati, etc., etc.; *honorable mention 1889*

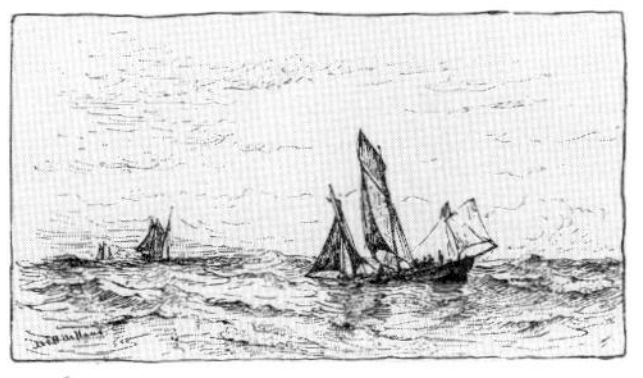
136.

136. On the Fishing Grounds. *Oil on canvas, 28 x 44".* *Engraving after the painting, from* National Academy Notes, *(1887), p. 77. Photograph courtesy The New-York Historical Society*

HAMILTON, E*dward* W*ilbur* Dean *1862/64–1948*
Born at Somerfields, Pa.; died Kingston, Mass. Masters: Bouguereau, T. Robert-Fleury

137. Sandy Plains at Cape Ann, Mass. *(unlocated)*

HAMILTON, Hamilton *1847–1928*
Born in England

138. A September Day *(unlocated)*

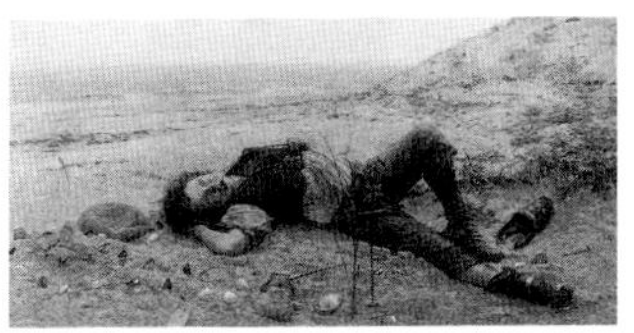
139.

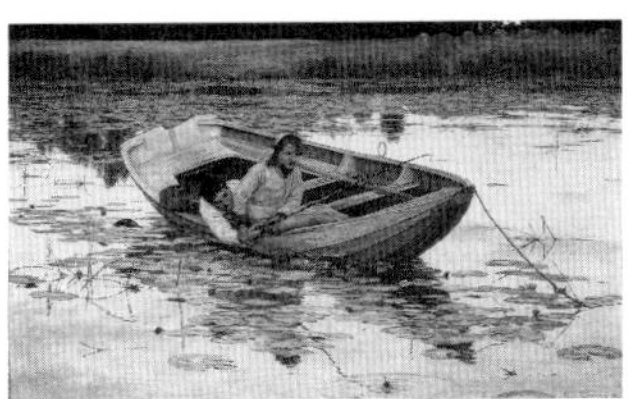
140.

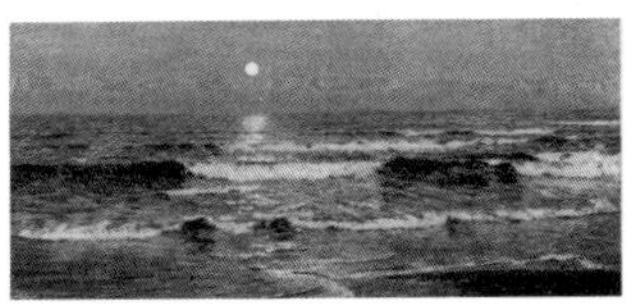
141.

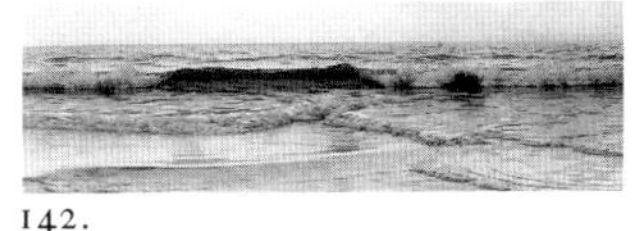
142.

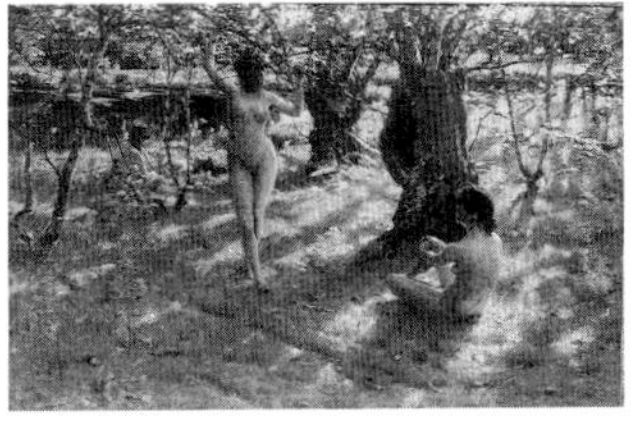
143.

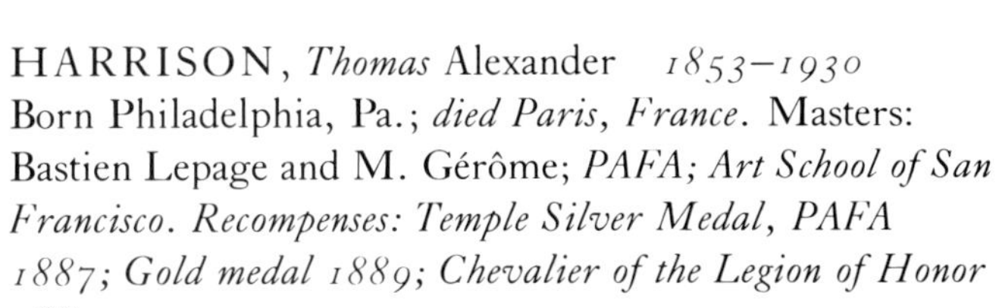

HARRISON, *Thomas* Alexander *1853–1930*
Born Philadelphia, Pa.; *died Paris, France*. Masters: Bastien Lepage and M. Gérôme; *PAFA; Art School of San Francisco. Recompenses: Temple Silver Medal, PAFA 1887; Gold medal 1889; Chevalier of the Legion of Honor 1889*

139. Castles in the air (Owner, J.G. Johnson). *Castles in Spain, c. 1882. See page 160.*

140. The Amateurs, *1882–83* (Owner, Chicago Art Institute). *See page 160.*

141. Twilight, *c. 1884* (Owner, St. Louis Museum of Fine Arts). *Engraving by H. Wolf after the painting, from* Century Magazine *(May–Oct., 1891), p. 576. Photograph courtesy The Library of Congress*

142. The Wave, *c. 1885. See page 160.*

143. In Arcadia, *c. 1886. See page 160.*

144. Evening *(unlocated)*

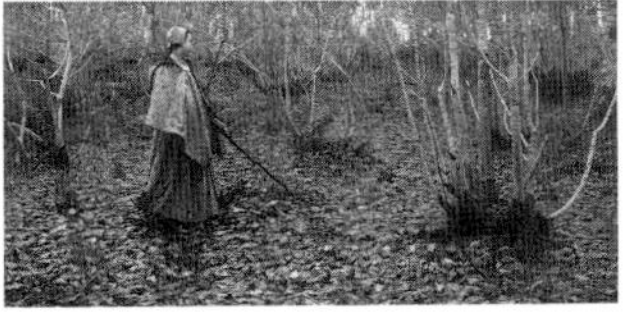
145.

HARRISON, *Lowell* Birge *1854–1928*
Born at Philadelphia, Pa. *Masters: Carolus-Duran, Cabanel. Recompense: Silver medal 1889*

145. Novembre, *1881*. Property of French Gov't. *See page 164.*

HARRISON, *Apollo* Butler *c. 1862–c. 1897*
Born at Philadelphia, Pa.; *died Plymouth, Mass.* Master: M.L.O. Merson

146. Landscape *(unlocated)*

HART, Jas. *McDonald* *1828–1901*
Born at Kilmarnock, Scotland; *died New York*. Masters: Wm. Hart and J.W. Shirm. Recompenses: Centennial medal, 1876; *bronze medal 1889*

147. The Rain is over *(unlocated)*
148. In the Autumn Woods *(unlocated)*

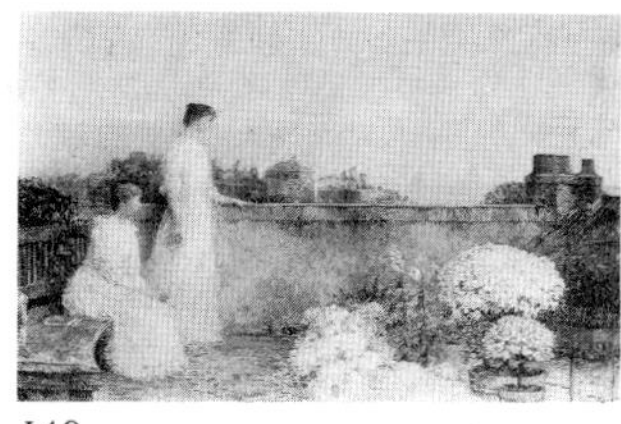
149.

150.

HASSAM, Childe *1859–1935*
Born at Boston, Mass.; *died East Hampton, N.Y. Masters: Dorcet, Boulanger, Lefebvre. Recompense: Bronze medal 1889*

149. Twilight. *Twilight in Paris, c. 1888. Oil on canvas, 50 x 77". Private collection. Photograph courtesy Hirschl & Adler, New York*
150. Rue Lafayette; winter evening *(unlocated). Oil on canvas, 20 x 26". Photograph Peter A. Juley & Son Collection*
151. After breakfast *(unlocated)*
152. Letter from America *(unlocated)*

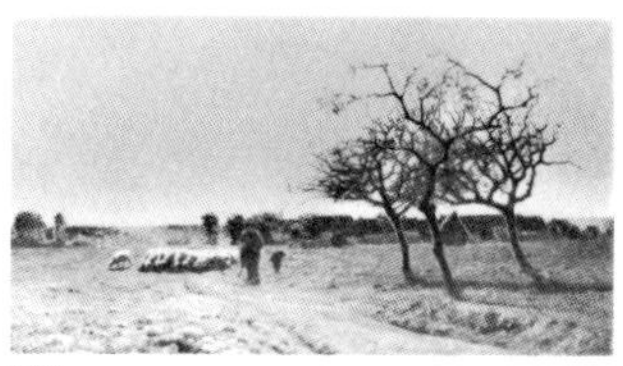
153.

HAYDEN, Charles Henry 1856–1901
Born at Plymouth, Mass. Masters: Boulanger, Lefebvre, Collin. *Recompense: Honorable mention 1889*

153. Morning on the plains. *Morning on the Plains, St. Leger, France, 1888 (unlocated). Oil on canvas, 22¼ x 36¼". Photograph courtesy Sotheby's, New York*

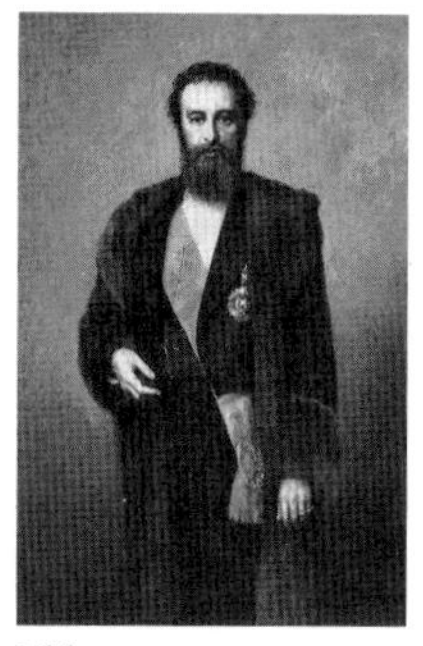

155.

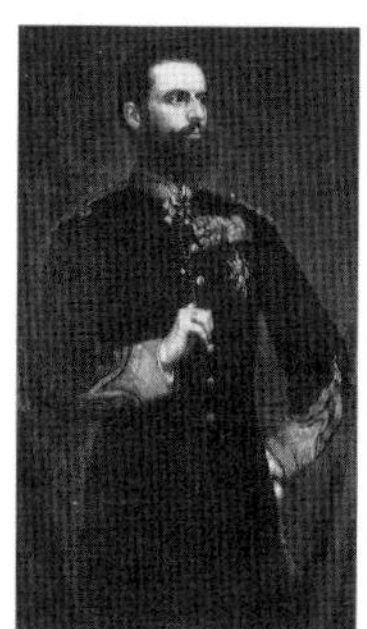
156.

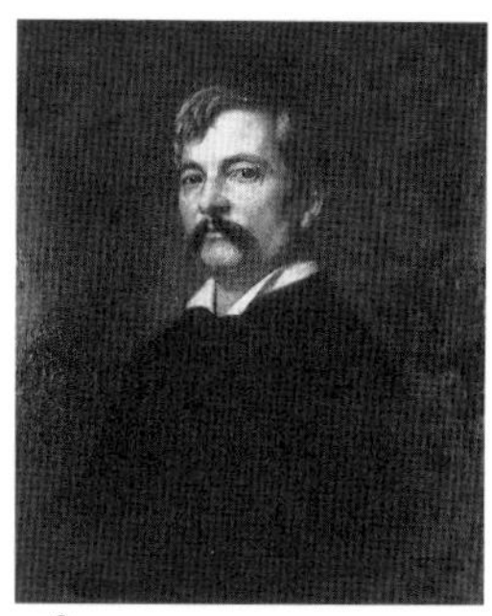
158.

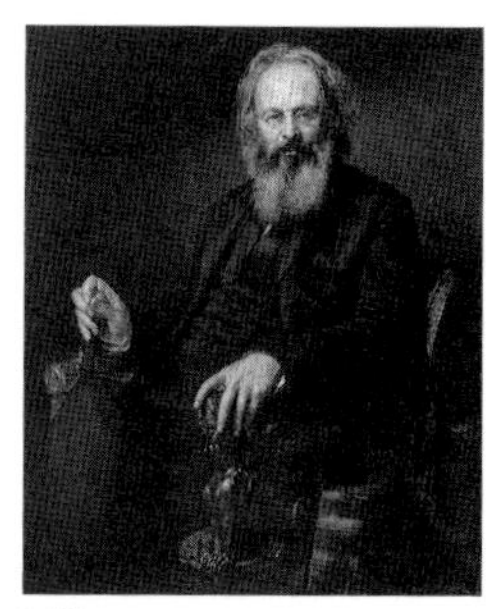
159.

HEALY, *George Peter Alexander* *1813–1894*
Born at Boston, Mass.; *died Chicago*. Masters: Gros and Couture. *Recompenses:* Med. 3rd cl., Salon 1840, 2nd class 1855 (E.U.)

154. Portrait of M. C. Bigot *(unlocated)*
155. Lord Lytton, *1888.* *See page 165.*
156. King of Roumania. *King Charles, 1881. Oil on canvas, 54½ x 30¾". The Newberry Library, Chicago*
157. Study at the harp *(unlocated)*
158. Stanley. *Sir Henry M. Stanley. Oil on canvas, 30½ x 24¾". The Newberry Library, Chicago*
159. Portrait of M. Brownson. *See page 165.*

HENNESSY, William *John* *1839–1917*

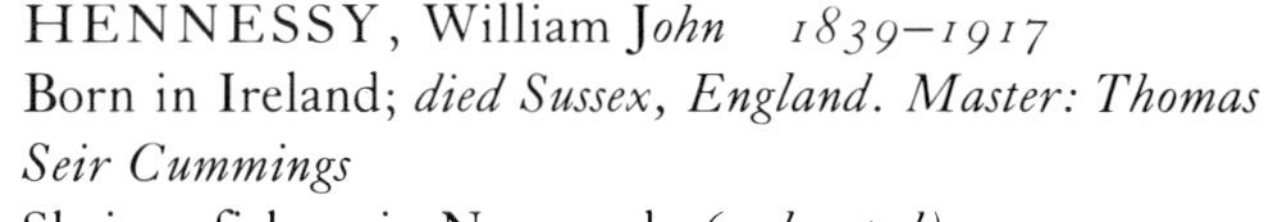

Born in Ireland; *died Sussex, England. Master: Thomas Seir Cummings*

160. Shrimp fishers in Normandy *(unlocated)*

161. Expiation pilgrimage, Calvados *(unlocated)*

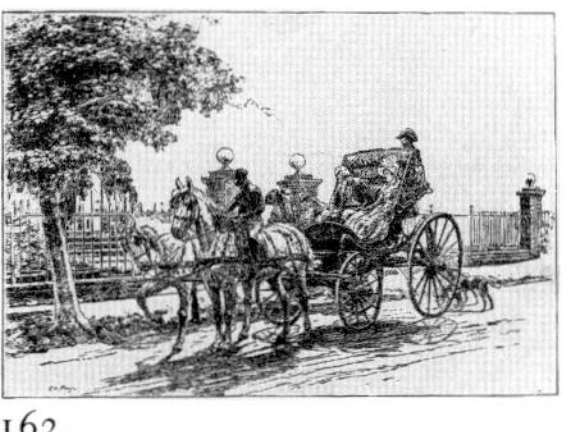

162.

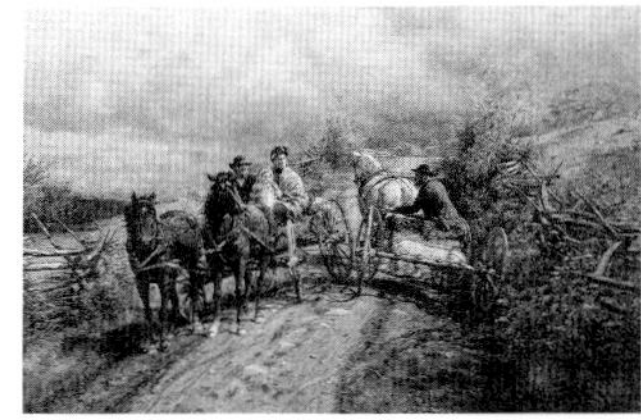

163.

HENRY, Edward *Lamson* *1841–1919*

Born at Charleston, S.C.; *died Ellenville, N.Y.* Masters: Paul Weber; *Gleyre*. Recompenses: medals, New Orleans and Chicago; *honorable mention 1889*

162. One hundred Years ago, *1887. Oil on canvas, 27 x 41". Engraving after the painting from* National Academy Notes *(1888), p. 73. Photograph courtesy The New York Public Library*

163. The latest Village Scandal, *1885.* *See page 168.*

HINCKLEY, Robert *1853–1941*

Born at Boston, Mass. Master: Carolus-Duran

164. Portrait of Mr. Clifford Richardson *(unlocated)*

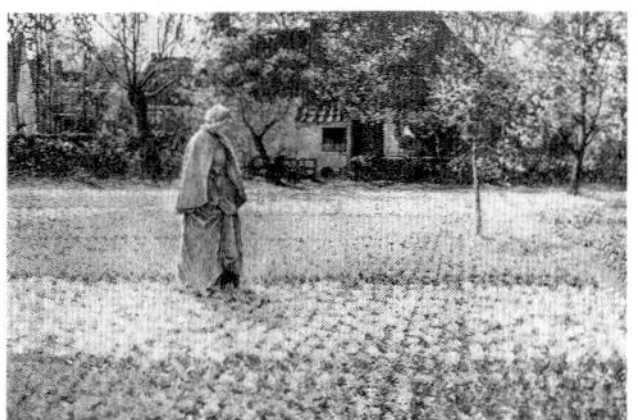

165.

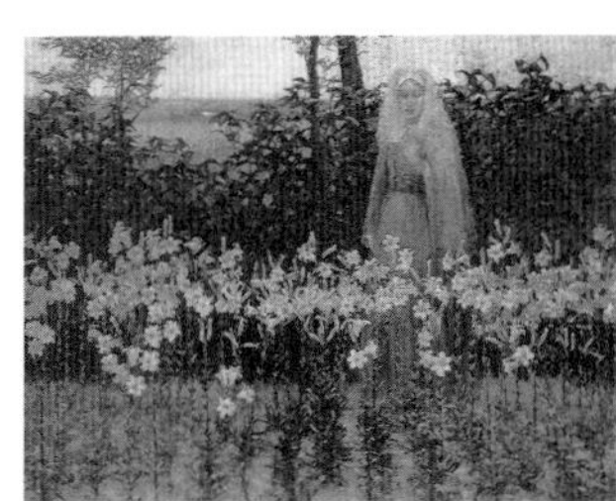

166.

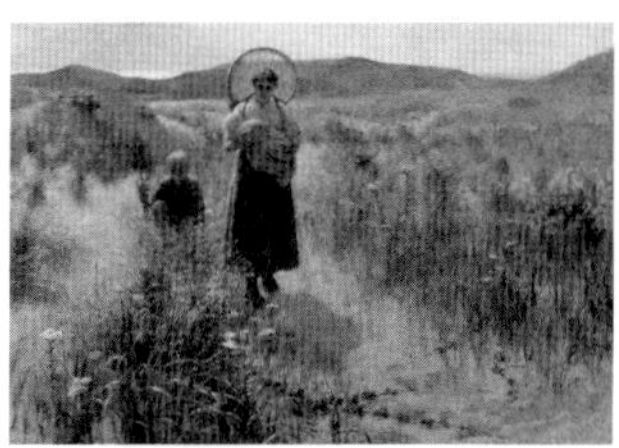

167.

HITCHCOCK, George *1850–1941*

Born at Providence, R.I.; *died Island of Marden, the Netherlands. Masters: Boulanger, Lefebvre, Mesdag. Recompense: Gold medal 1889*

165. Tulip Culture *c. 1887* (Owner, W.H. Tailer) *(unlocated). Ill. from* Salon de 1887 *(Paris), p. 207.*

166. Annonciation, *c. 1887.* *See page 169.*

167. Maternity, *1889.* *See page 169.*

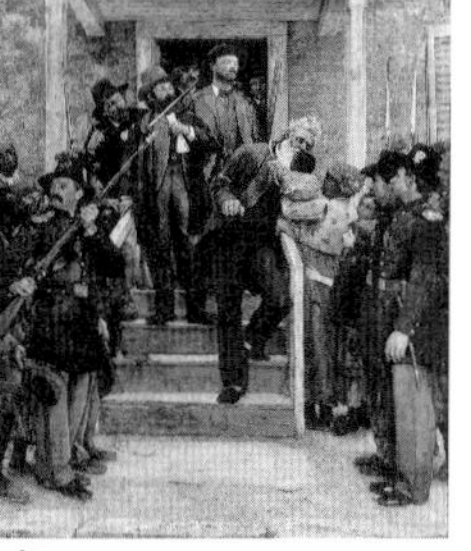

168.

HOVENDEN, Thomas *1840–1895*

Born in Ireland; *died Plymouth Meeting, Pa.* Masters: Cabanel; *Cork School of Design, Ireland; NAD*

168. Last Moments of John Brown, John Brown leaving the jail on the morning of his execution (Owner, Robbins Battell) *1884. Oil on canvas, 77⅜ x 66½". © The Metropolitan Museum of Art, New York, Gift of Mr. and Mrs. Carl Stoeckel, 97.5.* *See page 170.*

HOWE, William H*enry* *1846–1929*

Born at Ravenna, Ohio; *died Bronxville, N.Y.* Masters: de Thoven and de Vuillefroy; *Royal Academy, Düsseldorf.* Recompenses: Med. 3rd cl. 1888; *silver medal 1889*

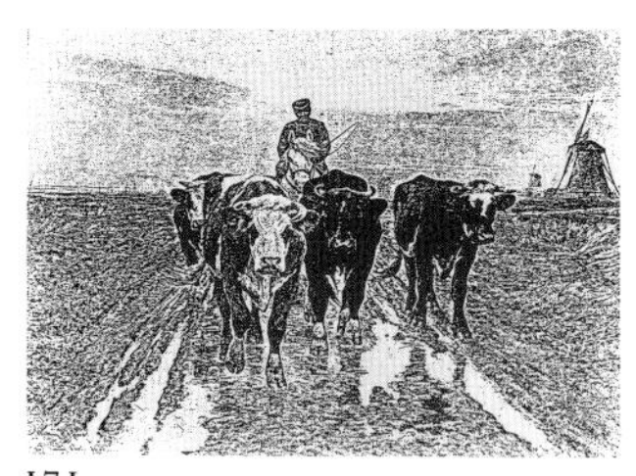
171.

169. At rest; September in Normandy *(unlocated)*
170. The Return of the cows; evening in Normandy *(unlocated)*
171. Departure for the market, souvenir of Holland.
Engraving after the painting; source of photograph unknown

HOWLAND, Alfred *Cornelius* *1838–1909*
Born at Walpole, N.H.; *died Pasadena, Calif.* Masters: Flamm of Dusseldorf, and Lambinet of Paris

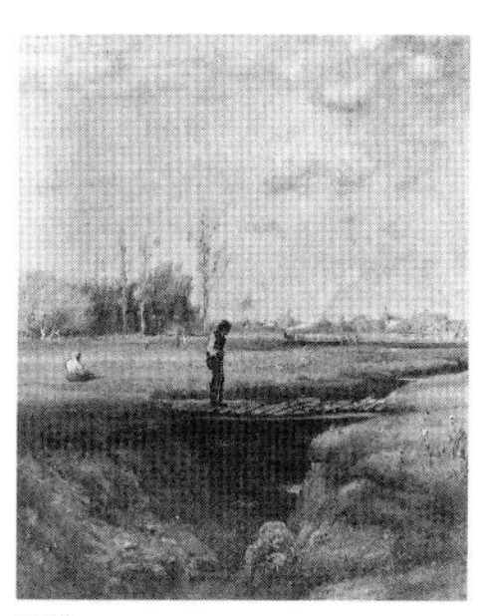

172.

172. A Day in June, *c. 1888. Oil on canvas, 18 x 24".*
Engraving after the painting, from National Academy Notes *(1888), p. 83.*

HUNTINGTON, Daniel *1816–1906*
Born at New York, N.Y.; *died New York.* Masters: S.F.B. Morse and G.F. Ferrero; *Couture.* Recompense: 1st class Medal, Centennial Exposition, 1876
173. A Burgomaster of New Amsterdam (New Amsterdam was the original name of New York). *Oil on canvas, 52 x 42¾" (unlocated). Sold Parke Bernet, New York, June 17, 1970, lot 100.*

HYDE, W*illiam* H*enry* *1858–1943*
Born at New York. Masters: Boulanger, Doucet, Harrison
174. The first Romance *(unlocated)*

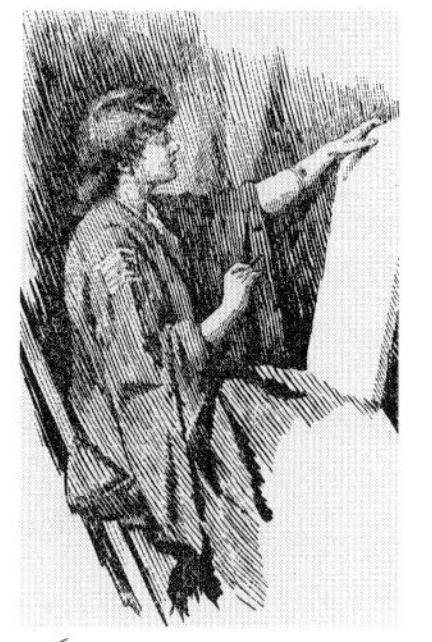
175.

INNESS, George *1824–1894*
Born at Newburgh, N.Y.; died Bridge of Allan, Scotland. Master: Régis Gignoux. Recompense: Bronze medal 1889
175. A shortcut to Wachung Station, *1883* (Owner, American Art Association). *See page 173.*

IRWIN, Benoni *1840–1896*
Born at Newmarket, Canada; died South Coventry, Conn. Master: Carolus-Duran
176. An Art Votary, *c. 1883 (unlocated). Engraving after the painting from* National Academy Notes *(1883), p. 28. Photograph courtesy The New-York Historical Society*

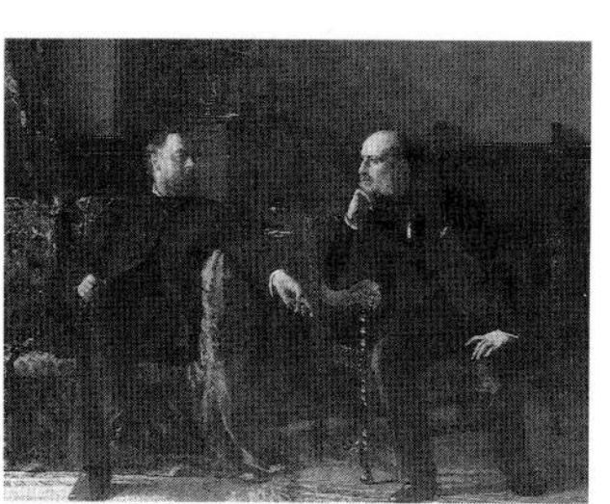
178.

ISHAM, Samuel *1855–1914*
Born at New York, N.Y.; *died East Hampton, N.Y.* Masters: Jacquessen de la Chevreuse, Boulanger and Lefebvre
177. Study for a Portrait *(unlocated)*

JOHNSON, Eastman *1824–1906*
Born in Maine *(Lovell); died New York. Masters: Leutze, Düsseldorf; Couture, Paris. Recompense: Bronze medal 1889*
178. Two Men. *The Funding Bill, 1881.* *See page 176.*

JONES, Hugh Bolton *1848–1927*
Born at Baltimore, Md.; died New York. Student at Maryland Institute; Horace Robbins. Recompense: Bronze medal 1889

179. The Old Pasture *(unlocated)*

KAVANAGH, John
Born at Cleveland, Ohio. Masters: Loefftz, Boulanger, Cormon

180. Washerwomen *(unlocated)*
181. Woman of Scheveningen *(unlocated)*
182. Shepherd *(unlocated)*

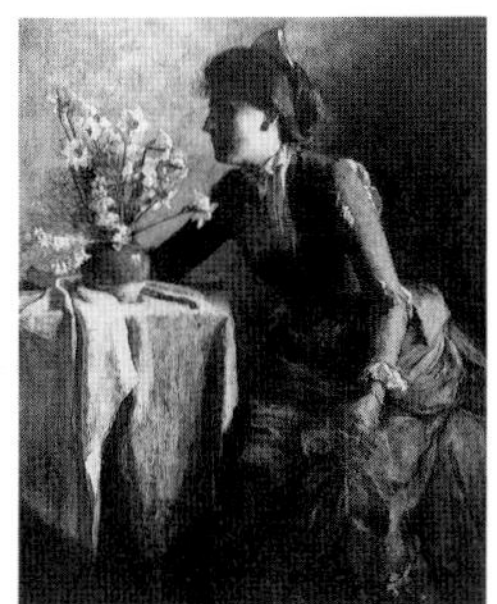
183.

KELLOGG *(Tyler)*, Miss Alice De *Wolf* *1862–1900*
Born at Chicago, Ill.; *died Chicago*. Masters: Boulanger, Lefebvre, Courtois; *Rixens, Dagnan-Bouveret, Robert-Fleury*

183. Portrait of Miss G.E.K. *Portrait of Gertrude E. Kellogg, 1888. See page 177.*

KING, Louise Howland *(Mrs. Kenyon Cox) 1865–1945*
Born at San Francisco, Cal.; *died Windham, Conn.* Student at the Academy of Design and Art Students League

184. The Lotos Eaters *(unlocated)*

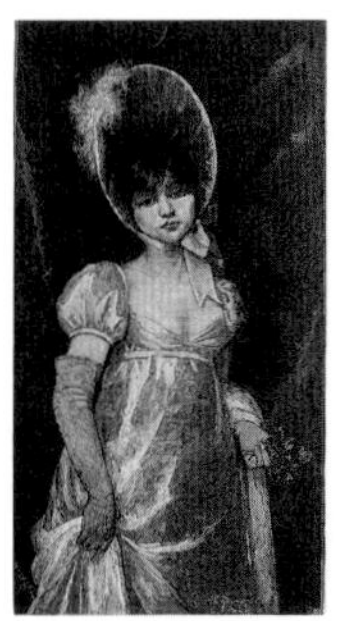
185.

KLUMPKE, Miss Anna E. *1856–1942*
Born at San Francisco, Cal., *died San Francisco*. Masters: T. Robert-Fleury, Bouguereau, and de Vuillefroy. *Recompense: Bronze medal 1889*

185. Portrait, *1887. Engraving after the painting from William Walton,* Chefs d'oeuvres, *Book 2, p. 11. Photograph courtesy The Library of Congress.*

KLYN, Charles F. de
Born at Tarrytown, N.Y. Masters: J. Lefebvre and Cormon

186. Women chatting *(unlocated)*
187. A Ray of Sunlight *(unlocated)*

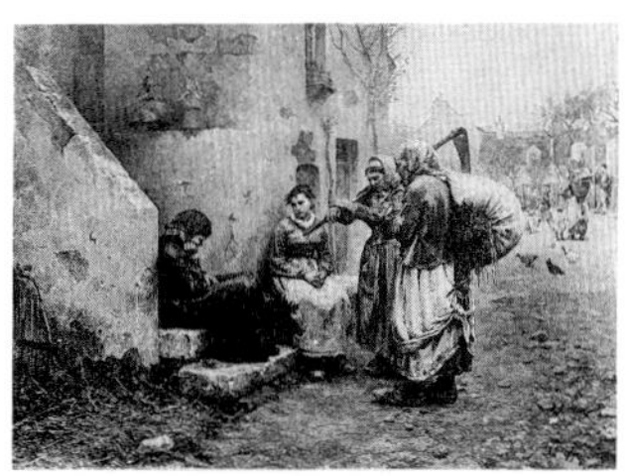
188.

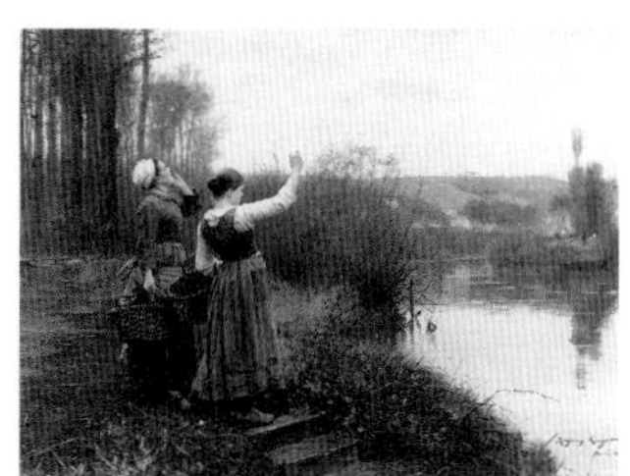
189.

KNIGHT, Daniel Ridgway *1839–1924*
Born at Philadelphia; *died Paris, France*. Masters: Gleyre and Meissonier; *Ecole des Beaux-Arts; Accademia di San Luca; PAFA. Recompenses:* Hon. Men. Paris, '82; Medal 3rd class, Paris, '88; Gold med. 2nd class, Munich, '88; *silver medal 1889; Chevalier of the Legion of Honor 1889*

188. Mourning *(unlocated). Engraving after the painting from G. W. Sheldon,* Recent Ideals, *p. 35. Photograph courtesy The Library of Congress.*
189. Hailing the Ferryman, *1888. See page 179.*
190. The Meeting *(unlocated)*

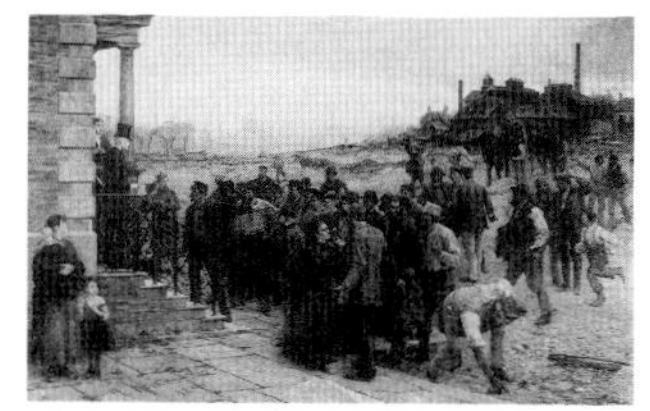

191.

KOEHLER, Robert *1850–1917*
Born at Hamburg, *Germany; died Minneapolis.* Masters: Defregger and Loefftz, *Royal Academy, Munich; NAD, ASL. Recompense: Honorable mention 1889*

191. The Strike, *1886.* *See page 179.*

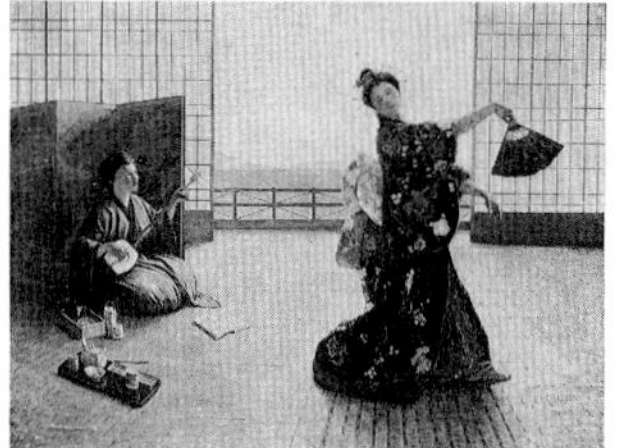

192.

LA CHAISE, Eugene *Armand*
Born at New York, N.Y. Masters: G. Boulanger and Lefebvre

192. Souvenirs of Japan, *1889 (unlocated). Ill. from G.W. Sheldon,* Recent Ideals, *p. 125. Photograph courtesy The Library of Congress*

LASAR, Charles *Augustus* *1856–1936*
Born at Johnstown, Pa. Master: M. Gérôme

193. On the coast of Britany *[sic] (unlocated)*

LASH, Lee *1864–?*
Born at San Francisco, Cal. Masters: Boulanger and M. J. Lefebvre

194. The Death-watch *(unlocated)*

LOCKWOOD, Robert W*ilton* *1862–1914*
Born at Wilton, Conn.; *died Brookline, Mass.* Masters: Schenck and La Farge

195. Portrait of M.C. *(unlocated)*

LOOMIS *(France)*, Eurilda Q. *1865–1931*
Born at Pittsburg*h*, Pa.; *died New Haven, Conn.* Masters: Boulanger and Lefebvre, *Carolus-Duran, Morot, Constant*

196. Rustic Life in Picardy *(unlocated)*

LORING, Francis William *1838–1905*
Born at Boston, Mass.; *died Theran, Tyrol (?)*

197. Autumn in the Valley of the Arno *(unlocated)*

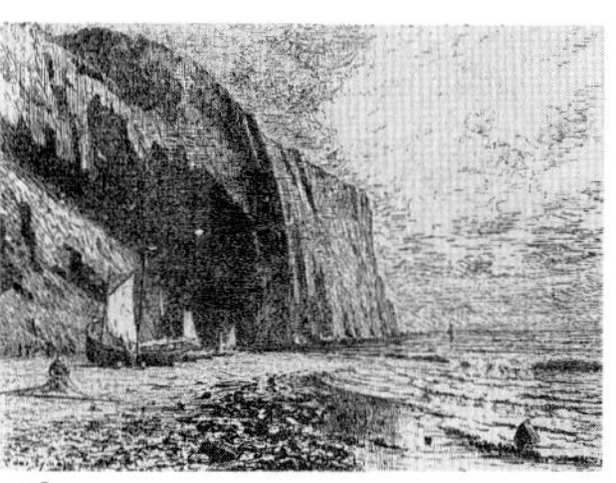

198.

LYMAN, Joseph, *Jr.* *1843–1913*
Born at Ravenna, Ohio; *died Wallingford, Conn. Masters: J.H. Dolph, S. Colman; studied in Europe*

198. On the Beach (at Percé, Canada) *(unlocated). Engraving after the painting, from American Art Association catalogue, 1885, cat. no. 164.*

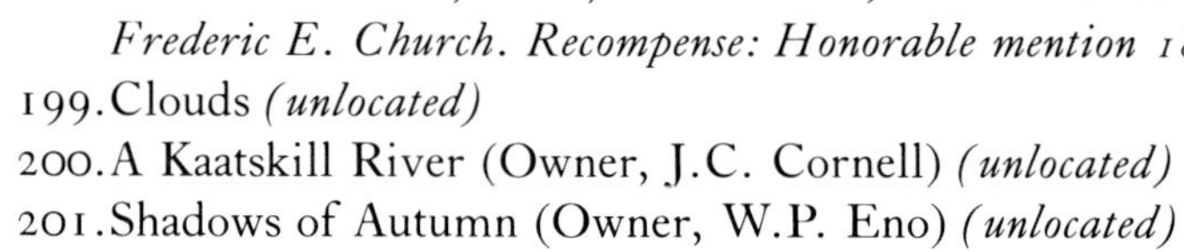

McENTEE, Jervis *1828–1891*
Born at Rondout, N.Y.; *died Rondout, N.Y. Master: Frederic E. Church. Recompense: Honorable mention 1889*

199. Clouds *(unlocated)*

200. A Kaatskill River (Owner, J.C. Cornell) *(unlocated)*

201. Shadows of Autumn (Owner, W.P. Eno) *(unlocated)*

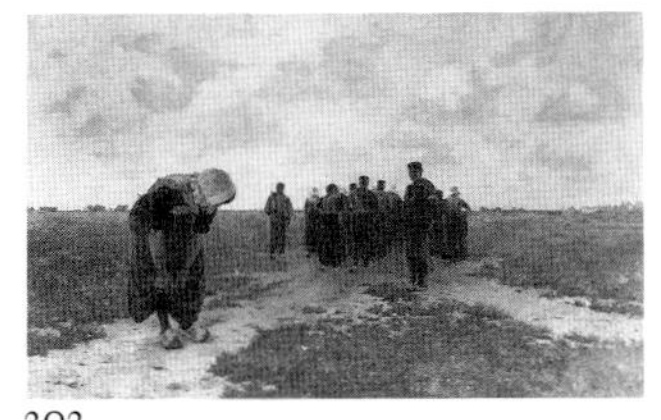
202.

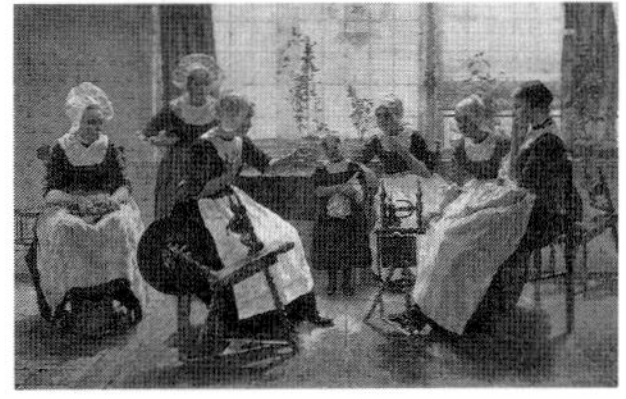
203.

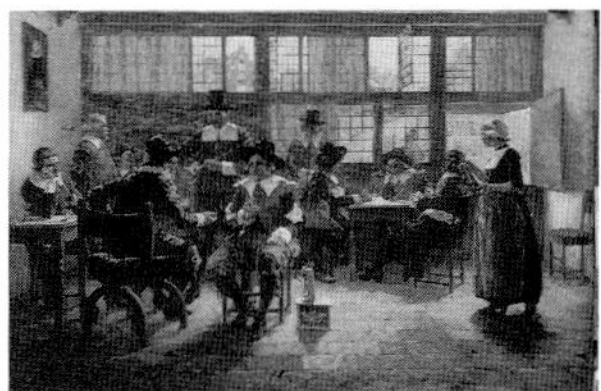
204.

MAC-EWEN, Walter *1860–1943*
Born at Chicago, Ill.; *died New York. Masters: Robert-Fleury, Cormon, Duveneck. Recompense: Silver medal 1889*

202. Returning from work, *c. 1885. See page 182.*

203. A Ghost story, *1887. See page 182.*

204. Stad Herberg, Nieuw Amsterdam (New York) 1650. *Town Hall of New Amsterdam (New York) 1650 (unlocated). Oil on canvas, 56 x 81 1/16". Sold at Christie's, New York, Dec. 5, 1986, lot 115. Photograph courtesy Christie's, New York*

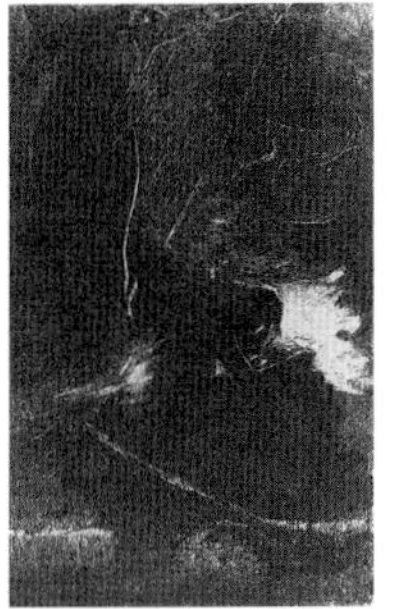
206.

MACY, William *Starbuck* *1853–1945*
Born at New Bedford, Mass. *Master: Van Velten, Munich*

205. The Shore of Meacham Lake *(unlocated)*

MATHEWS, Arthur F. *1860–1945*
Born in California *[Markesan, Wisconsin]; died San Francisco.* Masters: Boulanger and Lefebvre

206. Pandore, *c. 1888. Ill. from* Salon de 1888 *(Paris), p. 309.*

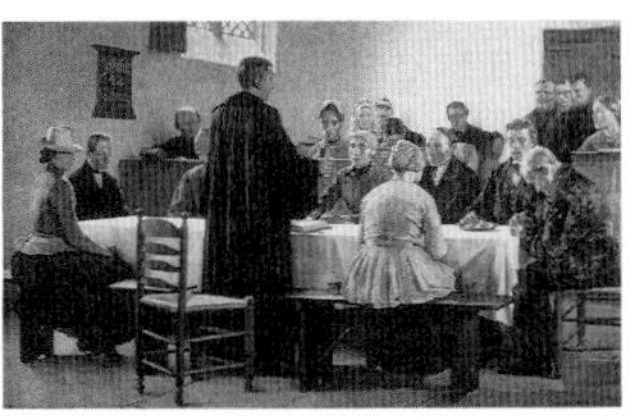
207.

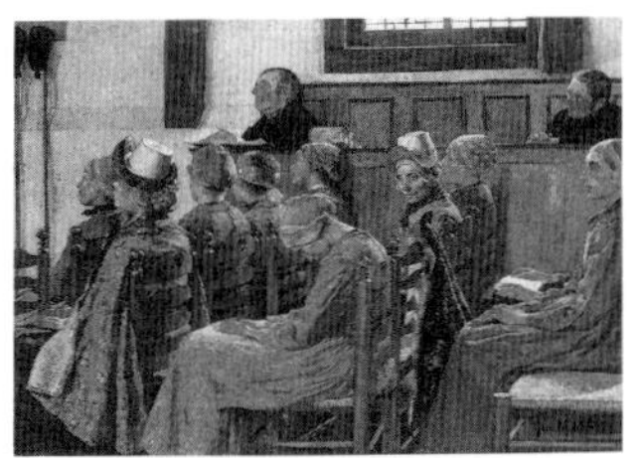
208.

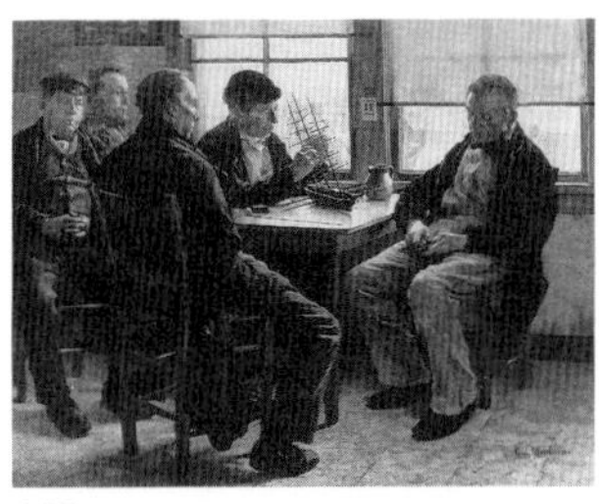
209.

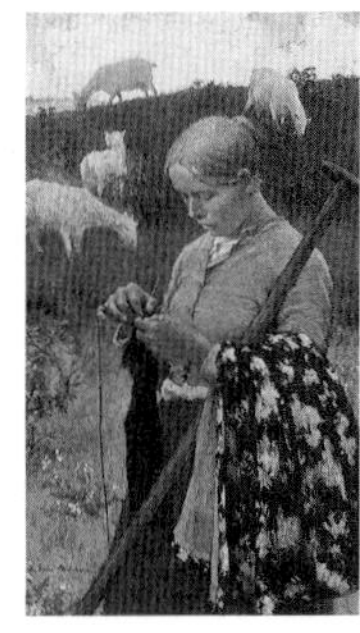
210.

MELCHERS, J*ulius* Gari *1860–1932*
Born at Detroit, Mich.; *died Fredericksburg, Va.* Masters: Boulanger and Lefebvre; *von Gebhardt, Peter Janssen, Düsseldorf. Recompenses:* Med. 3rd. cl., 1888; *Grand Prize 1889*

207. Communion, *1888. See page 183.*

208. The Sermon, *1886. Oil on canvas, 62 5/8 x 86 1/2". National Museum of American Art, Smithsonian Institution, Washington, D.C. Bequest of Henry Ward Ranger through the NAD*

209. The Pilots, *1887. Oil on canvas, 67 x 83 1/2". Charles and Emma Frye Art Museum, Seattle*

210. Shepherdess, *c. 1889. See page 183.*

MEZA, *Matias* Wilson de
Born at Tarrytown-on-the-Hudson, N.Y. Masters: Boulanger and Lefebvre. *Recompense: Honorable mention 1889*
211. Portrait of a Lady *(unlocated)*

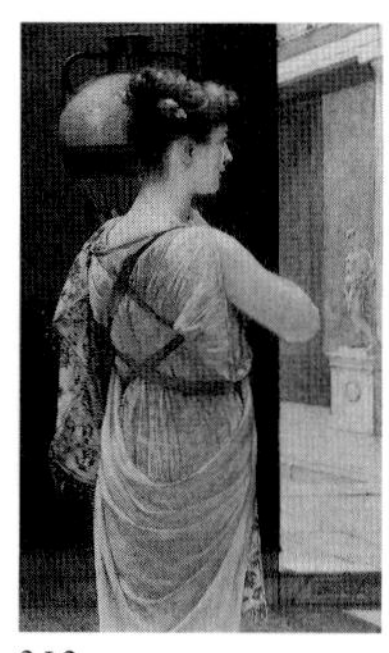
212.

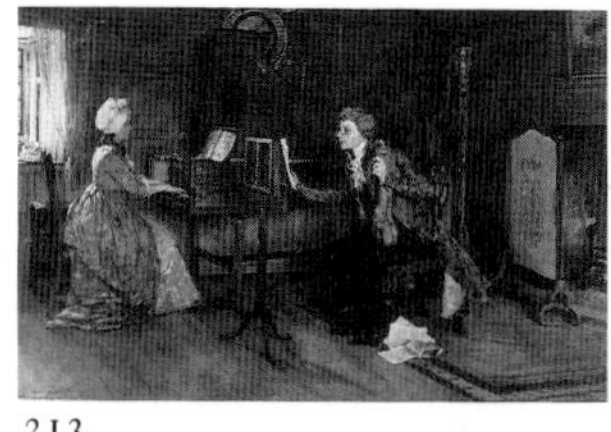
213.

MILLET, Francis *Davis (Frank)* *1846–1912*
Born in Massachusetts *(Mattapoisett); died at sea. Student at Royal Academy, Antwerp*
212. A Handmaiden, *1886* (Owner, George T. Seney). *See page 187.*
213. A difficult Duet, *1886* (Owner, Mrs. Raymond). *See page 187.*

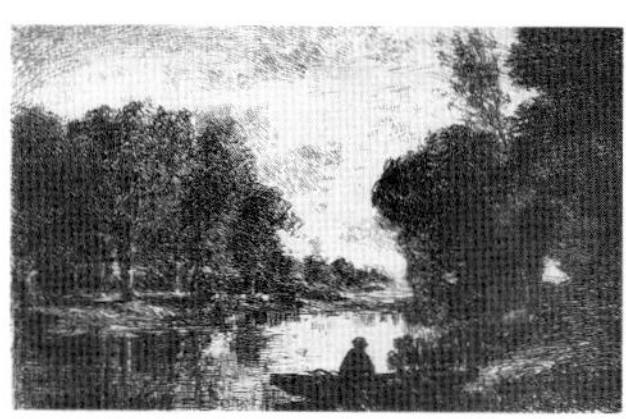
214.

MILLER, Charles H*enry* *1842–1922*
Born at New York, N.Y. Student at National Academy of Design, and Royal Academy of Bavaria. Recompenses: Gold medals, Boston, New Orleans and Philadelphia
214. A Bouquet of Oaks, near Jamaica, Long Island, N.Y., *c. 1884 Engraving after the painting from* National Academy Notes *(1884), p. 67. Photograph courtesy The New-York Historical Society*

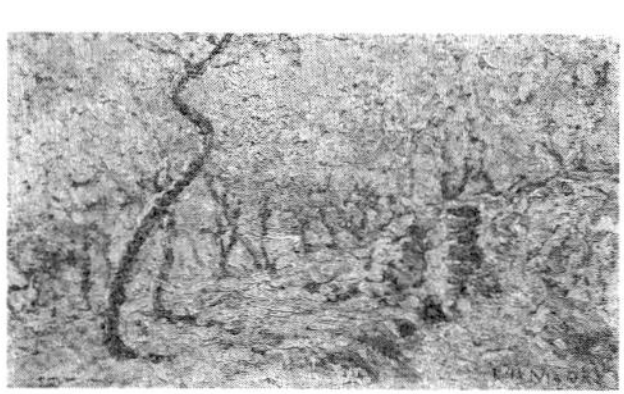
215.

MINOR, Robert C*rannell* *1839–1904*
Born at New York; died Waterford, Conn. Student of Alfred C. Howland; van Luppen, Antwerp; disciple of Narcisse Diaz. Recompense: Bronze medal 1889
215. Close of Day, *1886* (Owner, W.T. Evans) *(unlocated). Oil on canvas, 30 x 50". Sold to S.P. Avery in 1900. Etching after the painting, James Ruddach Collection of American Art. Photograph courtesy William Benton Museum of Art, University of Connecticut, Storrs, Conn.*

MOELLER, L*ouis Charles* *1855–1930*
Born at New York; died Weehawken, N.J. Masters: NAD, Wilhelm von Diez, Royal Academy, Munich. Recompense: Hallgarten Prize (NAD) 1884
216. A Doubtful Investment *(unlocated)*

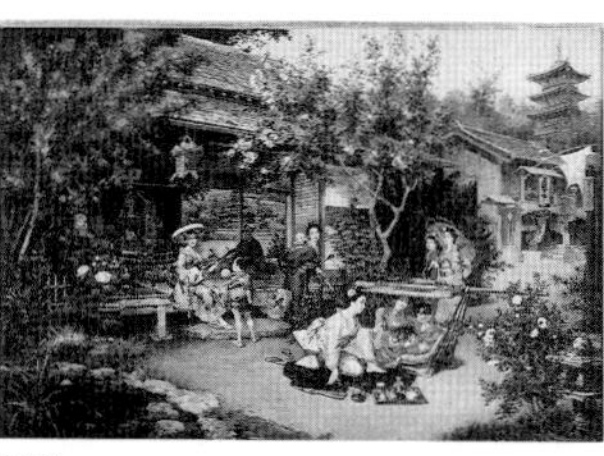
217.

MONKS, Robert Hatton *1856–1923*
Born at Boston, Mass.; *died Wellesley, Mass.* Masters: Bouguereau and T. Robert-Fleury; *Grundmann, Rimmer*
217. A Grey Day. *See page 189.*

220.

MOORE, H*arry* Humphrey *1844–1926*
Born at New York; died Paris, France
Student of Gérôme, Fortuny, Yvon, Boulanger; PAFA, Samuel B. Waugh. Recompenses: Medal at 1876 Centennial; bronze medal 1889
218. Japanese Views. *Glimpse into the Pleasure Quarters, Yoshiwara, 1887. See page 190.*
219. Japanese Views *(unlocated)*
220. Japanese Views *(unlocated)*

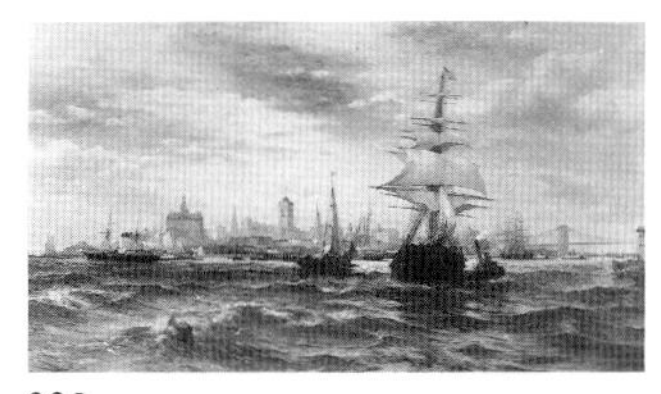
221.

MORAN, Edward *1829–1901*
Born at Bolton, England *[Bolton-le-Moor, Lancashire]; died New York.* Masters: James Hamilton and Paul Weber. Recompenses: Medal, Palette Club, Centennial Exposition, 1876

221. New York City from the Channel, *1889.* *See page 191.*

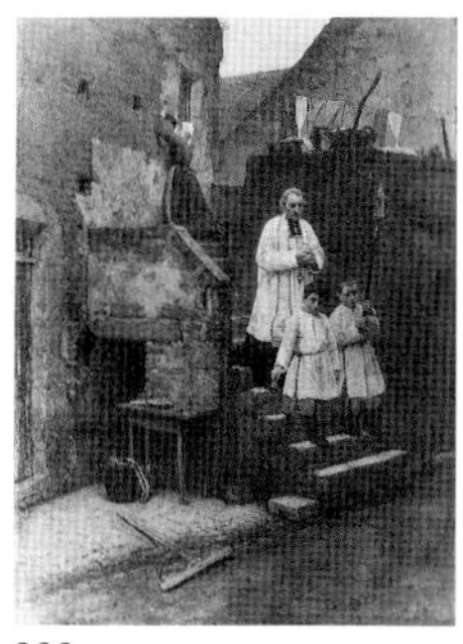
222.

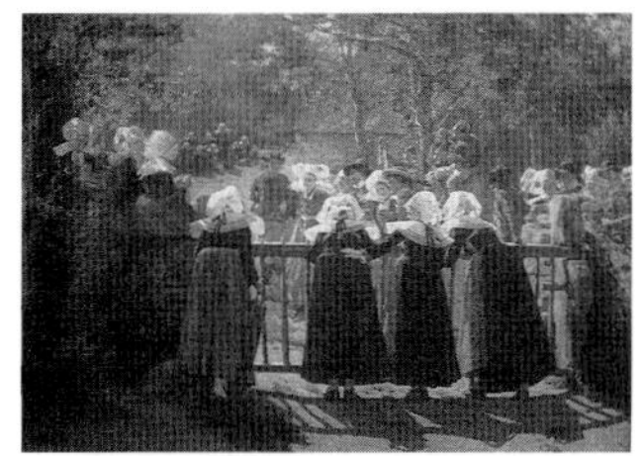
223.

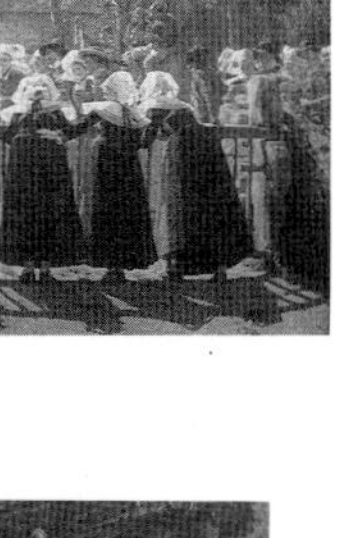
224.

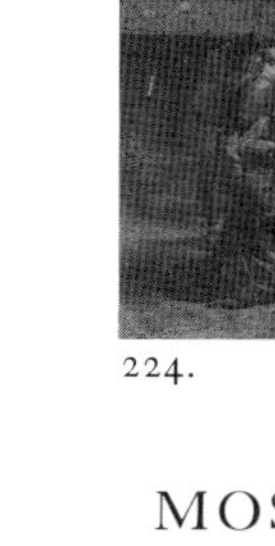

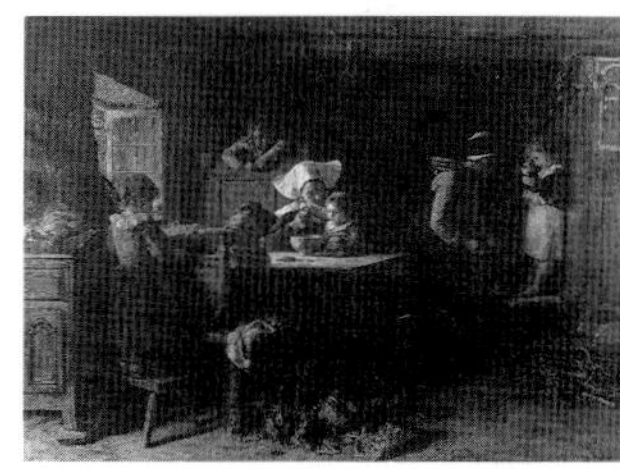
226.

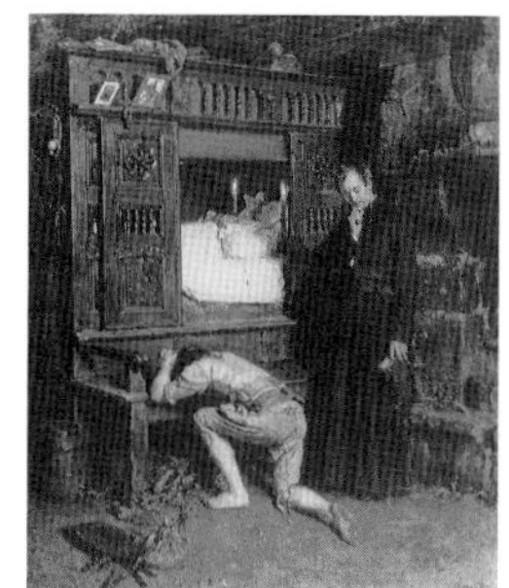
226A.

MOSLER, Henry *1841–1920*
Born at New York; *died New York.* Masters: M. Hébert; *Mucke and Kindler, Düsseldorf; Wagner and von Piloty, Munich. Recompense:* Med. 3rd cl., 1888; *silver medal 1889*

222. The last Sacraments, *1884* (Owner, Louisville, Polytechnic Ass'n.). *See page 194.*
223. Harvest Festival (Owner, Mrs. Haydock, Cincinnati). *Oil on canvas, 52 5/8 x 39 1/2". Cincinnati Public Schools*
224. The last Moments. *Oil on canvas; 47 5/8 x 63 5/8". Walker Art Center, Minneapolis*
225. The young Bag-piper (Owner, O.J. Wilson, Cincinnati) *(unlocated)*
226. New Year's Morning, *1888* (Owner, Phil D. Armour, Chicago.). *Oil on canvas, 44 x 59 1/16". Cincinnati Art Museum*
The Return, *1879* (To be seen at Luxembourg Museum.). *Oil on canvas, 47 1/4 x 39 1/2". Musée Départemental Breton, Quimper, France*

NETTLETON, Walter E. *1861–1936*
Born New Haven, Conn. Masters: Boulanger, Lefebvre

227. Winnowing; Finistère *(unlocated)*

NEWMAN, Carl *1858–1932*
Born at Philadelphia, Pa.

228. Portrait of Mme. X. *(unlocated)*

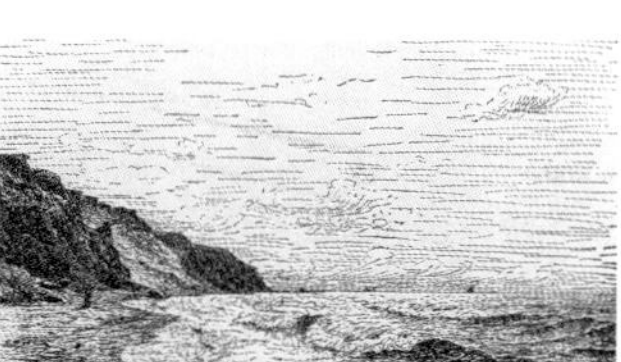
229.

NICOLL, James Craig *1847–1918*
Born at New York, N.Y. Masters: M.F.H. de Haas; *van Elten.* Recompense: First Class, New Orleans Exposition; *honorable mention 1889*

229. Sunlight on the Sea, *c. 1884. Engraving after the painting, from* National Academy Notes *(1887), p. 4. Photograph courtesy The New-York Historical Society*

O'HALLORAN, Miss *Agnes*

Born at St. Paul, Minn. Master: George Hitchcock

230. Study *(unlocated)*

231. Cottage on the Dutch downs *(unlocated)*

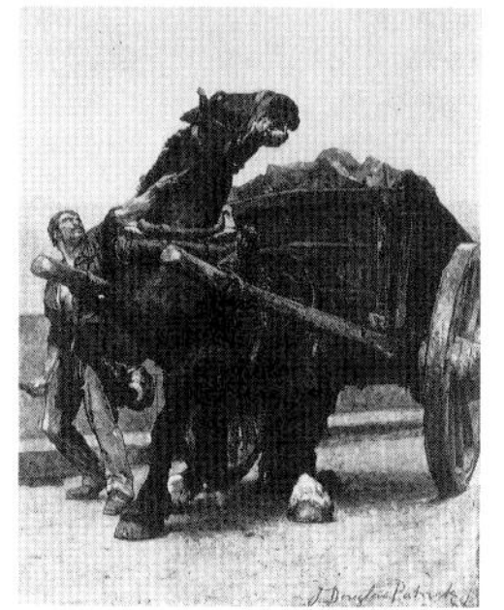

233.

PARKER, Stephen Hills *1852–1925*

Born at New York, N.Y.; *died in Florida. Student of Carolus-Duran*

232. Father Gaspard, *c. 1887 (unlocated)*

PARTON, Arthur *1842–1914*

Born at Hudson, N.Y.; *died Yonkers, N.Y. Masters: William Trost Richards and Barbizon School. Recompense: Honorable mention 1889*

233. In the month of May. (Owner, W. T. Evans.) *(unlocated). Oil on canvas, 26 x 36". Ill. from G.W. Sheldon,* Recent Ideals, *p.111. Photograph courtesy The Library of Congress*

234. Winter on the Hudson. (Owner, American Art Association.) *(unlocated)*

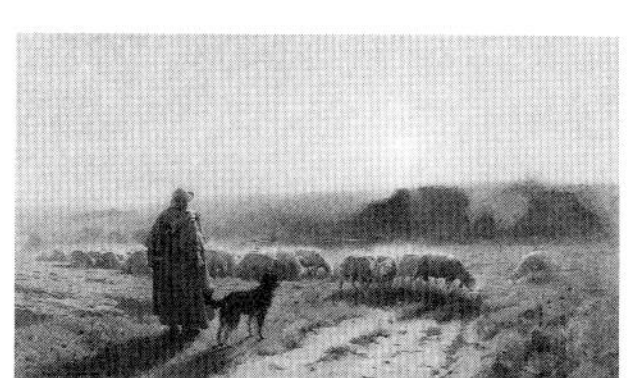

235.

PATRICK, J*ohn* Douglas *1863–1937*

Born at Hopewell, Pa.; died Kansas City, Kansas. Masters: Boulanger, Lefebvre, Chartran. Recompense: Bronze medal 1889

235. Brutality, *1888.* *See page 195.*

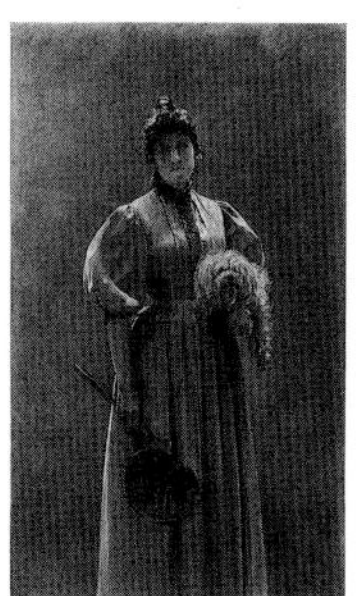

238.

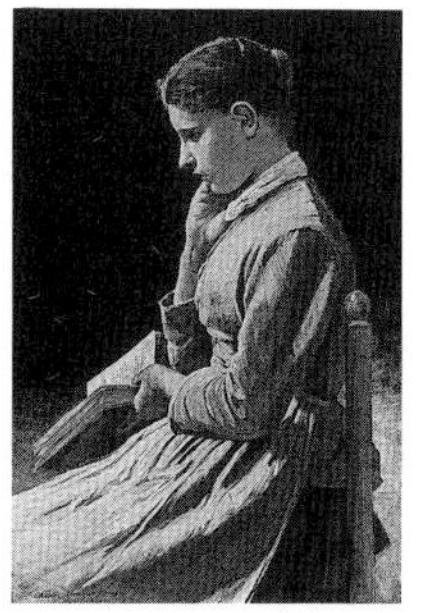

239.

PEARCE, Charles Sprague *1851–1914*

Born at Boston, Mass.; *died Paris, France.* Master: M. Bonnat. *Recompenses:* Honorable mention, Salon 1881; 3rd cl. gold med., 1883; gold med. 2nd cl., 1888 Munich; grand med. of honor Ghent, 1886

236. Shepherdess, *c. 1885* (unlocated). *Ill. from G.W. Sheldon,* Recent Ideals, *p. 27. Photograph courtesy The Library of Congress*

237. Evening. *See page 198.*

238. Portrait of Mme P., *1889 (unlocated). Ill. from G.W. Sheldon,* Recent Ideals, *p.128. Photograph courtesy The Library of Congress*

239. Melancholy. *A Reverie (unlocated). Ill. from G.W. Sheldon,* Recent Ideals, *p.15. Photograph courtesy The Library of Congress*

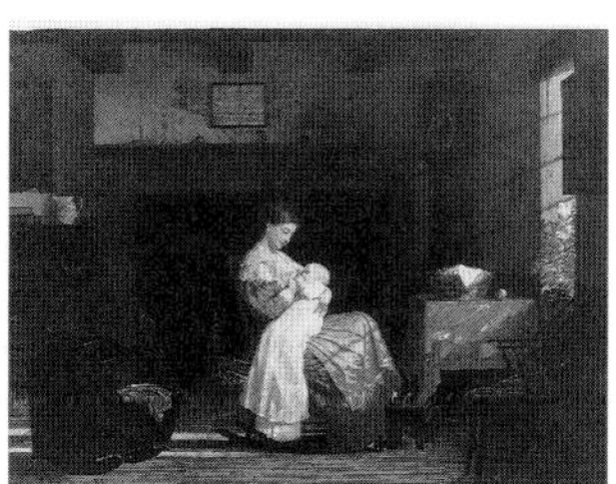

241.

PEARCE, Louise Catharine *(Mrs. Charles S. Pearce)*

Born at Paris, France. Master: Charles Sprague Pearce

240. Japanese nick-nacks *(unlocated)*

PERRY, Jr. E*noch* Wood *1831–1915*

Born at Boston, Mass.; *died New York.* Masters: T. Couture; *Leutze, Düsseldorf*

241. Mother and Child, *1881. Oil on canvas, 25⅝ x 36¾". Manoogian Collection*

PETERS, *Dewitt* Clinton *1865–1948*
Born at Baltimore, Md. Masters: Boulanger, Lefebvre, Gérôme, and Collin. *Recompense: Bronze medal 1889*
242. Portrait of Doctor G. J. B. *(unlocated)*

PLUMB, Henry *Grant* *1847–1935*
Born at Sherburne, N.Y.; *died New York.* Masters: Gérôme; *Yvon. Recompense: Honorable mention 1899*
243. The Orphans *(unlocated)*

244.

PORTER, Benjamin Curtis *1845–1908*
Born at Melrose, Mass. *Associated with Rimmer, Bicknell*
244. Portrait of a Lady (Owner, Mrs. Chas. Berryman). *Oil on canvas, 41½ x 29½" (oval). Collection Vera de Rham Photograph courtesy Frick Art Reference Library*

245.

POTTHAST, Edward *Henry* *1857–1927*
Born at Cincinnati, Ohio; *died New York.* Master: M. Cormon; *Marr, Gysis, von Loefftz; McMicken School of Design, Cincinnati*
245. Study: A young Britany *[sic]* Girl. *Sunshine, 1889.* *See page 199.*

REID, Robert *1862–1929*
Born at Stockbridge, Mass.; died Clifton Springs, N.Y. Masters: Boulanger, Lefebvre
246. Study *(unlocated)*

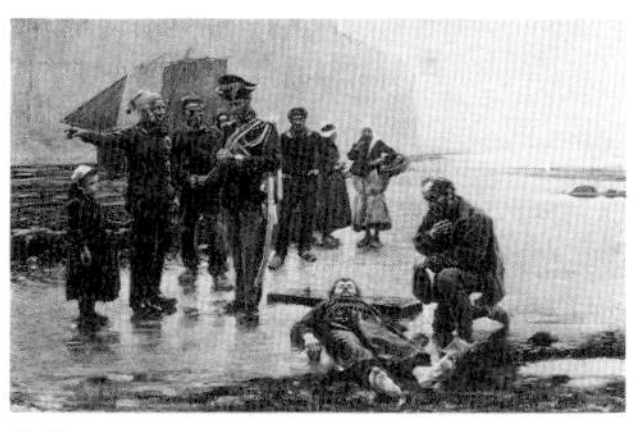
247.

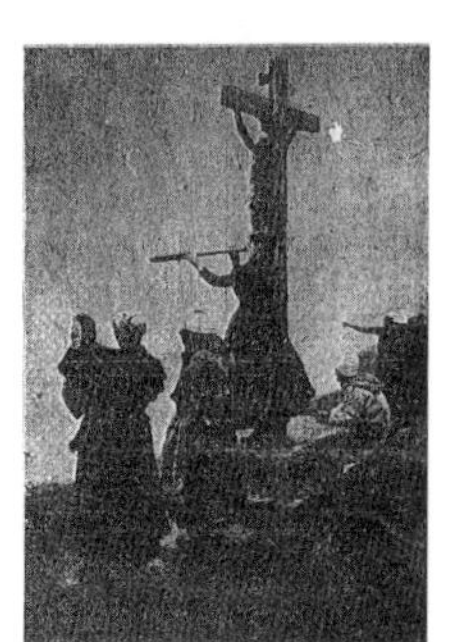
248.

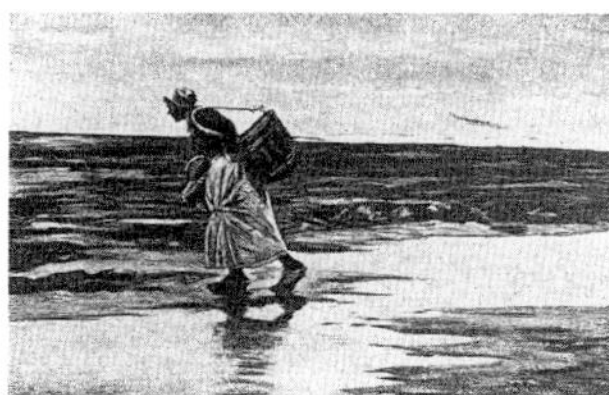
249.

REINHART, Charles Stanley *1844–1896*
Born at Pittsburgh, Pa.; *died New York. Student at Atelier Suisse, Paris; Royal Academy, Munich. Recompense: Silver medal 1889*
247. Washed ashore, *1887*
Engraving after the painting from G.W. Sheldon, Recent Ideals, *p.144. Photograph courtesy The Library of Congress*
248. Awaiting the Absent, *1888 (unlocated; formerly Carnegie Museum of Art, Pittsburgh). Oil on canvas, 107 x 72".* *See page 199.*
249. Rising tide *(unlocated). Engraving after the painting, from William Walton,* Chefs-d'oeuvre, *vol. 1, p.8.*
250. An Old Woman *(unlocated)*
251. The Sea *(unlocated)*
252. Fog Effect *(unlocated)*

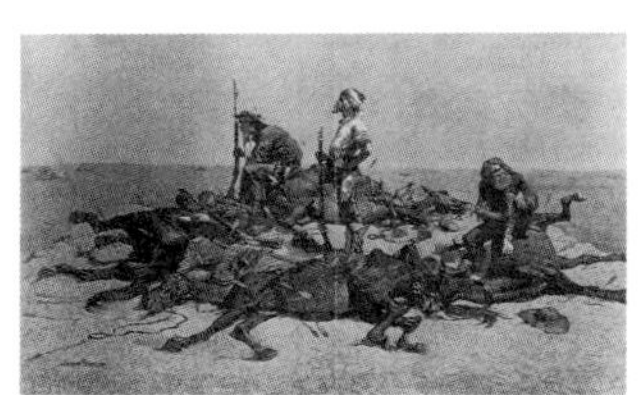
253.

REMINGTON, Frederic *1861–1909*
Born at Canton, N.Y.; *died Ridgefield, Conn. Studied: John Henry Niemeyer, Yale University; NAD*
253. A Lull in the Fight. Descriptive of an affair on the Staked Plain (Texas), in 1861, as told by a Comanche "brave" who participated, *c. 1889 (unlocated). Wood engraving after the painting, from* Harper's Weekly, *March 30, 1889, pp. 244–45. Remington Art Museum, Ogdensburg, N.Y.*

RENOUF, A. Vincent
Born at New York, N.Y. Masters: Max Thedy and Frillhot Smith
254. Portrait *(unlocated)*

RICE, William M.J. *1854–1922*
Born at Brooklyn, N.Y. Masters: Carolus-Duran and J. Carroll Beckwith
255. Portrait *(unlocated)*

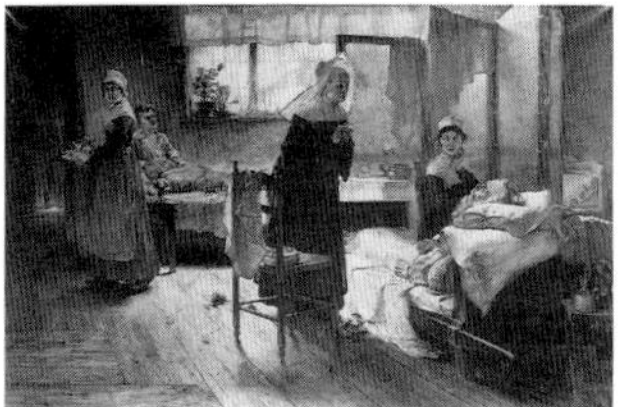
256.

RICHARDS, Samuel *1853–1893*
Born at Spencer, Owen County, Indiana; *died Denver, Colo.* Masters: Straehuber, Benczur, Gysis, Loefftyz *[sic]*
256. Evangeline. *Evangeline Discovering Her Affianced in the Hospital. Oil on canvas, 69 x 102." © The Detroit Institute of Arts, Gift of Bela Hubbard*

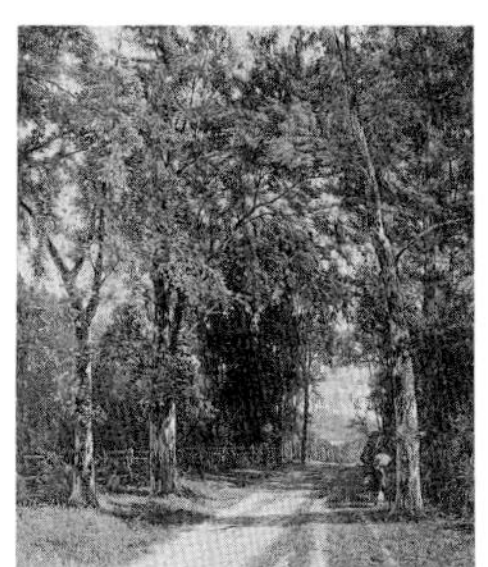
258.

RICHARDS, William T*rost* *1833–1905*
Born at Philadelphia, Pa.; *died Newport, R.I. Master: Paul Weber. Recompense: Bronze medal 1889*
257. After a Storm *(unlocated)*

ROBBINS, Horace W*olcott* *1842–1904*
Born at Mobile, Ala. Masters: James M. Hart; *Théodore Rousseau*
258. A Mountain Road *(unlocated). Ill. from G.W. Sheldon,* Recent Ideals, *p. 67. Photograph courtesy The Library of Congress*

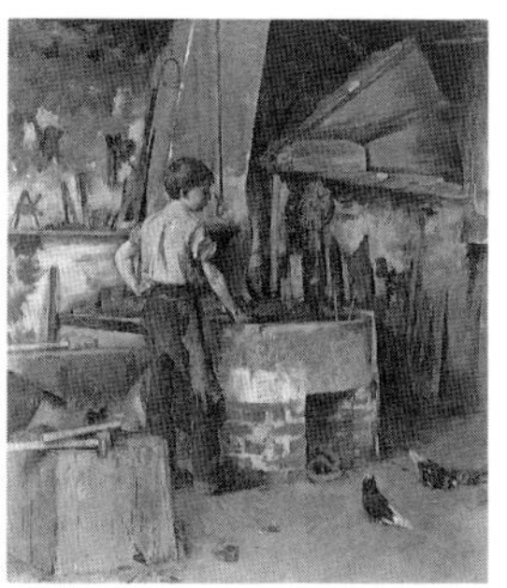
260.

ROBINSON, Theodore *1852–1896*
Born at Irasburg, Vt.; died New York. Masters: Carolus-Duran; association with Monet; NAD
259. The Bread Carrier *(unlocated). See fig. 21.*
260. The Forge, *1886. See page 202.*

RYDER, Platt P*owell* *1821–1896*
Born at Brooklyn, N.Y.; *died Saratoga Springs, N.Y.* Master: Léon Bonnat
261. A Game of Marbles (Owner, W.T. Evans.) *(unlocated). Oil on canvas, 17 x 16". Engraving after the painting, from* National Academy Notes *(1887), p.116. Photograph courtesy The New York Public Library*

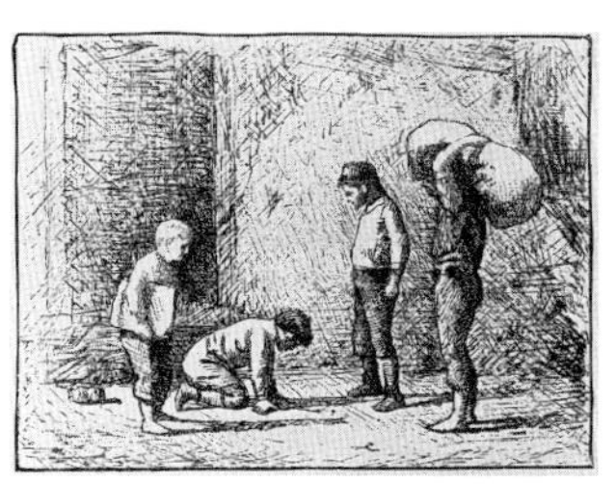
261.

SARGENT, John S*inger* *1856–1925*
Born at Florence, Italy; died London, England. Master: Carolus-Duran. *Recompenses:* 2nd med. Salon, Paris; *Grand Prize 1889; Chevalier of the Legion of Honor 1889*
262. Portrait of the Misses B. *The Daughters of Edward D. Boit, 1882. Oil on canvas, 87 x 87". See fig. 19.*
263. Portrait of Mrs. W. *Mrs. Henry White, 1883. Oil on canvas, 87 x 55" The Corcoran Gallery of Art, Washington, D.C. Gift of John Campbell White.*

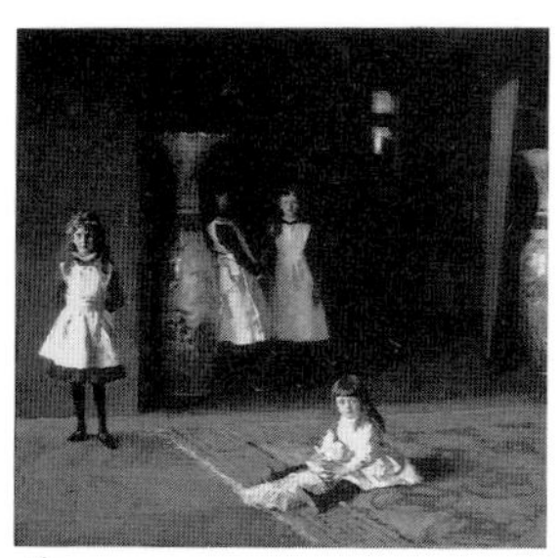

262.

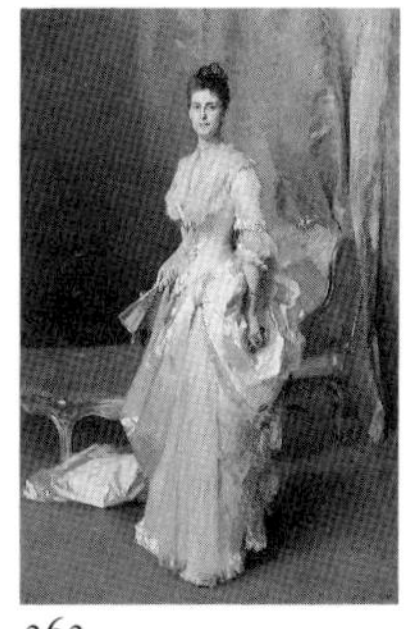

263.

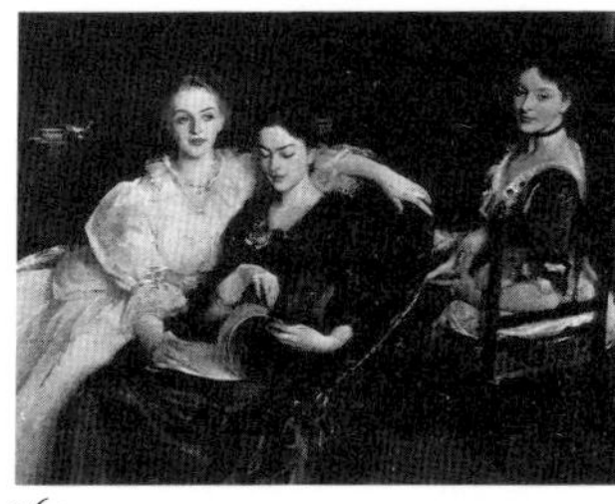

264.

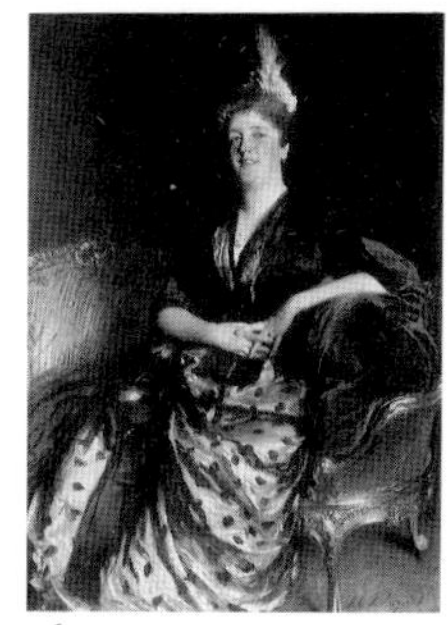

265.

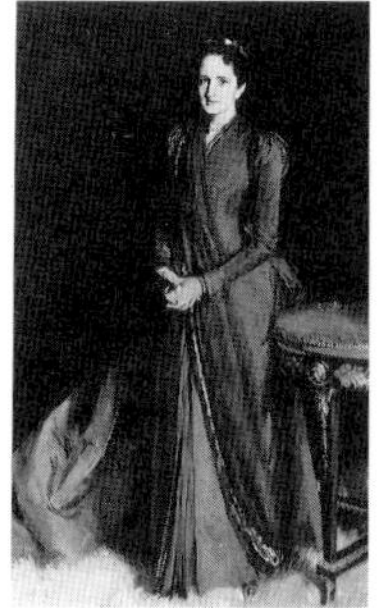

266.

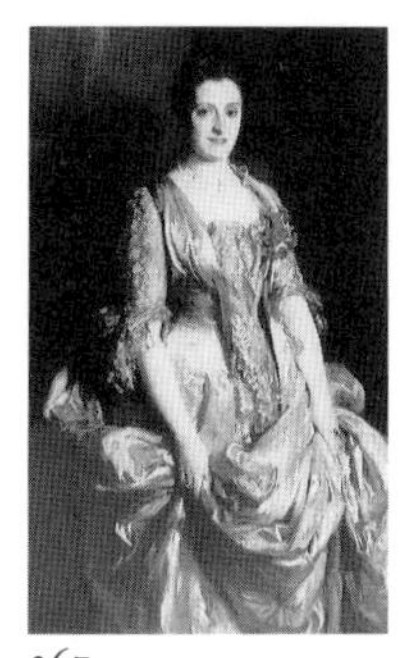

267.

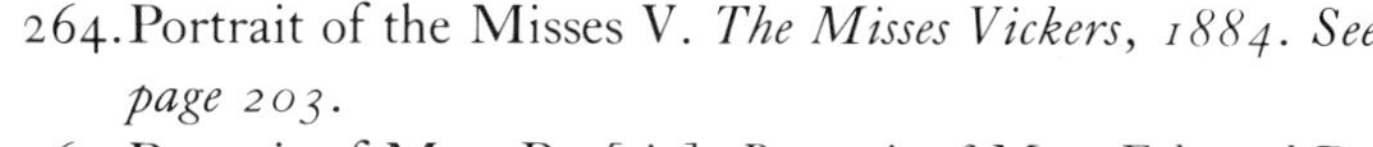

264. Portrait of the Misses V. *The Misses Vickers, 1884. See page 203.*
265. Portrait of Mrs. R. *[sic]. Portrait of Mrs. Edward D. Boit, 1888. See page 203.*
266. Portrait of Mrs. S. *Portrait of Mrs. Elliott Fitch Shepard, 1888. See page 203.*
267. Portrait of Mrs. K. *Mrs. Benjamin Kissam. Biltmore, Asheville, N.C.*

SAWYER, R*oswell* D*ouglas*
Born at Watertown, N.Y. Masters: Boulanger and Lefebvre

268. A Normandy Idyl *(unlocated)*

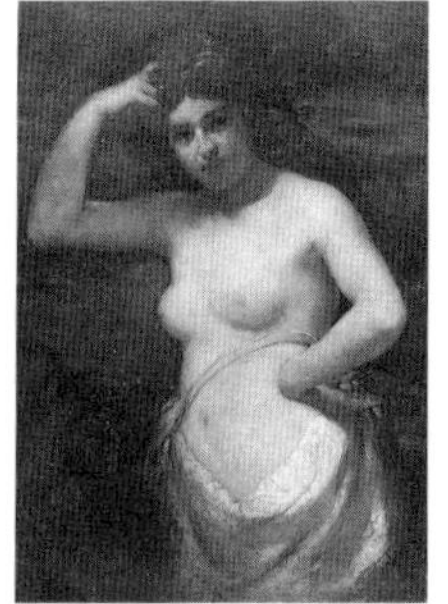

270.

SHERWOOD, Rosina Emmet *1854–1948*
Born at New York, N.Y.; *died New York.* Masters: Wm. M.Chase; *Académie Julian*

269. Portrait (Owner, J.N.A. Griswold) *(unlocated)*

SHIRLAW, Walter *1838–1909*
Born in Scotland *(Paisley); died Madrid, Spain. Masters: Raab, Wagner, von Ramberg, von Lindenschmit. Recompense: Honorable mention 1889*

270. Rufina. *See page 207.*

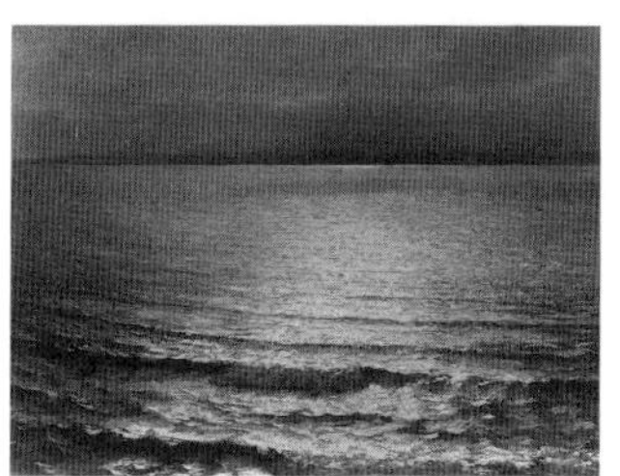

272.

SIMMONS, Edward Emerson *1852–1931*
Born at Concord, Mass.; *died Baltimore, Md.* Masters: Boulanger and M. J. Lefebvre; *Ecole des Beaux-Arts; Crowninshield, Rimmer. Recompense: Bronze medal 1889*

271. The Farmer, *1889.The Farmer: Moonrise over St. Ives Bay, Cornwall. Oil on canvas, 34 x 44". Sold Parke Bernet, New York, April 1, 1942, lot 99*
272. Night. *Night, St.Ives Bay, 1889. See page 210.*
273. Study *(unlocated)*

SMITH, de Cost *1864–1939*
Born at Skaneateles, N.Y. Masters: Boulanger, Lefebvre, Beckwith, etc.

274. Conflicting Faiths, representing an Iroquois holding a Shamanic mask, symbolizing Paganism, and a priest with

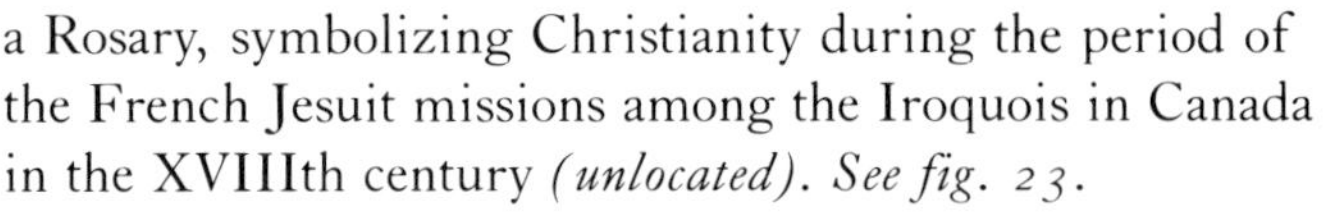

a Rosary, symbolizing Christianity during the period of the French Jesuit missions among the Iroquois in Canada in the XVIIIth century *(unlocated). See fig. 23.*

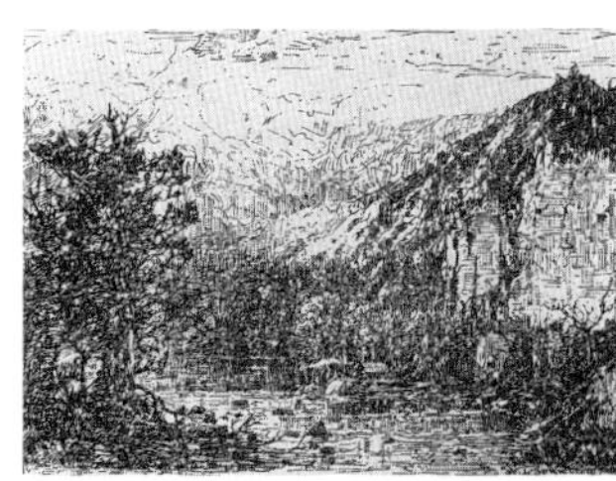

275.

SONNTAG, William L*ouis* *1822–1900*
Born at Cincinnati, Ohio *[East Liberty, now Pittsburgh, Pa.]; died New York*

275. A Mountain Stream from the foot of Mt. Carter, N.H. *(unlocated). Oil on canvas, 40 x 55". Engraving after the painting, from* National Academy Notes *(1888), p. 24. Photograph courtesy The New York Public Library*

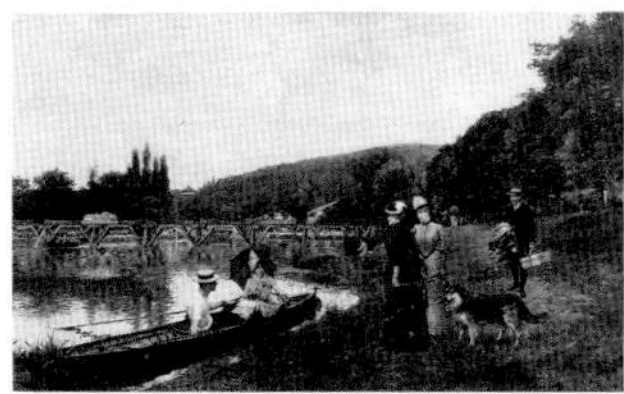

277.

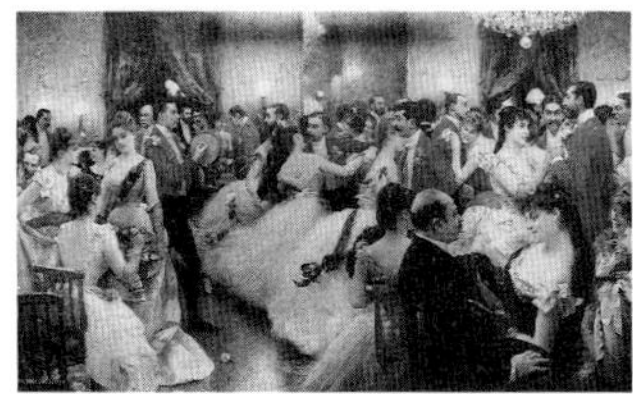

278.

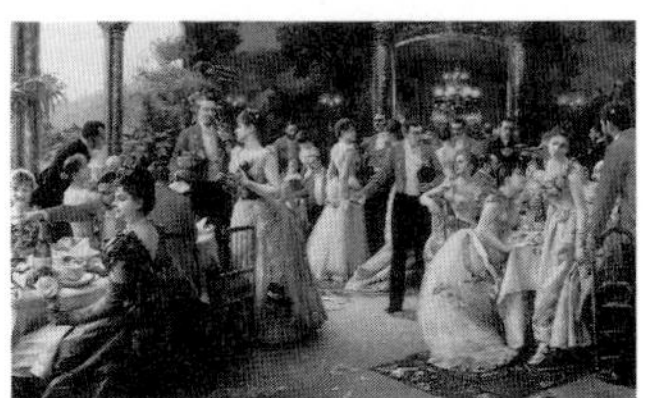

279.

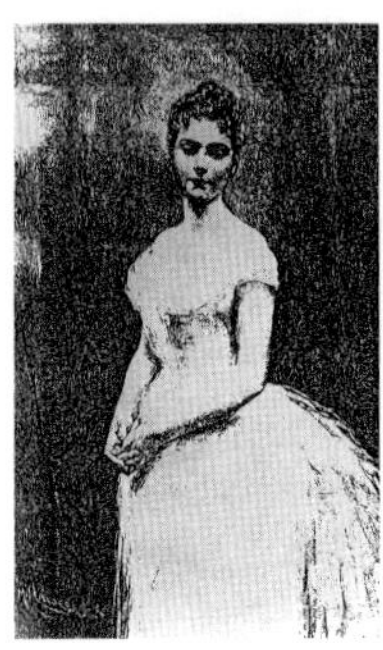

281.

STEWART, Julius L*eBlanc* *1855–1919*
Born at Philadelphia, Pa.; *died Paris, France.* Masters: Zamacoïs, Gérôme and R. de Madrazo

276. A Court at Cairo, *1883 (unlocated)*
277. The Seine at Bougival, *1885. See page 211.*
278. A Hunt Ball, *1885. See page 211.*
279. A Hunt Supper, *1889. Oil on canvas, 47 x 73". Private collection. Photograph by Biff Henrich*
280. Portrait of the Baroness B.M. *(unlocated).*
281. Portrait of the Baroness de B. *(unlocated). Engraving by M. Haiger after the painting, from* Harper's New Monthly Magazine, *vol. 79 (Sept. 1889)*

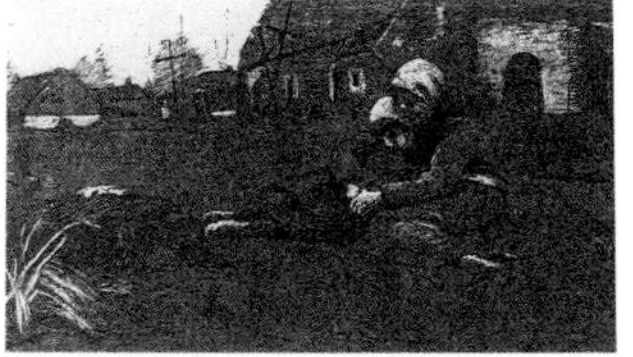

282.

STOKES, Frank Wilbert *1858–1955*
Born at Nashville, Tenn. Masters: Boulanger, Gérôme and J. Lefebvre

282. The Orphans, *c. 1888 (unlocated). Ill. from* Salon de 1888 *(Paris), p. 230*
283. A Good Sermon *(unlocated)*

STORY, Julian Russell *1857–1919*
Born at Walton-on-Thames, England; *died Philadelphia. Masters: Duveneck; Paris. Recompense: Bronze medal 1889*

284. The Black Prince finding the dead body of the King of Bohemia, after the Battle of Crecy (1346). *Oil on canvas, 135½ x 205¾". Telfair Academy of Arts and Sciences, Savannah. Ill. in* Art Works of Savannah and Augusta, Georgia *(Chicago, 1902), vol. 2*
285. Portrait; reign Louis XVI *(unlocated)*
286. Portrait of my father *(unlocated)*

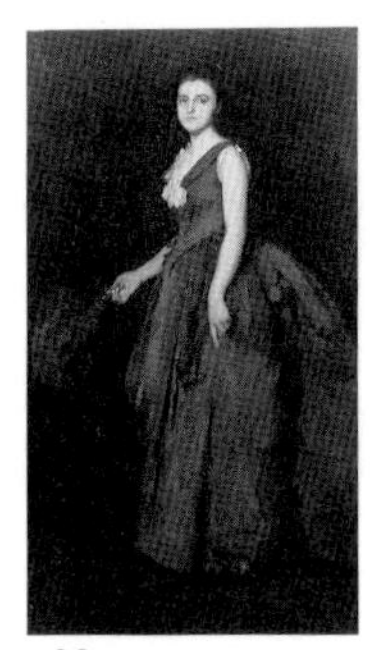
288.

STRICKLAND, Charles Hobart
Born at New York, N.Y. Masters: Bouguereau and Fleury
287. Portrait of Miss X *(unlocated)*

TARBELL, Edmund *Charles* *1862–1938*
Born at West Groton, Mass.; *died New Castle, N.H.*
Masters: Boulanger and Lefebvre; *Grundmann, Crowninshield.* Recompense: Silver Medal, Boston, Mass., 1887
288. Portrait of Mme. T. (Owner, Mme T.). *Portrait of Madame Tarbell, c. 1888. See page 214.*

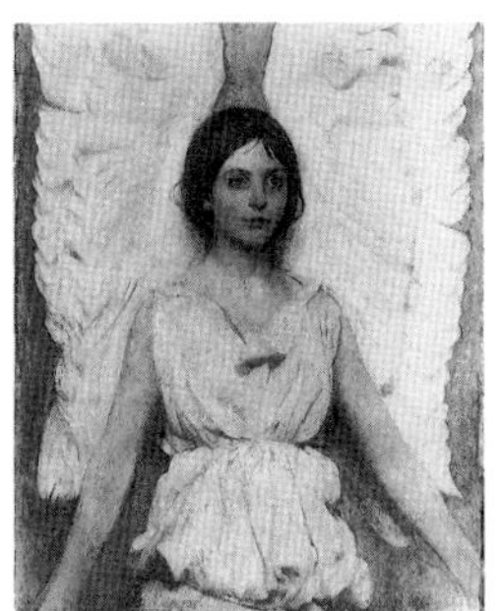
289.

THAYER, Abbott Handerson *1849–1921*
Born at Boston, Mass.; *died Dublin, Vt.* Masters: Gérôme; *Henri Lehman; Brooklyn Art School, NAD. Recompense: Bronze medal 1889*
289. Winged Figure. (Owner, A.A. Carey, Boston). *Angel, 1888. See page 215.*

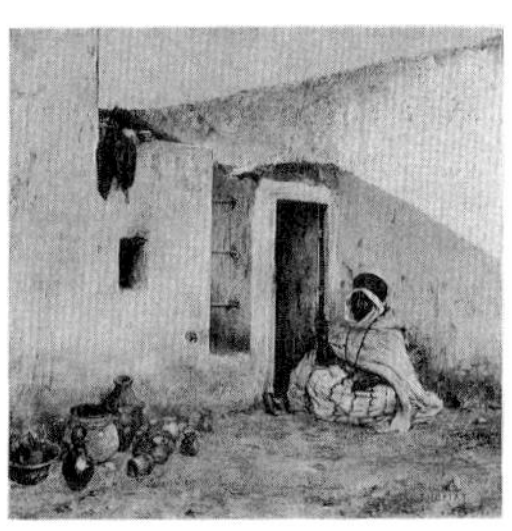
290.

THERIAT, Charles *1860–?*
Born at New York, N.Y. Masters: Boulanger and Lefebvre. *Recompense: Honorable mention 1889*
290. Souvenir of Biskra, *1888 (unlocated). Ill. from G.W. Sheldon,* Recent Ideals, *p.142. Photograph courtesy The Library of Congress*

THOMPSON, *Alfred* Wordsworth *1840–1896*
Born at Baltimore, Md.; *died Summit, N.J.* Masters: M. Charles Gleyre; *Emile Lambinet*
Recompense: Bronze medal 1889
291. A New England Farm House *(unlocated)*

THROOP, Frances Hunt
Born at New York, N.Y. Masters: J. Carroll Beckwith and Alfred Stevens
292. Portrait of Miss C. *(unlocated)*

TIFFANY, Louis C*omfort* *1848–1933*
Born at New York, N.Y.; *died New York. Master: Léon Belly, Paris*
293. Carrying the Boat at Seabright *(unlocated)*

TOMPKINS, Frank H*ector* *1847–1922*
Born at Hector, N.Y.; *died Brookline, Mass. Studied at Art Students League*
294. Memories, *1886. Oil on canvas, 29 x 39½". Sold by Parke Bernet, New York, June 21, 1940*

TRACY, John M. *1843–1893*
Born at Rochester, Ohio; died Ocean Springs, Miss. Masters: Carolus-Duran, Pils, Yvon
295. Chesapeake Bay Dog retrieving a Wounded Goose *(unlocated). See fig 23.*

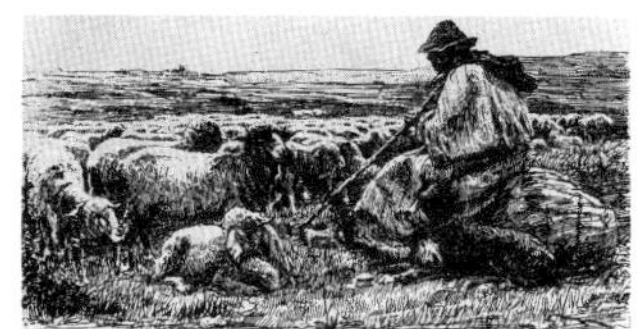
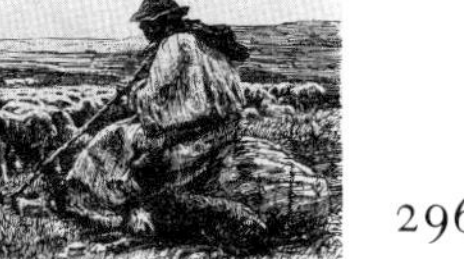
296.

TRUESDELL, *Gaylord* Sangston *1850–1899*
Born at Waukegan, Ill.; died New York. Masters: student at PAFA; Morot, Cormon. Recompense: Bronze medal 1889
296. The Shepherd and his flock, *1887 (unlocated). Oil on canvas, 24 x 34". Sold Parke Bernet, New York, January 22, 1965, lot 379. Engraving after the painting, from* Salon de 1888 *(Paris), p.195.*

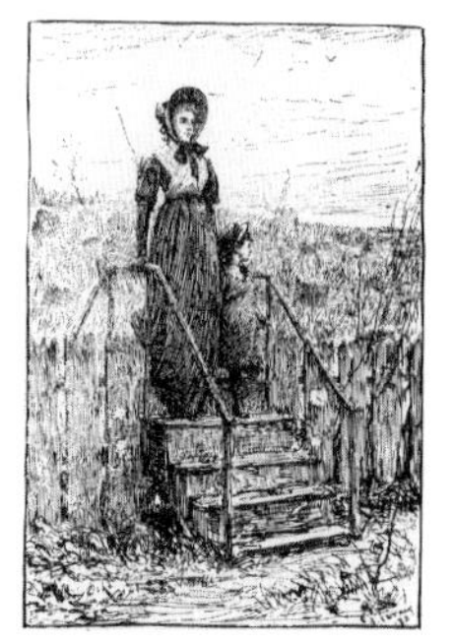
297.

TURNER, Charles *Yardley* *1850–1918*
Born at Baltimore, Md.; *died New York.* Masters: J. P. Laurens, M. Munckacsy, Léon Bonnat. *Recompense: Honorable mention 1889*
297. The days that are no more, *1882. Oil on canvas, 45 x 30". Engraving after the painting, from* National Academy Notes *(1882), p. 35. Photograph courtesy The New-York Historical Society*

TYLER, James *Gale* *1855–1931*
Born at Oswego, N.Y.; *died Pelham, N.Y.* Master: A. Cary Smith
298. Off Cape Ann *(unlocated)*

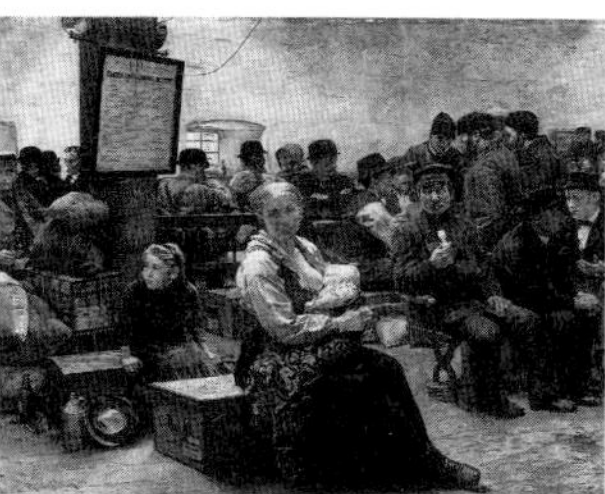
299.

ULRICH, Charles *Frederick* *1858–1908*
Born at New York; died Berlin, Germany. Masters: von Loefftz, von Lindenschmit. Recompense: Bronze medal 1889
299. In the Land of Promise, *c. 1884* (Owner, W.T. Evans.). *Oil on wood panel, 28⅜ x 35¾". The Corcoran Gallery of Art, Washington, D.C.*

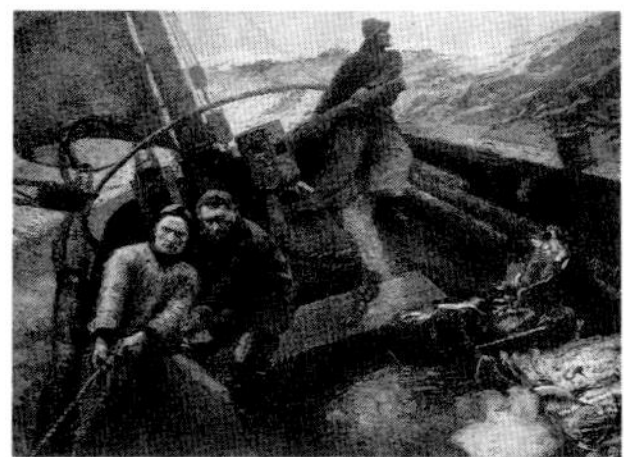
300.

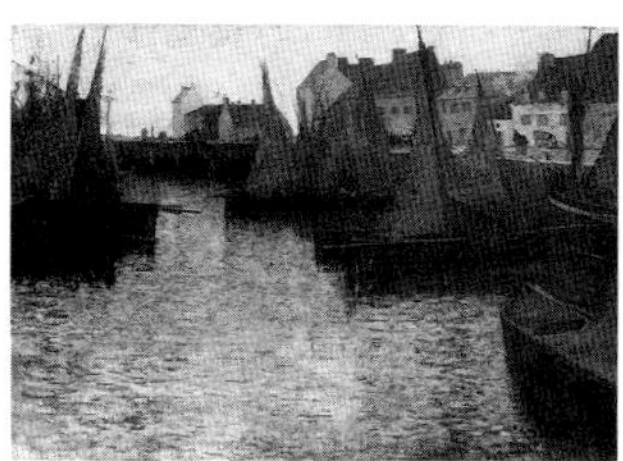
301.

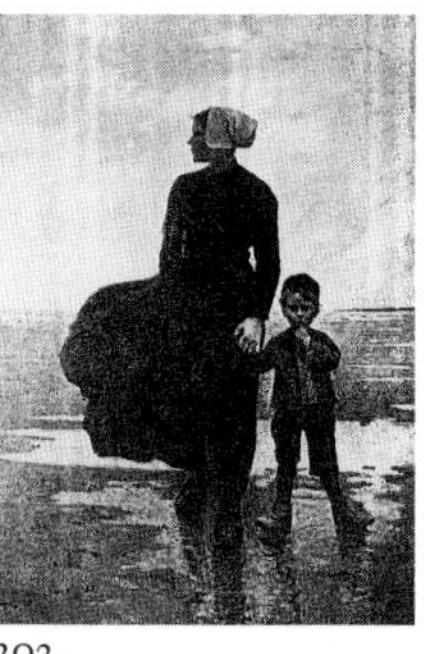
302.

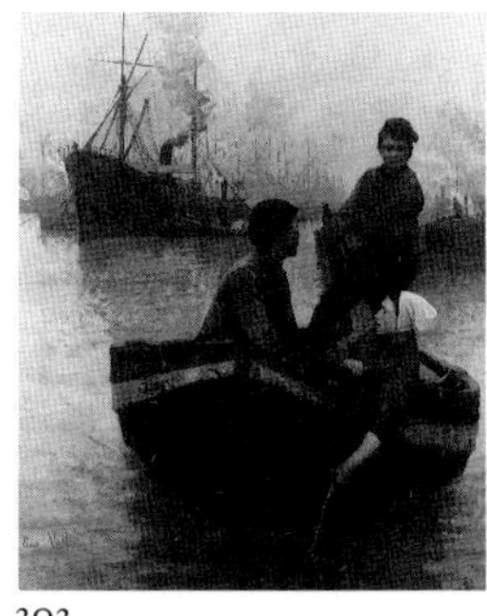
303.

VAIL, Eugene *Lawrence* *1857–1934*
Born at St. Malo, France. Masters: Cabanel, Collin, Dagnan-Bouveret; *Beckwith, Chase. Recompenses:* Med. 3rd cl. 1888; *gold medal 1889*
300. Ready About. *Oil on canvas, 84 x 124". Photograph courtesy The Corcoran Gallery of Art, Washington, D.C.*
301. Fishing harbour, 1884. *See page 216.*
302. The Widow *(unlocated). Ill. from* Eugene Vail Exhibition Catalogue, *Delaware Art Center, Wilmington, March 1940*
303. On the Thames, *1886. See page 216.*

VAN BOSKERCK, Robert W. *1855–1932*
Born in New Jersey. Masters: A.H. Wyant, R.S. Gifford
304. A Rhode Island River *(unlocated)*

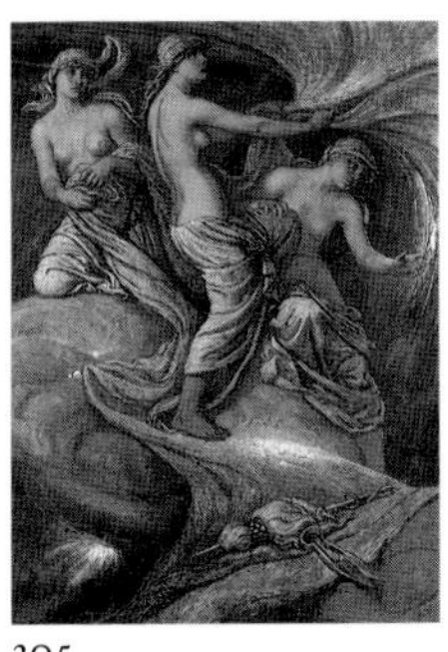
305.

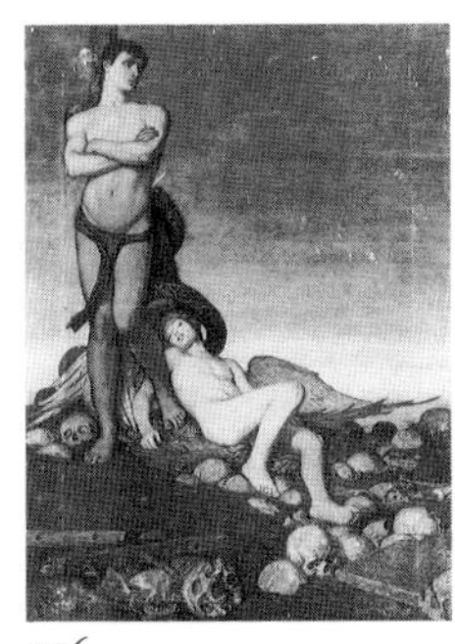
306.

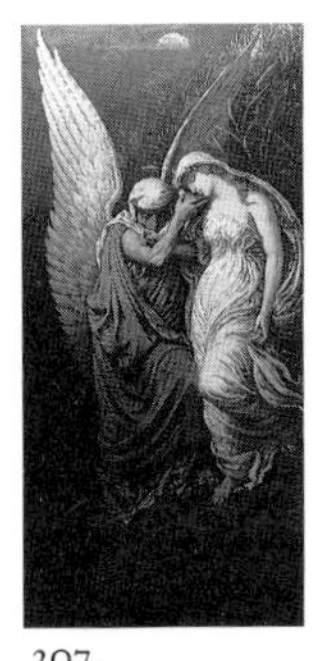
307.

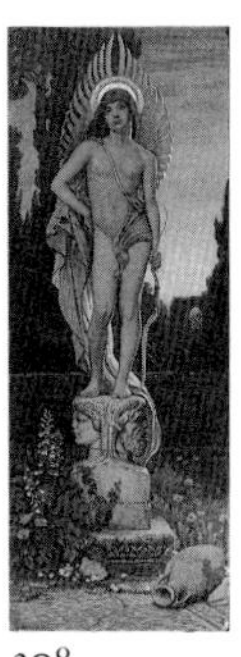
308.

VEDDER, Elihu *1836–1923*
Born at New York, N.Y.; *died Rome, Italy. Masters: Tomkins Matteson; Picot, Raffaello Bonaiutto (Florence). Recompense: Honorable mention 1889*
305. The Fates gathering in the Stars, *1887. See page 218.*
306. The Last Man, *1886 (unlocated). Oil on canvas, 36 x 25". Sold Parke Bernet, New York, June 2, 1983, cat. ill. p. 72*
307. The Death Cup, *1885. See page 218.*
308. Love always present, *1887–99. Oil on canvas, 34¼ x 12½". Collection James Ricau, on extended loan to The Brooklyn Museum, New York*

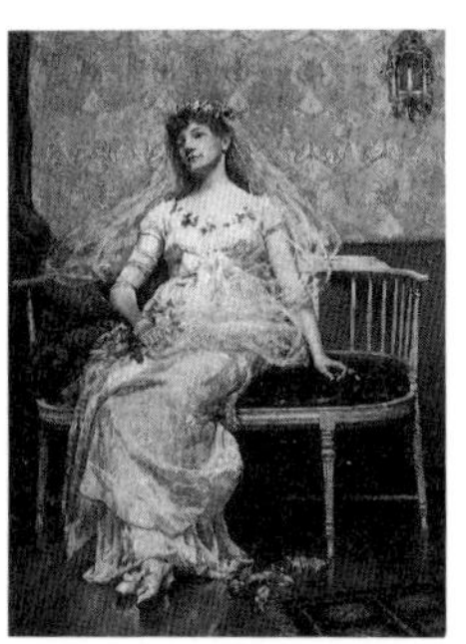
310.

VOLK, Douglas *Stephen 1856–1935*
Born in Pittsfield, Mass.; died Fryeburg, Maine. Masters: Gérôme; Ecole des Beaux-Arts; St. Luke's Academy, Rome
309. The Puritan Captives, *1882 (unlocated). Oil on canvas, 36 x 30"*
310. After the Reception, *1887. See page 221.*

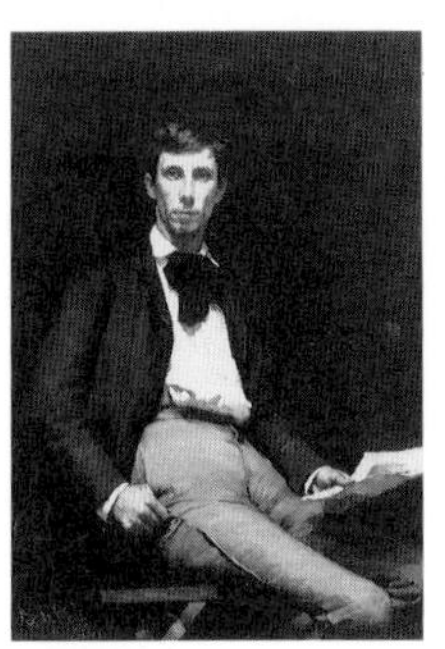
311.

VONNOH, Robert William *1858–1933*
Born at Hartford, Conn.; *died Nice, France.* Masters: Boulanger and Lefebvre. *Recompenses:* Gold medal for portraits at Mechanic's Institute, Mass.; *bronze medal 1889*
311. Studio Comrade, *1888. See page 222.*
312. Revery *(unlocated)*

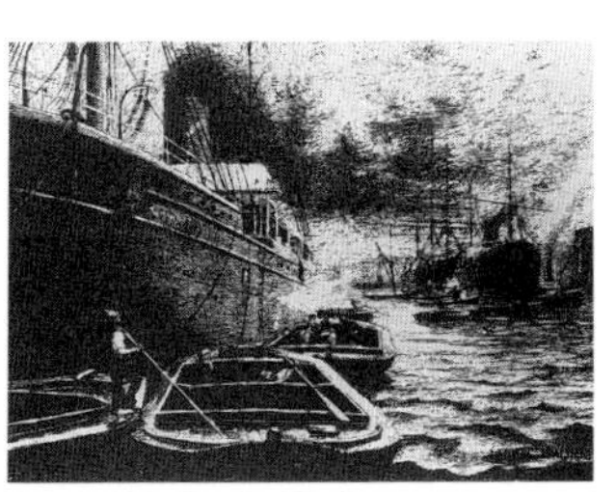
313.

WALDEN, Lionel *1861–1933*
Born at Norwich, Conn.; *died Honolulu, Hawaii.* Master: Carolus-Duran. *Recompense: Honorable mention 1889*
313. The Steamer "Shah" coming down the Thames *(unlocated). Engraving by Gillat after the painting, from* Salon de 1888 *(Paris), p. 304*
314. Fog on the Thames *(unlocated)*

WALKER, Horatio *1858–1938*
Born at Listowel, Ontario, Canada; died Quebec. Masters: John Fraser, Robert Gagen (Toronto). Recompense: Bronze medal 1889

315. A Stye. *A Pastoral—Swine (unlocated). Watercolor, 12 x 17½"*

WARD, Edgar M*elville* *1839–1915*
Born in Ohio *(Urbana). Master: Cabanel*

316. The Tack Workers *(unlocated)*
317. The Rest *(unlocated)*

WEBB, J. Louis *1856–1928*
Born at Washington, D.C. Master: W.M. Chase

318. A Studio Corner *(unlocated)*

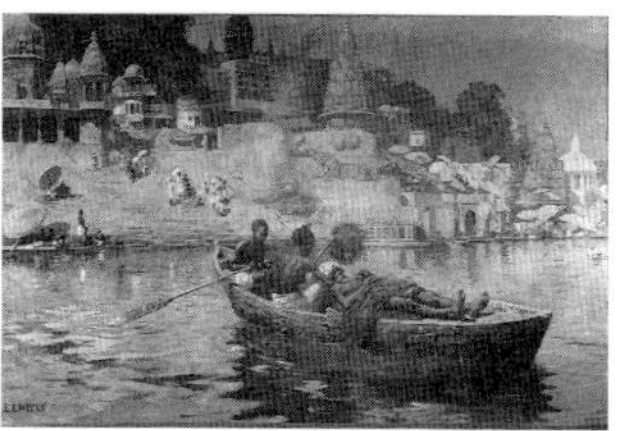
319.

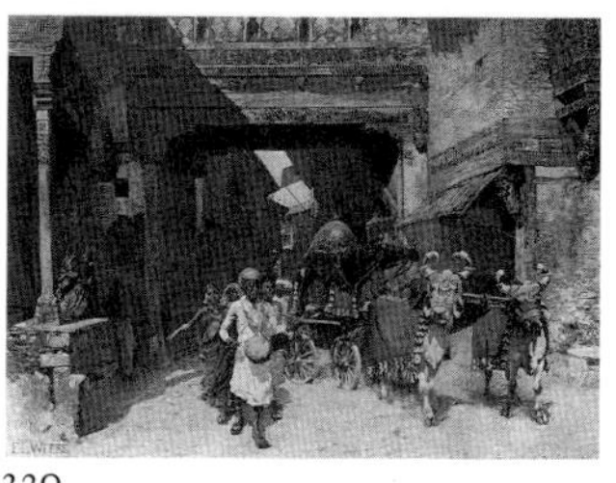
320.

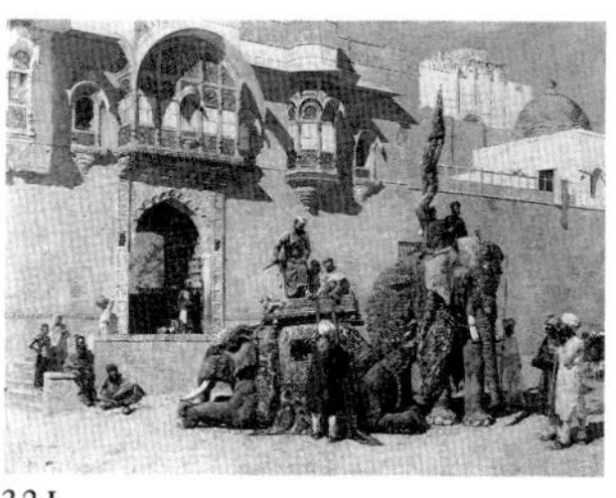
321.

WEEKS, E*dwin* Lord *1849–1903*
Born at Boston, Mass.; *died Paris, France.* Masters: Bonnat, *Gérôme. Recompense: Gold medal 1889*

319. The last Journey; Souvenir of the Ganges, *c. 1884. See page 223.*
320. Hindoo marriage Procession; Ahmedabad *(unlocated). Engraving after the painting, from G.W. Sheldon,* Recent Ideals, *p. 142. Photograph courtesy The Library of Congress*
321. The Rajah of Jodhpare *[sic] c. 1888. Oil on canvas, 56 5/16 x 74". Nationalgalerie, Staatliche Museen, Berlin*
322. Sacred Lake; Study *(unlocated)*
323. The Mosque of Vazin Khan, Lahore; Study *(unlocated)*

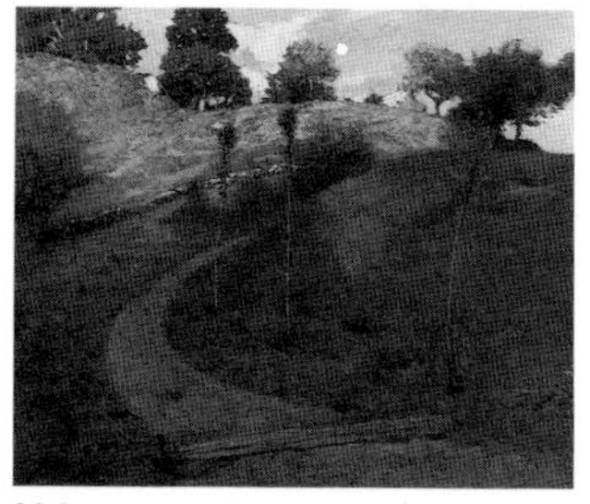
325.

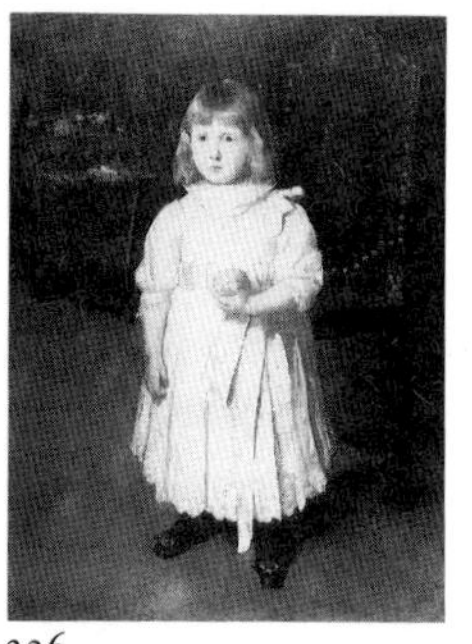
326.

WEIR, J*ulian* Alden *1852–1919*
Born at West Point, N.Y.; *died New York.* Masters: Gérôme, *Boulanger, Wilmarth.* Recompense: Honorable Mention, Paris Salon '82; *silver medal 1889*

324. Preparing for Christmas. *c. 1888 (unlocated). Watercolor*
325. Lengthening Shadows, *1887.* (Owner, W. T. Evans.) *See page 225.*
326. Portrait of Artist's Child, *1887. See page 225.*

WHITEMAN, Samuel Edwin *1860–1922*
Born at Philadelphia, Pa. Masters: Boulanger and M. J. Lefebvre. *Recompense: Honorable mention 1889*

327. Moonrise *(unlocated)*

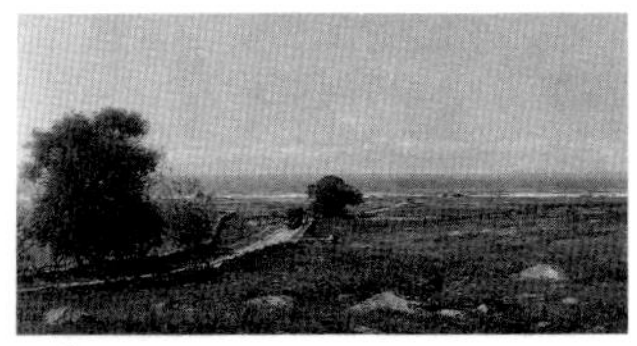
328.

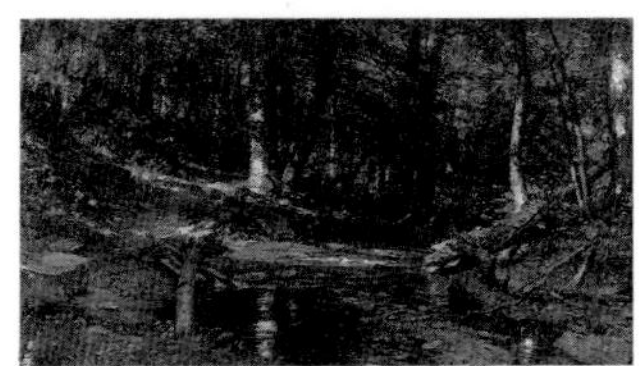
329.

WHITTREDGE, *Thomas* Worthington *1820–1910*
Born in Ohio *(Springfield); died Summit, N.J. Masters: Leutze, Düsseldorf. Recompenses:* 1st class Medal, Centennial Exposition, 1876; *honorable mention 1889*

328. The Old Road to the Sea, *1884* (Owners, Messrs. Pettus and Curtis). *See page 229.*

329. A Brook in the Woods, *c. 1889. See page 229.*

WICKENDEN, Robert John *1861–1931.*
Born at Rochester, England, *died Brooklyn, N.Y.* Masters: Carroll Beckwith, Chase, Hébert and Merson

330. Noon *(unlocated)*

WIGHT, Moses *1827–1895*
Born at Boston, Mass.; *died Boston, Mass.* Masters: Hébert and Bonnat

331. Portrait of Mrs. W. *(unlocated)*

WILES, Irving R*amsey* *1862–1948*
Born at Utica, N.Y.; *died New York.* Master: Carolus-Duran

332. Portrait of a Lady *(unlocated)*

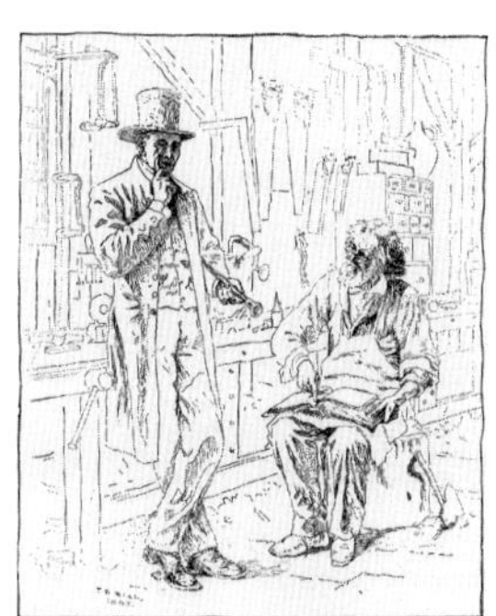
335.

WITT, J*ohn* H*arrison* *1840–1901*
Born at Dublin, Ind.; died New York

333. Planning an Apple Cutting *(unlocated)*

WOOD, Ogden *1851–1922*
Born at New York, N.Y.; *died Paris, France.* Masters: School of Fine Arts and M. Van Marcke

334. Pasture at the Sea-Side *(unlocated)*

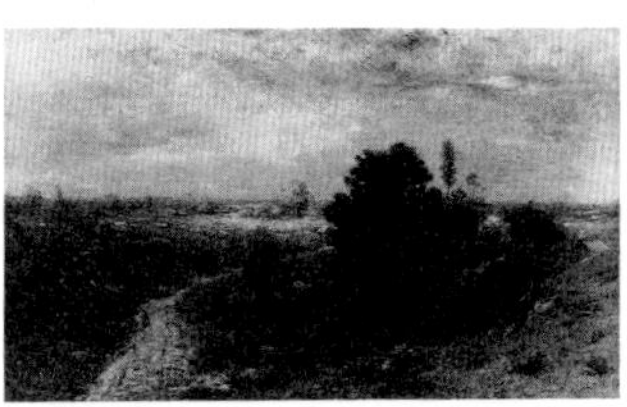
336.

WOOD, Thomas Waterman *1823–1903*
Born at Montpelier, Vt.; *died New York*

335. The Difficult Text, *1885.* (Owner, T.N. Vail.) *(unlocated). Engraving after the painting, from* National Academy Notes *(1885), p. 4. Photograph courtesy The New-York Historical Society*

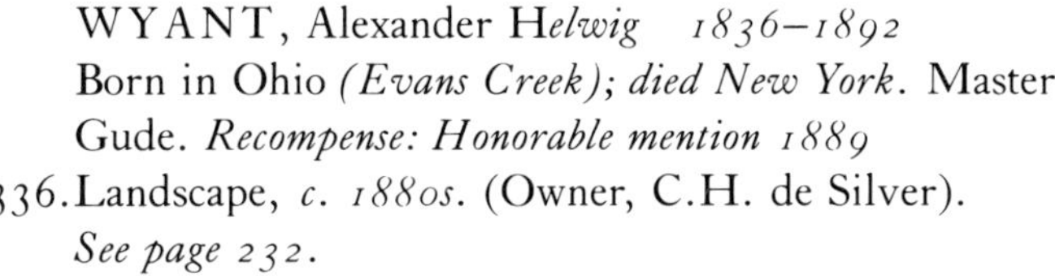

WYANT, Alexander H*elwig* *1836–1892*
Born in Ohio *(Evans Creek); died New York.* Master: Gude. *Recompense: Honorable mention 1889*

336. Landscape, *c. 1880s.* (Owner, C.H. de Silver). *See page 232.*

Index

Note. *Italic* page numbers refer to illustrations. **Boldface** page numbers refer to the catalogue entries for artists who appear in the present catalogue (pp. 111–251) and/or the 1889 catalogue (pp. 267–97).